ARCHAEOLOGICAL LANDSCAPES OF THE *Near East*

ARCHAEOLOGICAL LANDSCAPES

OF THE *Near East*

T. J. WILKINSON

The University of Arizona Press   Tucson

The University of Arizona Press
© 2003 The Arizona Board of Regents

www.uapress.arizona.edu

Library of Congress Cataloging-in-Publication Data
Wilkinson, T. J. (Tony J.)
Archaeological landscapes of the Near East / T. J. Wilkinson.
p. cm.
Includes bibliographical references and index.
ISBN 0-8165-2173-5 — ISBN 0-8165-2174-3 (pbk.)
1. Middle East—Historical geography. 2. Landscape archaeology—Middle East.
3. Landscape—Middle East. I. Title.
DS44.9.W55 2003
911'.394—dc21
2003005024

Manufactured in the United States of America on acid-free, archival-quality paper
containing a minimum of 30% post-consumer waste and processed chlorine free.

15   14   13   12   11   10   7   6   5   4   3   2

Contents

Figures

Tables

Preface and Acknowledgments

Despite landscape being virtually everywhere, nowhere is there a book on the ancient landscapes of the Near East. I have therefore written this book to give an overview of the archaeological landscapes of the Near East and by so doing to provide a context for the rise of early states and empires. Although some of what appears in the following pages is based upon my own work, a considerable amount is synthesized from what is a fragmented literature of regional studies and local surveys, not all of which were originally classified as landscape studies. To maintain some degree of balance, I have selected case studies from a very wide geographical range of studies rather than focusing upon just those areas that have been investigated in greatest detail.

The reader should also appreciate that I have walked a fine line between the pragmatic empiricism of geoarchaeology and archaeological survey on the one hand and the qualitative theoretical approaches of the post-processualist school on the other. Despite this balancing act, the volume as it stands has a decidedly empirical flavor. Indeed, parts of this book could be categorized as "landscape geoarchaeology." I make no apologies for this: a descriptive overview of the subject is much needed, and this book is intended to act as a basic foundation for more sophisticated studies in future. Overall, the geographical range of this book extends from southern Arabia to the Anatolian and Transcaucasian highlands, and from the Mediterranean coast of the Levant to Iran. Chronologically, it encompasses some ten

thousand plus years. By covering such a broad canvas, there should be something in this book to annoy everyone.

My first steps in landscape archaeology were inspired by the work of Robert McCormick Adams, whose truly seminal studies on Mesopotamian settlement and irrigation influenced me even before I became an archaeologist. In terms of the pragmatics of landscape survey, my early work benefited enormously from the influences of Andrew Williamson and Martha Prickett. Although both died at an early age, their innovative studies of landscape archaeology (of the Islamic and prehistoric periods respectively) greatly influenced my own work. I must also thank the following excavation directors who invited me, at the start of my career, to work on their field projects: Richard Harper, David Whitehouse, Tom Holland, Paolo Costa, and Lee Marfoe. All allowed me to develop my field methods without any promise of an immediate return; I am very grateful to all for their encouragement.

Others who have helped or encouraged my landscape approach through the years include David and Joan Oates, Nicholas Postgate, McGuire Gibson, Andrew Moore, Maurizio Tosi, Donald Whitcomb, Claudio Vita-Finzi, Malcolm Wagstaff, Peter M. M. G. Akkermans, Naomi Miller, Aslihan Yener, Mark Lebeau, Karel Vanlerberghe, Gil Stein, Guillermo Algaze, and Henry Wright. All these individuals had a considerable influence on my ideas and the development of my field methodology. In addition, I wish to

thank Nick Kouchoukos, Clemens Reichel, Michael Roaf, Jennifer Pournelle, Carl Phillips, Kris Verhoeven, Graham Philip, Roger Matthews, Charly French, Glynn Barrett, Paul Goldberg, Arlene Miller Rosen, Christopher Edens, John Bintliff and Adam Smith, all of whom have contributed to the way I understand processes of landscape development. A considerable vote of thanks must also go to our students at the University of Chicago (in Near Eastern Languages and Civilizations as well as in the Department of Anthropology), who have tested many of my ideas in both the field and the laboratory and who have also helped by providing illustrations for this book. Particularly, I must thank Jason Ur, Jesse Casana, Carrie Hritz, Mark Altaweel, Jerry Lyon, and Krista Lewis. Many of the graphics were produced in the CAMEL laboratory at the Oriental Institute, and I am grateful to Jason Ur and Carrie Hritz, who labored long and hard to produce the remote-sensing images illustrated as well as maps derived from them.

Many of the maps and illustrations were produced by Peggy Sanders, who is to be thanked for her considerable skill and patience throughout the production of this volume. Thanks also go to Eleanor Barbanes for additional fine drawings and maps.

I am particularly grateful to the recent directors of the Oriental Institute: William Sumner, Gene Gragg, and Gil Stein, during whose tenure this book was respectively dreamed up, written, and brought to completion. The Oriental Institute has been a marvelous place to write a book such as this. Not only did I benefit from the fine research archives and from the help of Chuck Jones, the research archivist (who guided me to many tomes I would otherwise have neglected to consult), but my research for this book was enhanced by numerous conversations with colleagues at the Oriental Institute. It was as a result of many discussions and occasional seminars with Mac Gibson, Aslihan Yener, Abbas Alizadeh, David Schloen, Donald Whitcomb, and John Sanders that I was able to start to draw some common threads from a mass of data. Ideas were also forged and tested by Oriental Institute seminars on "the Waters of Babylon" and "Comparative Irrigation Systems" that included faculty, staff and students from both the Oriental Institute and the Department of Anthropology.

My fieldwork has been conducted in many countries of the Middle East, and I particularly should thank the following individuals who helped or supported my fieldwork: Dr. Yusuf Abdullah (San'a) and Dr. Abdu Ghalab Othman (San'a), Ali Sanabani (Dhamar), Hatice Pamir (Mustafa Kemal University, Antakya), Sa'ad al Rashid (Riyadh), Salah al-Hilwa (Riyadh), Mu'ayyad Sa'id Damerji (Baghdad), Ali Shanfari (Muscat), and Sultan Muhesen (Damascus). I also benefited significantly from my several years associated with the British Archaeological Expedition to Iraq, and I particularly wish to thank Warwick Ball, Moslem Mohamed (Tell Afar), David Tucker, and Manhal Jabar (Mosul); without their help, no serious work could have been done in the North Jazira Project.

I am also most grateful to the numerous organizations that have funded my work or parts of it over the years: the British School of Archaeology in Iraq, the National Geographic Society, the British Academy, the National Endowment for the Humanities, the National Science Foundation, the Ameri-

can Institute for Yemeni Studies, the Oriental Institute, the Ministry of National Heritage and Culture, Oman, the Department of Antiquities of Saudi Arabia, and numerous private donors.

The editorial staff of the University of Arizona Press, especially Christine Szuter, Alan Schroder, Yvonne Reineke, Nancy Moore, and Anne Keyl, require a special vote of gratitude for patiently dealing with an unwieldy manuscript. In addition, two anonymous reviewers made suggestions that enabled the final text to be more cohesive and understandable. This book has benefited significantly from the advice of these reviewers and many of the above-mentioned colleagues, but I remain fully responsible for any of the mistakes or shortcomings in the text.

Special thanks go to Eleanor Barbanes, my wife, who has provided much help and commentary on my landscape studies and has been a wonderful companion during a succession of field campaigns.

Dating Conventions

Dating Conventions Employed in Text

Uncalibrated radiocarbon years before present	B.P.
Calibrated radiocarbon years before present	cal. B.P.
Conventional calendar or historical years B.C. or A.D.	B.C. or A.D.
Calibrated radiocarbon years B.C. or A.D.	cal. B.C. or cal. A.D.

No dates are given in the form uncalibrated years B.C. or A.D.

Chronological Charts

Dates A.D./B.C.	Syro-Palestine	Upper Mesopotamia	Lower Mesopotamia
2000			
1800	Ottoman	Ottoman	Ottoman
1600	Late Islamic	Late Islamic	Late Islamic
1400			
1200	Crusader & Ayyubid	Middle Islamic	Middle Islamic
1000			
800 A.D.	Early Islamic	Early Islamic	Early Islamic
600			
400	Byzantine	Sasanian	Sasanian
200			
0	Roman	Parthian	Parthian
200	Late Hellenistic	Hellenistic-Parthian	Hellenistic-Parthian
400	Early Hellenistic	Hellenistic/Seleucid	Hellenistic/Seleucid
600	Babylonian–Persian	Late Iron Age	Neo-Babylonian
800	Iron Age II	Late Assyrian/Iron Age	
1000 B.C.		?	
1200	Iron Age I	Late Bronze/Mid Assyrian	Middle Babylonian
1400	Late Bronze	Late Bronze	Kassite
1600	MBA (Middle Bronze Age)	Late MBA/Early LBA	
1800		Middle MBA	Old Babylonian
2000	MB I/EB–MB	Early MBA/Old Assyrian	Isin Larsa
2200	EB (Early Bronze) IV	Late Early Bronze Age	Ur III
2400	EB III	Mid Early Bronze Age	Akkadian
2600			Early Dynastic II/III
2800		Early Early Bronze Age/	Early Dynastic I
3000	EB II	Ninevite 5	Jemdet Nasr
3200			
3400	EB I	L. Chalcolithic/Uruk	Late Uruk
3600			
3800	Chalcolithic	L. Chalcolithic	Early Uruk
4000			
4200	Chalcolithic	Late Northern Ubaid	Ubaid 4
4400			
4600			Ubaid 3
4800		Early Northern Ubaid	
5000			
5200		Late Halaf	Ubaid 2
5400	Ceramic Neolithic	Middle Halaf	
5600		Early Halaf/Samarran	Ubaid 1
5800	Aceramic Neolithic	Ceramic Neolithic/	Ubaid 0
6000		Hassuna	
6200			
6400			
6600			
6800	Aceramic	Aceramic	
7000	Neolithic	Neolithic	
7200			
7400			
7600			
7800			
8000			

Dates A.D./B.C.	Anatolia	SE and SW Arabia
2000		
1800	Ottoman	Ottoman
1600	Late Islamic	Late Islamic
1400		
1200	Crusader & Ayyubid	Middle Islamic
1000		
800 A.D.	Early Islamic	Early Islamic
600		
400	Byzantine	Himyarite (Yemen)
200		Sasanian (Oman)
0	Roman	Parthian (Oman)
200	Late Hellenistic	
400	Early Hellenistic	Sabaean
600	Lydian	& Qatabanian (Yemen)
800	Phrygian/Urartian	& Iron Age Cultures (Oman
1000 B.C.	Syro-Hittite	& parts of Yemen)
1200		
1400	Hittite (Late Bronze Age)	"Late Bronze Age"
1600		
1800	Middle Bronze Age	"MBA" (Yemen)
2000		Wadi Suq (Oman)
2200	Early Bronze III	EBA (Yemen)
2400	EB II	Umm an-Nar (Oman)
2600		EBA (Yemen)
2800		
3000	EB I	Jemdet Nasr (Oman)
3200		
3400	Late Chalcolithic	Aceramic shell middens
3600		of the Arabian coastline
3800		&
4000		Arabian Bifacial Tradition
4200		
4400	Middle Chalcolithic	Arabian
4600		
4800		
5000		Bifacial
5200	Early Chalcolithic	
5400		
5600	Ceramic Neolithic	Tradition
5800		
6000		
6200		
6400	Late Neolithic	
6600		
6800	Aceramic	Aceramic
7000	Neolithic	Neolithic
7200		
7400		
7600		
7800		
8000		

ARCHAEOLOGICAL LANDSCAPES OF THE *Near East*

1 Introduction

Approaches to Landscape Archaeology

Many fundamental works on the origins of states (Wright 1994; Adams 1981) necessarily build upon landscape data, but the overall study of the Near Eastern landscape itself has not been laid out either empirically or theoretically. Moreover, the underpinnings of the state as manifest in exchange systems, "world systems," and alternative models (Stein 2000) are traditionally predicated upon the political economy and its social underpinnings, but these too implicitly require an understanding of the structure and distribution of settlement and landscape. The lack of systematic study of the Near Eastern landscape has, I believe, impeded the development of archaeological research.

The objective of this book is therefore to provide an overview of the Near Eastern landscape that can provide a framework for other studies requiring an understanding of the economic or physical infrastructure of this large and fundamental region. More specifically, this book attempts to describe the basic attributes of the ancient cultural landscape and to place its development within the context of a dynamic environment. This task, in turn, requires an understanding of the principles that underlie the preservation and recovery of landscape features, as well as how the cultural landscape was managed through time.

The term *landscape* has become increasingly popular in the last twenty years, and so its meaning has become stretched well beyond what was originally understood. Landscape archaeology has a long and distinguished history in western Europe for much of the twentieth century, but in the Near East it has been neglected, emphasis having been placed upon art historical and cultural historical approaches. Even when regional approaches to archaeology gained momentum during the 1970s, emphasis continued to be upon either settlement patterns or the physical landscape. The aim of this book is to describe and analyze the archaeological landscapes of the Near East by the use of key landscape types in the context of prevailing social, economic, and physical environments. Emphasis is upon the cultural landscape evident on the ground or from the air by means of remote sensing. These landscapes can be recognized from their characteristic signatures that comprise arrangements of features such as field boundaries, artifact scatters, archaeological settlement sites, roads, canals, temples, and inscriptions. In turn, the landscape itself changes through time as social, economic, political, and environmental circumstances vary to include a complex range of interactions between human factors and the environment.

A key theme of this book is that the development of different landscapes is contingent upon both local ecology and social or cultural factors. Antecedent conditions are especially important to landscape history because very few landscapes developed upon entirely virgin terrain. Moreover, landscape development also entails interactions between various driving and feedback mechanisms such as demographic growth, climatic fluctuations, human-induced degradation of the landscape, and a wide range of social, historical, and political factors. Finally, chance plays its hand in the development of settlement and landscapes, and it is crucial to allow for occasional "surprise" events. Therefore, although it is necessary to establish a rigorous record of the landscape within a theoretical framework, it is equally essential for such a framework to be flexible and to allow for a considerable degree of historical contingency.

When confronted with the range of complexity offered by ancient landscapes, the archaeologist may seek to obtain a range of complex histories from which can be distilled an understanding of general process. However, here I follow the opposite course by seeking a better grasp of general processes so as to understand an immensely complicated history (Stone 1996: 192).

Landscape Archaeology Defined

The following is a convenient working definition of landscape archaeology for the purposes of this book:

Landscape archaeology is concerned with the analysis of the cultural landscape through time. This entails the recording and dating of cultural factors that remain as well as their interpretation in terms of social, economic, and environmental factors. It is assumed that the "natural landscape" has been reorganized either consciously or subconsciously for a variety of religious, economic, social, political, environmental, or symbolic purposes. Evidence includes traces of earth-moving activities, patterns or sequences of vegetation, traces of fields or gardens, settlements, and various types of land-use practices. (Adapted from Metheny 1996: 384)

Fisher and Thurston (1999: 630) regard landscape archaeology as an outgrowth of regional landscape archaeology. They point out that it does not replace but is complementary to more traditional approaches such as excavation.

Landscape archaeology attempts to describe, interpret, and understand the development of the cultural features that occur on the surface of the earth. This includes both human settlements as well as the land between or beyond them. This study focuses upon the development of cultural landscapes, especially the economic infrastructure of fields, roads, canals, and so on, as well as symbolic, political, and religious landscapes. Emphasis is on how the cultural landscape itself relates to the natural environment, particularly on how the cultural and environmental spheres interact. Because landscape archaeology addresses both the cultural and the physical record over large geographical areas, landscape archaeology has the potential to be truly unifying. It can therefore bridge the gulf between "scientific" or positivist archaeologies on the one hand and those that approach from the perspective of social theory or the humanities (Thomas 1993: 20) on the other. Here I attempt to achieve an integrated study of landscapes in which ecological, economic, cultural, political, and symbolic features of landscapes are all treated to provide a broad and varied picture of cultural change through time. This picture is intended to complement that provided by more specific methodologies such as excavation, textual interpretation, or environmental archaeology.

There are problems, however, when a field attempts to be too inclusive, because such studies can become so vague or indeed so vacuous that their only advantage is that there is room enough for all (Thomas 1993: 20). This awareness of the potential vagueness of the subject is therefore reflected in the comment of Stoddart and Zubrow (1999: 688), who suggest that "the current diversity of landscape approaches is now too great to be encompassed in one definition or approach." That said, no attempt is made here to be comprehensive. Rather, this is a preliminary attempt to demonstrate the richness and complexity of the Near Eastern landscape record and to provide some insights into its development.

Why Undertake Landscape Archaeology?

Before examining the various approaches to the subject, it is appropriate to state why it is necessary to study the archaeology of the landscape (not listed in order of importance):

— The landscape provides the economic infrastructure and support system for settlements and society.
— It provides a receptacle for records of environmental change and contributes fundamental data concerning transformations of the earth's land surface.
— Landscapes provide evidence for long-term changes in settlement, economic patterning, and features that relate to social or religious changes. In addition, the landscape provides a fundamental context for features such as religious monuments or many inscriptions, monumental or informal.
— It provides the context for people's lives throughout history and therefore shapes their perceptions and way of life.
— Overall, landscape archaeology

provides evidence for long term human activity beyond the actual living areas themselves.

Approaches to Landscape Archaeology

Theoretical developments of landscape archaeology have followed the main trends of archaeology by shifting through a number of stages. These are not sequential stages, however, and different branches of the discipline practice a range of approaches. Often there is remarkably little cross-reference between the different strands of the discipline, with the result that in many recent post-processual studies there is, for example, scant reference to major foundation figures of the field such as W. G. Hoskins, whose seminal *The Making of the English Landscape* (1955) dominated the English school of landscape history. At risk of oversimplification, three broad strands of landscape archaeology can be defined as follows (for alternative narratives, see Anschuetz et al. 2001):

— The cultural-historical approach, or the school of landscape history.
— Processual approaches: Archaeological survey, off-site and quantitative studies, catchment analysis, settlement archaeology, and various ecosystem approaches.
— Post-processual approaches to phenomenological, ideational, and symbolic/religious landscape.

The Cultural-Historical Approach

This is well represented by the British school of landscape history, which draws on historical documents, archaeology, and the landscape itself (B. K. Roberts 1987). Because landscapes of the last millennium or so represent those that are most complete and well documented, the landscape-history approach provides more data on the medieval and post-medieval than for the prehistoric periods. From this standpoint, it is therefore entirely logical to start with "late" landscapes such as post-medieval field systems, which can then be peeled off to reveal a partial record of preexisting landscapes. Obviously, however, such an approach can result in a rather slender prehistoric record unless steps are taken specifically to seek out areas that are rich in prehistoric remains. For many areas, however, this is not possible, and so a volume such as Michael Aston's excellent *Interpreting the Landscape* (1985), contains only some ten pages devoted to the prehistoric period. For the Near East, the most complete landscape record may therefore be expected to remain from the Islamic or medieval periods. Consequently, we should look to the archaeologists of these periods for important breakthroughs in landscape archaeology; but at the time of writing, such work has hardly been started (see also chapter 3).

A key event in British landscape archaeology was the publication of Cyril Fox's *Archaeology of the Cambridge Region* published in 1923. This took a geographical perspective to settlement, rather than an artifact-based or antiquarian and site-based approach, and set the stage for the development of English landscape archaeology. This approach rubbed shoulders with the fields of landscape history and historical geography and often showed a bias towards the study of field patterns, place names, and historical sources such as the Domesday book. Few Near Eastern studies have produced a comparable range of material except perhaps for the fine reconstructions of Ottoman land use and settlement of Göyünç and Hütteroth (1997) or Norman Lewis (1987).

The Processual Approach

This approach embodies a much more self-consciously "scientific" methodology; thus Rossignol (1992:

4) draws a distinction between the "landscape approach," which incorporates geological and ecological variables into the investigation of past societies, and "landscape archaeology," which has an explicitly historical emphasis that excludes geological or ecological data. The adherence to scientific principles therefore looms large in the landscape approach, and there is often a rather dangerous tendency towards determinism, whereby the environment and ecology as well as factors such as population pressure can be seen to drive research. The processual school follows the methodological and theoretical canon of the 1970s "New Archaeology," with a resultant emphasis on environmental reconstructions as well as ever more detailed and increasingly sophisticated techniques of sample survey.

Methodologically, the processual school of landscape archaeology started to gain an enhanced definition with the introduction of the concept of the continuous landscape. This developed during the 1970s and reached the general academic community with the publication of a seminal article, "Frogs round the Pond," by John Cherry (1983). The concept of the continuous landscape, which is elaborated in chapter 3, has shown that as a result of ever more intensive archaeological surveys in many parts of the world, archaeological features or debris form an almost continuous spread across the terrain. Despite the technical success of the Mediterranean school of landscape survey, one criticism that can be leveled at its practitioners is that by focusing on small areas in minute detail, they sometimes tend to lose track of the broad sweep of history, as emphasis is placed upon the recovery of more and yet more data.

The Post-processual Critique

This school has reacted strongly to the positivist approach of the processual school, with its emphasis on the purity of space, the use of subsistence

models based upon the economically rational individual, and environmental reconstruction. Here subjective elements of the landscape such as memory, power, identity, human agency, or ritual are considered of fundamental importance. Building upon social theory, the sociosymbolic dimension of landscape is emphasized to narrate the way individuals perceive and experience the landscape (Ashmore and Knapp 1999: 1). During and since the 1980s a phenomenological school of landscape archaeology has developed and thrived, particularly in parts of Europe and increasingly in the United States.

Phenomenology, defined by Tilley (1994: 12) as involving the understanding and description of things as a subject experiences them, has an approach that is diametrically opposed to that of the processualists. Nevertheless, more recently there has been frequent appeal to the need to integrate and unify the two approaches. In some cases, however, these contrasting schools examine different aspects of the landscape, so that whereas processual landscape archaeologists deal with settlement pattern, land use, environment, and subsistence, post-processual approaches focus more on ideational landscapes and subjects such as ritual, power, or identity. This said, however, when dealing with the same landscape, the two fields will usually have divergent approaches and results.

By reacting against the most mechanistic and generalizing of the processualist traits, the post-processualists have enabled the processualist landscape archaeologists to modify some of their more rigid views such as the orthodoxy of applying aspects of economic maximization models to ancient settlement systems. Unfortunately, the post-processual critique has frequently entailed an underrepresentation of the environment, with the result that human-environment relationships have been woefully undertheorized

(McGlade 1997: 461). Clearly, both phenomenological and functionalist/positivist interpretations can be applied to landscape analysis, a point that becomes particularly evident in chapter 9.

There is undoubtedly a need for an integrated approach in which both phenomenological and positivist approaches are taken into account. Here Winston Churchill's crystal clear statement, "We shape our buildings and they shape us," is apposite. Churchill, although not generally regarded as a landscape archaeologist, articulated a concept that could be well applied also to the landscape. Landscape must therefore be seen as both actively influencing the lives of the inhabitants as well as being, in turn, heavily influenced by the activities of those inhabitants.

Historically my own work fits within the second, processual school of thought, but it also builds upon the work of the British school of landscape history as well. In this volume, I place emphasis on the complexities of landscape development that result not only from interactions between humans and the environment but from the recognition of fundamental historical and social factors, an approach that has much in common with settlement ecology (Stone 1996; Anschuetz et al. 2001: 177–178). An integrated approach is essential if we are really to understand landscape development rather than simply impose our own ideological constructs on past landscapes. Emphasis here though is very much on the empirical record of the landscape in the form of tangible features and their interpretation. Nevertheless, notions of the ideational landscape are incorporated where possible because this approach, which has enormous potential for Near Eastern landscape analysis, has hitherto been underemphasized.

The dichotomy between functionalist and phenomenological interpretations of the landscape is well illustrated by recent studies of terraced fields in Yemen. Dan Varisco (1982)

suggests that that most functional of features, the terraced field, was also imbued with a metaphysical presence in the landscape. In the al-Ahjar area of northern Yemen, according to local belief, a man or a woman must look out for spirits on the terraced fields, especially at night. Although the productive function of the fields is without doubt, it is of interest that there was also a spiritual presence as well (Varisco 1982: 139). In a similar vein, Serjeant observed that when a new well was being inaugurated in the Tihama plain of western Yemen, it was deemed appropriate to slaughter a sheep or a goat: first, before the well was started; second, when water was struck; and third, when the masonry lining was completed. Finally (to accommodate the modern world), a fourth sheep was sacrificed when a motor pump was installed (Serjeant 1988: 150). Thus the discovery of the remains of a ritually slaughtered animal does not imply that the monument itself was "ritual," rather that it was deemed necessary to enact a ritual before such a feature was inaugurated. In the ancient Near East even a brief perusal of cuneiform texts indicates that ritual was everywhere but also that ritual and function existed side by side.

Ideational aspects of landscapes do not simply constitute ritual and religion, and in a much quoted phrase, Simon Schama (1995) has asserted that "landscape is the work of the mind. Its scenery is built up as much from strata of memory as from layers of rock." This should not simply be seen as an eminently quotable phrase, but it is all too true in the Near East today. Thus in the southern Levant since the 1948 war, an entire social, political, and economic landscape of a traditional Arab society has been erased and supplanted by an new landscape of the Israelite state (Benvenisti 2000). Equivalent radical changes, which entail both physical restructuring of the land as well as the erasure of social memory, have probably occurred

numerous times in the Near East (the impact of Neo-Assyrian resettlement springs to mind: chapter 7). It is one of the tasks of the landscape archaeologist to try to recognize such significant transformations.

Rather than seeing developmental stages such as cultural historical, processual, and so on, Preucel and Hodder (1996) perceive four different approaches to landscape and culture that entail a gradation from landscape as a natural towards landscape as a cultural entity. These stages, to some degree, also incorporate a change from a regional scale (natural approach) to those that are grounded in the individual. The four approaches are

(1) Landscape as environment, which entails landscape reconstructions and palaeoeconomies. Such approaches are well exemplified for the Near East by the studies of Higgs and Vita-Finzi (1972) for the Eastern Mediterranean palaeoeconomy, and van Zeist and Bottema (1991) for the vegetation succession.

(2) Landscape as system, which building upon the pioneering work of Willey (1953), refers to the need to place sites within a pattern of off-site and settlement-based activities. For the Near East, Adams' surveys exemplify this approach, and his work retains a freshness because of his consistent incorporation of historical sources.

(3) Landscape as power treats a landscape that is ideologically manipulated. For example, studies of the Neo-Assyrian kings exemplify this approach because of their attempts to conquer and settle a vast territorial empire (Morandi 1996b; Smith 1996).

(4) Landscape as experience takes into account the degree to which the landscape was perceived by the original inhabitants and was imbued with meaning. Ironi-

cally, in the Near East, given the superb textual corpus that often refers to the metaphysical world or the world of experience, this area of research has been rather untapped (Preucel and Hodder 1996: 32–34).

Different Types of Landscape

From the above it is evident that no single unified approach is currently being applied to the landscape. Pragmatically, however, the cultural resource manager or archaeological administrator must be able to deal with entire cultural landscapes rather than simply those parts that suit his or her mind-set. The definition of UNESCO provides some general guidelines by recognizing three basic types of landscape as follows (from Cleere 1995; see also Ashmore and Knapp 1999: 9):

— Clearly defined landscapes that were designed and created intentionally, for example, parks and gardens and other monumental structures.
— Organically evolved landscapes, including relict or fossil features such as fields and quarries.
— Associative cultural landscapes such as sacred promontories and religious settlements.

Of these three categories, clearly defined (constructed) landscapes could include, for example, major canal systems, Early Islamic landscape parks, and Roman centuriated field systems. Organically evolved landscapes would include rural tracks, small-scale irrigation systems, and terraced fields (traditional types). In reality, however, intentionally (clearly defined) and organic landscapes merge into each another, and so the UNESCO definition is most appropriate to the imposition of single landscapes by individual empires or regimes. Associative landscapes, on the other hand, form the remaining category, which encompasses religious settlements such as monastic communities, shrines on hilltops, as well as "natural places" such as springs and roadside temples (see Bradley 2000).

The UNESCO definition, although useful, is not universally accepted, and Ashmore and Knapp (1999) prefer: (a) constructed landscapes, (b) conceptual landscapes, and (c) ideational landscapes. In this volume, emphasis is placed on landscapes that fall within the first two categories of the UNESCO definition, while aspects of the ideational landscape are included as appropriate. Interestingly, the role of ideational interpretations becomes stronger, in fact unavoidable, when interpreting desert or mountain landscapes, namely, in those areas where population densities are lower.

Some Basic Issues of Landscape Archaeology

Landscape as Palimpsest

Most cultural landscapes contain an almost daunting amount of complexity (B. K. Roberts 1987: 85; B. K. Roberts 1996) because different levels of preservation and loss of individual features through time have resulted in any given landscape comprising a wide range of features dating from different periods. Therefore, there is little chance of achieving any form of total landscape archaeology. Rather, at best we should expect only glimpses of the landscape where preservation of key features has occurred.

Fundamental is the notion of landscape as palimpsest (Stoddart and Zubrow 1999). This deals with the progressive superposition of one landscape on another and sometimes the selective removal of parts of the earlier landscapes by later landscapes. B. K. Roberts describes antecedent features and successor features (1987: 78, 80) to show that each generation uses a property or feature, changes it, adapts it to its new needs and demands, and then passes it on to the next generation.

As a result, the inherited landscape will contain a mix of features of different dates.

It is important to note that in this book the term *signature landscapes* refers to those landscapes that are sufficiently physically etched into the land to remain in some way to the present day. In reality, however, there are many landscapes in existence: some are lightly etched to the point of being invisible, whereas others are heavily etched and are therefore visible to the naked eye (or the satellite sensor). We are therefore only able to see part of the ancient landscape, for example, either those parts that were imposed by the heavy weight of imperial power or alternatively those that persisted for a sufficient length of time to leave a permanent record. This leads to the simple principle that a feature will remain in the landscape until there is a force or process that is strong enough to remove it. Therefore, in the landscape, the powerful hand of emperors or caliphs or the continuous movement of numerous individuals can leave a conspicuous imprint. Furthermore, if a feature is heavily etched into the landscape, it may well be perpetuated through long periods of subsequent use, although again this depends on the nature of the landscape or social system that follows. In some cases, landscape features can remain in the landscape, and their very persistence can dictate subsequent use of the land. This "historical path-dependence" is illustrated by roads that can frequently attract future phases of settlement even though alternative, more appropriate settlement locations may be available (McGlade 1997: 477).

A brief perusal of the landscape record of any region will indicate that certain areas are used more (or at least for different purposes) than others. *Persistent Places* can therefore be defined as "places that were repeatedly used during long-term occupations of regions" (Schlanger 1992: 97). Either these can be zones such as valley-bottom lands that have unique qualities for particular activities, or they can be smaller, more spatially defined places such as springs or unique topographic situations. Even though persistent places may not attract permanent settlement, they may attract long-term episodic use. For the Bronze Age of the Near East, this concept refers to alluvial lowlands, as opposed to fringing uplands of highlands. Notwithstanding the above, fertile lowlands should not necessarily be equated with cultivation, because (as will be discussed in chapter 9) such areas also provide valuable pastoral zones with land use and landscapes switching back and forth between cultivation and pasture. Conversely, the problem of "invisible" (or nearly so) occupations of the landscape becomes significant when we must deal with the record of the remains of pastoral/nomadic communities.

The partial nature of landscape remains is analogous to the problem of interpreting ancient texts in which only one sector of society is literate, thereby imparting a bias to the written record. The textual evidence that the scholar witnesses is frequently that part recorded by the hand of state, the ruling authorities, or the literate elites. The landscape record must therefore be critically assessed by the employment of principles equivalent to those of historiography.

To analyze past landscapes, it is necessary to build up a range of principles that can be used to assess the completeness of the landscape. This process, termed here *landscape taphonomy*, deals with the processes by which elements of the landscape become selectively removed by both physical and cultural processes, thereby leaving us with a biased and misleading record of earlier landscapes. When assessing the overall development of the landscape, it is therefore necessary to conduct a three-stage investigation (fig. 1.1). First, we must determine to what degree parts of the landscape may have

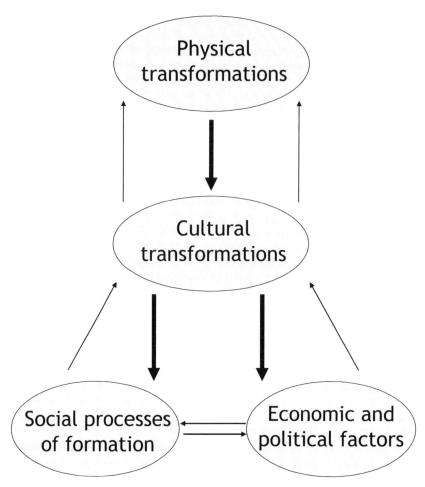

Fig. 1.1   Model of landscape formation processes. Solid arrows: main direction of analysis; thin arrows: feedback processes.

been lost or obscured as a result of physical transformations (Schiffer's n-transforms: Schiffer 1987). Second, cultural processes, which might have resulted in the selective loss of landscape features (c-transforms: e.g., the robbing of stones from previous field walls to build a dam) must be taken into account. Only after these two levels of analysis have been conducted can we move to the third stage, namely, examining the influence of social, political, and economic factors on landscape formation. Such analysis must not be seen as a simple progression from one stage to another, because each process can also feed back into the other stages, thereby causing further complications (fine arrows, fig. 1.1). A concrete example may illustrate the operation of this third stage.

Social and political factors do not operate in isolation, but they can themselves contribute to the development of the physical landscape. For example, the deliberate act of diverting a river either to thwart an adversary in battle or to deprive an enemy community of essential water (for example, in irrigated southern Mesopotamia) can then result in a complete change in the river-channel pattern and perhaps even the hydrology, which itself can further obscure or expunge the archaeological record (chapters 2 and 3).

Landscape Dynamics

Feinman (1999: 685) provides three tenets that he regards as central to the landscape approach. This approach

— entails a dedicated effort to examine the physical environment using a diverse range of natural science techniques, but with explicit social science questions guiding the research;

— recognizes human-environment interactions as historically contingent, dynamic, and accretionary, shaped by distinct cultural perceptions and past human actions; and

— includes the realization that human environments are in themselves partly products or constructions of dynamic interactions with human behavior.

These tenets were an attempt to guard against an unduly environmentally deterministic approach to the landscape, but by raising the image of "environmental determinism," there is an unwitting tendency to understate the significance of natural events. In reality, in cases such as the Holocene marine transgression over the continental shelf, or certain extreme climatic events, the environment clearly does have a major impact that may have determined the fate of vulnerable communities. Although this book does not intend to wade into these turbulent waters, some aspects of landscape dynamics are highly relevant to these issues, as will be discussed in chapter 10.

In contrast to an environmentally driven approach, the relevance of different cultural landscape signatures is evident in settlement ecology. The importance of culture is particularly apparent in the ways in which different communities or ethnic groups harness the productive capacity of the land. For example, in his study of Kofyar agriculture in West Africa, Glenn Stone contrasts the settlement signatures of the Kofya, who farm the land intensively, with the more mobile Tiv, who employ more extensive farming strategies (Stone 1996). Consequently, a switch from one land-use/settlement system to a contrasting one may take place simply when a new community acquires land from another. Consequently, evidence for a marked change in the archaeological landscape record does not necessarily imply that there has been a change in either the environment or the economy.

Recent discussions of landscape archaeology also focus on the dynamic nature of landscape development. The need to view landscapes as the product of long-term social-natural co-evolution is argued by McGlade (1997: 460), who sees landscapes as being nonlinear dynamical systems that result in occasional abrupt transitions between different stages of landscape development. Such transitions can result in abrupt "bifurcations" that entail very different pathways being adopted for settlement/landscape trajectories. Known as complex adaptive systems, such systems are not complex simply because they embody many components or behavioral rules but because of the nature of the global response of the system. Complex adaptive systems exhibit self-organization, which is a process in which the pattern at the global level of a system emerges solely from interactions among the lower-level components of that system (Camazine et al. 2001: 8). This process contrasts with pattern formation in which order is imposed from above in the form of some sort of blueprint (Camazine et al. 2001: 12). Clearly, both concepts are applicable to the organization of the landscape because some organically evolved landscapes (such as staircases of terraced fields in southwest Arabia) could well be evidence for self-organization, whereas many major irrigation systems unambiguously show the hand of human design and intentionality (chapter 10).

The rhetoric of human ecodynamics may unfortunately be lost on the landscape archaeologist who is plunged into a barren plain perforated by occasional tells or a pleasantly cluttered Mediterranean hillside, but careful study of landscapes over long periods of time can illustrate the relevance of such concepts. First, landscape complexity becomes particularly apparent when the landscape is viewed according to broad zones such as mountain landscapes or landscapes of tells (chapters 6 and 9). Each landscape zone often exhibits a "signature landscape," which is seemingly well adapted to local environmental conditions. For example, tell-dominated plains have an apparent stability through time. Nevertheless, this does not mean that long-term stasis was achieved, and so tells formed the sole type of occupation in perpetuity. Rather, a number of successor landscapes can be recognized, perhaps taking the form of traces of extensive cultivation followed by either mobile pastoral communities or increased evidence of irrigation systems. Each of these landscape and settlement systems may have been well adapted to the prevailing economic, social, and environmental conditions and were able to persist until replaced by another type of landscape. Signature landscapes should not therefore be viewed as static entities but rather as complex palimpsests themselves, each of which is conditionally adapted to prevailing conditions. Shifts, often abrupt, from one state to another are to be expected. Such shifting landscape patterns occur in every environmental zone discussed in this book and fall well within the definitions of human ecodynamics outlined by McGlade.

Similarly, Karl Butzer (1997a: 251) argues for the complexity of human-environmental relationships: "Human populations have always interacted with their environment in multiple ways, using it, shaping it, and devising alternate ways to bend its constraints—but also abusing it and sometimes degrading it. At the core of human history is a long tradition of persistence in the face of adversity and resilience in the throes of crisis." Inevitably, therefore, any study of the Near Eastern landscape must deal not only with the cultural features of the economic landscape but also with the effects of processes such as deforestation and soil erosion. This, in turn, entails the use of geoarchaeology, an approach that is all too frequently omitted from landscape studies.

Towards an Integrated Approach to Archaeological Landscapes

Today landscape archaeology can be seen to encompass cultural historical, processual and post-processual schools. Because there are so many approaches, however, there often appears to be little to unite the field except for the term *landscape* itself. Although processual archaeologists often appeal for the need for a scientific approach to landscape recording (see, for example, Rossignol 1992), one major advantage of landscape archaeology is that it does and should contain both cultural and physical components. Thus it should truly be an integrative discipline. A brief example (elaborated in chapter 9) should demonstrate this point.

In highland Yemen, the modern landscape includes great staircases of terraced fields that continue in use today. The sediments that have built up cover relict palaeosols that date back to a mid-Holocene moist period and that are amenable to analysis using an array of scientific techniques. Many field walls are monumental structures that date back to the Himyarite period some two thousand years ago and that overlie or cut the palaeosol. In places, these walls are associated with inscriptions, which require translation and interpretation. By remaining in the landscape, monumental walls also become enshrined in local memories, and so they retain their names and continue to contribute to the "social memory." Landscape features therefore form part of a grid of places that are well known to local people and form a complex non-Cartesian web of reference points on the landscape. Although observed

features are not "dated" according to western calendrical or archaeological systems, the local inhabitants are aware of their antiquity, and because such features continue to be used, they are part of the modern landscape as well. Furthermore, the local inhabitants can provide insights as to how certain features originally functioned. Such observations are extremely valuable and help us to extend our "scientific" observations on features such as buried soils. Ideally, landscape studies should therefore involve field mapping of archaeological sites and off-site features, scientific analysis of soil and environmental data, the employment of a linguist or ethnographer, a sense of phenomenological issues, and epigraphy.

Landscape in the Near East

In 1997 an entire meeting of the Rencontre Assyriologique Internationale was devoted to landscapes (Milano et al. 1999). This conference included significant contributions on both cultural landscapes and landscape archaeology. Chosen subjects included several papers on frontiers, developments of the physical landscape (sedimentation and geomorphology), urban and rural landscapes, Neo-Assyrian gardens, climate change, ecology, art history, archaeology, the frankincense road in southern Oman, oasis settlements in southeast Arabia, and so on. Although it is encouraging to see such a range of topics united under the term landscape, it is equally evident that there is little to unify such topics. This is partly because of the development of Near Eastern studies, which has tended to deal with the pragmatics of available data rather than broad synthetic approaches. To understand how such a situation may have come about, it is necessary to review the history of landscape studies in the Near East.

Studies of the Near Eastern landscape first appeared just after World War I, primarily as a result of the

development of techniques of aerial photography (for pioneers of aerial photography, see chapter 3). The flood of information that became available resulted in pioneering studies of the Near Eastern landscape by, for example, Stein (1938), Poidebard (1934), van Liere and Lauffray (1954), and Bowen (1958). Despite this early florescence, few formal studies had been made of the archaeology of the Near Eastern landscape until the 1970s and 1980s. In western Europe, parts of the Mediterranean, and the Near East, landscape archaeology often developed hand in hand with the growth of aerial photography. For example, Bradford's *Ancient Landscapes* (1957) used aerial photography and historical data in concert to analyze the development of centuriated landscapes of the Mediterranean.

Unfortunately, little attempt could be made to integrate these aerial studies with data from the ground surface because few archaeological surveys had been undertaken at that time. Kennedy and Riley's 1990 volume, *Rome's Desert Frontier from the Air*, represents a similar outgrowth from aerial photography, but because of its concentration on a single period, it can be regarding primarily as a monothematic approach to landscape archaeology. An important integrative step towards the development of a landscape approach was the publication of David Oates' *The Ancient History of Northern Iraq* (1968). This was a rare book-length attempt to analyze the development of a large region from the perspective of long-term historical trends and regional scale (as opposed to site-based) archaeological data. By taking a regional, environmental, and social perspective, this book has had a profound influence on the field.

In the Near East, archaeological settlement survey was born, almost prematurely, as a result of Robert Braidwood's pioneering Amuq Survey (1937). Important progress was made also in Mesopotamia, and Jacobsen's and later Adams' Diyala and Susiana surveys were fundamental because of their integration of historical, archaeological, and geomorphological data into broad synthetic studies (Adams 1965). These culminated in the collaborative volume with Han Nissen, *The Uruk Countryside* (Adams and Nissen 1972) and *Heartland of Cities* (Adams 1981). Similarly integrative in their approach (although not necessarily always landscape studies) were those emanating from the Michigan School and related projects, which resulted in the appearance of a series of classic monographs on the Deh Luran, Susiana, Hulailan, and Marv Dasht plains (summarized in Hole 1987; see also Hole et al. 1969; Johnson 1973; Sumner 1990). Although the works of Adams are not explicitly devoted to landscape archaeology, they have had a major impact on the development of the field.

In Palestine the pioneering surveys of Nelson Glueck (1934, 1935, 1959) were a great influence on the development of Levantine landscape archaeology, a field that became more attuned to environmental processes as a result of detailed studies of desert runoff systems in the Negev and adjacent areas during the 1960s and 1970s. During the final quarter of the twentieth century there was a boom in studies of the cultural landscape (Dar 1986; Gibson and Edelstein 1985), geoarchaeology (Goldberg 1998; Rosen 1986) as well as survey in general (Finkelstein and Lederman 1997). Owing to the lack of overall syntheses, however, these studies remained as isolated views of particular segments of landscapes or slices of time.

More historical than archaeological are the studies of the "Rome School" of social history. These practitioners, particularly Mario Liverani, Mario Fales, Carlo Zaccagnini, and Lucio Milano, have opened up the study of cuneiform texts to provide well-informed (albeit sometimes Marxist) perspectives on the ancient Mesopotamian economy, social history, and landscape

(Fales 1990; Liverani 1996). Not only are their studies historically informed, they also show an appreciation of the role of archaeology in the study of landscapes. Being a historian, Liverani cautions that the achievements of recent surveys by themselves alone do not and cannot provide a reconstruction of the rural landscape, but they do provide an overall framework for such constructions (Liverani 1996: 4).

The Approach Adopted in This Book

In the chapters that follow, emphasis is upon the development of the cultural landscape and its features in light of the physical, cultural, and historical context. It will be evident that geography and the physical landscape (chapter 2; figs. 1.2, 1.3, and 2.1) exert a considerable influence on landscape development at every stage, specifically by offering a range of possibilities. But rarely does it determine the actual trajectory of development. Before examining the landscapes themselves, the range of techniques for recovering ancient landscapes such as archaeological site survey, off-site archaeology, aerial photography, and satellite imagery are described (chapter 3).

Individual landscape features that form the basic elements in the landscape are summarized in chapter 4. When viewed together as coherent landscapes, these elements can be employed to describe the economic or social infrastructure for selected periods. Individual features or entire landscapes survive or are lost as a result of taphonomic processes, which include both cultural and physical process (chapter 3).

The Near Eastern landscape consists of component features such as tracks, fields, canals, agricultural installations, and religious features. Together, such landscape features may form a landscape "signature," which comprises a coherent group of features that can be shown to relate to a single entity or time period.

The signature landscape results from an amalgam of signals and activities conducted over hundreds or even thousands of years. Although individual features are difficult or impossible to date, the overall signature can be seen to belong to a broad phase of landscape history.

For example, a river channel, distributary canals, and settlements of roughly the same date and forming an alignment within the Mesopotamian plains provide an example of a "signature landscape." Such coherent systems are valuable because they contribute a wide range of information concerning the physical layout and infrastructure of ancient society. A range of signature landscapes are treated in chapters 5–9. It must be emphasized, however, that these signature landscapes provide only glimpses of the landscape of the period. Often entire phases of the landscape may be invisible or represented only by the settlements that were occupied, because the landscape features have either not survived or cannot be dated with any precision. Neither should the signature landscape approach employed be used to imply that ancient landscapes were static. The reconstructions described in the following chapters represent only particularly well preserved glimpses of the ancient landscape. Often one phase recorded (for example, intensive cultivation in the mid-third millennium) may have replaced an earlier phase of mainly pastoral specialization and in turn led to a subsequent phase of, for example, mixed pasture and cultivation. Such landscape systems may be represented only partly by landscape signatures.

There must also have been a considerable degree of spatial variation in landscapes from place to place. Just because one area exhibits a certain signature landscape, it does not follow that the adjacent region will exhibit precisely the same signature. By way of illustration, when surveys provide estimates of ancient population levels, one can infer that

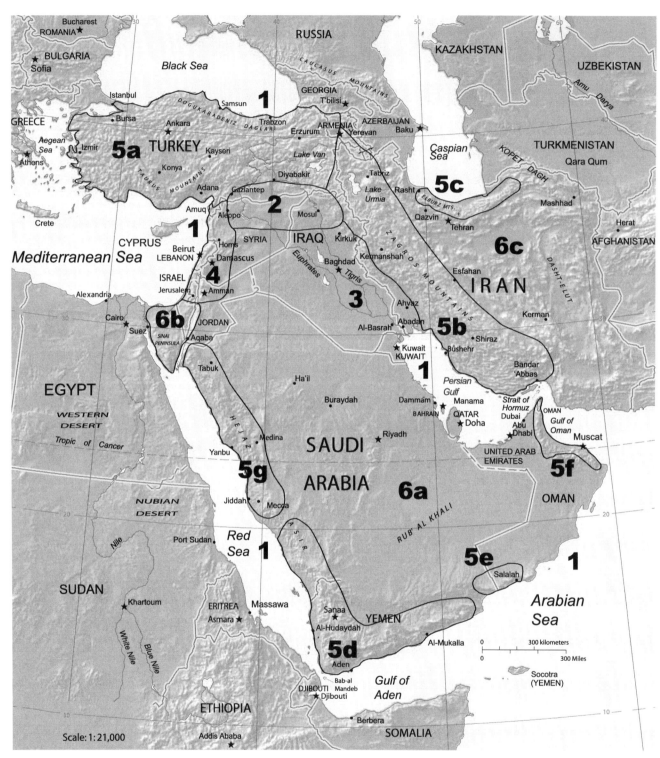

Fig. 1.2 The Near East, showing regional units referred to in the text. (Base map courtesy of The General Libraries, The University of Texas at Austin)

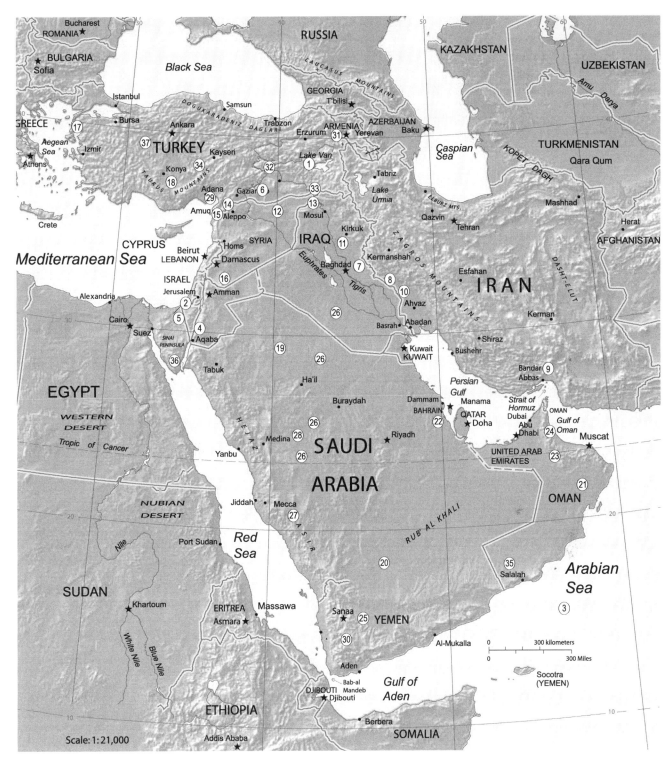

Fig. 1.3 The Near East, showing key places mentioned in the text: (1) Lake Van/Söğütlü, (2) Soreq Cave, (3) Core 74 KL, Arabian Sea, (4) Wadi Faynan, (Jordan), (5) Negev Desert, (6) Titriş Höyük, (7) Choga Mami, (8) Deh Luran Plain, (9) Daulatabad/Tepe Yahya, (10) Susiana Plain, (11) Nuzi, (12) Syrian Jazira, (13) Iraqi Jazira, (14) Massif Calcaire (Syria), (15) Amuq Plain (Turkey), (16) Hauran/Jebel Arab, (17) Troy/Kuçuk Menderes, (18) Konya Plain, (19) Great Nafud Desert, (20) Mundafan relict lakes, (21) Wahiba Sands, (22) al-Hasa (al-Ahsa; Saudi Arabia), (23) Bat (Oman), (24) Arja (Oman), (25) Sayhad oases including Marib (Yemen), (26) Darb Zubaydah pilgrim road from Kufa (Iraq) to Mecca (Saudi Arabia), (27) Taif, (28) Nejd plateau of Saudi Arabia, (29) Cilicia, (30) Dhamar (Yemen highlands), (31) Shirak/Tsakahovit Plain, (Armenia), (32) Altinova Plain, (33) Cizre Plain (Turkey), (34) Bolkadağ/Kestel, (35) Dhofar, (36) Mount Sinai, (37) Phrygia. (Base map courtesy of The General Libraries, The University of Texas at Austin)

settlement growth in one area was sometimes counterbalanced by decline in a neighboring area (Algaze 1999; Wilkinson 2000b). Such patterned growth and decline of settlement may also be paralleled by a similar patterning of the landscape.

Finally, chapter 10 examines various regional landscapes together by discussing their dynamics and how settlement, land use, and society may have changed through time in response to a range of economic, social, political, and environmental variables. Such dynamic landscapes are treated from the point of view of complex adaptive systems. Although archaeological studies have hardly developed to the stage where they can routinely be analyzed using such models, at present these concepts represent one of the most promising tools for analyzing complex and messy landscapes through long chronological spans of time.

2 Environmental Context

The natural environment provides the physical underpinning of the cultural landscape. Perceived in this light, the subject could be disposed of fairly quickly by cantering through geological structure, the environmental framework, and so on. Such an approach would, however, understate the importance of the environment to the development of the landscape. Consequently, I have chosen to summarize the basic environmental framework that is indispensable to an understanding of the landscape, and then I treat recent work that illustrates the historical progression of environmental change throughout the last 18,000 years or so. Finally, I briefly examine the dynamics of soil erosion and landscape degradation. This chapter therefore sets the stage for later chapters that elaborate on key issues as appropriate. For example, here I will move rapidly over the geomorphology of the great alluvial rivers, because this topic provides the underpinning of a later chapter devoted to landscapes of irrigation (chapter 5).

A major problem that has to be confronted during the analysis of Near Eastern landscapes is the difficulty of separating influences that stem from climatic change and those that can be attributed to human agency. Rather than seeing two separate forces, it is more likely that the two broad process fields operate in combination (Barker 1997: 274, 278). According to John Bintliff and Graeme Barker, one of the greatest challenges for regional landscape studies will be to bridge the gap between the ecological approach of

natural sciences on the one hand and the concerns of archaeologists and historians on the other (Bintliff and Barker in Barker 1997: 278).

When natural and human factors interact, the result may be either a cascade of responses or a complex sequence of feedback process. Consequently, the form or layout of the resultant landscape may be difficult to anticipate. For example, in a river basin surrounded by forested or well-vegetated hill slopes, if the population increases so that more vegetation must be cleared for fields, such clearance can expose soils that then become particularly sensitive to high-rainfall events. If major storms occur, they are more likely to produce high runoff, soil erosion, and valley-floor floods than if the vegetation canopy had remained intact. Such increased landscape sensitivity can result in greater valley-floor flooding, which in turn encourages people (perhaps) to abandon vulnerable valley-floor locations and move into the hills. This further exacerbates the loss of vegetation, which encourages more valley-floor flooding. However, if hillside clearance is conducted in conjunction with construction of terraced fields, then the land will become stabilized. Runoff and erosion may decrease, and so valley-floor flooding may actually diminish. Because there are innumerable combinations of these various types of landscape (forested, shrubland or *maquis*, cultivated fields, terraced landscapes), it can be difficult to predict how the physical system will change through time. This is especially so because various

combinations of landscape or land use will occur in different parts of different river basins.

Topography and Geology as a Framework for Landscape and Human Activities

Here I place emphasis upon topographic divisions that are particularly relevant to the examples discussed in this book; for greater details on the physical and human landscapes, the reader is referred to excellent general texts on the subject, such as Sanlaville (2000), Wagstaff (1985), and Beaumont and colleagues (1976), from which parts of the following summary have been drawn.

The physical geography of the Near East is dominated by mountains and high plateaus to the north in Turkey, Iran, and the Transcaucasus. Forming major east–west chains extending to elevations above 3,000 m above sea level are the Pontic mountains paralleling the Black Sea coast and the Taurus mountains, which parallel the Mediterranean. These mountains provide major barriers to human movement, and so occasional corridors such as the Cilician Gates north of Adana become especially significant. Between these highlands, plateaus from 500 to 1,000 m above sea level provide ideal conditions for agriculture and have become the bread baskets of Turkey. Such areas appear to have been occupied by tells from at least the aceramic Neolithic, and they formed particularly important centers of tell-based sedentary settlement during the Early Bronze Age (chapter 9). Further east where these mountain chains converge, mountains attain altitudes of 5,000 meters or more. Opportunities for farming become restricted as a result of the lack of cultivable land, short growing seasons, and the inability to keep animals grazing outside over winter. The Zagros and Elburz mountains in Iran, like the Taurus and Pontic ranges, provide similar barriers to movement, and again high intermontane plateaus occur between. The aridity of these basins can severely limit human occupation especially in the deserts of the Dasht-e-Lut and Dasht-e-Kavir.

The backbone of Arabia is formed by the Hejaz mountain range located immediately to the east of the Red Sea. Further south, the highlands of southwest Arabia rise to more than 3,000 m in the ʿAsir province of Saudi Arabia and 3,700 m in the highlands of Yemen. Extending to the east of this chain are the plateaus of the Nejd, which form an extensive dipping plateau interrupted only by occasional low curvilinear escarpments to the east. Further north, the mountains become attenuated into the hill country of the Levant, which attains nearly 3,000 m in the Jebel al-Shaikh (Mt. Hermon) range. Parallel to the coast is the faulted depression of the Dead Sea Rift, the continuation of which is the Beqaʿ, Ghab and Amuq Valleys occupied by the Orontes River to the north. The southeast corner of the Arabian peninsula is occupied by the United Arab Emirates, Oman, and southern Yemen, where coastal ranges of mountains attain a summit elevation in excess of 3,000 m in the Jebel Akhdhar of Oman. Although some of these mountain ranges such as the Hajar al Gharbi and Sharqi ranges in Oman and those bordering the Hadhramaut are too arid for sustained settlement, except in isolated oases, the Jebel Akhdhar and Jebel Qara of Oman, like their counterparts in Yemen and the ʿAsir,

intercept moisture-bearing westerlies and monsoonal air masses and receive moderate to high annual rainfall. Not only does this make these mountains more attractive for human settlement but also by shedding water to neighboring aquifers, this moisture can sustain oases around their flanks.

The above physical framework is founded upon the complex mosaic of the African, Arabian, and Eurasian tectonic plates. Plate boundaries are particularly conspicuous on maps of earthquake epicenters, which tend to concentrate along plate boundaries, as in southeast Iran (Beaumont et al. 1976: fig. 1.4). Especially vulnerable to earthquakes are parts of western Turkey and Greece, where the dynamic Aegean and Turkish plates and a number of active fault lines are found.

The Red Sea depression was formed partly as the result of tension from the movement away from each other of the African, Somalian, and Arabian plates as well as the associated uplift of the neighboring mountains. The associated mountains, which include those of southern Syria, Jordan, the Hejaz, and Yemen, feature enormous desolate areas of eruptive basaltic lava flows (*harra*), which date from Tertiary time until the last few centuries. This volcanic terrain includes the tribal areas of mobile pastoral groups in eastern Jordan and also includes the aquifers for settlements of western Arabia. In Yemen, eruptions associated with such recent volcanism have deposited ash horizons interstratified with basin deposits of late Pleistocene age, and in southern Syria, more recent volcanic activity has even resulted in Bronze Age land surfaces and fauna being overwhelmed. Plate movement, by producing overthrust zones in which the continental crust has been thickened and contorted, has contributed to the development of the highly folded chain of the Zagros Mountains.

Interior Arabia forms a low,

sloping, relict plain surface of great age that has developed upon Pre-Cambrian and Palaeozoic rocks. The western part of this low plateau comprises the Nejd of Saudi Arabia, above which younger sedimentary rocks outcrop to form the plains of eastern Arabia and occasional low escarpments such as the Jebel Tuwayq.

Of particular importance for mineral resources are complex zones of mineralization in the Taurus Mountains; obsidian outcrops in eastern Turkey, the Hejaz, and the southern Levantine mountains; and ophiolite zones of southeast Iran and Oman. The last-named zones, being rich in copper and certain workable stones such as steatite, provided important resources for the early complex economies of Mesopotamia. Obsidian was also an important item of exchange, and the Near East is positioned between four major source zones: eastern Anatolia, the Aegean, highland Yemen, and northeast Africa. Regional disparities of resource availability have contributed to the trade and exchange networks so that resources such as Anatolian obsidian were being exchanged with communities well to the south in Iraq, Syria, and the Levant as early as the late Pleistocene.

Similarly, limitations in the growing season of crops as well as the pasturing of animals outside will have encouraged some degree of human mobility, simply because it would have been difficult to maintain large communities and their animals year-round at such high altitudes. Although it is difficult to demonstrate the origins of vertical nomadic movements from high summer pastures in, for example, the Zagros or Taurus Mountains, to lower winter pastures along their flanks, the recent pattern of movement has a long history. Similarly the seasonal availability of winter pastures in the deserts of Arabia will have encouraged mobile strategies among the indigenous communities.

The single greatest integrating feature in the Near East is the basin of the Tigris-Euphrates rivers. Not only does this drain much of eastern Turkey, Western Iran, Syria, Iraq, and even parts of Jordan, during glacial episodes of low sea level, this basin would have extended to the southeast to take in much of Arabia and southwestern Iran. The catchment straddles the area of dominantly westerly airflow over the Anatolian plateau, whereas during the earlier Holocene, the southern parts of the basin would have fallen within the zone of monsoonal influence (el-Moslimany 1994). Consequently, at this time the basin would have received climatic influences from both the westerlies and the monsoons, which would have contributed rain in both winter and summer. Part of this enormous area of lowlands now consists of the arid sand seas of the Rub al-Khali, al Dahna, and the Nafud. Although seemingly unoccupied, these areas contain the archaeological imprint of past moist climates and associated human activity (see below). Even during the drier late Holocene, these were crossed by active caravan and pilgrim routes, and many parts of the area were routinely used by nomadic pastoralists (chapter 8).

The following topographical/geographical regions are discussed in text (see fig. 1.2):

1. The Coasts: Mediterranean, Black Sea, the gulf, the Red Sea, and Indian Ocean.
2. Upper Mesopotamia, the Jazira, and adjacent areas of northern Syria, Iraq, and Turkey; the semiarid steppe.
3. Major irrigated lowlands of Iraq, the Tigris-Euphrates valleys (within zone 2), and adjacent areas in the Zagros fringe.
4. The Levantine uplands and the adjacent rift valley.
5. The mountains consisting of the Taurus/Amanus, Pontic highlands of Anatolia (a), the Zagros (b), the Elburz (c) the 'Asir and Yemen highlands (d) the Jebels Akhdar and Qara of Oman (f and e), and the Hejaz of Saudi Arabia (g).
6. The deserts of Arabia (a), the Negev/Sinai (b), and Iran (c).

Climate Today and during the Last 20,000 Years

Owing to its location within the subtropical high-pressure belt, much of the Near East experiences an arid or semiarid climate (Roberts and Wright 1993). Northern areas, namely, Anatolia, Iran, northern Syria, northern Iraq, and the Levant, receive most of their precipitation in winter as a result of the passage of depressions moving from the west and whose tracks are steered by the subtropical jet stream (Wigley and Farmer 1982; Beaumont et al. 1976: fig. 2.2). Low-pressure cells and associated winter rainfall penetrate as far east as Afghanistan and as far south as Oman. In summer when moisture-bearing westerlies shift to the north, the subtropical high-pressure zone moves north, so that the typically subsiding air results in dry conditions over the Mediterranean and Fertile Crescent. In winter, however, very cold air masses can develop over the Anatolian and Iranian plateaus so that depressions are steered to the north and south of the plateaus, which experience dry winter conditions too (Beaumont et al. 1976: 52).

Southern parts of Arabia receive much of their rainfall as a result of monsoonal conditions that develop in the spring and summer. Typically, much of the Yemen highlands receives a split summer monsoonal regime, with an early rainfall in April and May and a later rainfall period in August–September, whereas southern Oman receives summer precipitation in the form of monsoon-generated mists. In addition, southern Arabia also receives some winter rainfall from occasional westerly air masses. Basically the monsoonal-driven rainfall pattern results from summer heating of the Asian landmass so that the resultant convection causes air to be sucked in to form the southwest monsoons. A counter current known as the northeast monsoon results from the development of cold high-pressure air over the Asian subcontinent.

The precipitation regimes that result from these circulation patterns are crucial to the development of agriculture and settlement. Moist conditions over the Anatolian coasts and mountains, parts of the Iranian mountains, the Levant, and the Jazira are the product of the movement of depression tracks from the west, whereas high rainfall in southern Arabia is a result of the above mentioned summer monsoonal conditions. On the other hand, low rainfall on the Anatolian plateau and parts of Iran results from the diversion of moisture-bearing air around these high plateaus as well as localized rain-shadow effects. The higher rainfall areas indicated on figure 2.1 provide conditions suitable for rain-fed cultivation, but where precipitation is between 300 and 200 mm per annum, conditions are marginal for rain-fed cultivation. This limit, however, varies from year to year and is contingent upon socioeconomic circumstances, the distribution of rainfall, and whether rainfall-enhancement techniques such as runoff collection are employed (chapter 8). Because the relative interannual variability of rainfall increases as mean rainfall decreases, human communities in marginal areas must accommodate themselves to greater year-to-year variations in rainfall than those in moister areas (Wallén 1967: fig. 1). Consequently, whether pastoral or sedentary, communities in the drier margins are more likely to experience greater instability of crop and animal production than those in moister regions.

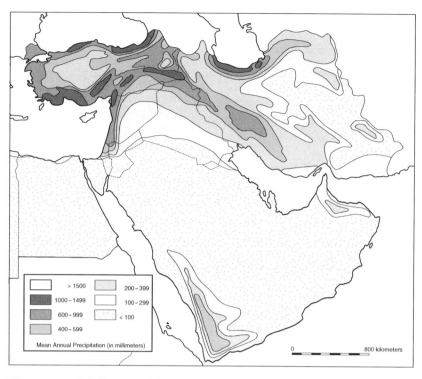

Fig. 2.1 Rainfall map of the Near East. (Modified from Beaumont et al. 1976: fig. 2.8.)

For the Near East in general, with the exception of areas of major population aggregation around the Saudi capital of Riyadh, oil fields of the gulf, and some irrigated areas, there is a broad correspondence between areas of higher rainfall and high population densities (e.g., compare Beaumont et al. 1976: figs. 2.8 and 5.2). In other words, higher levels of population usually exist in those areas where agricultural productivity is also relatively high. Although there are interesting exceptions, this relationship provides a hint of where prehistoric populations may also have been dense. Moreover, the identification of zones of long-term dense population and agricultural activity is fundamental to landscape interpretation because such areas are likely to have experienced greater overall transformation of the landscape (chapter 3).

Vegetation Conditions Today

As a result of the considerable degradation that has affected the Near East during the last ten thousand years, the vegetation evident today bares little resemblance to that sustainable during earlier interglacials, when human occupation was minimal. Nevertheless, there is still some relationship between climate and vegetation so that wooded or forested areas continue to be restricted to the wetter areas below 2,000 m above sea level as well as to less accessible refuge areas in the mountains. According to Zohary (1973), there are six main vegetation zones in the northern part of the Near East.

Desert occurs where rainfall is less than 100 mm per annum (region of winter maximum rainfall) or 250 mm (summer maximum). In addition to areas of rock or sand desert, this includes low-density xerophytic shrubs, herbs, and sedges.

Steppe is found where rainfall is in the range 100–300 mm per annum (winter maximum), and these areas are essentially treeless, although lines of trees occur along watercourses. Large areas of northern

Syria and northern Iraq fall within the steppic belt today, but owing to the considerable degradation that has resulted from the activities of both sedentary and pastoral nomadic communities, the region has taken on the appearance of a treeless agro-desert with extensive tracts of bare prairielike cultivation. On the other hand, in drier parts of the Nejd plateau of interior Saudi Arabia, where rainfall is only around 100 mm or even less per year, low-density scrub with scattered trees can extend along wadis. This apparently more well vegetated environment is probably partly caused by lower grazing pressures and little demand for wood fuel in these sparsely populated areas, as well as the practice of traditional restrictions on grazing within specially designated *hema* reserves (chapter 8).

Steppe forest forms a transitional zone where rainfall is today 300–600 mm (winter maximum). Vegetation consists of open xeric woodland to steppe with scattered shrubs and trees, which include pine, oak, and pistachio as well as juniper (for additional details for the Jazira, see chapter 6).

Eu-Mediterranean woodland occurs where rainfall falls in the range 300–1,000 mm (winter maximum) at altitudes up to around 400 m. The main tree species are deciduous and evergreen oak, pine, cedar, pistachio, and olive.

Oro-Mediterranean forest occurs in wetter areas with rainfall in excess of 600 mm (winter maximum) and at altitudes between 400 and 2,000 m above sea level. This zone is often dominated by deciduous oak with pine and cedar in parts of Turkey and Lebanon.

Mesic Euxinian forest (also known as the Pontic and humid deciduous forest zone) occurs where rainfall is greater than 600 mm. This includes areas specifically along the Black Sea coast and adjacent parts of Transcaucasia. Among the large number of species encountered are sweet chestnut, hornbeam, oriental spruce, alder, beech, fir, and pine (Dewdney 1971: 53).

Southwest Arabia falls within the Sudanian and Saharo-Arabian plant geographic zones and the rich flora, which shares links with northeast Africa, includes the presence of frequent succulents (Scholte et al. 1991). Again, degradation has resulted in the apparent loss of much woodland, although sparse *Ziziphus spina-christi* (Christ's thorn) and *Acacia* woodland are occasionally present, especially in the high western highlands more than 1,800 m above sea level. This area consists of a patchwork of xeromorphic woodland mixed with grass and bush savanna extending as far north as 22 degrees north latitude, which, in turn merges to drier areas with semidesert shrublands and xeric grasslands (TAVO map A VI 1).

In Oman, the Jebels Qara and Akhdhar are covered by various forms of dry xeromorphic woodland. Of these, the former area also has been made famous by the presence of frankincense *(Boswellia sacra)*. Within the deserts of interior Arabia, the dominant vegetation type is a xeromorphic open dwarf shrubland, which merges with xeromorphic grassland and desert with local *sabkha* (salt marsh) and salt deserts in the low relief coastal zone of the gulf. Very dry steppe is also found within parts of interior Anatolia as well as further east on the Iranian plateau.

Environmental Change

It is rarely possible to measure past climate or climate change directly, and the conventional alternative is to employ proxy indicators that can act as a substitute for climate and which are thought to correlate with it. For example, pollen (itself a proxy for vegetation), rising or falling lake levels, microfossils, and carbon or oxygen isotopes are all proxy indicators, each of which respond to factors that themselves reflect climate. Pioneering studies of environmental

change undertaken from the 1950s by Karl Butzer (1958, 1971), Hubert Lamb (1977), and others clearly demonstrate that Holocene climate was dynamic through time. Butzer recognized that the Near East was subdivided into climatic provinces, each of which had its own trajectory of climatic change through the period since the Late Glacial Maximum. Nevertheless, because of the dearth of detailed and well-dated studies, it was possible for some to assert that the Holocene was in fact a period of stable climate (Raikes 1967). Although Holocene stability is apparent from some ice-core data, this is relative to the instability of the Pleistocene cool periods, which showed wild swings in temperature and precipitation between ten thousand and eighty thousand years ago, and especially during the glacial-interglacial transition between twenty thousand and ten thousand years ago. In fact, recent high-resolution studies of ocean cores closer to human population centers in the Near East than the Greenland ice sheets demonstrate that Holocene climate (i.e., during the last 11,500 calendar years) was prone to significant fluctuations. This is well illustrated in the Indian Ocean, where annually laminated cores indicate variations in monsoonal circulation, salinity, and sea surface temperature of the order of one dry phase every one hundred–two hundred years (Doose-Rolinski et al. 2001). Other studies suggest that there were larger, fairly abrupt cooling events of the order of every one thousand to two thousand years (de Menocal 2001: 668). At a still longer timescale, broader climatic trends extending over millennia are distinguishable, as will be discussed below. What is less clear is to what degree moist or dry intervals occurred over the entire Near East or were simply restricted to certain climatic zones. Specifically problematic is the area of northern Syria and northern Iraq. This area (the Jazira) is well known for its well-developed network of large

Bronze Age settlements, but unfortunately it lacks high-resolution proxy records of fine temporal range. Recent soil micromorphological studies by Marie-Agnes Courty (1994) provide a framework for understanding environmental changes in this region, but it is difficult to compare soil micromorphological interpretations of soil environments (which relative to ocean cores exhibit rather weak chronological control), with the high-resolution micropalaeontological, isotope, and trace-element data from sedimentary cores or ice laminations. Further geoarchaeological evidence for environmental change in the Jazira region is supplied in chapter 6.

During the 1990s several new climatic proxy curves have increased our understanding of environmental change in the Near East. Especially valuable are the so-called multiproxy records that detail changes in a wide range of indicators such as pollen, diatoms, and other microfossils, carbon/oxygen isotopes, and sedimentary mineralogy. These are available for different parts of the Near East (fig. 2.2) primarily where deep silts and clays have accumulated in lakes and marshes.

First, the Lake Van core from the Anatolian Plateau in eastern Turkey is based upon annually laminated (i.e., varved) sediments accumulated over the last 13,700 years (Lemcke and Sturm 1997). This replaces an earlier series of cores that were missing key parts of the stratigraphic sequence. The Lake Van analyses were on autochthonous carbonates deposited in the lake sediments and a range of elements that can be indicators of different salinities in this sodic lake (Lemcke and Sturm 1997). Oxygen isotopes (δ^{18}O) strontium:calcium and magnesium:calcium ratios were used to construct a palaeohumidity curve (fig. 2.2b), the veracity of which is supported by the impressive negative spike corresponding to the Younger Dryas.[1] Following this short, intense, cold dry period, relative humidity

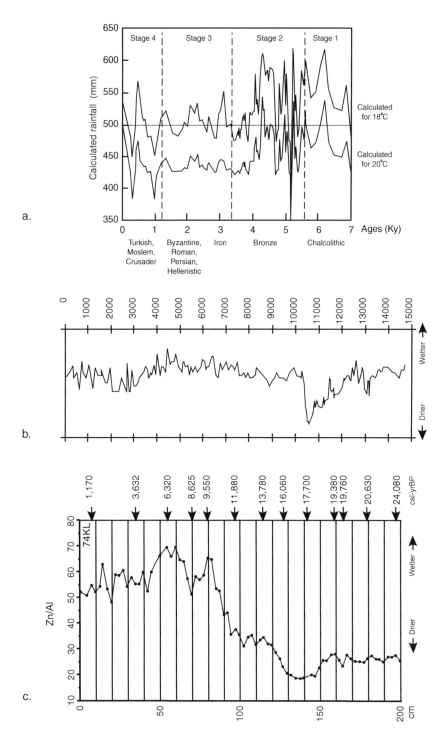

a.

b.

c.

Fig. 2.2 Climate proxy records from (a) Soreq Cave, Israel (modified from Bar-Matthews et al. 1998: fig. 9.5); (b) Lake Van, Turkey (modified from Lemcke and Sturm 1997: fig. 5); (c) the Indian Ocean (modified from Sirocko 1996: fig. 4e). Note that time scales are in (a) uncalibrated years B.P. (at 1,000-year intervals), (b) calendar years, and (c) calibrated years B.P.

increased erratically attaining maximum values for the Holocene between around 7500 and 4200/4400 years cal. B.P., with drier phases between 8000 and 9000 cal. B.P. which may correspond to a similar episode in the Soreq and Indian Ocean cores. From around 4400/4200 cal. B.P. (corresponding to the late Early Bronze Age) relative humidity declined over a number of cycles to reach minimum values between 3000 and 2000 cal. B.P., that is, during the Iron Age.

Unfortunately, some of the most impressive relict lake systems in Anatolia such as the Konya Plain system have been less forthcoming in providing detailed Holocene records. This is because the complexities of rises and falls of lake levels have resulted in parts of the sedimentary sequence being condensed by periods of soil formation or deflated away during episodes of desiccation (Fontugne et al. 1999; Roberts et al. 1999). Fortunately, a 16,000–year record from the crater lake of Eski Acıgöl in central Anatolia provides a more robust record from a wide range of proxy indicators (Roberts et al. 2001). Overall, diatoms, pollen, oxygen and carbon isotopes, and sedimentology demonstrate that the lake was deepest and was fresh water during the early Holocene until around approximately 6,500 years ago, after which the lake level became lower, and certain tree species such as pistachio, elm, and hazel diminished their relative contribution of pollen. The coincidence of lowered lake levels and decreased mesophilic tree species can most likely be ascribed to climatic drying. Significantly, however, oak woodland continued and even increased during and after this dry phase but then declined along with some anthropogenic plant species (hawthorn, *Plantago*) between ca. 4500 and 4000 cal. B.P. This lack of association with a decline in lake level, as well as the coincidence of oak decline with increased anthropogenic species and the appearance of large nucleated

Early Bronze Age tells in the region, implies that this decline was probably caused by human activity (Roberts et al. 2001: 733).

Proxy climate indicators from Lake Zeribar cores in western Iran indicate that the lake was significantly more saline and that atmospheric conditions were drier between 17,900 and 12,800 cal. B.P. as well as during the Younger Dryas around 11,600 cal. B.P. (van Zeist and Bottema 1977; Snyder et al. 2001; Stevens et al. 2001). Lake conditions then became less saline during the early to mid Holocene, that is, until around 4000 B.C. This suggests that atmospheric conditions were somewhat moister, after which the lake became slightly more saline as conditions dried during the late Holocene, especially between 4000 and 3000 B.P. That responses of lakes to climate or environmental conditions were not uniform, however, is indicated by the sequence from Lake Miribad further south in southwest Iran, which clearly indicates that lower lake levels during the earlier part of the Holocene were succeeded by higher lake levels after ca. 4000 cal. B.P. (Griffiths et al. 2001).

Second, in the southern Levant, a 60,000-year record from Soreq Cave near Jerusalem (recently extended to 185,000 years) is based upon analysis of carbon and oxygen isotopes from stalactite and stalagmites; dating is by ^{230}Th-^{234}U (fig. 2.2a; Bar-Matthews et al. 1998 and 1999). Again, the Younger Dryas is evident, in addition to earlier cold peaks, as well as a cool, dry event between 8200 and 8000 B.P. (not shown on fig. 2.2a). During the Chalcolithic and Bronze Age until around 4200 B.P., climatic conditions were moister than today, although the record is erratic. There followed over the next four hundred years a drying phase, which ushered in a late-Holocene dry period, which again exhibited considerable fluctuations around current rainfall values. In general, moister episodes in the isotopic records from Soreq cave,

as well as a second cave at Nahal Qanah, correspond to high stands of the Dead Sea as measured in the Mount Sedom caves (Frumkin et al. 1999).

Third, offshore records from Indian Ocean sediments provide a wide range of data from trace elements, oxygen isotopes, microfossils, sediment laminations (varves), and other indicators. Figure 2.2c, which shows just one of many trace elements signatures that were analyzed for a total record length of 24,000 years (Sirocko 1996), corresponds approximately to the record of oceanic upwelling of Zonneveld and colleagues (1997). Zinc:aluminum ratios are thought to reflect the intensity of ocean upwelling, which in turn is a function of the intensity of southwest monsoonal circulation; dates were provided by radiocarbon assay. This curve shows a marked increase in ocean upwelling between 16,000 and ca. 9500 cal. B.P. (ca. 14,000–7500 cal. B.C.). Ocean upwelling and co-related monsoonal rainfall then attained maximum values between 9500 and 6300 cal. B.P. (ca. 7500–4300 cal. B.C.) with a marked downturn at 8600 cal. B.P. There followed an episode of progressive drying from 6300 cal. B.P. until about 4000 cal. B.P. (ca. 2000 cal. B.C.), around which time there occurred a brief phase of dry conditions and increased dustfall from the north (Cullen et al. 2000; ca. 2200 cal. B.C.). The remainder of the Holocene then appears to have experienced drier conditions. That there is some degree of spatial variability within the monsoonal zone is illustrated by a high-resolution record taken closer to the Pakistan mainland, which shows a cooler and drier phase between 4600 and 3300 cal. B.P. (2600 and 1300 cal. B.C.), followed by warmer, moister conditions after 3300 cal. B.P. A noticeably drier downturn between 500 and 200 cal. B.P. is thought to correspond to the Little Ice Age (Doose-Rolinski et al. 2001).

The Indian Ocean proxy record

suggests that after the relatively cold and arid climate of the Late Glacial Maximum (ca. 18,000 B.P.), increased solar radiation in the northern hemisphere resulted in a broadening of the zone of tropical convectional rains, and so there was increased summer rainfall over parts of the Arabian desert, the highlands of southwest Arabia, and parts of northwest India (summarized in Roberts 1998: 119; Roberts and Wright 1993). Increased monsoonal circulation during the early to mid Holocene also resulted in increased ocean upwelling within the western Indian Ocean and Arabia. The early–mid Holocene intensification of monsoonal activity roughly follows the increased curve of solar radiation but with a moderate time lag (Zonnefeld et al. 1997).

In contrast to the Arabian environmental record, which closely follows monsoonal activity, that of the two northern sites (Van and Soreq) are in the pathway of the westerly depressions. Overall, there appears to be no correlation (either negative or positive) between Anatolian rainfall and the intensity of the Arabian monsoon (Cullen and de Menocal 2000: 861). As a result, there is no reason to expect moist phases in the Fertile Crescent to follow those in the south or Arabia; in fact, it is possible that the timing of moist phases is in opposite directions (Roberts and Wright 1993: 215). On the other hand, high rainfall in Turkey is correlated with patterns of circulation in the north Atlantic (namely, a negative index of the North Atlantic Oscillation). This is of immediate significance to the archaeology of the region because it means that flow in the Tigris-Euphrates headwaters (which derives in large part from precipitation on the Iranian and Anatolian highlands) is also correlated with the North Atlantic Oscillation (Cullen and de Menocal 2000: 860). Consequently, flooding events in the Mesopotamian lowlands, as well as stream changes that may result from them, may be linked with atmospheric circulation patterns in the North Atlantic that initiate crises in other areas within the same latitudinal zone. There may therefore be some degree of synchronicity of climatically induced crises in this zone of westerly flowing air.

In terms of human settlement and agriculture it is noteworthy that following a rapid increase in temperature and humidity both before and after the Younger Dryas there was a broad early to mid Holocene moist interval followed by drier conditions towards the end of the Early Bronze Age. Drier conditions then continued, albeit with considerable fluctuations, through the last four thousand years. Many of the landscape transformations dealt with in this book relate either to the tail end of the moist phase or to the subsequent drier periods, a point that will be elaborated in later chapters.

Holocene Lakes

Ocean cores usually provide continuous and incremental accumulations of sediments that are almost ideal for recording environmental change. This is not the case for many records on land, however, which provide an often incomplete and complex pattern of events that cannot always be simply resolved into "wet" and "dry" intervals. Nevertheless, in southern Arabia, support for the climatic sequences established by Sirocko, Zonneveld, and others comes from lakes in and around the deserts of Arabia as well as from dated organic palaeosols preserved below irrigated soils and sediments behind terraced fields. Increased mid-Holocene moisture is also recorded from northern Oman (chapter 9).

In Turkey and adjacent areas located in the zone of westerly circulation, some investigations suggest that mid-Holocene conditions were somewhat drier than today (Roberts and Wright 1993). On the other hand, more recent evidence summarized above suggests that the mid Holocene was also moister in parts of

the Levant. Increased mid-Holocene moisture is also provided by oxygen and carbon isotope analysis of land snails from the Negev and from salt caves relating to higher levels of the Dead Sea (Goodfriend 1990, 1991; Frumkin et al. 1994). In the Konya Plain in central Anatolia, lake sediments and shorelines provide a complex climatic signal that shows considerable variation from sub-basin to sub-basin. Nevertheless, lake levels were high and produced well-developed shoreline features around 23,000 B.P. There then followed a Late Glacial phase of arid conditions around 17,000–12,000 B.P., after which lakes and marshes developed in different parts of the basin at various time throughout the Holocene (Roberts et al. 1999; Fontugne et al. 1999). These Holocene moist phases (dated variously between 7000–5600, 4700–4200, and ca. 3300 B.P.; Fontugne et al. 1999) were followed by progressively drier conditions throughout the Konya basin.

The isotopic record from Soreq Cave, when calibrated against modern conditions, implies that the mid-Holocene moist phase was probably some 10–32 percent wetter than the last four thousand years (Bar-Matthews et al. 1998). This rather modest mid-Holocene peak in moisture (which is also evident in Anatolia, north Syria, and the Levant) appears to have been less marked than those in southern Arabia and the Sahara, where proxy indicators suggest a much moister early to mid-Holocene climate (chapter 8).

Rivers in the Desert

That Arabia was significantly moister during parts of the early–mid Holocene and late Pleistocene is evident from the system of ephemeral channels (*wadis*) that cross the peninsula from west to east. During moister phases of the Pleistocene, these often sand-choked channels must have once been rivers, if not flowing year round, at least with continuous channels down to the sea. In Saudi

Arabia, space-borne sensors of the shuttle imaging radar (SIR-C/X-SAR) system have enabled the original maps of Hötzl et al. to be updated (fig. 2.3; Hötzl et al. 1984; Dabbagh et al. 1998). The sensors, which have the ability to penetrate dry sand to a depth of around 1.5 m, reveal well-developed alluvial channels beneath thin sand veneers. Further east in Oman, palaeohydrological studies by Judith Maizels have shown that relict alluvial channels raised above the surrounding terrain as a result of sustained erosion and deflation of the fine-grained sediments were flowing throughout much of the Pleistocene, frequently with significantly greater flows than the current wadis systems (Maizels 1990). Finally, a French-Italian team has demonstrated that the Upper Wadi Jawf system in Yemen originally flowed through what is now an area of aeolian sand dunes of the Ramlat Sabat'ayn to link with the upper course of the Wadi Hadhramaut (fig. 8.6; Cleuziou et al. 1992). In this last-named area, enhanced flow also occurred during the early–mid Holocene moist interval. Although it is not currently possible to reconstruct palaeodrainage maps for a single time phase for all of Arabia, these channel systems suggest that during the Pleistocene, a much larger and more well integrated system of drainage channels flowed from west to east across the Nejd and Rub al-Khali areas to discharge into the Arabian/Persian Gulf (fig. 2.3).

Sea-Level Change and Holocene Coastal Landscapes

That spectacular rise in sea level was a consequence of the melting of the high-latitude ice sheets has long been known, but recent data have brought both precision and a more refined theoretical understanding to this issue (Lambeck 1996a, 1996b). For the Near East this rise in sea level of 120–130 m had a number of consequences. First, the entire area of what is now the Arabian/Persian Gulf was

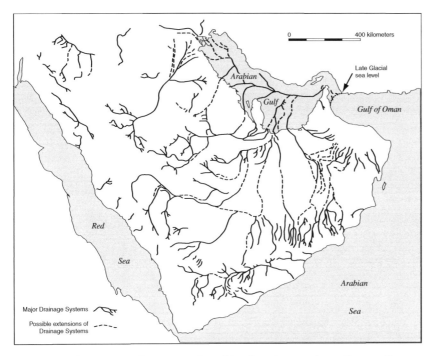

Fig. 2.3 Pleistocene drainage of Arabia showing major relict wadis recorded from existing flow channels and radar imagery. Note that channels beneath the gulf relate to a low Late Glacial Maximum sea level located by the Musandam Peninsula, near the head of the Gulf of Oman. (From Dabbagh et al. 1998 and others)

flooded, thereby dramatically changing the geography of the region. This same Holocene transgression resulted in large areas of the continental shelf elsewhere in the Near East being flooded together with their archaeological landscapes. Unfortunately little is known about what has been lost, but off the coast of Israel, prehistoric sites remain associated with their relict old land surface as well as various archaeological installations. Together, these provide part of an emerging picture of submerged landscapes that is appearing worldwide (Masters and Flemming 1983; Fulford et al. 1997). Sites like Atlil Yam (late seventh–early sixth millennium B.C.) are providing fascinating insights into the pretransgression landscapes at depths between −12m below sea level and present sea level (Galili and Weinstein-Evron 1985; Galili et al. 1993). Sites occur in conjunction with a dark clay associated with the freshwater swamps that developed between now sub-

merged Kurkar ridges (consolidated sand dunes). Atlil Yam has revealed a Pre-Pottery Neolithic well and a massive grain hoard, whereas Kfar Samir (at −1 to −5 m depth) yielded extraordinarily well preserved olive-processing areas dated from 5700 to 4400 cal. B.C. (Galili et al. 1997).

Around the Red Sea and gulf coasts, the main source of evidence for ancient marine communities are shell middens dotted along a raised shoreline some 1–2 m above present sea level (Zarins and Zahrani 1985; Tosi 1985; Biagi 1994). These raised beach lines and associated salt flats (*sabkhas*), which can be traced around the coasts of Oman (Hanns 1998), throughout eastern Arabia, and to Kuwait (al-Asfour 1978), have now been dated in numerous locations. In Oman such shorelines fall mainly within the range 6000 to 4000 B.P. Shell–midden settlements that date mainly in the range 4000–2000 B.C. (ca. 5300–3500 B.P.) appear to have developed in a more verdant

maritime fringe environment than currently exists (fig. 2.4; Biagi 1994; Lézine et al. in press). Estuaries, lagoons, and mangrove swamps were all more extensive than those of today's coast. A proxy indicator for mangrove woodland exists in the form of the large marine gastropod *Terebralia palustris*, which during the mid Holocene had a more widespread distribution around the coasts of eastern Arabia, apparently in association with more mangrove coastal woodlands, a higher sea level, and increased rainfall (Glover 1998). Unfortunately, there is no archaeological record of the submerged prehistoric landscapes in these areas. Shell middens represent the maximum stage of a marine transgression that rapidly encroached inland to obscure and partly obliterate any preexisting settlements.

A slight rise in sea level also occurred in Oman between 2600 and 1900 B.P. (Hanns 1998: 25), as well as further east along the Saudi coast of the gulf, where the same event may have created extensive coastal embayments (now remaining as *sabkhas*) that penetrated well inland. As a result, during the first millennium B.C. "inland" sites such as Thaj may have been much closer to the coast than the present geography might indicate (Barth 2001).[2]

Despite the lack of tangible information on the flooded landscape, the wealth of off-shore drilling that has taken place in the gulf has provided abundant indirect information on the submerged natural land surface. During the Late Glacial Maximum around 21,000 to 18,000 B.P., when sea level was around 120 m below present sea level, the entire floor of the gulf was dry. Teller and colleagues (2000) suggest that the extension of the Tigris and Euphrates rivers formed part of a marshy, lake-dotted environment for some 1,000 km from southern Mesopotamia to the Straits of Hormuz. This vast lowland must have included large areas of desert, because palaeoclimatic proxy data is unanimous in

Fig. 2.4 Relict *sabkha* evident as broad salt flat extending between coastal storm beach (to right) and modern palm gardens (to left and center). The raised mid-Holocene sea level of ca. ± 1.5 m is approximately the boundary between the palm gardens and the *sabkha*. Located to north of Sohar on the Batina coast of Oman.

demonstrating that conditions were both colder and drier at this time. Consequently, these deserts provided a source for the extensive dune fields of the United Arab Emirates (UAE) and adjacent areas. These dune sands were derived from carbonates and bioclastic remains that originally formed in shallow marine waters and were then exposed in the floor of the gulf to be blown inland towards the present Arabian landmass. The progressive decrease in calcareous debris inland appears to be a result of this dispersal from the exposed floor of the gulf. As is now well known, the Holocene transgression was at times rapid. When the modest vertical rise is expressed in terms of the very gentle gradients of the Gulf floor, this translates into a horizontal shoreline movement of as much as 1 km per year (a little after 10,000 B.P.) and a longer-term average of 140 m per year (Teller et al. 2000: 303). Viewed at face value, this suggests that coastal communities would have needed to have been mobile and followed a way of life that was a hybrid

between the current nomadic pastoral strategies and those of marine hunter-gatherer communities.

Needless to say, the dramatic pace of the transgression in the gulf has encouraged claims for this being the original Noah's flood (Teller et al. 2000). There is no shortage of other claimants for this event, however, and a catastrophic marine transgression across the Black Sea floor has been suggested (Ryan et al. 1997) but disputed by others (Aksu et al. 2002). Furthermore, mega floods that occurred along the Euphrates and Khabur River could also have had a drastic impact on the alluvial lowlands of southern Iraq. Therefore, although the association of the gulf rapid transgression with Noah may be questioned, there can be little doubt that this was a dramatic event that would have had far-reaching impact on the communities that occupied what was then the floor of the gulf. The impact of this rise must have continued until 4000–6000 B.P., at which time the sea had penetrated some 200 km or more

inland into the Mesopotamian plains (chapter 5).

Around the Aegean coasts of southwest Turkey the interaction between rising sea level and increased riverine sedimentation can be recognized in considerable detail. This has resulted in historically attested coastal settlements being marooned well inland of the present coast. This is a clear indication that the human population has been influenced by environmental change, but equally that the infilling of these extensive delta plains can partly be blamed on erosion resulting from human activity (but see Grove and Rackham 2001: 350). In other words, this region provides evidence indicating that changing environments influenced the human population and conversely that human populations impacted the environment.

In southwest Turkey, sea level attained its present level around six thousand or seven thousand years ago. In this area of deeply serrated coastlines backed by mountains rising to elevations of 1,000–

2,000 m, the Holocene sea first penetrated well inland of the present marine limit. For example, in the valley of the Büyük Menderes river, Brückner (1996) notes that thick marine sediments of the transgression extended more than 30 km inland. In the Büyük Menderes valley after 7000–6000 B.P., the shoreline then extended seaward and to the west as a result of alluvial aggradation and deltaic accumulation, so that by around 500 B.C. the riverine deltaic deposition occupied a position only 12–20 km inland (Eismer 1978: fig. 2; Erinç 1978: fig. 5; Brückner 1996). Similar processes obtained around many parts of the coast, so that, for example, in the Küçük Menderes valley, the shoreline of 750 B.C. may have been around 9.5 km inland. Although none of these figures compare with the 200[+] km transgression inferred for the Mesopotamian plains, the alluviation effected profound changes on the coastal geography. This resulted in major cities such as Ephesus and Miletus that were referred to in classical sources as being on the sea now being well inland. Similarly, on open coastlines such as the Altinova plain the earlier Holocene beach zone was some 2–3 km inland of its present limit (Kayan 1999).

Ilhan Kayan and colleagues have made some of the most detailed palaeogeographic reconstructions in the region of ancient Troy (Kraft et al. 1982; Kayan 1999). These show that an estuary 12 km long was in existence around 7000 B.P., at which time sea level was still −20 km below present. This was followed by progradation, so that around 4500 B.P., the coast was only ca. 8 km inland. Troy cities I and II were on a broad estuary, which extended to around 6 km inland at 3250 B.P., and 2–3 km around two thousand years ago (fig. 2.5; Kraft et al. 1982). Although the broad outlines of these reconstructions are clear, there is some questioning by Zanggar and colleagues of certain details specifically on the grounds that landscape recon-

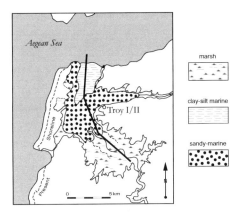

a.

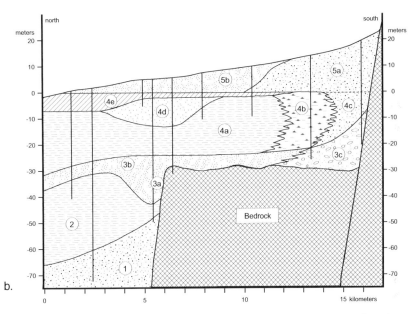

b.

Fig. 2.5 Section through the Scamandar floodplain near Troy showing the location of the settlement of Troy I/II in relation to the marine embayment ca. 4500 B.P. (based on Kayan 1999 and Kraft et al. 1982: figs. 10, 15). (1) Pre-Holocene coarse fluvial deposits; (2) late Pleistocene (ca. 40,000–20,000 B.P.) sandy marine sediments; (3) deposits of early Holocene marine transgression (a and b), (3c) alluvial fan of Karamenderes River; (4a) early- to- mid-Holocene marine sediments, (4b) coastal swamp or delta progradation, (4c) alluvial fan deposit, (4d) marine deltaic lobe, (4e) transition between marine and fluvial sediments; (5) middle- to late-Holocene floodplain aggradation, (5a) sand and gravel, (5b) sand-silt alluvium.

structions should not rest exclusively on the drilling of cores (Zangger et al. 1999: 95). It is therefore argued that by incorporating a more broad-based methodology, more cultural features such as quays and canals may be recognized to form a more humanized palaeogeography. Although there may be a need to

extend the breadth of landscape reconstructions, the coastal reconstructions by Kayan and colleagues provide an essential initial step for understanding changing coastal landscape.

The rapid infilling of coastal embayments with 10[+] m of riverine and alluvial deltaic sediments evidently results from the high rate of sedimentation of rivers draining the adjacent lofty and erodable mountains. Eismer blames the rapid alluvial infilling on soil erosion, which in turn was initiated by colonization and devastation during wars that followed the conquests of Alexander the Great (1978: 77). Brückner (1996) is more specific by attributing blame to the human degradation of a former open deciduous oak forest to an open maquis bush landscape, a point supported by Bilal Bey and colleagues, who estimate that the 20–50 km^3 of suspended sediment accumulated in the embayment during the late Holocene is four times greater than the geological "norm" (Bilal Bey et al. 1997). These reconstructions make a compelling case for the significance of human impact on the environment and landscape degradation. Nevertheless, a cautionary note should be added because such interpretations are, as yet, based on relatively little geoarchaeological data from key areas of sediment supply located inland.[3] Furthermore, rapid progradation would be expected to increase as sea level attained its present level around 6,000 years ago, and the volume of deep estuaries that could accommodate the incoming sediments decreased through time.

Holocene Vegetation Change and Landscape Degradation

Pollen analysis has provided our best evidence for changing patterns of vegetation during the Holocene period, and as a result of long-term programs of investigation by palynologists, it is possible to make tentative reconstructions of the distribution of woodland and steppe (van Zeist and Bottema 1991). However, because good pollen profiles depend upon the availability of deep sequences of usually lake or marsh deposits that are both continuous and well dated (Roberts 1998), these palaeogeographic reconstructions

reflect the availability of suitable sediments. Consequently, because well-preserved pollen sequences do not occur uniformly throughout the Near East, these reconstructions should be regarded more as models of vegetation belts than accurate reconstructions.

Furthermore, vegetation reconstructions do not necessarily provide a good idea of whether the woodland cover was "natural" or influenced by human activity, because it is often arbitrary and artificial to distinguish between these two states. Instead, in many parts of the Near East the colonization of the former Late Glacial dry steppe by woodland took place in the presence of significant human populations who had some impact on the vegetation cover before it could stabilize. Thus the woodlands evolved and developed in the presence of human interference, and in the vicinity of human habitats, woodlands have probably been managed for millennia (Roberts 1998: 189; Grove and Rackham 2001: 48–49). Such coevolution of the biotic and human environments should therefore be taken into account when pollen diagrams and palaeogeographic maps are interpreted.

Using the distribution of present-day vegetation, rainfall and temperature levels, and other indicators, Gordon Hillman and colleagues have reconstructed the potential vegetation cover for northern Syria (Moore et al. 2000: fig. 3.7). They suggest that park woodland and woodland steppe extended into what is today semiarid steppe denuded of virtually all vegetation (see chapter 6). If these reconstructed vegetation zones are approximately correct, they indicate that massive loss of natural vegetation has taken place during the Holocene and that grasslands and park woodlands have been replaced by an essentially desertified steppe.

Similarly, the most recently available pollen profiles provide valuable reconstructions of the main trends

in Holocene vegetation history, further details of which are supplied in the following chapters. In particular, three recent pollen cores have clarified earlier vegetation sequences, especially by providing refined chronologies. Here emphasis is on three diagrams, from north to south (fig. 2.6): (a) Söğütlü (near Lake Van: Bottema 1995), (b) Lake Hula in the Jordan Valley (Baruch and Bottema 1999; but see Rossignol-Strick 2002 for a reassessment of the dating evidence), and (c) a recent core drilled in the Ghab plain of the Orontes Valley (Syria: Yasuda et al. 2000). For the Ghab and Hula cores, tree pollen increased rapidly between thirteen thousand and ten thousand years ago as global temperature and moisture increased. There was then an early to mid-Holocene phase of mixed evergreen and deciduous woodland between approximately 10,000 and 5000 B.P. which corresponds to the Pre-Pottery Neolithic until the early part of the Early Bronze Age. Of importance for interpretation of human activity is the evidence, in the Hula core, of cycles of expansion of olive woodland during the pottery Neolithic, the early Chalcolithic, the Early Bronze Age, and Iron Age/Byzantine. Baruch and Bottema ascribe these cycles to cultivation of domestic olive trees rather than gathering from nondomestic stock (1999: 82). Similar increases in olive growth appear in the Ghab, during the ceramic Neolithic and variously during the Chalcolithic, Early Bronze Age, and especially from the Middle Bronze Age through Byzantine periods. At both core sites these indicators suggest that humans were having a significant impact on the landscape by cultivating olive groves. In both the Hula and Ghab sequences there was a stepwise decrease in woodland during the Early Bronze Age (Hula) or the later part of the Chalcolithic (Ghab), with the deciduous varieties of oak being totally reduced, whereas the evergreen increased, apparently at the

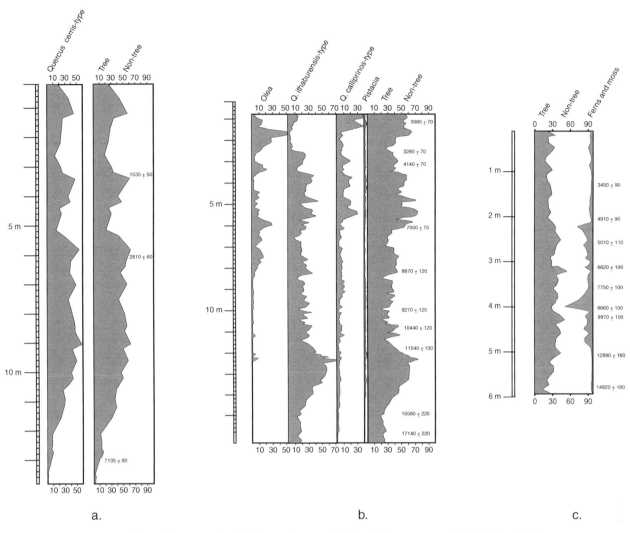

Fig. 2.6 Summary pollen diagrams for (a) Söğütlü, east Turkey (Bottema 1995), (b) Lake Hula, Jordan Valley (Baruch and Bottema 1999), and (c) Ghab Valley, Syria (Yasuda et al. 2000). Radiocarbon dates in radiocarbon years B.P.

expense of deciduous oak. This shift appears to represent the onset of the classic Mediterranean maquis type of degraded shrubland environment.

The trajectory of forest growth and decline in the highlands of eastern Turkey and western Iran provides a marked contrast with the Levantine lowlands because forest developed relatively late in the Holocene. This is evident in the Söğütlü pollen sequence taken from a marsh at the west end of Lake Van (Bottema 1995). Here woodland cover, represented by deciduous oak, increased from around 7100 B.P. to reach a peak around 5000 B.P. and despite

some diminution during the Bronze Age remained high, dipping only a little after 2810 B.P. (chapter 9). Therefore, although the advance of forest during the Holocene was complete by 8000–9000 B.P. in the Levant and parts of western and central Anatolia (Woldring 2002), in the eastern Anatolian highlands, a complete cover had not been achieved until around 5000 B.P. This delayed growth in woodland cover may be blamed on the late appearance of humid conditions on the eastern Anatolian plateau (van Zeist and Bottema 1991), a situation that accords well with the relative humidity

curve of Lake Van, which did not attain present levels until a little before 7000 B.P. (Lemcke and Sturm 1997; but see Roberts 2002).

Whereas the advance of woodland appears to reflect climatic factors that allowed forest growth to take place, the phases of woodland degradation are in part or largely blamed on human activity. Despite the recognition of early impacts on the woodland cover during the Pre-Pottery Neolithic (Köhler-Rollefson and Rollefson 1990; Yasuda et al. 2000), evidence for widespread deforestation does not appear in pollen diagrams until around 2000 B.C.

(Bottema and Woldring 1990; Baruch 1990), and it is not clearly visible until the Iron Age (Willcox, cited in N. Miller 1998: 205). Human impacts on the environment in the Near East seem remarkably late for a region that claims to be a hearth of domestication and urban civilization. These contradictions may occur because the early structure of settlement was such that human impact was fairly localized. Only during the later phases of history did settlement structure change so as to result in widespread degradation of vegetation beyond the lowlands (chapter 7).

This lack of evidence of early impact on vegetation contrasts with the situation in northwest Europe, where there is abundant evidence for woodland clearance by humans before the third millennium B.C. Given the massive scale of many Near Eastern communities in the third and fourth millennium and the fact that significant human impact on the environment has been inferred at earlier date from carbonized plant remains and other evidence (McCorriston 1992 and Köhler-Rollefson and Rollefson 1990), the pollen evidence appears to provide an unusually late record of human impacts on woodland (Walker and Singh 1993). Unfortunately, however, some of the most intensively occupied areas of the Near East such as southern or northern Mesopotamia are without good pollen sequences, and it is only in the Levant and parts of Turkey that pollen sequences are available in areas where evidence for evolving settlement trends is available from archaeological surveys.

The Beyshehir area of southwest Turkey now has a wealth of pollen sequences derived from several lake basins located within the catchments of large classical cities (van Zeist et al. 1975; Roberts 1990; Eastwood et al. 1998; Vermore et al. 2000). These studies demonstrate that in wooded mountains at elevations between 1,000 and 2,000 m above sea level, a distinctive phase of woodland

clearance known as the Beyshehir occupation phase took place in the later second millennium B.C. This phase appears in several pollen diagrams around 1450 B.C. or somewhat later and continued until around A.D. 600–700 (Eastwood et al. 1998: 70), at which time it seems to have been terminated by a phase of renewed forest growth dominated by pine. The Beyshehir phase therefore appears to represent "a full cycle from woodland clearance, through farming to abandonment and apparently back to woodland once again" (Bottema et al. 1990, Roberts 1990; Eastwood et al. 1998). In terms of the settlement record, the evidence is less clear, but by the Hellenistic, Roman, and early Byzantine periods, when both urban and rural scale settlements were common, human impacts on the environment were considerable, especially around the Roman Sagalassos (Vermore et al. 2000). Unfortunately, the record for human occupation during the early part of this phase is rather scant, although textual evidence attests the existence of small states in the region (Vermore et al. 2000: 592). Rather than being associated with a phase of colonization by sedentary settlement, this phase appears to coincide with the collapse of the Mycenean state and the empire of the Hittite Old Kingdom (Eastwood et al. 1998: 81). After this general phase of settlement growth and extension, which appears to have terminated after the Early Byzantine period, the organized and well-managed landscape then went into an apparent abrupt decline.

A simple increase in sedentary population cannot satisfactorily account for this distinctive occupation phase. Neither can environmental change be an explanation for the appearance of so many indicators of cultivation, of both food and orchard crops. The most expedient and necessarily tentative explanation for such a clearance horizon is either that Late Bronze Age settlement has eluded discovery by survey

because their remains are small scale, subtle, or buried beneath later occupations, or that clearance relates to a structural change in settlement that was caused by a breakdown of the earlier states. Such a breakdown may have been associated with a shift from long-term settlement on the plains during the Bronze Age to the more widespread settlement on hill slopes and more erodable uplands, as occurred in parts of the Levant (chapter 7). On the other hand, more recent analyses of three cores in the area of Sagalassos show that deforestation that starts around the mid first millennium BC and is fully underway by the third century B.C. correlates closely with a phase of abundant Hellenistic and Roman settlement in the territory of Sagalassos (Vermore et al. 2002). The above examples demonstrate that pollen sequences and human activity do not always correspond closely and only under ideal or fortuitous circumstances can they be seen to provide a close correlation.

A complementary picture of long-term landscape change comes from the Anatolian coast around Troy. Here, carbonized plant remains suggest a gradual shift from a predominantly open woodland and maquis in the fifth millennium B.C. to a more open agricultural environment, with cultivation and pasture extending on to the silted-up prehistoric estuarine valley floor, by the late second millennium B.C. (Riehl 1999).

One of the strongest cases for human removal of woodland comes from textual evidence, and Mikesell has assembled a wide range of written records to demonstrate how the original woodland of Mount Lebanon was probably destroyed, in part as a result of deliberate expeditions for cedars and other large conifers by the Assyrians and the Akkadians before them (Mikesell 1969; see also Rowton 1967). Overall, however, it would be misleading to depict vegetation history of the Near East as being one of forest clearance alone. In the Levant, summer-dry woodland spread at the expense of subhumid forest (Roberts 1998: fig. 6.10), and on uplands it is possible to discern various forms of savanna or maquis that exist in dynamic equilibrium with both browsing animals and fire and have been subjected to a considerable degree of management by humans (Grove and Rackham 2001: 45–71). Unfortunately, because archaeological surveys and vegetation studies have rarely been integrated, it is difficult to see precisely how the development of human settlement and vegetation change were interrelated through time.

The Geoarchaeological Record

Geoarchaeology does not supply a neat quantified record of proxy climate data but instead gives the impression that there is often a rather disorderly accumulation of deposits. These deposits, although reflecting a distinctive range of environmental and cultural processes, are frequently temporally interrupted and spatially separated. Nevertheless, the sometimes frustrating records of valley fills are fundamental to an understanding of landscape change because they not only include the actual sediments that were eroded during various climatic or human-induced phases, they also frequently encapsulate archaeological materials and even archaeological sites. Here I simply provide a conceptual framework for the more detailed geoarchaeological sequences that are occasionally referred to in the remainder of the book.

Geoarchaeological studies of alluviation frequently polarize between two extremes: those that interpret changes in terms of fluctuations in climate and those that consider human interference with the landscape as being of prime importance. To break this impasse it is better to analyze the geoarchaeological record within a broader framework as in the following conceptual stages (Frederick 2000: 57). First, it is nec-

essary to recognize a stratigraphic sequence; second, stratigraphic sequences must be fixed or constrained by a chronology; and third, the sequence so formed should be related to a number of proxy records for external variables. Such proxies may include vegetation change, isotopic records of climate change, indicators of land use, settlement, tectonic activity, and sea level change (if appropriate).

The stratigraphic record will normally comprise a range of alluvial, colluvial, lacustrine, and aeolian deposits (Waters 1992). Alluvial deposits, which are laid down by running water, include coarser bed load, and silt and clay that were carried in suspension. Colluvial deposits are normally laid down as a result of slope processes and comprise poorly sorted slopewash and downslope creep as well as mass wasting deposits from landslips and slope failures (Bell and Walker 1992: 187–202). Many geoarchaeological studies in the Mediterranean and Near East recognize the importance of soil erosion in the production of valley fills. Butzer (1974) has provided an overall assessment of the basic processes of soil erosion as well as the main factors that influence them. Sheet and rill wash, gullying, mass movements, and deflation all result in the loss of soil. Human-induced factors that exacerbate these processes are loss of vegetation, ploughing, overgrazing, the development of tracks and settlement on uplands, as well as cultivation, whereas environmental factors include the amount and intensity of precipitation, the latter being dependent upon the climatic regime (Butzer 1974; Redman 1999). Hence, tropical monsoonal climates, for example, can exhibit particularly high rates of erosion.

Vita-Finzi's influential studies of the Mediterranean valleys (1969) recognized regional climatic change as being a dominant factor in valley alluviation, whereas later studies not only emphasized the complexity of the alluvial record but also demon-

strated the significance of human factors on the alluvial record (van Andel and Zangger 1990). Subsequently there has been a swing back towards factoring climate into the record, with emphasis on the effect of extreme events such as very heavy rainfall (Bintliff 1992). The latter is well illustrated by Grove's study of the Little Ice Age, which demonstrates that there were major "deluges" at times when Alpine glaciers were advancing around A.D. 1320, 1600, 1700, and 1810 and that the ensuing floods had a catastrophic effect of the landscape, not only in terms of alluviation but also because slope failure and mass wasting occurred to a considerable degree (Grove and Rackham 2001).

For the archaeologist, such swings in academic opinion are as confusing as the sedimentary record itself, which is why it is necessary to place such analyses within an overall conceptual framework that relates to overall processes of soil erosion in the Mediterranean and Near East. Mediterranean-wide studies show that erosion and sediment yield under shrubland increases to attain a peak value in the rainfall range 280–300 mm per annum and thereafter decreases with any increase in rainfall above that figure (fig. 2.7a). This result is parallel with that derived by Inbar (1992), which suggests that under seminatural vegetation conditions ground cover will inhibit erosion as rainfall increases. In the case of Israel, Inbar has shown that sediment yield attains a peak value at around 300 mm of rainfall per annum, and at higher rainfalls it decreases (fig. 2.7b; Inbar 1992: fig. 3; cf. Langbein and Schumm 1958).[4] In other words, sediment yield attains a maximum within the semidesert fringe. This relationship therefore demonstrates that under natural conditions, as rainfall increases, denser vegetation cover inhibits erosion. This is not the case though for cultivated conditions because for any one class of land use, those years with higher rainfall experi-

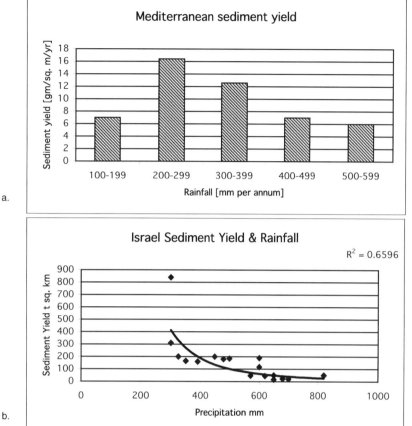

a.

b.

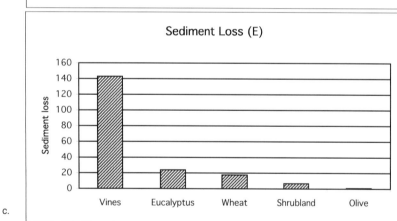

c.

Fig. 2.7   Relationship between sediment yield, climate, and land use in the Mediterranean basin: (a) Sediment yield according to annual precipitation measured at four sites in the Mediterranean basin under shrubland (based on Kosmas et al. 1997: fig. 5). (b) Sediment yield (in tons per sq. km) according to mean annual precipitation in Israel (based on data in Inbar 1992). (c) Average sediment loss (in tons per sq. km per year) for various land-use types in the Mediterranean basin (based on data from Kosmas et al. 1997: table 2).

ence higher runoff and sediment yield (Kosmas et al. 1997). However, because lithology, soil cover, and vegetation cover also influence sediment yield, the above relationship must be considered to be an ideal one. Because of the crucial role that vegetation plays in the process of soil erosion, it is necessary to incorporate assessments of land use into the interpretation of sediment yield data. For example, in a Mediterranean-wide study, Kosmas and colleagues (1997) demonstrated that the greatest rates of soil erosion occurred in hilly areas under vines, areas under wheat show intermediate levels of erosion, whereas olives grown under seminatural conditions exhibit much lower rates of erosion (fig. 2.7c; table 2.1). The low erosional rates under olives occur because the well-developed understorey of plants can inhibit erosion.

Unfortunately, generalized principles cannot be applied uncritically to the geoarchaeological record of valley fills because alluvial basins operate as complex systems. The response of individual basins can deviate widely from any norm. As a result of storage of sediments within "sinks" in various parts of the basin, sediments accumulate or are released with no obvious relationship to such driving factors as climate or human activities (Dearing 1994; Walling 1996; Trimble 1981). Such sinks occur in the form of, for example, colluvial or alluvial accumulations. As a result, there is often very little relationship between the quantity of material eroded from an individual field (or runoff plot) and that which is transported out of the basin.

Bearing these factors in mind, geoarchaeological studies from the Near East do, however, show an overall trend. At a general level there has been a trend from mainly climatic influences on valley fills during the late Pleistocene and earlier Holocene towards a dominantly human influence during the later Holocene (Goldberg and Bar-Yosef

Table 2.1 Average Sediment Loss in Terms of Tons per Square Kilometer per Annum from Eight Sites Around the Mediterranean

Land Use	Sediment Loss
Vines	142.8
Eucalyptus	23.8
Wheat	17.6
Shrubland	6.7
Olive	0.8

Source: Kosmas et al. 1997: table 2

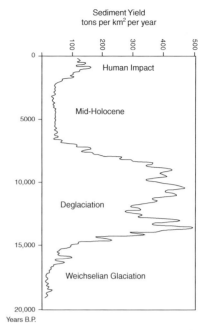

Fig. 2.8 Sediment yield into the Black Sea over the last ca. 18,000 years (after Degens et al. 1991, in Walling 1996). Note that sediment yield from the Black Sea drainage basin was high during the period of deglaciation, when ice sheets were melting and continental vegetation cover was low. Sediment yield was also increasing when human activity resulted in increased loss of woodland.

1990). For the central plateau of Jordan, Cordova (1999, 2000) makes a similar observation and also notes that during the last seven thousand years, human intervention has created a "noise" that obscures the evidence for climatic fluctuations. When proxy data for natural and human factors are related to the alluviation record for part of the northwest Fertile Crescent, it appears that during the early and mid Holocene, valley-floor conditions were fairly stable, and there was evidence for increased perennial flow (Wilkinson 1999b: fig. 8). By the third millennium B.C., wadi flow was more erratic, and perennial water flow had declined, with a tendency towards more "flashy" flood regimes. Overall, there is increased evidence for soil wash in alluvial sequences. From the second millennium B.C. this situation was exacerbated by increased withdrawal of water via canals (chapter 7).

In contrast to the episodic sequences of alluvial valleys, the marine record provides a more continuous and coherent view of long-term sediment yield. This is clearly shown for the Black Sea, where the sedimentary record demonstrates a low input of sediment during the Weichselian glacial period, massive increases during the deglaciation phase between roughly 15,000 and ca. 10,000 B.P., a rapid decline as vegetation cover became established during the early to mid Holocene and finally a rapid rise during the

last two thousand years as humans increasingly interfered with the landscape (fig. 2.8, based on Degens et al. 1991, cited in Walling 1996: 46). Similar records from lake sediments show that in areas that have experienced much less human impact on the landscape than the Near East, there have been considerable changes in sedimentation through time. These relate to varying degrees of human activity as well as specific factors such as the stripping of topsoil or erosion of subsoil (Dearing 1994).

In the chapters that follow, examples will be provided that illustrate various parts of this sediment supply system. Efforts are made to link the record of long-term settlement to the geoarchaeological, vegetation, and climatic record and to infer interactions between different sectors of the record. Just as land use is an important influence on sediment yield, features of the cultural record that relate to land use are also fundamental. For example, certain features such as ploughed fields will increase sediment yield, whereas other features, field walls, terraces, quarries, dams, even buildings will trap eroded soils and therefore act as temporary sediment sinks. Roads and tracks (or hollow ways) and threshing floors will all increase runoff, although changes in sediment yield will vary. Similarly, some canals and trackways provide foci for gully erosion, and their presence in turn can operate to extend the "natural" drainage network and in-

crease drainage density. Interaction between human and natural systems is therefore the norm rather than being a special case. This is also the case for the basic dichotomy between human and environmental influences. Although it is true that a radical change in land use from forest to cultivated field will result in an increase in erosion and sediment yield, such changes will also increase the sensitivity of the landscape. As a result, the impact of extreme events will be felt more strongly.

Environmental Change in Its Broader Context

The clearest signal of climatic variation comes from the Arabian peninsula and the Sahara, especially at lower latitudes where conditions were significantly moister during the early to mid Holocene, after which there was a significant climatic drying around six thousand years ago. These changes resulted from a northerly shift in the zone of summer monsoonal rainfall during the early Holocene, which then shifted to the south again as a result of variations in the receipt of solar radiation caused by changes in the geometry of the earth's orbit around the sun (the so-called Milankovitch effect). Reduced solar radiation in the summer produced a southerly shift in the monsoonal zone, which in turn contributed to the progressing desiccation between around 6,000 and 4,000 years ago. On the other hand, the early Holocene moistening of Anatolia as demonstrated at Eski Acıgöl seems unlikely to be explained simply by the expansion and subsequent retreat of the monsoonal belt (Roberts et al. 2001: 735).

Overall, many of the changes in Anatolia and western Iran may be explained by variations in the easterly movement of the tracks of depressions and storms (Stevens et al. 2001), as well as by different local catchment responses to climate as filtered by local variations in vegetation and hydrology. For Anatolia, a key conclusion to be drawn from the new multiproxy sequences is that Neolithic communities at sites such as Çatal Höyük and Ashikli developed when climatic conditions were at their most moist, whereas Early Bronze Age sites grew and then declined during a phase of progressive desiccation (Roberts et al. 2001; Wilkinson 1999b). However, that there is no simple linear relationship between atmospheric moisture and the development of complex society should be apparent from the coincidence of some major changes in societal development, for example, Neolithic domestication and Bronze Age urbanism, within periods of increased climatic stress, namely, the Younger Dryas and mid-Holocene

drying respectively. However, this should not be used to understate the importance of the environment, and some of the complexities of these interrelationships will be elaborated in chapters 5–10.

3 Recording the Ancient Near Eastern Landscape
Techniques and Analysis

The idea of recording the landscape of the ancient Near East is not new, and during the early decades of this century, rapid strides were made as a result of the development of aerial photography. Consequently, by the time that Bradford's book *Ancient Landscapes* was published in 1957, the field was already some three decades old. We should not therefore pretend that studies of the archaeological landscape are entirely new. Nevertheless, what distinguishes the modern school of Near Eastern landscape archaeology is that there is now much more systematically recorded ground control as a result of surveys and excavations. In addition, more is known about geomorphology and environmental change than formerly, and we also have a broader theoretical base with which to assess the results of aerial reconnaissance.

It is necessary to emphasize that different archaeological methodologies result in different kinds of archaeological data (Barker 1997: 277). In the Levant the original driving force behind many landscape studies was, for example, the study of the Roman frontier, the recording of Byzantine religious buildings, or simply the ability to undertake aerial reconnaissance. Such specialized monothematic approaches have been an important part of landscape studies in the Near East, but they are undertaken at the expense of a wider range of topics that are frequently neglected. Ideally, regional landscape archaeologies should treat the full range of available data (for an example of a good broad spectrum investigation, see the discussion of

the Wadi Faynan Project in chapter 8), but unfortunately this is not always possible.

Landscape prospection falls into three basic stages: first is the analysis of maps, aerial photographs, satellite images, and other data sources prior to fieldwork. Second is the recovery of data in the field using various forms of archaeological or geo-archaeological survey; ideally, this part can provide ground control for the first stage. The third stage entails the analysis of samples taken in the field by various techniques such as geochemical analysis, as well as the process of combining data collected in the field with that from the initial reconnaissance stage. Ideally, because Geographic Information Systems (GIS; see below) have become a fundamental tool for manipulating spatial data sets as well as the visualization of ideational landscapes and perception of the terrain, GIS analysis can proceed from the initial stages of a project. In addition, however, it is vital for the landscape archaeologist to understand the processes of landscape formation that may have been in operation in the chosen field area. Such "taphonomic processes" do not necessarily provide the field archaeologist with any dramatic new discoveries, but they do make it possible for the field and remote-sensing records to be interpreted in a more meaningful way.

Data Sources and Techniques
Data Recovered before Fieldwork

Maps provide a fundamental data source for landscape analysis and

should not be underestimated because in many parts of the Near East they show numerous features of relevance to landscape archaeology. These include field terraces, *khirbeh* (low ruin mounds of usually post-Hellenistic settlements), ruins (often later in date than *khirbeh*), water reservoirs (*birkeh*), dams (*sedd*), and wells (*bir*) (fig. 3.1). In addition, place names such as Khirbet al-Fulan, Tell Brak, or Bir Halu (sweet water) supply information on earlier phases of settlement and water supply before one even sets foot in the field. The availability of specialized project maps (such as maps for irrigation schemes) can supply detailed topographic information that, in turn, can help define mounded sites. The availability of maps at scales as large as 1:5,000 with contours at 0.5 m intervals, can be invaluable not only for recognizing sites but also for defining quarry pits, ancient routes, and canals (fig. 6.9; Wilkinson and Tucker 1995). Geographically corrected maps or satellite images provide a key base for plotting landscape data and can be used for geo-rectifying less geographically precise aerial photographs or CORONA satellite images. Therefore by the use of image analysis software, aerial photos, or CORONA images, can be warped onto a preexisting map base.

Air photography has long been a tool for archaeological mapping. In the Near East the first steps in landscape archaeology were taken as a result of aerial photography missions flown during and immediately after World War I (Kennedy 2002). Probably the first aerial photograph was taken by Mr. Felix Tounachon over

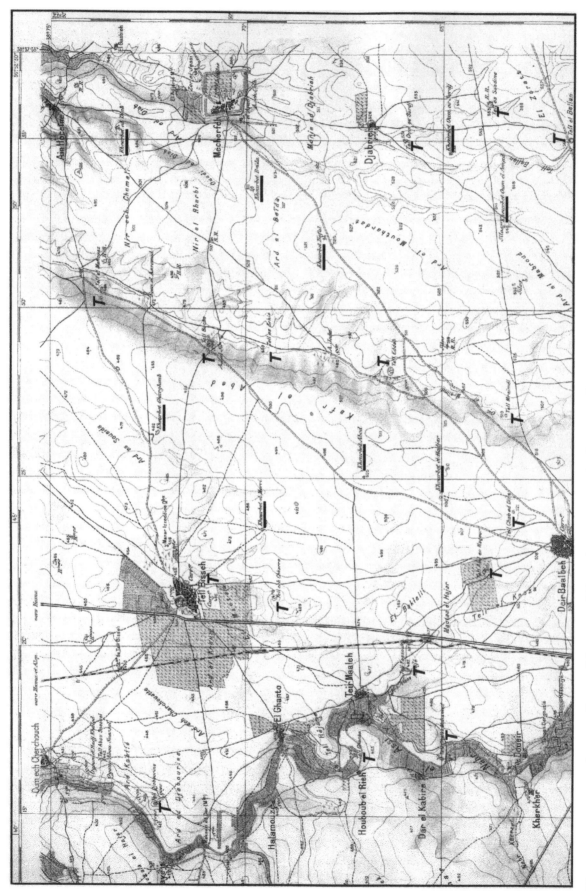

Fig. 3.1 1:50,000 scale map of part of the area of Homs in western Syria showing tells (T), mainly (but not exclusively) along rivers and wadis and in more low-lying areas, and dispersed *khirbet*-type sites (*kheurbet*) mainly occupying the intervening uplands. Note the massive square enclosure of Early/Middle Bronze Age Mecherfeh/Qatna along the eastern margin of the map. Each grid square measures 5 km. (From Service géographique de l'armée 1931 [Paris]).

Paris in 1858 (Verhoeven and Daels 1994: 519), and further progress in the art was made between 1877 and 1887 (for a summary, see Crawford 1923 and 1954). However, it was not until a German aerial photography unit was pioneered by Dr. Theodor Wiegand during World War I that serious advances were made in landscape archaeology. Wiegand's pioneering efforts made noteworthy photographs of Byzantine villages, forts, and monasteries as well as run-off agricultural systems in the Negev Desert of Palestine (Crawford 1954; Kennedy and Riley 1990: 28). These campaigns were published in 1920, at around the same time as a flurry of other publications appeared from Lieut. Col. G. A. Beazeley, Sir Aurel Stein, and others (Beazeley 1919; Stein 1919).

The great potential of aerial photography was also evident to some Near Eastern archaeologists, and James Henry Breasted undertook a number of photographic missions over Egypt, Iran, and the Fertile Crescent between 1919 and 1931 (Breasted 1933: 36, 85, 93). Unlike modern landscape studies that concentrate on ground surveys to provide a detailed record of cultural and physical landscapes, earlier aerial reconnaissances were usually more sparing in the use of ground control. Although ground control was frequently undertaken, often by simply landing the airplane or even by conducting quick trial excavations, these earlier surveys were dominantly aerial photographic reconnaissances (for overviews, see Gregory and Kennedy 1985; Schmidt 1940). Certainly, the massive potential of aerial photography for landscape analysis was rapidly appreciated, and the results of field campaigns during the 1920s, 1930s, 1940s, and 1950s provided a substantial body of data and theoretical insights. This has been well summarized by Bradford (1957), whose book used a wide range of Near Eastern and Mediterranean examples. More recent works on the

use of aerial photographs include D. R. Wilson (2000) and Kennedy and Riley (1990), the latter concerning applications of aerial photography to the specialized study of the history of the Roman frontier. To fully appreciate the impact of aerial photography, however, it is necessary to look at the huge increase of known sites in areas where aerial photographs have been used as a means of reconnaissance. This is particularly evident in northern Jordan, where a dense rash of new sites has appeared as a result of the interpretation of 1953 aerial photographs (Kennedy 2001:2).

In theory, the use of satellite remote sensing should have revolutionized landscape mapping in the Near East, especially because it provides terrain data on areas for which aerial photographic coverage is often unavailable for reasons of security. Although these new technologies supply valuable new data on the terrain, they have not entirely supplanted aerial photographs that provide a historical record of the landscape as it was before modern developments erased many earlier features (Kouchoukos 2001: 82). In addition, aerial photographs are capable of recognizing individual archaeological features such as field walls and also are more readily viewed stereoscopically. Thus by using overlapping stereo pairs taken along a single plane run, it is possible to view the landscape in three dimensions (D. R. Wilson 2000: 210–217). This is especially advantageous in the Middle East, where individual sites as well as landscape features such as canals have a topographic component that can be exaggerated on 3-D aerial photographs.

Despite their sluggish adoption by many archaeologists, orbital observation satellites now provide valuable data on the landscape of the Near East (table 3.1). In these systems, satellites rotate around the earth in sun-synchronous orbits at altitudes of around 750 km. They

provide views of swathes of terrain that can then be analyzed by means of a range of imaging software (Lillesand and Kiefer 1999; Donoghue 2001). There are two forms of earth observation systems: first are so-called passive systems that monitor electromagnetic radiation reflected back naturally from the earth's surface. This spectrum includes not only visible light but also longer wavelength radiation such as infrared and thermal infrared radiation. Second are "active" systems that send out their own impulse (such as radar) and then receive the reflection back as digital data. Today passive systems find the greatest use in archaeological remote sensing, although in recent years increased use has been made of radar imagery. Frequently used passive systems are the American LANDSAT, the French SPOT, and the recently released American CORONA images, but more recently IKONOS, ASTER, Indian IRS, and Russian Soyuz and KVR-1000 systems have become available (Kouchoukos 2001). The advantage of multispectral image data is that by providing a wide range of the electromagnetic radiation spectrum, these images enable features that are not necessarily visible to the naked eye or regular photographic techniques to be perceived. This is particularly valuable for the recognition of archaeological sites that include in their composition ash and refuse that differ from the surrounding soils and that can provide a distinctive signature on wide spectral range images such as the LANDSAT TM (Thematic Mapper) series. By combining high resolution with a broad spectral range, the new generation of imaging systems should make significant contributions to the recognition and mapping of archaeological features.

On the other hand, there is a distinct advantage for the archaeologist in the earlier CORONA images because these were taken during the 1960s and 1970s, before the appearance of much modern clutter such

CHAPTER 3

Table 3.1 Some Basic Imaging Systems Useful for Landscape Archaeology

Imaging System and series	Pixel Size and/or resolution m	Bands	Frame Size	Comments
Air photographs	< 1 m	Normally visible light only*	Stereo pairs; frequently 23 × 23 cm prints	3-D capability. Shows most sites and landscape features: fields, ancient tracks, canals, etc.
CORONA	ca. 2 m, 3 m	Visible light (photographic)	Long strips (negative or positive)	Main period of data collection 1959 (KH-1) to 1972 (KH-4B). Good for recognition of sites, canals, ancient roads, and field systems. Some 3-D capability. Best missions with KH-4B camera.
LANDSAT MSS 1–5	79 and 82 m	4 bands visible + near infrared	185 × 170 km	Introduced 1972. Useful for general land-use and geomorphological mapping.
LANDSAT TM and LANDSAT 7	28.5 m (15 m for panchromatic)	4 bands visible + near/mid infrared	185 × 170 km	Sites as small as 1 ha or less and some off-site features such as canals are detectable.
SPOT	10 m and 20 m	Panchromatic and near infrared	60 km × 60–80 km	Canals and some landscape features visible as well as many sites. Stereo-mapping capability.
IKONOS	1 m (panchromatic and color) and 4 m (multispectral)	Multispectral and panchromatic	Variable	Introduced 1999. Capable of showing details of archaeological sites down to the scale of individual buildings.
ASTER	15 m, 30 m, 90 m	14 bands multispectral	60 km	Introduced 1999. Shows a wide range of archaeological sites.
Russian KVR 1000	1–3 m	Visible light (black and white)	40 × 40 km	Introduced 1984.
Russian TK 350	10 m	Visible light (black and white)	200 × 300 km	Introduced 1987. Includes stereo-mapping capability.
Indian IRS	5 m (black and white), 23.5 m (multispectral)	Visible (5 m) and multispectral (23.5 m)	70 × 70 km (5 m pixel); 140 × 140 km (23.5 m pixel)	Introduced 1988.

*Because cameras can use infrared as well as conventional films, air photography has a capability extending beyond the range of visible light.

as houses, industrial areas, military bases, reservoirs, and irrigation systems (Kennedy 1998; Philip et al. 2002a). These images, which were taken for the Central Intelligence Agency of areas deemed as potentially a threat to U.S. security, cover a wide area of the globe (McDonald 1995). They were earmarked for general release by President William Clinton in 1995 and are available for viewing over the World Wide Web (http://edcwww.cr.usgs.gov/). Being photographs, these lack the wide spectral range of the more recent satellite images, but they do provide remarkably high-quality views of the Near Eastern landscape. Not only are archaeological sites frequently readily visible, but specific landscape features such as canals, some field systems, and ancient routes can also be recognized (fig. 3.2).

Emerging techniques include radar images that generate a pulse, which is then received by a radar antenna to construct an image. By detecting variations in surface roughness or by penetrating, for

Fig. 3.2 Representative views of part of the landscape to the west of Tell Hamoukar (Syria) showing differing image quality according to imaging system and time of year. Left: SPOT image (taken between 1992 and 1995). Center: CORONA photograph (December 1969). Right: CORONA photograph (May 1972). Note that the strong dark lines running from top right to bottom left are linear hollows (see chapters 4 and 6); the diffuse gray feature trending from the top to the bottom left corner appears to be the course of a relict wadi infilled with plough wash. (By Jason Ur; courtesy of U.S. Geological Survey)

example, dry sand, radar can provide an image of subsurface terrain. This technique has given remarkable views of early drainage channels such as the recent images of relict drainage systems in Saudi Arabia (fig. 2.3; Dabbagh et al. 1998). The wide spectral range of LANDSAT and especially specialized sensors such as ASTER and MODIS are particularly valuable for assessing modern land use and vegetation, which, in turn, can be used as a baseline for estimating past land-use systems (Kouchoukos 2001: 83).

Although remote sensing is proving to be a valuable technique for the recovery of landscape data, the Middle East continues to be rather poorly served by archaeological remote sensing studies. There are few publications that can be compared with satellite and aerial photographic studies undertaken on,

for example, Mayan land-use systems (Adams et al. 1981; Pope and Dahlin 1989), pre-Hispanic fields in Peru (Moore 1988), and New World roads (Trombold 1991). Nevertheless, the work of Robert Adams (1981) and Verhoeven and Daels (1994) on Mesopotamian settlement patterns; Brunner (1997) and Gentelle (1998) on South Arabian irrigation; Tate (1992) and Gentelle (1985) on Syrian field systems; van Liere and Lauffray (1954) on north Syrian landscapes (Ur 2002, 2003); Kennedy (1998) and Kennedy and Riley (1990) on the Roman frontier all demonstrate the potential of remote sensing for recording ancient landscapes.

Data Recovery by Field Work
Archaeological Site Survey

Archaeological survey, which aims to locate and analyze the distribution

of ancient settlements, usually according to period, supplies the basic data framework for the landscape archaeology of a region. Archaeological survey does not, however, always supply information on the landscape features themselves, unless the survey is of the "siteless" variety that investigates both the sites as well as the land in between. Traditional Near Eastern archaeological surveys frequently record only the mounded sites, whereas smaller unmounded occupations or more dispersed sites of low relief are often underrepresented (chapter 4). This is unfortunate because not only can low sites extend over large areas, but also smaller settlements (say those less than 1 ha in area) frequently form the bulk of settlement for certain periods; therefore, to omit such sites can severely bias the survey.

In recent years the archaeologi-

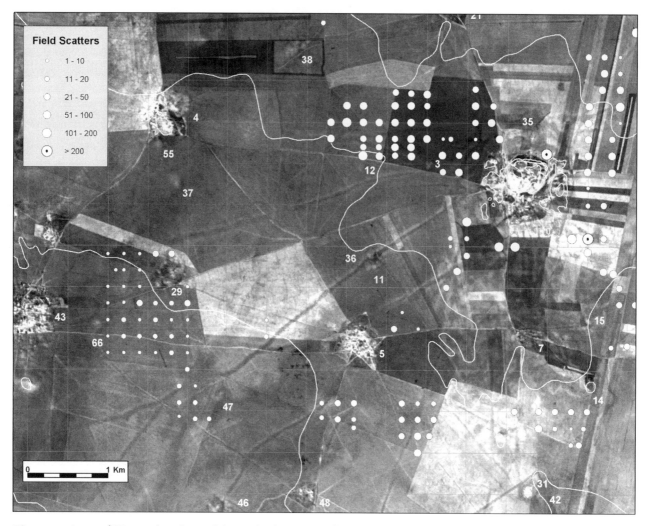

Fig. 3.3   Area of Hamoukar (THS 1) in Syria showing off-site collection areas (field scatters) in relation to archaeological sites and superimposed on a CORONA image. Note the well-developed linear hollow leading southwest from the major Early Bronze Age site of Hamoukar. Contour lines (at 5 m interval) are derived from a 1:50,000 topographic map (photograph courtesy of the U.S. Geological Survey; data compiled by Jason Ur).

cal landscape has been perceived as forming an almost continuous record, with off-site activity being represented by cultural features such as quarries, roads, tracks, artifact scatters, irrigation systems, fields, wine or olive presses, and threshing floors (chapter 4).

A basic tenet of off-site survey is that the notion of a site is a subjective construct and would better be replaced by a more rigorous definition that allows for the sparseness or poor spatial definition of human activities (Dunnell and Dancy 1983; Cherry 1983). Nevertheless, in many parts of the Near East, archaeological

sites of sedentary settlement are well defined, and often are mounded, so that a real distinction can be made between "site" and "off-site" areas. On the other hand, the presence of sometimes dense artifact scatters off site can blur the picture. Such scatters can be explained as resulting from a range of agricultural process, as well as locally intermittent settlement or other activity (see below, chapters 4 and 6). To obtain robust off-site data, surveys should be designed to supply a continuous record of the landscape in the form of transects across the terrain, or there should be a sample between

sites by means of sample squares (Banning 2002). Before 1990 the positioning of transects was impeded by the limited availability of good maps or the relative inaccuracy of hand-held mapping systems (such as the prismatic or Brunton compass). Now with the widespread availability of hand-held GPS (global positioning systems) units, it is possible to walk to specific sample locations positioned on, for example, a grid of 100 or 200 m to fix points within ± 5 m or even less. At each location a sample square or circle is laid out and all surface artifacts are collected (fig. 3.3; Ur 2002).

Despite the application of off-site techniques to landscape survey since the 1970s, Near Eastern surveys still lag behind those in the Mediterranean in terms of technique and quality of data recovery. The methodological differences are well expressed in recent volumes in the series *Archaeology of the Mediterranean Landscapes* (Barker and Mattingly 2000), which provide numerous insights into how methods of intensive survey and integrated survey practice can be applied to the archaeological landscape to provide enhanced levels of data recovery. With the advent of new GPS technology and geographically corrected satellite images, it is now possible to recognize and target features on images and employ the "go to" capability of the GPS to find precisely and visit key features.

Existing databases for survey in the Near East remain scanty, but some government databases provide information on archaeological site locations and distributions. These include the Atlas of Archaeological Sites in Iraq (Iraq Department of Antiquities 1976), archaeological maps of Jordan, the TAVO (Tübinger Atlas des Vorderen Orients) maps of Tübingen, and the TAY (Türkiye Arkeolojik Yerlşmeleri) series from Turkey. In addition, some of the most intensively surveyed parts of the Near East are found in the southern Levant, where the archaeological survey of Israel has built upon earlier surveys of Palestine undertaken by the British Mandate.[1]

Recent critiques of settlement survey often regard past surveys as being inadequate at representing the dynamics of settlement change because they provide only a staccato development of settlement history, subdivided into arbitrary stages (Brück and Goodman 1999). However, this factor is inherent in the very problem of representing potentially unstable systems such as settlement patterns (Roberts 1996: 120–128), and attempts are being made to take such considerations into account (e.g., Bintliff 2000). The incorporation of a dynamic element into settlement survey using the techniques of Dewar (1991) goes some way towards demonstrating that settlement history does not simply progress in somewhat arbitrary chronological stages. The recognition of persistent features in the landscape that often hark back to earlier time periods, or relict features or sites that continue to have meaning to the local people, can also provide insights into long-term perspectives on settlement change that are not dealt with by earlier surveys.

Preoccupations with capitalist-type economic models are also rightly subject to criticism, although this is less a problem for Near Eastern archaeological surveys because there, the basis for comparing the archaeological record has been a persisting and often vigorous traditional way of life. Ethnographic or ethnoarchaeological studies of the social and economic systems of traditional village or nomadic communities over the past two hundred years has supplied a wealth of data for unraveling past landscapes (Kramer 1979; Sweet 1974). Although it would be naive to regard the modern communities as linear descendents of the ancient communities, they can provide a basis for comparison with the archaeological record that is very different from our own fully capitalist economies. Substantial insights into landscape history can therefore be obtained from ethnoarchaeological studies or simply by discussions with local people, who frequently have an intimate knowledge of the way installations such as threshing floors, terrace walls, or dams actually operated. The uncritical extrapolation of the ways of life of present-day traditional societies into the past can, however, be misleading. This is especially the case if the population has arrived fairly recently and is not well acquainted with the landscape, as is the case for those parts of the Fertile Crescent that have experienced the recent resettlement of population groups.

Geochemical Prospection

Geochemical prospection provides a spatial record of human activity in the form of a fixed anthropogenic signal superimposed over that of the soil chemical environment (Heron 2001: 565). Soil samples are analyzed to provide a spatial patterning of chemical properties that yield a signature of both the original soil record as well as a signal of later human activities. Key indicators include phosphates, lead (Pb), zinc (Zn), copper (Cu), manganese (Mn), and nickel (Ni) (Heron 2001; Taylor 2000; Rimmington 2000). Phosphate analysis has been employed in archaeology for some forty years to record various geochemical forms of phosphate that result from activities such as pasturing or bedding of animals, ancient manuring, modern fertilizer practice, burial of the dead, as well as settlement middens. Most surveys attempt to detect the inorganic phosphate (P_2O_5) component of the soil, which gradually accumulates by means of transformation from an initial input of organic phosphates. In addition, more sophisticated methods such as phosphate fractionation have been used, for example, to demonstrate the accumulation of phosphates in irrigated soils in southern Arabia (Eidt 1977; Brinkmann 1996). Trace metals also accumulate in the soil over the millennia to produce complex patterning around occupation sites (Bintliff et al. 1992). Like phosphates, trace metals can be related to patterns of past activity such as the intensity of land use, disposal of rubbish, and other processes.

Geochemical indicators can then be related to patterns of off-site artifacts to produce a composite interpretation of ancient activities in the region (Wilkinson 1990a; Bintliff et al. 1992). The combination of such signatures in concert with the assay of biomarkers (e.g., lipids) provides a specific impression of activities such as manuring or even the presence of certain animal species (Bull et al. 1999, 2001). Unfortunately, unlike artifact scatters, most geochemical patterns can rarely be dated, with the result that they provide a signature of long-term activity rather being specific to any particular period of occupation.

Geoarchaeology

Geoarchaeological studies form an essential part of landscape archaeology and enable landscape surveys to be placed within a dynamic physical context. Field surveys should therefore endeavor to record as many cuts and sections as possible to obtain sequences through Pleistocene and Holocene sedimentary accumulations. The application of earth science techniques also allows the landscape record to be assessed in terms of natural transformation processes (Schiffer's n-transforms: 1987: 235–262). By undertaking geoarchaeological studies simultaneously with archaeological surveys, it is therefore possible to determine what proportion of sites and landscapes have been lost through erosion, whether features may have been buried by sedimentation, or whether sites lie on relatively stable terrain (Kouchoukos 1998: 100–103). In addition, geoarchaeological studies such as soil micromorphology, particle-size analysis, and soil-profile description provide essential information on the development and dynamics of landscape features such as buried land surfaces, infilled quarry pits, and terraced fields (Groenman-van Waateringe and Robinson 1988; Miller and Gleason 1994).

Geoarchaeological techniques form a key element in the interpretation of many landscape features. For example, if a surface mound contains abundant gravel, it is necessary to determine the source of that gravel, which may indicate whether the mound comprised material cast up from the excavation of a well that penetrated to a specific geological substratum (fig. 4.1). Similarly, geoarchaeological techniques can be used to assess the size, sorting, and depositional environment of sediments transported along the beds of irrigation canals. Where sediments have accumulated behind terrace walls, analysis of soil properties and their inclusions aid in the recognition of episodes of soil stabilization in the form of palaeosols (Waters 1992; Courty et al. 1989; see also chapter 4 and following chapters).

Geophysical Techniques

Geophysical techniques have been applied to the investigation of ancient landscapes in many parts of the New and Old Worlds, but relatively little use has been made of them in the Near East (Sarris and Jones 2000; Bevan 1994). On the other hand, during the last ten years, geophysical prospection has been applied to settlement sites in Turkey with impressive results (Summers and Summers 1998; Matney and Algaze 1995; Becker and Jansen 1994). Proven techniques include resistivity survey, which measures the electrical resistance of the soil; magnetometry survey, which measures variations in the earth's magnetic field or the magnetic susceptibility of the subsurfaces; electromagnetic survey; ground-penetrating radar; and seismic survey. Insightful recent applications of geophysical prospection include resistivity survey for defining site boundaries at Tell al-Amarna, the recognition of tombs or tunnels using resistivity survey (Sarris and Jones 2000: 18–19), and the location of mudbrick structures at Neolithic Çatal Höyük using magnetometry (Shell 1996).

Most of the foregoing have been undertaken as part of settlement-based studies, but both ground-penetrating radar and seismic techniques show considerable potential for the recognition of canals and buried channels (Sarris and Jones 2000: 36–40; Karastathis and Papamarinopoulos 1997). The underutilization of geophysical techniques for landscape analysis will surely change in the near future, however, because ground-penetrating radar and soil-resistivity survey are of considerable value for providing supplementary records of features that appear on satellite images. In the future it should therefore be possible to test whether, for example, a dark mark crossing the landscape represents a canal or a shallow feature worn into the terrain by prolonged use (such as an ancient trackway). Although such questions are only just starting to be resolved by geophysical survey, the combination of excavation with geophysical survey should provide a basic signature for a verified feature, so that in subsequent investigations geophysical surveys will be capable of demonstrating the likely origin of such features.

Other Environmental Data

Ideally, landscape investigations should take place in tandem with excavations, and indeed they should be conceived as part of one overarching investigation. For example, Naomi Miller's investigations of carbonized plant remains show that during the fourth and third millennia B.C., the landscape along the Turkish Euphrates was becoming increasingly degraded. The landscape analysis supports this point, since it demonstrates that as more trees were removed from the region, it was necessary to burn more dung as fuel. The consequent lack of dung meant that fields could not be fertilized with animal dung and that recourse had to be made to the spreading of household ash on the fields. Geoarchaeological surveys also showed that there was parallel evidence for landscape degradation after around 2000 B.C. (Wilkinson 1990a: 26–29). In some cases, rather than conducting surveys in a given area to answer specific cultural or historical questions, it can be advantageous to conduct surveys in areas where good pollen sequences exist to examine how settlement and vegetation change through time in relation to each other.

Data Integration Using GIS

Geographic Information Systems (GIS) have become a buzzword in archaeology, and although not a panacea, they do provide a convenient and powerful way of integrating different data sets from large-scale regional investigations. GIS enable different types of mapped information to be stored as a series of "layers" that can then be analyzed and manipulated together so as to display them in new ways or to provide new data combinations. It is therefore possible to superimpose distributions of archaeological sites on soil maps to determine favored locations for settlement development, calculate the areas of archaeological sites, estimate the amount of cultivated land around sites of a given period, as well as to ask questions about, for example, distance to the nearest water sources or nearest neighbors. When employed in conjunction with data on the physical environment, GIS provide an excellent way of manipulating the large spatial data sets gathered during survey. For this reason alone they will prove to be indispensable in landscape analysis in the future.

Inevitably, because early applications involved the use of data derived from soils, topographic maps, and land use, there has been a tendency for GIS applications to become deterministic so that site locations, for example, can be predicted on the basis of the physical potential of the landscape alone, rather than combining these with a range of social factors. However, recent innovations that treat landscapes as being perceived from the perspective of the viewer provide a novel component to GIS that has considerable potential (see papers in Gillings et al. 1999). By way of illustration, Gaffney and colleagues (1995) argued that the

GIS modeling of the topographic area visible from any site provides a measure of the cognitive environment. Michael Given (2001) has successfully applied viewshed analysis in Cyprus to show the landscape that was perceived during the daily round of work by the inhabitants of individual settlements. Related techniques such as those that place Australian rock-art sites within their cognitive environment could readily be used for equivalent problems in Arabia or for the recognition of intervisibility of burial monuments or tombs on ridge tops.

Landscape Taphonomy

Even during the earlier stages of landscape archaeology there was an awareness that the cultural landscape had suffered progressive attrition of features through time, with some elements being added whereas others were lost. During his assessment of centuriated landscapes of the Mediterranean region, John Bradford described the progressive attrition of field boundaries (Bradford 1957: 208). More recently, Schiffer (1987) has formalized landscape transformation processes into those resulting from cultural and those resulting from environmental processes (c- and n-transforms respectively). Christopher Taylor's recognition of landscapes of destruction and survival in Britain (Taylor 1972) was a landmark statement because this conceptual framework enabled archaeologists to take account of the likelihood of feature survival when assessing the landscape record. For example, above the limit of cultivation in the uplands there was an increased likelihood of landscape features or entire landscapes surviving, whereas in the lowlands where processes of settlement and cultivation had endured over millennia, there was a much greater chance of earlier landscapes being lost. This simple conceptual framework received less attention than it deserved, but in a revised and more detailed

form, Tom Williamson has applied it for the British Isles. Despite the fact that Taylor's neat conceptual framework oversimplifies what is in reality "a particularly complex kaleidoscope of patterned creation and structure destruction" (Williamson 1998: 6 and fig. 3), it is clear that landscape transformations have played a fundamental role in the preservation or loss of landscape data.

Strictly speaking, the term *taphonomy* applies to the processes that act upon biological materials after death and before they become fossils, but I have adapted the term to landscape studies because similar principles apply. This is illustrated by the progressive removal of, for example, stones from a wall to build a new one or the wholesale removal of some features when they become redundant. Similarly, geomorphological processes either can erode parts of the landscape away or can entomb landscape features beneath an obscuring blanket of sediment.

Suitably amended, the Taylor model can be effectively applied to the ancient Near Eastern landscape. Landscapes with the greatest probability of feature survival occur in deserts and high mountains, whereas progressive loss of features is at its maximum in areas of long-term cultivation and rather less so in marginal zones of settlement. The coastal zone experiences a patterned loss and survival depending upon coastal sedimentation and currents. Major taphonomic zones in the Near East can be suggested as follows, although it requires emphasis that the patterning of landscapes of destruction and survival can be extremely complicated.

Zone 1: Zone of Preservation in Deserts

Because most deserts lack the potential for cultivation, they are not normally occupied by long-term sedentary settlement. Nevertheless, if settlement did take place, there is little likelihood that their remains would be erased by subsequent settlement. Consequently, archaeological remains can be remarkably well preserved in deserts. Indeed some of the first steps in landscape archaeology were conducted in the hyperarid regions of the Gobi and Takla Makan deserts, where relict canals, off-site sherd scatters, and fossilized orchards, dating from the first millennium A.D., were all recorded in fine detail (Stein 1921).

Probably the best examples of zones of preservation occur where economic, environmental, or political factors have encouraged the extension of settlement into otherwise marginal areas. For example, a remarkable pattern of prehistoric fields near Tepe Yahya in southeast Iran remained for some seven thousand years because of the lack of subsequent settlement, but they were then lost from view by the extension of cultivation during the late twentieth century A.D. (Prickett 1986; Lamberg-Karlovsky personal communication; chapter 5). Similarly, the deserts of Jordan, Saudi Arabia, and southern Israel, with rainfall of less than 200 mm per annum, provide numerous examples of landscapes of preservation. Despite the high quality of preservation of surface features, establishing a date for them is frequently difficult because of the lack of associated dating evidence. Hence, in Jordan various field systems near Nabatean, Roman, or Byzantine settlements remain difficult to date with confidence (Kennedy and Freeman 1995: 39; Barker et al. 1997).

Zone 2: Zone of Preservation in Mountainous Areas

At the other extreme, mountains provide conditions that are unsuitable for sustained human activity, with the result that permanent settlement rarely occurs above a certain limit. When it does occur, for example, if the area suddenly becomes important for mining or as a source for stones such as obsidian, or high-

land pastures are adopted for upland camps (equivalent to the Turkish *yayla*), then archaeological remains may be preserved with remarkable clarity. Such preservation can occur as long as the characteristic geomorphological processes of mountain areas (mass wasting, talus development, and so on) have not destroyed them. By way of example, forming an island within an otherwise well-watered part of northwest Syria near Aleppo, the limestone uplands of the "Massif Calcaire" present an almost complete relict landscape of Late Roman/Byzantine date. Settlements, oil presses, trackways, and fields are all preserved with remarkable clarity because there has been little subsequent settlement since the ninth century A.D. to remove their remains (chapter 7). The record from this small area therefore forms a remarkable island of archaeological preservation that stands in stark contrast to the nearby lowlands, where the remains of the same period usually take the form of rather anonymous tells or low mounds. Off-site features in such landscapes of destruction are usually lacking unless they are particularly robust.

Zone 3: Intermediate Zone (Marginal Rain-Fed Steppe, with Fluctuation Settlement Levels)

The Jazira region of northern Syria and Iraq is dominated by tells that attained their maximum size often during the middle part of the third millennium B.C. For landscape archaeologists, this marginal zone of rain-fed cultivation in Upper Mesopotamia holds special significance because it houses an unusual combination of important sites together with related landscape features that provide valuable insights into Bronze Age economic activities (Wilkinson 1994; Kouchoukos 1998).

With a mean annual rainfall ranging from ca. 200 to 500 mm, Zone 3 can register well-preserved,

off-site features such as linear hollows (of ancient tracks), off-site sherd scatters, and relict canals (chapter 6). Other landscape features such as ancient relict fields are usually absent, except where "windows" of the landscape of preservation may be visible on localized uplands (fig. 3.4). In the Jazira the retreat of settlement from around the fifteenth century A.D. until the nineteenth and twentieth centuries resulted in a large area of tells and their associated landscapes remaining beyond the limits of the settled areas. As a result, archaeological landscape features appear to have survived particularly well (fig. 6.6). Overall, optimum landscape preservation may occur in the intermediate zone. This is because in wetter areas, sustained human settlement has increased the loss of early features or sites by attrition or by burial below later sites. In drier areas to the south, however, even though landscape transformation processes are less marked, long-term settlement has not been sufficiently heavy in its imprint to cause features to be embedded into the landscape.

Through the millennia this area has experienced several cycles of settlement rise and decline. The cause of this pattern of rise and decline continues to be debated, but it appears to result from a combination of climatic, social, economic, and political changes (see papers in Dalfes, Kukla, and Weiss, 1997). In such areas the retreat in the margin of settlement has allowed the early phases of settlement and landscape to be visible. Feature survival in the intermediate zone has also been encouraged by the nature of the subsequent settlement pattern (roughly post Late Bronze Age), which was dispersed and consequently left a lighter print on the landscape than the nucleated pattern of the Bronze Age. As a result, occasional hiatuses or declines in settlement have resulted in diminished attrition of landscape features.

Fig. 3.4 Small "taphonomic window" on edge of basalt plateau near Tell Beydar, Syria. Preserved features include lynchetlike terraced fields on scarp slope of basalt in center, and circular stone settings of nomadic huts (mid–late first millennium A.D.) left of center; the ploughed land forming the landscape of attrition is along the right-hand margin of the photograph.

Zone 4: Zone of Attrition

Whereas Zone 3 exhibits a partial landscape record in which occasional earlier features remain, in the "zone of attrition" there is decreased chance of feature survival because long-term settlement has been virtually continuous over some nine thousand years. This vast zone includes the Levantine coastal plain and much of Israel, Lebanon, western Syria, as well as parts of Turkey, Jordan, and Yemen. Although it is impossible to do justice to such a complex zone, the following example illustrates that processes of landscape transformation in Zone 4 have operated to deplete significantly the Roman landscape over the past two thousand years.

In Syria several examples of Roman centuriation have been recognized as relict patterns within the modern field systems (chapter 7). The presence of a few remaining relict field boundaries on an apparent grid within a pattern of recent field systems implies that existing field systems hold traces of earlier systems in them, just as in other parts of the Mediterranean (Wirth 1971: 375, 412; Bradford 1957, Alcock 1993: 139–140 for Roman; Gaffney, Bintliff, and Slapsak 1991 for Hellenistic). If such systems can be dated archaeologically, they can then supply a datum for estimating the ages of yet earlier field systems and landscape features, as has been possible in, for example, East Anglia (Williamson 1987).

Zone 5: The Coastal Zone

The small tidal range of the coastal waters surrounding the Near East restricts the potential for the discovery of sites in intertidal locations. Nevertheless, following from pioneering studies assembled by Masters and Flemming (1983), shallow underwater survey has now yielded impressive amounts of prehistoric occupation (chapter 2). Sites on the coast of Israel (Galili et al. 1993) and Greece (Flemming 1983) indicate that the level of preservation is often considerable, and this zone itself has its own processes of taphonomy that encourage or discourage preservation. Coastal geomorphological processes are obviously of greater importance than cultural transformations. According to Flemming (1998: 134), discovery of a submerged marine site is most likely to occur when a site that has been buried in sediment is slowly re-eroded as a result of a change in sediment supply or related circumstances. When investigated using geoarchaeology, geophysical prospection, and underwater archaeology, such landscapes can provide results that complement the record from adjacent dry lands. As in coastal sites in northwest Europe, feature preservation is often extremely good. In the future, this zone should provide valuable control for the heavily degraded record from adjacent drylands.

Conclusions

The foregoing pages argue that there is no such thing as a complete landscape record. Not only do taphonomic processes operate so that there is a progressive loss of landscape features through time, but also the quality of feature recovery will change through time. Hence, despite the availability of modern satellite sensors of unsurpassed precision (especially because of their wide spectral range), aerial photography taken earlier in the twentieth century can still provide results of remarkable quality, in part because they were taken under better taphonomic circumstances with less landscape disturbance. In reality, there is no single formula for the maximum recovery of early landscape data. Rather, it is necessary to harness a combination of remote-sensing techniques, detailed field survey, and local information, together with a certain amount of luck. Once the landscape record has been recovered, it can then be interpreted in terms of feature elements and systems of features, as will be attempted in the following chapters.

4 Elements of Landscape

The elements of the landscape discussed in this chapter are those features that form the fundamental components of the overall landscape. These elements (ancient settlements, roads, fields, canals, and so on) when assembled together do not make the complete landscape, but they do enable us to start to recognize a structure for the landscape for certain periods. Emphasis here is on those features that can be recognized in the field or by remote sensing. This may seem obvious, but many phases of landscape use (perhaps even most) will have been lost from view as a result of the taphonomic processes described in chapter 3 or because they failed to leave a tangible imprint in the first place. By recording and assembling the basic features of the landscape, we can start to recognize features or groups of features that can then act as a yardstick against which earlier or later phases can be assessed.

This chapter provides a skeletal classification of landscape features that provides the foundation for chapters 5–9, which then give a more contextual view of regional landscape development. Of course, many individual features do not have a single function. For example, in addition to their role as a water supply for irrigation systems, canals also are used for transport. Similarly, fields have a primary use for cultivation, while at certain times of the year, they also function as pastoral resources. Even when features such as threshing floors have a single obvious function, namely, to thresh or process cereal, they can also have a social function serving,

for example, as meeting places within or outside villages. A similar line of argument follows for village wells or water holes that serve as social meeting places, especially for the women of the community.

Types of features that constitute the landscape can be subdivided into four basic classes: first, those that correspond to features that were created to satisfy the physical needs of the inhabitants; second, those that were created to satisfy their spiritual needs; a third class consists of features that were used, but not created, to satisfy spiritual needs; these "natural places" (see Bradley 2000) are not described in this chapter but will be alluded to where necessary in later chapters. Fourth, we must not neglect pleasure. Whereas Mesoamerica can offer ball courts as evident of game-playing activities, there is little remaining in the Near Eastern landscape of game playing or pleasure seeking in general. The obvious candidates: Hellenistic/Roman theaters mainly form part of the urban landscape and are beyond the scope of this book, but for the early Islamic period, we have magnificent remains of racecourses such as those at Samarra (Iraq). These elaborate but subtle features, which were amongst the earliest landscape features recorded from the air (Beazeley 1919), have more recently been the subject of more detailed scrutiny (Northedge et al. 1990). Formal gardens of the Assyrians and Persians also come into this category.

Those features that were used to satisfy the physical needs of the inhabitants form the basis of the archaeological landscape to be dis-

cussed here (fig. 4.1), and these are most readily interpreted from a functionalist perspective. When they can be seen to form a functionally related group, they might then be described as forming a system. For example, features of ancient mining complexes can frequently nest together in interrelated groups as follows: the mine shaft supplies the ore, furnaces contributed the smelted material, fields supplied food for the miners, and canals or conduits supplied water to irrigated fields, as well as the drinking needs of the mining community and perhaps even some industrial functions. Despite the obvious functions of mining features, one should not lose sight of their ideational aspects, and mining sites can frequently exhibit a ceremonial or ritual function as well (Knapp 1999). Similarly, water-supply features can usually be classed together as a system of interrelated elements that capture and distribute water to fields (Doolittle 1990: 13). Again, such systems are interpreted from a functionalist perspective, but often they also include religious features such as the ablution areas of mosques, and these can then be seen to form part of an economic-social-ritual system.

Religious or sanctified features cannot be dealt with from a functional perspective, but their location with respect to the functional agricultural landscape can be significant. It is therefore important to determine how these two landscape domains relate to one another. Because churches, mosques, and temples possess distinctive architectural features that enable them to be distinguished from other buildings, they have often been comprehensively studied in the past (e.g., Butler 1929). Rarely though have they been placed in their landscape context (chapter 7).

The primary aim of this chapter is to describe what particularly features look like, to determine how they functioned, and to suggest means of dating them. The systems themselves as well as many details concerning their landscape context will be left for the later chapters devoted to "signature landscapes."

Settlements (Places of the Living)

Although the tell is often regarded as the archetypal Near Eastern settlement, the landscape includes a much wider range of site types. To recover these requires carefully structured and (usually) intensive surveys. Table 4.1 summarizes the basic types of settlement sites, classified from the most to the least conspicuous features.

Settlement sites should not be viewed simply in isolation because frequently they provide hints as to the date of associated features. In suitable cases, landscape features may be physically related to sites, either being built into them so that their constituent stones are interleaved or radiating out from them, as is the case for certain types of roadways.

Water-Supply Systems

Water supply is crucial to settlement, and in drier regions the modes of water supply become more conspicuous because of the need to supply not only drinking water but also irrigation water for crops. Because irrigation provides the lion's share of water demand for any given community, irrigation canals can be large and conspicuous.

There are two basic classes of natural water-supply systems in desert areas: endogenous, namely, those that originate from within the area of the desert itself, and exogenous, those that have their source outside the desert, such as, for example, the Nile river (Goudie and Wilkinson 1977: 55). Endogenous systems can, in turn, be subdivided into groundwater and overland sources of supply. Many irrigation systems can be subdivided into four basic zones (fig. 4.2).

— A water-gathering area, in the form of a river, a dam and its upland catchment, or an alluvial fan (in the case of a *qanat*). Rivers and dams are simple water-gathering areas, but in the case of a qanat, the alluvial fan itself will have its own catchment in the form of a tributary valley or wadi. Because the hydrological properties of such compound water-gathering areas depend on the properties of both fan and the contributory valley, the flow characteristics of the qanat can themselves be complex.
— A water-transmission or water-transport zone. This usually takes the form of a canal, which either can be plaster-lined or simply made of mud.
— The irrigation zone, namely, fields or gardens.
— An outflow zone, namely, the area that receives surplus water from the irrigation system. In southern Mesopotamia this might be a lake or marsh or the river itself further downstream.

Water-supply systems tend to be constructed in accordance with the topography and hydrology of the region, but there are also regional cultural traditions in water supply. For instance, Neil Roberts recognized a zone of runoff agriculture extending from the southern Levant, through the Hejaz mountains of Saudi Arabia, and to Yemen in the south. Further east in Iran and Oman, a zone of qanat irrigation is based around groundwater captured mainly from alluvial fan systems (Roberts 1977). This patterning, in part, recognizes that historical factors such as the diffusion of technological knowledge of qanat construction also influenced the configuration of these zones. Although qanat and runoff systems are both endogenous systems, even within the endogenous zone there is often a rather complex patterning of irrigation systems depending upon local geomorphological and hydrological conditions. Hence in Saudi Arabia, where runoff might be considered to be the primary means of water supply, qanats, wells, springs, and runoff can all be used, depending upon local circumstances, whereas within the qanat zone of Iran, alternative technologies such as dams, runoff, and riverine irrigation systems can occur. Water-supply systems therefore are sensitively engineered to suit local hydrogeological conditions. Because of this, the same class of water-supply systems should not be expected to occur over extensive areas unless hydrogeological and cultural conditions have been particularly uniform for extended periods of time.

Ancient Near Eastern water systems can be grouped into the following hydrological classes:

Groundwater Supply Systems

Wells and Water Holes. Wells can be deep, cylindrical in form, and usually are lined with stones, baked bricks, or an organic framework. Water holes, on the other hand, are irregular holes dug down to a rather shallow water table and lack visible reinforcement. Because ancient wells will usually have been abandoned for long periods and have therefore been infilled with sediment, they can sometimes be recognized only from the gravel that has been dug out from them and cast up from deeper geological strata. Once transmogrified by long-term geomorphological process, such well-mounds may be almost indistinguishable from small settlement mounds. Nevertheless, if a well mouth is exposed

a.   b.   c.

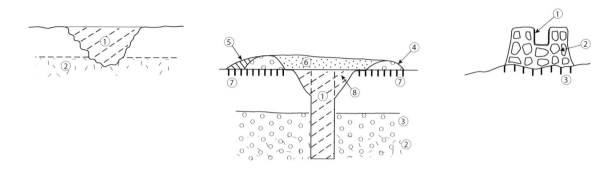

d.

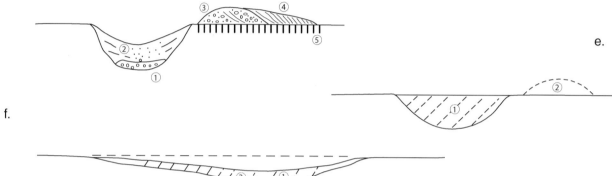

e.

f.

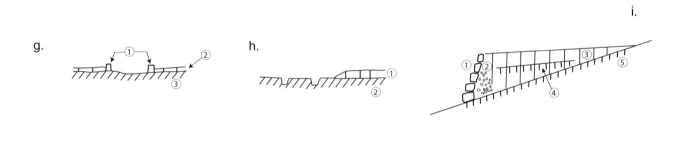

i.

g.   h.

j.

k.   l.

by excavation or there is abundant gravel on the surface of the mound, it is possible to diagnose the feature as a well (Costa and Wilkinson 1987). Wells are normally associated with the collection of groundwater, but in certain desert areas, shallow wells collect and intercept runoff from rainwater (chapter 8). In the Near East, water holes have been traced back to the ceramic Neolithic (Hassuna/Samarran periods) (Wilkinson and Tucker 1995) and wells to the Halaf (Miller 1980) and in Cyprus, even to the Pre-Pottery Neolithic (Peltenburg 2000). Later developments included wells that could be accessed via underground staircases (for example, at Megiddo) or post-Roman wells that include an inclined plane dug beneath the ground and down which an oxen walks to draw water.

Qanats. Qanats, or in southern Arabia *falaj* (pl. *aflaj*), derive their flow from groundwater. This is effected by the excavation of vertical shafts down to a water table or submerged spring in an alluvial fan system (chapter 8). The intercepted water is then led away downslope via underground channels and then an open conduit, until it arrives at the area to be irrigated. Qanats are thought to have originated in northwest Iran, whence the technique may have been spread by

Sargon II of Assyria (721–705 B.C.), who claims to have learned the technique during his campaign against Urartu. From this region qanats are thought to have been spread by the Achaemenids as far as Oman and Egypt (Lambton 1989; J. C. Wilkinson 1977; Lightfoot 2000; but see chapter 8) as well as Spain and ultimately Mexico (Woodbury and Neely 1972: 148).

Wells and water holes, especially those for irrigation, tend to be restricted to areas of accessible groundwater. When used for irrigation, wells are often less than 20 m deep, but in desert areas, much deeper wells have been dug for the supply of drinking water for humans and animals. Wells allow settlements to disperse, because their presence means that communities are not tied to a single source of water such as a spring or a perennial river. Qanats on the other hand, by leading water to a focal point in the landscape, can result in nucleated settlements with rather constrained areas of gardens (chapter 8).

Perennial Flow Systems

The basic perennial flow systems are canals or open water channels that lead water from a year-round source of water such as a spring, from permanent pools in a wadi bed, or from a large perennially flowing

river. Springs usually supply a reliable but relatively minor flow, and as a result, water can be dispersed by means of small conduits. Perennial flow can be used direct for supplying drinking water for humans or domestic animals, or alternatively excess water can be led downslope via a canal to be used for irrigation. Because perennial rivers can have high rates of flow and high flow variation, canals from these sources can be as large as or larger than the water requirement of the communities that are being supplied. Such canals can be in excess of 100 km in length (chapter 5).

A fundamental principle of water distribution is that there is an optimum "design gradient" for the construction of canals so that their beds should be neither too steep (which would result in erosion)[1] nor too gentle (which would encourage the accumulation of excess sediment). If the terrain is too steep for a canal to be constructed directly down gradient, the channel can be constructed to flow oblique to the slope or almost parallel to the contours. Canals can therefore be constructed to "rise" with respect to the river systems, which tend to have gradients that are steeper than the design gradient of canals. By the use of these basic principles, the ancient engineers were capable not only of building more sustainable irrigation systems

Fig. 4.1   Sketches of some characteristic landscape features. (a) *Water hole*: (1) fill, (2) water table (chemically reduced soil). (b) *Well*: (1) fill in shaft, (2) water table within gravel (chemically reduced), (3) bed of gravel, (4) initial gravel upcast, (5) clean-out silts, (6) wind-blown sand, (7) buried soil, (8) cone of collapse. (c) *Open channel*: (1) waterproof plaster, (2) masonry with large cobbles, (3) buried soil. (d) *Canal with spoil banks*: (1) primary sand and gravel fill of channel, (2) secondary and tertiary fills, (3) primary spoil from initial excavation, (4) secondary siltation (clean-out), (5) buried soil. (e) *Canal with spoil banks deflated*: (1) fill, (2) clean–out spoil banks (deflated). (f) *Linear hollow*: (1) loam (plough wash) infill, (2) fine gravel washed by concentrated overland flow. (g) track with stone boundary "fences", (1) line of large stones, (2) field soil, (3) bedrock. (h) *Wheel ruts*: (1) soil (partly eroded), (2) limestone bedrock. (i) *Terraced field*: (1) terrace wall, (2) wedge of stones for subsoil drainage, (3) accretionary deposits, (4) weak palaeosol within sedimentary build-up, (5) pre-terrace palaeosol. (j) *Field clearance mound*: (1) stones cleared from fields, (2) original level of ground surface, (3) buried soil with contained rocks, (4) plough-scarred rock, (5) depth of soil lost by erosion. (k) *Mud-brick extraction pit*: (1) soil, (2) infill deposits, (3) cut face (note asymmetrical profile). (l) *Stone quarry*: (1) original ground surface, (2) quarry face after removal of stones (subsequently weathered back to curvilinear face), (3) stone-working debris, (4) buried soil, (5) abandoned cut stones.

Table 4.1   Means of Distinguishing Settlement Sites in the Near East

(a)	Tells (mounded sites)	Tells comprise multiple layers of building levels and accumulated wastes built up through time, in part because the locus of occupation has remained stationary. Tell settlements frequently are defined by an outer wall that both contained and constrained the accumulated materials, thereby restricting their spread (Rosen 1986; Butzer 1982). The tell is by no means the sole locus of occupation in the Near East. Early surveyors such as Von der Osten (Anatolia) and Glueck (Jordan) were well aware of and recorded low or flat sites as well. But it was not until the 1970s and 1980s that many outer or lower towns were fully recognized. These secondary occupations often appear as low humps or simply artifact scatters around tells, and they can extend the total occupied area of a site several fold.
(b)	Low mounds	Low mounded sites may have been occupied for a brief range of time, but some comprise many minor occupations. Low mounds include the small straggling *khirbets* that are common in the Levant and Fertile Crescent. Smaller sites of this class can be defined by microtopographic surveys with contour intervals as little as 20 cm.
(c)	Nonmounded sites	When building materials are primarily of stone, mounding can be minimal. In such cases, stone foundations or lower courses of walls remain, so the original building layout can be recognized and drawn. Sites of this type are common in deserts and mountains where stone predominates over mudbrick. Where buildings were of perishable materials such as wood or reed, only artifacts will remain on the surface. Care must be taken to define the perimeters of such sites because of the "continuous landscape" (see text). Because of the tendency for artifacts to stretch as a seemingly continuous carpet across the terrain, it can sometimes be easier to recognize settlement sites from their scatter of stone foundations than from their artifacts. This is especially true if settlement occurred, for example, on deep loam terrain, in which case any stones evident on the surface probably derive from wall foundations. This is because the geology dictates that there would be a minimal presence of stones on the surface. Stone scatters of this type are frequently associated with large ceramic fragments, grinding stones, or door-pivot stones, all of which provide support for domestic occupation.
(d)	Soil color	Where natural soils have a distinctive hue, such as the "*terra rossa* soils" of the Eastern Mediterranean, settlements can be distinguished by their contrasting color. This is exemplified on the red-brown soils of the Euphrates terraces of southern Turkey and northern Syria, where settlement sites exhibit grayish hues derived from included ashy midden material. This contrast is discernible by recording Munsell colors of soils sampled from transects made across sites (Wilkinson 1990a) as well as on satellite images, where the settlement material exhibits a different spectral signature from surrounding soils.
(e)	Cut features	Features dug into the subsoil are also diagnostic of occupation. If sections have been exposed by modern earth-moving activities, storage pits or extraction pits for mudbrick are recognizable (see below).
(f)	Caves	Natural caves were occasionally used as living areas, especially during the Palaeolithic, but they also retain a use into later periods, often serving a ritual function. Deliberately cut caves are more likely to have been used as burial chambers.
(g)	Nomad settlements	Despite their seemingly light imprint on the land, nomadic settlements can be distinguished by means of artifact scatters as well as the presence of tent rings and other structural foundations (Rosen 1992; Cribb 1991). The scatter of artifacts is less dense than on sedentary sites. If a site has been visited over a long period of time, the range of dates inferred from both pottery and radiocarbon may span a long period of time. Avner, for example, while investigating agro-pastoral sites in the Uvda valley of the Negev, demonstrated that one site was occupied from 8200 to 3500 B.C. (Avner 1998: 178–179).

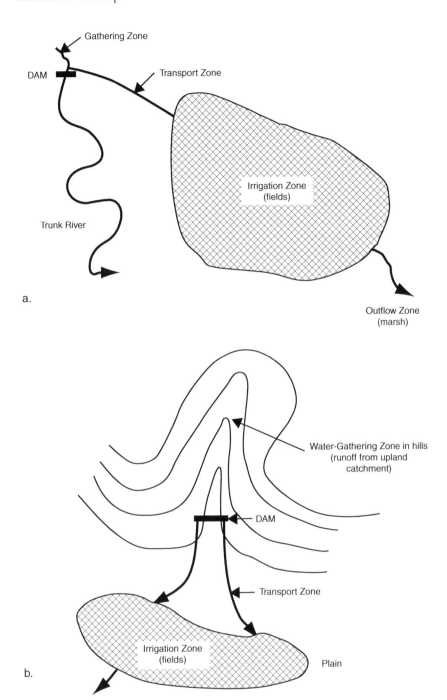

a.

b.

Fig. 4.2 Main elements of irrigation systems: (a) in alluvial lowland such as southern Mesopotamia, (b) on edge of highland area, as in western or southern Arabia.

the most sophisticated examples of such technology are post-Roman in date, a well-attested aqueduct was constructed by Sennacherib in the seventh century B.C. to convey water down to the vicinity of Nineveh (Jacobsen and Lloyd 1935).

Springs and minor perennial flows can be tapped by clay- or masonry-lined open channels, and because such water sources usually conduct relatively little sediment, these often have little in the way of spoil mounds alongside them. Small masonry open channels, which can be followed for long distances across country, provide an important element of the landscape behind Roman/Parthian and later settlements in the Near East. In the Roman world aqueducts enable water to be transported from its source to where it is needed, whether this was for irrigation or for urban use. Aqueducts therefore serve a function similar to the open channel falaj of Oman (fig. 4.3a) and related systems found elsewhere in the Near East (Hodge 2000). At their most impressive, major aqueduct bridges were constructed to enable water to be transported across valleys of various scale,[2] and similar techniques have been used by modern falaj builders to circumvent tributary valleys. Related to aqueducts are closed pipelines of stone or ceramic, which allowed water to cross depressions on the way to supply settlements with water (Peleg 1991).

Large open channels usually tap perennial rivers of variable size and are usually considerably more than 100 cm wide and 50 cm deep. Their channels are usually of mud except at key points, and their high sediment load requires frequent cleaning, which results in large clean-out mounds alongside (fig. 4.3b). These types of canals are particular common in the irrigated lowlands of southern Iraq (chapter 5).

Water channels can be notoriously difficult to date, but there are a number of ways of securing dates under favorable circumstances.

but also of directing water laterally across the terrain away from the water sources.

To maintain a reasonable design gradient, canals need to be engineered to negotiate obstacles such as tributary valleys or inconvenient hills. Side valleys are negotiated by directing the channel along the contour around the valley, across it by means of an aqueduct, or beneath it be means of an inverted siphon. Siphons, which are usually sealed pipes dug beneath the river or wadi floor, can be recognized by the presence of masonry penstocks both upstream and downstream of an obstacle such as a wadi. Although

Fig. 4.3 The size range of different types of canal. Top: Small perennial flow channel of the Falaj al-Mutaridh near Sohar (Oman). Note that the large rounded cobbles used for construction are just peeping through the waterproof plaster (*saruj*) of the channel; scale 30 cm long (photo by the author). Bottom: Upcast mounds (ca. 50 m in width) alongside the Sasanian/Early Islamic Nahr al Qaʿim, Samarra (Iraq). Note that the canal is to the right of the photograph.

— Canals frequently transport pottery as part of their bedload, and by careful stratigraphic excavation, any diagnostic pottery recovered can be used to provide a date, providing care is taken to use only the most recent sherds recovered from any given layer.

— Freshwater mollusks frequently live in canals, and radiocarbon assay of their shells can provide estimated dates for the later phases of the channel. A sequence of dates on charcoal or shell from both the channel and the banks may therefore provide an outline chronological framework for the canal.

— Calcium carbonate coatings (flow stone or tufa) commonly occur on the insides of masonry and mortar channels (Gardiner and McQuitty 1987: fig. 4) and also indicate points where open channels have leaked. Such flow stones can provide radiocarbon or other radiometric dates.

— Frequently, dams or water tanks are made of mortar that includes ash; consequently, the contained charcoals can then be used for radiocarbon dating (Bruins 1986).

— The excavation of installations such as lime kilns, mills, or cisterns along the channel can provide indirect dates for the construction of the canal. For example, lime kilns can supply charcoal for radiocarbon assay, whereas watermills or cisterns may yield artifacts that can be dated.

— Techniques of optical luminescence dating now make it possible for the dates of deposition of the sedimentary fills of channels to be estimated (Aitken 1997).

Episodic Flow Systems

Runoff from hill slopes or wadi floods sustains episodic flow systems. The former systems simply direct slope runoff onto fields (see chapter 8), whereas the latter gather water from the wadi channel during floods to lead it downstream via canals to fields. Because such systems usually exhibit very wide fluctuations of flow discharge, artificial channels must be sufficiently large to accommodate the maximum flow, or steps must be taken to allow for the evacuation of excess water. Therefore, even though they may supply a relatively modest area of fields, canals receiving water from wadis or other episodic flow channels can give the impression that they belong to much larger systems. Unlike perennial flow systems such as springs, which are clean and clear, episodic flow systems often conduct very muddy water, with the result that canals, sluices, and fields accumulate large quantities of silt and gradually rise in level above the surrounding terrain (chapter 8). This is also the case for perennial river systems like the Tigris and Euphrates, but in such cases, irrigation water was usually tapped from the low winter flow regime, before the spring flood brought in large quantities of silt and clay.

Episodic flow systems also include temporary storage features such as reservoirs and water tanks (birkehs) that are characteristic of desert landscapes (chapter 8; Lancaster and Lancaster 1999: 144). Of smaller scale, and tailored to the needs of single households, are rock-cut, bottle-shaped cisterns that derive their water as runoff from adjacent hill slopes (Evenari et al. 1982: 148–178; Oleson 1991: 56; Lancaster and Lancaster 1999: 139). Although reservoirs are usually too large to be roofed, smaller cisterns can be roofed or tunneled into the bedrock, thereby minimizing evaporation.

For episodic flow systems it is often more important to get rid of excess water than to maximize the amount of flow gathered. Thus ancient engineers frequently located water tanks or dams away from the wadi, rather than in its main path, where deflecting walls could be damaged. Masonry dams were typically located in the narrowest defiles of a rock-cut valley, but in other cases, dams were built of impermanent or perishable materials so that a peak flood, rather than damaging key installations such as sluices, would break through the system and continue downstream. This appears to have been the case with the main part of the Marib dam in Yemen, which being constructed of earth, required frequent rebuilding (chapter 8).

Water-supply installations can be recognized by a number of key diagnostic features (table 4.2). Their preservation within the landscape depends upon whether they are located in a dynamic high-energy zone or were constructed in more stable areas. Thus any barrier built across a river or wadi to deflect flow into a canal will usually be eroded away, as will much of the transport section of canals or conduits. On the other hand, if canals cut through large areas of stable land surface, they will be preserved for centuries or millennia. Those parts of the system designed to conduct high-energy or turbulent flow—sluices, some dams, key parts of canals—will usually be manufactured of robust masonry or baked brick and are more likely to survive than structures of impermanent materials. Stones with rectilinear grooves to house sluice gates can sometimes be recognized, even if the original canal has been removed by erosion or obscured sedimentation or agricultural activities. In the case of an irrigation system in the Syrian Balikh Valley, large sluice stones of limestone noted at regular intervals across the landscape were all that remained of a post-Roman canal system (Wilkinson 1998).

Landscape transformations almost invariably impede our ability to recognize all parts of an irrigation system, and it is common to find that a considerable portion of any canal system has been eroded away by the vigorous flow of wadis or obscured

Table 4.2   Selected Diagnostic Features of the Main Types of Water Supply in the Near East.

Water Source	Water-Supply Feature	Some Diagnostic Features (fig. 4.1)
Ground water-supply systems	Wells and water holes	The well void, sometimes evident as depression; ring of upcast sediments, frequently consisting of gravels excavated from deeper geological strata; elongated depression of animal walkway; upstanding masonry of well-head lifting device and small water-catching tank and distribution channels.
	Qanats	Alignment of circular access shafts (fig. 8.2) and surrounding upcast; further downstream open channel within ditch.
Perennial-flow systems	Small open channels	Frequently of masonry alignments (fig. 4.3a); sometimes remaining as low embankments, alignments of stones, or faint depressions across country, < 100 cm wide and 50 cm deep. Patches of shells (cleaned out of channel) or lime-burning kilns (from masonry construction) are occasionally found alongside.
	Large open channels	Usually > 100 cm wide and > 50 cm deep. Can take the form of shallow linear depressions or soil or moisture marks (fig. 5.7) and/or can be identified by large clean-out mounds alongside (fig. 4.3b).
Episodic-flow systems	Dams	Can be of masonry (as in Urartian systems of Anatolia; or highland Arabia: fig. 9.8b) or of soil (as in the Marib Dam in Yemen). Earthen dams often have conspicuous remains of upstanding masonry sluices (fig. 8.7). Small valley-floor check dams and wadi-floor terraces are equipped with spillways (fig. 8.12).
	Canals	Earthen channels, reinforced by masonry or stone structures where water flow has high energy. Frequently cleaned out, resulting in large amounts of upcast spoil.
	Water-gathering areas	Water-gathering enhanced by low walls oblique to contours (*saghiyas* in Yemen: fig. 8.12), sometimes by removal of stones from water catchment as in Negev systems (Evenari et al. 1982).

by sedimentation. Alternatively, irrigated fields may be unrecognizable because their boundaries consisted of perishable materials, because they have been obscured by sedimentation, or because they have been incorporated into more recent landscapes. The recognition of upcast and clean-out features is, however, the most immediate way of recognizing many types of ancient water-supply systems. Canals are typically flanked by upcast banks (figs. 4.1d and 4.3b), unless as in lower Mesopotamia, these have been removed by deflation or obscured because ground level has risen as a result of sedimentation. Alternatively canals can be recognized by the presence of scatters of freshwater mollusks, which result from the cleaning out of silts or weeds.

The lifespan of wells or canals can

be estimated from the number of cleaning episodes evident in the secondary silt deposits piled up around or adjacent to them. Frequently, such upcast can produce a patchwork of different mounds. In principal the excavation of such mound complexes may provide a more secure chronological sequence for the well, canal, or water tank than excavation of the feature itself. This is because the fill of a well or canal may relate only to the final phase of the features' use, whereas upcast mounds relate to the entire history of the feature in question. Ideally, of course, both the well shaft and its upcast should be excavated.

There is frequently considerable evidence for the cleaning out of canals and water systems not only because muddy flows accumulate much sediment but in theory be-

cause, to extend the irrigation capacity of a canal system, they can be expanded only by rebuilding the entire existing network (Doolittle 1990: 151). In other words, to increase flow for an expanded area of fields, it is necessary to increase the size of the channel, which then results in a change of the hydraulic parameters, which in turn can result in either increased erosion or sedimentation. These principles have important implications for the construction of Mesopotamian irrigation systems (see chapter 5).

Fields

Ideally, fields can be recognized in the landscape by means of the boundaries that enclose them, although as will become apparent below, not all fields are bounded on all sides. Bounding a field is usually a deliberate act that entails the laying out of cultivated land often using techniques of geometry to determine the form of the field parcel. The origins of this practice are clearly ancient. Herodotus ascribed the origins of geometry to the ancient Egyptians who had to lay out the land along the Nile Valley where annual flooding obliterated field boundaries (cited in Gleason 1994: 5). The formal process of bounding fields extends to earlier periods though, and from Jemdet Nasr in Mesopotamia, cadastral texts belonging to the late fourth millennium B.C. (Uruk III period) record actual field measurements of a range of rectangular, square, as well as thin, striplike fields (Liverani 1996: 10–12). Unfortunately, because such field plots were bounded with temporary materials, they are unlikely to be recognized by archaeological techniques, unless the fields correspond with the meshwork of irrigation (or drainage) canals or have been buried and thereby preserved. Elsewhere, field systems may have been of varying degrees of permanence so that part of the record may have survived. For example, in Anatolia, the Hittite landscape of the mid second millennium B.C. often comprised a mixture of rain-fed and irrigated fields, some of which were "open," whereas others were enclosed by walls and fences. In such circumstances, the latter imprint would have a greater chance of survival, thereby giving a biased view of the landscape of the time.

The discovery of relict fields in the landscape is usually a function of the robustness of the materials that were used to construct the walls as well as the taphonomic circumstances of preservation. Because most fields either consist of impermanent boundaries or are found in areas where there has been much subsequent activity, the discovery of pre-Roman fields systems is relatively rare. Nevertheless, skeletal remains of relict systems can survive, and as in the Wadi Faynan (Jordan), parts

of earlier field systems can be encapsulated within later ones (Barker et al. 1999). Arguably some of the earliest fields in the Near East may remain because they take the form of terraced fields bounded on one side by high multiphased terraced walls. Such fields, with their deep sedimentary accumulations upslope, often appear to have been in use for extended periods of time (chapter 9). In lowland areas, field boundaries are usually of perishable materials and are marked by little more than occasional boundary stones, whereas in rock terrain where stones are abundant, fields are walled and therefore have a much higher likelihood of survival (chapter 9).

Classes of fields found in the Near East include

— Fields bounded with permanent walls on all sides.
— Formal fields of gardens with monumental terrace or boundary walls. Usually these are more geometric than the more informally shaped fields of the long-term agricultural landscape.
— Partly bounded fields with terrace wall on one side.
— Lightly bounded fields in which the field boundary was of soil or some other impermanent material that was easily removed. These are more likely to be found on extensive areas of lowlands.
— Fields aggraded by irrigation silts and defined by rectilinear erosion patterns.
— Sunken fields dug down to the level of a qanat, canal, or water table.

Other features that can be related either to fields or to agricultural usage include sherd scatters, field clearance mounds, and cultivated soil horizons.

The following examples indicate the range of morphological features of fields that remain in the Near Eastern landscape:

Fields Bounded with Permanent Wall. These are common in the marginal rock deserts of Jordan and southern Syria, although the illustrated example is from Oman (fig. 4.4) (e.g., Villeneuve 1985; also fig. 7.8). Such fields often include stone clearance mounds and are frequently Roman/Byzantine in date. Optimum conditions for preservation of bounded fields are found in climatically marginal areas, but relict fields are becoming increasingly scarce as a result of disturbance arising from recent extensions of cultivated land.

Similar systems, but formalized into a large rectangular grid, remain in areas of former centuriation. For many years centuriation was considered to be absent from the Near East, but possible examples have been recognized by van Liere (1958/59), Dodinet et al. (1990), and Wirth (1971) in long-cultivated areas of western Syria. As a result of sustained use, the original field divisions have been eroded by later cultivation so that only occasional linear elements remain as witnesses to the preexisting grid (Wirth 1971: 375, 412).

Estates or other more formal agricultural units can also be fossilized, in which case the monumental boundary or terrace walls appear as a distinct physical presence imposed on a preexisting more organic or informal system of fields.

Partly Bounded Fields. These usually remain because one element, usually a terrace wall, comprises a main defining element. The other field boundaries, being minimally defined, would be less likely to survive, although they may be recognizable where the loam wedge of accumulated soils upslope of the terrace wall dwindle to nothing. Such fields are usually bounded by terraced walls up to 5–6 m in height and are associated with varying degrees of soil accumulation upslope, depending upon the amount of post-abandonment erosion or deliberate

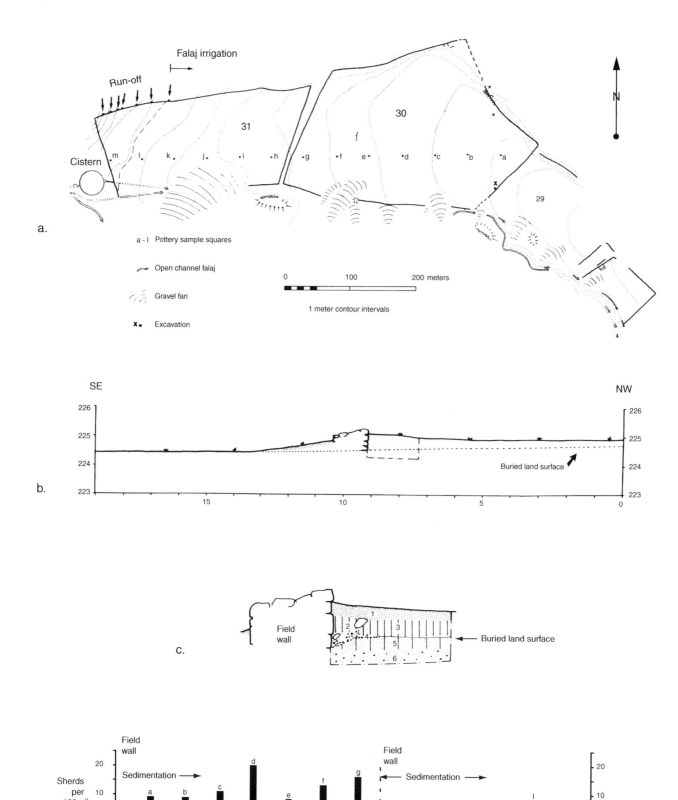

Fig. 4.4 Elements of Early Islamic fields at Arja (Oman). (a) Overall field area with boundary wall, passageway for goats between fields (between h and g), inlet for perennial irrigation water via cistern, to west, and supplementary runoff (arrows). (b) and (c) Section and detail across field wall at X showing depth of accumulated soils. (d) Pottery density per 100 sq. m on the field surface (i.e., field scatters). Note that lower pot counts occur in the area of alluvial fan sedimentation (h, i, j, k) (Costa and Wilkinson 1987: figs. 46, 47).

infill. Terrace walls frequently have a foundation of small stones as well as a wedge of accumulated sediments behind, and sometimes the remains of a relict buried soil are sealed beneath the wedge of sediment (fig. 4.1i). Terraced fields are common in upland areas of the Near East, especially in western Syria and the Levant (Ron 1966). In Yemen, valley floor terraced fields can be traced back to the fourth millennium B.C. (chapters 7 and 9).

Terraced fields are constructed to take advantage of the topography, runoff from slopes, and slope gradient. Their morphology also depends on local architectural tradition, and owing to the wide range of combinations of these factors, the range of morphological classes of terraced fields is potentially large. No classification has therefore been attempted here, but the following classes of terraced fields have been recognized elsewhere:

Mediterranean terraces (Grove and Rackham 2001: 107–110) include (1) step terraces (with straight wall), (2) step terraces along contours, (3) braided terraces, (4) "pocket terraces," (5) terraced fields (i.e., bounded on 3–4 sides), (6) check-dam terraces in wadis/gullies, (7) check-dam terraces on gentle terrain, (8) false terraces (cut out of slopes by bulldozers), (9) lynchets, and (10) terraces of Ligurian type (with uppermost part of wall being a grassy bank).

Andean mountain terraces (Denevan 1987; Treacy and Denevan 1994; see also Donkin 1979) consist of (1) bench terraces, (2) contour terraces, (3) linear terraces, (4) broadfield terraces, (5) valley bottom walled terraces, (6) upland walled terraces, (7) wet-field terraces, (8) sloping dry-field terraces, (9) barrage terraces, and (10) weir terraces.

Fields with Impermanent Boundaries. In those parts of the Near East typified by loam or clay plains, fields are usually bounded by per-

ishable or impermanent materials, and they rarely remain unless they are fortuitously buried by later sediments. On the other hand, in deserts and other landscapes of survival where preservation conditions are ideal, field traces can be recognized. For example, in the proximity of a Chalcolithic site in the Negev, low earthen embankments may have been in use in the fourth millennium B.C. as part of floodwater agriculture (Avner 1998: 170). Because of their scarcity in the archaeological record, however, the best record of this class of ancient fields comes from cuneiform texts (Liverani 1996; Zaccagnini 1979; Zettler 1989).

Aggraded Silt Fields. A conspicuous type of relict field pattern occurs where flood runoff agriculture has resulted in the aggradation of great depths of silt within fields. Such fields are further defined by the presence of a meshwork of rectilinear gullies that trace out roughly the pattern of within-field irrigation gullies. As with terraced fields, long-term aggradation of sediments has favored the preservation of ancient agricultural soils as well as related features, and aggraded fields form probably the best examples of spatially and temporally resolved fields in the Near East (chapter 8).

Field Clearance Features. When fields are constructed in stony terrain, it is necessary first to remove the stones and pile them into stone clearance mounds. These often occur as alignments within fields. Because part of the original ground surface can be preserved beneath, the survival of clearance mounds enables the amount of soil erosion to be estimated and pre-clearance soils recognized (figs. 4.5 and 4.1j). In addition to preserving the underlying ground surface, in Yemen, field stones can be piled up over preexisting buildings, thereby encapsulating them within a multiperiod cairn. Although field-clearance mounds can be difficult to date, different degrees of lichen growth or desert varnish on

stones provide a rough estimate of their age (Innes 1985) and therefore the age of the fields. For example, in deflation-prone southern Syria and Jordan, stones of clearance mounds exhibit an upper coating of lichens below which occurs a clean rock surface (Philips et al. 2002b). The clean surface appears to have been that part of the rock that was covered by the former plough soil and that has been subsequently lost as a result of deflation. In similar areas, rocks now exposed within bounded fields bear scars from ploughing (Barker et al. 1999: 269–270), again implying that the soil had once been much deeper than at present. In particularly fortuitous circumstances where deflation has removed the soil matrix, stone field boundaries can even be inferred from the difference in stone size between the cleared fields (surface lag of small stones) and the uncleared area beyond where stone size is both larger and more variable.

Sunken Fields. Where irrigation water is below the level of the fields to be irrigated, farmers occasionally undertake the herculaean task of digging fields down to the level of the water-supply channel. Although rare, traditional sunken fields of this type have been recorded in Oman and the United Arab Emirates, where they result in distinctive and often enormous upcast mounts around the perimeter of palm gardens (Costa 2000: 77; chapter 8 and fig. 8.4). Alternatively, Hehmeyer (1998) suggests that around the city of San ʿa in Yemen sunken fields were laid out in the base of pits dug for the extraction of mudbrick for housing.

Indirect Evidence of Ancient Cultivation. During the 1970s and 1980s, field archaeologists became acutely aware that many landscapes in Europe, the Near East, and the New World could not simply be divided into site and off-site areas. Instead, surveys had to contend with what was an essentially continuous archaeological landscape consisting of scatters of artifacts and other

Fig. 4.5   Stone clearance mounds in relict fields at roughly 2,000 m above sea level, near the Early Bronze Age mine of Kestel, Turkey.

features occurring apparently without discernable limit across the land (Cherry 1983). The definition of such scatters and their interpretation have become a major preoccupation of surveys in the Mediterranean zone, but rather less so in the Near East. Nevertheless, the ground surface in many parts of the Near East can be covered by a sparse scatter of small battered sherds, occasional tile fragments, small pieces of stone, and other artifactual materials. On fields, artifact visibility depends upon the state of ploughing, sherds being more obvious when fallowing has allowed them to become washed and concentrated, whereas they are less obvious after ploughing.

By increasing background noise, "field scatters" interfere with the visibility of sedentary settlements. For example, where sites of nomad encampments occur,[3] their recognition will be hampered by the presence of sherds across the entire area. Moreover, "off-site" sherd scatters can blur site boundaries. Intensive surveys in the Mediterranean region and Near East suggest that such scatters derive from five main sources (not listed in order of importance). First, debris associated with small buildings, nomad tent sites, and other minor occupations. Second, upcast from robbed graves that originally contained ceramics. Third, random pot drops. Fourth, ploughed-out middens around larger sites. Fifth, the remains of composts and settlement-derived manure, which were spread on the fields as fertilizer. Such settlement-derived refuse includes various artifacts, and following the decay of the organic components, the resistant material such as pottery and vitrified clay from the cleaning out of kilns remains in the soil. When viewed in thin section, such soils exhibit distinctive traces of charred material and microartifacts that were introduced by the manuring. It is the presence of cultural material within relict soil horizons that represents one of the most effective ways of recognizing ancient cultivation (Courty et al. 1989; Davidson and Simpson 2001: 175). In Mediterranean lands where topography is complex and field terraces and other built features are common, numerous cultural and geomorphologic processes often disturb field scatters. In such areas, artifact scatters probably consist of artifacts from a range of sources, only some of them from manuring (Bintliff 2000). Surprisingly, given the prosaic nature of this process, the topic of "manuring scatters" has led to an impassioned debate in the literature (see, for example, Alcock et al. 1994 and response by Snodgrass 1994). Nevertheless, soil micromorphology, the analysis of chemical inclusions in the form of trace metals (Rimmington 2000), as well as lipid biomarkers (Bull et al. 2001; Evershed et al. 1997) provide support for the antiquity of manuring and its tendency to concentrate geochemical traces in the topsoil. In the Near East, scatters can be dense, especially where they have been concentrated by the aeolian removal of topsoil (Costa and Wilkinson 1987; see chapters 5 and 8). The densest off-site scatters have been recognized in irrigated and deflated areas of the Near East and central Asia (Wilkinson 1982; Bintliff and Snodgrass 1988).

Although "field scatters" can impede the recording of small archaeological sites, the presence of ceramics on fields should not be regarded as a random event. Instead, they can contribute to the dating of periods of cultivation, especially if the sherds occur in buried soil horizons (Wilkinson 1988). In addition, because their distribution relates to an inner zone of intensive cultivation rather than the entire cultivated area, field scatters are most useful for determining the development of rings of varying land use intensity around sites rather than total cultivated area (chapter 6).

Agricultural Installations

The presence of agricultural installations lends depth to the interpretation of the rural landscape, but their survival is very variable. Whereas entire monographs have been written on specific features such as Hellenistic, Roman, and Byzantine oil presses (Frankel 1999), much less is known about such features in earlier landscapes. The following is just a summary of some commonly recurring installations.

Threshing Floors

These form surfaces, upon which cereals and other grains are separated from the chaff or where straw is reduced to fragments. They are normally platforms of laid stones, bare rock, or beaten earth, sometimes with a low wall surround. Threshing floors are rarely preserved on alluvial plains or areas of deep soft sediments and are more common in rocky places where there are abundant stones for the construction of stone platforms. Sumerian texts indicate that from the third millennium B.C., threshing was effected by beating the grain with a stick, by domestic bovids trampling around the threshing floor (so that the action of their hooves would separate out the grains from the chaff), or by means of threshing sledges (Civil 1994: 95). Precisely when threshing floors became formalized is not clear, but numerous mainly circular threshing floors have been recorded in the Uvda valley of the southern Negev, where they were either dug down to a rock surface or made of beaten earth. These are thought to date to the fourth millennium B.C., the Middle Bronze Age, Iron Age, and Nabatean periods (Avner 1998: 162–169). The presence of what appears to be a ceremonial threshing sledge on an Uruk style cylinder seal from Arslantepe (Littauer and Crouwel 1990) suggests that threshing with sledges can be traced back to at least the fourth millennium B.C.

Thanks to their robust construction, threshing floors can survive for millennia, but because they rarely occur in stratified contexts, they are difficult to date. In the highlands of Yemen, relict threshing floors (known as *megran* or *mejran*; cf. Akkadian: *magrattu* = threshing floor or grain pile) are constructed of lines or curvilinear alignments of dressed stones that over the centuries have becomes coated with dark brown or black "desert varnish" (fig. 4.6). They are clearly ancient

features and are often located near to sites of Iron Age and Himyarite date (1000 B.C. to A.D. 600). For these reasons, and because they are described as "Himyari" by the local inhabitants, it is reasonable to interpret these floors as Iron Age or Himyarite in date. When circular threshing floors are bordered by stone walls or "fences" but the interior becomes infilled by wind-blown soil, they can easily be confused with "prehistoric" stone circles, because the circular stone fences can remain as upstanding features.

Scatters of flint, chert, or small fragments of basalt around suspected threshing floors supply supporting evidence that platforms were used for threshing because lithics were frequently inserted into the base of threshing sledges. As a result of repeated threshing, the inserts received a punishing battering recognizable by use-ware analysis (Chabot 2001).

Wine Presses

Wine presses are best known from the southern Levant, where a wide range of types has been recorded (Åhlström 1978; Dar 1986; Gibson and Edelstein 1985: 145–149). An early example from Tell Ta 'annek was beautifully preserved below a Middle Bronze Age glacis and is therefore either EB–MB or EB II/III in date (Lapp 1969: fig. 8). Normally, wine presses are cut in bedrock and consist of two elements: a treading floor and a small rock-cut basin to catch the grape juices that flow from the treading floor via a narrow channel or rock-cut pipe. Treading floors can be either square or circular (Hirschfeld and Birger-Calderon 1991: figs. 15 and 18). Although they appear to be much less common in Syria and Jordan, perhaps because there has been less intensive survey in these countries, examples have been recorded in the limestone uplands of northern Syria (Tate 1992) and along the Euphrates Valley near Tell Sweyhat (fig. 4.7).

Fig. 4.6 Stone threshing floor on Yemen high plains, probably of Himyarite date (1st century B.C.–6th century A.D.).

Olive Presses

In the field these are easily confused with wine presses (Frankel 1999: 26), and it is understandable therefore that similar terms are used for them in the Biblical literature. Levantine oil presses are of various sizes, up to industrial-scale features. Callot (1984) and Frankel (1999) provide detailed classifications of oil presses, which aid considerably in their field recognition. Frankel's classification, which recognizes a range of improved and pre-industrial installations, consists of six classes: (1) simple lever and weight presses, (2) olive-crushing devices, (3) improved lever presses, (4) beam weights, (5) lever and screw presses, and (6) rigid frame presses with various types of screw press (Frankel 1999: chapter 6).

Field Towers

Typically, these remain as foundations of stone usually of square or nearly square ground plan. They are relatively common in the Levant (Dar 1986, 1999; Gibson and Edelstein 1985), the Eastern Mediterranean (Cherry et al. 1991: 285–298), and Yemen, in all cases dating back until the early first millennium B.C. Their simple ground plans are ambiguous, and so their precise function is not always apparent, but they were probably used for storage of agricultural produce and implements or as observation points to watch over vineyards or olive orchards. As pointed out by Cherry and colleagues (1991), probably no single function can be attached to field towers. They probably served a multitude of purposes that included temporary living accommo-

dation, storage, and watchtowers. In Yemen where field towers form a conspicuous part of the present rural landscape, they are used as guard posts over high-value crops such as *qat*. It is depressingly common while on survey to be greeted by an enthusiastically savage dog, tethered to a watchtower, and it is quite clear that the dog, at least, is in no doubt that towers form part of a guardianship strategy. Larger tower-like features around and within third millennium B.C. oasis settlements in Oman also appear to have played a combined defensive, habitation, and watchtower role (chapter 8).

Water Mills and Windmills

These enable cereals to be ground beyond the village. From the first century B.C., water mills become an element of the landscape (Wikander

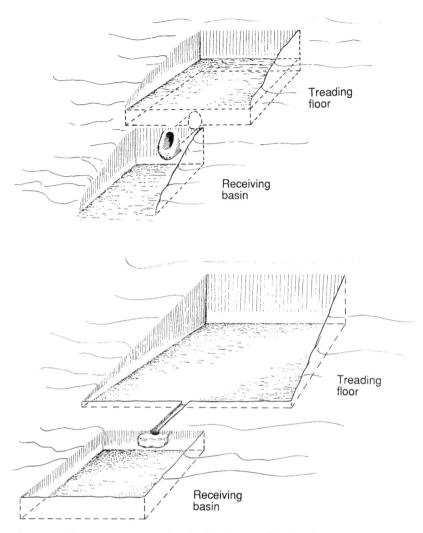

Fig. 4.7   Two wine presses by the Euphrates floodplain near Tell Sweyhat, Syria.

2000: 398). Most common are "drop tower" mills also known as arubah penstocks (Avitsur 1960), Norse, or horizontal mills. In most cases, the power to turn the millstones was generated by leading a small flow of water into a vertical pipe enclosed in a sturdy stone and masonry penstock. Having filled the pipe, a jet of water issued under pressure from a spout in the base (normally some 5–8 m below the inlet channel) and struck a horizontal paddle wheel set on a vertical axis, which in turn rotated the millstones. Drop-tower water mills form a dramatic component of the landscape because of their conspicuous penstocks that jut out of hillsides as large masonry walls. Despite the small flows required, they are capable of generating in the region of 400–1,200 kg of flour per day (Harverson 1993: 167–168) as well as copious dust. Numerous watermills of Roman/Byzantine/Early Islamic date have been recorded from the eastern Mediterranean, the southern Levant, the Amuq plain in southern Turkey, Jordan, and Oman (Schioler 1989; Gardiner and McQuitty 1987; Avitsur 1960; Wilkinson 1980). The largest concentrations, however, have been recorded from Iran, where their siting can range from large rivers (as at Shushtar) to along underground qanats (Harverson 1993: 153; Neely 1974).

Other types of water mills, such as those utilizing the kinetic energy of water flowing down an inclined chute, or vertical (Vitruvian) mills (Harverson 1993), as well as windmills, are less common and have had less impact on the development of the landscape than the drop-tower mill.

Pasturelands

Because pasturelands include few built remains, their imprint on the landscape is usually slight. Probably the most straightforward way to recognize early pasturelands is first to define the area that was not used for pasture for most of the year, namely, the cultivated land. Then by default, the land beyond that was capable of being grazed can be inferred to have been devoted to pasture (see chapter 6). Former pastures may also be inferred from the presence of built structures that are normally associated with pastoral activities. For example, a circular corral-like structure associated with a sparse ceramic scatter of Late Roman/Byzantine date occurred in a broad zone of what is today upland pasture in southern Turkey (Wilkinson 1990a: 118, 174–175). Both corral and surrounding steppe could therefore be inferred to have belonged to pastoral lands that were in use during the first millennium A.D. Other built structures providing evidence for pastoral communities include stone-walled compounds or semisubterranean structures that probably supplied shelter for animals that over-wintered on higher, cooler pastures (Yakar 2000: figs. 71, 82). Although the latter structures may resemble domestic structures in form, the lack of artifacts and the presence of accumulated dung (archaeologically detectable as phosphate signatures) imply that they were used for stabling animals.

Both of the above classes of information rely to a considerable degree on inference verging on guesswork, but recent geoarchaeological studies in Yemen suggest that pasturelands may be recognizable in palaeosols. Traditional pasture reserves in Arabia develop mollic horizons in areas where pasture is protected from overgrazing. Consequently, similar deep dark, humic horizons preserved beneath cultivated or eroded soils may therefore be interpretable as relict pastoral soils. In such pastoral horizons, diagnostic soil micromorphological features of cultivation must be absent, whereas features such as faecal spherulites[4] may be expected to accumulate.

Roads and Tracks

Roads and tracks are fundamental to an understanding of the economic landscape. Their routes can be inferred on the basis of textual evidence that refers to named places on cuneiform itineraries (e.g., the Sippar itinerary of Goetze 1953; Hallo 1964). Alternatively, routes can be inferred more deterministically from the overall topography of a region, that is, from the location of through valleys, mountain passes, and similar features. Field evidence for actual roads can sometimes be recognized, as described in table 4.3 (see fig. 4.8).

Additional features, such as milestones (carved with Roman or Arabic lettering), stone road-marking cairns, bridges, paved fords (French 1981: fig. 5; Oates and Oates 1990), and gateways within sites, allow the trajectories of routes to be reconstructed. Roads are important not only because of their economic role but also because sites or individual landscape features often form alignments along them, as is the case along the Darb Zubaydah pilgrim road across the Arabian desert (chapter 8).

Moreover, roads play an important role in determining overall landscape structure. For example, if a landscape has been subdivided by centuriation, Roman roads should form part of such alignments. Consequently, if individual roadside features, such

as Roman milestones, can be recorded in place, these can then be used to estimate the overall centuriation grid. Thus a single feature can (ideally) provide a key to the layout of the entire landscape.

Boundaries in the Landscape

Landscape boundaries in the Near East are difficult to fix, and usually they can be defined only by default, that is, by the recognition of large areas of open space between settlements or settled areas or by the presence of natural boundaries such as mountains, ridges, or watersheds. Nevertheless, some landscape-scale features illustrate that boundaries were sometimes constructed to ward off threats that were either real or perceived or simply as statements of power and control. Interestingly, both boundary walls cited below have been misattributed either by popular legend or in later historical sources to the wrong builder or external threat.

For example, Alexander's wall (Sad-i Iskander located near Iran's border with Russia) extends for some 100 km east of the Caspian Sea as a bank 5 m wide, interrupted by small forts at intervals of ca. 6 km. Despite its name, this appears to have been constructed during that great period of imperial construction, the late Sasanian period, when the king Anushirvan in the sixth century A.D. constructed a wall as defense against tribes from Central Asia (Matheson 1976: 67). Similarly misnamed is the so-called Median wall (Habl as-Sahr) that was constructed during the sixth century B.C. in the reign of Nebuchadnezar II. This extends as a bank 1 m high 30 m wide for some 15 km across the northern plains of the Mesopotamian alluvium from near Sippar towards the east. The inclusion within its makeup of baked bricks with the stamp of Nebuchadnezar II confirm its date (Black et al. 1987), and its present degraded state results from recent cultivation, as well as the construction of irriga-

tion canals, drainage ditches, roads, and villages.

These activities have all served to diminish this feature to a fraction of its former state (Black et al. 1987: 3). Now the wall, which originally served as a boundary to keep people out, acts as a raised causeway used by local people to traverse low-lying, flood-prone areas. To interpret the role of this wall in the landscape, it is necessary to understand its relationship to the changing fluvial geomorphology of the area. Significantly, the curving course of the wall parallels roughly that of the ancient Euphrates through Sippar, not that of any modern river. Despite the original massive scale of the Habl as-Sahr, which must have extended for some 45 km from the Euphrates to the Tigris, historical records provide no convincing motive for its construction. While it might have been conceived as a deterrent against perceived threats, it could simply have been constructed as a massive and spectacular statement of the power of Babylon and the majesty of its king Nebuchadnezar II (Black et al. 1987: 29).

Although the former provides a convincing example of a large boundary earthwork, the latter is difficult to distinguish from one of the many levees that remain in the area. These two remarkable earthworks underscore the need, wherever possible, to undertake integrated studies of texts, the physical landscape, and control excavations.

Even more elusive in terms of their archaeological remains are boundary stele such as the Pazarcik and Antakya stele erected by Adad Nerari III (810–783 B.C.) to define the borders between Kummu· and Gaugum, and Arpad and Hammath respectively (Wazana 2001: 699, 701). More often that not, these will have been removed from their original landscape context, but we can understand their original function from Hittite texts as given in the following verdict of Muršilis: "He (referring to the Uriyannu priest) selected the

Fig. 4.8 Two types of road trace in the Near East: (top) Wheel ruts incised in limestone, Amuq Plain, Turkey (scale 30 cm). (bottom) Ancient roadway in Yemen, marked by boundary walls of stone.

Table 4.3 Main Classes of Roads and Tracks

Formal and paved roads	Usually of Roman date (Kennedy and Riley 1990: 77–94; French 1981: 15–22). To prevent travelers from sinking into the (often muddy) soil in antiquity, it was sometimes necessary to provide a paved surface. Remains of pre-Roman paved roads are, however, unusual in the Near East, either because more informal roads were in use or because the stones have been robbed out. Frequently, only the edge stones, spine, or part of the surface remain (French 1981: figs. 1–4). Construction methods vary according to terrain. Fischer and colleagues (1996) describe a range of states, including well-paved roads with intact pavement, areas where only the kerbstones remain, roadways in partial cuttings, rock-cut steps, and roads between parallel stone walls.
Informally paved tracks	These are more common in mountainous terrain, e.g., in Saudi Arabia, Yemen (Thenayian 2000), and Turkey (von der Osten 1929: figs. 175–178), and are similar to Roman roads but exhibit more variable paving.
Cuttings	Usually made through mountain passes. Sometimes cuttings are referred to in Neo-Assyrian texts (e.g., Liverani 1992). Excellent examples also occur along the Roman road between Damascus and Beirut.
Linear hollows	Shallow, straight valleys aligned or radiating from sites, usually in the rain-fed steppe of Upper Mesopotamia (chapter 6; Van Liere and Lauffray 1954; Wilkinson 1993) or aligned erosional gullies and related hollows (Tsoar and Yekutieli 1993). These have numerous parallels through the Old and New Worlds. In the United States, equivalent features have been associated with Anasazi settlement (Trombold 1991a) as well as the European settlement of the western United States.
Rural tracks	Informal rural roads or tracks frequently demarcated by parallel lines of stones or fences (fig. 4.8b; Dar 1986).
Stepped tracks	Cut in bedrock or of masonry along certain routes, specifically those used by foot passengers (Fischer et al. 1996: pls. 63, 77). Found in both Palestine and Yemen, their presence demonstrates that wheeled transport was not in use along the route in question (Kloner 1996: 117).
Wheel ruts	Areas of bedrock incised by grooves worn by wheeled vehicles. An example recorded in the Amuq of southern Turkey (fig. 4.8a) resembles the well-known cart tracks of Malta (Zammit 1928). Although aligned along a Roman route, this distinctive feature could be as early as the Bronze Age in date.
Desert tracks	Sometimes evident as broad lineations cleared of stones through the desert (Al-Rashid 1986) or similar alignments along ancient caravan routes (Clapp 1998: 175). Where thousands of camels or other pack animals have passed through areas of ancient gravel or rock desert that have developed a patina or "desert varnish" over the millennia, paths are recognizable as lighter trails through the dark patinated ground surface. Alternatively, stones may have been scraped to one side to produce a cleared trail along the route. Finally, the passage of camels may have compressed the soil sufficiently so that it registers as a different soil or vegetation mark on satellite images. In Dhofar (southern Oman), satellite-borne radar has distinguished trampled clay and sand along trails. Such features can also be rendered more visible by the use of satellite sensors that are sensitive to infrared radiation. As a result, satellite images provide a more distinctive image than would be obtained by more conventional air photography (Aspaturian 1992).

areas between the king of Ugarit and the king of Siyannu, and established stones on the borders between them" (Wazana 2001: 702).

Mineral Extraction and Processing

Quarries

These form a ubiquitous part of the landscape, but because they are simply "holes in the ground," they are easily overlooked. Alternatively, they can become infilled by sediments and lost from view. They serve a variety of purposes, providing either a source of supply for everyday building stone or for more specialized purposes such as for statues or for high-status, carved stone implements. Probably equally common as stone quarries but less obvious, are the large mudbrick ex-

traction pits that are found next to most mounded sites in the Middle East (chapter 6).

Quarries for ashlar building blocks can be recognized by the distinctively cut backwalls from which blocks have been removed as well as by the detachment grooves of the removed blocks, which also perhaps provided template for the blocks that were removed next (fig. 4.9; Abu Dayyah 2001). Ac-

Fig. 4.9   Quarry for limestone blocks along the Euphrates, near Tell Sweyhat, Syria.

cording to Waelkens, the cutting of such grooves had already been developed by the Hittite period in the thirteenth century B.C. (Waelkens et al. 1992: 12). Quarry faces are frequently marked by drilled holes that demarcated the blocks to be removed (Sumaka'i Fink 2000). In the Near East, stone quarries are known from at least the third millennium B.C., but they increase markedly in the Roman period, at which time there appears to have been a greater demand for ashlar blocks.

More subtle are the spoil heaps that remain from the dressing of the blocks themselves (see Reade 1983: fig. 50). Near Titrish Höyük in southern Turkey, spoil mounds of limestone chips form conical heaps some 20–40 m away from the cut face of a quarry. Almost certainly, this quarry supplied the neighboring 40 ha Early Bronze Age site of Titrish Höyük with building stones, an inference that is supported by

calculations by Jennifer Pournelle (2001a). Her calculations suggest that the quantity of stone quarried approximates the amount of stone required for the construction of the foundations. In the case of specialized quarries such as those for soft stone vessels or millstones, roughouts of the original stone artifacts or millstones may remain scattered among quarry debris.

On the other hand, if spoil dumps of quarrying waste are absent, this may be because the waste material had an intrinsic value. For example, in the case of limestone quarries, the limestone chippings could have been burned for the manufacture of lime.

Mines

Although the actual trace of the mine shaft itself may be minimal (simply a hole cut in the rock large enough to take a man or boy), mines can act as focal points for entire

landscapes. Mining landscapes can include ore-crushing areas and their waste, smelting areas, slag fields, villages for the miners, as well as their associated fields, water-supply systems, pasture areas (for working animals), and sanctuaries or religious areas and cemeteries (chapter 9; Knapp 1999). Other industrial installations associated with mining include those for the washing of ore to separate out the metalliferous particles (Andrew Wilson 2000: 135). Where Near Eastern mines occur in dry areas, ore washing is precluded, but where water is sufficient, water separation or even crushing by means of water mills may have taken place. Because mines often occur in isolated rocky areas with minimal potential for agriculture, the appearance of mining can result in the imposition of a completely new agricultural landscape on the area. The most significant and recognizable features of mining complexes are ore-crushing areas with their characteristic crushing stones, dumps of waste slag, and other waste materials. In the case of copper smelting, slag can form extensive dark signatures recognizable on aerial photographs. Sustained weathering can result in the slag becoming disaggregated into small fragments, whereas specialized processes of extraction result in much less slag remaining on the surface. Furnaces with vitrified linings are diagnostic of smelting, and under ideal circumstances (as is the case of Early Islamic mining in desert areas), entire working units for copper extraction can be recognized (chapter 9).

In the Near East, salt has always been a major item of exchange and in southern Arabia, some ancient tracks are referred to as "salt roads." Salt can be extracted by means of evaporation from saline estuaries or coastal embayments. Alternatively, the extraction of saline soil may result in extensive areas of pitting, as has been recorded in parts of northern Iraq and Syria. Such pits are surrounded by spoil heaps, which indicates that the objective was not the recovery of the soil itself. Instead, these distinctive areas may have been associated with the production of salt. The location of such pit complexes in areas of probable saline groundwater, or where gypsum occurs, suggests that these pits were for the extraction of either mineral. Salt extraction can also be quarried from rock-salt sources such as salt plugs. In this case, they are recognizable as conventional mines, except that the host rock is crystalline salt.

Lime Kilns

Burning of lime to make plaster can be traced back to the Pre-Pottery Neolithic period (8700–7000 B.C.; Hauptmann and Yakin 2000). Actual lime kilns have been recorded in the mid-third-millennium levels of Khafaje (Forbes 1955: 59). Because high temperatures are required to reduce lime to quick lime, the baked clay linings of lime kilns become melted to produce conspicuous olive green slaglike coatings. It is common to find lime kilns in association with aqueducts and open channels that require a waterproof lime-based plaster to hold and conduct water. Thus lime kilns occur at regular intervals along open channels in Oman (Costa and Wilkinson 1987: 55–56), adjacent to plaster-lined reservoirs in Syria and Saudi Arabia (chapter 8), and adjacent to mid–late Islamic dams in Morocco. Alignments of kilns along water channels also aid in the tracing of the channels themselves, especially where the channels are heavily eroded. Moreover, the excavation of kilns adjacent to dams or channels can yield charcoal for radiocarbon dating, thereby providing an indirect date for the dam or channel itself. Lime kilns are also common in the Levant, where they have been recovered by landscape surveys both inland (Gibson 1984) and around the coast.

Religious Places

Religious places in the landscape can be difficult to recognize unless they exhibit buildings with distinctive sacred architecture. For example, churches and mosques have been recorded in rural parts of the Near East for a century or more, although rarely have they been studied within a landscape context (but see chapter 7). Pilgrimage lends another dimension to religious landscapes because of the need for pilgrims to traverse entire regions, including deserts, to attain the holy place in question. This requires large numbers of pilgrims and their animals to be supplied with food and water in often unrelentingly harsh environments. Hence the entire Hajj routes of Arabia can be regarded as religious landscapes, and, like mining landscapes, they come with their own infrastructure or support systems (chapter 8). Christian pilgrimage also produced its own distinct landscape as, for example, the hermitages and other features found in association with St. Catherine's monastery and Mount Sinai in the Sinai Desert (chapter 9).

Often of greater antiquity, and now attracting considerable attention, are natural places in the landscape. Most prominent among these are mountains and high places, which from time immemorial played a venerated role in people's lives (Bradley 2000). In the Near East, sanctified places are marked by temples on prominent hills because many deities are regarded as being located therein. It is not uncommon to find inscriptions or rock art that relates to religious or sanctified hills (chapter 8 and 9). Because temples can simply be formalizations of pre-existing holy mountains, it may be expected that rites, deities, or architecture have evolved through time as the sanctified place has adapted to changing religious practices (Steinsapir 1999). It is therefore necessary to examine rural temples or sanctuaries for evidence of religious activity that may predate the formalized adoption of a religious building. In this way, it may be possible to recognize the local origins of religious places.

More problematic in terms of landscape investigation are sanctified places such as springs that also represent an economic resource. Although such features can remain in the landscape for millennia, if they are located in areas of water deficiency or population expansion, they may be absorbed within the secular or economic landscape, at which time they could experience a change in function from holy place to domestic water supply. For such a transformation to take place, however, it may have been necessary for there to have been a change in religious practice. However, few landscape studies in the Near East have examined both the religious and secular landscapes together; therefore, the way such mutual competition plays out in the landscape remains unclear (but see Dar 1993).

Landscapes of Pleasure

In contrast to religious or functional places, landscapes devoted simply to sport or pleasure are scarce. In the Near East, gardens have a long history extending back to the third millennium B.C. (Gleason 1994, 1997). In many places, gardens form a subset of landscapes of irrigation. Nevertheless, they also exhibit a dual function: on the one hand, representing the ultimate degree of domestication or taming of the landscape; on the other hand, the introduction of the wildscape into the urban milieu. Gardens testify to the power of the ruler, a point well exemplified by the Neo-Assyrian gardens and hunting parks of Nineveh, where trees, landscapes, and fauna were introduced from far-flung parts of the empire specifically for the king's relaxation.

Most distinctive are the immense racecourses in the vicinity of Abbasid (i.e., Early Islamic) Samarra. These elongated or cloverleaf traces of low banks in the desert near this Abbasid capital are the result of extensive landscaping in pursuit of pleasure (Northedge 1990). Because of their fragility, however, such features are readily erased from the landscape, and it is likely that such features have a much longer history than existing field evidence indicates.

Landscapes of the Dead

At the other end of the human/landscape life cycle are landscapes of the dead. Because burial and disposal of the dead is so culture-specific, no single body of data can be seen to represent these practices adequately. Nevertheless, it is possible to sketch some basic themes concerning the position of the dead within the Near Eastern landscape.

In the Near East in the last century or so, landscapes of the dead have become painfully obvious because of the sheer scale of plundering that has resulted in entire cemeteries being turned into little more than pockmarked debris fields. From their new-found visibility it is evident that necropoleis were frequently separated some distance from the settlements to maintain "an acceptable degree of physical and psychical distance between the living and the dead" (Greene 1997: 18). This principle is well exemplified along the Euphrates in Syria, where Early Bronze Age tomb fields extend as discrete patches along the Pleistocene river terraces at some distance from contemporaneous settlements. Although some cemeteries can be assumed to belong to neighboring sedentary sites, others may have been associated with settlements that had once existed on the flood plain but have subsequently been eroded away. Yet others may have been the chosen burial areas of nomadic pastoral groups that used the area as seasonal pastures.

A clearer association with nomadic pastoralists can be posited for dolmens and tumuli found in the Levant and southernmost Turkey, where these monumental features appear either to act as territorial markers or to be positioned on specific topographic features such as escarpments (Ilan 1997; Prag 1995; chapter 8). With these monuments the range of interpretation of individual features is also expanded. Not only are dolmens not necessarily associated with formal burials, but also these landscape features may be a monumental indicator of how some communities signify their long-term ties with the land.

In parts of the central Anatolian plateau there is a marked partitioning between the sedentary realm of höyüks (tells) and food production lands on the one hand and waste or upland areas on the other, the latter including landscapes dedicated to the dead. This is obvious in the Alishar region (east of Ankara) as well as in Phrygia, where noncultivated uplands often become the primary location of tombs and monuments for the dead (chapter 9). Partitioning between the dead and the living is evident also at Gordion (central Turkey), where the huge early first-millennium B.C. tumuli of an elite mortuary cult have been constructed above the level of the flood plain, perhaps along a ceremonial way. At Gordion there was a decent separation of burial grounds from the main settlement, but the tombs were sufficiently close to demonstrate their overriding power; other less impressive tumuli then are found in less-prominent locations around or near the edge of the cultivated zone.

These examples imply that although no formal rules apply to the location of burial grounds in the subhumid areas, under certain circumstances there is frequently some degree of physical separation of settlement and burial areas. Moreover, although cemeteries often are located on land that is unfit for cultivation, this is hardly sufficient grounds to explain the presence of a burial area. Usually the dead play a more privileged role in the landscape, and it is necessary to place them in a context that may be meaningful in terms of the social conditions of the contemporaneous societies. This is much more difficult than placing functional systems such as irrigation canals within their economic milieu, and to date, there have been few well-theorized studies of landscapes of the dead in the Near East.

On the other hand, some of the most impressive landscapes of the dead are found in deserts where grave fields become especially conspicuous (chapter 8). Particularly instructive are those graves whose appendages are preferentially oriented along routes, a situation reminiscent of, for example, chambered cairns in the Welsh Black Mountains (Tilley 1994: 203). To force a cross-cultural (and diachronic) parallel on these disparate monuments would be unrealistic, however, but it is evident that analysis within a landscape context can help explain such otherwise enigmatic features.

Some Principles of Landscape Analysis

In addition to recognizing landscape features using key diagnostic attributes (summarized on table 4.4), it is necessary to provide a context and date for them within the overall landscape. It is usually possible to hazard some sort of date for the landscape features, so that it is then possible to order features in terms of their age relative to one another. More important, however, is to build up a dating framework that provides a wide range of date estimates on individual features as well as both cross-checks, tests, and relative dates for as many features as possible. The following principles can be employed to date landscape archaeological features:

— Passive association of feature with dated sites. In this case, a feature such as a relict field may simply be physically adjacent to a site of a given date. If the field then appears from other attributes to be early in date, it can be inferred that it might have been in use when the site was occupied. This associative dating, although suggestive of a date, is of a low order of reliability.
— Active association. In this case, if a feature such as a hollow-way road leads directly to another feature (e.g., a gate) that forms part of a site the occupation phases of which are known, then the hollow way and the gate were likely, but not necessarily, in use at the same time.
— Cutting relationship. If a given feature is cut by a later (frequently linear) feature such as a canal, then the feature that has been cut is the earlier feature.

It is advisable to verify such relationships by the application of support criteria such as the relative degree of development of weathering, desert varnish, or lichen cover (see below) on either or both the cut feature and that which does the cutting.
— Superimposed relationship, in which an earlier feature is overlaid by a later feature or stratigraphic unit. For example, if a threshing floor is overlaid by sediment accumulated upslope of a later field terrace, then the threshing floor is earlier in date than the soil of the field. Such relationships are useful because sedimentary accumulations have the potential to provide datable materials such as ceramics or charred material for radiocarbon dating.
— Surface relative dating. Landscape features constructed of stone can acquire coatings, either of Fe/Mg compounds (i.e., desert varnish) or lichens that accumulate with time. Thus the thickest and darkest desert varnishes, or the thickest lichen accumulations with most species, will be the oldest (Lev-Yadun et al. 1996; Innes 1985). Despite recent doubts about the veracity of desert varnish dating, there continues to be optimism regarding the future of this medium (Broeker and Liu 2001). Desert varnish and lichenography both provide a useful means of qualitatively dating landscape features in arid or semiarid landscapes.
— Structures associated with aggraded sediments. Cisterns, reservoirs, canals, and terraced fields all accumulate a stratigraphic record of sediments. If their contained sediments can be dated, then it is possible to provide an estimate of the date of the feature in question. Due caution must be paid to the presence of earlier artifacts reworked into later deposits

(see above, for other methods of dating perennial flow channels). Ideally, age estimates should be arrived at by the excavation of both the features themselves and their upcast or clean-out sediments.
— Sedimentary deposits contained within landscape features or sediments that overlie them can be dated from the development of soil horizons, the recognition of multiple soil profiles, or horizon features such as well-developed calcium carbonate concretions (Waters 1992).
— Intrinsically dated features. Off-site sherd scatters should, in theory, be of approximately the same date as the contained diagnostic sherds. In such cases, however, the field archaeologist should be confident that the scatters were not caused as a result of the artifacts being dug out of a preexisting site. Whenever possible, it is advisable also to record buried exposures that provide a stratified context for the layer in question.

The following case from highland Yemen exemplifies some principles of dating landscape features. Figure 4.10 illustrates a complex palimpsest of fields, linear stone-lines, occupation sites, cisterns, and other features. Two cisterns are dated by inscriptions that explicitly state that they were constructed by named individuals in the Himyarite or late pre-Himyarite periods. Because stone-lined tracks both converge on the dated cisterns and lead from them to a well-attested Himyarite site (of the first centuries A.D.: Harwarwah, fig. 4.10), the tracks are actively associated with both site and cisterns and can therefore be inferred to have been in use during the same (Himyarite) period. In the detail of the southwest area, a small subcircular hut can be dated by its architecture and associated pottery only to the Bronze Age (ca. 3000–1200 B.C.). However, the rectilinear structures

Table 4.4 Off-Site Landscapes: Classification and Diagnostic Features

Class	System	Diagnostic Features
Water Supply (see table 4.2)		
Groundwater	Wells	Mounds of gravel cast up from deep strata. Small distributary channels. Basins for receiving water. Postholes at well head. Animal walkways, in some cases.
	Water holes	Inverted cone form. Reduction-oxidation mottling in lower parts.
Groundwater flow	Qanats, kariz, falaj	Mounds of sediment cast up around access shafts. Cut-and-cover channels locally collapsed.
Spring or wadi pools	Channels	Narrow channels, often cement lined, to accommodate usually small but constant flow. Built installations along routes, or channels, including mills, construction stations, lime kilns, cisterns, inverted siphons, rest places. Shells from clean-out of weeds.
Rivers	Major Canals	Linear upcast levees from (a) initial digging (i.e., geological substrata), (b) clean-out (channel silt and sand). Canals are usually lined with mud. Sluices, etc., are of stone or baked brick.
Episodic flow	Runoff systems	Large channels to accommodate large flow variations, but size depends on scale of catchment. Catchments include hillslopes (sometimes cleared of stones), small valley basins, and runoff areas, wadis, enclosed basins. Field terraces along wadis often equipped with spillways. Flow can go directly to fields, into temporary storage (for fields), or into long-term storage (for travelers).
	Dams	Can be associated with runoff systems or perennial flow. Scale varies but equipped with spillways and sluices. Can be of stone or earth.
Fields	Irrigated terraces	Receive low sedimentation if perennial flow, high sedimentation if flood runoff or from muddy river.
	Soil (or bench) terraces	Receive soil from upslope. Minor additions of water and soil introduced from elsewhere.
	Stone-clearance fields	Stone-clearance mounds and perimeter stone walls.
	Centuriated fields	Rectangular net of fields bounded by walls or roads, usually of Roman date.
	Excavated fields	Dug down to water level of a channel such as a *qanat*; alongside are large upcast "*nudud*" mounds.
	Field scatters	Low-density scatter across large areas. Pottery, kiln waste, other artifacts. Usually abraded.
	Silt fields	From runoff irrigation. Eroded by gully networks. Field soils include plough furrows, root casts of plants, and bowls of trees (in former orchards).

Table 4.4   Continued

Class	System	Diagnostic Features
Routes and roads (see table 4.3)	Hollow ways, sunken lanes	Relates to enclosed land. No evidence of cutting, no upcast mounds. Oriented on sites. Local (radial) or long-distance systems. Wheel ruts occur on limestone.
	Formal paved roads	Roman roads.
	Lanes in rocky hills	Stone fences, banks, or kerbs.
		Stepped Roman roads.
	Cuttings	Found on Assyrian and Roman roads.
		Milestones.
		Bridges.
		Route markers (stone piles, etc).
		Khans and caravansaries along routes.
Quarries and Mines	Limestone quarries	Waste piles.
		Impressions of removed stones.
	Salt mines	Tunnels in salt plugs; water-evaporation basins.
	Soil pits for mudbrick	Large depressions without upcast waste soil.
	Pits for lime, gypsum, and other minerals	Large heaps consist of waste materials.
	Lime kilns	Presence of vitrified slaglike clay and pieces of kiln wall.
	Metaliferrous mines	Slag dumps.
		Furnaces, roasting pits.
		Tuyeres, ore-crushing stones.
		Miners' villages.
Areas of pleasure	Racecourses	Layout can be demarcated by low soil banks. Also include prominent mounds for spectators.
	Game parks	Same as for racecourses but enclosed by boundary mounds.
	Gardens	Usually bounded by walls, fences, or hedges. Can include monumental features recognizable as ornamental terraces, pavilions, water-supply channels, or bedding trenches. Often include imported plants or trees (Gleason 1994, 1997).
Agricultural installations	Wine press	Rock-cut treading floor and collecting basin.
	Olive press	Similar to wine presses, including press weights.
	Threshing floor	Paved surfaces with perimeter wall. Features of compressed earth are more likely to be lost by subsequent activity.
	Field towers	Small structures with foundations of stone.
Cemeteries	Ridgetop graves, tomb fields, tomb towers, underground necropoli	Cairns of stones, circular stone structures as in Umm an-Nar graves of Oman peninsula. Sometimes towers or truncated tombs, with or without "tails." Dolmens with capstones. See also chapter 8.
Religious sites	Churches and ecclesiastical complexes	Stones with cruciform figures in relief, apsidal structures, and various other ecclesiastical architectural elements. *Mihrab* along *qiblah* wall.
	Mosques and *massalah*s	Ablution area. Temples show distinctive orientation, often exhibit well-cut stones (in contrast to rough-cut stones of dwellings); specialist pottery assemblages. Distinctive inscriptions.
	Temples: roadside, natural hilltop sanctuaries	

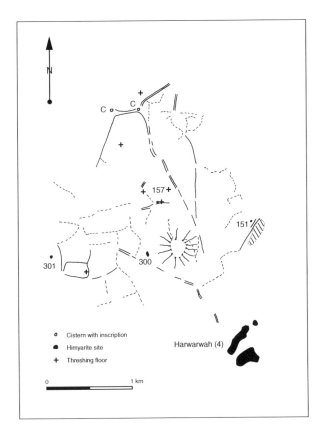

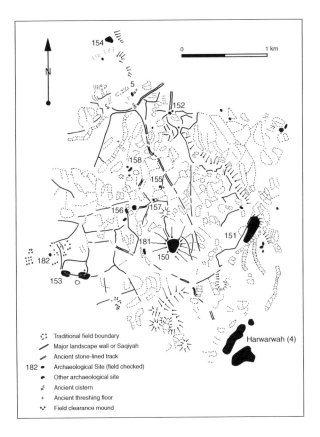

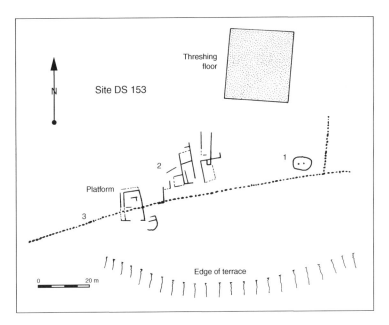

Fig. 4.10 Palimpsest of landscape features at Harwarwah, Yemen highlands. Top right: full range of landscape features and archaeological sites. Top left: selected features that are associated with Himyarite sites or cisterns. Bottom: detail of Site 153, showing relationships between houses and landscape features.

appear to relate to the Iron Age component of the pottery scatter. These buildings are cut by the large linear feature, which must therefore be post–Iron Age in date. Finally,

this stone line is clearly of some antiquity because it is covered with a thick coating of desert varnish, which in this part of the Yemen highlands tends to occur to this degree

of intensity on structures older than about a thousand years. This links the detail with the larger mapped area. In addition, the small, partially bounded terraced fields contain a sedimentary wedge upslope that is amenable to dating by contained ceramics, by radiocarbon dating of contained flecks of charcoal, or directly by optical luminescence. Age estimates of the fields can also be obtained from the architectural phases of the terraces themselves and from the soils backed up against the terrace walls. Finally, the threshing floor is typologically of Himyarite/Iron Age date.

This example demonstrates that despite the rather low reliability of estimated dates for many individual features, by analyzing a wide range of features within their landscape context, a corpus of dates of various degrees of reliability can be built up, some of which can be used to test, refute, or cross-check other estimated dates.

Landscapes of Irrigation

Irrigation, probably more than any other technology, is capable of providing a structure for the landscape. By forming alignments of water supply, irrigation channels determine the pattern of settlement and even in some cases the internal street and building plan of a settlement. Irrigation channels, in turn, can form part of a "natural" system of rivers, and the processes that result in the development of such channels can contribute to the pattern of irrigation and settlement that follow. Moreover, when irrigation systems outgrow the scale of the natural environment or result in the neglect of natural processes such as drainage, the society that built such systems must suffer the consequences. This chapter examines how natural channel systems could have allowed for earlier systems of irrigation to develop, how such irrigation systems then interacted with natural geomorphic systems, and eventually how the mightiest systems were configured to form some of the most impressive, but ultimately transitory, landscapes in the Near East.

Emphasis is placed on the landscapes of southern Mesopotamia, which have been so central to discussions of the growth of early civilization. No attempt is made to discuss the history and development of Mesopotamian irrigation; for this, a wide range of excellent overviews are available (e.g., Postgate 1992a; Charles 1988; Hunt 1988; Potts 1997: chap. 1). Instead, this chapter provides a series of snapshot views of selected landscapes of irrigation that developed from the formative stages of early civilizations until the

peak of imperial investment in canal construction during the Sasanian period. Interpretations are based upon observations of the physical and cultural landscape derived from field studies and geoarchaeology. Archaeological surveys demonstrate how landscapes developed from initially small-scale systems to larger, more organized state-level systems and finally to the extraordinarily large-scale systems that were characteristic of the early empires. Key features of each landscape are described, after which I will discuss just how such systems functioned and could be maintained in the face of both a capricious environment and increased food demands from rising populations. The environment not only influences irrigation by supplying varying amounts of water, it also influences the topographic framework that guides the river channels across the plain as well as the morphology and dynamics of channel movement. Human actions are obviously fundamental to the shaping of the riverine irrigated environment. For example, in addition to excavating canals, humans contribute eroded soils to the sediment supply by clearing woodlands or establishing settlements on upland basins that supply runoff to the river systems. As a result, channels located downstream become clogged with silt, thereby increasing the probability that they will overspill their banks and form new channels. Moreover, the withdrawal of water for upstream irrigation works can diminish the flow of rivers. Such removals, although minor (or even trivial) during the early states, probably as-

sumed significance in the years of the later empires.

Where rain-fed agriculture is impossible due to low annual rainfall, irrigation is necessary for crop production. The pattern of canals and irrigation channels so formed results in distinctive linear landscapes that are best exemplified by those presented in the seminal studies of Robert Adams of the Mesopotamian plains. The sheer magnitude of such settlement systems is only now becoming apparent as more of the original surveys are being combined into databases by means of Geographic Information Systems (fig. 5.1).

More recently Guillermo Algaze has argued that the primacy of southern Mesopotamian civilization was due to a combination of economic and environmental factors. He asserts that the environment, although not determining the trajectory of development, did allow development to take place, first by conferring greater resiliency as a result of the varied subsistence resources, second by allowing higher agricultural productivity because of irrigation, and third by encouraging greater efficiency in the form of a riverine transport system (Algaze 2001a). All three factors are either directly or indirectly the result of the distinctive circumstances that resulted from this riverine environment. Of these factors, the role of rivers as arteries of transportation is particularly important to the socioeconomic development of Mesopotamia, especially because they would have made intraregional commerce much more efficient than in

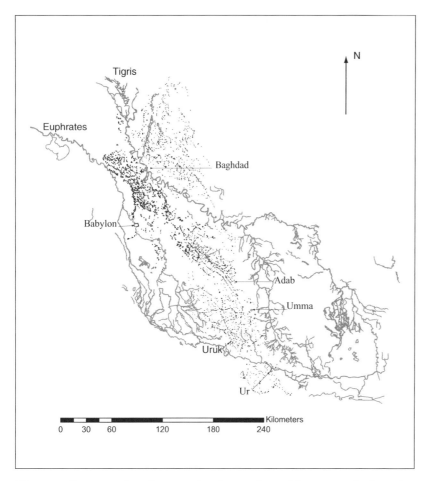

Fig. 5.1   Pattern of settlement sites in southern Mesopotamia, based on data originally surveyed by R. Adams (1981), replotted as part of a GIS (by Carrie Hritz, with thanks also to K. Verhoeven, University of Ghent). Note that sites form alignments along former watercourses.

the north, where overland transport was the primary means of transport. Algaze is careful to avoid a deterministic argument. He does point out the fundamental role that the Tigris-Euphrates river system played in the development of civilization, one that is often underplayed in other recent works on state development. Ironically, there is little in the way of a truly natural environment in southern Mesopotamia. Rather, we are confronted with the results of constant interactions between human and natural processes that have resulted in a landscape that was both managed (by humans) but also subject to natural catastrophes, some of which may have been triggered by human mismanagement, others by external environmental factors.

Formative Stages of Irrigation

Landscapes of irrigation are therefore fundamental to an understanding of the rise of the state, but how did such sophisticated settlement-irrigation systems develop and flourish?

Some form of irrigation is necessary for successful crop production in all parts of the Near East where rainfall is less than 200 mm per annum (Oates and Oates 1976: 111). Therefore, irrigation is a crucial factor in the development of cultural landscapes in Mesopotamia. Irrigation technology probably was not introduced as a total package but rather underwent a series of developmental stages from initial relatively simple, small-scale, and

undemanding forms towards larger and complex systems at a later date (Doolittle 1990: 18). Thus with Meso-American systems in mind, Doolittle recognizes that there existed three schools of thought for the development of irrigation technology. First, as suggested by William T. Sanders, canals may have been developed to carry water from springs to agricultural plots. Second, irrigation originated where drainage ditches were employed to convey water away from habitation sites (Flannery and Marcus 1976: 378). Third, fields were positioned where excess water could be directed away from natural stream flow, usually as a result of flooding (Smith 1965, cited in Doolittle 1990: 137–138). Although these schools of thought should not be viewed as a template for the evolution of irrigation, they are relevant to the development of irrigation systems in and around Mesopotamia.

The presence of early irrigation can be inferred from a variety of evidence, both indirect, in the form of ecofacts that relate to irrigation agriculture, and direct, which is shown by the canals themselves. Indirect evidence for early irrigation can also be inferred from the location of archaeological sites. If archaeological sites are situated beyond the limit of rain-fed cultivation, in areas where irrigation is required to produce a viable crop, then it is reasonable to infer that some form of irrigation was practiced around those sites. Nevertheless, care must be taken to ascertain whether the region has experienced a marked climate change, because as Kouchoukos has argued for parts of southwest Iran, during the initial phases of irrigation development it is possible that the present winter rainfall regime may also have been supplemented by some summer rainfall (Kouchoukos 1998). This could have resulted in a markedly different environment than that of today, with the result that the irrigation requirements of early crops could have been significantly different.

In many long-settled areas the actual channels can be elusive because processes of landscape transformation may have erased the earlier evidence for irrigation canals. In such cases, indirect evidence for the earlier phases of irrigation can be sought from the carbonized remains of plants that were associated with enhanced water supply in an otherwise arid environment (Neely and Wright 1994: 183–185; Helbaek 1972 and references therein). For example, paleoethnobotanical information implies that irrigation was employed certainly in the Sabz phase of southwest Iran (5200–5000 B.C.; Hole et al. 1969) and at Chagha Sefid (Hole 1977), and it probably can be traced to as early as 6000 B.C. (Helbaek in Hole et al. 1969: 424). In terms of the landscape itself, despite promising breakthroughs in the recognition of early irrigation in the 1960s and 1970s, the direct evidence for the remains of unequivocal early canals themselves remains frustratingly elusive.

Specific evidence for the development of irrigation during the sixth millennium B.C. comes from the prehistoric mound of Choga Mami in eastern Iraq, where relict channels have been exposed in archaeological sections as well as on the ground surface, and irrigation is implied from carbonized plant remains. Choga Mami is located where the reliable rainfall is about 200 mm per annum, within a small oasis situated on an alluvial fan between the Zagros foothills and the edge of the Mesopotamian plain (Oates and Oates 1976). The initial phase of irrigation appears to have taken advantage of the fan morphology, with the result that small prehistoric settlements were aligned up and down slope along what were essentially natural watercourses. Profiles of small channels, some 2 m in width, filled with water-laid clay and associated with Samarran ceramics[1] were exposed in sections and were shown to be stratified within deposits at the edge of the mound (Oates 1969:

124). The position of these Samarran channels, being below the inferred plain level of the period, suggests that they were not used for irrigation (unless the fields were some way downstream). On the other hand, similar channels at higher elevations in the mound (E and F of Oates 1969: 127) were above contemporaneous plain level and therefore cannot have functioned as natural watercourses. Later irrigation was also evident in the form of a channel 4–6 m wide associated with sherds of Ubaid 3 date (ca. 5000–4500 B.C.).

The initial irrigation system, which was established in the Samarran period not long after 6000 B.C., probably entailed the artificial manipulation of river flow or floods. The smaller early channels, which appear to have been in use when the land surface was aggrading (Oates and Oates 1976: fig. 5), were probably part of an early phase of canal irrigation that directed water down the main slope of the fan. This is in the manner of natural drainage, but it was at a higher level so that water could have been raised on to the higher surfaces of the fan itself. Only later, but still associated with Samarran ceramics dated before 5000 B.C., were wider lateral canals established in the form of channels that followed the contours. Because of their spatial extent across wide areas of the plain, such canals could be constructed only when drainage was not incising into the fan surface (Oates and Oates 1976: 109). Analysis of the palaeobotanical remains, which included six-row barley, provided indirect evidence that irrigation was practiced (Field in Oates 1969: 140–141).

In southwest Iran the judicious use of a range of both indirect and direct evidence suggests that irrigation technology was introduced to the Deh Luran plain during the Choga Mami transitional phase (i.e., ca. 5400–5200 B.C.: Neely and Wright 1994: 194), a phase that ushered in a change in the economy as well as an increase in the total number of sites in western Iran (Hole 1987:

35). The introduction of—six-row hulled barley (a grain that is frequently associated with irrigation), free-threshing hexaploid wheat, large-seeded lentil, flax, and domestic cattle all appear to have been associated with changes in social organization and irrigation agriculture. More direct evidence has been adduced from the Deh Luran plain, where early canals were apparent from the presence of broad, shallow depressions, sometimes with low spoil banks, and from the pattern of denser, greener vegetation (Neely and Wright 1994: 186). No canals have been found in stratigraphic sequence between dated sedimentary deposits, nor have they been directly dated by ceramics or radiocarbon. Instead, their date has been inferred from the placement of sites alongside. In other words, an irrigation canal or channel was inferred to have been in use at a given time if two or more archaeological sites containing the occupation phase in question were present (Neely and Wright 1994: 186).

The employment of such indirect methodologies suggests that in the Deh Luran plain, canal technology evolved from smaller channels up to 2 m wide and 50 cm deep and perhaps 4–6 km in length during the Choga Mami Transitional phase to larger features of 10–12 km length by Early Dynastic time (Neely and Wright 1994: 196–199). This increase in the scale of the canal systems corresponds approximately with increased population levels, as inferred from aggregate site area.[2] Whether such an association between increased population and longer canals is due to more people being needed to dig the longer canals, or because higher populations could be supported by the increased food production from such canals, or a combination of both, is unclear. Nevertheless, this observation does point out that canal systems are likely to become longer and more complex as population increases. In terms of social organization, the larger canals of the Early Dynastic period were probably beyond the scale that was easily managed within immediate kin groups of a community (Neely and Wright 1994: 199; see also Fernea 1970). The relevance of such observations will be taken up later in this chapter.

Unfortunately, as compelling as the evidence is from these two areas, many landscape features appear to be later in date than the formative phases of irrigation. These landscapes must therefore be seen as complex palimpsests of later and earlier features rather than as single-phase landscapes.

This is not the case, however, for the Daulatabad region of southeast Iran, where Martha Prickett's work around Tepe Yahya provides some of the earliest discernable evidence of relict landscapes in the Near East. In this arid part of southeast Iran, rainfall is insufficient for cultivation, and agriculture could not benefit from the presence of a large perennial river. Instead, the prehistoric communities were dependent upon flow from probably ephemeral wadis. Recourse had to be made to the use of runoff and spates for irrigation.

This remarkable prehistoric landscape is an excellent example of a landscape of survival. Here the entire landscape of low archaeological mounds, fields, and water channels all survived until the 1970s and 1980s, in part because there was no settlement subsequent to the fourth millennium B.C. to erase them. The Chalcolithic settlements that dotted this landscape developed upon a series of gravel fans deposited by the Rud I Gushk river a little above a dry lake depression. Fields were small (0.06–0.8 ha), usually 30–40 m apart, and were bounded by low ridges of cobble and stones, alignments of cobbles and stone, low silt ridges, or rarely low walls two courses wide (fig. 5.2; Prickett 1986: 696–712). Floodwater runoff fields initially appeared in southern, lower, or distal part of fans and the best examples of these were mapped over

some 300 ha in the north fan area (Prickett 1986: 728). This is where the best soils, namely, the most moisture-retentive silts, occur and where conditions would have been most favorable for the development of flood-runoff agriculture (cf. Fogel 1975, cited in Brown 1997: 255).

By the latter part of the sixth millennium B.C., runoff agriculture must therefore have supported a thriving system of settlement (Prickett 1986: 655). By the mid fifth millennium B.C., settlement and cultivation then shifted to the mid fan, where fields were preserved on stable enclaves within the alluvial fan system (Prickett 1986: 656–657). These fields received water from both local sheet flood and floodwaters from the Rud I Gushk river. At one site (R37), two possible canals were recorded in section. These took the form of a later straight-sided channel 1.4 m wide by 0.7 m deep containing sherds and other cultural debris, and a lower, smaller presumably earlier canal. Being stratified between silts of the underlying silt plain and having some 4.5 m of prehistoric cultural deposits above, there is no doubt about the date of the channel, although Prickett is careful to point out its artificial function is not proven. Irrigation canals that were difficult to distinguish from natural drainage channels eroded into the surface of the gravel fans, usually consisted of shallow depressions 1–10 m wide, the straighter examples of which are thought to be humanly constructed.

The irrigation canals probably received their water via temporary dams of stones across valley floors, which conveyed water to fields downslope, that is, in the same manner as the water-deflection structures (*garbabands*) of southeast Iran and Pakistan. Plant remains included einkorn and emmer wheat, hulled two- and six-row barley, millet, as well as capers and dates (Prickett 1986: 670). The occurrence of dates, if they were not imported, suggests that irrigated palm gardens were

present as early as the mid sixth millennium B.C. Although irrigation must have formed a mainstay of the local agricultural economy, it is significant that this settlement system terminated during the fourth millennium B.C., at a time when ocean cores suggest that the effect of monsoon rains was declining (Prickett 1986: 651; Roberts and Wright 1993). It therefore seems likely that the immediate area of the Daulatabad fan was more verdant during the Chalcolithic than today, both as a result of greater seasonal moisture and because of the use of irrigation. Conversely, the environment appears then to have become significantly drier as a result of both the collapse of irrigation and climatic drying after the fourth millennium B.C.

In summary, irrigated landscapes must have been in existence at least as early as the sixth millennium B.C. These systems were of modest size, however, being less then 6 km in length. Initially they employed the most rudimentary technique of channeling water along existing ground slopes or down alluvial fan gradients. Nevertheless, by 5000 B.C., more sophisticated lateral distribution systems such as that Choga Mami canal were in existence. Of the three examples discussed two, namely, those from Choga Mami and Daulatabad, show that early irrigated landscapes developed on alluvial fans. This is hardly surprising because as has been demonstrated in the New World, the lower slopes of alluvial fans provide optimum loci for the development of natural irrigation. For example, in areas of Ak Chin–type farming in Arizona, this is where flow becomes unconfined and can therefore be spread across the fan surface (Waters and Field 1986).

Irrigation on the Mesopotamian Plains

The austere environment of the Mesopotamian plains played a crucial role in the development of early

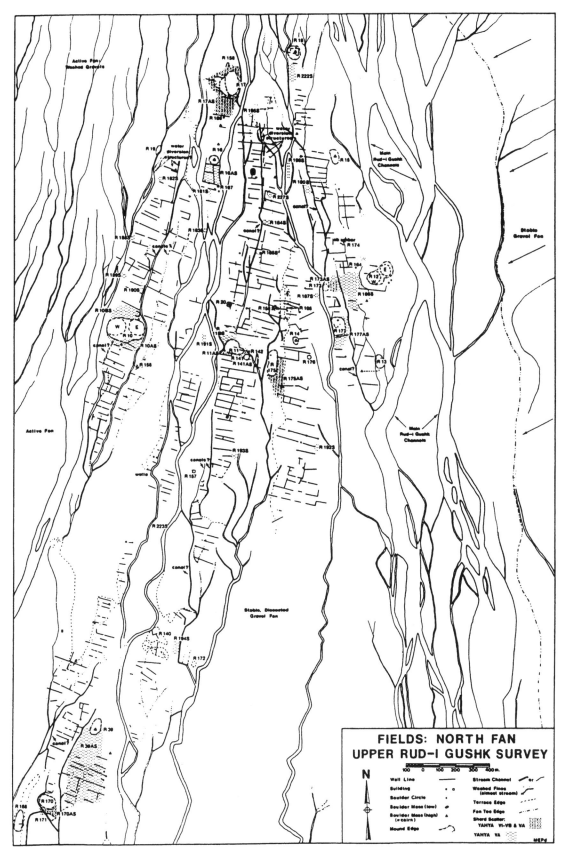

Fig. 5.2   Prehistoric fields in area of Chalcolithic sites near Daulatabad, Iran (from Prickett, 1986: fig. 9.5, with permission from The Tepe Yahya Project, Harvard University).

civilization. Because riverine water supply is so fundamental to the well-being of Mesopotamian society, it is appropriate to discuss this in more detail, so that we can understand just what problems the inhabitants of the plain had to cope with.

First, the water supply of the Tigris-Euphrates rivers is not infinite. For example, although the gross area of cultivated and cultivable lands amounts to some 51,000 sq. km, the supply of irrigation water is only sufficient to irrigate some 30,000 sq. km (Ionides 1937: 5). Adams (1981: 6) provides an even more conservative figure and estimates that at least 8,000 and not more than 12,000 sq. km were capable of being irrigated by the available water. This means that a significant portion of the plains would have been un-irrigable, with the result that some of this land would have been available as steppe pasture. As Adams has emphasized, the contribution of pasture and pastoral communities is therefore important for understanding Mesopotamian civilization.

Although appearing to be flat and featureless, the Mesopotamian plain includes a wide range of distinctive physical landscape units (fig. 5.3). The plain forms a structural trough between the high folded mountain range of the Zagros Mountains of Iran to the northeast, with their fringing zone of alluvial fans that have accumulated from tributary valleys of the Adhaim, the Diyala, and Karun rivers as well as numerous minor valleys. To the west, the plains are bounded by the low plateau of the western desert developed upon Tertiary sedimentary rocks of the Arabian Shelf. The Tigris-Euphrates plain is sandwiched between these two regions. In the recent past, the plain comprised a mosaic of environments that included marshes and lakes, dune fields, sinuous and sometimes extensive gardens of date palms, as well as cultivated fields and of course wind-swept alluvial desert. That the ancient landscape was also patterned in this way is supported by

textual evidence for ancient marshes (many of which were produced by humans [S. Cole 1994]) as well as dunes (Brandt 1990). It should not therefore be assumed that during Ubaid through Babylonian times the Mesopotamian lowlands simply formed an austere agricultural plain. Rather, they probably comprised a complex pattern of low levee ridges, levee slopes, flood basins, low "turtle backs,"[3] and sometimes very extensive marshes, which together provided a complex of ecosystems that could have been exploited for a wide range of agricultural, garden and aquatic resources.

The physical landscape of southern Mesopotamia can be subdivided according to geomorphological provinces as noted below (fig. 5.3; based upon Verhoeven 1998: fig. 1), or as was preferred by some Islamic authorities, according to irrigated zones (Ibn Khurradadhbeh, cited in El-Samarraie 1972: 15–19). Here, the former has been adopted because it relates to physiographic regions that can be recognized on maps and satellite images:

1. Relict flood plain and terraces north of Baghdad.
2. The flood plain of the meandering channels of the Tigris and Middle Euphrates.
3. The Tigris-Euphrates flood plains: (a) lower Tigris downstream of Kut, (b) anastomosing flood plain of the Euphrates from near Hillah to Nasiriyah.
4. (a) Irrigation fan apron of the Diyala River, (b) Zagros and Karun fans, (c) Wadi al-Batin.
5. Zone of marshes and lakes: The limit of the marine transgression at ca. 4300 B.C. is derived from Sanlaville 1989, updated by the recent information on the marine transgression derived from Aqrawi (2001). But as Adams (1981: 16) has warned, there may never have been a well-defined shoreline but rather a progression of swamps and brackish or saline lagoons.

6. The estuarine zone downstream of (5).
7. The abandoned flood plain of the Tigris/Euphrates: 7a being the main survey area of Adams (1981), and 7b being the area east of the Shatt al-Gharraf.
8. Pleistocene terraces remain as occasional "islands" within the alluvium upstream towards Sippar[4] (Verhoeven 1998; Buringh and Edelman 1955: 47–48).

The Physical Development of the Plain

Geologically, the Mesopotamian plain forms part of a broad basin (or geosyncline) that has accumulated many hundreds of meters of sediment eroded from the upland basins within Syria, Iraq, Turkey, and Iran. These have accumulated over much of the Quaternary whereas folding has continued since the Late Tertiary period (Larsen and Evans 1978: 231). The present topography is determined, in part, by the underlying Pleistocene valley floored by deposits of sand and gravel that underlie a later complex wedge of sediments deposited over the last eleven thousand years (i.e., the Holocene). This Holocene sedimentary wedge is derived mainly from the Tigris, Euphrates, Diyala, and Karun river channels that cross the plain and have deposited their load via a series of sinuous channels.

The classic study of Mesopotamian soils continues to be Buringh's monograph (1960) and related papers (Buringh 1957; Buringh and Edelman 1955), which provide the foundation for some overall generalizations about landscape development. First, at the macrolevel and relevant to the history of channel development, it is possible to differentiate between sediments from the Tigris (with a pinkish brown hue and containing more epidote and alterite, and less green hornblende and augite) and those of the Euphrates (grayish brown with less palygorskite clay mineral). In addition, the mol-

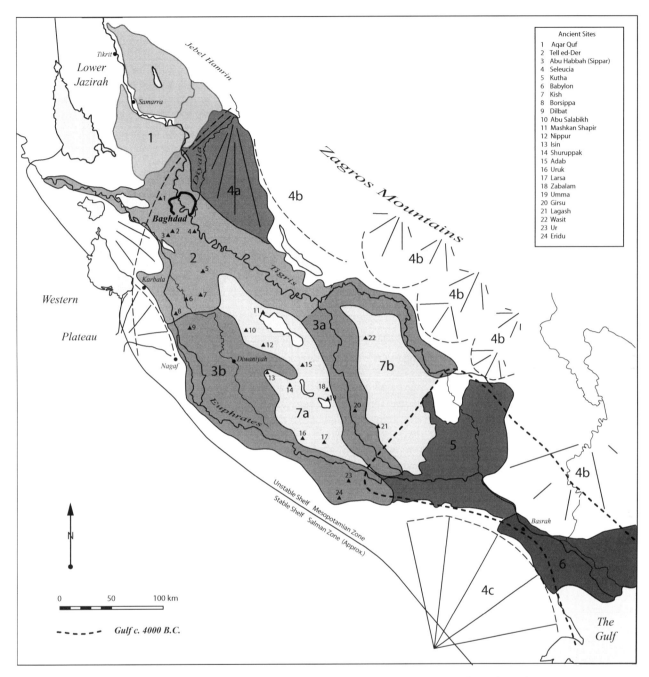

Fig. 5.3 Physiographic regions of the Mesopotamian plains. For description of numbered regions, see text. Modified from Verhoeven 1998: fig. 1.

lusk *Anadon* species appears to be confined to the waters of the Euphrates (Harris and Adams 1957: 158). The difference in mineral composition and color is in part the result of the different geological sources of sediments for the two rivers as well as the weathering regimes of the parent materials that form the source of the sediments (Buringh 1960: 116; al-Rawi and Sys 1967). This difference is complemented by the assertion that the soils of Euphrates sediments are more fertile than those of the Tigris (Postgate 1992a: 174).

That there was a contrast in potential fertility between soils of different types was well known to the Sumerian farmer (Postgate 1992a: 176), and it is necessary to counter the observation that Mesopotamian soils were either very fertile (cf. Herodotus, *History* I.93) or of consistently low fertility (Potts 1997: 14–15). Rather, the potential fertility of the soils varied considerably, depending upon topographic and geomorphological location. The soils of levees range from fine sand to silty clay loam, and being raised some 2–3 m above flood basins, these are well drained with relatively low water tables. On such levees, conditions for crop growth are good, and these nonsaline levee soils are ideal for date and fruit gardens with multicropping of vegetables and other plants. Fundamental to an understanding of landscape development is the microclimate and soil climate that is associated with the palm gardens on levees. The advantage of providing ample shade for a lower story of plants was already well known to the Sumerians as far back as Early Dynastic times, and the tradition has been kept up until the present day (Nemet-Nejat 1998: 255). According to Buringh, these well-shaded soils have a low soil temperature, high moisture content, a high level of biological activity, and little development of surface crusts, and they are homogenized by biological and soil-forming processes through the upper meter or so. This makes these soils of exceptional quality for agricultural use (Buringh 1960: 149) and provides a stark contrast to the soils developed on similar parent materials in neighboring desertified areas, which suffer extreme moisture and temperature fluctuations, are crusted, and become heavily deflated with a surface crust of shells, potsherds, and other cultural debris.

In contrast to the levee soils, those of the riverine basins are fine textured (silty clay loam to clay), occupy topographic lows, suffer a high groundwater level, are poorly drained, and are usually saline, sometimes markedly so (Buringh 1960: 150–151). The lowest locations within the basins are variously occupied by *haur* and lake bottom soils, both of which experience inundation for at least part of the year and are therefore even less well drained than other parts of the basins. Overall, however, most Mesopotamian soils are low in organic matter,[5] nitrogen, and phosphorus but have an adequate level of potassium. Such deficiencies have been countered by the application of manure or ashes, and Islamic authorities were well aware of the value (as well as drawbacks) of both simple and

compound fertilizers. Manures and fertilizers were classified as "hot" or "cold," depending upon their effect on plants, and much was written on the various sources of manures as well as their relative merits (el-Samarraie 1972: 74–75; el-Faiz 1995: 263–268). Because application to hot, dry soils results in rapid oxidation of the organic matter (see below), it was preferable to apply them to soils that were moistened by irrigation and at best were well shaded.

Remarkably little has been published on the sedimentary sequence of the plains, but the overall pattern of deposition and the associated topography can be gleaned from three sections from the northern, central, and southern parts of the plain. The northern sequence in the Sippar area was first established by the Belgian geomorphologists Paepe and Baeteman (1978) and subsequently by K. Verhoeven (1998). Verhoeven hand-drilled cores across the present course of the Euphrates (to the southwest on fig. 5.4a) as well as across the levee of the ancient channel. The second sequence, recorded briefly from the third river drain near Nippur, benefited from the presence of an open section that provided details of individual features such as occupation deposits and canals as well as potentially datable artifacts. Finally, near the head of the gulf a crucial sequence for the Holocene history of the plain has been built up over the last fifty years as a result of petroleum exploration and related geological work (Aqrawi 2001).

Typically, the extensive alluvial tracts of the central and upper plains exhibit a low relief topography with a vertical interval of some 2–5 m. This masks an underlying geology that is both subtle and complex. For example, in the two type areas, which are representative of much of the Mesopotamian plain, long sinuous levees consist of sandy channel deposits, sand and silt overbank deposits, as well as silt and clay that accumulated within irrigation canals and on fields (Buringh 1957: 41). De-

pressions beyond or between the levees form broad often enclosed clay-filled basins that are frequently either saline or marshy because they accumulate the overflow water from floods or excess irrigation water. Their usually waterlogged status limits their potential for cultivation (but see below), and instead, many flood basins provide reeds, salt, areas for hunting and fishing, as well as pasture for the local communities.

Both the northern and southern sections (fig. 5.4a and b) illustrate the fundamental geoarchaeological feature of the alluvial plains, namely, the development of levees. They also show the presence of a complex succession of superimposed sedimentary units, which include channel bed and point bar sands deposited in large alluvial channels; fine sands, loamy sands, and silts relating to low-energy canals; riverine levees or irrigation levees, as well as silts and clays deposited in flood basins or as a result of low-energy flow on the flood plain itself. In addition, one encounters deposits of relict marshes such as that of the first millennium B.C. recorded in a deep stratigraphic sequence near the Musaiyib project (Harris and Adams 1957). The northern (Sippar) sequence demonstrates that a major Euphrates channel, which originally flowed through the area, was raised above the contemporaneous terrain represented by a humic relict land surface (fig. 5.4a, based on Verhoeven 1998: figs. 18–20). This channel was succeeded, probably at some time during the second or early first millennium B.C., by sands and loamy sands accumulated in a more sluggish canal as well as lenses of similar deposits accumulated in minor channels.

The third river drain section exposed a similar levee sequence, as well as at least one small canal and a wide channel (fig. 5.4b: 4 and 5). The latter feature, being sunk slightly below the contemporaneous flood-plain level (3), appears not to have been an artificial channel. This is because the lack of obvious upcast

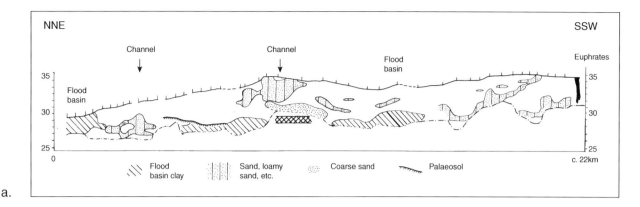

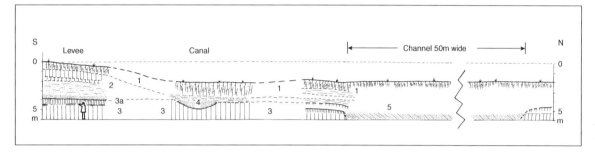

Fig. 5.4   Representative sedimentary sections across the Mesopotamian plains: (a) Auger transect, approximately 22 km long, through sedimentary accumulations of the levee of the old Sippar branch of the Euphrates (simplified from Verhoeven 1998: figs. 18–20). Auger holes are represented by vertical lines; deposits left blank are silts, silty clays, and silt loams. Cross-hatching refers to the "complex A sands" that were probably deposited within the channel and on point bars of the former Euphrates. They appear to be associated and contemporaneous with the flood basin clays to the southwest and northeast. Note that the base of occupation of Tell ed-Der (ca. 2300 B.C.) is at 29.5 m above sea level, and Sippar (3300 B.C.) is 28.5 m above sea level. The elevation of these sites suggests that the channel complex A was in existence roughly within this time interval, if not earlier. (b) Third River Drain section, near Nippur, Iraq, showing alluvial deposits and relict channels.

deposits alongside the channel implies that it had not been subjected to large-scale cleaning-out operations. A thin layer of cultural deposit of Ubaid/Uruk date (3a) at the south end of the section suggests that the flood plain (3) then ceased to aggrade around Early Dynastic times and was followed by the accumulation of the deposits of a major levee (2). Finally, the upper gray-brown blocky silty clay (1) represents an irrigated soil, which apparently blanketed the entire terrain from levee to flood basin. The stratigraphic position of this soil is late, and it can be inferred to be the result of Sasanian–Early Islamic irrigation that distributed water across the entire plain in the area rather than being restricted to the better-drained levees.

Whereas the Sippar section demonstrates that much of or even the entire Euphrates flow passed through the Sippar area until the second millennium B.C., in the central Nippur section the northern channel (5) can only have conducted a small proportion of the Tigris or Euphrates discharge. From its stratigraphic relation to the main dated sequence on the levee (fig. 5.4.1–3), both the canal (4) and the alluvial channel (5) can tentatively be dated in the range Ubaid through Early Dynastic, whereas the levee (2) postdated the Early Dynastic and appears to correspond to the large channel system that persisted from Early Dynastic through to Early Islamic times. This follows a line to the northeast of Nippur through Adab on figure 5.11.

The shift from a low-energy floodplain environment (fig. 5.4b: 3) to higher-energy sands (2) was clearly abrupt, and it may have resulted from either the abrupt shift to a new river course along this line (i.e., an avulsion) or the construction of a new canal.

Opinion on the precise history of the head of the gulf has fluctuated over the past century, with opposing views being taken by, for example, De Morgan (1900), who argued for the extension of the gulf well inland into the Mesopotamian plain. Lees and Falcon suggested that there had been little change in the shoreline of the gulf because the downward settling of the plain was balanced by the incoming sediments (Lees and Falcon 1952). Today, however, there is a consensus in favor of a maximum marine incursion that extended inland to the vicinity of Nasiriyah/Ur, that is, perhaps as much as 250 km upstream of the present coastline near Fao on figure 5.3 (Larsen and Evans 1978; Sanlaville 1989). Geomorphological studies in the vicinity of Tell Oueli demonstrate that during the Late Glacial Maximum around 18,000–20,000 years ago, the Euphrates had incised at least 4 m into its preexisting plain level and that there followed a progressive rise in the sedimentary surface during the Early and Middle Holocene that corresponded in part to the rise in sea level (Geyer and Sanlaville 1996: 394–396, 406).

The sedimentary sequence from boreholes indicates that between Nasiriyah and Basrah during the early–mid Holocene, the sea transgressed inland across an earlier Holocene alluvial plain to deposit the gray marine clays known as the Hammar formation. This formation was then overlain by silty clays, evaporites, and then again silty clays, which resulted from the progradation of coastal marshes, sabkhas, and riverine deposits respectively. This post-Hammar phase of marsh and alluvial accumulation resulted in the infilling of the preexisting embayment (Aqrawi 2001). Although the details of infilling and the contribution of tectonic activity to the development of the basin continue to be debated, it now appears that around 6000 B.C., sea level rapidly encroached up the Lower Mesopotamian/gulf plain so that by 4000 B.C., a marine limit of 1–2 m above the present probably existed close to Ur or Eridu (Geyer and Sanlaville 1996: 396). Whether this marine embayment took the form of a broad bay, a narrow estuarine inlet, or a patchwork of lagoons of varying salinity remains unclear, but recent boreholes suggest that for at least part of this transgressive phase, the inlet was both broad and open (Aqrawi 1995: fig. 2).

Dynamics of Sedimentation

The hallmark of the sedimentary sequence of the plains is its considerable chronological and spatial variability. Recent studies of the depths of burial of the lowest occupational levels of archaeological sites support earlier observations that sedimentary accumulations were greater in the Diyala fan and upper alluvial plain than further to the south (Adams and Nissen 1972: 9; Reichel 1997). According to Clemens Reichel (1997), who has estimated the overall depth of sedimentation at excavated sites from the depth of burial of the lowest levels below the level of the adjacent plain, the sedimentation on the Diyala plains has been 8–11 m since the Uruk/Jamdat Nasr period. This compares with figures of 6.2 and 9 m in the Sippar and Kish areas respectively, 5.2 m at Nippur, and 1–1.80 m further to the south at Fara and Adab. These figures eloquently demonstrate that the bulk of sediment deposition has occurred in the upper part of the plains and Diyala fan. This is probably because, first, there was increased sediment transport into the rivers from the upper basins; second, irrigation has diminished water discharge in the downstream direction; and third, more silt load was intercepted by low-gradient canals and ditches.

The high spatial variability of deposition is further complicated by the dynamic nature of the processes of erosion and sedimentation that have prevailed at different times. Such patterns are crucial to landscape interpretation because in any given area of the plain, one site may be buried by several meters of alluvial sediment, whereas another of roughly the same date may sit on a pedestal of sediment above plain level. Such anomalous patterns appear to result from the patchy and localized nature of alluvial sedimentation combined with the removal of sediments by episodes of intense aeolian degradation. In addition, compaction of the underlying sedi-

ments may have resulted in some sedimentary sequences being compressed.

Erosional/aggradation cycles in the alluvial plains are illustrated by the following model (fig. 5.5), which assumes the existence of a broad alluvial plain crossed by narrow riverine or channel belts (natural or artificial) and interspersed with zones of alluvial desert that do not receive irrigation or flood water from the rivers. If there are no major declines in sediment input to the rivers, and if sea level has remained at a roughly comparable level since the mid-Holocene high stand, riverine areas would progressively aggrade as a result of sedimentation within and alongside the channels as well as from increments of silt/clay associated with both irrigation canals and fields. Palm groves, which usually form linear belts along the channels, would exhibit stable, aggrading, fertile soil environments with their own relatively cool and moist microenvironments, whereas fields further down the levees beyond the palm groves would lose sand-sized silt/clay aggregates as a result of deflation. These particles would then be deposited elsewhere as "parna" (or clay) dunes. In extreme cases, entire depositional units such as marsh clays can be removed by deflation. Elsewhere in the alluvial desert, soils will aggrade if they receive episodic floods. Otherwise, they will degrade as a result of aeolian activity, which removes the unvegetated soil, unless or until a protective armor of coarse materials (potsherds, fired clay, etc) develops.

Thus during periods of channel stability, riverine areas will aggrade, and cereal fields will undergo alluvial aggradation but will also act as supply zones for developing dune fields down wind (Brandt 1990), whereas desert areas will degrade. However, should there be a complete channel shift as a result of either a natural avulsion event (see below) or a deliberate diversion, and if water is not maintained in the original chan-

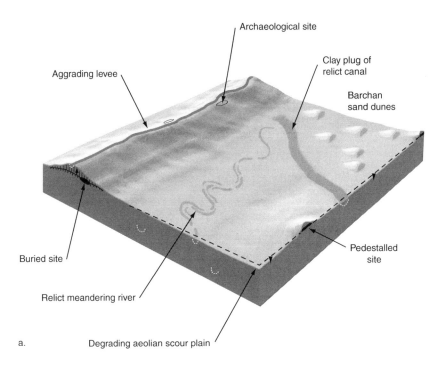

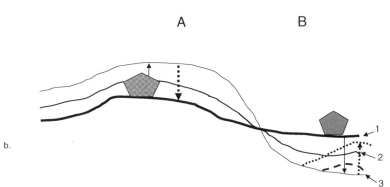

Fig. 5.5 Aggradation and degradation cycles in the Mesopotamian plain: (a) Model of aggradation/degradation cycle on the Mesopotamian alluvial plain showing an aggrading alluvial ridge (to the top left) and a degrading scour plain (lower right). The latter is exposing relict meandering and low sinuosity channels, as well as pedestaled archaeological sites. (b) Schematic view of the same area showing potential cycles of aggradation and degradation: (1) shows an initial ground surface with sites represented by pentagons; (2) phase of aggradation along a river channel system (A) and associated deflation in the nearby desert (B); (3) represents the final stage of aggradation (in A) and deflation (in B) prior to a channel shift. The direction of the initial stage of aggradation and degradation is shown by solid arrows, and the onset of degradation in Zone A and aggradation in Zone B is indicated by broken-line arrows. As a result of this process, sites on surface 1 will either be buried (in Zone A) or pedestaled (in Zone B). In theory (although confirmed cases of this are not known), buried sites in Zone A could be eventually exhumed as a result of the later phase of degradation.

nel, the palm groves will die, soils will desiccate, sediment input will drop to zero, and surface degradation will commence. Even new dune fields will develop as a result of increased supply of silt/clay aggregates derived from the deflation of relict irrigation and garden areas (Armstrong and Brandt 1994). Meanwhile, if the riverine zone has shifted to the desert (as a result of canal construction or channel avulsion), a new cycle of aggradation will begin.

The complexity of landscape traces that remains today is evident from the sketch map of a small area near Abu Salabikh and Nippur (fig. 5.6). Here, the main Ubaid/Uruk channel traces are obscured by what appears to be a mainly post–Early Dynastic irrigation levee (see also fig. 5.4b). A broad northwest–southeast band of plain scoured by sand transporting winds (aeolian scour plain) shows evidence not only of relict meanders but also of archaeological sites, sand dunes, relict marsh (evident as olive-green silts in auger holes east of Abu Salabikh), and relict canals. Forming a broad tract to the west and southwest is the zone of modern cultivation comprising irrigated fields and canals as well as a number of archaeological sites that have been buried (11, 16, and parts of 15; fig. 5.6 inset). Of these, two sites (15 and 16) date to the Uruk period and are therefore contemporaneous with several sites in the area of relict meanders. This example therefore illustrates how in an arid alluvial landscape a land surface of a given date may be close to the modern surface in one locality (at A), be deeply buried, as along the levee (B), near the surface or pedestaled (at C), and buried at D. In area D, not only are sites buried but also the entire landscape seems to have been blanketed beneath irrigation silts. Hence, early channels can be traced between the mounds of both Abu Salabikh and Nippur, although today these are masked by a blanket of alluvium (Wilkinson 1990b).

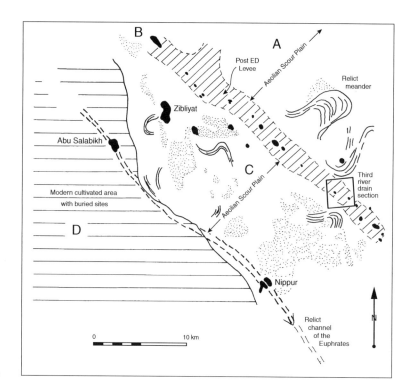

a.

b.

Fig. 5.6 Details of the Mesopotamian plain near Nippur/Abu Salabikh: (a) Sketch map of Nippur/Abu Salabikh area showing landscape taphonomic zones with selected sites (based on Adams 1981 and surveys by the author). The aeolian scour plain (A, C) includes relict meanders (those indicated being of fourth millennium B.C. date; Adams 1981: 62); sand dunes are stippled. Sites in these two zones are of various periods and have been partly denuded and perhaps pedestaled by aeolian activity. The post Early Dynastic levee (B), shown in section in the third river-drain section (fig. 5.4b), has partly buried the pre-third-millennium B.C. land surface. The relict river channel of the Euphrates is based on auger transects at Abu Salabikh (Wilkinson 1990b), the Nippur map (ca. thirteenth-century tablet) and CORONA image interpretation (see also fig. 5.8). The western landscape zone (D: horizontal lines) was under irrigated cultivation at the time of Adams' survey.
(b) Archaeological sites visible on the surface (solid black) and buried by alluvial/irrigation sediments (broken lines) in area of Abu Salabikh.

Channel Patterns of the Alluvial Plain

Today the Tigris and Euphrates river channels exhibit three contrasting morphologies.

— Upstream of the alluvial plain in Syria, Turkey, and northern Iraq river channels are braided or a combination of braided and meandering; they transport bed loads of sand and gravel and flow down relatively steep gradients.

— In the upper alluvial plains where the host sediments are fine (i.e., silt and clay), the channels of both rivers adopt a single-thread meandering pattern.

— Finally, in the lower courses (fig. 5.3) the two rivers bifurcate into subsidiary channels, thereby forming an anastomosing trace, the branches of which are often less sinuous than the main channels further upstream. Although today such bifurcations occur downstream of Hindiyah on the Euphrates, and al-Kut on the Tigris, in earlier times they may have occurred as far upstream as Falujah and Samarra. Bifurcation usually results from the abrupt shifting of a river channel to produce a new branch. If there has been a breach in the riverbank or levee, a new channel is formed as an offshoot of the main channel. This process of bifurcation, known as avulsion, is crucial to the interpretation of both alluvial hydrology and the development of irrigation systems, as will be discussed below.

Although little is known about the Pleistocene rivers of the Mesopotamian lowlands, from the sedimentary geomorphology of the Pleistocene alluvial terraces alongside them it can be inferred that during Pleistocene cold spells, Mesopotamian rivers would have flowed via braided channels separated by sand and gravel islands.

Satellite images and aerial photographs show numerous traces of relict channels, some of which can be associated with ancient settlement (Adams 1981: 1–51). Relict meanders take various forms: (a) bedded alluvial deposits of sand and silt, (b) patterns of differential growth of vegetation that exploits soil moisture within buried channels (Gibson personal communication; Harris and Adams 1957: 161), (c) fine, silt/clay channel fills that retain moisture after rains (fig. 5.7; Geyer and Sanlaville 1996: pl. IV), and (d) field patterns that reflect the topography and sediments that were in existence when the fields were laid out. Although relict channels are frequently difficult to date without recourse to dating the actual sediments or contained organic

Fig. 5.7   Trace of a relict canal or channel near Abu Salabikh, Iraq. The channel course has been accentuated by the clay fill, which has retained moisture from recent rains; in addition, any bank of upcast soil has been blown away by wind action.

materials, the presence of sites of known dates in association with such channels can indirectly suggest when the channels were in use. This of course assumes that the inhabitants of the later settlements did not by chance build upon a preexisting river channel. The best example of a dated channel occurs to the north of Nippur. By assuming at that site that river meanders predated a group of key sites of Late Uruk date, Adams was able to suggest that meander morphology evolved from a low sinuosity to a meandering form. This implies there was a shift from a channel with a higher gradient during an earlier Ubaid phase to a mature, meandering channel that was mainly associated with a silt and clay flood plain during the Uruk (Adams 1981: 62). Such a change can also occur when a channel shifts from transporting more bedload to one in which finer silt or clay is transported as suspended load.

Such well-developed relict channel traces, although sporadically occurring in many parts of the plain, are not uniformly present, in part because the sedimentary deposits and

vegetation are not always favorable to their preservation or because the accumulations of later levees have obscured them (Adams 1981: 31).

Recent mapping of the plains by Robert Adams and Jennifer Pournelle at the University of California at San Diego has revealed, in addition to large areas of hitherto unknown field and irrigation systems (see below), numerous traces of ancient relict meanders of various dates. Because some areas, such as that to the west of Tell Oueli, consist of relict late Pleistocene deposits (e.g., Geyer and Sanlaville 1996: fig. 5) into which the Euphrates incised during the Late Glacial Maximum, some meander traces may be of pre-Holocene date. Unfortunately lack of information on Quaternary stratigraphy of the plains precludes our being able to differentiate between Holocene channels and those of Pleistocene date.

To understand the capricious behavior of Mesopotamian channel systems, it is necessary to examine the mechanics of channel movement. Specifically this entails an understanding of the process of "avulsion" in which a river course is suddenly abandoned in favor of another course, usually at a lower topographic level (Allen 1965). A characteristic feature of an avulsion is that an old meandering channel flowing along the crest of its own alluvial ridge or levee of accumulated deposits spills over its banks or exits them via an existing gap or crevice. As a result, the new channel ultimately flows down the levee slope and across the flood basin, after which it either disappears into swamps or finds its way back into the main channel further downstream (Jones and Schumm 1999). Such new channels, which frequently exhibit a low sinuosity (i.e., are less meandering), usually leave part of their flow continuing along a sinuous old channel (Stouthamer and Berendsen 2000: 1053). If both new and old channels were observed in relict form, it might, however, be concluded from their contrasting geometries that each had been formed under different environmental conditions (Brizga and Finlayson 1990: 395, 399).

Avulsion therefore results in multiple channels that follow often markedly different courses across the plain; these are termed "anastomosing" if they are low-energy channels associated with fine sediments (Nanson and Huang 1999: 478). By creating new channels, anastomosing systems can provide opportunities for the local communities to extend the existing irrigation network. Nevertheless, the abrupt shift of a channel to a new course, by removing the water supply from some areas and devastating settlements and their fields in others, can be a catastrophe for the local inhabitants (Gibson 1973). I argue, however, that both opportunities and catastrophes are offered by this mode of channel development, and an understanding of both processes is crucial to an assessment of settlement and economy of southern Mesopotamia (Schumm 1992). But before discussing possible human responses, it is necessary

to examine why avulsion may have been such a characteristic feature of the plains.

In general, the diminishing gradient of the Mesopotamian plains downstream is associated with a progressive decrease in riverine discharge in the same direction (as a result of irrigation and evaporation). This is a characteristic feature of anastomosing rivers (Nanson and Huang 1999: 489). Furthermore, where a river enters a very low gradient plain, the reduction in gradient can increase aggradation to such a point that overbank spillage becomes more probable. Although sediment accumulation is not a primary cause of avulsion, the tendency of a river to clog with sediment can destabilize the river or push it towards a threshold condition in which a periodic flood may serve as a trigger for avulsion (Jones and Schumm 1999: 175–176). Specifically, very high "megaflood" events such as those recorded in the third millennium B.C. in the valley of the Syrian Euphrates would almost certainly trigger avulsions (Tipping in Peltenburg et al. 1996). Triggers other than floods can include tectonic events, breaches of the levees by animal trails (Jones and Schumm 1999), or of course human activities (Stouthamer and Berendsen 2000: 1062).

In the case of the Euphrates, there is good evidence for severe bank-bursting floods in the first half of the second millennium B.C. In addition, several important watercourses became choked with silt and vegetation (Cole and Gasche 1998: 9–10). This combination of channel clogging with high peak floods provides ideal conditions for avulsion to take place, and it is particularly significant that the major branching point of the Euphrates near Sippar is located where the long profile of the river abruptly decreases in gradient. Because this provides ideal conditions for avulsion, such a major branching area could be described as a "node of avulsion" (Stouthamer and Berendsen 2000: 1053; Morozova and Smith

1999: 242). Avulsion is not simply a hypothetical situation in Mesopotamia: Gibson has described in some detail the human response to a late nineteenth- and early twentieth-century shift in the Euphrates at Hilla (Gibson 1972). Similarly, a medieval Islamic avulsion appears to have diverted the Tigris near Samarra (Northedge et al. 1990). Areas that are particularly vulnerable to avulsions are those at the head of the plains (such as Faluja/Sippar), where there is an abrupt change of gradient, and areas near the head of the gulf, where a rising sea level would have decreased channel gradients thereby encouraging within-channel aggradation and potentially pushing the river towards the threshold of avulsion. For example, in the Rhine delta, an avulsion zone has been recorded within some 40 km of the mouth of the estuary at about 7500 B.C. This zone then moved inland over the next four thousand years as sea level rose (Stouthamer and Berensen 2000).

The Mesopotamian plain not only exhibits an anastomosing channel pattern and provides evidence of avulsions during the period of the historical record; it also exhibits numerous conditions that would increase the likelihood of channel avulsion. But whether such avulsions became an opportunity or a problem would depend partly on the scale of the floods that initiated avulsions and also on the response of the local communities and administrative systems.

Because the breaking of riverbanks or levees by natural floods or by human action (i.e., for irrigation) must have been frequent events, there would be numerous weaknesses in the channel banks that would encourage avulsion. Any increase in the total length of channels by subdividing the water of one channel into two would provide circumstances that would eventually allow population to increase in direct proportion to channel length. One might therefore expect settlements to be established along the new channel. Nevertheless, it is unlikely that the old branch would be deserted because avulsions do not necessarily result in the immediate drying of the old bed upstream of the point of avulsion. Instead, flow tends to be maintained in both new and old channels, thereby constituting a partial avulsion (Stouthamer and Berendsen 2000). Being on a raised levee, and because all the irrigation facilities would have been in place, the old channel would have continued to be the most advantageous area for irrigation; on the other hand, the new channel may have invaded a flood basin, with the result that opportunities for gravity flow from the channel itself would have been limited. Also because the older preavulsion channel is often more sinuous than the new one (Brizga and Finlayson 1990: 394–395; see fig. 5.8), the newly developed channel may have provided an advantageous route for boats. With the development of a new channel, and the growth of some new settlements along it, it would have been in the interest of the inhabitants to maintain the point of avulsion so that both old and new communities would have received flow. Therefore the management and maintenance of key bifurcations would have been important foci of public works.

Thus the question arises as to what extent the elongated channels that flowed from north to south through the entire length of the Mesopotamian plains were natural river channels, excavated canals, or a combination of both. In other words, were they simply anabranches of rivers that required maintenance only at key points such as bifurcations or where sedimentation was most problematic? It has been suggested that by the third millennium B.C., greater parts of the Mesopotamian channels were essentially canalized and artificial (Nissen 1988: 96, 130). Postgate points out that although there are frequent mentions in cuneiform texts of the cleaning

of canals, there is little evidence for them being dug in the first place (Postgate 1992a: 179). This problem has been stated by Adams (1981: 144) in the context of the apparently rapid development of irrigation works during Early Dynastic times: "Precisely this kind of [rapid] growth would be needed if there were to be a transition from localized, ad hoc, generally small-scale irrigation concentrated along the back slopes of particular natural levees to extensive increasingly artificial intercommunity systems."

The channel system of southern Mesopotamia may not therefore be the result of the massive organization of huge teams of labor to excavate megacanals along the entire length of the plain. Instead, the very longest channels may simply have been the result of channel management in which key points such as nodes of avulsion, other channel junctions, excessively weedy or silty stretches, and so on were the subject of focused teams that cleaned, dug, and maintained the system at only those points that required attention.

By simply cleaning and managing natural channels, some of the problems of canal modification pointed about by Doolittle for Meso-American canals would have been avoided (1990: 153). Although it is natural to assume that with population growth or increased food demands existing channels would be extended, such a simple policy could have run into considerable problems:

Extending canals or adding new ones to existing irrigation networks is . . . a task more complex than many researches have assumed. Not only do new segments have to be added, but all the canals upstream of the new sections have to be enlarged and reshaped. In quantitative terms, doubling the size of an irrigation system involves much more than simply doubling the lengths of canals. In terms of materials alone, the earth moved in expanding even a simple

system would be at least three times as great. (Doolittle 1990: 153)

On the other hand, Fernea notes that around the modern town of Dagharah the local communities gradually extended the canal system. Similarly, second-millennium B.C. texts refer to the modification of canals or channels (see van Driel 1988: 137). Both of these instances indicate that the principles of good canal design can be violated, albeit not without problems (cf. Doolittle 1990).

Overall Channel Shifts during the Holocene

Whereas much information concerning the riverine environments can be gleaned from soils and geomorphology, the overall geography of changing river channels has been assembled from the careful compilation of information from cuneiform texts, aerial photographs, archaeological surveys, and satellite images. As a result of the rapid pace of development of satellite imaging, there has been a surge of new information since about 1990, and a number of new models of riverine geography have recently been proposed. Earlier reconstructions, building upon Jacobsen's model (1960), suggested that most of the alluvial plain received its water from the Euphrates, which split into a number of branches (Gibson 1972: fig. 69). This river episodically shifted to the western part of the plain so that by the Kassite period, much settlement was probably outside the realm of those areas surveyed by Adams (Brinkman 1984). In fact, analysis of satellite images by Adams and Pournelle now suggest that there was a major westward deflection of Euphrates flow as early as the Ur III period, or even earlier, and that this course can be traced as far south as the city of Ur.[6]

Effectively, the Tigris, which has a higher and more variable discharge than the Euphrates and today flows through an incised channel, was

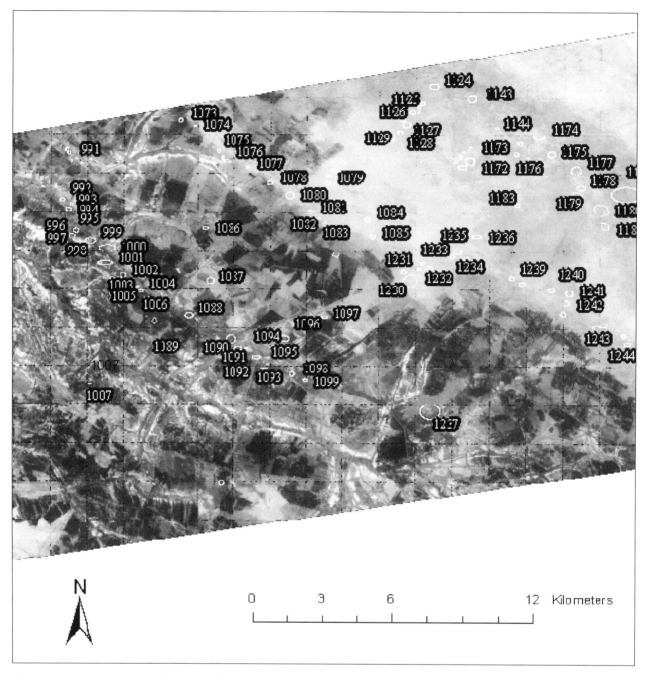

Fig. 5.8 CORONA image showing relict channel system to south of Nippur, together with the branching network of an irrigation system (near Site 1237). Light areas adjacent to the channels represent levees and sediments cleaned out of channels; the pale area to the northeast is alluvial desert, the dark variegated terrain representing recent cultivation; sites (numbered) are taken from the surveys of R. McC. Adams 1981. (Compiled by Carrie Hritz; photograph courtesy of the U.S. Geological Survey)

thought to have been little used for irrigation until around the Hellenistic period. At this time the main centers such as Seleucia developed on the Tigris, and subsequently, massive imperial irrigation systems were constructed (Adams 1981: 7). Although

Adams considered the likelihood of the existence of a joint Tigris-Euphrates channel (Adams 1981: 16; see also Paepe 1971), this was difficult to prove. In more recent years, a number of scholars have accepted the possibility that large parts of the

plain were watered from the Tigris itself or perhaps from a combined channel of the Tigris/Euphrates (e.g., Algaze 2001, fig. 1). Building upon an earlier study of Heimpel (1990), Steinkeller makes a compelling case that suggests that during Ur III times, a course of the Tigris flowed east of Nippur through Adab and Zabalam, that is, well to the southwest of the modern Tigris (fig. 5.11; Gersche et al. 2002; Steinkeller 2001).

The Development of Irrigation Systems

Existing models for the earlier stages of the development of irrigation systems in the Mesopotamian plains build upon ecological arguments (e.g., Buringh's model summarized below). Three further stages supply more complex reconstructions based upon information gleaned from cuneiform texts, archaeology, and geomorphology.

Three methodological approaches can be recognized for the historical interpretation of irrigation:

— The first was made during the Diyala project, initially by Jacobsen during the 1930s and later by Jacobsen and Adams, both of whom attempted reconstructions on the assumption that alignments of settlements must have fallen on the same watercourses (Jacobsen 1958).
— More sophisticated reconstructions were then made possible by the judicious use of cuneiform texts, which referred to sites being located on named watercourses. This resulted in Jacobsen's reconstruction of the Waters of Ur (1960, 1969). Using these principles, additional reconstructions of channel systems were then made by Adams (1965; Adams and Nissen 1972; Adams 1981), Gibson (1972), and Wright (1969).
— The third stage utilized detailed topographic maps to reconstruct the actual levees. Cole and Gasche then employed textual sources that were employed to link those levees and the sites along them with named channels and their associated sites (Cole and Gasche 1998). Types of evidence include topo-

graphic levees and flood basins, channel traces on the ground (Adams 1981: 27–37), sluices (e.g., Tello), auger profiles across channels (Verhoeven 1998), physical traces of channels on aerial photographs, and satellite images. As a result of the work of Gasche and colleagues, it has become clear that some levee systems did not correspond to channel systems inferred by Adams and instead, in some cases, earlier reconstructions result in channels flowing up and over levees.

A total of five stages are recognizable in the development of Mesopotamian irrigation systems. Of these, the initial stage is inferred from slender and elusive evidence, the following three stages are inferred from a combination of historical, archaeological, and geomorphological data.

(a) Initial Developments. Evidence from soil development and geomorphology, as well as the observation that most archaeological sites (as recorded by air-photo analysis) were located on soils of highest quality, led Buringh to suggest an evolutionary trajectory of irrigation agriculture as follows: "Early cultivation" would have taken place in those parts of flood basins that dried out in time for sowing. The timing of this would partly determine the types of crops to be grown, so that supplementary soil moisture would be supplied via flood gullies that channeled water through levee breaks. Potential locations for these early stages of irrigation can be recognized as the distinctive deposits of "crevasse splays" that fan out over the levees (fig. 5.9 left; Verhoeven 1998) or dendritic channel patterns radiating out from levee breaks (fig. 5.9a–c; Buringh 1960). Water flow through levee breaks could be adjusted by human activity, and with increasing scale of settlement and population growth, the channels themselves could be manipulated

and lengthened until they too developed levees. Formative stages of irrigation may also have included flood recession (i.e., *décrue*) agriculture during which certain crops were sown after the retreat of the flood (Kouchoukos 1998: 224). Supplementary water could come from rainfall or have been applied later in the cropping season. Furthermore, in the perimarine zone near the head of the gulf, agriculturalists could have taken advantage of the daily tidal fluctuations that would raise the water to the level of fields (Nelson 1962; Kouchoukos 1998: 229). Although none of the above ecological models has independent support from archaeological evidence, it is clear that in Lower Mesopotamia during the earlier Ubaid period, a wide range of environmental niches would have existed. These included levees, moist flood basins with marshes, levee break areas subject to flooding, areas subject to recession, and tidal fluctuations, all of which would have provided a complex mosaic of opportunities for the original settlers (Algaze 2001).

Sustained erosion and sedimentation over the millennia appear to have erased or obscured traces of the earliest canals. Nevertheless, Ubaid and earlier Uruk sites in the area of Warka (Uruk) form approximate alignments that might result from the sites falling along the line of a single canal (Adams and Nissen 1972: fig. 2). Alternatively, more recent satellite-image studies suggest that Ubaid sites may have been located upon slight rises in the underlying plain surface (turtle backs) within an otherwise deltaic, marshy environment (Adams 2001; Pournelle 2001b). Unfortunately, the lack of detailed geoarchaeological field studies makes it difficult to determine the environmental context of such sites, and it is possible that other sites may be buried at lower levels. The agricultural support system of Ubaid sites in the lower plains may have taken the form of flood-recession agriculture, or alternatively, small

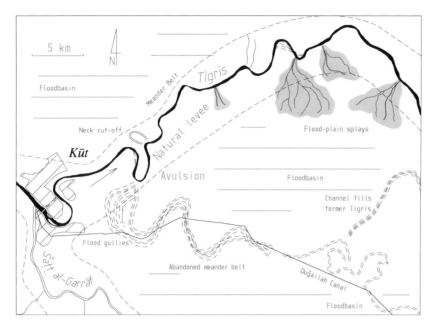

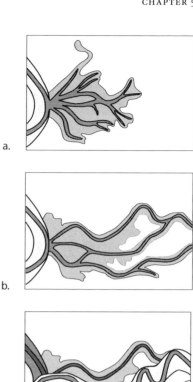

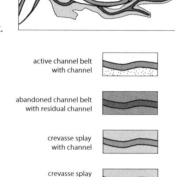

Fig. 5.9   Left: Alluvial geomorphology of the junction of the Tigris and Shatt al-Gharraf, near Kūt. Note the recent splays of alluvial deposits on the floodplain; also the point of avulsion that resulted in a shift in the channel belt from one leading to the east southeast to a new course (in black) leading to the northeast (Verhoeven 1998: fig. 2). Right: evolution of channel pattern from crevasse splay (a) to a new avulsion channel (b), and a fully developed avulsion channel (c). (Modified from Makaske 2001: fig. 4)

canals or channels could have supplied water via breaks in the levee (Roberts 1998: 174–175). Levee breaks appear to take advantage of so-called crevasse splays, which can result in a fan of coarse channel sediment being deposited on the flood plain, lower levee slopes, and nearby parts of the flood basin (Waters 1992: 134–135). Such breaches form a common feature of natural flood plains. Because they form an opportune way of leading water on to the flood plain, they presumably would have been manipulated by Mesopotamian communities to supply water when required. Such practices would have resulted in a weakening of levee channels, and so preexisting breeches could have been enlarged by high flood levels. Evidence of such breaches getting out of control and being enlarged comes from third-millennium B.C. texts that refer to the filling of channel breaches with dirt (Steinkeller 2001: notes 80, 117).

The excavated record of Ubaid sites provides indirect support of early irrigation agriculture in the form of carbonized plant remains and animal bones; no actual Ubaid-period irrigation canals have been recorded on the surface. Nevertheless, according to the results of a French team working at Tell Oueli (Huot 1989, 1996), carbonized *Triticum monococcum* and *Hordeum vulgare* from Ubaid 0 levels (ca. 6000–5500 B.C.) provide the earliest known evidence for agriculture in the southern plains, with Hordeum vulgare becoming the principle crop of irrigated cultivation (Huot 1989: 26–27). Communities appear to have practiced a mixed animal husbandry, with sheep/goats providing 17 percent, pigs 38 percent, and cattle 45 percent of animal bones. Although practically no fish are found in Ubaid 0 levels, brackish, estuarine, and freshwater species were all present in Ubaid 4 levels, that

is, at a time when sea level reached maximum. Therefore, from the geological data, global eustatic sea level curves, and the faunal remains, it can be inferred that an estuarine or brackish environment had probably penetrated close to Oueli by Ubaid 4 (ca. 4500–4000 B.C.).

Sanlaville sees the environment as having been both verdant and variegated, with faunal remains suggesting that a great reliance was placed on domestic animals such as pig and cattle, which thrive in rather moist conditions. Arguing from satellite images and a reinterpretation of Adams' and Wright's survey data, Pournelle goes further to suggest that communities sustained by marshland biomass and a combination of farming, fishing, and (animal) husbandry provided the foundation of Sumerian society, which preceded the development of formalized irrigation in the third millennium B.C. (Pournelle 2001b).

(b) The Formative Stage. The fourth and early third millennia B.C. were crucial times for the development of early Mesopotamian cities. During this time, the area of southern Mesopotamia was transformed from a predominantly rural pattern of small settlements to an urban one that by Early Dynastic I times was dominated by the ca. 400 ha city of Uruk (Adams and Nissen 1972: 87). During the Uruk and Jemdet Nasr periods, channels were probably mainly natural systems of bifurcating and rejoining river branches. As in the initial stages, irrigation probably continued to take advantage of crevasse splay breaks in the edge of riverbanks, but because such locations themselves can promote avulsion, these can, in turn, result in the diversion of the main flow of a channel (Slingerford and Smith 1998; Makaske 2001: 161–162). The extension of an elongated avulsion course across the former crevasse splay zone would therefore create an entirely new channel, with the result that the settled and agricultural area would be extended (fig. 5.9c).

Irrigation presumably entailed the management of natural channels as well as the damming of distributary channels so that water was conveyed to fields via small dug canals or localized flooding (Adams 1981: 245). There is little evidence for the construction of large-scale artificial canal systems during the fourth millennium B.C., but by Jemdet Nasr times, there is a suggestion of at least one canal 15 km in length (Adams and Nissen 1972: 18; Adams 1981: 245). Marshes continued to play an important role in the landscape and economy. The presence of what appears to have been marshland settlements during the Jemdet Nasr period

some 10 km to the north of Uruk provides hints that marshland exploitation continued to be important (Adams and Nissen 1972: 25).

(c) Third, Second, and Early First Millennium B.C. Developments. Cuneiform texts show that during the third millennium B.C., channel cleaning was taking place, and we now find unequivocal evidence of the presence of major excavated canals (Nissen 1988: 96). Archaeological surveys also provide a tangible record of the landscape of the central alluvial plains, although much of the western part of Lower Mesopotamia remains unexplored by surveys. During the third millennium, the number of channels appears to have been sharply reduced, and the belt of irrigated cultivation became broader (Adams and Nissen 1972: 12). As a result, the overall landscape structure was determined by the few major watercourses that existed, as well as bulges along them that were caused by branch canals that locally extended the limits of cultivation. According to Nissen, we therefore get a picture of an early Dynastic landscape in which irrigation oases were "threaded like pearls along the main water courses" (Nissen 1988: 141; see, for example, Adams and Nissen 1972: fig. 6). Adams and Nissen make the important point that the major watercourses were derived from earlier natural channels but that they gradually assumed a more canal-like regime as a result of increased human management that took the form of channel straightening (1972: 12). The latter practice was, in part, intended to accommodate the increased passage of boats. Moreover, Adams (1981) asserts that this configuration was not the result of overall planning by the rulers but was a piecemeal outgrowth of centuries of small-scale modifications. By the second millennium B.C., evidence from cuneiform texts suggest that large canals, such as ambitious schemes by Hammurapi and Rim Sin, were indeed underway

by Old Babylonian times (Renger 1990: 34–35). During Kassite times, a large series of east–west canals was constructed to the south of Nippur (Armstrong and Brandt 1994).

A fundamental contribution to the reconstruction of the Mesopotamian landscape has come from an integrated assessment of geomorphology, archaeology, and philology by a Belgian-American team (Cole and Gasche 1998: 53). This collaborative enterprise entailed mapping the physical remains of fossil levees of old branches of the rivers, which then formed a topographic framework by providing a platform for later channels (fig. 5.10). This illustrates a process of "path dependence" in which earlier features can then determine the pattern of later landscape elements (see chapter 1). Textual information was then employed to identify the various river branches that flowed between sites identified by various archaeological surveys. The results demonstrate that most archaeological sites were indeed located along levees but that not every site alignment consisted of a former levee or channel. In the northern alluvium, a series of channels bifurcate from the Euphrates between Faluja and Sippar. One of these channels extends a considerable distance to the east, so that it may have intersected the former Tigris course to form a channel known from cuneiform texts as the Zubi (Cole and Gasche 1998: 16–23). This channel, by comprising a mixture of Tigris and Euphrates waters, may explain the ambiguity in the interpretation of channel systems further downstream, some texts of which describe them as being of the Euphrates, others the Tigris. As can be seen on figure 5.11, at least some eastern channels formerly recognized as being exclusively fed by the Euphrates may in fact have received water from both sources. Such reconstructions should, however, take into account that the Tigris did not occupy the present incised channel but probably a rather more elevated

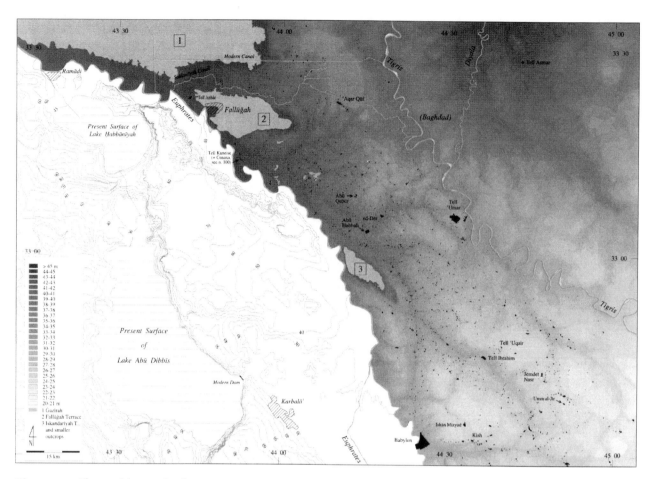

Fig. 5.10 Channel levees in the upper Mesopotamian plains near Sippar (Abu Habbah), evident as subtle variations in the elevation of the terrain. Sites from the University of Ghent site inventory can be seen to lie mainly at various points across the raised levees (although some do occur in flood basins between the levees). Note that the Sippar/Abu Habbah system derives its waters from the Euphrates, whereas those to the east through Tell ʿUmar may relate to a former course of the Tigris. (From Cole and Gasche 1998, map 3, with permission)

one located a little to the north and that such a channel must predate the medieval avulsion near Samarra (Northedge et al. 1990).

One explanation for the development of such multiple channels in the alluvial plains is that abrupt shifts of channels take place at intervals. Thus Gibson (1973) has posited an abrupt shift in the Euphrates from a position east of Nippur in the Uruk period to a line further west by Jemdet Nasr times. Nissen (1988) suggests an abrupt shift in the course of the Euphrates from a line through Nippur, Shurrupak, and Uruk in Early Dynastic I to a more eastern course through Umma in Early Dynastic II (Nissen 1988: 131–

134). The relevance of this process is considered below (and see fig. 5.11).

The structure of the landscape appears to have arisen from both the overall morphology of the elongated levees that followed the major channels, as well as from the construction of local irrigated modules nourished by small branch canals. The pattern of the main settlement systems, which would have been distributed along the levees and higher ground, has been successfully captured by the extensive surveys of Adams. At a local level, however, it seems that some smaller settlements may have been overlooked by surveys. For example, analysis of Ur III texts relating to the Umma

area by P. Steinkeller suggests that there were originally 150 small settlements, a number far in excess of the count in the survey by Adams and Nissen (1972). Such a mismatch may have resulted because the original settlements were small, were made of perishable materials, or had a function (e.g., as a threshing floor) that does not show up well in the survey record. Also, some of these settlements may have been buried below alluvial sediments.

Local irrigation modules would probably have been nourished either by small watercourses led off each bank of the river channel at successive points or by means of a new channel dug from the river from a

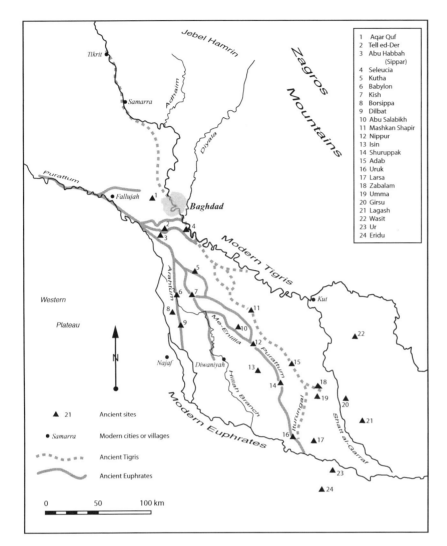

Fig. 5.11 Tentative reconstruction of major ancient channels in the Mesopotamian plain from geomorphological, archaeological, and textual sources. Note the bifurcating nature of these anastomosing channel systems (based on Gasche et al. 2002: carte 1).

Even the layout of some cities was determined, in part, by the pattern of water channels, which served both as communication routes within the city and as dividers between quarters (Stone 1995: 239). Thus the various mounded quarters of Nippur and Abu Salabikh were both arranged around axial canal systems, with the former site being flanked to the west by the channel of the Euphrates and bisected by an unnamed canal, both of which appear on the famous Kassite-period map of Nippur (see, for example, van de Mieroop 1999: 64). In addition, a fourth- or third-millennium B.C. canal existed to the east of Nippur. Similarly, the Old Babylonian city of Mashkan Shapir was subdivided into functional districts by its canal systems. At Larsa the canals delimited the administrative-religious and habitation zones (Stone 1995: 239).

As in Upper Mesopotamia, the majority of buildings in southern Mesopotamian towns were constructed of mudbrick, which usually had to be excavated from the adjacent plain. Although the actual archaeological evidence is lacking, the mention in the *Epic of Gilgamesh* that the city of Uruk (Warka) was subdivided into one square mile of city, one square mile of gardens, one square mile of brick pits, and a half square mile of Ishtar's dwelling (Foster 2001: 3) suggests that large areas of southern cities or their outskirts were perforated by pits dug for the extraction of mudbrick. Because such pits would rapidly silt up with water-laid or aeolian sediments or garbage, it is hardly surprising that they are not evident today. But before they silted up, extensive water-filled pools close to the main occupied towns could have been transformed into ideal harbors. Therefore one might expect to see reference to such features in the textual record and this may explain the curious intramural "harbors" at sites such as Mashkan Shapir (Stone and Zimansky 1994: 454).

point well upstream to flow roughly parallel to the main channel (Postgate 1992a: 174). A small irrigated module (figs. 5.8, 5.12) might have consisted of settlements together with date-palm orchards and other trees along the crest of the levee, cultivated plots at more distant locations on the backslope of the levee, and finally marginal fields, marshes, and desert grazing beyond (Postgate 1992a: 173–190). Unfortunately, there is scant information on the configuration of larger-scale irrigation land-use systems, but at a finer-scale Liverani, using mainly the record of Early Dynastic and Akkadian cadas-

tral texts, suggests that there were two fundamentally different landscapes in the Mesopotamian plains. In the south the landscape was dominated by large, open fields parceled into narrower fields, whereas in the northern plains the fields were more blocklike and less elongate (Liverani 1996: 15–18). Because field parcels had to be in such a position that they could receive water from the canals and that water could be distributed over all parts of the field, it is clear that the overall pattern of fields was determined by the layout of channels as well as the local gradient of the terrain.

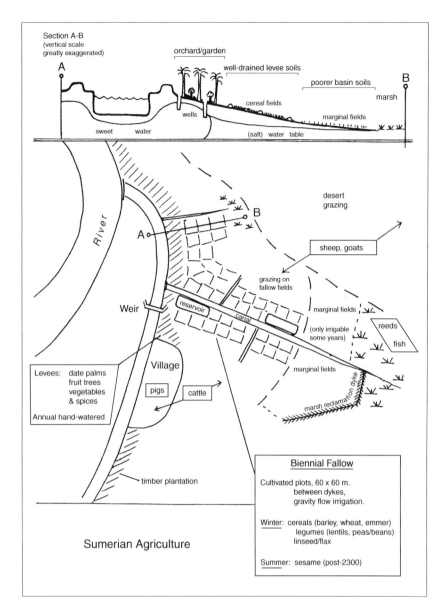

Fig. 5.12 Hypothetical sketch of an irrigated agricultural cell in the southern Mesopotamian plain; compare with fig. 5.8 (from Postgate 1992a: fig. 9.1, with permission).

(d) Large-Scale Irrigation Systems. Starting in the Kassite period and clearly from Neo-Babylonian times on, the construction of massive region-scale canal and irrigation systems, frequently under the sponsorship of state authorities, resulted in the opening up of huge new areas for settlement as well as the expansion of existing populations. Such schemes entailed the parcellation of substantial tracts of land (Adams 1981: 245) into what were effectively enormous estates. Thus at roughly

the same time as territorial empires had grown to administer vast areas of the Near East and Eastern Mediterranean we can also discern the scale of irrigation systems becoming even larger than before. According to the surveys of Adams, population density attained its apogee in the Diyala and Lower Mesopotamian plains during the Sasanian period.[7] A similar pattern of growth was also evident in the area north of Baghdad, where the Dujail canal resulted in substantial settlement growth. In

this case, however, the number of settlements apparently peaked during Parthian times, with those of urban proportions attaining a peak during the Sasanian period (Adams 1972: 187–188; Gibson 1972: maps 6–9).

Similar population increases can also be discerned in neighboring areas of Iran, such as in the Deh Luran plain, where Neely has described a landscape that was both densely and patchily settled during the Sasanian period (Neely 1974). On the other hand, in the Susiana plain, settlement and overall population climaxed in either the Late Parthian (Wenke 1975–1976) or the Sasanian periods (Adams 1962: 116; Christensen 1993: 305). According to Wenke, whereas the Parthian period showed a peak in rural settlement, during Sasanian times there was a marked increase in the scale of urban settlement at the same time as certain rural areas became depopulated (Wenke 1987: 256).

Despite minor contradictions in the interpretation of population trends, throughout much of Mesopotamia and adjacent regions, the Parthian and Sasanian periods (i.e., between the second century B.C. and the sixth century A.D.) can be seen to have witnessed a tremendous expansion of settlement and irrigation (Christensen 1993: 247). The landscape transformations of the Sasanian period were particularly ambitious and were in part a result of Sasanian imperial policy, which comprised three main elements: (1) the construction of large irrigation systems, (2) the founding of new towns, and (3) forcible deportations of large populations and their resettlement in areas that were deemed to benefit from agricultural investment (Adams 1981; Christensen 1993: 107). In the Susiana plain Sasanian policy was manifest in the form of massive investments in weirs and bunds across the deeply incised rivers. Thus near the town of Shushtar, Shapur I (A.D. 240–272) constructed a weir 600 m long across the Karun River that raised water to sufficient height to flow down the Mashruqan canal (now the Qar Qar river; Adams 1962: 116; Christensen 1993: 107–108). As a result of such investments, agricultural productivity was substantially increased, presumably as a result of the extension of both wheat and barley cultivation as well as that of rice (Adams 1962; Wenke 1975–1976; Christensen 1993). In turn, the increased food production was capable of supporting the substantial urbanization of this phase. As a result of such prodigious growth, towns such as Ivan-I Karkhah, Jundishapur, Shushtar, and perhaps Susa together must have housed at least one hundred thousand people or more (Wenke 1987: 255).

Although archaeological surveys have mainly focused on the recording of settlements rather than the landscapes in between, it is evident that by the Sasanian period, the construction of massive irrigation systems had also transformed the countryside (Adams 1962: fig. 5). This expansion culminated in the Nahrawan system, 230 plus km long, which conveyed water from upstream of Samarra through the Diyala plains to the Tigris (Adams 1965). This huge gash through the earth, some 30–50 m wide, comprised an upstream segment north of the Diyala known as the Kātūl al-Kisrawi, and a downstream segment, the Nahrawan. The waters from this channel, which was probably constructed by Chosroes I (A.D. 531–579), when combined with those of the Diyala, enabled some 8,000 sq. km of land to the northeast of Baghdad to be irrigated and cultivated (Adams 1965: 74). Not only did total settlement reach its peak at this time but the total area of urban settlement also attained its maximum. As in the Susiana plain, sophisticated irrigation technology enabled obstacles to be negotiated and water to be distributed. This entailed the construction of massive weirs of baked brick, various types

of headworks for diverting water, as well as numerous bridges, all of which are known either from field evidence or from later texts (Adams 1965: 79).

The Nahrawan system was complemented to the west of Baghdad by a series of transverse canals flowing from the Euphrates to the Tigris. Although constructed as early as the fifth century B.C. (Christensen 1993: 57), these are best known for the Early Islamic period (Le Strange 1905: 67–68; El-Samarraie 1972: 14). These canals illustrate the problems created by the introduction of too much water into a poorly drained alluvial area. It has been suggested that irrigation from these canals raised water tables between Baghdad and Babylon to excessively high levels, so that there was acute salinization over large areas. Consequently, lands around the southernmost canal, the Shatt al-Nil, were abandoned by A.D. 1250, and by A.D. 1500 virtually the entire area was deserted (Gibson 1974: 15).

Because much of the Diyala as well as the northern alluvium irrigated by the transverse canals has been cultivated for a long period of time, it is necessary to look to more marginal areas for evidence of the Sasanian landscape. In the Deh Luran Neely recorded a variegated landscape consisting of isolated farmsteads and cultivated fields dispersed across the piedmont areas, in contrast to irrigated homesteads on the alluvial plains (Neely 1974). A combination of qanats, which collected water from raised water tables along the rivers, as well as conventional irrigation canals, supplied water not only for irrigation and domestic purposes but also for turning the millstones of water mills. Settlements in the irrigated area formed stringlike arrangements along canals, whereas in the dry-farmed piedmont zone, staircases of check dams followed the watercourses with agricultural terraces occupying the rolling land in between (fig. 5.13). This episode of settlement expansion was achieved

probably by the Sasanian kings of Kavadh (488–531) and Chosroes I Anosharwan (531–579), who initiated the repair, planning, and construction of large-scale public works such as roads, bridges, and irrigation systems. In addition, they also probably undertook the building of towns, the resettlement of entire communities (which included the incorporation of large numbers of prisoners of war), and the encouragement of population growth. Although it is possible that the Deh Luran area may have been earmarked as a "breadbasket" for the Sasanian state, Neely favors the notion that it became an area to which surplus population was transferred.

From its earliest days, irrigation has entailed the development of technologies that were specifically capable of manipulating water and distributing it across the landscape. During the first millennia B.C. and A.D., however, these technologies became much more sophisticated and could be applied to a wider range of tasks. For example, in the Khuzistan plain Sasanian engineers frequently cut through ridges of rock or dug tunnels with vent holes to provide a hydraulically efficient course for canals. In one case, water was diverted from the Diz River to lands adjacent to the Karun, which were too high to be irrigated by that river (Adams 1962: 116–117). Such approaches to the landscape are reminiscent of those recorded in other parts of the Middle East where, for example, Islamic engineers reconfigured the landscape thereby overriding its disadvantages to redistribute water when new needs arose (chapter 9). The technology also harks back to earlier traditions such as those of the Assyrian canal builders who diverted water across watersheds to supply Nineveh with irrigation water (chapter 7) or to the earliest qanat builders in the Iranian highlands. It has also been claimed that by capturing the Roman emperor Valerian, Shapur I was able to apply advanced Roman

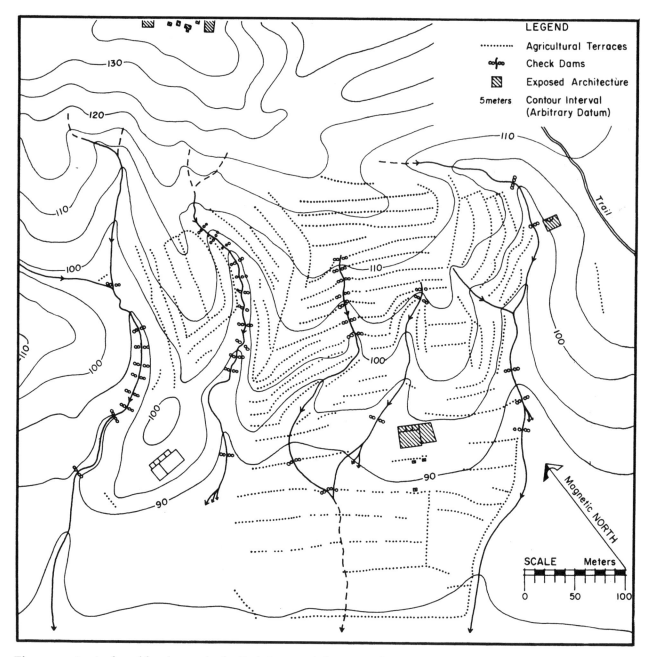

Fig. 5.13 Agricultural landscape in the Deh Luran piedmont with Sasanian homestead, relict fields, and check dams (from Neely 1974: fig. 3.7, with permission).

technology to the construction of canals. Although one might question whether the Iranians really had much to learn from Romans about the technology of irrigation (Christensen 1993: 109), there seems little doubt that the availability of some seventy thousand Roman legionnaires, some of them skilled in building crafts and technology, would have been a remarkable boon to the Sasanian program of canal building.

Although the use of innovative technology was not original to the Sasanians, the wide-ranging application of such technologies represents a significant advance over what earlier polities had accomplished. Specifically, irrigation technology was not restricted to the distribution of water but was also extended to a wider range of uses such as milling. This is well exemplified by the tower water mills (i.e., water mills

equipped with a tower-shaped penstock), which formed a prominent part of the Deh Luran landscape. These were the result of a technology that had spread rapidly throughout the Near East during the Roman/Parthian and Sasanian periods (Avitsur 1960), with the result that such mills, both above- and belowground varieties, are known to have spread by Early Islamic times as far east as Oman (Wilkinson 1980). The presence of such technologically sophisticated installations highlights an important factor in the development of the later irrigated landscapes of Mesopotamia. Investment in agricultural schemes together with the application of the appropriate technology had become a major factor in landscape development, and this entailed the construction of sophisticated installations that could have been built only by or with the aid of engineers.

Thus the Sasanian policy of expansion entailed not only investment and the mobilization of vast quantities of labor, including captives, but also the employment of skilled engineers, diviners, and artisans. Much of the Sasanian irrigated area was probably brought under cultivation as a result of the policies of Sasanian rulers, but smaller-scale systems of Sasanian or Islamic date found in more peripheral locations around the gulf may have been instigated by prosperous merchants or land owners, much in the way that Persian landlords have been prime investors in qanat technology. Overall, these ambitious schemes, whether state sponsored or private, resulted in massive areas of land being brought under the plough, so that during the Sasanian and Early Islamic periods, even economically and politically marginal areas, such as those around the Deh Luran plain, were producing agricultural products seemingly to their full capacity (Neely 1974: 40). Nevertheless, it would be erroneous to caricature such developments as being simply indicative of population pressure, because not all cultivable parts of the Susiana plain were under cultivation during the Sasanian period. Rather, there appears to have been a tendency to concentrate agriculture around certain urban centers, in areas of abandoned land, or in areas within the reach of irrigation systems.

In the alluvial plains, the massive extension of settlement that occurred during the Parthian, Sasanian, and perhaps Early Islamic periods was characterized by numerous low sprawling settlements that extended often as linear mounds along canals (Adams 1965: 73). Such configurations, according to Adams, are not suggestive of a "feudal"-type society in which peasant villages hugged the flanks of the highly fortified seats of a landed nobility. Rather, they imply that there was a considerable degree of peace and control in the landscape, presumably thanks to the Sasanian authorities. These settlement and landscape configurations of the Diyala and the Deh Luran too, therefore, provide a marked contrast with the tell landscapes of Bronze Age Upper Mesopotamia. These, if not strictly feudal, must have possessed some of the operational characteristics of feudal society (Schloen 2001), with the result that settlements remained highly nucleated and in one place.

On the ground, obvious remains of the great Sasanian and Early Islamic field systems are difficult to discern. Even some of the canals and their flanking spoil mounds have been planed off by the scouring and abrasive winds. Only occasionally is it possible to witness the totality of the results of landscape transformations wrought by the Sasanian or Early Islamic rulers in the Mesopotamian plains. However, to the south of Basra, Nelson (1962) recorded extensive field systems defined by linear boundaries, separated by intervening basinlike fields. Fed by means of an intake canal from the Khor al-Hamma, this configuration of fields covered some 57,000 ha of land. Although not dated archaeologically, they could plausibly be the remains of Early Islamic fields that became salinized and were forcibly cleared of the salt rich horizons by the Zanj slaves during the ninth century A.D. (Nelson 1962). The evidence of clearance is strong, being in the form of salt-rich field-boundary ridges, which presumably were constructed of the salt dug by the slave laborers from the intervening basins. In addition to the Basra fields, which were recorded using aerial photographs, recent analysis of CORONA series satellite images by Robert Adams has recognized extensive grid patterns of fields, canals, and settlements. Occasional field control in the form of earlier surveys suggests that these systems are Sasanian or perhaps Early Islamic in date. Presumably, such landscapes would have been much more evident before the boom in agriculture and population that occurred during the twentieth century A.D.

In addition, parts of the plain are veneered by scatters of potsherds and broken shells, which can extend over many square kilometers. The scatters, which primarily comprise sherds of Parthian to Early Islamic type, can form remarkably dense carpets across the desert between sites as a result of deflation that has removed the matrix of topsoil that contained the sherds. Although these field scatters presumably include traces of individual dwellings, middens, and other structures, the presence of sherds within soil horizons as well as scatters distributed across terrain between grids of field canals suggests that they also include artifacts remaining from fertilization with settlement-derived refuse (fig. 5.14; see chapter 4). Scatters of shell fragments, on the other hand, are the remains of mollusks that lived in the irrigation canals and ultimately became reworked into the irrigated soils and canal fills. After this, if the soils were then deflated, shell fragments were then resorted into dunes of sand and clay aggregates (*parna*).

By the Sasanian period the estimated settlement and cultivated area of the Mesopotamian lowlands exceeded that of the Ur III period and had attained an all-time high (Adams 1981: 180–181). As a result, cultivation must have been virtually continuous over the entire plain. The above-mentioned sherd scatters were therefore arguably the result of the need to maximize agricultural

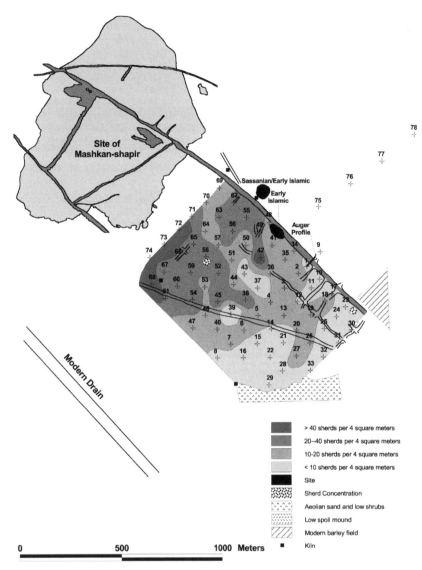

Fig. 5.14   Small area of the central Mesopotamian plain near Abu
Duwari, Iraq (second millennium B.C. Mashkan Shapir), showing
density of sherd scatters, archaeological sites, an undated canal
(through sample point 39), and a grid of small post-Hellenistic canals
(from Stone and Zimansky forthcoming).

production. Such was the demand
for soil enhancements that by the
Islamic period, plant ash and night
soil were imported by barge from the
city of Basra in Lower Mesopotamia
to Khuzestan to be used as fertilizer
(Adams 1962: 119). Significantly, the
approximate coincidence of maximum settlement density and estimated population with evidence for
the application of settlement-derived
fertilizers supports the model of
Ester Boserup that high population

levels can necessitate an increase in
both agricultural production and the
level of intensity (Boserup 1965). In
this context, the construction of extensive, large-scale canal systems (including massive labor mobilization)
and the introduction of intensified
fertilization are both indicative of
agricultural intensification. Although
precisely what crops were fertilized
and irrigated remains unclear, for
the Susiana plains Wenke (1987: 259)
has suggested that local subsistence

systems gave way to the cultivation
of rice, sugar, and orchard crops (see
also Adams 1962: 118).

The imposition of massive canal
systems, which entailed the construction of branch canals that extended a long distance from the levee
crests, created numerous ecological
problems. As discussed by Adams
(1974: 5), the low gradients of parts
of these canals would have encouraged excessive siltation. The presence
of canal levees, often transverse to
the traditional drainage net, would
have interrupted natural patterns
of drainage and encouraged salinity
(Adams 1974: 5; Gibson 1974: 15).
Consequently, what was in the third
and second millennia B.C. a variegated landscape in which cultivation
exploited higher-quality levee soils
and flood basins were left as marshes
or pasture had been transformed
by the first millennium A.D. into
a single agroecological zone. As a
result of the extension of irrigated
cultivation over the levees and down
into flood basins (fig. 5.4), lands of
very different qualities would have
been cultivated, and crop yields
would have been commensurately
variable. In addition to increased
salinization, the extension of agriculture into more ill-drained lands must
have contributed to the loss of vital
pastures. These losses, in turn, must
have had an adverse effect upon the
rural economy by physically pushing
potential pastures to more distant
locations.

In contrast to settlement phases
of the fourth, third, and second millennia B.C., canal systems of the first
millennium B.C. or later were of
truly regional scale. It is therefore
in this context that Wittfogel's arguments for a relationship between
hydraulic administration and system
scale appear to be more appropriate
(Adams 1974: 5). Regional-scale canal
systems in greater Mesopotamia can
therefore plausibly be argued to have
been constructed mainly, but not
exclusively, when large-scale territorial empires were in existence. The

adoption of large-scale canals from the first millennium B.C. and later throughout Mesopotamia may therefore have occurred only when it was possible to gather water and distribute it on a regional scale. In other words, it was the presence of an administrative structure over large areas that provided an opportunity for irrigation systems to extend over very large hydraulic catchments, rather than the needs of hydraulic administration being the driving force behind the development of empires.

Overall, the Sasanians managed, probably more than any preceding society, not only to reshape the landscape itself but also to effect changes in the landscape that were capable of overriding the natural environment. Moreover, in many areas, the social landscape was radically changed as a result of the huge transfers of populations that had occurred as part of the resettlement schemes. Although such resettlement schemes were hardly new (see chapter 7 for Assyrian resettlement), the introduction of alien populations and advanced technologies into specific localities must have had a profound impact on the way that humans interacted with and perceived the land itself. In contrast to land-use systems where local knowledge of the soil landscape would have been in place for long periods of time, deliberate resettlement would introduce foreign populations who lacked local knowledge. Decisions made by such communities could easily result in agronomic failures that would compound some of the negative effects of large-scale irrigation.

(e) Local Demise and Partial Abandonment. As a finale to the massive growth of irrigation systems in the Parthian, Sasanian, and Early Islamic periods, the Mesopotamian plains then witnessed a steady decline in population. This was first evident in the form of the abandonment of large areas of the southern

plains (Adams 1981), which became the domain of great swamps that formed in the fifth and seventh centuries A.D. as a result of flood waters pouring through breaches or the overflow of excess irrigation water (Le Strange 1905: 27). Gradually, as a result of neglect, disease, natural disasters, and war, including the Mongol invasions, much of Mesopotamia became depopulated (Christensen 1993). Once demographic decline had set in, it must have been virtually impossible for any one ruler to resuscitate the dying canal system, in large part because the labor supply did not exist in sufficient quantities to effect the tremendous amounts of work required. The region then witnessed the partial depopulation of vast areas of the southern plains. Nevertheless, despite the demise of large-scale irrigation systems, life continued. Irrigation systems operated primarily on the fringes of the Tigris-Euphrates rivers, the oases between remaining as desert. Such systems continued at a level that could be administered by local communities very much in the manner described by Fernea (1970).

Discussion

The management of what were originally natural watercourses appears to have been a key factor in the development of the alluvial landscape of the Mesopotamian plain. Although natural channels that existed in the fifth and early fourth millennia B.C. must then have become progressively more artificial or controlled through the remainder of the fourth, third, and second millennia B.C., precisely to what degree new channels were excavated is less clear. Texts occasionally allude to significant interference by rulers in the flow of major channels. Thus Sin-iddinam, king of Larsa (ca. 1849–1843 B.C.), states: "In order to provide sweet water for the cities of my country. . . . (An and Enlil) commissioned me to excavate the Tigris (and) to restore it (to its

original bed)" (Frayne 1990: 158–160; Steinkeller 2001).

This action of river diversion into a preexisting bed is common to "natural avulsions" as well. The Sin-iddinam text and others like it suggest that humans were capable of changing the courses of entire rivers to their own advantage. However, of probably greater importance than simply viewing channels shifts as a catalyst for change is to explore the tension between natural channel development on the one hand versus artificial canal construction on the other. That is:

— The tendency for new channels to be created by avulsion, perhaps assisted by human actions, would result in the extension of the channel network, thereby allowing or encouraging growth of new settlements and population along the new branch channel. In addition to allowing population growth, this would extend the all-important network of transport arteries.

— In opposition to the first point is that enormous labor forces would have been required for the excavation of longitudinal canal systems. This would almost certainly have taxed the available pool of labor who would already have been extremely busy in cleaning and maintaining the existing canals as well as conducting normal agricultural tasks. The increased labor demand would have increased local populations, either temporarily or in the long term.

Before discussing the relative merits of these two opposing processes, it is necessary to examine briefly the labor required for the excavation of major canal systems.

The work required to excavate ever-longer canals is suggested by simple calculations that employ information derived from Old Babylonian mathematical texts and administrative tablets of the Ur III period

(Renger 1990: 35). Thus a canal 50 km long, 2 m deep, with a surface width of 7 m and a basal width of 4.2 m that Rim Sin claims to have dug from Larsa to Ur, would have required around 1,925 men working for sixty days simply to dredge (Renger 1990: 36) and between 1,555 and 4,150 men sixty days to excavate. This rate depends of course on the volume of soil excavated per worker, a figure that can vary but that here has been taken to range from 2.25 to 6 cu m per day per worker, with the lower estimate being applied to canal cleaning (Renger 1990: 35). For yet larger canals, namely, (a) 100 km × 20 m wide × 5 m deep, and (b) 200 km long, 40 m wide and 6 m deep, between 4,761 and 12,700 men working for one year would be required (canal a), with between 22,900 and 61,000 men working for one year (canal b). Excavations of such magnitude, although feasible (witness the prodigious enterprises of the Sasanians discussed above), would require either the loss of a significant portion of the agricultural workforce or the importation of large quantities of labor, perhaps as captives.

On the assumption that these workers would be required also to maintain such megacanal systems, a process of positive feedback would be set in motion, because additional workers would not only be required to dig the canals but would also create a demand for food that, in turn, would increase the need for more irrigated farmland. This process would therefore contribute to population growth, urbanization, and (potentially) further growth of the irrigation system.

It is therefore significant that if either of the above-mentioned processes operated, they would have created opportunities for the settlement system to expand, perhaps in unanticipated ways (witness the revolt of the Zanj in the south in the tenth century A.D.). At one extreme, humans could make opportune use of the natural avulsion of river chan-

nels so that after a natural split in the channel had occurred, the point of avulsion could be managed so that both channels would remain open. Not only would this extend the potential irrigable area of the plain but the new channels would also operate as a safety valve by receiving surplus flood water from the original channel. At the other extreme, one could imagine extremely long canals being dug the length of the plain by corvée labor. In this way, southern Mesopotamia would suck up surplus labor from fringing areas as well as from nomadic groups living both within the lowlands and in adjacent regions. Unfortunately, at present it is difficult to suggest precisely where such populations may have come from (Pollock 1999: 68–69).

In contrast to the rain-fed zone of Upper Mesopotamia where local rulers would have had few opportunities to manipulate the local environment, in the south, the river systems would have provided numerous opportunities for rulers to exert their power by providing water for their communities (as quoted above) or by depriving others of their needs (Cooper 1983b, cited in Pollock 1999: 76; see also Nissen 1988: 135). In fact, one of the key roles of the Sumerian ruler was to ensure the flow of water to the lands of his subjects (Nemet-Nejat 1998: 254). Always, however, there lurked the threat of catastrophe resulting from an exceptional flood that could trigger an avulsion or sweep away both settlements and their support systems, as has been noted for the Sasanian period in Babylonia (Gibson 1973: 456). Communities in southern Mesopotamia were therefore poised between (1) opportunities for great growth presented by natural channel shifts, especially if these were astutely managed, (2) slow starvation of resources as a result of diversion of water from key channels during political conflicts, or (3) naturally occurring catastrophes that could wipe out entire regions. Because these variant pathways probably

existed as long as there were avulsions (and people!), there would have been a tendency for the settlement and landscape system to shift from one state to another, sometimes with little warning. It would certainly be misleading to characterize these landscapes as being environmentally determined at one extreme, created by vast labor demands and economic considerations at another, or simply being landscapes of power under the control of a series of powerful kings. Probably all three factors came into play, but to a different degree at different times.

As Adams has emphasized, the Mesopotamian plains have experienced a series of demographic cycles, which in turn must have been roughly in phase with changes in the configuration and scale of land use. One major factor in these cycles appears to have been the well-known process of salinization, which resulted in large-scale declines in productivity, so that by the Ur III period, cereal yields were almost 50 percent those of Early Dynastic time and even lower by 1700 B.C. (Adams 1981: 151–152). As in the northern dry-farmed zone, violation of fallow may have contributed to the productivity of the soil, in the case of southern Mesopotamia, resulting in less leaching of the salts from the soil profile and a commensurate build up in salts (Jacobsen and Adams 1958; Gibson 1974). This story is well known,[8] but bears repetition because it underscores how a change in land-use practice (i.e., from biennial to annual cropping) can itself influence changes in landscape at the regional level (chapter 6). At a still later date, the radical reorganization of channels in the Sasanian period may have contributed to salinization and large-scale land abandonment (Adams 1981: 213), so that again, attempts to increase total crop production ultimately contributed to the decline of the total system of crop production.

It should come as no surprise that over the last seven thousand or

eight thousand years of irrigation in
Iraq and Iran there has been a general evolutionary trajectory towards
more large-scale and complex systems of water supply, transmission,
and irrigation. At the same time,
however, it is also possible to discern
that certain agricultural techniques
appear hardly to have changed. Consequently, if we compare the Chalcolithic runoff irrigation systems of the
Daulatabad area with those of the
Deh Luran plain (compare figs. 5.2
and 5.13), we can discern relatively
little change either in the scale of the
system or in the complexity of its
operation. The significant difference
between the two systems may, however, lie in their context: in the later
Deh Luran system, runoff agriculture
was harnessed in a more marginal
area, whereas the earlier Daulatabad
case was situated, arguably, closer
to the main focus of settlement activity of the period. Therefore, even
though an evolutionary trend can
be discerned in the development of
major irrigation systems, at the same
time (as in the case of the Sasanian
systems of southwest Iran) large
complex systems and small simple
ones can coexist within what is apparently the same societal and political context. This suggests that the
face of the landscape has undergone
transformation by the combined
action of both evolving systems as
well as systems that have remained
in a seemingly undeveloped state for
millennia.

6 Landscapes of Tells
The Fragile Crescent in the Bronze Age

To many people, even some archaeologists, the Near East is a landscape of tells. This chapter outlines some of the basic components of these landscapes of tells and will suggest how they enable us to draw greater insights into early societies and economies.

In the Near East the tell has often been the principal focus of archaeological research to the point that it is possible to refer to "the tyranny of the tell." As a result of this focus, early surveys are often seriously biased, especially for the record of early prehistoric as well as the Iron Age and later periods (see also Banning 1996). Although this criticism of tell-based survey is true to a certain degree, detailed and locally intensive surveys have demonstrated that for some parts of the Near East, and specifically for the Early Bronze Age, the tell does form the basic unit of settlement and furthermore that this feature provides the fundamental organizing structure for the landscape as well. In fact, as Andrew Sherratt (1997: 276) has stated: "Few prehistoric phenomena are more concrete than a tell; it makes sense to see the appearance of such substantial habitation residues as the critical indicator of a substantial commitment to farming." Therefore, despite the potential bias of tell-based analyses, early studies such as Lloyd's "Mounds of the Near East" (1963) continue to have their relevance. On the other hand, for the first millennium B.C. and later periods, an emphasis upon tells provides a highly misleading view of the landscape (chapter 7).

In the Near East, areas characterized by tells include northern and eastern Iraq, those parts of Syria with rainfall greater than 200 mm per annum, the Levantine lowlands, as well as many parts of Turkey and Iran. Beyond what might be described as this nuclear zone, low tells also occur in southeast Europe, for example, in the Hungarian plain and Greece; they are less common in Arabia but still occur as far south as the desert fringes of Yemen and the United Arab Emirates. Here I concentrate on the steppelands of upper Mesopotamia to provide the basic landscape signature and then briefly compare these with equivalent landscapes of the Levant.

The Physical Landscape of Upper Mesopotamia

In northern Iraq, Syria, and southern Turkey the rolling steppe is peppered by seemingly huge numbers of prominent mounds of varying size and up to 30 m or more in height (fig. 6.1). Such conspicuous features have obviously been known to western antiquarians for centuries. In the early 1800s Layard, while at Tell Afar in northern Iraq, was able to count "above one hundred mounds, throwing their dark and long thinning shadows across the plain" (Layard 1849: 315). Archaeological investigations since the time of Layard have demonstrated that such mounds represent occupation over usually thousands of years. As a result of such longevity, tells must have formed a major focal point in the landscape so that off-site features have become virtually incised into the terrain.

Because it forms an island between the Tigris and Euphrates rivers, the rolling steppe of northern Syria and Iraq is known in Arabic as the Jazira. Most of the terrain falls between 200 and 600 m above sea level, and rainfall decreases from around 700 mm per annum in the north (within southern Turkey) to around 150 mm per annum in the south (at Deir al-Zor on the Euphrates; fig. 6.2). Until the recent introduction of pumps for irrigation, the predominant form of crop husbandry was rain-fed cultivation of wheat and barley. In the wetter areas to the north and west, there is increased cultivation of lentils, vines, olives and even nuts, whereas towards the south and east, barley cultivation predominates. Although the conventional limit of rain-fed cultivation is between 250 and 200 mm per annum, cultivation of cereals can extend further south, especially where rainfall and soil moisture are concentrated along wadis. The southern limit of cultivation is both ragged and diffuse (Jas 2000: 249–251). Recent studies emphasize that towards the south, where barley becomes the main cereal crop, pastoralism, perhaps with some seasonal cultivation, becomes the viable option (Wachholtz 1996). Throughout the Jazira, however, the pasturing of flocks is important so that everywhere the agricultural landscape is one of mixed farming; but moister lowlands show more emphasis on cultivation of a wider mix of crops, and in drier areas or near the uplands, pasture becomes more important.

Although the inhabitants of the region often continue to live on or around tells, low sprawling vil-

Fig. 6.1 Tells in the eastern part of the Amuq plain: Tell al-Judaidah is to the right; Tell Dhahab is the small tell to the left of center; Chatal Höyük is on the extreme right in the background. The photograph was taken in September 1932 just before the excavations of the Oriental Institute commenced (Braidwood and Braidwood 1960: pl. 1; courtesy of the Oriental Institute of the University of Chicago).

lages, some nucleated and others dispersed, predominate. Nowhere do we find densely populated walled settlements such as must have been characteristic of the region in the Bronze Age. Because of this difference, it would be misleading to use the present settlement record as a direct analogue of that of the Bronze Age. Nevertheless, it is possible to suggest parallels between traditional forms of land use and similar practices that might have occurred in the Bronze Age.

Geologically most of upper Mesopotamian Jazira consists of younger sedimentary rocks—mainly limestone, sandstone, and marls—that were deposited during the Cretaceous and Tertiary eras. In addition, parts of the Euphrates, Khabur, and Balikh valleys contain up to 150 m

of unconsolidated Quaternary and Pliocene sediments that often form valuable aquifers. The terrain is broken by two upfolded (anticlinal) ridges: the Jebel Sinjar, predominantly within northern Iraq to the east, and the Jebel Abd al-Aziz, wholly within Syria to the west, while the northern edge of the steppe is defined by the low Taurus foothills. In addition, a number of Pleistocene and Holocene volcanic peaks such as Jebels Kawkab and Mankhar (to the east of Hassakeh and Raqqa respectively) break the topography. Other outcrops of Quaternary period igneous rock occur in the form of broad, flat-topped basalt lava plateaus, in the Khabur basin to the south of the Jebel Abd al-Aziz, and to the northeast of the Syrian Jazira near Jerablus. In the Turkish Jazira, simi-

lar outcrops of basalt occur between Urfa and the Euphrates to the north.

Most wadis in the west and central Jazira drain towards the Euphrates, and only in the east do they drain into the Tigris. The main perennial channels are the small north–south rivers of the Balikh and Khabur, which in the earlier twentieth century A.D. supplied some 0.6 percent and 6 percent of the flow of the Euphrates respectively (Kolars and Mitchell 1991). As a result of overpumping for irrigation water in both Syria and Turkey, both rivers have experienced massive declines of flow in recent years so that the Balikh is today virtually dry, except for some spillover water from Turkish irrigation schemes, and the Khabur is but a fraction of its former self. The Khabur and Balikh both

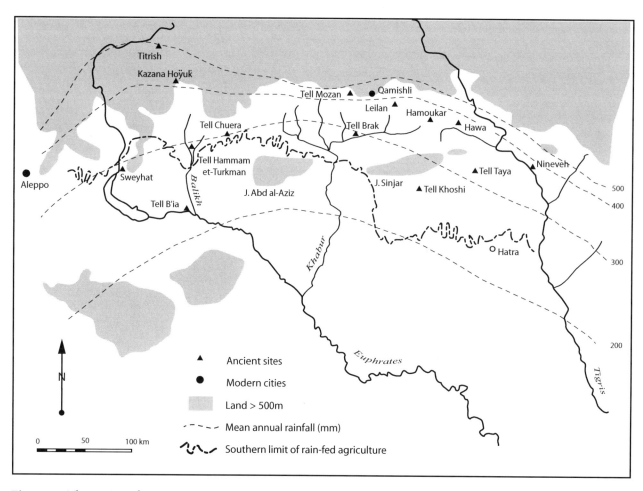

Fig. 6.2 The Jazira of Syria, Iraq, and southern Turkey, showing mean annual rainfall (mm), selected archaeological sites, and the southern limit of rain-fed agriculture.

appear to have conducted greater flows during the Pleistocene so that their valleys are much larger than the size of the present rivers would imply. In the case of the Khabur, quarry sections to the southeast of Qamishli and near Tell Brak have exposed deep accumulations of coarse, well-rounded gravels of eastern Anatolian provenance, together with interbedded palaeosols. The gravels appear to have been deposited by braided channels. With their associated palaeosols, they form a broad sediment sheet across much of the eastern Khabur basin. The varied rock types represented in the gravels, their high degree of roundness, and their contrast with the later Pleistocene and Holocene gravels (which are of local limestones and

other sedimentary rocks) indicate that during the earlier Pleistocene or Pliocene, major rivers comparable in scale to the Tigris flowed from the eastern Taurus mountains along the present Tigris to pass through the gap between the Jebels Abd al-Aziz and Sinjar near Hassekeh and thence to the Euphrates. At a more general level, the ancestors of the Tigris-Euphrates system may once have flowed as a series of subparallel streams from north to south from the Taurus mountains through the Wadis Tharthar, Khabur, and Balikh. Only at a later stage of the Pleistocene did the present deeply incised and locally downfaulted channels of the Euphrates and Tigris Rivers form.

In such a climatically marginal

environment, water supply is crucial for survival. In addition to the Tigris-Euphrates rivers and their tributaries, a large number of freshwater springs were once active, that is, before modern well drilling resulted in a rapidly declining water table. These springs, which receive their water via recharge into Tertiary dolomite and limestone, issue at various points along the modern Turkish/Syrian border, around the Jebel Abd al-Aziz, as well as in the area of Lake Khatuniye (Kolars and Mitchell 1991: 168–175). Although many of these springs provide rather meager discharges, major springs at ʿAyn al-Arus on the Syrian Balikh and Ras al-ʿAyn, at the head of the Khabur, once provided a significant proportion of the flow of these rivers.

Holocene Landscape Evolution

The Holocene environmental history of the Jazira continues to be little understood (for reviews, see Courty 1994; Rosen 1998; Wilkinson 1999b), but there is an emerging picture that suggests that following a Late Pleistocene stage characterized by episodically high flow along braided channels, river discharges continued to be higher than in recent times throughout the early to mid Holocene. In the Khabur this manifests itself as a shift from an early- to mid-Holocene braided sand-bed channel, towards (around 3000 B.C.) flow in a meandering silt channel (Ergenzinger 1991). In tributaries of the Turkish Euphrates and in the upper Balikh valley (Turkey), higher flows resulted in the deposition of riverine gravels during the mid Holocene. A phase of nonerosion or channel incision that followed was then infilled, in turn, by Late Roman to Early Byzantine aggraded sediments (Rosen 1998). That water tables were higher in the mid Holocene can be inferred from valley sediments in the Wadi Awaij (western Khabur), the Wadi Jagh Jagh (central Khabur), and the Balikh valley (fig. 6.2). Early- to mid-Holocene environments were also more verdant, according to Courty (1994), who recognized episodic moist intervals that gave way, in the later part of the third millennium B.C. and later, to a phase of late-Holocene aridification. The moist phase recorded by geoarchaeologists roughly parallels the early- to mid-Holocene moist phase evident in the palaeoclimatic proxy data from Lake Van (Lemcke and Sturme 1997). But despite the evidence of large accumulations of both valley fills and alluvial fan deposits in conjunction with considerable degrees of human activity and forest removal, it is still difficult to establish a neat separation of alluvial sequences into a climatic or human component. Rather, it seems that during the mid to late Holocene,

just as climatic conditions were getting drier, population in many places was increasing considerably so that there was a dual stress on the natural vegetation that could have led to landscape destabilization (chapter 2). Moreover, many of the smaller rivers in the Jazira exhibit late-Holocene channels that are narrow, deep, and meandering, in contrast with those of the early to mid–Holocene, when channels were broader and shallower (fig. 6.3). During the late Holocene, not only were regimes destabilized by the removal of woodlands but also increasing amounts of water were abstracted for purposes of irrigation. These two factors resulted in increased runoff and soil erosion on the one hand, and decreased base flow of rivers on the other. Together, these two factors, as well as the climatic drying that can be inferred from proxy climate records, must have contributed towards greater instability of channel flow.

Vegetation Landscape Zones

Despite its archaeological importance, Upper Mesopotamia has a meager record of vegetation history derived from pollen analysis (chapter 2; Bottema and Woldring 1990). Therefore, to produce a model of vegetation history, it has been necessary to combine data from carbonized plant remains with palynology and other evidence.

Particularly instructive are the vegetation reconstructions of Gordon Hillman and colleagues, which build upon late-Pleistocene and early-Holocene pollen sequences, carbonized plant remains from Neolithic Abu Hureyra in the Syrian Euphrates, modern vegetation (especially that within protected areas), climate parameters and terrain type, the density of modern settlement, and water courses, as well as early traveler's accounts (Moore et al. 2000: 49–91).

The map of potential vegetation illustrates what might be expected

to have existed in the absence of vegetational degradation resulting from dense human activity. After the spread of agriculture in the ninth millennium B.P., it is then difficult to distinguish climatic effects from those of human activity (Moore et al. 2000: 84). Fortunately, as will be discussed below, information concerning the degradation of woodland vegetation can be inferred from carbonized plant remains. In terms of the pollen record, however, unequivocal evidence for large-scale loss of woodland does not appear until the second or even first millennia B.C. (see chapter 7; also Bottema and Woldring 1990).

Bearing in mind the fragmentary nature of the database, Hillman's reconstructions forcefully point out that much of what is today a degraded upland steppe in Turkey would have been a moderately dense deciduous woodland of oaks, various types of wild plum or rose, hawthorn, and almond (Hillman's zones 3a and 3b). In fact, most of the Jazira considered here, namely, the rain-fed zone of dense Bronze Age settlement, would have fallen within the terebinth-almond woodland steppe comprising drought-tolerant pistachio trees, shrubby almonds, cherries, and hawthorns (Hillman's zones 3 and 4; Moore et al. 2000: 60). It was probably the northern part of zone 4 and the southern more xeric parts of zone 3 that would have supported extensive stands of wild wheats and rye prior to domestication (Moore et al. 2000: 80), which then went on to provide the agrarian foundations for the later Bronze Age city-states.

Overall, the early- and mid-Holocene environment appears to have been significantly more verdant and well wooded than the late Holocene, namely, the period after 2000 B.C. Nevertheless, carbonized plant remains from the Khabur basin suggest that during the Halaf period in the northern, moister part of the basin, vegetation had become some-

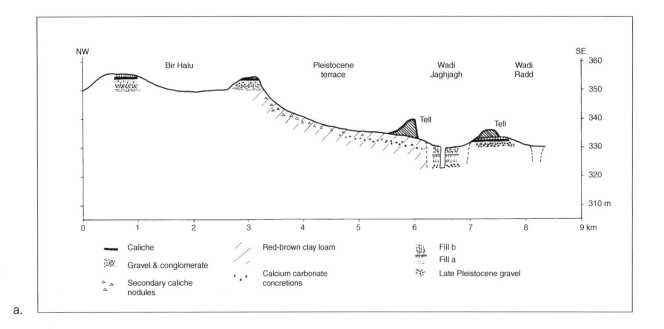

a.

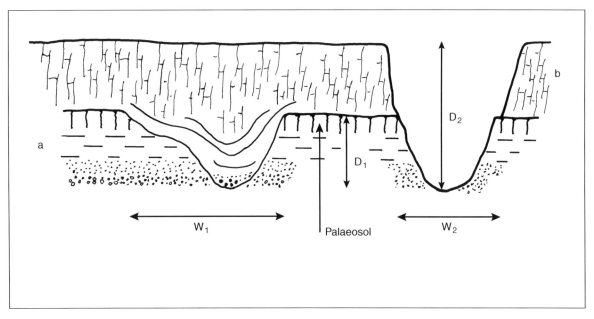

b.

Fig. 6.3 Top: some major geomorphological units of the upper Khabur basin illustrated by a northwest–southeast section near Tell Brak, Syria. Below: detail of sedimentary units in the valley of the Jaghjagh near Tell Brak. Fill a, of early- to mid-Holocene date, probably terminates in the second millennium B.C. Fill b is post–1000 B.C. Note the decreased width:depth ratio associated with the later channel fill.

what degraded, whereas south of Hasseka, in an area that is today desertified and beyond the realistic limits of rain-fed cultivation, the flora and fauna were all significantly more diverse and richer than today (McCorriston 1992: 329). This implies that even by the Halaf period,

the well-populated northern Khabur basin had already become significantly degraded to the point that the inhabitants had limited woody resources to burn and therefore had to resort to the burning of animal dung for fuel.

Further details on progressive

landscape degradation come from the work of Naomi Miller, who has spent two decades on the systematic analysis of carbonized plant remains from archaeological sites located in southern Turkey and northern Syria. Miller's investigations (Miller 1997a, 1997b; Miller in

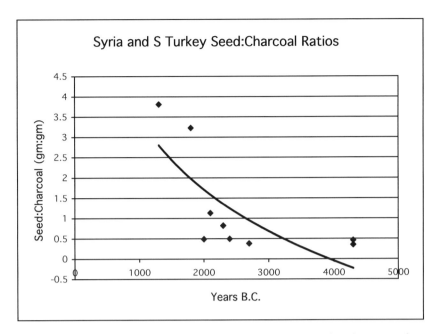

Fig. 6.4   Increase in seed:charcoal ratio through time for the sites of Kurban Höyük, Tell Sweyhat, Umm al-Marra, and Hacinebi Tepe along the Turkish–Syrian Euphrates and in the Jabbul Plain (based on data in Miller 1997a and b, and Miller in Schwartz et al. 2000).

Schwartz et al. 2000) suggest that vegetation and landscape degradation occurred throughout the Chalcolithic to Middle Bronze Age. In a nutshell, seed:charcoal and wild-seed:charcoal ratios provide a relative measure of tree cover, with the numerator (top) mainly indicating seeds that relate to the burning of dung as fuel (fig. 6.4). Consequently, as the burning of dung became more common, seed counts rose; conversely, lower values, indicative of more charcoal in the samples, suggest that there was more wood available for fuel. When data from a range of sites is combined, there is a discernable trend from more charcoal in the fourth millennium B.C. to more seeds in the second millennium B.C. (fig. 6.4). There is also a tendency for higher seed:charcoal ratios in drier locations (e.g., at Tell Sweyhat and Umm al-Marra) as well as in the second millennium B.C. This implies that first there was a greater use of the steppe for grazing; second, there was less reliance on wood fuel through

time and more reliance on dung as fuel; or third, the environment may have become slightly drier. In the last-named case, the drier areas tend to have higher seed:charcoal ratios and therefore, according to prevailing reconstructions, would have been less wooded.

This tendency towards increased environmental degradation attained an all-time high in the last one hundred years with the increased ploughing of marginal steppelands for barley cultivation and the extension of farming into marginal "high risk" zones (Kouchoukos et al. 1998: 482, fig. 9). This has resulted in the present-day prairielike landscape in which the occasional patches or strips of verdancy result from irrigated cultivation around deep-drilled wells or from large riverine dams.

The Prehistoric Prelude

Despite the large number of prehistoric excavations conducted in recent years, our knowledge of the prehis-

toric cultural landscape continues to be little understood. Consequently, I limit my comments to a summary of the basic factors that enable the more distinctive patterns of the Bronze Age landscapes to be understood.

For the north Mesopotamian plains, the early Holocene was ushered in by the descent of settlement from the uplands and a concomitant colonization of the plains, a process that must have been linked with processes of plant and animal domestication (Matthews 2000: 114, 116). The process is exemplified around the Jebel Sinjar of northern Iraq, where aceramic Neolithic settlement was (with a few exceptions) primarily on rocky outcrops and ridges, whereas during the subsequent ceramic Neolithic (the Proto-Hassuna and Hassuna), settlement developed rapidly on the potentially cultivable (and rich pastures) of the lowlands to the south (Kozlowski 1999: fig. 2). Nevertheless, aceramic settlement was present in the lowlands. Witness the presence of aceramic Neolithic sites along the Balikh valley (Akkermans 1993: 168–169) as well as along the Syrian Euphrates (Moore et al. 2000). The evidence for aceramic settlement might be lacking simply because such occupations are deeply buried beneath later occupations. The visibility of such occupations along the Balikh Valley may be due to a shift in the river channel that resulted in a change in the locus of later settlement, thereby leaving those of Neolithic date exposed to view (fig. 6.5).

In both the Balikh and Khabur valleys, following a period of relatively sparse settlement during the ceramic Neolithic and earlier Halaf periods, by the mid–Halaf, settlement occurred in the form of a scatter of small villages north of about the 300 mm per annum *isohyet*. South of this limit along the Balikh, settlement dwindled to a straggle of smaller sites (Akkermans 1993) but was virtually absent in the Khabur

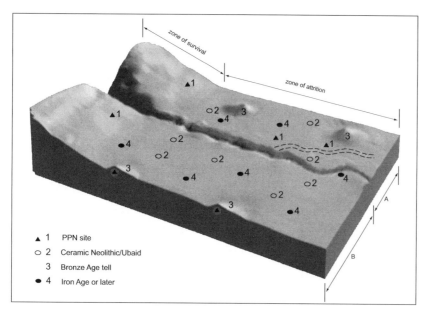

Fig. 6.5 Block diagram of landscape zones in the Jazira, showing the effect of the burial of early settlement below tells, based on the Tell Afar plain (Iraq) and the Balikh Valley (Syria). Note the presence of Pre-Pottery Neolithic (PPN) sites on the ridge (1) and the lack of them in taphonomic Zone B. In the latter area, rare PPN sites are likely to be buried and completely encapsulated within the Chalcolithic and Bronze Age occupations of tells (3). In Zone A, however, where a wadi channel has been abandoned, the locus of settlement has shifted so that PPN sites have not been buried by later occupation. In Zone B, it appears that PPN settlement is confined to the ridge (zone of survival), whereas ceramic Neolithic sites (Hassuna and Halaf) represent an explosion of activity on the plains. In contrast, there probably are PPN sites on the plain, but these will only be evident either as a result of excavation or where there is a lack of post Neolithic occupation. Post Bronze Age settlement dispersal is shown in solid black ovals (4).

south of Umm Qseir (Nieuwenhuyse 2000: 180). Further east in the Iraqi north Jazira, settlement was moderately dense throughout the Hassuna (ceramic Neolithic), Halaf, and Ubaid (Wilkinson and Tucker 1995; Campbell 1992). During the early-Holocene Hassuna and proto-Hassuna phases there was a remarkable lobe of small, dispersed villages that extended as far south as Hatra in the Wadi Tharthar (Hijara 1997; J. Oates 1982). Such an extension of settlement may have been a response to moister conditions in the early to mid Holocene, after which settlement retreated some way to the north. As a result of this retreat, the Neolithic settlements were not ob-scured by later occupations. In the verdant Euphrates valley of Syria, on the other hand, early ceramic and Halaf sites are sparse. This dearth may be a victim of the main river that eroded the flood plain away, along with any sites on it, thereby leaving only the marginal sites on terraces beyond.

Although most sites were small, low mounds of less than 2 ha, in recent years it has become evident that large Halaf settlements of 10–20 ha occurred at sites such as Domuztepe (Campbell et al. 1999), Tell Kurdu (Yener et al. 2000), Kazana Höyük (Bernbeck et al. 1999), and Takyan Höyük (Algaze et al. 1991: 195) in Turkey, as well as at Mun-bata (Akkermans 1993) and Nisibis (Nieuwenhuyse 2000) in Syria. Whether these large sites were really towns or simply expanded villages is a matter for debate, but it is likely that the presence of large population concentrations in such settlements would have had an impact on the environment. This is especially the case for Munbata, located near the limit of rain-fed cultivation in the Balikh (Akkermans 1993). The marginal location of this site, ca. 20 ha in size, suggests that it may have functioned as a gateway community that was involved in exchange of goods between communities of the steppe and those of the village zone further north (Akkermans 1993). The presence of such large settlements may have resulted in significant degradation of the fragile local environments, and to guarantee crops yields (even under the more verdant conditions that prevailed), it may have been necessary for the inhabitants to practice irrigation.

In the central Balikh valley around Sabi Abyad the pattern of cropping appears to have shifted from a mixed range of pulses and wheat during the Halaf period towards the monocropping of barley by the Early Bronze Age (Van Zeist et al. 1989; Wilkinson 1998). Whether this was due to cultural, demographic, economic, or environmental factors is not entirely clear, but it appears that the Halaf agricultural landscape was more heterogeneous than at later times.

During the Ubaid, settlement appears to have been patchy, with only occasional settlements along the Syrian and Turkish Euphrates, the Balikh, and the upper Khabur basin, and virtually none around the Jebel Abd al-Aziz (Hole 1998b). In contrast, the North Jazira of Iraq showed evidence for numerous small hamlets and villages, and there is even the suggestion of a settlement hierarchy (Wilkinson et al. 1996). The apparent lack of visibility of Ubaid sites may be due to the development of nucleated settlements from this time on, which buried the Ubaid levels below

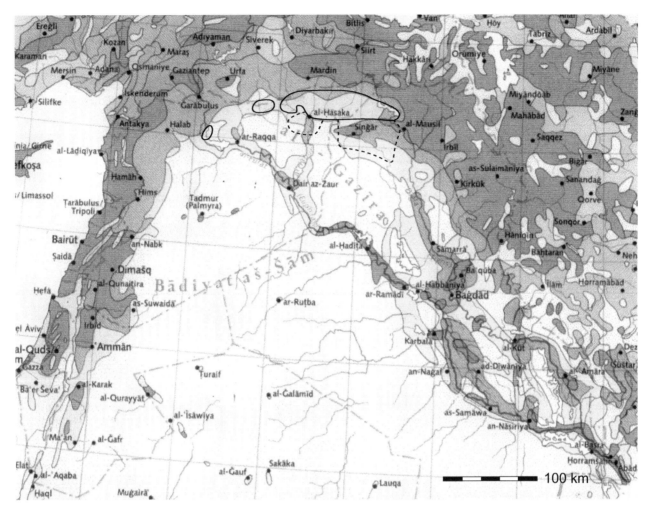

Fig. 6.6   Late phases of settlement (i.e., post–World War I) in the Near East with areas of linear hollows superimposed. (Modified from TAVO Map A IX 1)

vast accumulations of Chalcolithic and Early Bronze Age deposits. It is therefore possible that the foundations of the strongly nucleated pattern of settlement of the Early Bronze Age were set in the fourth and fifth millennia B.C. The initial stages of some of the landscape features to be discussed below may therefore have been during these millennia. Nevertheless, it was not until the third millennium B.C. that we can start to distinguish a distinct signature of landscape features.

Landscape Transformations and Recent Settlement

As discussed in chapter 3, processes of landscape transformation are crucial to an understanding of land-scape development. Consequently, before considering the features of the Jaziran landscape it is necessary to sketch how the dynamics of settlement may have impacted the landscape. In the recent past, as a result of a complex range of social/political and environmental factors, settlement colonized the steppe during the seventeenth century A.D., re-treated during the eighteenth and nineteenth centuries, and then expanded again in the twentieth century (fig. 6.6; Lewis 1987; Hütteroth 1990). Archaeologically these periods of agricultural colonization may have resulted in the archaeological record being eroded away or destroyed by ploughing or earth-moving activities, whereas in lightly settled areas, archaeological features are more likely to have survived. Therefore, on figure 6.6 the distribution of one class of landscape features (the zone of linear hollows) can be seen to correspond closely to the zone of "recently settled lands" as mapped by the Tübingen Atlas. Whether this means that in the moister areas north and west of this zone off-site land-scape features have been expunged by long-term settlement is unclear. What is clear is that the preservation or visibility of the archaeological record in the Jazira is partly a re-sult of process that followed their formation.

The Bronze Age Landscape

The tell is not only the fundamental archaeological feature of the landscape of Upper Mesopotamia but it is also the most conspicuous. In part because of this conspicuousness, tells may have played a role as a memory bank for local communities, and John Chapman (1997: 40) has pointed out that in the Hungarian plain, tells have a strong presence of public symbolism. The longevity of the tell, combined with its visibility and its "place-value," contribute to a sanctity of place that flat sites cannot match. This sanctity increases the social power of those in place to deal with ritual and ceremony. More prosaically, tells show considerable time depth, and their surrounding landscapes may be expected to show signs of long-term degradation as well as "embedded" features that result from long, continued use of selected areas (such as paths or routeways). Because tells provide such prominent and immobile features in the landscape, they provide a classic example of "path dependency": once they are in place, even after they have been abandoned they will continue to be reoccupied. thereby continuing to structure the landscape. For example, they may be revisited by nomadic groups and will therefore continue to attract settlement or in some way function as landscape features. Whether one accepts a post-processual or a processual perspective, tells are special features that should exhibit a longterm role in the perspective of local communities.

The distinctive form of the tell results from the progressive accumulation of superimposed building levels. Processes of tell development are complex and beyond the scope of this book (Rosen 1986), but the accumulated sediments can be classed into (1) organo-cultural refuse, (2) collapsed masses from built structures, (3) water-laid sediments, (4) biogenic and geochemical alterations, and (5) aeolian sediments (Butzer 1982: 89–90). In addition, episodes of prolonged stabilization can result in the development of various levels of soil development

over the site (Wilkinson 1990c). An important cultural factor in the formation of many mounds is the presence of an outer defensive wall that inhibits the erosional spreading of the sediments, thereby damming them up within the tell itself (Rosen 1986: 14). As a result, not only will the outer wall determine the basic form of the tell but the location of gates within the wall can become foci of erosion that will ultimately develop into major gullies.

In theory, tells can extend laterally and can build up vertically. For the latter to take place, there must be some reason for accumulation to be focused at one point: either there is a reason for the inhabitants to remain nucleated in one place (perhaps because of the need to stay within a defensive wall) or the place itself holds a special significance, perhaps for religious reasons. The latter point is important because it is likely that one of the reasons that settlement continues on tells is that by virtue of their being the site of religious buildings, they retain sanctity through time (van de Mieroop 1999: 77). Probably the best example of continuity of religious buildings on a site occurred in the form of the well-known stack of temples at Eridu in southern Iraq (Safar et al. 1981; see Postgate 1992: fig. 2.2), and although such continuity is not so well attested at tells in upper Mesopotamia, it is likely that similar factors rooted settlement to a single location.[1] Of course, other reasons could encourage settlements to remain fixed, and these, in turn, could encourage temples to remain in place. These include, defense, family ties, proximity to administrative buildings and palaces, or land redistribution. The process of land redistribution is particularly important because the holding of land in common, which may have been the predominant practice in the Bronze Age Jazira, results in the fields of any one family being redistributed from year to year, often according to a system of lots (Adams 1982: 10–11;

Renger 1995: 306). This would inhibit farmers from living by their fields and would encourage occupation to be confined to a central nucleated settlement. The above-mentioned processes of sanctity, defense, kingroup affiliation, administration, and field allotment would therefore all contribute to the fixed position of settlements (B. K. Roberts 1996: 35–37).

In those parts of the Fertile Crescent where settlements have stayed fixed often for millennia, cultivation must have been concentrated on the same lands, with the result that nutrient loss and soil degradation were probably concentrated in the same zone, thereby leading to longterm soil degradation. Although it is probably an oversimplification to state that tells remain fixed only because of the need to retain continuity of religion and for defensive and administrative needs, this does raise the fundamental point that cultural factors such as these, if they contribute to settlement stability, must also therefore ultimately influence the physical state of the land by contributing to the development of zones of soil degradation.

The Scale of Tells in the Jazira

In Upper Mesopotamia, tells are more prominent features than the often elongated, straggling features of the southern Mesopotamian plains. However, the tells of the Jaziran rain-fed farming zone usually extend over a smaller area, so that they generally range in size from less than 1 ha to a maximum in the order of 100 ha. This maximum size does not appear to represent an arbitrary tailing off of the upper limit of settlement area but rather may reflect a real constraint, being perhaps the size larger than which it was difficult for settlements to grow under the prevailing economy and technologies (Wilkinson 1994). Although there are a large number of smaller sites, the upper size limit of tells trends asymptotically towards a figure of

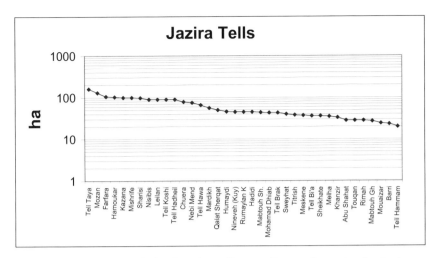

Fig. 6.7 The size (in ha) of major tells or tell complexes in the Jazira and north central Syria. Most, but not all, saw their main phases of occupation in the Early Bronze Age.

little more than 100 ha, of which there are eleven sites in the range 90–110 ha (fig. 6.7).

As may be expected, the large tells of Upper Mesopotamia usually have long histories of occupation, but with a few exceptions, most attained their maximum size during the mid centuries of the third millennium B.C. More generally, tells were the characteristic settlement type in the Jazira during the Bronze Age and to a lesser degree for many other parts of the Near East as well.

This pattern is well demonstrated for the area of Tell Beydar in the western Khabur basin. If sites *of all periods* are plotted according to their gross morphology (i.e., their height:diameter ratio), they fall into three distinctive classes: tells, small low sites, and extensive low sites (or lower towns; fig. 6.8a). When plotted according to chronological period, the smaller low sites are predominantly either post Bronze Age or Chalcolithic/Neolithic in date; nearly all tells were occupied in the third millennium B.C. (fig. 6.8b). A similar pattern is evident in the north Jazira of Iraq, where large nucleated sites (mainly tells) were again occupied in the third millennium B.C. This pattern has been recognized qualitatively in other parts of the Fertile Crescent, but not in all. Neverthe-

less, in general, for many parts of the Jazira, a significant proportion of tells were occupied in the third millennium B.C., and conversely, most third-millennium B.C. sites are tells.

A Modular Early Bronze Age Landscape in Northern Syria or Iraq

The monotonous undulating steppe of north Syria, southeast Turkey, and Iraq seems on first sight reluctant to give away many secrets. Nevertheless, the judicious use of high-resolution satellite imagery, detailed off-site surveys, and topographic analysis has demonstrated the presence of a rich, albeit subtle, range of landscape features (described here from the tell outwards): broad depressions adjacent to the sites, linear hollows, cemeteries, and field scatters. These features are not always found together at the same site, but their absence can often be explained as a result of processes of landscape transformation or because of social or demographic factors. Taken together, these landscape features can be used to provide a modular reconstruction of the agricultural landscape as indicated on table 6.1.

Enclosed Depressions Adjacent to Sites. Detailed topographic sur-

veys demonstrate that what often appear to be virtually flat plains are in fact broken up by various types of depression. For example, in the immediate vicinity of mounds, one or several shallow enclosed depressions can be evident, especially in the wet season when they frequently become filled with water (fig. 6.9). At first glance, these often appear to be water holes. Indeed, they frequently continue to function as such, but like many landscape features, they probably had a primary as well as a secondary function.

In the north Jazira of Iraq, many small low mounds have visible depressions immediately adjacent, and more recent sites are associated with more and larger depressions (Wilkinson and Tucker 1995: figs. 28, 30). Moreover, where the presence of modern canals and other cuts provided sections through mound peripheries, infilled pits are also apparent. For example, at Mowasha (northern Iraq), a depression 3.5 ha in size extended to at least 5 m below plain level and was infilled with 3 m of occupational debris. Cuts through other sites showed that completely infilled depressions were associated with sites of all periods back to the prehistoric. Usually such pits had accumulated sediments showing the characteristic traces of waterlogging in antiquity, namely, olive green and gray "gleyed" mottling. Similar depressions have been demonstrated by excavation at Proto Hassuna (early sixth millennium B.C.) Tell Kashkashok II in the western Khabur (Matsutani and Nishiaki 1998), as well as in the vicinity of Tell Brak (Wilkinson et al. 2001b).

The following model may account for the development of enclosed depressions in Upper Mesopotamia. When constructing mudbrick buildings, it is customary to excavate soil, usually from a convenient nearby area that also is close to a water supply. Such excavations result in deep and extensive brick pits adjacent to the site itself. Because such pits are dug from the very first stages

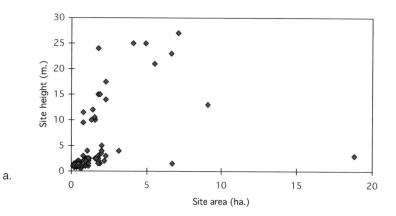

a.

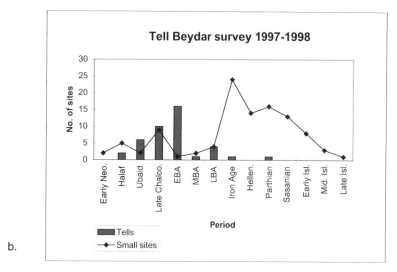

b.

Fig. 6.8 Site morphology in the Tell Beydar area, Syria: (a) site area:height ratios, (b) number of tells and small sites, according to archaeological period.

Table 6.1 Land-use Zones around a Tell in Upper Mesopotamia

Zone	Features
Tell	Living, administrative, religious, and manufacturing areas; water from wells; intramural burials.
Outer tell zone	Quarry pits, threshing, stalling sheep/goats; kilns; water from wells, quarry pits, or springs; additional manufacturing areas.
Proximal fields	Intensive cultivation of garden crops, cereals; manured land.
Distant fields	Lower-intensity cultivation of cereals, probably fallowed.
Beyond the cultivation	Steppe and pasture; routes to other sites; extramural burials.

Note: In western Syria, southern Turkey, and moister parts of Upper Mesopotamia, grape and olive orchards would also be found within or just beyond the field areas.

of the site, they can also be found below the later cultural layers of the mound. When enclosed depressions are evident as coherent measurable features, estimation of their original volume suggests that the soil removed from them frequently approximates to the volume of soil employed in the construction of the constituent buildings (Wilkinson and Tucker 1995), allowance being made for the inclusion of large amounts of waste discarded by occupation and other debris.

Although the excavation of mudbrick adjacent to the settlement conserves effort, more distant sources of mudbrick can also be used. For example, analysis of mudbrick at Tell Lachish in Palestine by Arlene Miller-Rosen showed that soil for mudbricks may have been obtained from the mound itself or even from communities in nearby areas, perhaps being received as some form of tax (Rosen 1986: 84). Although such examples may be unusual, they are nevertheless instructive. At the Neo-Assyrian capital of Dur-Sharrukin, large numbers of new bricks were produced according to a quota system by the villages around the new city (Lanfranchi and Parpola 1990: no. 296; cited in van de Mieroop 1999: 54). In such cases, the brick pits of those communities might have been larger than the size of the village mounds might predict. Such a case is hinted at by the large pits at Mowasha. Furthermore, clean soil, often of distinctive hues would be required for certain high status or public buildings (Rosen 1986: 65, 78–91); such pits again would need to tap fresh clean soils beyond the detritus of everyday life. However, allowing for all these variables, it follows that a significant amount of mudbrick for every day construction purposes would have been obtained in close proximity to the settlement itself (McClellan et al. 2000).

In theory, such pits should attain their maximum size in the proximity of the largest tells, but this is not always apparent probably be-

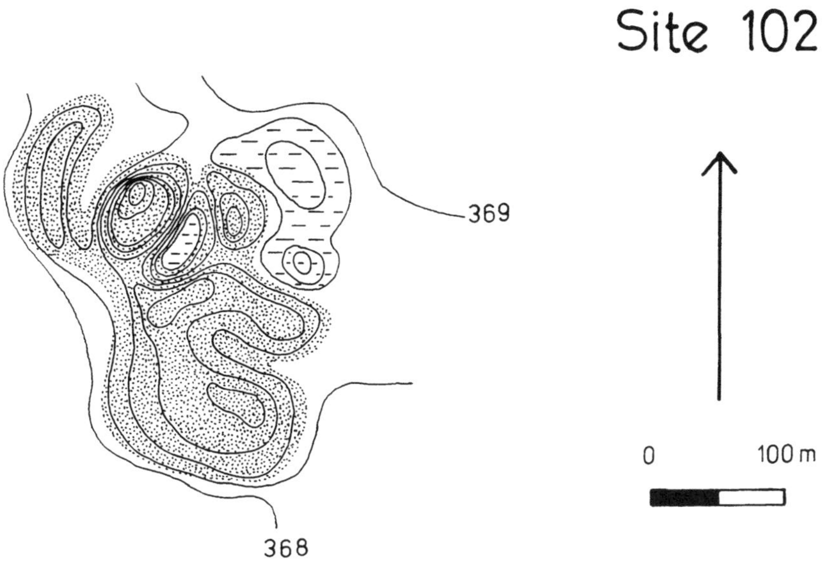

Site 102

369

368

0   100 m

Fig. 6.9 Topographic map (contour interval of 0.5 m) of a typical small site in the north Jazira of Iraq; stipple = mounded area, horizontal lines = enclosed depressions (NJP site 102).

cause erosion of mound deposits will approach a maximum around the biggest and highest mounds. This is well illustrated around Brak, where the main mound has been dissected by numerous massive erosional gullies, each of which debouches into a large alluvial fan at the point where the gully reaches the plain (fig. 6.10). These often substantial accumulations can therefore infill or obscure the quarry pits that once surrounded the mound.

Linear Hollows. In Upper Mesopotamia, dark linear features were first recognized from the air by Poidebard, a pioneer of aerial photography (Poidebard 1934). His initial observations were then followed by a classic study undertaken by van Liere and Lauffray (1954), as well as by Buringh in his study of the soils of Iraq (1960). There was then a long gap in the observation of these features until recent years, which have witnessed a renewed flurry of activity.

Linear hollows usually form broad dark lines radiating from archaeological sites, generally tells. They are most obvious on aerial photographs or on high-resolution satellite

images of the CORONA series, are less obvious on SPOT images, and are normally not evident on those of the LANDSAT series. On the ground they are elusive, but sometimes they appear as a line of dark vegetation, usually dwarf mesquite (*Prosopis farcta* or *shauk* in Arabic) or as broad shallow hollows up to 1–2 m deep. Most are broad, ranging from 20 m to over 100 m wide (Ur 2002), although owing to their subtle cross sections, their original width prior to erosion can be difficult to estimate. In the north Jazira of Iraq they normally extend some 3–4 km away from the central tell, and frequently they feature bifurcations roughly 1–2 km from the central sites (Wilkinson and Tucker 1995). According to an analysis of the van Liere and Lauffray system of the Khabur basin, there were some 573 lines radiating from 106 hub sites, which gives an estimate of some 5 lines per site (McClellan et al. 2000). Overall, these features have been recorded over a wide extent of the Jazira of northern Iraq and Syria (fig. 6.6), as well as part of the northern Negev (Tsoar and Yekutieli 1993). Van Liere and Lauffray were able to distinguish them from canals, which would nor-

mally be expected to show linear banks of excavated upcast along side.

Linear hollows are well developed around Tells Brak and Cholma Foqani in the upper Khabur basin (fig. 6.11). At the latter site more than a dozen prominent hollows occur around the central tell. Subparallel sets of hollows to the west and northeast suggest that the hollows may have developed with respect to a rectilinear net of field boundaries. Relatively few linear hollows have been exposed in cross section, but in the north Jazira, linear hollows cut by a modern irrigation canal were wide and shallow, with infilling sediments less than 1 m deep overlying reddish soils enriched in calcium carbonate concretions indistinguishable from the locally developed calcic xerosols. At Brak a feature ca. 50 m wide was infilled with up to 140 cm of loam fill containing occasional potsherds (fig. 6.12). The basal fill, a fine gravel of locally derived sediments, attests episodic flow of moderate energy along the hollow. This is to be expected in view of the role that roads can have in concentrating overland flow (Cooke and Reeves, 1976: 33, 186). Such is the close relationship between roads and the "natural" drainage network that in the Negev and parts of the Jazira, erosional gullies follow road networks to form what Tsoar and Yekutieli term "road (or path) originated" gullies (1993: 214). The Brak cross-section indicates that the smooth profile on the surface comprised a subsurface hollow some 25 m wide, which was probably the original feature. This subsequently became modified by erosion or ploughing of the slopes to form the much broader feature evident today. There was no sign that the hollow had been deliberately dug nor that it included any sediments upcast from excavation or cleaning.

By intercepting flowpaths of water across the landscape, linear hollows also play a hydraulic role. Tom McClellan and colleagues (2000: 144) point out that the contributing area

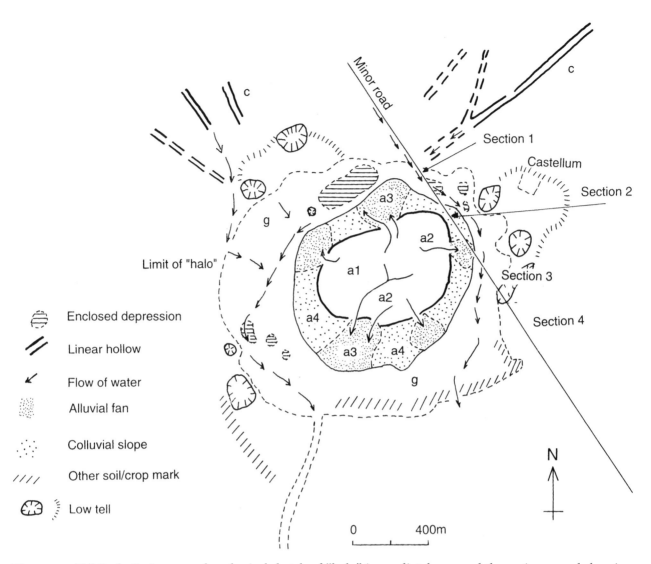

Fig. 6.10   Tell Brak, Syria: geoarchaeological sketch of "halo" immediately around the main mound showing probable lines of water flow, incoming linear hollows, and infilled enclosed depressions. From Wilkinson et al. 2001: fig. 9.

for Tell Brak was increased considerably by the linear hollows. Also by capturing additional overland flow, any features on the upstream side of a tell would conduct more flow than those radiating from downslope (Wilkinson 1993: fig. 8). Applying these principles to a hypothetical system of tracks around a tell, a full radial system could then become enhanced by increased overland flow upslope of the tell and minimally developed downslope. Therefore, in contrast to landscape features such as canals that are initiated as deep cuts through the landscape, and then

get progressively infilled or erased by geomorphic or cultural process of landscape transformation, linear hollows consist of a network on the landscape, some elements of which are passive, and develop minimally or not at all, whereas others become amplified because they are situated in an optimal location for overland flow and erosion.

Interpretation of both aerial photos and satellite images indicates that linear hollows can cross the landscape between tells, thereby hinting at the presence of cross-country systems, or form radial configurations

around them. In the latter case, they frequently form star-shaped patterns, occasional limbs of which lead to other (usually subsidiary) sites.

Figure 6.6 shows the distribution of linear hollows in the Jazira (see Wilkinson 1993; Ur 2003). They are noticeably lacking west of the Euphrates in Syria, but smaller, narrower examples have been recognized both on the ground and on satellite images in the area of the Turkish Euphrates (Wilkinson 1990a; Pournelle 2001) as well as to the east in Syria (Ur 2002). Elsewhere, hollow ways have been recorded in

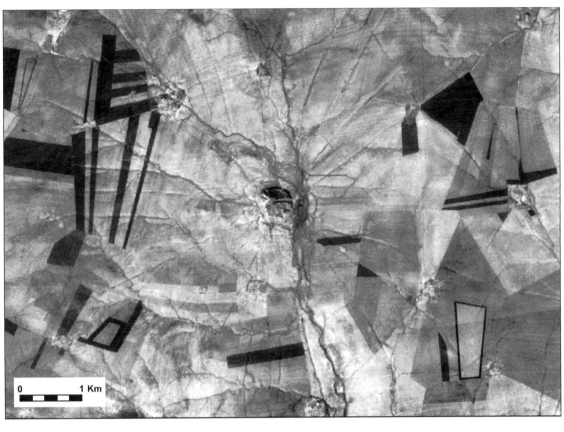

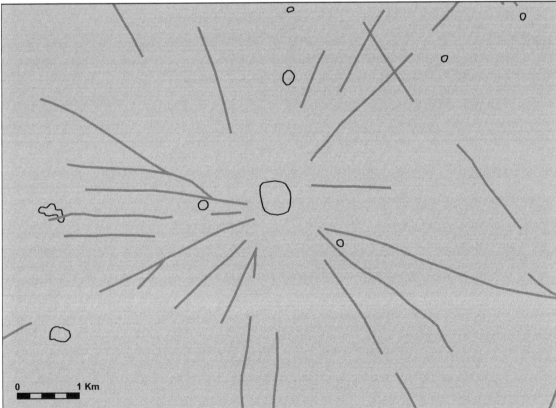

Fig. 6.11 CORONA image and map of linear hollows around Cholma Foqani in the upper Khabur basin, Syria. Note that the shadow on the northern side of the tell emphasizes its elevation (by Jason Ur; photograph courtesy of the U.S. Geological Survey).

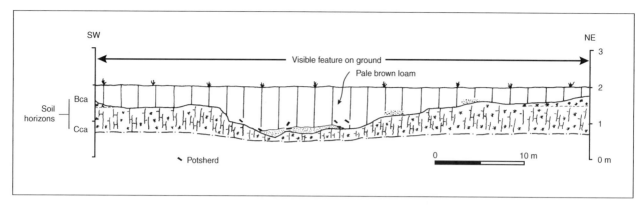

Fig. 6.12   Section through linear hollow to north-northeast of Tell Brak, Syria, showing the profile of the buried ground surface. Note the presence of fine–medium gravel along the floor of the hollow (stippled), which presumably results from localized wash along the hollow. The hollow appears to have been eroded through the preexisting A and B horizons of the soil into the subsoil "C" horizon (Cca) of the local calcareous reddish brown soil. Note the presence of occasional potsherds in the fill of the hollow and their absence in the underlying Cca horizon of the natural soil. (Vertical exaggeration × 4).

various locations in the New World (Trombold 1991) and in many parts of western Europe (Jager 1985; Aston 1985; Fowler 1998).

In terms of their function, Van Liere and Buringh (both of whom specialized in mapping soils and land-use systems from aerial photographs), provided a confident interpretation of linear hollows, an interpretation followed by David Oates, this author, and more recently Jennifer Pournelle (2001a). This interpretation sees the features as being the result of the persistent movement of humans and animals along fixed tracks so that the soils become compressed and preferentially eroded. In addition, high winds can entrain the fine soil and remove it as atmospheric dust. Soil disturbance would be exacerbated by wheeled vehicles that etch deep wheel ruts, especially during the typically wet winters of the Jazira (Hughes 1999). Sledges employed as primitive forms of overland transport (Yakar 2000: fig. 61) would also have contributed to the development of linear hollows. Experimental studies of trail formation by hikers or horse and rider show that not only does the ground become rapidly bare of vegetation after only a few hundred passes but after 1,000 passes on level ground, a trail

would be hollowed to a depth of some 4–5 cm on gentle slopes and 10 cm on a 15 degree slope (Forman 1995: 173; Weaver and Dale 1978). Any hollow initiated by such traction would then result in the concentration of overland flow, which would further enlarges the features.

Tsoar and Yekutieli (1993: 211) on the other hand see linear features on loess in the northern Negev as resulting from a process termed *hydrocompaction*. In this interpretation, the traction and compression of loess results in the disturbance and rupture of the fine soil material, which then initiates the formation of a linear gully.

Sustained movement along tracks is therefore likely to result in hollowing. Because such movements to and from central tells are likely to have entailed many hundreds or even thousands of people moving over thousands of years, the effects can reasonably be expected to be considerable (Wilkinson 1993).

By analogy with traditional land-use patterns such as around the town of Qara Qosh in Iraq (fig. 6.13), it is evident that the geometry of linear hollows resembles that of traditional tracks, down to details such as the forks that develop to provide greater accessibility to fields in the more

distant parts of the cultivated area. Similar radial patterns have also been noted in the form of church paths radiating from medieval parish churches in Cornwall (Aston 1985: fig. 89–after Maxwell 1976) as well as around Iron Age, Roman, Islamic sites in the Levant (chapter 7 and Guérin 1997).

An alternative explanation by Tom McClellan, which views linear hollows as water-harvesting devices, although compelling, is rendered problematic for a number of reasons. First, the hollows show no sign of having been dug, and there is no upcast as would be expected alongside a canal. As has been demonstrated for parts of the north Jazira in Iraq, linear hollows often run up and over watersheds in direct contradiction of canal design (fig. 6.14; Wilkinson 1993: fig. 6). Finally, the layout of the hollows would result in most flow being directed towards the site itself, where only limited amounts of water were required, with the result that the site would be flooded and outlying fields would be deprived of water. On the other hand, the geometry of the systems, including bifurcations, closely resembles that of radial track systems around central settlements in various parts of the Near East (figs. 6.13 and 7.6; Roberts

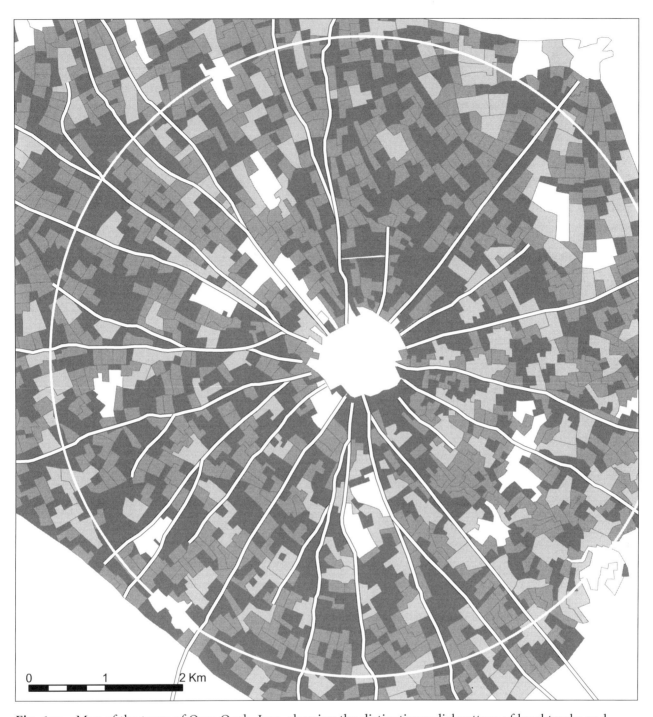

Fig. 6.13   Map of the town of Qara Qosh, Iraq, showing the distinctive radial pattern of local tracks and associated fields. Note the highly nucleated nature of the settlement. Compare with figs. 6.11 and 7.3 (compiled by Jason Ur).

1996: fig. 2.5). Finally, analogous features can be seen being formed today. For example, tracks across irrigated silt terrain in Morocco and volcanic ash in Yemen frequently exhibit deep U-shaped profiles, which in turn encourage gully development. These further enlarge the

features until a fully articulated gully network develops. In such ways, trackways must also contribute to the degradation of the landscape.

Estimating a date of use for landscape features is never easy, and linear hollows are no exception. Van Liere and Lauffray (1954) pointed

out that the radial features were focused upon tells and were likely to have been in use during the Bronze Age, whereas the narrower examples appeared to be post Hellenistic in date. This basic observation is borne out by more recent studies by the author, McClellan and colleagues

Fig. 6.14 Three-dimensional view of terrain around Tell Beydar, Syria (left foreground) looking along cross-country linear hollow trending toward the northeast (top right). Note the tendency of the hollow to rise up and over the raised ground in the mid-ground. This image was produced by draping a CORONA image over a digital terrain model of the area (compiled by Jason Ur; photograph courtesy of the U.S. Geological Survey).

Chalcolithic as well as the Middle and Late Bronze Ages. Consequently, if tells predominantly fall within this temporal range, then it follows, by association, that the radial hollows are approximately contemporaneous. Other features, such as those that cross the terrain between sites, are more likely to be dated by the age of the sites along them. The substantial scale of the hollows as well as the sedimentary accumulations within them suggest that the features developed over a long period of time. For example, the loam fill of the feature exposed in cross section near Tell Brak (fig. 6.12) contained potsherds of pre-Hellenistic type. In addition, flecks of calcium carbonate within the soil matrix require a few centuries to form; therefore, their presence rules out a very recent date for the fills. There is little doubt though that massive increases in ploughing over the last century or two has resulted in the hollows being infilled by soil wash.

The archaeological context also suggests an early date, as in the case of Early Bronze Age Tell Beydar, where hollow ways focus on what may have been gateways, or pre-Hellenistic, as can be deduced from the case of a Parthian mound that encroached into and partly infilled a preexisting linear hollow near Hamoukar, northeast Syria (Ur 2002: fig. 26).

Linear hollow tracks frequently fade out between 3 and 5 km from the central site. Observations of traditional village tracks in the Middle East show a similar fading effect primarily because most tracks are used to gain access to the fields rather than to reach neighboring settlements. As pointed out by Aston (1985: 145), this is such an obvious point that it has hardly been studied. Consequently, because most traffic leaves the track to enter fields well before the village boundary, traffic decreases rapidly away from the settlement so that tracks become less and less clear. In general the "fade-out" point approximates to

(2000), and Jason Ur (2003), all of whom recognize that the broad dark linear features (irrespective of their interpretation) radiate from tells whose main phase of occupa-

tion was in the Early Bronze Age. This dating is also supported by the observation that tells were primarily occupied in the Early Bronze Age, with lesser occupation in the

the point where, if there is still traffic on the track, it has reached the
open steppe/pasture, at which point
people and humans fan out so that a
hollow way ceases to form. Thus the
fade-out point may provide a rough
proxy for the limit of cultivation
around a central tell (for a medieval
analogy, see Roberts 1996: fig. 2.5).

The existence of forks in tracks
can be inferred from cuneiform
land-sale documents from Nuzi,
which show that in one or two cases
a field will be bordered by a road
leading to a *dimtu* (small settlement) on each side. As pointed out
by Zaccagnini (1979: 89–90), the unlikely configuration of two parallel
tracks bordering opposite sides of a
field may instead refer to a field that
was located between the two component tracks of a bifurcation. That
such a configuration can frequently
be expected can be deduced from the
numerous occurrences of forks on
hollow ways.

Finally, in some cases hollow ways
provide cross-country links between
sites. By way of illustration, in the
northern Jazira of Syria and Iraq,
in addition to the common radial
patterns around tells, hollow ways
also appear to form cross-country
links, at which time they may have
functioned as long-distance routes
(fig. 6.14).

Field scatters. Increased intensity
of survey in recent decades demonstrates that archaeological materials
do not simply concentrate upon
the sites themselves but also occur
off site. In the Jazira, field scatters
usually consist of occasional small
battered sherds scattered over the
surface of cultivated fields, attaining densities of around 100 sherds
per 100 sq. m or even more in some
areas (Wilkinson and Tucker 1995).
Scatters include fragments of vitrified kiln slag, occasional fragments
of basalt (either from broken quern
stones or from threshing sled inserts), and, rarely, chipped stone.
Pottery predominates, however,
and those sherds that remain are

usually the more resistant parts
of the vessels or more highly fired
pieces. Scatters tend to be concentrated in the topsoil and decrease
rapidly downwards in the soil except
in those cases where they are contained within a buried soil horizon,
in which case they peak within that
horizon (Wilkinson 1988: fig. 7.3).

The date of field scatters can be
estimated from the diagnostic type
of ceramics contained within them.
For example, in the northeastern
Khabur basin and adjacent parts of
northern Iraq, field scatters contain numerous sherds of metallic
ware dated to the third quarter of
the third millennium B.C., as well as
occasional other sherds of the same
chronological range (Wilkinson and
Tucker 1995: 15–23; Ur 2002). Also
probably of third-millennium B.C.
date is vitrified kiln slag, which is
characteristic (but not exclusively so)
of the high-temperature kilns that
made highly fired Akkadian beakers
and bowls. Further west along the
Syrian Euphrates, pottery scatters
dating to the mid–late third millennium B.C. have been recorded
around Tell Sweyhat, Kurban Höyük,
and Titriş Höyük (Wilkinson 1982,
1990a; Algaze et al. 1992) as well
as in the Biricik area (Algaze et al.
1996). In the western and northern
parts of the Jazira and west of the
Euphrates, Early Bronze Age sherds
are less common in field scatters, and
instead diagnostic artifacts include
larger quantities of Hellenistic, Roman, and Early Byzantine pottery
(see chapter 7).

At the most general level, the term
field scatter refers to background
noise that occurs in off-site locations
(chapter 4). Large areas of field scatters in the vicinity of Tell al-Hawa
have been cut by tens of kilometers
of modern canals, and only in exceptional cases could the scatters be seen
to be the remains of occupation sites.
By analogy with traditional agricultural practice in parts of the Old
World, field scatters are interpreted
as being the remains of composts
and ash cast on the fields in antiquity

to maintain fertility. Because the ash
becomes mixed with domestic refuse
and potsherds in the midden, these
inorganic inclusions become incorporated into the field soils, thereby
enabling the "manuring" episode to
be dated. In addition to an origin
from within domestic hearths, the
presence of kiln waste in significant
quantities in some field scatters suggests that pottery kilns were also
cleaned out for their fertilizing ash.

Exceptions to this model do occur
though. This is especially the case
in Egypt, where *sabakh* digging of
occupational refuse from ancient
sites results in the spreading of archaeological debris on fields as fertilizer. As a result, the sites disappear,
and the fields get covered with archaeological debris (Bailey 1999).
However, such excavation appears
to be indiscriminate, and the sabakh
diggers do not target specific cultural horizons for their fertilizer. In
contrast, field scatters in the Jazira
contain very battered sherds that
have clearly been in the fields a long
time, and they belong to specific cultural periods. Because it is unlikely
that when confronted by multiperiod
mounds, sabakh excavators would
target specific strata, it follows that if
recent sabakh digging had occurred
in the Jazira, the field scatters would
contain less-battered sherds of a
wide range of periods. Furthermore,
the occasional presence of field scatters in buried horizons, both in the
north Jazira, Iraq (Wilkinson and
Tucker 1995), and in the Tell Sweyhat area (Wilkinson 1988: fig. 7.3),
suggests that they were spread a
relatively short time after the date
suggested by their ceramic type.

Although there is a substantial
literature attesting the use of settlement refuse as fertilizer back to the
classical period (Wilkinson 1982;
Alcock et al. 1994), earlier references
remain elusive. Akkadian terminology from Mesopotamia rarely
refers to the specific practice of
manuring or fertilization, but this
may simply result from problems of
translation or because the practice

was considered unworthy of official record. Akkadian terminology includes two possible contenders for manure: compost or fertilizer. The first is *eperu*, which, according to the *Chicago Assyrian Dictionary* (Oppenheim and Reiner 1958: 184–190), means dust, earth, loose earth, debris. From its context in such phrases as "*eperu* from the city gate," "*eperu* from the front threshold (of the house)," "*eperu* from the kiln," the term might refer to loose ashes sometimes applied as a soil conditioner. A second word, *ziblu*, *zibli*, although listed in the Chicago Assyrian Dictionary as having an uncertain meaning, has been taken by Pfeiffer and Speiser (1936) and Kwasman and Parpola (1991) as relating to the use of manure. Because of its low value or esteem, manure is hardly expected to be a hot topic of royal dispatches, but in a more pedestrian Nuzi text of the late second millennium B.C. we learn: "The manure for one imer five aweharu of land the gardener of Kushshiharbe took away (from me)" (Pfeiffer and Speiser 1936: 67). Installations relating to manuring are also implied, for example, Late Assyrian (earlier first millennium B.C.) land-purchase texts refer to land adjoining a "manure house" and an estate with a "manure house" (Kwasman and Parpola 1991: 27, 216).

By applying manure or compost to fields, the farmer will arrest the long-term decline of nutrients withdrawn by sustained cropping. Under normal circumstances, dung from animals would be applied directly to the fields, but if all available fuel wood had been removed from the vicinity of the home, farmers would have resorted to the burning of dung, thereby diminishing the source of manure (Miller and Smart 1984). Because the loss of woodland for fuel would occur during times of maximum population, it follows that this is precisely the time when manure would also be required to increase crop production. As a result of this competition for dung, it would have

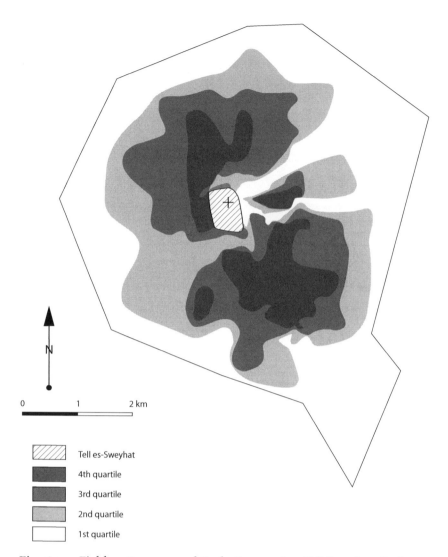

Fig. 6.15 Field scatters around Early Bronze Age Tell Sweyhat, Syria. Quartile ranges for sherd-scatter densities are the following: fourth quartile: 56–146 sherds per 100 sq. m, third: 34–55, second: 20–33, first 1–19.

0   1   2 km

Tell es-Sweyhat

4th quartile

3rd quartile

2nd quartile

1st quartile

been necessary to apply ash from burnt dung and other fuels to the fields. Such applications appear to result in a halo of higher-density field scatters around larger sites, which then gradually decrease from the site until they become very low density scatters, or none at all occur between 2 and 5 km away from the central site, depending upon its size (fig. 6.15). Similar, small-diameter scatters are found around the smaller sites. It should be recognized, however, that the zone of sherd scatters does not reflect the total area of cultivated land but simply the area of intensive cultivation and manuring.

This can then be combined with the limit of cultivation inferred from linear hollows to produce an estimate of land-use patterns around the site.

Archaeological and Textual Records Compared. Cuneiform texts, in the form of land-sale transactions, provide a complementary view of the Bronze Age agricultural landscape. Although these records are sparse for the third millennium B.C., a detailed study by Zaccagnini of the large number of texts from mid second millennium B.C. Nuzi (Yorgun Tepe) in the land of Arraphe (Kirkuk) provides a convenient synthesis of a

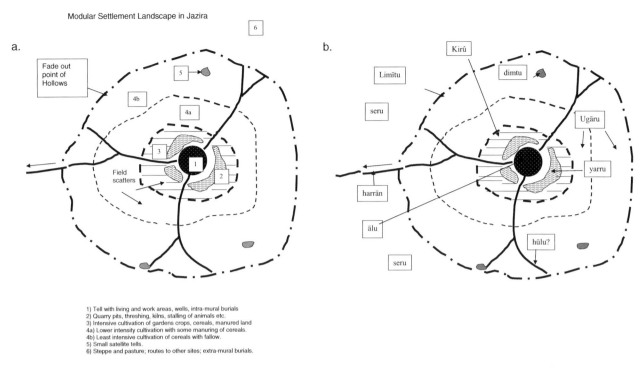

1) Tell with living and work areas, wells, intra-mural burials
2) Quarry pits, threshing, kilns, stalling of animals etc.
3) Intensive cultivation of gardens crops, cereals, manured land
4a) Lower intensity cultivation with some manuring of cereals.
4b) Least intensive cultivation of cereals with fallow.
5) Small satellite tells.
6) Steppe and pasture; routes to other sites; extra-mural burials.

Fig. 6.16   The landscape of tells: (a) according to field data from surveys in northern Syria and Iraq, (b) inferred from Nuzi texts. (b is based on data in Zaccagnini 1979)

community located near the limits of the rain-fed farming belt in eastern Iraq that parallels those already described in the Iraqi and Syrian Jazira (Zaccagnini 1979; Fincke 2000).

Despite uncertainties in the translation of several terms, what is remarkable is the number of features in the text for which we can recognize a plausible landscape feature in the field (table 6.2 and fig. 6.16). For example, at the most general level, because houses are normally stated as bordering on other houses and fields on fields or tracks, Zaccagnini deduces that houses were closely grouped together. This supports the observation that Bronze Age settlements in Upper Mesopotamia were nucleated rather than consisting of farmsteads dispersed within fields. At a higher degree of specificity, of the two classes of roads noted to occur outside the town (*harrānu* and *hūlu*), the former appears to refer to those linking settlements (e.g., linking *alu* with *dimtu*). On the other hand, the huīlu, rather than simply being wagon roads, as Zaccagnini suggests, might be roads that led to

fields or the outlying steppe. Alternatively, the *limitu*, which seems to represent some form of boundary or perimeter may be equivalent to the limit of cultivation that can be inferred from the fade-out point of hollow ways. The *seru*, being open country or steppe, should logically be the outer pastoral lands. However, in the Nuzi texts, although the seru is recognized, they usually seem to lack references to the pasturing of animals. Zaccagnini infers the zone of cultivation to be the *ugaru* (also Fincke 2000: 156), but there is no textual information to indicate whether or not this was manured. However, a second zone of gardens (*kiru*) appears to form a zone of smaller land parcels closer to the settlement, usually around the larger *alani* (*alu*) rather than *dimati* (*dimtu*). Hence, this garden belt might be equivalent to the more intensively manured and cultivated land immediately adjacent to the settlement. More tenuous is the presence of *yarru*, translated as pools or ponds. Because the mudbrick extraction pits eventually fill with water,

these might refer to such features, although the texts do not seem to provide any consistent reference to their location adjacent to the sites.

In contrast to the above, a number of features mentioned in the text cannot be recognized in the field. Thus the *magrattu* (threshing floor) cannot be recorded in the archaeological record of Upper Mesopotamia, presumably because threshing floors were made of compressed earth and have been destroyed and ploughed away. Similarly, sheepfolds and stables have not yet been distinguished in the landscape record, presumably because they were of perishable materials and failed to leave a tangible material record. References to canals and irrigation, on the other hand, are more frequent in the Nuzi area than might be expected in the Jazira. From the textual records at Nuzi, Zaccagnini deduces that hardly 20 percent of the land can have been irrigated; therefore, even in this climatically marginal area, some 80 percent of the land would have consisted of rain-fed fields (1979: 110–113). Similarly in

Table 6.2 Landscape Features and Their Possible Equivalents in Late Bronze Age Nuzi Texts

Landscape feature	Interpreted function[1]	Akkadian Term	Interpreted function[2]
Medium–large tell	Central settlement	*Alu*	Central settlement
Small tells	Satellite settlement	*Dimtu*	Minor settlement, its district; fortified farmhouse
Linear hollow between sites	Through route	*harranu*	Road linking *alu* with *dimtu*
Linear hollow that fades out	Route to fields and/or pasture	*huīlu*	"Wagon road"
Fade-out point of linear hollows	Territorial boundary	*Limitu*	Perimeter of district, border
Field scatters	Intensive cultivation	*kiru* *ugaru*	Gardens Cultivated land
Area beyond fade-out point of linear hollows and without field scatters	Steppe/pasture	*seru*	Open country, steppe
Enclosed depressions	Mudbrick extraction pits	*yarru*	Pond or pool

Note: See figure 6.16.
[1] Based on field evidence.
[2] Based on Zaccagnini (1979).

the Jazira there may have been a narrow belt of irrigated land extending perhaps a few hundred meters away from the central wadi. The Jazira, however, unlike the area of Mari (Lafont 2000), lacks evidence for dug canals with banks of upcast alongside. Therefore, if irrigation did occur in the Bronze Age Jazira, it was probably effected by means of small-scale canals that did not leave a significant landscape record.

Pastoral Resources and Regional Variations in Land Use. The estimation of pastoral zones is difficult because of the lack of direct evidence for this activity (chapters 4 and 8), but textual evidence eloquently demonstrates the importance of pasture resources to the Bronze Age economy (Gelb 1986). To counteract the paucity of direct evidence, the likely

availability of pasture and its significance to the economy can be estimated first by defining the probable areas of cultivation as described. By default, the land beyond the cultivation zone may then be inferred to have formed the pasture lands, an inference that can be cross-checked by current or traditional land use. For example, in the western Jazira, many Bronze Age settlements would have had ready access to steppe pasture on adjacent uplands (fig. 6.17a; see also Wilkinson 2000a: figs. 5–8). The situation would have been more constrained, however, in areas such as the Khabur basin and parts of northern Iraq, where large populations centers like Tell al-Hawa and Hamoukar (ca. 66 and 104 ha respectively) developed within extensive cultivated areas. In the case of Tell al-Hawa, an area of undulating land

that had been occupied by numerous small villages in the late Chalcolithic was abandoned by the early third millennium and continued to be virtually unoccupied by sedentary settlement for the rest of the millennium. This large area of open space (fig. 6.17b) may therefore have become a pastoral reserve for the large flocks that must have existed during the Akkadian period (Gelb 1986). The situation is less clear around Tell Hamoukar, but again it seems that most of the area would have been devoted to cultivation, and there would have been only a limited area available for pasture.

Steppe beyond the zone of cultivation, when available, would have supplied some pasture resources, but this may not have sufficed to feed large flocks of sheep and goats. Michael Danti argues, therefore, that to support large numbers of sheep and goats, winter and early spring feed would have been necessary as a supplementary food source (Danti 2000: 42). This would have required animals to be fed on grain, straw, or chaff, a practice confirmed by texts of the Akkadian period at Beydar (Van Lerberghe 1996: 120–121) and possibly recorded in the archaeobotanical record of the Khabur by a dramatic increase in barley products at third-millennium B.C. sites (McCorriston and Weinberg 2002). Consequently, the pastoral sector was partly dependent upon the production of the cultivated zone for straw fodder and barley, with the result that the domestic animals may have been in competition with the human population (McCorriston and Weinberg 2002: 57). The alternative practice of making animals fully reliant upon steppe grazing would have inflicted greater pressure on the steppe, with the result that there would have been increased landscape degradation. Either way, increased animal holdings would have imparted a stress on the land or human populations.

At a regional scale, the relative distribution of plough and pasture can

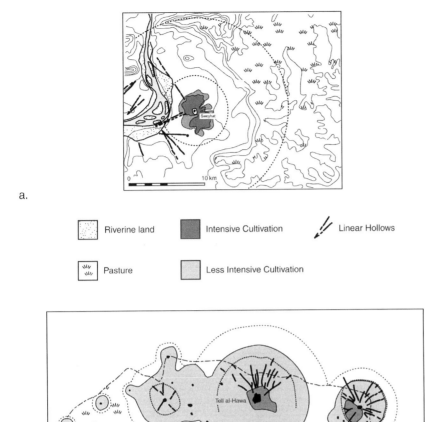

a.

Riverine land   Intensive Cultivation   Linear Hollows

Pasture   Less Intensive Cultivation

b.

Fig. 6.17 Agricultural territories reconstructed from intensive surveys: (a) Tell Sweyhat, Syria, (b) Tell al-Hawa, Iraq. Intensive and less-intensive cultivation zones are based on off-site field-scatter densities as indicated on fig. 6.15.

be inferred for the greater Khabur basin by combining faunal analyses with schematic views of the regional landscape inferred from archaeological surveys and satellite-image interpretation. According to a recent syntheses by Melinda Zeder (1995, 1999), animal-bone assemblages from excavated sites within the Khabur Basin demonstrate that during the fourth and third millennia B.C. there was a transition towards a specialized pastoral economy based upon the herding of sheep and goats. This grew out of long-established local traditions that

had placed greater reliance on less-specialized animal husbandry and wild animal resources. Zeder's work supports textual records that demonstrate that the Bronze Age city-states maintained large holdings of sheep and goats (Gelb 1986). What is less clear, however, is how these communities apportioned their cultivated and pastoral resources. It is relatively straightforward to suggest that the large areas of sparsely populated steppe south of the Jebel Abd al-Aziz provided extensive Bronze Age pasture, but within the Khabur basin itself, pastoral resources may have

been more limited. By estimating the Bronze Age settlement pattern for the entire basin, the cultivated zones can be estimated so that, by default, the land left over can be used as a proxy for the potential pasture that was in use.

To reconstruct the cultivated zones around the settlements, it is necessary first to establish the distribution of Early Bronze Age settlement. Because there have been no overall surveys of the Khabur basin, an initial approximation must be made by recording the tells, which, as established for the Beydar area, represent the majority of Early Bronze Age settlement. This approximation is derived from the CORONA satellite images because tells are recognizable as pale features that throw a slight shadow and often exhibit radial erosional gullies. The smaller, lower sites can therefore be neglected in this region because they are less likely to date to the Early Bronze Age. Where possible, these estimates can be cross-checked using conventional surveys such as that of Meijer (1986) for the northeast Khabur, as well as surveys around the Jebel Abd al-Aziz (Kouchoukos 1998).

Next, the pattern of cultivation is estimated to be proportional to the area of each site (e.g., Stein 1994) or each site is assumed to have required around 3 km radius of cultivated land (i.e., 28 sq. km; fig. 6.18). Finally, by default, areas beyond the cultivated zone are those that most likely would have remained as pasture. Although only a rough estimate, this simulation suggests that cultivated land was so extensive that there was little space for pasture except along the watersheds between major wadis. Consequently, large areas of cultivated land must have been separated by narrow roughly north–south pastoral corridors that linked the Tur ab-Din mountains to the north with the more open and sparsely settled steppe lands to the south. Clearly pastureland, although present, was rather scarce. Not only would this open land have been

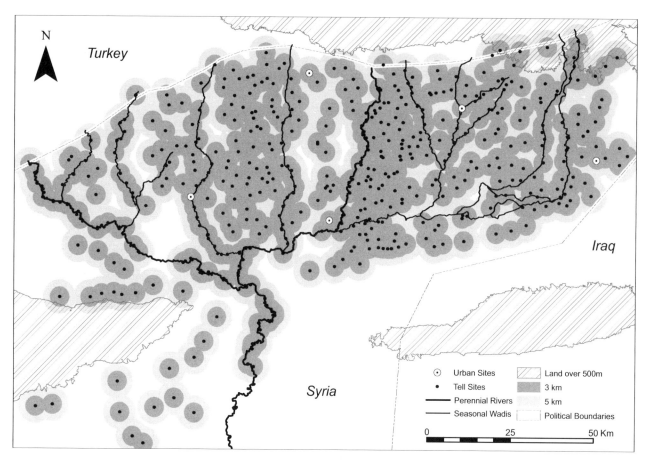

Fig. 6.18 Reconstruction of land-use zones in the upper Khabur Basin of Syria. Shading indicates the likely cultivated areas around tells; the white areas between, the inferred pasture lands (by J. Ur and C. Hritz).

subjected to competition between adjacent communities but overgrazing could have led to increased soil erosion within the basin.

On the other hand, as noted by Kouchoukos (1998), the open steppe to the east and west of the lower Khabur and around the Jebel Abd al-Aziz would have formed an ideal pasture zone. This would have served the inhabitants of the nearby kranzhügel mounds and other smaller tell sites and also the city-states in the Khabur basin to the north. How such flock management was operationalized is unclear, but it appears that there was a distinct trend towards specialized sheep and goat husbandry (Zeder 1998: fig. 4) during the fourth and especially the third millennium B.C. That these open lands to the south of the Khabur basin would have formed an ideal resource for pastoral usage has also

been suggested by Zeder: "What we are likely witnessing then is the development of an animal economy focused on caprines raised by pastoral specialists, who took advantage of this relatively untouched grassland to pasture their flocks, while relying on stored grain in riverside sites to tide them through leaner seasons on the steppe" (Zeder 1999: 13).

The foregoing analysis suggests therefore that the Bronze Age landscapes of Upper Mesopotamia were variegated and included lands that were densely settled with numerous towns (the largest accommodating perhaps ten thousand people or more) but relatively little pasture. To the south of the upper Khabur Basin the steppe with its occasional *kranzhügel* settlements would have provided vast open pastures, whereas west of the Khabur and along the Euphrates and Balikh rivers, open

steppe pasture would have been readily available, so that even at times of maximum urbanization, the local inhabitants of these areas would have placed considerable reliance upon pastoral resources or hunting (Danti and Zettler 1998).

Cult Sites and Cemeteries

Whereas the agricultural and pastoral landscapes can be perceived primarily via a functionalist lens, the ideational and funerary components require a different approach. Apart from the presence of the Early Bronze Age extramural cemeteries (chapter 4), the ideational landscape remains elusive. In part this is because formalized religion was often situated within the settlement itself, with the result that relatively few Early Bronze Age rural sanctuaries are known in the Jazira. Of particular significance therefore is the site of Jebelet al-Beidha, discovered by Baron von Oppenheim on a western extension of the Jebel Abd al-Aziz. This group of four basalt sculptures up to 3.5 m in height set on a small 20 × 15 m platform atop a low limestone hill must have formed an imposing monument within the relentless semiarid steppe southwest of the Khabur. The stylistic parallels of the sculptures are Sumerian, and given the lack of settlement in the vicinity, the monument can probably be interpreted either as a place of worship or perhaps as some sort of victory monument (Moortgat-Correns 1972). If the monument was primarily religious in purpose, it could have served for mobile pastoralists in the region, perhaps during a transitional stage towards sedentary settlement (Kouchoukos 1998: 433–435), for travelers passing along east–west routes through the region, or for a regional pilgrimage center, as appears to have been the case at Pre-Pottery Neolithic Gobekli Tepe in southern Turkey.

Equally enigmatic is the massive Early Bronze Age conical monument at Tell Banat north, which forms an impressive mound 100 m diameter and 20 m high in the landscape of the Syrian Euphrates. The Banat monument, like a similar pair in the Balikh valley and another at Tell Hadhail in northern Iraq, is located just within the long-term limit of rain-fed cultivation. As Ann Porter has argued, although the monument is positioned near the boundary between two ecological or resource zones, this is probably not a sufficient explanation for the location of the monument, and she suggests that such features may relate to territorial definition of pastoral groups, in which the role of genealogy and ancestors plays a key role (Porter 1998: 424–425; Porter 2002). Whether temple platform, sanctified high place, or monumental tomb, according to Tom McClellan, the Banat mound is part of a long tradition of cultic high places in the Levant,

and it clearly represents a display of power and prestige of an elite class capable of mobilizing the large labor force required to erect a monument comprising some 52,360 m^3 of soil (McClellan 1998: 246).

In the case of the mounds of both the Jebelet al-Beidha and the Banat type, major visible monuments have been placed in areas where sedentary and pastoral groups came into contact or where during certain periods, pastoral groups held sway. In the case of the prominent hilltop site of Jebelet al-Beidha within the pastoral nomadic steppe, this monument clearly has more parallels with the standing stone monuments of the desert than with the religious places of the sedentary zone (chapter 8).

Other "Landscapes of Tells" in the Near East

There is a considerable amount of regional variation in the type of settlement. In many parts of the Near East, an undue emphasis on the tell has resulted in a misleading perception of the pattern of ancient settlement. Not only must allowance be made for the existence of small non-mounded settlements, but, as in the Wadi Ziqlab, Jordan, parts of the settlement record may be missing. As a result of detailed geoarchaeological studies in the Wadi Ziglab, Banning argues that gaps in settlement, such as occur in Jordan during the late Neolithic, Early Bronze IV (Early Bronze–Middle Bronze or Middle Bronze I), and Persian eras, may in part be the result of our failure to deal with buried sites along wadis (Banning 1996: 38).

An immediate contrast is apparent if we compare the Jazira with the area of Ebla in central Syria. Here it appears that landscape features such as linear hollows are not present, whereas field scatters are either not present or have gone unrecorded because of the general low intensity of archaeological survey (but see Philip et al. 2002b: 13). The lack of linear hollows in western

Syria and the neighboring parts of the Levant may be because over the centuries, an overlay of later Seleucid, Roman, Byzantine, and Islamic field systems erased more archaeological features than in the Jazira. On the other hand, the textual evidence derived from the Ebla tablets (ca. 2400–2300 B.C.) implies a rather different landscape than that prevailing in the Jazira. Within the kingdom of Ebla (which may have extended some 200 km from Carchemish in the north to Hama in the south), it is clear that outlying villages farmed not only large areas of cereals but also numerous olive groves, and occasional vineyards were present (Archi 1990: 16–17). This is hardly surprising, given the present land use of the region, which is given over to significant amounts of olive and vines. As Archi suggests, those villages that appear to have had more olive groves than grain were probably located on the more hilly lands of the kingdom. In addition, the huge holdings of sheep attributed to the palace (some seventy to eighty thousand, according to Archi 1990: 19) cannot have been pastured on the immediate land that surrounded the town but must have been taken for at least part of the year to pastures around the marshes of the river Quoueiq (located some 15 km to the east) as well as to the semi-arid steppe beyond. East of Ebla, tell-based settlements are associated with small, flat plains (*faidhas*) that occur at intervals between low hills to the west and the climatic margin of cultivation to the east (Geyer 1998: 6–7).

In the Biqaʿ valley of Lebanon (Marfoe 1979) and the Amuq plain of southern Turkey, tells again provide a major locus of occupation. For the Amuq, Braidwood's pioneering survey of 1937 showed a characteristic tell-based settlement pattern, but as in many parts of the Levant, landscape features such as hollow ways and Bronze Age field scatters are absent.

The landscape of the southern

Levant, on the other hand, rarely exhibits Bronze Age tells of the scale found in Syria, Iraq, and southern Turkey. Following the disintegration of Chalcolithic settlement, there was a new cycle of settlement growth during Early Bronze I in which a range of open and unwalled settlements developed into a hierarchical system of compact and fortified settlements indicative of a more urbanized and stable society (Joffe 1993: 68; Gophner and Portugali 1988; Harrison 1997). Settlements of Early Bronze II date, which frequently formed tells usually up to 25 ha in area (Joffe 1993: 70), although often described as urban, may not have been truly urban, and they certainly do not rival the massive towns that eventually developed in Upper Mesopotamia. The process of Early Bronze II tell nucleation in the Mediterranean zone of the southern Levant appears to have been associated with a reduction in the total number sites compared to the previous Early Bronze I; but at the same time, there was a significant increase in settlement in the arid zones (Joffe 1993: 73). In the uplands west of the Jordan, Early Bronze II settlements include a significant number of tells, although none were greater than 10 ha in area. In contrast, in the Golan (Jawlan), fortified "enclosure" sites often built upon mountain spurs appear (Joffe 1993: 76). Overall, Joffe recognizes two patterns of rural settlement, the first in which smaller sites occur as satellites around major tells, and the second characterized by small, seemingly independent sites in the valleys of upper Galilee, northern Samaria, and northern Gilead. These sites, which are significantly smaller than the lowland tells oriented along apparent trade routes, appear to anticipate the pattern of settlement that becomes typical of the Middle Bronze Age and Iron I (see chapter 7). Meanwhile in the deserts of the Negev and Sinai, hundreds of sites from the Chalcolithic and Bronze Age have been recorded. The communities that occupied

these usually small, straggling settlements appear to have combined both sedentary and pastoral strategies.

Further south, settlements in climatically marginal areas such as Jawa and those of the Uvda valley appear to have derived their sustenance by collecting water using techniques of water harvesting (Joffe 1993; Helms 1981). On the uplands west of the Jordan, where tells are scarce, small and low Early or Middle Bronze Age sites continue to be rare, and a brief perusal of the survey record suggests that relatively few of the low or scattered "khirbet" type sites were initially occupied during the Early Bronze Age (Finkelstein and Ledermann 1997).

Following this period of nucleated Early Bronze II/III tell-based settlement, there was a major devolution of settlement, which resulted in a major phase of "ruralization" in which settlement became much less hierarchical and urbanized and the economy shifted along the sedentary–pastoral continuum towards a greater concentration on pastoralism (Dever 1992). In the hill country west of the Jordan there was a substantial decline into a much small number of total settlements, which in the Early Bronze IV were smaller unwalled villages (Finkelstein 1988: 42).

From the foregoing it is evident that the settlement pattern of much of the southern Levant in the Early Bronze II/III (3000–2200 B.C.) resembles that of Upper Mesopotamia except that the scale of the tells and the associated settlement hierarchy are smaller and distinctively less "urban" (Falconer and Savage 1995). The small Bronze Age settlements that developed in the uplands west of the Jordan appear to have no obvious equivalents in Upper Mesopotamia; neither does the rash of desert settlement that has been recorded in various phases of the Early Bronze Age. On the other hand, the southern Levantine landscape lacks many of the features that enliven that of Upper Mesopotamia. Thus

field scatters, although recorded, seem to be mainly of the Late Roman/Byzantine type (R. Frankel personal communication Nov. 1999), and linear hollows, although well represented in parts of the Negev, seem to be limited to the loessic areas (Tsoar and Yekutieli 1993).

This lack of Bronze Age field scatters and linear hollows may be due to the significantly larger size of settlements in Upper Mesopotamia than in the Levant. This would have resulted in increased intensity of land use and considerably more traffic from settlement to field and beyond in Upper Mesopotamia so that linear hollows became more deeply etched. Also of significance are taphonomic factors resulting from the long and perhaps more continuous history of settlement that prevailed in the Levant after the Bronze Age. Such sustained land use may have resulted in linear hollows being ploughed or eroded or infilled with soil wash more rapidly than in Upper Mesopotamia. Alternatively, the concentration, in the Negev, of hollow ways on loessic soils vulnerable to "hydrocompaction" may be relevant to the Jazira, where soils also include an admixture of loess. Because soils in northern Iraq and northern Syria include 50–75 percent silty loess,[2] Jaziran soils may also be vulnerable to hydrocompaction and hollow development. The concentration of hollows ways within this rather specific zone illustrated on figure 6.6 may therefore reflect the distribution of silty soils occupying a broad belt of terrain adjacent to the Syrian desert.

Other landscape features appear to have been better developed in the Levant, specifically where they are found within the landscape of survival of the deserts. Thus the water-harvesting systems of Avdat and Jawa, which show a highly developed technology for the time, have no known equivalents in the deserts of northern Syria and Iraq.

Despite the evidence that sites in the southern Levant attained their maximum size during the Early or Middle Bronze Age, their impact upon the natural environment is not particularly obvious. Nevertheless, a pollen diagram from Lake Kinneret shows a minor impact of forest clearance during the Early Bronze Age (Baruch 1990; see also chapter 7), whereas the Hula Lake core shows a larger reduction in deciduous and evergreen oak and a pronounced olive peak (Baruch and Bottema 1999).

Just as the above reconstructions of land-use patterns suggested a rather variegated landscape, archaeological surveys indicate that settlement did not necessarily evolve in terms of uniform cycles of rise and fall. Instead, settlement in northern Mesopotamia from the late Chalcolithic onwards is characterized by its patchiness, so that for any given period, certain areas appear relatively densely settled, whereas others may have been relatively deserted (Algaze 1999; Wilkinson 2000b).

Discussion

In Bronze Age Upper Mesopotamia the system of nucleated tell-based settlement existed within a variegated and patchy landscape comprising intensive cultivation around settlements with zones of pasture beyond and even occasional valley-floor marshes. In such a landscape, agriculture formed the main means of sustenance of the inhabitants to the point that most urban dwellers were probably primarily reliant upon their crops and flocks for support (Schloen 2001: 101, 198).

Although this pattern of settlement exhibits a scalar hierarchy, there is no evidence for a single primary administrative settlement that stands out physically above all the others. Rather, there are a significant number of large settlements in the range of 50–150 ha that seem to show some measure of parity, at least in terms of size and apparent population. Whether this means that no single settlement had primacy

in terms of administration over all others is not clear, but it appears that the region comprised a series of small city-states or equivalent modular settlement systems, each of which had its own ruler or petty king (see chapter 10).

A preliminary model of agricultural production for nucleated Bronze Age towns suggests that the main agricultural zone within 10–15 km distance was just capable of provisioning the estimated population with food but that such settlement systems would have been vulnerable to climatic or socioeconomic perturbations (Wilkinson 1994). Although such settlement clusters may have provided the basic units of food production for major settlements, these probably did not constitute the primary political units. Textual records from Ebla and Mari imply that emergent kingdoms probably comprised larger and more fluid aggregates of tells (with their surrounding territories) that resulted from one king subjugating neighboring polities into larger compound units. The apparent uniformity of maximum settlement size over large areas, which resulted in there being no dominant prime settlement, suggests that Early Bronze Age towns may have reached a regional equilibrium of size. This could have been the result of a balance of positive and negative feedback processes as follows.

Because tells acted as centers of power, defense, religion, economic concentration, and storage, they grew partly as a result of the aggregation of population into them. Any nonproducers within the urban population needed to be primarily supported from the local supplies of food. In the rain-fed farming zone, areas with higher rainfall and agricultural productivity (in terms of kg per ha) were capable of supporting more nonfood producers in addition to those who actually produced the food. Conversely, where yields were lower, more food producers would have been required to grow sufficient

food to feed each additional non-food producer.[3] Consequently, any positive feedback mechanism that resulted in more people concentrating in the growing centers would have resulted in an increased labor requirement, especially in the more arid parts of Upper Mesopotamia. Under such circumstances, in drier areas more individuals would be drawn into the system as labor (perhaps as transients), a situation that would reinforce population growth and also the demand for food. The potentially destabilizing growth arising from this positive feedback could have been counteracted by negative feedback processes that served to constrain their growth. Such processes include the inability to supply sufficient food from the areas immediately surrounding any large center (Wilkinson 1994). Therefore, as a result of these two counteracting processes, one might expect settlement populations to attain a plateau in tell sites in rain-fed farming areas, whereas in drier areas where the counter-acting feedback mechanisms were out of balance, the level of population would have been potentially unstable.

The tendency for sites to be highly nucleated during the Bronze Age appears to result in landscape features such as linear hollows and field scatters becoming oriented around major tells. Moreover, the sustained agricultural use of fields in the vicinity of tells over millennia has probably resulted in some degree of restructuring of soil chemistry. Hints of this come from the Euphrates terraces around Kurban Höyük, where the main long-term occupied terrace was preferentially enriched with phosphates, compared with the much more sparsely occupied upper terraces (Wilkinson 1990a).

Particularly noteworthy is that landscape features do not seem to function in isolation. For example, by gathering runoff from the surrounding fields, tracks (or linear hollows) would have directed water towards the tell and any surrounding mudbrick extraction pits. These pits would then have filled with water during the winter rainy season, which for the inhabitants would have been a double-edged sword. By providing valuable water, perhaps even through the summer dry season, this would have been a bonus, but by contributing to the development of potentially fetid swamps that could have concentrated human and animal wastes through time, such pits could have become a vector for infectious diseases. Although the natural drainage around the tell would help drain such areas, at sites like Tell Brak, where a natural system of through drainage was less well developed, the accumulation of stagnant water near the living areas may have created health problems.

During the third millennium B.C., at least in parts of the Jazira, the landscape may have become truly zoned, with large sites being surrounded by areas of greater and lesser degrees of intensive cultivation. Beyond, where areas with limited or no settlements have been recorded, specialized pasturelands may have accommodated the excess sheep and goat population from the more densely settled areas.

The presence of field scatters concentrated around major tells such as Hawa, Hamoukar, Brak, and Sweyhat may result from a simple processual relationship, namely, that with increasing population, or population concentration, there was a need to maximize agricultural production by the application of large quantities of fertilizer. This argument, based on the work of Ester Boserup (1965, 1981), has its attractions and superficially can be seen to fit the limited field-scatter data available. However, as Glenn Stone has pointed out for traditional west African societies, concentric land-use zones associated with refuse manuring are related to nucleated villages and moderate regional population densities; thereafter, with further increases in population density, population tends to disperse as farmers move beyond

the initial settlement zone (Stone 1996: 46–47). It should not therefore be assumed that the Early Bronze Age population concentration represents the all-time demographic peak.

Second Millennium Transition

By focusing upon specific landscape signatures and themes, the above narrative may give an erroneous impression that the tell-dominated landscape of the third millennium B.C. was stable or static. Although more finely divided chronological sequences are required for the details of settlement shifts to be evident, in most areas there is either a cyclical shift from more dispersed towards nucleated settlement and back again, or with episodic development of satellite settlements, as in the area of Tell al-Hawa and Titrish Höyüks (Wilkinson and Tucker 1995; Algaze 2001b), satellite communities switch on and off like traffic lights through much of the third and second millennium B.C. Overall in many parts of the Jazira during the final quarter of the third millennium B.C. there was a major transition that witnessed a partial breakdown or even a complete collapse of the nucleated settlements of the mid third millennium B.C. and the development of dispersed communities and/or areas of abandonment. Such a pattern has been recognized in parts of the Khabur basin (where it has been described as a major collapse: Weiss et al. 1993), in the Turkish Euphrates (Wilkinson 1990a; Algaze et al. 1992; Algaze 1999), in the Levant and the Aegean (for discussion, see Hole 1997; Butzer 1997b; and Peltenberg 2000; chapter 10). Whatever the cause of this restructuring, it represents the beginning of a complex period of transition that ultimately resulted in the breakdown of the configuration of third millennium B.C. "city-states" and their replacement by a much more dispersed pattern of settlement (chapter 7).

Some elements of this broad tran-

sitional period can be summarized for the Jazira region as follows (from east to west):

— In the north Jazira (Iraq), following a period of early second-millennium growth, there was a general thinning of settlement, so that by the Middle Assyrian period, although the main sites were sometimes still occupied, there had been an overall decline in settlement.

— In the western Khabur, the development of open space (pastures?) contrasted with a concentration of settlement in the eastern Khabur (Meijer 1986). Around the middle of the second millennium B.C. in the western Khabur, many tells were resettled by means of sprawling lower towns or localized dispersed settlement. Abandonment may have coincided with a phase of nomadism during the early second millennium B.C., a phenomenon well attested in, for example, the Mari texts (Matthews 1979; see also Lyonnet 1998).

— Around the Jebel Abd al-Aziz area, collapse of the kranzhügel mounds during the later third millennium B.C. ushered in a period of sparse population in the second millennium (Hole n.d.: 6).

— In the Balikh valley, settlement was sufficiently dense for there to be competition for water as well as a general decline in the flow of the Balikh River (Wilkinson 1998). Although by the mid second millennium B.C. both settlement and irrigation had declined significantly, recolonization by the Middle Assyrian empire was already underway (Curvers 1991; Akkermans et al. 1993; Lyon 2000; Wiggermans 2000).

— West of the Euphrates in the Jabbul plain, a significant decline of settlement during the second millennium attained a minimum in terms of settlement numbers during the Late Bronze Age (Gerritsen and Macormak, in Schwartz et al. 2000).

The series of changes described above resulted in an overall decline of settlement throughout the second millennium B.C., which ultimately set the stage for the establishment of a landscape that provided a total contrast with that of the third millennium B.C. (chapter 7).

7 The Great Dispersal
Post-Bronze Age Landscapes of the Fertile Crescent

During the Late Bronze and Iron Ages there was a remarkable dispersal of settlement in many parts of the Near East. This resulted in patterns of landscape features that together provide a view of the subsistence economy, commercial farming, and religious activities dating back some two thousand to three thousand years. Referring to the Mediterranean basin during the classical and Roman periods, Lloyd (1991: 234) asserted that "over the past three decades archaeological survey has provided spectacular evidence for a wealth and diversity of rural settlement in classical times that were entirely unsuspected from the written sources" (also Barker 1997: 268). This chapter will examine an equivalent phenomenon for Upper Mesopotamia and the Levant and will place it within the context of the prevailing political economy and environment. Although it is possible to make some generalizations about settlement and landscape over the three millennia of concern here, it should be emphasized that the archaeological record for this variegated area of uplands and lowlands is extraordinarily complex. Whereas early surveys often proceeded along thematic lines (witness the studies of Christian architecture by Butler [1929], Roman/Late Antique communities by Tchalenko [1953], or specialized studies of oil manufacturing by Callot [1984]), later surveys have provided a more complex multiperiod view of the landscape (e.g., Dar 1986, 1993; Finkelstein and Ledermann 1997). The progression toward intensive landscape survey probably attained its peak in terms of survey intensity with the Wadi Faynan project, which by the time of the 2000 report had recorded no fewer than one thousand "sites" within 30 sq. km of terrain (Barker et al. 2000). Recent multidisciplinary projects have produced a vast amount of material, and in this chapter I take the opportunity to distill some fundamental themes from the published data and to draw contrasts and comparisons between Upper Mesopotamia and the Levant.

Landscapes of the desert margin are treated in this chapter rather than the deserts themselves (see chapter 8) because this keeps a group of consistent case studies together and allows a uniformity of approach. The history of desertification, as well as the discussion of hunting/pastoral features of the desert margins will be treated in chapter 8.

The Assyrian Urban Core

The Assyrian rulers of the Late Assyrian empire inherited a landscape that had undergone considerable settlement reorganization during the second millennium B.C. Consequently, by the late second millennium, the Jazira had experienced both Middle Assyrian colonization and an Aramaean presence (chapter 6). Following a major administrative reorganization by Tiglath-Pileser III in the eighth century B.C. (Postgate 1979), the empire was transformed by the establishment of Assyrian power bases in the capital cities at Assur, Kalhu (Nimrud), Dur Sharrukin (Khorsabad), and Nineveh (Ninua). These were supplemented by local administrations such as at Til Barsip on the Euphrates and slightly later at Harran (Morandi 2000: 357). Not only did the capital cities dominate the empire administratively, but also their massive area exceeded the cities of the preceding Early Bronze Age by a considerable degree (van de Mieroop 1999).

The area immediately around Sennacherib's capital of Nineveh illustrates how the landscape must have been restructured within the context of a growing empire. Assyrian policy entailed the construction of large-scale systems of water management and, during Sennacherib's reign, the loss of a significant part of its former agricultural hinterland to newly created parks and gardens.

Although historical or Biblical sources for the population of the Assyrian capital cities vary and are potentially disputable (Oates 1968), these estimates can be cross-checked using the area of the city as measured within the city wall as well as by the expected population densities for ancient cities. An estimate population of 63,000 for ninth-century Kalhu (Oates 1968: 43–44; 630 ha: Nimrud) would result in a population density within the total site area of 100 persons/ha. Similarly, in the seventh century B.C. the 750 ha city of Ninua (Nineveh: Oates 1968: 48–49) held, according to an estimate in the book of Jonah, some 120,000 people. This gives a population estimate of 160 persons/ha (but see Oates 1968: 49). Although both population density estimates are rough, they fall within the range of 100–300 persons per ha expected for traditional Near Eastern cities. The populations of such cities together with the massive demands of the palace sector for banquets and other needs would have placed a huge demand on the agricultural resources of the region. Therefore, in contrast to the third millennium B.C. when the food supplies of Upper Mesopotamian cities could have been satisfied by an immediate catchment of 5–20 km (see chapter 6), during the Iron Age a much larger area would have been brought into play to supply Nineveh with its essential supplies. Commodities required by the capital would have included not only cereals and orchard fruits but also animals and their products as well as stone for the manufacture of monumental reliefs and buildings.

Despite the lack of comprehensive surveys, textual sources together with a range of archaeological investigations (Oates 1968; Reade 1978; Bagg 2000; Jacobsen and Lloyd 1935) enable four broad landscape zones to be sketched around Nineveh (fig. 7.1):

1. An inner zone around the walled city itself consisting of gardens, irrigated fields, and various earthworks. This area may originally have been devoted to rain-fed agricultural production when the population of Nineveh was smaller, but later, this zone became incorporated into the expanded lower town and various game parks and gardens around the city. The Assyrian king played a major role in the development of this cultured landscape, but that this was not solely the realm of the king is brought out by inscriptions of Sennacherib, which state that orchard plots were also disbursed to the people of Nineveh (Jacobsen and Lloyd 1935: 33). Hints about the land use of this zone can be gleaned from the names of the gates of Nineveh and other textual sources: the Gate of Shibaniba was the gate of choicest flocks and grain (i.e., good farm supplies), the gate of Halahhu was the product of

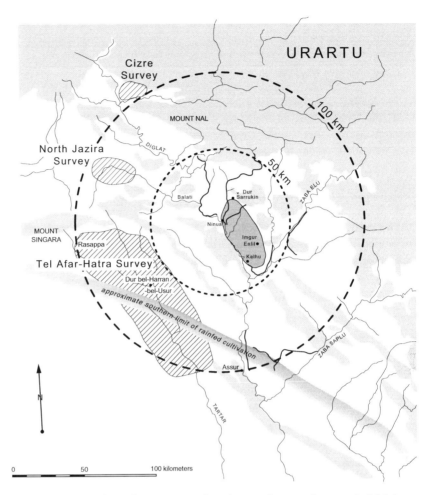

Fig. 7.1 Nineveh and its region, showing major canal systems (thick lines), the Assyrian capitals (Assur, Kalhu [Nimrud], Dur Sharrukin [Khorsabad], Ninua [Nineveh]), and areas of rural settlement mapped by surveys mentioned in the text (based on Oates 1968; Reade 1978; Barbanes 1999).

the mountains, the Adad gate faced the game preserve, Kirate was the gate of the gardens, there was a gate of the watering places, another gate of the garden, a gate of the quay, and the gate of the desert (Reade 1978: 51–54).

2. Forming an intermediate zone within some 50 km of Nineveh are the plains east of the Tigris containing the three Assyrian capitals, as well as Imgur Enlil (Balawat) and the quarries at Balatai. David Oates (1968: 44–45) estimated that Nimrud would have required some 100 sq. km to produce the requisite crops to sustain its population,

whereas Nineveh, at roughly twice the size, may have required a little more than 200 sq. km of cultivable land. However, if rural populations around the capital were also dense, then more food would have been required to sustain these inhabitants, and the food production area would have increased accordingly. Zone 2 not only functioned as the main area of food supply for the Assyrian capital cities but also included the catchment area of a series of massive canals. The seventh-century B.C. Assyrian king Sennacherib, who claimed to be the "one who caused canals to be dug" and who "puts irrigation water inside of Assyria" (Radner 2000: 237), was responsible for the construction of many of the canal systems that brought water to irrigate the lands around Nineveh as well as to supply the needs of the city's inhabitants. Oates (1968: 49–51) described how this program was accomplished in four stages, and entailed cutting water-diversion channels from rivers leading away from Nineveh so that the water could be led to where it was needed.

Even when water was in the right valley, it was frequently necessary to lead it across the valleys, a feat of engineering that is best illustrated by the superb Jerwan aqueduct that conducted water across a tributary of the Gomel River into the Khosr valley some 40 km north–northeast of Nineveh (Jacobsen and Lloyd 1935). In the time of Sennacherib, water gathered from the Gomel and Khosr Rivers as well as a northeast tributary (the Wadi al-Milh), was used to water orchards in the summer and cereal fields in the winter below and around the city. This area even included an artificial swamp as well as fields of cotton (Oates 1968: 51). The gardens of the Assyrian capitals are rightly famous, and they represent a clear attempt to replicate landscapes from other parts of the empire in what is basically a rain-fed environment. This attempt at introducing "alien" landscapes, which included the importation of trees, can be traced back to the time of Tiglath-Pileser I (1114–1067 B.C.). Sargon II of Assyria (721–705 B.C.), when constructing gardens around Dur Sharrukin (Khorsabad), imported trees from the Amanus mountains near the Mediterranean coast of Turkey, whereas to create an

irrigated paradise, Sennacherib tried to emulate the landscape of Babylonia (Radner 2000: 239–240).

3. A more distant zone of alternating plains and frequently hilly or rocky areas could, if necessary, be called upon to supply food to the capital. It also included the source of the fossiliferous *pindu* stone of Mount Nipur, which is most likely the Judi Dagh near the Iraq/Turkish border (Reade 1978: 60). Only three parts of this large region have been systematically surveyed, but all showed significant increases in rural population during the Iron Age (Ibrahim 1986; Oates 1968; Algaze et al. 1991; Wilkinson and Tucker 1995; Barbanes 1999). Changes in the economy of the Near East toward the use of a more flexible and fungible system of quasi-monetary exchange may have enabled grain surpluses in these more distant areas to be used to alleviate shortfalls at the center. The Cizre area, surveyed by Guillermo Algaze (Algaze et al. 1991), was particularly conveniently located because it was linked to Nineveh by means of the "low friction" transport artery of the Tigris.

That such economic supply zones may have existed is suggested by Assyrian texts that allude to prices of grain being lower in the "desert," moderate in intermediate areas (such as Halahhu, Khorsabad area), and most expensive at the city of Nineveh (Saggs 1959; Postgate 1974; Fales 1990). This suggests that grain could have been moved between the hinterlands and the main city, as long as it was possible to turn a profit (Wilkinson 1995: 158).

4. The mountains provided an additional source of agricultural supplies such as specialized fruit or tree crops, as is implied by the title for the Hallahu Gate:

"bringing the products of the mountains" (Reade 1978: 51).

Overall, therefore, agricultural surpluses from the surrounding areas could have been used to redress any food imbalances in the capital (fig. 7.1).

By initiating great public works such as the canal systems of Nineveh's hinterland, the productivity of the capital region could have been significantly raised. Nevertheless, as David Oates (1968: 47–52) has pointed out, the increase in productivity was probably insufficient to supply the inhabitants of the city and its region with all their food needs. This therefore begs the question whether the canals were primarily required for the irrigation of food crops. As an alternative, Julian Reade has suggested that the principle aim of the irrigation projects around Nineveh may have been to improve the quality and beauty of the landscape (Reade 1978: 174). This raises the fundamental issue that canal and irrigation systems, although functional at a basic level, should not be viewed solely in that light. In reality, despite the large effort that was expended on canal construction, much of the agricultural productivity probably came from the rolling plains to both the east and the west of the Tigris, where a very different manifestation of Assyrian landscape policy was in evidence.

Areas around Nineveh, especially those west of the Tigris and throughout the Jazira, experienced a substantial increase in rural settlement in the form of small, dispersed villages, hamlets, and farmsteads (fig. 7.2; table 7.1). This process of settlement was first observed archaeologically by the surveys of David Oates (1968), and it has now been verified in a number of areas (summarized in Morandi 2000 and Wilkinson and Barbanes 2000): the Upper Tigris in the Cizre plain (Algaze 1989; Algaze et al. 1991; Parker 1997); the Sinjar/Afar plain (Oates 1968; Ibrahim 1986); the north Jazira of Iraq (Wil-

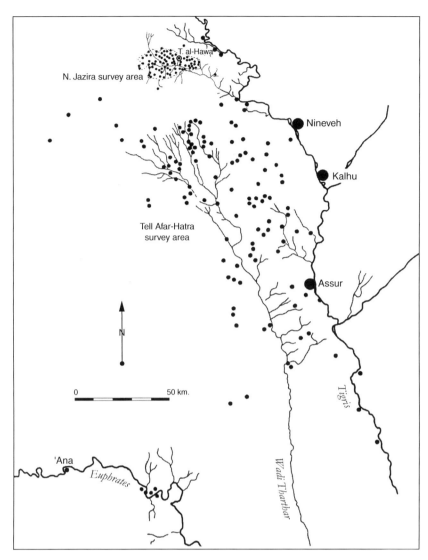

Fig. 7.2 Late Assyrian settlement to the west of the Tigris, as determined by the North Jazira, Tell Afar-Hatra, and other surveys (modified from Barbanes 1999: figs. 7, 8).

Table 7.1 The Number and Aggregate Settlement Area of Early Bronze and Iron Age Sites in Northern Iraq and Northern Syria

Survey	Area (km²)	Total Sites	Early Bronze Age*	Iron Age*
North Jazira survey	475	184	20 sites 146 ha	78 sites 123 ha
Tell Beydar survey	450	82	17 sites 98 ha	35 sites 97 ha
Tell Hamoukar survey	125	67	9 sites 114 ha	20 sites 64 ha

Note: Although the number of settlements dramatically increases in every case, the aggregate settlement area (roughly proportional to total population) either remains the same or declines. Data are derived from surveys by the author, Eleanor Barbanes, and Jason Ur.

*Number of sites and aggregate area.

kinson and Tucker 1995); the Wadi Ajij (Bernbeck 1993); the lower Khabur valley (Morandi 1996a; Ergenzinger et al. 1988); the Jebel Abd al-Aziz (Hole and Kouchoukos in press); the Tell Beydar area (Barbanes 1999); the Tell Chuera area (J.-W. Meyer, personal communication Jan. 2001); the Balikh valley (Wilkinson 1995; Wilkinson and Barbanes 2000); and the Turkish Euphrates (Algaze et al. 1994). Related trends are evident west of the Euphrates in the Jabbul plain (Schwartz et al. 2000) and in the Amuq (Yener et al. 2000).

The Tell Beydar area in the western Khabur well illustrates how the landscape was transformed during the Iron Age. Following the collapse of tell-based settlement in the later part of the third millennium B.C., much of the area was deserted during the early second millennium. There followed a phase of resettlement in the Late Bronze Age that took the form of small "lower towns" that developed at the bases of tells, with some smaller sites in the countryside. Resettlement coincided in part with a phase of Middle Assyrian colonization that established fortified strongholds (*dunnu*) and their satellite communities between the Khabur and Balikh valleys and that seem to represent an official Middle Assyrian presence in contrast to the indigenous non-Assyrian communities (Akkermans et al. 1993; Lyon 2000; Wiggermans 2000). In the Tell Beydar area there then appeared during the Iron Age numerous small settlements that were dispersed across the landscape, between tells, across the rolling steppe beyond the valleys, and even on the isolated basalt plateau to the west (fig. 7.3). In addition, small Late Bronze Age lower towns then developed into sprawling settlements during the Iron Age, the largest being the lower town, 30–40 ha in size, at Tell Beydar (Bretschneider 1997). Of the 82 sites recorded in the 450 sq. km survey area, 35 were small Iron Age villages of 1–2 ha, of which 8 were lower towns below tells. This phase

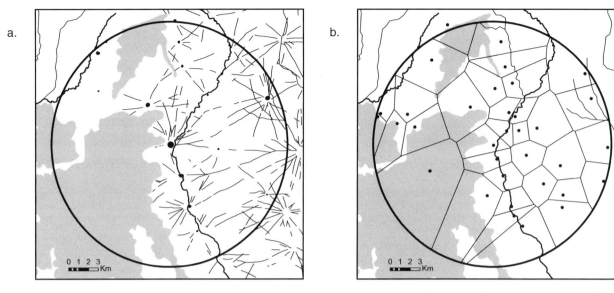

Fig. 7.3   The distribution of (a) Bronze Age and (b) Iron Age sites around Tell Beydar, Syria. Linear hollows on the Bronze Age map are plotted from CORONA satellite images. Iron Age territories have been estimated using Thiessen polygons. The shaded area is the sparsely occupied basalt plateau. (Modified from Barbanes 1999; compiled by Jason Ur)

of settlement does not simply represent a movement off the tells but also entailed the settlement of land that during the Early Bronze Age was cultivation, marginal land, or steppe pasture. The presence of settlements on what was probably steppe pasture underscores that this phase of settlement actually extended the total amount of cultivated area. This settlement cannot yet be subdivided into phases, but it is evident that it occurred over several episodes. Equally, it is unclear how many of these sites were occupied at the same time, but from ceramic parallels, it is clear that occupation was concentrated in the period between around 1000 and 600 B.C. (Wilkinson and Barbanes 2000).

In addition to settling previously occupied lands, Neo-Assyrian policy entailed the colonization of new lands between preexisting settlements (Wilkinson 1995: 146–147), marginal land virtually within the desert (Bernbeck 1993), as well as riverine landscapes in the Khabur (Morandi 1996a) and on the Tigris (Parker 2001). The scale of this settlement was such that no single process can suffice to explain it.

That the Neo-Assyrian kings were active in resettlement of the steppe is evident from texts that boast of their achievements in reclaiming the desert (Oded 1979). One particular statement by Sargon of Assyria enunciates this policy of landscape transformation with crystal clarity:

> The well versed king, who constantly considers plans of good things and who directs his attention to the settlement of desolate steppe, to the cultivation of fallow land and to the plantation of fruit groves, contemplated causing steep rocks, from which never before green had sprouted, to produce yield. He had in mind to let furrows arise in waste barren land which had not known the plough under the previous kings, to let the work song resound, to open a spring as a *karattu* in an area without well and have (everything) irrigated in abundance from top to bottom (with) water, like with the masses of the flood (of a river in spring). (Radner 2000: 238 citing Fuchs 1994: 37 and 292)

In such resettlement schemes, entire communities appear to have

been taken from their homes (e.g., in Palestine) and resettled in the Syrian or Iraqi steppe, often in underpopulated areas (Oded 1979: 71). Such policies, which raised both agricultural production and imperial revenues, are attested on the stelae of Adad Nirari III from Tell Rimah (Page 1968), which may explain the large increase of settlement in the neighboring Afar-Sinjar plains. On the other hand, dispersed settlement patterns elsewhere may be accounted for by more spontaneous processes. It is well attested from textual studies that during the second and early first millennium B.C., marginal steppe-lands and the desert were populated by pastoral nomadic Ahlamu and Aramaeans. The spontaneous settlement of members of these groups may account for some areas of rural settlement. Nevertheless, whether state directed or spontaneous, it seems likely that conditions of political stability in Upper Mesopotamia during much of the first millennium B.C. provided conditions favorable to the creation of small rural settlements dispersed across what had been steppe.

Support for the archaeological

record is provided by the "Harran census" (Johns 1901), which gives a remarkable record of settlement and land use for a region under Neo-Assyrian administration. These records derive from the central archives of Nineveh but actually relate to the land of the Harran region in the upper valley of the Balikh (Fales and Postgate 1995: xxxi). Typically, the tablets list the family members of the farmstead or holding as well as the real estate itself, giving the quantity of cereal land (expressed as yield in *homers*), vineyards (as shoots of vines), orchards, gardens, the number of animals (sheep, goat, oxen), and the geographical location in relation to the steppe, to neighboring places, or to provinces. Altogether, the census lists provide a remarkably specific view of the Neo-Assyrian landscape of parts of upper Mesopotamia that confirm that the small village, hamlet, or farmstead was a common form of settlement in the upper Balikh valley. Vineyards are mentioned only in some of the listings, which may indicate that those that do not mention vineyards may be south of the zone of cultivation of the vine. Also, some lists note the amount of poplars and willows, trees that traditionally tend to be associated with ditches or watercourses.

Other landscape features are less well documented for this period than for the third millennium B.C. For example, the only evidence for increased intensity of cultivation is a secondary peak of Iron Age pottery within field scatters in the Iraqi North Jazira area (Wilkinson and Tucker 1995: fig. 51e). Linear hollows rarely form radial patterns around Iron Age sites, but in the North Jazira, several Iron Age ("Late Assyrian") sites are located on longer interregional linear hollows (Wilkinson and Tucker 1995: fig. 41). Further west in the Syrian Balikh valley, a north–south linear hollow and associated Iron Age sites coincide with a postulated Assyrian route referred to in the annals of Ashurnasirpal II (883–859 B.C.). This provides useful archaeological corroboration for the operation of long-distance routes during the Neo-Assyrian period (Wilkinson 1995).

Within the Neo-Assyrian settlement zone between the Tigris and Euphrates there was little Iron Age settlement actually on tells. This may be because Neo-Assyrian policy specifically forbad the inhabitants from living on the higher mounds (Fales 1990: 111), perhaps for the reason that tell summits, being defensible and potentially fortified locations, were regarded as positions of power. On the other hand, west of the Euphrates, in an area that also experienced increased settlement during the first millennium B.C., settlement was frequently on previously occupied tells (Sader 2000: 68), although small dispersed sites also exist. That there was continued settlement on tells during the early first millennium B.C. is well illustrated for the Amuq on the Balawat gates (Shalmaneser III mid ninth century B.C.), which show Unkians bearing tribute from a moated fortified settlement in the land of Unqi. The land of Unqi most likely equates to the Amuq (or perhaps the Ghab to the south), and it is even possible to select a possible candidate for the illustrated settlement, namely, the moated tell of Yer Köy (AS 99) located within the central Amuq (Wilkinson 1997b: fig. 2).

The presence of Iron Age occupation on tells in the outer provinces implies, therefore, that local communities were allowed to occupy such positions of power, perhaps because there was some degree of local autonomy in the provinces. This contrasts with the "home provinces" comprising the Jazira and the core area east of the Tigris, which were under the direct rule of the Assyrian capital cities near Mosul (Postgate 1992b).

In many parts of northern Syria and Iraq the overall structure of the pattern of settlement and the surrounding landscape appear to have changed relatively little between the Iron Age and the present day.

There were, however, many changes in settlement locations, and so the settlement pattern shows localized instability with cycles of growth and collapse. Moreover, in marginal areas or near to favorable watercourses, irrigation systems were dug to improve agricultural productivity (Geyer 1990; Ergenzinger and Kühne 1991). Extensive areas of Upper Mesopotamia continued to be a landscape of villages and small towns well into the Partho-Sasanian period (Hauser 1999). In contrast to the period of Bronze Age "city-states," major seats of administration were either widely distributed or even located outside the area.

Settlement Dispersal in the Levant, ca. 1200 B.C. and Later

In the Levant, post–Bronze Age settlement underwent changes not unlike those found in Upper Mesopotamia. However, the historical context is usually expounded through the prism of Biblical archaeology, which gives the narrative a political emphasis that is today the subject of some debate. Illustrative of the Biblical perspective is the situation described by Oded Borowski (1987: 15), namely, that when the Israelites arrived in Canaan around the end of the Late Bronze Age, they found the fertile soils in the valleys to be controlled by strong Canaanite cities. Realizing that they could not overpower the city-states, the Israelites started colonizing previously unsettled lands. Such resettlement resulted in the cutting down of forests, well illustrated in Joshua 17: 14–18, which states that people of the house of Joseph were told by Joshua to "go up to the forest, and clear there ground for yourselves. . . . The hill country shall be yours, for though it is a forest, you shall clear it and possess it to its farthest borders" (Stager 1975: 238; Borowski 1987: 15).

Archaeologically this provides a compelling case for both deforestation and settlement in the hill country as well as implying that such deforestation would have resulted in the erosion of any soil cover. Archaeological surveys provide a more prosaic reading of the changes in settlement, but one that parallels the above statement. There is, though, one difference, namely, that the pattern of settlement that is described as the "Israelite settlement" is in fact part of a much broader phenomenon that can be traced throughout much of the Fertile Crescent.

Following the marked settlement nucleation of Early Bronze I–III and Middle Bronze II, there was a significant decline or settlement transition in the Late Bronze Age, which also paralleled those further north in Upper Mesopotamia. According to Broshi and Finkelstein (1992), whereas during Early Bronze II–III about 63 percent of the population lived in settlements greater than 5 ha, in Middle Bronze II this figure amounted to 49 percent, and in Iron II this percentage had declined to only 34 percent. On the one hand, these data indicate the intensity of the urbanization process during the Early Bronze Age, while on the other, they suggest that the Iron Age II settlement pattern reflects a period that opened the way for the foundation of many small and undefended settlements (fig. 7.4). That settlement dispersal was also matched by settlement extension is illustrated by a rise in the proportion of the total population of Palestine that resided in the hill country to the west of the Jordan River. This percentage increased from 35 percent during Early Bronze II–III, to 40 percent in Middle Bronze II, and to 52.5 percent in Iron Age II. Similar trends have been observed in the Akko region, where Frankel (1994) and Lehmann (2001) have demonstrated that whereas in the Late Bronze Age, settlements were predominantly in the plains or fringing outcrops, by Iron I a significant number of settlements had grown up in the hills and mountains. The foregoing statistics may underrepresent the degree of Bronze Age settlement,

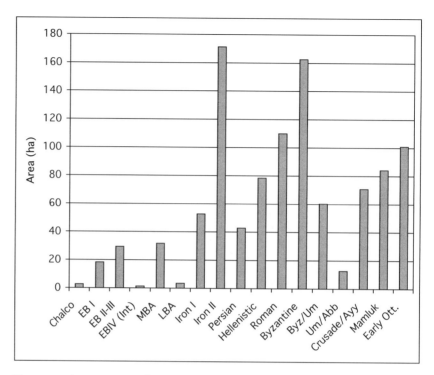

Fig. 7.4 Aggregate settlement area in southern Samaria (from Lev-Yadun 1997: table 5.1).

because recent surveys indicate that the highlands of Canaan were not as empty in the Bronze Age as was formerly believed. Nevertheless, as in Upper Mesopotamia, a substantial phase of settlement was clearly underway during the earlier part of the Iron Age, and this can be seen to have continued and even gained momentum through to the Byzantine period. In fact, such was the scale of this phase of settlement that the Southern Samaria Survey implies several waves of population growth from an estimated 700 people in the Late Bronze Age, 10,500 in Iron I, 34,250 in Iron II, and 32,500 in the Byzantine period (Lev-Yadun 1997: 91; Levy and Holl 2002: 98).

This process of settlement dispersal occurred over a wide area of the Fertile Crescent and appears to represent an actual extension of the frontier of settlement into areas that had not previously been inhabited by sedentary communities. Although it is feasible that similar mechanisms underlie the spread of settlement in various parts of this large region, there are clearly also specific local mechanisms that account for this phase of settlement. Rather than becoming embroiled in a detailed discussion of the various factors that contributed to the dispersal of settlement during the first millennium B.C. and later, using the southern Levant as a case study, emphasis here will be upon examining the resultant landscape and key processes that made it so distinctive.

According to Finkelstein (1998: 364), three technological factors have regularly been cited as being crucial to the development of Iron Age settlement in the uplands west of the River Jordan. These are

— The development of terraced agriculture.
— The availability of technology for making lime-plastered cisterns.
— The invention of iron tools for digging cisterns and clearing woodland.

In addition, a number of sociopolitical models have been suggested for the emergence of the Israelite state (for discussion, see Finkelstein

1998: 363; Bloch-Smith and Nakhai 1999; Levy and Holl 2002).

— According to William F. Albright, this took the form of a military conquest of the Canaanite city-states by nomadic Israelites.
— On the other hand, Albrecht Alt considered there to have been a peaceful infiltration of migratory nomadic groups from the steppe, perhaps by the *shasu* (nomads) of the deserts between Egypt and Canaan.
— Finally, George Mendenhall saw this phase of settlement as resulting from a social revolution against a stratified old order, which resulted in a sector of the population fleeing to the uplands west of the Jordan.
— Related models assume various degrees of settlement of nomadic groups as well as symbiosis between seminomadic tribes and the town-dwelling Canaanite population (see Bloch-Smith and Nakhai 1999: 66–70). These models must be supplemented by evidence indicating that economic circumstances were changing in the eastern Mediterranean during the late second and early first millennia, with the result that there was a shift toward a more commercialized production of olive and vines that were ideally suited to the Levantine uplands.

These models for the emergence of the Iron Age pattern of dispersed settlement are tailored specifically for the uplands west of the Jordan. Elsewhere in the Levant, different factors may apply. For example, the dispersal of small settlements into the hills east of Akko that took place between the Late Bronze Age and Iron Age I may, according to Lehmann (2001: 94), relate to the increased wealth generated by the Phoenician city of Tyre. By encouraging the production of cash products such as wine and olives, this

economy would have opened the door for a new wave of colonization into the neighboring hills.

Most of the elements of the cultural landscape present in the Roman-Byzantine landscape can already be recognized in the Iron Age. These include rural roads and tracks, terraced fields, other indicators of cultivation, field towers, wine and olive presses, agricultural buildings, and cisterns. In marginal areas such as the Negev highlands, it is even possible to recognize probable threshing floors that date back to the fourth millennium B.C. (Avner 1998: 164). Detailed surveys undertaken over the past two decades or more (Dar 1986, 1999; Gibson et al. 1985, 1991, 1999) have enabled these disparate elements to be assembled into what may be described as a "Roman landscape mosaic." Although antecedent features extending back to the Iron Age or earlier have been recognized, these seem sporadic, and it appears that the Roman-Byzantine periods may have obscured and/or locally displaced those of the earlier Iron Age.

Landscape Features

Terraced Fields. Terraced fields form an integral feature of the highland landscape, and in parts of the hill country some 50–60 percent of the land is covered by terraced fields (Ron 1966). It would be misleading, however, to assume the development of field terracing was an essential precondition for settlement in the hill country. Overall there are relatively few absolute dates for terraced fields, and many Israelite settlements were located in areas where terracing was not essential for cultivation to take place. Therefore, terracing should not be postulated as a prerequisite for settlement. Moreover, terracing, rather than being an Iron I innovation, was developed earlier in the Early Bronze Age (Gibson et al. 1991), Middle Bronze II (Finkelstein 1988: 309), or most prominently in Iron Age II (Hopkins 1985: 185, 266).

It seems clear therefore that although terraced agriculture is an important feature in the development of the Levantine landscape, it was not crucial to the spread of this wave of Iron Age settlement (Gibson 2001).

As in other parts of the world, terraced fields are difficult to date directly. In the uplands of the southern Levant, wall morphology suggests that Iron Age terrace walls were usually of large triangular stones, infilled with smaller stones between. Later Roman/Byzantine terraces, in contrast, were of smaller rectangular stones laid in rows (Edelstein and Gibson 1982: 52–53). Otherwise, dating evidence for the development of terraced fields is meager and ranges from the Early Bronze to the Roman/Byzantine period (Gibson 2001; Dar 1999: 118), but based on the recent evidence from Yemen (chapter 9), an earlier inception is possible. Hopkins' review of the subject of terraced agriculture in the uplands of the southern Levant shows that there is little evidence for the introduction of terraced farming during Iron I, that is, at a time when terracing might be expected to have been a causative factor behind the extension of settlement. Instead, a significant amount of terracing seems to have appeared by the eighth century B.C., that is, in Iron II (Hopkins 1985: 185, 266).

Field terraces in Palestine frequently take advantage of the natural form of the underlying bedrock, particularly in those areas where Cretaceous limestone and dolomite rocks are configured in the form of natural steps. In such cases, the terrain provides a natural foundation for terraces. With the exception of terraced systems that were constructed in conjunction with small-scale irrigation systems, most Levantine terraced fields receive their moisture from rainfall. In the southern Levant, where cut sections have revealed the original techniques of terrace construction, field benches often appear to have been artificially constructed, first by the addition of a layer of gravel, followed by soil, and then with more stones and gravel, with an upper level of more humic soil laid over the top (Edelstein and Gibson 1982: 53; Edelstein and Kislev 1981: 54). The presence of a fill of gravel behind the terrace wall resembles the use of a similar technique in Yemen (see chapter 9). The introduction of soil from elsewhere implies that there was insufficient soil on the hillsides before terrace construction (perhaps because of prior erosion), thereby necessitating the importation of soil from the vicinity. In addition, Edelstein and Kislev (1981: 55) suggested that where entire hillsides appear to have been terraced in one fell swoop, levels of organization larger than the family would have been necessary.

Along the same lines, Hopkins suggests (1985: 269): "The building of terrace systems, construction of storage facilities, and the installation of irrigation works all demand supra household planning as well as greater quantities of labor than can be supplied ordinarily by even the most viable family." Although such large-scale landscape works is often taken to imply the hand of a centralized authority or state, Hopkins' alternative suggestion is that the criss-crossed social relations of small-scale communities were frequently called into play during terrace construction. Presumably, such relations would have provided the requisite labor for these large programs of public works.

Such planning and construction of terraces over large blocks of land contrasts with fields in the Yemen highlands, where the soil fill of terraced fields appears to have been built up by accretion and where both construction and maintenance of individual fields was probably effected by individual households, except in the case of special terraces belonging to Himyarite "estates" (chapter 9).

Other Landscape Features. In the rain-fed parts of the southern Le-

vant there are few signs of coherent relict landscapes until the Iron Age. In the uplands west of the Jordan, rural roads and tracks, like their counterparts in Yemen, consist of parallel lines of stones usually 3–4 m wide, which fringe a "road surface" frequently worn or excavated down to the local bedrock (Dar 1986: 251). Although these features cannot be dated by stratified artifact assemblages, associated surface ceramics suggests that they were in use back to the Iron Age (Dar 1986). Other early features of the rural landscape include individual houses dating to the sixth–eighth centuries B.C. (Gibson and Edelstein 1985: 143), wine presses dating to the Early and Middle Bronze Ages (Gibson and Edelstein 1985: 149) and Iron Age II on the Samarian uplands (Dar 1986; see also Frankel 1999: 164), oil presses as early as Chalcolithic (Frankel 1999: 51), and stone quarries from the Late Iron Age (Gibson and Edelstein 1985: 151–153).

Although intrinsically interesting and important for studies of the development of agricultural technologies, these features rarely form a coherent landscape. It is therefore the desertic landscapes to the south, in the Negev and Sinai, or to the east, in Jordan, that are more likely to supply evidence for a continuous landscape (chapter 8).

The complex palimpsests of agricultural and settlement activity in the Wadi Faynan, Jordan, provide a classic example of a multiphased landscape. Phases include a classical/Nabataean period system of some thirty fields demarcated by walls that are associated with dense scatters of Bronze Age pottery suggestive of earlier activity (fig. 7.5; Barker et al. 1999: 268–269; Barker et al. 2000: 31). Later surveys and excavations demonstrated that a Bronze Age landscape consisting of walls of large boulders extended over an area of some 500 × 300 m. Moreover, Bronze Age rectilinear buildings were also incorporated

into later field walls, and in certain cases, the component boulders were scored by vertical lines resulting from ploughing. Such plough marks suggest that a soil had been present over the scarred stones and that subsequently around 20 cm of soil had been lost by wind erosion (Barker et al. 1999: 269). That such occurrences are not unique is suggested from similar examples in the Homs area, where Roman fields show similar scars and evidence for deflation (Graham Philip personal communication Sept. 2000). Such deflation, by removing the soil matrix, has probably concentrated the pottery scatters, which might account for their very high density (Barker et al. 2000: 31). The Wadi Faynan pottery scatters appear to result from the ploughing of artifact-bearing midden deposits of a large Bronze Age site in combination with manuring during the Roman/Byzantine period. In the Wadi Faynan, although it is not always possible to make a clear distinction between agricultural landscapes and the habitation areas themselves, what is clear is that an early (that is, Bronze Age) landscape was present, and it was then altered progressively to be incorporated into the later fieldscape of the classical/Nabataean period.

In yet more arid areas such as the 'Uvda valley of the southern Negev (mean annual rainfall around 28 mm), long-relict embankments thought to date back to Chalcolithic times provide "unequivocal evidence for the existence of agricultural flood water engineering and soil improvement during the Chalcolithic period" (Avner 1998: 170–173). The presence of Chalcolithic adzes support this early date for flood-water farming, and overall, such evidence attests the importance of seeking early landscapes not in the core areas of the moister rain-fed cultivated zones but in arid areas where chance survival within taphonomic windows can provide optimal conditions for preservation. Nevertheless, in the Levant land was also increased (Kingsley 2001: 44). The proliferation of rural settlements, wine and olive presses, and other installations all testify to the prosperity of this period. This landscape was clearly developed in the context of a flourishing economy, which encompassed both local commerce with Levantine cities as well as a Mediterranean-wide demand for wine and olive oil.

Despite the Levant under Roman rule providing us with some of the best evidence for ancient agrarian landscapes in the Near East, it is essential to grasp that this record is conspicuous only where subsequent human activity has been limited, thereby allowing for the preservation of landscape features. In some cases, such "taphonomic windows" were conspicuously colonized only during Graeco-Roman times. As a result, surveys that concentrate on uplands fringing the Mediterranean within Turkey and northwest Syria frequently yield little more than Graeco Roman/Byzantine settlement (Casana in press; Blanton 2000: 57). On the other hand, where settlement occurred on lowlands or on deep soil-covered riverine terraces, buildings would have been of mudbrick and would remain as small, low mounds. Moreover, subsequent settlement or agriculture would have caused earlier buildings to be disturbed, thereby diminishing their trace. In such lowlands, the evidence for the late phase of settlement is more muted than on the hills or within the desert margins. As Warwick Ball has noted, this landscape of rural communities must originally have been much more extensive than is evident today (Ball 2000: 243–245).

This expansion of settlement appears not only to have partly obscured or replaced traces of Iron Age landscapes but also to have resulted in a more durable landscape imprint. In part, this is because many regions have experienced little subsequent occupational activity that would have erased the Roman-

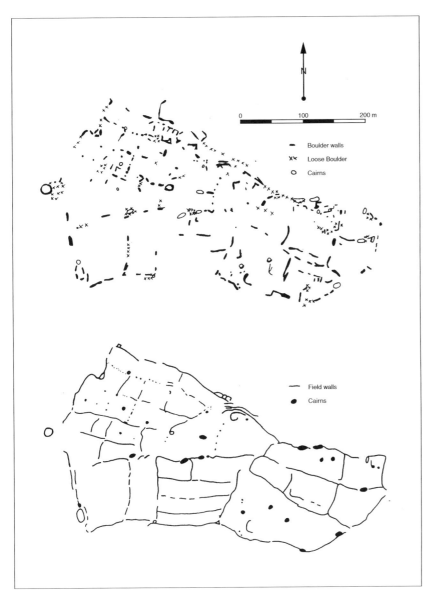

Fig. 7.5   Fields in the Wadi Faynan, Jordan, from the Early Bronze Age and Classical periods (from Barker et al. 1999: fig. 10, with permission).

it is the Roman/Nabataean period that provides us with the most impressive remains of landscapes in their entirety.

Roman/Nabataean Landscapes

Archaeological surveys and aerial photo interpretations of the uplands and desert fringes of the Levant provide tantalizing glimpses of Nabataean, Roman, Byzantine, and Islamic landscapes (Tchalenko 1953; Tate 1992; Kennedy 1982; Barker et al. 1999; Dar 1986, 1999). Following the surge of Iron Age settlement, many rural areas of the Levant attained a peak in settlement during the Roman-Byzantine period that was of greater magnitude than any that had gone before (Safrai 1994; Graf 2001). Overall, during the Byzantine period in Palestine, hundreds of new towns and villages were established. The landscapes in between were further transformed: swamps were drained and replaced by cultivation, new water-diversion structures were introduced, and it appears that the amount of terraced

Byzantine landscapes. It would be wrong, however, to characterize settlement trends as being synchronous over the entire region. In parts of the uplands west of the Jordan, settlement apparently declined just before the Islamic era. In the Massif Calcaire of northwest Syria, settlements such as Dehes continued to be occupied into the ninth century A.D. (Sodini et al. 1980), whereas in the Homs area, a second phase of dispersed rural settlements occurred between the eleventh and fourteenth centuries A.D. (Philip et al. 2002b: 19 and 20). Similarly, in the Biqaʿ valley of Lebanon, Marfoe recognized a complex pattern of Hellenistic, Roman, Byzantine, and Islamic settlement, which resulted in a widespread encroachment into the adjacent uplands that had formerly been sparsely settled (Marfoe 1978: 620–692). Such was this encroachment that mountain forests were denuded up to altitudes of 1,500 to 2,000 m, the Roman limits being recognized by a series of boundary markers erected during the reign of Hadrian (A.D. 117–137). These defined the protected imperial domains of the main tree species: cedar, fir, pine, and perhaps cypress (Marfoe 1978: 663; Mikesell 1969).

Despite the temptation to relate cycles of settlement growth and decline to shifts in climate (Netser 1998), sociohistoric events such as disturbed conditions relating to the Jewish revolts of A.D. 66 and 132 (Anderson 1998), or local variations in economic conditions, taxation and changes in demand for products, are as important or more important (Marfoe 1978; Rosen 2000). Such cultural factors may therefore have frequently overridden declines in agricultural production that were related to moisture stress caused by climatic variations. The following examples serve to illustrate the important role that landscape archaeology can play in the reconstruction of the early agricultural economy.

In the Cretaceous limestone uplands to the west of the River Jordan,

Shimon Dar and co-workers have reconstructed the rural landscape over an area that includes numerous windows of landscape preservation within which the fossilized remains of almost complete village territories can be discerned (Dar 1986). Many sites in these uplands bear a striking resemblance to those in the Yemen highlands (chapter 8): within settlements, walls of individual buildings occur in a matrix of later fields or terraces, and it is evident that the more recent agricultural areas often threaten to engulf the remaining archaeological sites (e.g., Finkelstein and Lederman 1997: 198, 551). A significant part of the semiarid uplands of the southern Levant are covered by soils of *terra rossa* and locally *rendzina* type, but much of this topsoil has been lost presumably as a result of prolonged erosion.

The region receives a mean annual rainfall in the range 500–800 mm (Horowitz 1979: 22–23). This was sufficient for the original natural vegetation of oak woodland, which has now has been degraded to an often dense open scrub (*maquis*) or an open, low, thorny scrub (*garigue* or *garriga*; for discussion, see Lev-Yadun in Finkelstein and Lederman 1997; also Roberts 1998: 187). According to the historian Josephus, writing in the first century A.D., these uplands formed a fertile and populous region, that although possessing "thirsty" soil and relatively few springs, was blessed with running streams, extensive pastures, and numerous trees, both fruit bearing and wild (cited in Dar 1986: 248).

The Hellenistic, Roman, and Byzantine settlement landscape of the Levant ranged from occasional towns capable of housing some fifteen hundred to two thousand people (Dar 1986: 248) to a large number of smaller villages and farmsteads in the countryside between. In addition, textual sources indicate the presence of rural markets, villas, churches, shrines, temples, and industrial settlements (Graf 2001). Grossman and Safrai described the

central villages as "mother" communities, with the smaller settlements being "daughter settlements that grew as secondary offshoots from them (Grossman and Safrai 1980). Satellite "daughter" settlements were frequently situated near the inferred territorial boundary. In Late Byzantine times, these communities can be seen to have been linked to the mother settlement for the payment of taxes (Brand 1969, cited in Safrai 1994: 70, 74). In the clearest examples, such as those around the sites of Kufr Thulth and Azun (fig. 7.6), a central "mother" settlement can be seen to have been surrounded by a territory of some 3–4 km radius within which occur about 5–6 satellite settlements (*kharaba*). This compares with modular village territories of traditional Palestinian communities in the region, with territories that range from 7.5–25 sq. km, in other words, equivalent to radii of 1.5 to 2.9 km (Finkelstein, in Finkelstein and Lederman 1997: 126). Some Roman/Byzantine territorial modules exhibit a series of routes that radiate from the central settlement (fig. 7.6). Stone-fenced tracks have been cut away in areas of rough ground, and occasionally grooves have been worn as a result of the passage of carts or wagons (chapter 4). The road network falls into two groups: those that linked the main village-sized sites, and a second group of local tracks that provided access to the fields themselves or to the satellite communities. These local routes either disappear after a distance of less than 3–4 km or terminate at a point inferred to be the former territorial boundary of the village (fig. 7.6). If routes continued into the territory of the next village, this point is marked by a distinct change in direction (Grossman and Safrai 1980: 449–450; Dar 1986: 134–135).

This configuration of radial routes with their bifurcations and fade-out points resembles rural routes in Roman/Byzantine Syria (Tate 1992: figs. 262–264) and Iron Age Himyar-

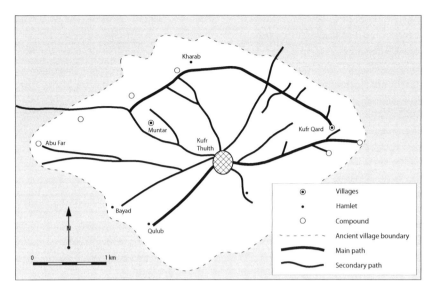

Fig. 7.6 Radial tracks around the Roman-Byzantine site of Kufr Thulth in the Samarian uplands (from Grossman and Safrai 1980: fig. 3; drawn by Peggy Sanders).

ite Yemen as well as the radial hollow ways of the Bronze Age Jazira (chapter 6). In the uplands west of the Jordan, the fade-out zone of the local tracks has been employed to infer not only that a territorial boundary was present but also that the local roads were all under one authority, presumably one that was vested in the central village (Dar 1986: 135). Alternatively, and by analogy with traditional usage in Yemen, such route systems may be inferred to have evolved organically to service the needs of the village in general. They may not have been conceived of as a single planned entity.

In the hill country of Palestine, each territorial/settlement module provided a wealth of landscape features. These included numerous small (ca. 3–5 m square) field towers, thought to have been used for wine production and storage or alternatively for watching over fields, orchards, and vineyards. Of the twelve hundred recorded towers, the earliest dated to the Iron Age, but most were in use during the Hellenistic and Early Roman occupations (Dar 1986: 248). In addition, settlements ranging from houses, rural farmsteads, or hamlets to small towns remain to form small

ruinfields or *khirbets*. In general in the southern Levant, agricultural production is evident in the form of hundreds of rock-cut wine and olive presses that ranged from small presses associated with households to larger presses that probably handled the production of the multiple tenants of larger estates (Dar 1986: 251; Frankel 1999). Threshing floors, unlike their paved counterparts in Yemen, were mainly rock cut or rock floored; they ranged in diameter from 8 to 20 m, were fenced (Dar 1986: 191), and located where consistent breezes could be of use during winnowing of the crop. Rather than being located near to the best soils, threshing floors were in the vicinity of those of second and third quality located a little further away from the main settlement (Dar 1986: 19). This implies that cereals were grown beyond an inner zone of cultivation, which was probably devoted to olive orchards. Analogous land-use configurations have also been observed around traditional villages in the region (Finkelstein in Finkelstein and Lederman 1997: fig. 7.4).

Although the surveys of the uplands west of the Jordan provide no published record of off-site artifact scatters, at Sumaqa in the Mount

Carmel area, pottery from trenches excavated within terraced fields yielded ceramics ranging in date from the late third to sixth centuries A.D. Shimon Dar interprets these scatters as resulting from manuring, with waste material being brought from the neighboring settlements (Dar 1999: 122, 124). This suggests not only that agriculture was intensive but also that the removal of potential wood for fuel from the surroundings had necessitated that the inhabitants use dung as a substitute fuel (chapter 6).

In addition to rain-fed cultivation, local irrigation systems comprised spring catchment areas, water-conveyance channels, and terraced fields. In such locations where irrigation systems had been constructed as a single module, Ron inferred that levels of labor organization were larger than the household (Ron 1966: 111–113). Additional water-gathering techniques included check dams for enhancing soil moisture as well as reservoirs (Dar 1999: 125).

Overall, the agricultural economy consisted of four main sectors of production, namely, viticulture and wine production, olive growing and oil extraction, cultivation of cereals, and the husbandry of sheep and goats (Dar 1986: 253). It is assumed that there was pasture in every village and that flocks were mainly confined to the territory of individual villages. The huge quantity of remains of wine and olive production led Dar to conclude that the southern Levant produced a surplus of wine and oil for export (Dar 1986: 253). This increasingly commercialized economy appears to have attained its peak between the fourth and seventh centuries A.D., as is suggested by the recognition of 899 Byzantine wine presses (Kingsley 2001: 49). By this time, a vigorous system of wine and olive oil production formed part of a Mediterranean-wide system of distribution of Palestinian amphorae (Kingsley 2001: fig. 3.4).

More dramatic in their architectural traces are the deserted villages of the limestone hills of the Massif Calcaire, to the north and west of Aleppo in Syria. According to Tchalenko (1953; also Callot 1986), the Roman/Byzantine villages of northwest Syria were involved in the large-scale commercial production of olive oil, the demand for which, from both urban centers and the networks of East Mediterranean trade, was prodigious (Mattingly 1996: 224). Nevertheless, as Georges Tate has pointed out for the same region, although the raising of olives was important, the economy was indeed a mixed one and must have included viticulture; the growing of wheat, legumes, and vegetables; and the raising of sheep and cattle (Tate 1992: 191–271; Tate 1997; Foss 1997). The works of both Tate (1992) and Tchalenko (1953) provide an intimate view of a congested upland landscape, in this case, occupied by some seven hundred towns and villages that formed a dense network, despite the apparently low agricultural potential of the thin and stony soils. The population appears to have grown explosively over some five hundred to six hundred years, starting in the first century A.D. but with a decline in the third century, followed by further growth until around the sixth century A.D., after which population stabilized and then declined (Tate 1992: 335–342). Like their equivalents in Palestine, these upland communities are fossilized within their own agricultural landscapes, thereby providing a classic example of a landscape of preservation.

Villages, with their individual buildings preserved up to roof level, were usually some 3–5 km apart. Territorial boundaries were indicated by boundary markers or boundaries of stones cleared from the fields. These enabled territorial areas to be estimated from 3–10 sq. km or slightly less.

The agricultural economy of the Massif Calcaire compares well with similar local variations in production that are evident in the traditional economy of Palestine. According to records of the British Mandate, not only was there considerable variation from region to region but surpluses and deficits of production could also have been satisfied by trade or exchange at a local level (Finkelstein and Lederman 1997: 118). A fundamental point that emerges from the work of Tate in Syria is that this tremendous growth in settlement was probably partially dependent upon the presence of urban centers such as Apamea and Antioch, which provided a major market for the products of the Massif Calcaire. This pattern emphasizes the degree of interdependence that existed between the urban and rural sectors of the Levantine landscape (Foss 1995: 221).

That there was a truly widespread (albeit locally variable) expansion of settlement during Roman/Byzantine times is evident from surveys in the Biqaʿ Valley, Lebanon (Marfoe 1978; 1979), the Hauran to the southeast of Damascus (Gentelle 1985; Villeneuve 1985; Foss 1995: 220; Braemer et al. 1996), the Amuq Plain (Yener et al. 2000), the Jabbul Plain (Schwartz et al. 2000), and southeastern Turkey along the Euphrates near the site of Kurban Höyük. In the last area, where building and landscape features were less well preserved than in the uplands of northwest Syria, similar settlement land-use modules could be reconstructed, albeit from the more prosaic remains of low khirbet-type mounds, off-site sherd scatters, occasional linear hollows, and a single Roman milestone (Wilkinson 1990a: 118–119). Late Roman and Early Byzantine settlement expansion is evident in the form of two tiers of small sites on river terraces overlooking the Euphrates. This left a third upper tier of land free for pasture, the evidence for which consisted of a well-preserved, small, pastoral enclosure together with Late Roman/Early Byzantine artifacts situated in an area of rocky, upland steppe. The Kurban Höyük

survey suggests that settlement and population again attained its peak during the Late Roman-Early Byzantine period (Wilkinson 1990a: fig. 6.2). However, that there was no consistent trend in such settlement dispersal is evident to the south in the Balikh Valley in Syria, where Bartl recorded a pronounced peak in dispersed khirbet-type settlement during Early Islamic times (Bartl 1996).

The foregoing discussion suggests that within the frontier of Roman rule as well as within the client states that formed a buffer zone along the frontier, there was a significant increase in settlement and agriculture. In marginal areas that were abandoned during the Early or Middle Islamic periods, one can witness (or could until recently) extensive spreads of these earlier landscapes. To what degree the Roman landscape was formally parceled into a cadastral system or *centuriation* is less clear. Clearly, the recognition of major phases of field parcellation is crucial for the study of the landscapes of the Near East because the imposition of a single cadastral system over a large area can provide a distinct datum against which both earlier and later landscapes can be measured. Centuriation, which consists of a grid of land divisions made in Roman units of land measurement, was usually imposed around settlements that were given the status of *colonia*. Large-scale systems of orthogonal field networks defined by individual walls up to several kilometers in length (*cadasters*) have been recognized by Tchalenko and Tate in northwest Syria (e.g., Tate 1997: 60–61). Although the history and function of these is debated, they appear to have been laid out as single entities, perhaps to provide land for resettled veterans. In which case, as Tate has suggested this implies large-scale expropriation of the local peasantry. Although such systems have been recognized elsewhere around the Mediterranean (Bradford 1957: figs. 42, 43), in the

Near East it is thought they are less likely to occur because the landscape was already parceled out prior to the imposition of Roman rule (Bradford 1957: 146). Nevertheless, possible centuriated landscapes have been recognized around Damascus (Dodinet et al. 1990), in southern and northern Syria (Wirth 1971: 375, 412), and in the area of Homs (ancient Emesa: Van Liere 1958/1959).

The Desert Margins

The desert margins of the Levant comprise three main zones: the *Bādiya*, a zone of dry steppe forming a southward arc from the great bend of the Euphrates in Syria; the stony steppe and desert of the *hamad* to the south, which in turn merges into the basalt lava fields of the *harra* that form the hills and low plateaus in southern Syria and northern Jordan (Gawlikowski 1997: 37–39; Betts 1998). Further south extend the desert margins of the Negev (Israel) and the Sinai (Egypt), together with the Jordanian desert, which merges southward into the deserts of Saudi Arabia (chapter 8). A complex *limes* frontier system defines the outer limits of the settled zone (Parker 1986; Kennedy and Riley 1990), and within this, various local communities were incorporated. As Warwick Ball has pointed out, these communities, rather than being truly Graeco-Roman, were part of a long tradition of locally administered villages belonging to the Semitic East (Ball 2000: 243).

Although survey and landscape studies have mainly concentrated upon the patterning of settlement and the landscape features themselves, Banning's analysis of settlement within the area of the Wadi al-Hasa suggests that areas within the Pax Romana, rather than being of uniform ethnicity or reflecting settlement groups that were in hostile confrontation with one another, may instead reflect a state of "mutualism" between various social groups. Thus a dense pattern of sedentary villages, hamlets with water mills, and farms was interspersed by smaller settlements that probably represent camps of mobile groups or agro-pastoralists. The distribution and proximity of sedentary settlements to camps suggest that the sedentary and mobile communities may have exploited only the resources required for their own needs. As a result, both communities were able to coexist in a form of symbiotic relationship (Banning 1986: 45). Although this study relates only to one particular area, it demonstrated that the landscape evidence can also shed light on the context of social relationships (if not on the relationships themselves).

If data from the various surveys are comparable and are not due to differences in the recognition of diagnostic ceramics or the delimitation of the sites themselves, settlement trends can be seen to vary from place to place. For example, following the well-attested Early Bronze II–III phase of settlement growth and nucleation, there was a marked decline during the Late Bronze Age in the hill country in general (Lev-Yadun 1997: table 5.1; Finkelstein 1998: fig. 2) as well as in Jordan in the Hesban (Ibach 1987), Wadi Hasa (Clark et al. 1998: 168), and southern Ghors (MacDonald 1992: 7) survey areas. A Late Bronze Age trough is not evident on the Kerak plateau, however, where the number of Late Bronze Age settlements (>100) is almost double that of the Early Bronze II–III (Miller 1991).

Such disparities suggest that although there was clearly a diminution of settlement and population in the Late Bronze Age, in certain areas there was population growth at the expense of other areas. Overall, the southern Levant appears to have experienced major cycles of landscape growth or abandonment, with the Hesban, Kerak, Wadi al-Hasa, and Southern Ghors survey areas to the east of the River Jordan (within the ancient kingdoms of Ammon, Moab, and Edom) all showing growth of settlement in the Iron Age II. That this growth extended into different terrain is illustrated by the Hesban area, where there was a general expansion of settlement. This was away from the lower, flatter terrain favored during the Early Bronze Age onto neighboring plateau areas in and after the Middle Bronze Age (Ibach 1987: 199–200).

Despite the differences between the four survey areas (for example, Nabataean is numerically represented by a massive phase of settlement in the Kerak area, but is not present as a cultural phase at Hesban), it is clear that between the first century B.C. and seventh centuries A.D. these areas were heavily populated. Moreover, in the southern Ghors and Hesban areas, settlement numerically attained its maximum during the Byzantine period.

Turning to the land between the settlements, some of the most dramatic remains of agrarian landscapes persisted until recently in the Hauran of southern Syria and northern Jordan. In this volcanic terrain, landscape studies utilizing a combination of air-photo analysis and ground-based survey demonstrate that extensive settlement and agricultural remains were in existence until the recent reexpansion of settlement threatened such landscapes with destruction. Fortunately the existence of air-photographic archives[1] has preserved a record of these dramatic landscapes as they appeared in the early and mid twentieth century A.D. Prior to the final phase of destructive extension of modern agriculture, much of the volcanic terrain of north Jordan and southern Syria could therefore be classed as landscapes of preservation.

In both the Syrian and Jordanian Hauran the patchwork of stone field boundaries (and in some cases even plough furrows) was evident to early twentieth century investigators (Butler 1949, vol. II.A2: 145, cited in Kennedy 1995: 278). Today, however, as a result of the extension of modern agriculture, such features

Fig. 7.7 Ancient fields near Umm el-Quttein, Jordan (from Kennedy et al. 1986: pl. XXIV.2 with permission).

are more evident on aerial photographs than on the ground. For example, around Umm el-Jemal, sites of the Roman/Byzantine period are associated with animal corrals, cross-wadi walls, rectilinear meshes of field systems, stone clearance mounds, reservoirs, water holes, dams, and qanats (*foggaras*) (Kennedy in de Vries 1998). Field systems are demarcated by lines of boulder heaps or by distinctive alignments of large stones (fig. 7.7; e.g., Kennedy et al. 1986: pl. XXIV.2). In certain cases, they are distinguished by a morphology that either is much narrower than modern fields (e.g., Kennedy and Freeman 1995: fig. 17) or were organized into a blocklike pattern across the landscape (Gentelle 1985: contrast fig. 5 and pl. IX). Such field systems, which form a dramatic meshwork across the landscape in both the southern and northern Hauran, relate to a major phase of settlement that occurred both during the Roman period and the immediate pre-Roman period. Communication systems take the form of either local routes marked by parallel lines of stones or Roman roads (Gentelle 1985: pl. XI), along which occur military sites and milestones (Kennedy in De Vries 1998; Kennedy and Riley 1990; Parker 1986).

The remarkable landscapes of northern Jordan and southern Syria may give the impression that there was only a single phase of expansion of Roman agriculture and settlement, but closer scrutiny shows there is a palimpsest of traces dating from different periods. Thus in the region of northern Jordan a loose grid of rectilinear fields marked by boundaries of stone alignments occurs within a scatter of field-clearance mounds (fig. 7.8a; Kennedy 1982: fig. 43B). Within this scatter and also near Umm al-Quttein occur the curvilinear walls of three kite structures, which are considered to have been used to trap wild animals (chapter 8; fig. 7.8b). The presence of such kites within a Romano-Byzantine field system suggests either that the kites predate the field systems and have been incorporated into them (fig. 7.8b) or that they are contemporaneous and represent installations designed to corral domestic livestock (or at least adapted to such a use). Other glimpses of multiperiod landscapes occur in the area of Quttein, where the main occupation phases were Middle Bronze Age, Iron Age, and Nabataean through Early Islamic. This agriculturally marginal area, with rainfall averaging 200 mm per annum, showed that in addition to the ruins of low, extensive Roman settlements, more enigmatic settlements occur. These comprise dense scatters of Roman sherds that merge into building rubble and scatters of Middle Bronze pottery (fig. 7.8a; Kennedy and Freeman 1995: 52). In these cases, a preexisting Middle Bronze Age landscape appears to have been overrun and transformed by later Roman settlement, thereby leaving the Middle Bronze Age sites as "ghosts." The true scale of such landscapes emerges only in other parts of the Hauran such as in the Wadi ʿAjib, where Middle Bronze Age sites and farmsteads associated with small canals and valley-floor fields appear to have extended into areas that were previously marginal grazing lands (Betts et al. 1996).

In the Syrian Hauran the considerable chronological depth of the landscape can also be discerned from the spatial relationships of certain features to each other. For example, near the Roman site of Siʿa, a well-attested Roman road deviates around two tombs verified by excavation to belong to an earlier phase (Gentelle 1985: 40–41). Southwest of the same site, the Roman road cuts a patchwork of fields that must therefore predate the road (Gentelle 1985: 39). Such relationships between apparently early field systems and later Roman roads that cut through them is analogous to what has been observed in multiperiod landscapes in eastern Britain (Williamson 1987). In yet drier areas of the Hauran the remains of extensive irrigation canals form coherent landscape systems that enable large units of the landscape to be related chronologically (Braemer et al. 1996; Newson 2000).

Observations on soils within such field systems suggests that in contrast to the aggraded soil profiles evident in irrigated landscapes of Iraq and Yemen, these marginal desertic soils have undergone considerable erosion. For example, in the southern Hauran, Kennedy and colleagues (1986: 153) infer from the abundance

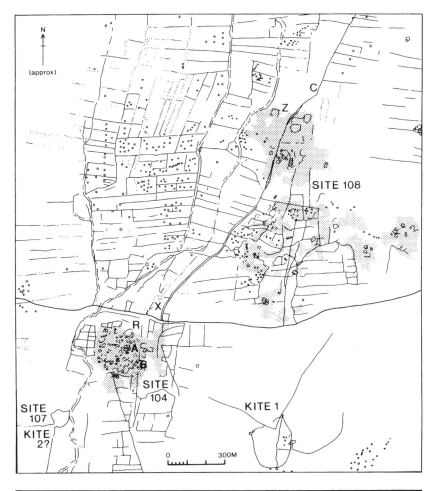

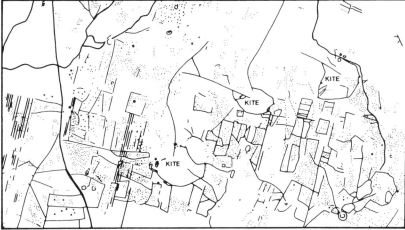

Fig. 7.8 (top) Fields with clearance mounds in the southern Hauran, Jordan (from Kennedy and Freeman 1995: fig. 17). (bottom) Field systems containing kites near Umm al-Quttein, northern Jordan (from Kennedy 1982: fig. 43b).

of large stones that would act as a major impediment to cultivation, that around 30 cm of soil has been removed since the fields were in use.

Human-Environment Interactions

Over the past seventy years there has been a shift in the assessment of the Levantine landscape from an earlier perception that decried the massive degradation that the region had suffered at the hands of human activity. The more measured tones of later works point out that both climatic change and human activity must account for the existing degraded landscapes. Whereas Reifenberg saw soil erosion as having a devastating effect on the landscape (1936: 146), more recent studies of alluvial fills recognize that both climatic and anthropogenic processes have been in operation. Although human activity is thought to be the overriding factor in shaping the Levantine landscape over the last five thousand years (Goldberg and Bar-Yosef 1990: 84) as in other areas of the Eastern Mediterranean, there continues to be much debate as to the relative significance of human versus natural environmental change (Grove and Rackham 2001).

Recent palaeobotanical studies inform this debate by indicating that although there were significant impacts on the vegetation in the Early Bronze Age, irreversible effects on the plant cover have occurred only during the past 3,700 years, and most notably since 2,400 years ago. Here discussion is restricted to key issues relevant to the development of the Levantine landscape over the past 5,000 years, specifically combining results from archaeological surveys with geoarchaeology and palaeobotanical studies.

Vegetation

The retrieval of pollen cores from Lake Kinneret, Lake Hula, and the Dead Sea over the last twenty years

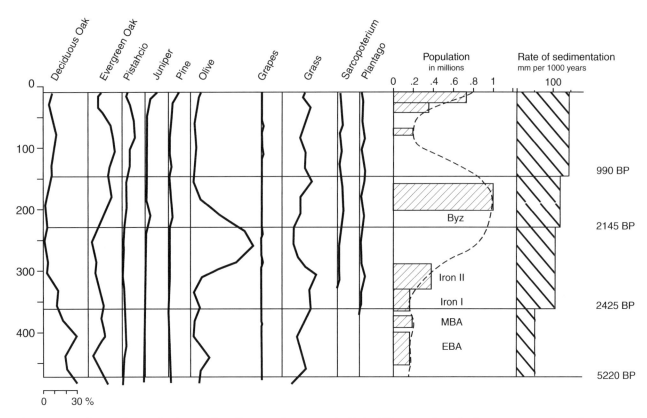

Fig. 7.9 Estimated population and sedimentation rates in Lake Kinneret in relation to vegetation change, as inferred from pollen trends (expressed as percentage of total pollen, excluding aquatic types) through the last 5,000 years from Lake Kinneret. Vertical scale in cm, horizontal scale = 30%. Note that the olive peak represents about 55% of total pollen minus aquatics. (Based on Baruch 1986: fig. 4; Goldberg and Bar-Yosef 1990; Broshi and Finkelstein 1992: fig. 2)

has provided a better record of vegetation and land-use changes than has been possible from either the northern Levant or Upper Mesopotamia. Consequently, it is now possible to compare changes in the vegetation, soil erosion, and archaeological settlement.

According to the synthesis of van Zeist and Bottema, by 5000 cal. B.P. (Early Bronze I) the hill country west of the Jordan was dominated by evergreen broad-leafed forest (*Quercus calliprini*), whereas broad-leafed deciduous forest (including deciduous oak) extended to the north around Lake Kinneret. In drier terrain the vegetation cover would have thinned out to form a shrub steppe, with *Pistacia atlantica* (pistachio), *Amygdalus korschinski* (almond), and *Crataegus aronis* (hawthorn) forming a localized forest steppe between the wooded uplands and the Jordan

valley (van Zeist and Bottema 1991: 109–110). Meanwhile, a combination of xeromorphic scrub and broadleafed deciduous woodland would have covered the coastal plain.

One of the clearest records of human-induced vegetation change from the southern Levant is from Lake Kinneret (the Sea of Galilee), analyzed by Uri Baruch (1986; see also Falconer and Fall 1995: 94–95; Redman 1999: 187–189). This record shows that a mixed oak woodland was gradually reduced, presumably as a result of clearance by humans during the late fourth and early third millennia B.C. This phase of woodland removal corresponds to, or is slightly earlier than, the phase of urbanism that occurred during Early Bronze II–III. Significantly, a minor peak in olive pollen at the same time suggests that olives may have been planted at the expense of woodland.

Following regrowth of oak woodland during the later third millennium B.C. (Early Bronze IV), which also corresponded to a slight decline in olives, there was continued reduction of woodland throughout the second millennium. This climaxed in a substantial decline of oak trees after ca. 1000 B.C. (that is, during the Iron Age) together with a dramatic increase in olives spanning the period between around 700/800 B.C. and the fourth–fifth centuries A.D. (fig. 7.9). The expansion of olive trees corresponds rather well with the major Iron Age II colonization of the hill country as well as with the development of the Roman/Hellenistic landscape described above. In the Kinneret area, following this main olive phase there was a rebound in the oak-pollen rain, specifically that of evergreen oak, as the area shifted towards a more Mediterranean vegetation. This later phase of increased evergreen oak and pine, together with significantly more *Artemisia*, *Sarcopoterium*, and *Plantago* (all good indicators of anthropogenic activity and disturbed soils), is also clearly evident in the less well dated Ein Gedi core taken from the western shores of the Dead Sea (Baruch 1990).

The results of Baruch build upon and support earlier analyses by Horowitz (1979), which suggest that a rising olive curve occurred after around 2370 B.P. in Lake Kinneret. An increase in olive pollen from the Iron Age is also supported by a recent analysis from Lake Hula to the north of Lake Kinneret (Baruch and Bottema 1999: fig. 2: zone 9; Horowitz 1979: figs. 6.22, 6.20). The replacement of deciduous oak by evergreen oak following the abandonment of widespread olive cultivation seems to have ushered in the vegetation that today forms the typical feature of the East Mediterranean landscape (see Willcox 1999; Roberts et al. 2001). Overall, the dramatic phase of olive growth (Baruch's Kinneret zone Y) provides the most convincing evidence to date for the impact of Iron Age through Byzantine settlement on the hill country and adjacent areas.

In the vicinity of Petra in Jordan, Patricia Fall has traced the progressive desertification of the environment through the analysis of pollen from fossil hyrax middens. The Syrian rock hyrax (= *Procavia capensis*) constructs middens composed of plant fragments, faecal pellets, and faunal parts, the plant remains being the result of the animals' browsing forays around the burrow. The resultant mass of biological refuse then becomes cemented by the crystallized urine of the hyrax. Because the middens contain pollen from the immediate area, they can be subjected to pollen analysis (Falconer and Fall 1995). These analyses suggest that the area around Petra in Jordan had become a degraded Mediterranean steppe

forest by the Roman–Byzantine periods and that by Early Islamic times, the total tree pollen had decreased to the level of that of the modern desert-steppe vegetation.

Evidence for increasingly desertic conditions is also supported by palynological and other environmental studies conducted in the Wadi Faynan. There, a significantly moister early-Holocene period was followed by a "diverse steppic landscape" in the fourth and third millennia B.C., which was then succeeded by a very degraded steppeland during the Nabataean period (first century B.C.) and an even more desertic environment in the Roman period (Barker et al. 1999: 261–262). Overall, in the Wadi Faynan it was the combination of copper smelting together with intensive human occupation that resulted in a highly degraded landscape by the post-Roman period (Barker 2002). The analyses of vegetation records therefore demonstrate that human impact on the vegetation has been considerable over the last three thousand years but that desertification itself has been patchy and also can be blamed, to some degree, on climatic drying, a conclusion that is in line with those of Bar-Matthews and colleagues (1998; chapter 2).

The Record of Valley Fills

Early studies of sedimentary valley fills around the Mediterranean appeared to provide evidence for a phase of Roman/Byzantine (but not Iron Age) alluviation that could be traced as a coherent entity from Spain to the Levant and indeed even further to the east (Vita-Finzi 1969: fig. 101). This "younger fill" was suggested by Vita-Finzi to have resulted from shifts in climatic patterns rather than human settlement, but Vita-Finzi's seminal contribution appears to have oversimplified a rather more complex sedimentary record (see Butzer 1974: 68; Wagstaff 1981).

For example, Arlene Rosen's interpretations of valley fills near Tell

Lachish, located west of the hill country, suggest that following an Early Bronze Age characterized by moist valley-floor wadi flow environments, a phase of Middle Bronze Age alluviation was followed during the Iron Age and Byzantine periods by increased levee sedimentation and colluviation (Rosen 1986: 57–69). Of these, the two later phases consisted of sediments that were less well sorted than those of the Bronze Age and also provided evidence of increased soil erosion and colluviation. These later Iron Age and Byzantine fills may therefore have been caused by increased soil erosion resulting from the extension of settlement on the uplands within the basin of the Nahal Lachish.

Because valley-floor alluvial sequences are usually interrupted by long phases of stability or incision that do not always leave a clear sedimentary record, their interpretation is not straightforward. This is especially the case because soil eroded from upland catchments can be intercepted by a variety of sedimentary "sinks" in the landscape (chapter 2). In contrast, the sedimentary records of lake cores are usually much more continuous. Thus the Lake Kinneret record clearly demonstrates that through the late Holocene there has been an increase in the rate of sedimentation from low rates during the Early/Middle Bronze Age, followed by a significant jump around Iron Age I, followed by even higher rates in the Roman/Byzantine periods and later (fig. 7.9; based on Thompson et al. 1985: fig. 7, and Goldberg and Bar-Yosef 1990: 82).

Unfortunately, as with riverine basins, lakes receive sediments that have been stored in different parts of often complex basins, and so their sedimentary record may not reflect the actual amount of soil eroded within the catchment. This complexity is illustrated by cores from Lake Hula and the Ghab Valley, which although demonstrating a general increase in rates of sedimentation during the Holocene, also show a considerable degree of variability. Despite such variability between cores, the late Pleistocene/initial Holocene phase (characterized by low population levels and increasing deciduous oak woodland) exhibited low sedimentation rates of 0.63 and 0.33 mm per annum for Hula and the Ghab respectively. In contrast, after the Younger Dryas, when human populations were increasing rapidly, mean sedimentation rates increased 1.33 mm per annum to 0.54 in the same cores (i.e., almost double).

The increased rate of sedimentation during the later phases at Lake Kinneret is likely to be the outcome of the expansion of settlement on to the highlands, combined with the establishment of *maquis* and *garrigue* vegetation. Together, these may be ascribed to the degradation of the environment resulting from increased human activity combined with late Holocene aridification. The contribution of the latter factor is particularly interesting because the carbon/oxygen isotope record from Saruq cave shows that the climate was somewhat drier following 2000 or 2200 B.C. and that there were at least two very dry phases during the last millennium (Bar-Matthews et al. 1998: 209). Nevertheless, when all three cores are compared, the lack of a clear and unequivocal increase in sedimentation rate throughout the Holocene underscores that the relationships between sedimentation rate, human activity, and climate are not always straightforward.

In the southern Levant during the first millennium B.C. many areas witnessed the extension of settlement to more erodable slopes, cycles of olive production (in the ceramic Neolithic, Chalcolithic, Early Bronze Age and Roman/Byzantine: Baruch and Bottema 1999), clearance of natural woodland, and the development of a more Mediterranean vegetation. These tendencies, all of which occurred in the face of a somewhat drier late Holocene climate, must have contributed to increased stress on the vegetation and more degraded, perhaps desertic, conditions. Although it is tempting to interpret the alluvial record as being solely caused by the extension of settlement and agriculture on to the uplands and into semiarid areas, one must not assume that all human activity simply results in increased valley-floor sedimentation. Following an initial pulse of erosion, terracing can result in landscape stabilization, as discussed in chapter 9, whereas the development of olive orchards can result in fairly low rates of erosion (chapter 2). It is of considerable significance, however, that anthropogenic activity appears to have been increasing in more vulnerable and sensitive environments as well as in the face of a drying climate. The combined effect of extension of settlement and climatic drying, together with the complex range of feedbacks that occurred between different parts of the human–environmental system, probably best accounts for the degraded conditions that we observe today.

The northern Levant provides a less well documented record, because fewer detailed geoarchaeological studies have been made of valley fills. Generalizing from sequences in southern Turkey and northwest Syria recorded by Arlene Rosen, Paul Goldberg, and others, it appears that as in the southern Levant there was a transition from a moister valley floor and also more wooded environment with more steady stream flow during much of the third millennium B.C., toward more erratic and less stable flow regimes during the later third and early second millennium B.C. (Rosen 1998; Rosen and Goldberg 1995; Wilkinson 1999). It is common to link such a shift of flow regime either to climatic drying or to degradation of the vegetation. The removal of woodland could have increased runoff, reduced the recharge of water tables, and caused springs to dry up as well as leading to a more flashy episodic flow regime (Rawat et al. 2000). Alter-

natively, in much of the northern Levant and Upper Mesopotamia, the episode of third-millennium settlement nucleation and population increase occurred in the face of a climatic regime that was becoming both dryer and more prone to variation. This trend becomes evident when the climate proxy record from Lake Van (Lemcke and Sturm 1997) is combined with plots of long-term aggregate settlement area (Wilkinson 1999b: fig. 8f). The combined index of atmospheric drying plus aggregate settlement area starts its upswing in the late third millennium and continues to increase, albeit erratically, until two thousand years ago, at which time it levels out but remains erratic. This implies that the combined effects of climatic drying with the loss of vegetation and habitat disturbance by human activity may together provide a more realistic mechanism for changing flow regimes in valley floors than either factor on its own.

The increased trend towards unstable landscapes over the last two thousand to three thousand years is exemplified by the sedimentary record from the Amuq plain of southern Turkey. The geoarchaeological record demonstrates that a transition from a low-energy and stable flood plain environment during the Chalcolithic and Bronze Age was succeeded during Roman/Byzantine times by the accumulation of sand and silt levees along the Orontes river, high-energy fan aggradation along the Amanus Mountains, and other valley fills in the Hellenistic Roman (fig. 7.10), as well as the development of a major lake and fringing marshes during the Iron Age or Roman periods (Yener et al. 2000). These sedimentary events in the Orontes flood plain and Amanus alluvial fans relate to increases in flow energy that might have been caused by human-induced land-use changes such as clearance of woodlands within the respective hydrological catchments, to an increased intensity of rainstorms, or

Fig. 7.10 High-energy gravel fan deposits overlying a Roman palaeosol (dark zone at base of upper gravels) and earlier Holocene fan gravels (behind figure), in the Amuq plain, southern Turkey.

to a combination of both. The presence of lake sediments overlying Early Bronze Age sites demonstrates that later phases of the lake occurred after the third millennium B.C. (Yener et al. 2000), and textual evidence indicates that a lake was in existence by the Seleucid period. Growth of the lake may result either from increased storm runoff or from increased frequency of overbank spills from the Orontes river. Evidence for increased flow energy and lake development all fall within the phase of the first millennium B.C. and A.D., when settlements dispersed on to uplands and sensitive vegetational environments would have been disturbed (Casana in press).

Although upland land-use changes and associated woodland clearance may account for such valley-floor changes in hydrological regime, anthropogenic changes in the lowlands themselves also complicate the environmental picture. Thus in the Amuq plain, the presence of Byzantine/Early Islamic canal systems may have resulted in increased marsh development as a result of the discharge of large volumes of overflow water on to the plain. Upstream on the Orontes in Syria, however, major hydrological changes were effected by Roman or Iron Age dams (e.g., the Homs barrage) that would have trapped flow in the headwaters (Calvet and Geyer 1992), or conversely large-scale marsh drainage and the excavation of new channels in the Ghab, which may have resulted in increased flow of water and associated flooding downstream in the Amuq. Although it is not possible to equate precisely the extension of settlement on both uplands and lowlands with downstream transitions in hydrology and sedimentation, it is clear that large-scale human landscaping projects, both on the uplands and within the valley floors, must have had a significant influence on hydrology and sedimentary regimes.

In the Levant, although human impact on the environment can be inferred as early as the Neolithic (Köhler-Rollefson and Rollefson 1990; Yasuda et al. 2000: 131), the most significant environmental transformations were not evident until probably the second millennium B.C. and later. This appears to be remarkably late in comparison to much of Europe and parts of southern and eastern Asia, where dates from the earliest palynological evidence for human impact on the landscape fall between five thousand and nine thousand years ago (Walker and Singh 1993: fig. 9.1). Therefore the relatively modest magnitude of Early Bronze II/III "urbanism" in the Levant appears to have had a relatively minor impact on the environment.

In part, this is probably because much of the activity was confined to the lowlands, where energy gradients of runoff were relatively low. Of major significance, however, was the extension during the early first millennium B.C. of dispersed settlement onto the hill country on both sides of the Jordan river as well as at a slightly later date in the northern Levant. The expansion of human activity onto steeper slopes made these areas more sensitive to high-rainfall events, which in turn would have encouraged increased erosion.

There has been a tendency in the past to view the erosive effect of human activity in rather simplistic terms: what I would call the goat-and-clearance syndrome. Although not denying the major impact of caprid grazing and fuel gathering on the landscape, it is also necessary to take into account the complexity of the cultural landscape. This comprises a patchwork of activity areas and sediment sinks that are linked by sediment transport routes in rather complex ways that are significantly different from those of the natural environment. In terms of sediment supply, cultivated fields, forest clearings, quarries, and degraded pasture areas would be expected to show rates of sediment yield that were higher than those of the natural vegetated environment, whereas fields would have provided high but variable supply rates, depending upon their state of ploughing or being fallow. Moreover, the presence of numerous quarries, with their heaps of quarry waste, would increase the supply of coarse debris to drainage systems but would also trap sediments where the quarries formed enclosed pits. Threshing floors and tracks could generate increased runoff, which could in turn initiate localized gully incision. On the other hand, terraced fields, cisterns, and wine presses would trap sediments for various durations, depending upon how they were maintained. Each of the above cultural patches would be linked by a conveyance

network for sediment and runoff that would have been significantly enlarged as a result of the development of systems of tracks and routes across the landscape. According to Dar's studies, for example, the total length of village tracks would approximate to some 30–35 km per major village (Dar 1986: 134). This could result in an increase in drainage density in the region by as much as 1 km per sq. km. The significance of such an increased channel length per sq. km would have varied considerably from place to place, in part depending upon their relation to the natural drainage network. In some places, tracks would increase sedimentation downslope by conveying large quantities of sediment from high-yield areas such as cultivated fields, whereas in other areas, by concentrating overland flow, tracks could encourage incision, gully development, or the stripping of soil cover and its transport downslope. In addition, of course, the settlements and their adjacent activity areas would contribute significantly to the sediment and erosional budget of the region.

The extension of a multitude of human activities into the hilly lands would be expected to exacerbate the transport and supply of sediments above the levels that would have pertained when the uplands formed only a mosaic of hill pasture and woodland. The wide range of different types of land use would, however, result in a nonlinear response to any rainfall event. In some localities, sediment yields would be increased; in other areas much sediment would have been trapped on the slope; and in other areas it would find its way down to the valley floor sinks, thereby obscuring landscape features in the lowlands. Therefore, although the proxy records for past vegetation show an increasing loss of woodland and a shift towards a more Mediterranean environment, including garrigue and maquis, the sediment records are more complex. There remains no unequivocal

evidence that degradation of the vegetation was responsible for the geomorphic shifts that have been recognized (Goldberg and Bar-Yosef 1990: 82).

Moreover, the record of valley fills is not uniform geographically: in the loess-covered areas of the northern Negev, the alluvial record is dominated by episodes of alluviation and erosion, while in the moister areas to the north, colluviation dominates (Goldberg and Bar-Yosef 1990: 80). At least in the Nahr Lachish area, the latter process was more pervasive during the Iron Age and Byzantine periods (Rosen 1986: 67), which again provides some support for increased slope erosion during the last three thousand years.

Some of the key chronological and spatial interrelationships between cultural process and landscape changes can be discerned from table 7.2 and figure 7.9. In the Lake Kinneret record the Chalcolithic and Bronze Age coincides with a significant but declining woodland cover, relatively nucleated and primarily lowland settlement (Broshi and Finkelstein 1992: 56–57), and a drying climate. Although the radiocarbon sequence is coarse, it is supported at a general level by more rigorous analyses (Thompson et al. 1985). In this case, the largest jump in sedimentation rates coincides approximately with the expansion of settlement in both the lowlands and the uplands, a situation that coincided with increased development of partially commercialized agriculture on the hills and a continued, rather dry climatic regime. The high rate of sedimentation in Lake Kinneret of 117 mm per one thousand years also coincides with maximum settlement and agriculture of the hill country during the Roman-Byzantine period. Finally, the highest sedimentation rate, rather than corresponding to the maximum extension of settlement, appears rather to relate to a wider range of annual rainfall and some reversion towards woodland in the uplands. That in-

Table 7.2 Settlement and Environmental Trends along the Jordan Valley and Neighboring Areas to the East

	Estimated Rainfall[1]	Settlement[2]	Kinneret[3]	Wadi Faynan[4]	Petra[5]	Jebel Arab[6]	Environmental Trends
Islamic	450–570 mm	Settlement decline	Increase in evergreen oak woodland	Desertic	Desert steppe	Mediterranean vegetation with evergreen oak	Late phase of degradation
Roman/ Byzantine	470–530 mm	Byzantine commercial agriculture and dispersed settlement	Olive orchards	Degraded steppe	Degraded Mediterranean steppe forest		Major phase of settlement and clearance with widespread human impact
Hellenistic/ Roman	470–530 mm	Hellenistic-Roman commercial agriculture and dispersed settlement	Olive orchards	Degraded steppe		Mediterranean vegetation with evergreen oak and some vine	
Iron Age	470–530 mm	Iron Age expansion of settlement	Olive orchards	—			Significant human impact
Late Bronze Age	470–530 mm	Decline	Oak decline	—			Local impact
Middle Bronze Age	470–530 mm	Middle Bronze Age polities	Oak decline	—			of humans
Early Bronze Age–Middle Bronze Age	470–570 mm	Decline	Low olive	—		Wooded steppe with olives	on the
Early Bronze Age	425–610 mm	Early Bronze Age urban centers	Oak decrease; olive increase	Steppe		Forest steppe with deciduous oak	environment
Chalcolithic	520–620 mm	Minor polities	Oak woodland	—			Minor
Early Holocene (10,000–7000 B.P.)	675–950 mm	Pottery Neolithic villages and Pre-Pottery Neolithic communities	Broad-leafed woodland	Moist steppe			Local human impact
Late Pleistocene (15,000–12,000 B.P.)	550–725 mm	Epipalaeolithic complex hunter-gatherers	Shrub steppe				

[1] From Soreq cave (Bar-Matthews et al. 1997, 1998). Note that mean annual rainfall at Soreq Cave (500 mm) is slightly higher than at Lake Kinneret (ca. 400 mm), therefore the trend in the rainfall figures is more significant than absolute amounts.
[2] Generalized trends in settlement to the west of the Jordan.
[3] From Baruch (1986).
[4] Wadi Faynan, Jordan, based on Barker et al. (1997, 1998, 1999, 2000).
[5] Petra, Jordan, based on the work of Patricia Fall in Falconer and Fall 1995: 95–97.
[6] Jebel Arab (formerly known as Jebel Druze) in southwest Syria, by Willcox (1999)

creased sedimentation should take place during a phase of settlement decline is not surprising, because the abandonment of terraces and the neglect of field walls can equally result in increased erosion (chapter 9; Butzer 1982: 130–131). Additional factors that must have contributed to high rates of erosion include the increased range of variation in annual rainfall in recent centuries (Bar-Matthews et al. 1998), continued aridity that would place stress on the vegetation cover, and a reversion to uncontrolled pastoral activity that would exacerbate erosion by the removal of vegetation and the development of animal trails.

Although increased settlement and vegetation removal on the hills must have contributed significantly to degradation, there is no "smoking gun." Rather, the patterning at this coarse grain of resolution are imprecise, and correlations are not always clear cut. Hence there is no dramatic change in sedimentation within Lake Kinneret during the late Early Bronze Age phase of drying (although the Nahr Lachish record does suggest a shift of regime around or slightly before 2000 B.C.). Rather, the relatively well wooded environment may have buffered the impact of the late Early Bronze Age drying event as well as the very wide range of climatic variation experienced during the third millennium B.C. Furthermore, it is crucial not to underestimate the degree of landscape degradation that has prevailed over the last century, when population levels have exploded in many parts of the Levant. As the record of the early travelers eloquently testifies, much of the now desertified areas to the east of the Jordan were much more verdant during the nineteenth century (Harlan 1982).

Conclusions

Despite the considerable variation in levels of preservation of settlement sites and their agrarian landscapes,

one can discern a remarkable dispersal of rural settlement throughout many parts of the Fertile Crescent during the first millennium B.C. (or somewhat earlier in places), but the causal mechanisms underlying this phenomenon vary from place to place.

In the first place it should be emphasized that the physical landscapes of the Levant and Upper Mesopotamia differ in their topography and soil resources. In the Levant, Iron Age settlement was associated with colonization of the hill country, some degree of woodland clearance, and the construction of terraced fields. In Upper Mesopotamia the analogous settlement phase in part comprised colonization of the semidesertic steppe, where agriculture appears primarily to have entailed traditional rain-fed cultivation, probably with an alternate year of fallow. With the exception of the construction of local irrigation canals and wells, technological innovations appear to have been relatively minor in the Jazira. In other words, the development of similar patterns of settlement resulted in the evolution of different rural landscapes because the communities involved had to deal with a different terrain and operate within a very different political economy. Moreover, these processes of settlement dispersal were not contemporaneous throughout the Fertile Crescent but rather were spread out over a thousand years.

In the Levant there is good evidence in support of increased removal of woodland and the development of maquis and garrigue vegetation as well as desertification in drier areas, but such degradation is less readily demonstrated in the Jazira. This is in part simply because of the lack of long-term pollen cores and geoarchaeological studies. Nevertheless, the extension of settlement and intensification of cultivation in the semiarid margins during the first half of the first

millennium B.C. appears to have resulted in a serious deterioration of the environment along the Khabur river (Frey et al. 1991: 106; Morandi 2000: 383). The bare and degraded landscape that is currently visible in the Jazira, although having its origins in the Neolithic period and Bronze Age, may therefore have been most devastated by the extension of settlement that took place under the suzerainty of the Neo-Assyrian and later empires.

8 Sustenance from a Reluctant Desert

Not only is the desert the quintessential Near Eastern landscape, it is also a "landscape of survival" and is therefore capable of providing some of the best-preserved landscapes. On the other hand, the environment of arid lands is not static, and climatic fluctuations have resulted in deserts undergoing numerous cycles of change. Desert formation (desertification) results in some marginal steppe lands becoming desert, in part because of misuse by humans. Alternatively, as will be shown for the Negev desert, human ingenuity results in marginal areas being periodically colonized. Despite the great interest in the desert over the past thirty years, the processes that underlie desert formation continue to be debated, with some factions regarding climate as driving desert formation, while others view human activities as being fundamental. In reality, the two processes should be viewed as operating hand-in-hand with complex interactions taking place between an episodically drying climate and long-term degradation by humans.

The deserts of the Near East form a complex of environments ranging from semiarid steppe in parts of Jordan, Syria, Iraq, and Israel to hyper-arid conditions in parts of Iran, Saudi Arabia, Yemen, and Oman. In terms of human perceptions, one can recognize at least two types of desert landscape. From the point of view of the sedentary occupants of the desert fringe and the oases, there are the settled zone and adjacent grazing areas, beyond which lies the inhospitable desert. On the other hand, to the nomads, the desert represents a variegated landscape of wadis, dune fields, mountains, steppe, extensive pastoral areas, even occasional areas of wooded savanna.

Such a varied landscape is not necessarily perceived by the dweller of the oases. Although it would be unwise to exaggerate such differences of perception, it is well to realize that they are to some degree present and are fundamental to the assessment of landscapes. Therefore, as will be described in chapter 9, landscapes differ according to the eye and experience of the beholder. Such differences are crucial when assessing human adjustments to the environmental record: for example, to the sedentary oasis dweller, a change toward drier conditions either could be catastrophic or could be counteracted by investment in more water-gathering technology. From the point of view of a nomadic pastoralist, the same climatic shift might simply be dealt with by changing the pattern of movement or by extending the size of the tribal territory to enclose more water sources or pastures. Alternatively, the resultant stresses might be met by a shift from a sedentary to nomadic way of life or vice versa.

Because water is fundamental to life and deserts lack water, evidence for the procurement of adequate water forms a significant part of this chapter. Water supply in deserts can typically be classed into two groups: exogenous, that is, employing water from rivers that have their source in wetter areas beyond the desert (Goudie and Wilkinson 1977), and endogenous, that is, water procured from local sources within the desert. In this chapter, only endogenous sources are discussed.

The dichotomy between the sensibilities of the sedentary and the nomadic inhabitants provides a useful organizational framework for discussing cultural landscapes of the desert. Therefore, following a discussion of environmental change and ecological conditions that relate to the formation of the deserts of interior Arabia, the landscapes of sedentary settlement such as oases and routes that lead through the desert between populated centers will be discussed, followed by the very different record left by nomadic pastoralists.

Environmental Change and the Deserts of Interior Arabia

The deserts of interior Arabia comprise a wide range of terrains that have formed under the influence of long-term environmental changes. Desert terrain includes functioning wadis and relict drainage channels, coastal and inland salt flats or sabkhas, extensive areas of dune sands, and cemented sand dunes known as aeolianites (Glennie 1998). The dominant fluvial channel systems flow from the Hejaz mountains to the west toward the Persian-Arabian Gulf in the east, and of these, many are relict features that date back to earlier moist intervals of the Pleistocene (chapter 2). Similarly, many dune systems reflect either modern northerly or southwesterly blowing winds or ancient wind

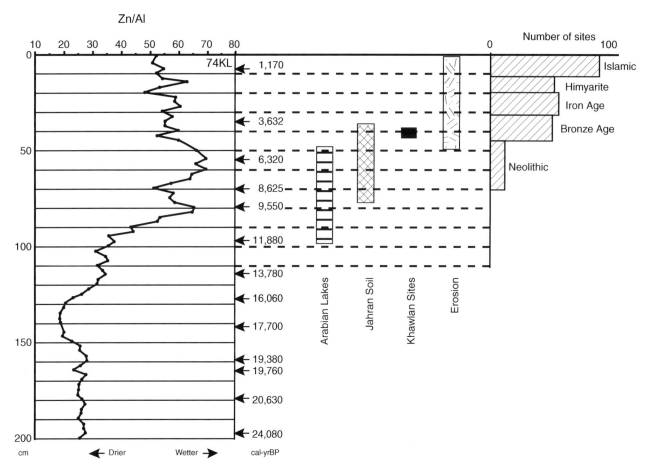

Fig. 8.1 Monsoon strength inferred from zinc:aluminum ratios from Indian Ocean core 74KL, off the Oman coast (from Sirocko 1996: fig. 4), chronology of Arabian lakes, buried soils, erosion sediments, and the number of archaeological sites in the highlands of Yemen.

patterns. It is now clear that the desert areas of Arabia were significantly moister during the early and mid Holocene and that this can partly be ascribed to changing patterns of solar radiation and resultant patterns of global circulation, as discussed in chapter 2.

The most tangible evidence for the early- to mid-Holocene moist interval comes in the form of temporary lakes found in the interior deserts. Deposits of such lakes, usually as cemented sands, rarely diatom-rich marls or shelly silts, have been described from as far north as the Nafud desert at 28 degrees north (Garrard and Harvey 1981; Schultz and Whitney 1986), as well as in Mundafan in southwest Saudi Arabia (McClure 1978), and in the Ramlat Sabat'ayn desert of Yemen (Lézine

et al. 1998). They also occur on the intermontane plains of Yemen at elevations between 2,300 and 2,600 m above sea level (chapter 9). In addition, the early to mid Holocene was a period of increased wadi flow throughout the peninsula (Hötzl et al. 1984: 307–308) and raised water tables in eastern Saudi Arabia. The bleak aeolian plains fringing the gulf were, during the sixth and fifth millennium B.C., dotted with numerous springs and saline embayments adjacent to which developed occasional Ubaid-period settlements (Masry 1997). The overall range of dates on lake development is from around 10,000 to 7000 cal. B.P. in southern Saudi Arabia. Lake development continued slightly later in the Nafud, where moist condition apparently lasted until around 5700

cal. B.P. (Lézine et al. 1998: 298) and may have commenced earlier in the Yemen highlands, where the earliest date is in the range 12100–11280 cal. B.P. Humic buried soils (palaeosols) also formed during this moist interval, and both on the highlands and in the arid interior, these continued to form to as late as 4000 cal. B.P., as discussed below.

The moist interval indicated by the lakes and palaeosols corresponds remarkably closely to the peak of oceanic upwelling, which acts as a proxy for intensified monsoonal activity (fig. 8.1; Zonneveld et al. 1997; Sirocko 1996). Between around six thousand and four thousand years ago, the monsoon started to weaken, and summer rainfall declined. But desiccation was not immediate, and rather, atmospheric drying appears to have continued in a series of steps, culminating perhaps in an abrupt desiccating event around 4300 cal. B.P. (Cullen et al. 2000).

During the early to mid Holocene, rainfall in the currently hyperarid Rub al-Khali has been estimated to have been in the range 100–400 mm per annum (Hötzl et al. 1984: 314). This is less than in the Sahara, where recent estimates suggest that rainfall may have been as high as 460–600 mm per annum at this time (Hoelzmann et al. 2001: 214). The deposits and biological remains of the Arabian lakes show them to have been ephemeral features, the sediments of which were often blown away by desiccating winds. Much of interior Arabia was probably a savanna or steppe environment (Hoelzmann et al. 1998: 43), with scattered occurrences of *Acacia* and *Commiphora* trees, as for example in the Hawa sequence of Yemen (Lézine et al. 1998: 296). Nevertheless, the presence of beds of *Typha* and *Phragmites* suggests that the presence of reedswamp must have supplied a locally luxuriant element to the landscape (Schultz and Whitney 1986: 181).

The Arabian moist interval corresponds to a period of considerable human activity within Arabia (Hassan 2000), the type fossils of which are Fasad points and related artifacts of the Arabian Bifacial Tradition (Edens 1982, 1988a). These points are occasionally found around the desiccated lakes of Saudi Arabia, where charcoal fragments in sedimentary beds are also related to human activity. Bones of cattle, sheep/goat, gazelle, and a form of equid are the remains of animals that presumably were hunted, although a wider range of animals can be inferred from rock art of mid-Holocene date (Edens 1982: 119–121). In the Wahiba sands of Oman, following the mid-Holocene burst of activity, the next dated phase of human presence occurred in the Late Islamic period. This corresponds to the onset of complex political economies asso-

ciated with the integration of coastal and inland economies and more general patterns of regional commerce (Edens 1988b: 128). There is therefore an apparent gap in significant settlement between the Neolithic and Islamic periods, with the cessation of Neolithic hunter-gatherers in the desert interior being associated with considerably drier conditions. This has led Zarins to posit that Neolithic cattle herders abandoned the entire Rub al Khali and adjacent areas of the Nejd (Zarins 2000: 42). As a consequence of this, Zarins postulates the development of three major patterns of life by the first millennium B.C.: (1) transhumant pastoralism by ancestors of the modern south Arabian linguistic groups, (2) mobile pastoralists associated with camel nomadism, and (3) sedentary settlements on the plateau and adjacent highlands. On the basis of rock art, Newton and Zarins suggest that occupation of the interior of Arabia fell into a phase of cattle nomadism coeval with the so-called Realistic-Dynamic style of rock art from around 7000 B.C., which then terminated in stages between 2300 and 1900 B.C. (2000: 226, 234). This stage was followed, in the second and early first millennium B.C., by the so-called Oval-headed style of rock art (see Rock Art, below).

Bedouin traditionally spend their summers around wells, waterholes, or oases and then venture out into the desert for the winter rainy season from roughly October to May. During the early- to mid-Holocene wet interval, however, when monsoonal summer rainfall extended as far north as the northern Nafud, year-round occupation of the desert may have been possible. Nevertheless, it may have been necessary for the inhabitants to incorporate some degree of mobility to follow pasturelands of herds of game such as gazelle.

The model of Zarins does not imply that climatic desiccation necessarily initiated the total desertion of the interior and a complementary rise of small-scale polities in

the moist uplands. Rather, patterns of life may have changed to adjust to prevailing conditions so that an earlier hunter-gather way of life, with more limited mobility based around episodically available animal and plant resources, was replaced by a more mobile lifestyle that not only could cope with more desertic conditions but also entailed residence during part of the year in neighboring moister areas. That stresses resulting from climatic desiccation might have contributed to such sociopolitical and demographic developments is implied by figure 8.1, which shows that agro-pastoral settlements in the semiarid Khawlan uplands near Marib (de Maigret 1990) were occupied from 2600 and were deserted by 2000 B.C., that is, during the drying episode. During this period there was an increase in sedentary settlement on the moist uplands where conditions for long-term settlement were more propitious (Edens and Wilkinson 1998). Settlement then continued on the high plains through the second and first millennia B.C. and later periods.

Although compelling, this scenario of a climatically driven adaptation to progressively drier conditions requires more data from both highlands and lowlands before it can be upheld. Perhaps more convincing is that the settlement of the intermontane plains, themselves a marginal semiarid area, appears to have taken place and continued in the face of drying conditions. Moreover, although the aridification of the fourth and third millennia B.C. may have resulted in considerable stress on the Neolithic agro-pastoral communities of the interior, it did not necessarily lead to the interior becoming deserted. Instead, rock art, standing stones, and other features of the third and second millennia suggest that there was some adaptation to the drier conditions. On the other hand, evidence for the abandonment of parts of the desert fringe such as the Khawlan, as well as significant increases in population that have been recorded in the highlands, do suggest that both the dry margins were losing population and the moist highlands were gaining them during the mid to late Holocene transition. In this way, interior Arabia seems to resemble the Sahara region, where an ebb and flow of population from the deserts to neighboring semiarid regions or oases apparently coincided with cycles of drier climate.

Ecology and Desertification

Desertification as both a term and a process has generated considerable controversy during the last few years, but basically it refers to a complex of processes of land degradation in arid or semiarid areas that involves the loss of productivity of the land as a result of both human-induced and climatic causes. Primary human agencies involved in arid land degradation are overgrazing, deforestation, and unsustainable agricultural practices (UNEP 1992: iv). Although the climatic proxy data that delineate the pattern of Holocene climatic change are sufficiently convincing to demonstrate that changing global atmospheric circulation was a major driving factor behind the development of the Arabian desert, human communities must also have exerted a long-term impact on the vegetation. That human-induced loss of vegetation is important is apparent when areas of desert are fenced and enclosed and livestock have been excluded. For example, at Jubail in northern Saudi Arabia vegetation cover inside recently fenced enclosures was 3–5 times greater than areas outside that were subjected to animal grazing (Barth 1999). Such acute vegetation loss causes increased movement of sand as well as the reactivation of fossil dunes.

The fundamental role played by loss of vegetation is illustrated by the work of ecologists who have demonstrated that removal of vegetation results in a downward spiral of negative feedback processes that ultimately can result in a desertified environment. For example, William Schlesinger and colleagues working in New Mexico have shown that long-term grazing of semiarid grasslands leads first to the soil and vegetation becoming patchy, with the result that desert shrubs invade. Between the shrubs, barren areas develop and grow, and these areas become less fertile as a result of rapid erosion from the impervious soil surface. This process then results in less water infiltrating into the soil so that there is less moisture to support plant life. As a result, patches of desert extend between the shrubs (Schlesinger et al. 1990). In a similar manner, the removal of vegetation, for example, by excessive grazing, reduces the amount of vegetation and biomass that can be incorporated into the soil, thereby reducing essential water retaining humus. The decline in humus then reduces the water-holding capacity of the soil, which further reduces its capacity to support plant life. This downward spiral results in the gradual spread of desertlike conditions, without any climatic drying actually taking place (Safriel 1999: 119–122).

Despite the tendency to exaggerate the spread of deserts and place undue blame on human agencies such as agro-pastoral communities, it is nevertheless evident that there has been a tendency for desertified areas to extend as a result of *both* climatic fluctuations and human factors. Certainly, the late Holocene desiccation referred to above has substantially contributed to the development of the Arabian desert. The apparent extension of deserts is frequently, however, the result of the degradation of steppic areas that surround the true deserts rather than the result of the actual growth of the desert areas themselves. Degradation varies depending upon the nature of the land use; thus in the case of pastoral nomads, many traditional nomadic systems, by spreading grazing pressure over the terrain, result in a more even impact on grassland and natural forage than occurs when grazing is concentrated around selective points (Schlesinger et al. 1990: 1047). The latter effect is well illustrated by the so-called pyosphere phenomenon in which zones of degraded vegetation develop around wells drilled in semiarid grasslands (Mainguet 1999: 73). These zones are constrained to mainly 3–4 km (but can extend up to 7 km) away from the well-head because livestock cannot move too far from their source of water. As a result of this dispersal of degradation with distance, areas close to the well become trampled but enriched with nutrients from dung; areas within a few hundred meters lose vegetation and become heavily degraded; in a third zone, bushes invade and take over from the grassland; while beyond 2–3 km steppe or savanna, grazing extends in a zone that is least affected by degradation. Although it may be true that nomadic pastoral groups spread their impact over a wide terrain, this is not the case under all circumstances nor with all traditional communities. Consequently, under appropriate circumstances such as around wells or cisterns used by bedouin, as well as around sedentary oases where specific zones are reserved for the grazing of local livestock, zones of degradation are to be expected.

Because they depend upon the desert for a living, both sedentary and mobile communities are remarkably knowledgeable about desert ecology. Only in recent years have ecologists started to catch up with the knowledge base of indigenous inhabitants. Now there are a number of theoretical models that help explain not only how desert plant communities develop or survive but also how ancient communities have tapped and applied such principles. Of fundamental importance is the source-sink model. This conceptualizes desert land surfaces as comprising a mosaic of patches, some of which shed water, and others of which receive water from those that shed it (Safriel 1999: 121). The raised soil water in localized sinks promotes denser plant cover, more litter, and increased organic matter, which in turn encourage increased infiltration and reduced runoff. By increasing the scale of this process, ancient communities have increased source areas to supply runoff water to sinks, which then can supply either increased forage or more normally field crops (Shachak et al. 1999). Related techniques have also been applied to water gathering. Although it is unclear how long such techniques have been formalized into runoff agriculture and cistern engineering, the utilization of such applied knowledge has been fundamental to the adaptation of communities to the desert (see below).

The Landscape of the Oasis

The quintessential settlement of the desert is the oasis. This has been succinctly defined by Paolo Costa as "where water and cultivable land meet" in the desert (Costa 1983) or alternatively as an "agricultural enclave in or on the edge of a desert" (Mainguet 1999: 209). Because they occur in areas where no rain-fed agriculture is possible, oases are entirely dependent upon available water, and of this, a considerable portion goes towards irrigated agriculture. For example, for oases in the Maghreb (north Africa) some 70–90 percent of the water supply is contributed to agriculture (Mainguet 1999: 223). Oases play a crucial role in the desert landscape and social systems because they provide not only support for their inhabitants but also supplies and form centers of exchange or markets for bedouin groups from the desert. Thus in late pre-Islamic times, gatherings for purposes of exchange of goods (i.e., fairs) occurred throughout the Arabian peninsula, and in many instances these were also associated with a shrine or some form of pilgrimage route (Wheatley 2001: 242).

For Oman, Paolo Costa and Stephen Kite have illustrated a number of oasis settlements in both the mountainous zone and adjoining plains (Costa 1983). Most receive their irrigation water today from underground falaj channels, a system that was probably introduced in the first millennium B.C. (see below). Because the underground channel is fundamental to an understanding of the traditional oasis, it is appropriate to understand the structure of these settlements before attempting to interpret the earliest oasis settlements.

The Landscapes of *Qanat* and *Falaj*

Today and in the recent past, underground water channels have supplied numerous oases in the Near East, and these systems have contributed greatly to the development of the structure of the rural landscape. Iran provides the best examples of such qanat systems, but variants are found in Oman (falaj), Afghanistan (*karez*), Egypt, Libya, Algeria (*foggara*), and Morocco (*khettara*). Their wide distribution throughout the Near East, and indeed into the New World (Lightfoot 2000), is thought to have taken place since the earlier part of the first millennium B.C. The apparent existence of underground channels dated to this time period in Oman and the southern Levant, however, suggests that the date of discovery and its dispersal may be rather earlier (Al-Tikriti 2002). Qanat-fed oases are found in many parts of the Arabian peninsula (Lightfoot 2000; fig. 4). Archaeological examples have been described in Saudi Arabia (Nasif 1988), the United Arab Emirates (Cleuziou 1996), Bahrain (Larsen 1983: 91), and Oman (Jeffrey Orchard 1999). In a typical qanat, water is collected from an alluvial fan or from river gravels and transported via underground tunnels linked by vertical ventilation and access shafts so that the rate of descent of the main channel is less than that of the ground surface. Because these tap ground-

water, flow is continuous, with the result that its distribution can entail time shares that run throughout night and day (fig. 8.2; Dutton 1989; Beaumont 1989). Qanats can determine the structure of both the neighboring rural landscape and the villages and towns that receive its water. For example, in Iran the main street often follows the qanat channel (Roaf 1989), and many social activities become focused upon the point where the water emerges at the surface (i.e., the *mazhar*). The place of water withdrawal is frequently located in the main village square around which some of the more prominent inhabitants have their houses (Honari 1989: 65). According to Bonine, there is often a striking correspondence between the field systems and settlement form so that the shape and orientation of courtyard houses follows and develops along the pattern of field systems (Bonine 1989). This field pattern is, in turn, established by the pattern of distribution canals, which follow a roughly rectilinear grid (Bonine 1989: 49). In parts of Iran, qanats dominate the landscape, and they appear almost like swarms across the face of alluvial fans. Most qanats are only 1–5 km long, with mother wells 10–50 m in depth, which makes them capable of irrigating a mere 10–20 ha, but in parts of Iran, they can be up to 50 km in length, with mother wells up to 290 m deep (Beaumont 1989).

In Oman, features equivalent to qanats are referred to as falaj (pl. *aflaj*), which for convenience have been classified by John Wilkinson (1977) into two classes: the qanat falaj, which is the equivalent of the Iranian qanat, and the *ghayl* falaj, which transports water across the surface usually from perennial pools in wadis or from springs. In a typical falaj village, water irrigates a main area of date palms with an understorey of fruit trees and vegetables, plus a peripheral area sown to field crops such as wheat and alfalfa (fig. 8.3; Dutton 1989: 248). In

Fig. 8.2   *Falaj* leading to palm gardens in southeast Oman.

an Omani falaj, oasis water is allocated sequentially downstream so that drinking water for a village is accessible first via an opening where the channel emerges at ground level. The water then flows through the village, often via a covered channel, along which occur special access points for drinking water, personal washing (men upstream, women further downstream, the dead furthest downstream); finally, water is led to the fields where it supplies the main palm gardens and other fields. A crucial part of the water's journey is through the village mosque (or mosques), where it supplies water for ablutions. In fact, the building of a mosque is often related to the construction of a new water channel (Costa 2001), and in this way, the religious landscape becomes tied in to the broader landscape. In certain years, excess flow can then be allocated to periodically farmed lands

known as *awabi* lands (J.C. Wilkinson 1977: 97–98). Supplementary water traditionally comes from shallow hand- or animal-operated wells and more recently from pumped wells. Larger oasis settlements receive water from more than one falaj.

A striking feature of some falaj landscapes is that gardens can be dug into the ground, thereby forming extensive sunken areas around which appear large mounds of spoil termed *nadd* (pl. *nudud*: fig. 8.4). The need to excavate the garden arises when a falaj issues at a level that is too low for the water to be brought by gravity flow to the surface; consequently, the field surface must be established at the level of the water rather than, as is customary, for the water to be "raised" relative to the terrain until it attains the level of the fields. For the archaeologist, these upcast mounds can be misleading because of their resemblance to

tells. Moreover, if the sunken garden was cut through buried archaeological strata, the upcast mounds can also exhibit a surface scatter of artifacts. Sunken gardens bear witness not only to the way that accessible water levels can determine the location of gardens but also to the extraordinary labor that traditional communities will expend to irrigate their land.

On historical grounds it has been suggested that the qanat falaj was introduced to Oman from Iran by the Achaemenid administration (J.C. Wilkinson 1977), but the recent discovery of falaj channels of probably Iron Age II date at al-Maysar in Oman (Yule 1999: 101), as well as Hili and al-Madam in the United Arab Emirates (Boucharlat 2001: 164; Benoist et al. 1997; Al-Tikriti 2002), suggests that a date in the early first millennium B.C. or even slightly earlier can now be accepted.

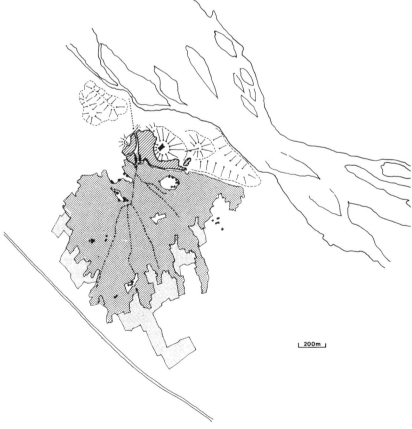

Fig. 8.3   An Omani oasis:
(top) Oasis of Mudhayrib in
Oman from the air (photo by T. J.
Wilkinson).
(left) Map of Mudhayrib showing
the *falaj* (dotted line), garden
area (stipple), and settlement
(hatched)
(from Costa 1983).

Fig. 8.4 Oasis in inner Oman showing mounds of soil (*nadd*) upcast during the excavation of sunken fields.

The evidence for an early Iron Age date is most compelling at the site of Hila 15 (Al-ʿAin, United Arab Emirates), where a series of excavations have revealed stone-lined channels, distributary channels (presumably leading to gardens), a point for the drawing of water (*shari ʾa*), and the well-like access shafts of the underground channel (Al-Tikriti 2002: 344–348). Excavated ceramics in association with the channel supply convincing evidence for a date of the aflaj in the range sixth to eleventh centuries B.C. An early first-millennium date is also supported by radiocarbon determinations of falaj channels (Falaj Jill) near Nizwa, which are approximately 2560 B.P. and 1735 B.P. (Clark 1988). Therefore, it now seems that the history of the qanat can be traced to an earlier date in southeast Arabia than in Iran, and its development appears to have contributed to the rapid increase in the number and scale of irrigated

oases that are found in Oman and the United Arab Emirates from the early first millennium B.C. (Magee 2000: 34).

Pre-Iron Age Oases

Today oasis settlements receive their water supply either from raised water tables (which can result in the emergence of springs) or from the perennial flow in wadis. Should the groundwater come sufficiently close to the surface it can be extracted by means of shallow wells. In particularly fortuitous circumstances, artesian water can even emerge from below sea level, as in Bahrain, where Larsen has described the historical sequence of oases that developed around artesian springs (Larsen 1983). Alternatively, some oases (for example, the Tafilalt oasis of Morocco) are positioned on major rivers that supply water for flood irrigation (see below for a Yemeni

example). Finally, oases can be artificial entities that receive their water via qanats or similar underground channels, as described above.

Probably the earliest oases recorded in the Arabian peninsula are those of eastern Saudi Arabia, where Ubaid settlements developed in the vicinity of springs, salt flats (sabkha), and relict shorelines near the al-Hasāʾ and Jabrin oases (Masry 1997). The large and complex oasis of al-Hasāʾ originally received its water from some 50–60 artesian springs. During the Ubaid, the third millennium B.C. and the Seleucid periods, oasis settlements were apparently situated on the edges of sabkhas and near wells, springs, or wadis (Adams et al. 1977: pl. 2). Extensive areas of gardens were eventually irrigated, and many of these were founded in the Early Islamic period (Adams et al. 1977: 28; Whitcomb 1978). Despite its aridity, Saudi Arabia is blessed with a number of oases where

Table 8.1 Amount of Garden Area Required to Support a Given Number of People in an Omani Garden Irrigated by a *Falaj*

A	B	C	D	E	F	G
Number of palms irrigated by 1 liter/sec. flow	Area of palms	No. of people supported per ha*	Assumed number of people per ha of occupied site	Area of site occupied by 100 persons	Area of garden to support 100 persons	Ratio of F:E
200	1 ha	20–25	100–200	0.5–1 ha	4–5 ha	1:4–1:10

*Increasing the area of garden per family so that each ha of garden was capable of supporting 10 persons would increase the field to settlement ratio to 1:10–1:20.

springs or pools supply sufficient water for irrigation. For example, large irrigated field systems have been recorded near the Jebel Tuwayq to the south of Riyadh, where the Comprehensive Survey of Saudi Arabia recorded a system of channels that distributed water from pools in the wadi bed (Zarins et al. 1979: 28–29). Water was then led to field systems surrounding a tell, both settlement and fields being dated by surface sherds to the local equivalent of the Hellenistic period. Similar field systems were noted by Ingraham et al. (1981: 72–73) in western Saudi Arabia, where channels and qanats supplied irrigation water to fields strewn with pottery that diminished in density away from the main settlement. Such a pattern suggests that intensive manuring was practiced in antiquity and that the sherds have been concentrated as a result of the deflation of the surrounding soil matrix, a common process in the arid Near East (see chapter 4).

A common natural source of water occurs where the water table along a wadi is elevated either behind a rock bar or where a major ridge obstructs the flow of groundwater. This is illustrated at the village of Sulayf (near Ibra, Oman), where a north-south ridge has been cut through by the Wadi Sulayf (Letts 1978). By acting as a partial barrier to groundwater flow, the level of the water table rose toward the gap to such a degree that surface water issued immediately downstream of the gap. In

antiquity such water sources could have been employed to irrigate fields either at the gap or at some distance downstream.

Before the introduction of falaj systems, oases would have harnessed a combination of perennial surface flow from wadis, hand-operated wells, and flood runoff, the last being gathered by so-called *garbabands*. Because climatic conditions in southern Arabia were probably moister in the early third millennium B.C. when the first Omani oases developed, discharge from wadi beds would have been greater than today. But in the absence of estimates of such discharges, it is appropriate to use a model of falaj settlement presented by John Wilkinson as a yardstick against which earlier oasis settlements can be measured. Assuming that 1 liter/second of flow is capable of irrigating around 200 palm trees on 1 ha, the number of people that could be supported by 1 ha of gardens, as well as the ratio of fields to settlement area, can be estimated (table 8.1).

As a Durham University team has shown (Letts 1978), falaj discharges in the area of Bāt (Oman) range from 2.5 to 153.7 liters/ha, which gives a feasible irrigated area for single falaj oases in the range 2.5–154 ha, a figure that would be exceeded if there were multiple water sources. If a family of five requires around 0.25 ha of palms and associated cultivation, then a garden 40 ha in area would be capable of supporting some eight hundred to one thou-

sand people (J. C. Wilkinson 1977: 92), which conforms to a ratio of garden to settlement of between 10:1 and 4:1 (table 8.1). Relaxing these constraints to allow for a more generous holding per family of 0.5 ha (i.e., ten persons per ha of garden), the garden:settlement ratio would be increased to between 10:1 to 20:1, which accords roughly to the pattern of traditional oases as illustrated on figure 8.3 (in this case, roughly 1:15). Because this ratio is not specific to falaj irrigation, but rather is applicable to Omani irrigated gardens in general, it provides a useful measure for comparison with the record of early oases.

To date, the most impressive evidence of an Early Bronze Age oasis settlement comes from Hili, located in the modern oasis of Buraimi. This site complex, which dates from the early third millennium B.C., has suffered considerably from attrition by later agricultural activities that, over the last four or five thousand years, have obscured or erased much of the landscape evidence. Nevertheless, within the oasis, large mudbrick towers, major tombs, and other monumental structures remain. Excavation suggests that already by the third millennium B.C., agriculture entailed a mixed husbandry based around palm gardens, with three types of barley, two varieties of wheat, and possibly sorghum (Cleuziou 1997: 400). Today palm trees form a fundamental part of the oases of Arabia, and these were also present at Hili during the third

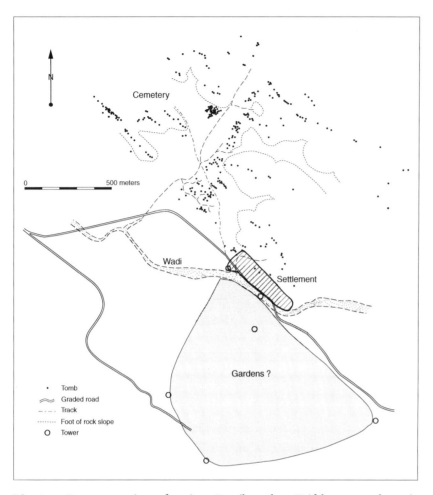

Fig. 8.5 Reconstruction of oasis at Bāt (based on Frifelt 1976 and 1985).

millennium B.C. (Cleuziou 1996: 160). By providing shade for a lower understory of plants such as peas and possibly melons, palm trees in Arabian oases, like their counterparts in ancient Iraq, played a vital role in providing a suitable microclimate for agriculture. Such palm gardens clearly required frequent irrigation, and support for this practice was found stratified within the archaeological levels of Hili 8 in the form of a ditch 4–5 m wide and 2.5 m. This provides convincing evidence for gravity-flow irrigation in the area (Cleuziou 1997: 402–403).

A broader picture of the landscape can be sketched from the site of Bāt excavated near Ibri by Karen Frifelt during the 1970s (Frifelt 1976; Frifelt 1985; Brunswig 1989). Here four or five ringwall towers defined an area of some 40–60 ha, which is bounded to the north by a wadi flow-

ing along the foot of a range of low hills (fig. 8.5). A roughly 4 ha Umm an-Nar period settlement (ca. 2500 to 2000 B.C.) occurs as a scatter of wall foundations along the foot of these hills. Small cross walls by the wadi suggest that wadi flow may have been captured by means of flood runoff deflection to irrigate a narrow terraced garden along the wadi edge (Brunswig 1989: 20). Extending over about 1 square km of rocky hills beyond the settlement was the realm of the dead. Here hundreds of tombs dating from the Bronze Age and later contain the remains of the inhabitants of the settlement, as well as presumably later inhabitants who may have belonged to different perhaps mobile communities. By around 2800 B.C., burial within single-chambered cairns had given way to large multichambered monumental Umm an-Nar tombs, which

served for collective burials. With the establishment of Umm an-Nar tombs closer to the settlement, this left the earlier ancestral tombs as territorial markers on the surrounding ridges, where they dominate the landscape (Gentelle and Frifelt 1989: 121; Cleuziou 1996: 161).

If the area enclosed by the towers (40–60 ha) was primarily devoted to palm gardens and ancillary agriculture, this area could support some eight hundred to twelve hundred people accommodated within a settlement of 6–12 ha (twelve hundred people) or 4–8 ha (eight hundred people), depending upon whether settlement densities of one hundred or two hundred persons per ha of site are employed. As rough as these figures are, the estimated population that could be supported by the production of the gardens accords approximately with the population calculated to have resided in the neighboring settlement. These areas of agricultural oases are also of approximately the same scale as modern falaj-irrigated oases in the region, as well as with the scale of Bronze Age towns in other parts of Arabia, where occupied areas are typically 3–5 ha. Only at Qalat al-Bahrain was a Bronze Age town unambiguously demonstrated to be in excess of this (Edens et al. 2000; Højland and Andersen 1997).

During the third millennium B.C., oasis settlements of interior Oman may therefore have consisted of enclosed gardens, peripheral domestic settlements, and hilltop necropoli. Together, these would define a landscape not unlike that of traditional Oman, with the exception that irrigation probably came from a combination of wells, perennial wadi flow, and floods rather than falaj systems. As with modern oasis settlements, the garden areas probably included occasional buildings, but one would not expect the valley bottom lands to be entirely built up to form a continuous built-up area.

Beyond the traditional oasis, it is possible to recognize a tripartite land-use zone along the mountains of inner Oman: an outer camel-herding zone furthest from the mountains; and an intermediate zone of mixed sheep/goat herding, which in turn merges with the agricultural zone along the edge of the mountains and within the foothill zone (J. C. Wilkinson 1977: 64). Given the lack of evidence for large-scale domestication of the camel during the third millennium B.C., it is unclear what form such an outer zone would have taken. On the other hand, the intermediate zone was probably well used by the flocks belonging to the village settlements, and we would therefore expect to see each oasis surrounded by a pasture zone, which would be equivalent to the *haram* of the traditional village. By analogy with the modern day, this pasture zone would degrade considerably from the depredations of sheep grazing and goat browsing.

Iron Age Oases of Southern Arabia

Around the fringes of the mountains of southwest Arabia and dependent upon these highlands for their water supply are spectacular irrigation systems that provide their own distinctive landscapes (namely, the Sayhad and Hadhramaut). Within the areas of the former Sabaean, Qatabanean, and Minaean states that fringe the interior deserts of the Rub al-Khali (or the "Empty Quarter"), agricultural systems are entirely depended upon irrigation, and here valley after valley is dominated by major systems of flood-irrigation agriculture.

Geoarchaeological investigations demonstrate that the two main wadi systems draining the Sayhad and Hadhramaut areas today—the Wadi Hadhramaut to the east and the Wadi Jawf to the west—were, during the early- to mid-Holocene moist interval, probably joined into a single, large, integrated channel system that connected through the intervening Ramlat Sabat'ayn desert (fig. 8.6; Cleuziou et al. 1992).

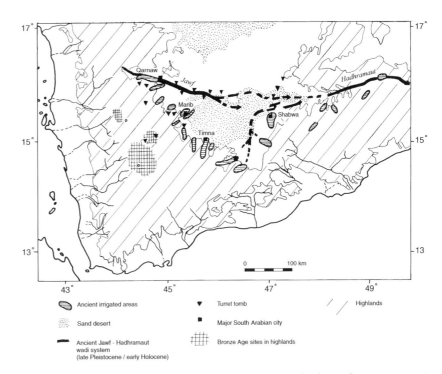

Fig. 8.6   Southern Arabia showing main oases, the late Pleistocene–early Holocene wadi system, the distribution of turret tombs, and major areas of Bronze Age settlement in highlands (based on Brunner 1997; Cleuziou et al. 1992; De Maigret 1996: fig. 13).

During the late second millennium B.C. and the early first millennium A.D., there developed in southern Arabia a brisk trade in frankincense and myrrh between the source area in present southern Oman and eastern Yemen and recipient areas to the north, namely, the Levant, Mesopotamia, and the East Mediterranean (Groom 1981). Profits generated from this trade stimulated the development of a series of large, thriving oasis towns along the route, both within southern Arabia and also along the chain of the Hejaz mountains of western Arabia. The agricultural systems that developed relied on the generation of flood runoff from the highlands, but in contrast to agricultural systems of the adjacent highlands, they were wholly reliant upon irrigation. In fact, Doe (1983: 102) goes so far as to suggest that the area of field systems recognized was so far in excess of the needs of the local inhabitants that the oases probably exported staple crops to the Mediterranean area. Al-

though there is no reason to support such an optimistic statement, the scale of these irrigated field systems was such that they have generated legends such as the tradition that a horse could travel in green pasture for seven days in each direction from Marib (Brunner 1997: 199).

The first formal mapping of these oases and their irrigation systems was undertaken in the Wadi Hadhramaut by Caton-Thompson and Gardner (1939) during the 1930s, followed by Bowen for the Wadi Bayhan area during the early 1950s (Bowen 1958). Since then, these oases have produced major geoarchaeological and landscape studies. Oases mapped to date include (from west to east: fig. 8.6): (a) the Marib area (Brunner 1983, Hehmeyer and Schmidt 1991, Hehmeyer 1989, Wagner 1993, and Schaloske 1995); (b) Wadi Bayhan (Bowen 1958; Breton et al. 1998; Marcolongo and Morandi 1997), and Wadi al-Jubah (Grolier et al. 1996; Overstreet et al. 1988a; both near Timna on fig. 8.6);

(c) Shabwa (Gentelle 1991) and (d) Hadhramaut (Caton-Thompson and Gardner 1939 and Caton-Thompson 1944).

The common factor in the recognition of these irrigated landscapes is the presence of large areas of silt terrain, which are conspicuous from the air by virtue of their distinctive pattern of gullies eroded on a rectangular grid. This erosional pattern has enabled the silts to be effectively mapped using aerial photographs. Because these silts encapsulate many agricultural features they can be described through time (that is, stratigraphically in the vertical plane) as well as in space. Deposits are up to 30 m or more deep in the Marib area, in excess of 11 m in the Wadi Marha (Brunner 1997), and from 15–18 m in the Wadi Bayhan (Bowen 1958: 65). Although initial studies suggested that such massive valley fills resulted from natural aeolian and alluvial sedimentation (Caton-Thompson and Gardner 1939), further study demonstrated that all are indeed the product of deposition resulting from former irrigation. Because the silts have aggraded by the gradual accretion of mud deposited from the silt-laden waters of the floods (at rates of 0.7–1 cm per annum), they have caused the gradual burial of parts of the archaeological record (Jocelyn Orchard 1982; Brunner 1983). Consequently, major structures such as the lower parts of the Bar'an temple at Marib have been obscured, and isolated hamlets and farms appear to have been completely buried (Breton 1998: 17).

The silts accumulate as the result of the redistribution of silt-rich floodwaters (the *sayl*) over irrigated fields. The main periods of flooding usually take place following the spring (April) or summer (July/August) monsoons. During the first millennium B.C., water was gathered either by dams, such as the great Marib Dam, or by temporary deflector walls constructed in the wadis, to be directed into a network of primary, secondary, and tertiary canals that led water onto the fields (for description of traditional flood agricultural systems, see Serjeant 1988). Channels were of silt, but where strong erosional flow was expected, they were reinforced by stone. Such masonry installations were constructed where water was released from canals, where it was necessary to prevent erosion at bends, within secondary distribution systems, and at drop structures where water was conducted from higher to lower levels (Bowen 1958: 45). Irrigation could be by submersion in which floodwater was directed on to fields enclosed by silt walls (Hehmeyer 1989: 36–37). As a result, the field became completely immersed until the water drained away. Alternatively, "controlled flooding" resulted in floodwater flowing through each field to the next. Finally, more long-lived systems of water supply were tapped from wells or cisterns, and these probably provided supplementary nourishment for selected plants. Of these three systems, the first two predominated and caused the rapid aggradation of the silt fields.

One byproduct of such rapid siltation was the preservation of agricultural features that include furrows (30–35 cm apart and indicating that the depth of ploughing was 10–15 cm), root casts of various plants, and ghosts of the bowls of trees. The last were evident in the form of concentric circles of silt and clay that sometimes projected as much as 50 cm above the silts (Hehmeyer 1989: 39; Hehmeyer and Schmidt 1991: 18–20). Root casts (fossilized root systems) became infilled with soil particles that were originally in contact with roots as well as sediments that trickled down subsequently from above. Root-cast morphology suggests that three types of plant were present: first, roots of a regular, uniform diameter are apparently of monocotyledons, probably date palms. Second, larger irregular casts of dicotyledons could be of fruit trees, 'ilb trees (*Ziziphus spina-christi*), ban trees (*Moringa aptera*) cultivated for their oils, or grapevines. Third, casts of fine root hairs appear to indicate the cultivation of garden crops, cereals, and fodder (Hehmeyer 1989: 41). Although root casts have been recorded only from the Marib silts, the tree circles, which normally occur in rows as would be expected in orchards, have been noted from the Wadi Bayhan (Bowen 1958), Marib (Hehmeyer and Schmidt 1991), and Wadi Mahrar (Brunner 1997: fig. 7). Because rectangular erosional patterns are caused by the development of gullies along less-resistant sand-filled irrigation channels, they allow the size and shape of fields to be estimated. Most were rectangular, ranging in size from around 0.35 ha to 2 ha (for Wadi Bayhan: Bowen 1958: 53; Marib: Hehmeyer 1989: 35; and Wadi Mahra: Brunner 1997: 196).

Fertilization was effected first by the high mineral and organic content of the floodwaters and second by fertilization, which was apparent in the form of horizons of ash within the sediments. Alternatively, darkened humic horizons may have resulted from the applications of organic manure (Hehmeyer 1989: 36), whereas stray sherds in the soil result from the application of artifact-rich refuse to the fields (Toplyn 1988: 98–99).

Sayl irrigation systems of the Sayhad appear to be an evolutionary development of traditional systems of flood irrigation. In most cases, the dams are not formal storage dams but rather were designed to deflect water into the canals or to raise it to the height required by the fields. The best example is the Marib Dam, which was built in probably the fifth or sixth century B.C. to replace earlier water-deflection structures extending in date back to the third millennium B.C. The main dam is an earthen structure some 16–20 m high and with a length of ca. 600–680 m (Brunner and Haefner 1986: 80; Breton 1998). Only the sluices are of masonry, and these rise like mas-

Fig. 8.7 Southern sluice of the Marib Dam, showing the strong ashlar superstructure of the sluice, with the sluice channel to left. Originally, the earthen dam was to the right (courtesy of McGuire Gibson). For location, see fig. 8.8:2.

sive fortifications to the north and south of the Wadi Dhanah (fig. 8.7).

Although inscriptions supply dates for some of these dams or deflectors, the early history of irrigation must be inferred from the sediments themselves. The Holocene stratigraphy of valley fills in the Sayhad is similar to that of the highlands. A black organic-rich palaeosol serves as a convenient stratigraphic marker for the mid Holocene (Grolier et al. 1996: 15) and is dated by radiocarbon determinations to the range 9520 ±280 B.P. to 5270 ± 90 B.P. (Grolier et al. 1996: 363) or slightly later. Above this horizon are silty sediments accumulated under a flood-irrigation regime (the anthrosols), whereas below occur alluvial and colluvial deposits. Therefore, as in the highlands, the dark palaeosol serves to differentiate the late Holocene sediments that accumulated in conjunction with significant human activity from the early Holo-

cene and late Pleistocene deposits that were deposited prior to significant human interference with the environment. At Marib, using the measured sedimentation rate of 0.7–1.1 cm per annum, irrigation is estimated to have extended back to around 2400 B.C. (Hehmeyer and Schmidt 1991: 11–12). Such an early date for the initiation of irrigation is supported by radiocarbon assay on charcoal obtained from within irrigation silts some 7 m below a water distributor in the Wadi Marha (3640 B.P.; Brunner 1997: 196). The date at which irrigation ceased varies from place to place depending upon social, economic, political, and environmental conditions, but by the time of the collapse of the great dam at Marib in the sixth or seventh century A.D., most irrigation systems had fallen out of use. Nevertheless, total collapse should not be assumed, and in some areas, such as the Wadi Marha, there was a continuation of

sayl irrigation, albeit at a smaller scale into the Islamic period.

Between the oases of Marib and Shabwa irrigated sediments are estimated to cover some 44,500 ha (i.e., 445 sq. km; Brunner 1997: 199). Although this area was not necessarily all in use at the same time, most was under cultivation during the first millennium B.C. At Marib the total area of some 9,600 cultivated hectares (or some 8,000 ha, according to Hehmeyer 1989) can be apportioned as 5,300 ha in the southern oasis and 4,300 ha in the northern oasis (fig. 8.8). This compares with an occupied area of the Iron Age town of Marib of about 100 ha. Although population estimates based on site areas are very coarse at best, the likely population of the town of Marib (10,000 to 30,000 people) overlaps with the potential number of people that could be supported from the estimated field area, but at the lower end of that range (26,400

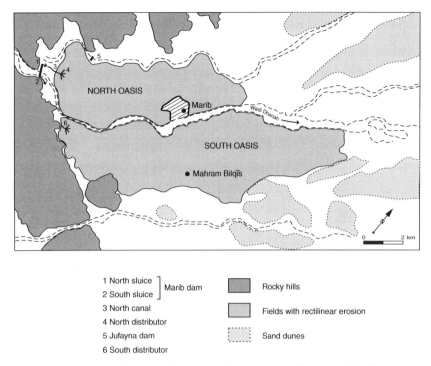

1 North sluice ⎫ Marib dam
2 South sluice ⎭

3 North canal

4 North distributor

5 Jufayna dam

6 South distributor

Rocky hills

Fields with rectilinear erosion

Sand dunes

Fig. 8.8   The Marib oasis, the dam, the town, and irrigated field areas (modified from Brunner 1983: fig. 24).

to 96,000). This assumes that the level of intensity was comparable to irrigation systems of the Tihama, where 0.5 ha of multicropped land can support a family (around 5–7 people). Allowing for a more generous holding per family of 1 and 1.5 ha gives supportable populations in the range 26,400 to 31,600, but if levels of intensity were equivalent to an Omani oasis (see above), the irrigated field area would support an even higher population.

Therefore, within the range of available land-use parameters and allowing for a reasonable area of gardens per family, the Marib oasis could comfortably support the population of the town but with a potential surplus. This could have been used to supply passing caravans, other nonurban communities around the oasis, or crucial stocks of reserve foods.

Water from a Reluctant Desert

Ultimately, water is the key limiting factor for human life in the desert, and if there is to be any long-term settlement, it is necessary to collect or gather water, ideally from as many water sources as possible. This provides insurance so that if one system fails to yield water, another can be employed. Such "belt-and-braces" tactics might entail the construction of both wells and runoff systems to supply water, but because in some locations physical conditions limit the amount of available water, such strategies are not always practicable. For example, in northeast Saudi Arabia local water tables fall within 7 to 25 m of the surface, that is, within the reach of hand-dug wells, but further west (i.e., to the west of Rafha), depths to water in the 1970s were greater than 160 m and even 350–500 m, thereby precluding the excavation of any wells using traditional techniques.

Where it is impossible to extract groundwater or it does not rise to the surface, it therefore becomes necessary to utilize some form of runoff-collection technique or wadi floods for building up reserves of water for travelers, nomads, or small local desert communities. In 1977

Neil Roberts defined a major zone for harnessing runoff throughout much of western Arabia, from Yemen to Jordan (Roberts 1977: fig. 1). Although this model can be upheld at a general level, more detailed analysis demonstrates the existence of many potential sources of water in this runoff zone. Consequently, communities have tailored their techniques to local hydrological conditions with a considerable degree of subtlety.

Desert communities frequently make use of the ecological principle of sources and sinks discussed above to yield an enhanced water supply for any given installation. In northern Saudi Arabia the bedouin have traditionally utilized so-called *mahfurs* (i.e., excavated depressions) to collect water either from enclosed depressions (*khabras*) or at the junction of two wadis (Vidale 1978: 115; Lancaster and Lancaster 1999: 135–137). Unfortunately, of the 730 mahfurs noted by Vidale (1978: 118), none could be convincingly dated. An analogous but more sophisticated system was recorded in the eastern Jordanian desert within an enclosed depression in basalt terrain where mean annual rainfall is ca. 150 mm per annum (Betts and Helms 1989). Two features, a pool and a well, were situated in a broad depression and received water guided into them by low walls or canals. Well 1 and pool 1 each received water from a catchment that captured water from areas of 21,500 and 4,700 sq. m respectively. Using principles developed in the Negev desert by Evenari et al. (1982), Betts and Helms estimate that the catchments would yield some 6,200 cubic m of water, of which around 5,500 would be available for storage in the pool and well (Betts and Helms 1989: 8). As with many desert features, this water-gathering system could not be dated except to broad possible ranges such as either Pre-Pottery Neolithic or Roman/Byzantine. It is noteworthy, however, that the overall layout and hydraulics of this system closely resemble more formalized systems of cisterns devised for the supply of pilgrims who passed along one of the main Hajj routes from Kufa in Iraq to Mecca in the Hejaz mountains.

Landscapes of the Desert Hajj Routes

Passage through the desert can offer innumerable privations for the traveler, and ancient route systems provide a unique insight into coping strategies that were developed for the provisioning of travelers. Rarely can true roadways be discerned such as are commonly associated with the Roman routes of the Levant (e.g., Kennedy and Riley 1990). Instead, as a result of the prolonged passage of humans through the desert, the rather indistinct traces of tracks are more common, and such traces can even be revealed by suitably enhanced satellite imagery (Clapp 1998).

Probably the best examples of desert route systems are those of the Hajj routes. The Hajj has always occupied a central role in Muslim life, and it is expected that each Muslim should visit Mecca at least once (Petersen 1994: 47). This was no easy matter, however, because for most pilgrims, this entailed an arduous journey through the deserts of Arabia en route for Mecca, which became the focus for Hajj routes from Egypt, Damascus and Bilad ash Sham (Syria), Iraq, Oman, and Yemen (see fig. 1 in Petersen 1994). To ease the privations of the original pilgrims, a number of individuals endowed the route with way stations, the best-known benefactor being the wife of the Abbasid caliph, Queen Zubayda, hence the name of the route: the Darb Zubayda (Al-Rashid 1980). By providing a major thoroughfare through the deserts (albeit sometimes building upon pre-Islamic routes), hajj roads became a major structuring element in the desert landscape. The robust and formalized water tanks found along these roads have survived in good condition since they were con-

structed, mainly in the ninth and tenth centuries A.D., so that with a little cleaning out, they have kept the bedouin well supplied with water through the last millennia. This has perpetuated the use of the way stations along the Darb Zubayda well beyond their originally intended use, so that now they service bedouin communities who have very different patterns of movement and agendas than the original pilgrims.

The route taken was arduous in the extreme, following a course 1,400 km long south–southwest from Kufa in Iraq, across the deserts of western Iraq and northern Saudi Arabia, between two elongate fingers of the Nefud desert, across the Nejd plateau of Saudi Arabia, to follow alongside the Hejaz mountains until Mecca was reached (Al-Rashid 1980; Finster 1978). Pilgrim roads were rarely paved, but in Yemen, the Hajj road from San ʿa to Mecca included a number of paved sections as well as lengths that consisted of "shouldered" tracks flanked by walls or banks of stones (Thenayian 1999: 142–148; cf. fig. 4.8b). Where it was necessary to negotiate mountains or ridges, the route was cut through rock and took the form of either paved steps (mudarrajat) or rock-cut passes (Thenayian 1999: 138–142). In most cases, the Darb Zubayda was simply a broad tract of land across the desert along which the caravans would pass, using landmarks (where present) to guide them. Near way stations the routes became more formalized, with cairns of stones and other alignments providing guidelines to the cisterns. Rarely it is possible to discern broad tracts of land that have been cleared of stones and demarcated by walls of cleared stones, or soil marks of disturbed ground along the routes (Musil 1928: 189). Milestones are also occasionally reported. According to Saad Al-Rashid, who originally surveyed the route in Saudi Arabia, there were some fifty-four major stopping places en route, with smaller way stations between (Al-Rashid 1979,

1980). Water was supplied by means of wells, water tanks (birkehs), qanats, and dams, depending upon local conditions. Additional facilities included khans (buildings designed for perhaps officials or more high-status individuals), mosques, palaces, occasional forts, rare settlements, and cemeteries, for the inevitable victims of the harsh travel conditions. This route was a conduit not only for people and commerce but also for disease (the shells of snails known to carry the disease bilharzia occur in some tanks).

Before illustrating the landscape of an individual station it is appropriate to discuss the variety of water systems along the route and how these in turn contribute to the development of the landscape. The Darb Zubayda in Saudi Arabia crosses a wide range of terrain types (fig. 8.9), all of which receive low and highly variable mean annual rainfall, around 100 mm per annum or less. It was therefore the task of the Abbasid engineers to position the water tanks (which formed the bulk of the water storage devices) where best advantage could be gained from the capricious rainfall and least damage would be incurred by floods.

At the northern end of the Darb Zubayda within Saudi Arabia, the route is aligned north–south to aim the travelers so they could pass through the narrow gap between the aeolian sand fingers of the Nafud and ad-Dahna deserts (A–B: fig. 8.9). The route mainly crosses a seemingly limitless plateau of Cretaceous and Tertiary sedimentary rocks of the Arabian Shelf. Most water tanks are located within enclosed silt-floored depressions (khabra or faydah) that form natural water-gathering basins (see below) or by weakly developed seasonal channels of wadis. Occasional wells, such as the massive ancient and deep masonry wells at Zubalah, supplied supplementary water. Between B and C (fig. 8.9) the route picks its way between the linear dune fields of the Nafud, which appear to have had a similar general

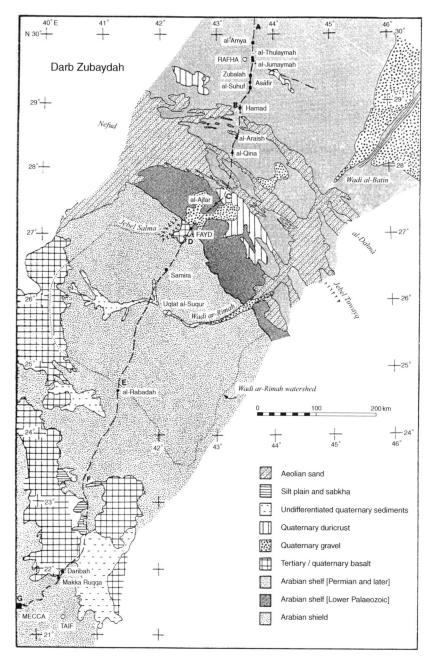

Fig. 8.9 Major way stations along the Darb Zubaydah in Saudi Arabia in their geological context.

water tanks derived their water from short wadis that crossed the Ordovician and Cambrian sandstones of the plateau. Continuing to the south—southwest, the route then tackled the vast but majestic Nejd plateau developed upon the ancient and mainly Pre-Cambrian metamorphic and granitic masses of the Arabian Shield (D–E: fig. 8.9). Here wadis become the main source of water. These vary in scale but include the bed of the major Wadi al-Rimah, a now partly relict Pleistocene channel that once crossed the entire Arabian peninsula (Dabbagh et al. 1998). Although larger wadis might supply higher-flow discharges for the tanks, they would also suffer considerable losses of flow into the sand and gravel channels. Because small tributary valleys can supply as many and certainly less destructive flows than large wadis, there is some flexibility in the location of the water tanks, which can frequently be positioned along smaller distributary or on tributary channels of the main wadis. If a distributary channel forms the source of supply, then water can flow directly into a water tank, through a small sediment trap or *misfah*, but on medium-sized wadis water would be directed into the tank via small masonry dams built across the wadis (see examples from Kutayfa, Hurayd, and al-Jaffālyya south in Wilkinson 1980b).

After arriving at the small town of al-Rabadhah (Al-Rashid 1986) travelers continued to enjoy the majesty of the Nejd (E–F: fig. 8.9), which would eventually be enlivened by two masses of forbidding black basalt plateau (*harrat*) through which the Darb continued (F–G: fig. 8.9). Birkehs between E and F appear to have captured water in a similar manner as those further to the north within the Nejd. In the final part of the route, where Tertiary and Quaternary basalts crop out, rainfall is slightly higher (in places in excess of 150 mm per annum) and contributes to the recharge of basalt aquifers that provided perennial

location and morphology during the Abbasid period. Again water is captured either from weak and localized wadi flows or from small, enclosed basins. Having made it through the hazards of the Nafud, travelers would then follow a southwest–northeast alignment towards the halfway station at Fayd. Unlike most stations along the route, Fayd is an oasis that grew up around springs and wells nourished by groundwater from the

adjacent basalt terrain (Mackenzie and al-Helwah 1980).

Fayd was an important place even prior to Islam, and in the Early Islamic period there were markets there. For an agreed fee, pilgrims would frequently leave part of their stores there under the care of the inhabitants (Musil 1928: 216–220). With the exception of Fayd and a few stations that received supplementary water from shallow wells, most flow for tanks and reservoirs. Thus from at least the station of al-Dariba to Mecca itself, water either came from wells or was channeled to the way stations via underground conduits (qanat) or occasional surface channels. This is the most verdant part of the Darb Zubayda, and here large settlements such as al-Dariba, al-Aqiq, and Umm al-Damīrān developed (al-Dayel and Helwah 1978). Some even included irrigated gardens such as at the site of Umm al-Salim, where a grid of canals constructed of small stones and mortar supplied several hectares of gardens to the west of the reservoir (Knudstad 1977: pl. 35). Elsewhere reservoirs were equipped with outlets so that surplus water could be used to supply irrigated gardens (Knudstad 1977). In addition, as with a number of different locations along the Hejaz mountains, Early Islamic dams such as that at Wadi Harād provided additional water (al-Dayel and Helwah 1978: 57).

Way stations along the Darb Zubayda vary in size from small towns to little more than a building or two around a water tank. An example of the latter can be seen at the site of al-Jumaymah located to the north of figure 8.9 (fig. 8.10; see also al-Helwah et al. 1982). Here a square birkeh ca. 33 m × 30 m and 6.2 m deep (fig. 8.11) was positioned within a broad oval depression 2 km E–W × 0.65 km N–S and 6 m deep. The birkeh was cut into sandy limestone, with the upper part being of stone-and-mortar construction. Water entered from the west, guided by two antennaelike collection walls into the tank, and pilgrims could gain access to the water via stairs from the east. Additional water supply came from well, 10 m deep (16: fig. 8.11), that was mentioned by the Muslim traveler al-Harbi in the ninth century A.D. Only two buildings (2 and 3) were present, and each was located just above the possible flood level of the basin to east and west respectively of the inferred course of the pilgrim route, which was marked by

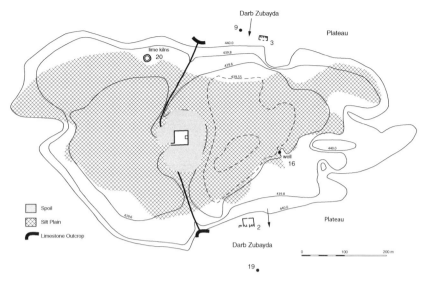

Fig. 8.10   Birket al-Jumaymah, Saudi Arabia, within its immediate catchment (north to top; for location, see fig. 8.9).

way markers (at 9 and 19: fig. 8.10). A kiln (20) had presumably been used to burn lime for the manufacturer of the plaster employed in waterproofing the tank. The basin comprised a western area of some 71 ha, which provided the runoff catchment for the birkeh, whereas the larger eastern area of the depression is today covered in shrubs. This would have supplied an ideal grazing area for pack animals well away from the water catchment for the cistern. Spoil mounds around both cistern and well attest periodic cleaning operations.

A perplexing question for the Darb Zubayda is why tanks and reservoirs are so frequent when a smaller number further apart could have adequately serviced most pilgrims and their pack animals. One reason may have been that they were designed to cater to the different lengths of travel before and after meal breaks. In addition, Queen Zubaydah is credited with commissioning the construction of smaller intermediate stations such as Jumaymah, which would have been inserted between larger stations to service the foot traveler (Al-Rashid 1980: 33). In addition, by provisioning the traveler with more tanks and stopping points than were absolutely

necessary, it was possible for tanks to collect the capricious and patchy rainfall of the Arabian desert and to increase the likelihood of at least some tanks retaining water. Recent records of rainfall from the nearby town of Rafha demonstrate that for the seventeen years (from 1967 to 1983), eight years supplied significant rainfall; of these eight, four rainfall years yielded sufficient runoff to fill or nearly fill the cistern. Consequently, under current climatic conditions, the cistern would have filled (or nearly so) only one year in four. By positioning more cisterns than were required, one could therefore take account of the spatially patchy desert rainfall and the differential response of different catchment basins to that rainfall. Therefore, Queen Zubayda, by claiming to have the interests of the poor foot traveler at heart, could also provide a more flexible and pragmatic water supply system than would be possible by spacing way stations more in keeping with the travel times of pilgrims.

In addition to short-term stopping places there were also settlements that acted as foci for long-term settlement and that included garden areas both to provision residents and to supply the pilgrims. Gardens often show up as walled and

Fig. 8.11   Birket al-Jumaymah, looking toward the western inlet.

irrigated areas (Knudstadt 1977), but elsewhere, as at the small site of Samira to the south of Fayd, they are invisible, except for the presence of sparse, dispersed scatters of potsherds that occur over the desert downstream of a reservoir located at the terminal point of an irrigation canal (Wilkinson 1980b: 62). These sherds probably represent all that is left of the settlement-derived refuse that was spread on the fields as fertilizer. Overall, however, there is little evidence for the production of food along the Darb Zubayda.

On the other hand, it was crucial to take care of the food requirements of the pack animals, and it was as important to locate way stations near good areas of forage as it was to position them with respect to water resources. By way of illustration, of fourteen way stations in the Nejd (i.e., zone D-E of fig. 8.9) only two areas showed evidence of zero or poor shrub forage, whereas twelve exhibited either moderate or high density of shrub forage. In other words, because it is fairly straightforward to extract water from many

different topographic or hydrological locations, in part because small wadis have a higher yield of water per unit of catchment than large wadis (Evenari et al. 1982; Bruins 1986: 42), there are many opportunities for the location of birkehs. Forage opportunities, in contrast, are more limited, and it may be expected that pasture areas would be equally or more important as a locational factor for way stations than the potential for gathering water.

Because of the importance of pasture resources for pilgrims traveling with large numbers of pack animals, pasture areas often became formalized. Witness the large areas of *hima* grazing lands that occurred at al-Rabadhah and five other stations along the Darb Zubayda (Al-Rashid 1986: 2–3). Overall therefore, pilgrim routes such as the Darb Zubayda resulted in the development of an alignment of "oases" through the desert, which thereby created not only a distinctive landscape but also one that was perpetuated through time by the very utility of the water-retaining cisterns.

Agriculture in the Desert Margins

Archaeological surveys undertaken in recent years demonstrate, rather counter-intuitively, that in the drier areas of the desert margins where rainfall is usually insufficient to sustain normal rain-fed agriculture, the number of archaeological sites (and associated features) per sq. km can be greater than in the moister areas where conditions are more suitable for human life and agriculture. This is illustrated by the Uvda valley in the Negev (rainfall ca. 30 mm), where Avner has recorded some 8 sites per sq. km (Avner 1998: 148), and around Umm al-Jimal in Jordan, where 2.5 sites per sq. km were recorded (Kennedy 2001: 41). Both figures are well in excess of, for example, site densities recorded in the fertile and relatively well watered lowlands of the northern Jazira (Iraq). Although it is clear that we are not comparing like with like (because sites in the Negev and Jordan are frequently small and dispersed, often including features that were occupied by transient populations), this statistic eloquently demonstrates that dry desert margins can harbor a considerable range of archaeological information. In addition, desert margins also form part of the landscape of preservation, because the episodic nature of settlement has allowed for greater preservation of landscape features.

The cyclical nature of desert occupations has been succinctly illustrated for the Negev, where distinct peaks in settlement occur in Early Bronze I–II, Middle Bronze I (i.e., the Intermediate Bronze Age at the end of the third millennium B.C.), and the Iron Age, culminating in a rapid succession of increasing settlement during Nabataean, Roman, and Byzantine times (Rosen 1987: figs. 6 and 7; for similar cycles, see Finkelstein 1995: fig. 2.1). Of these, the peak of greatest magnitude, namely, that of the Nabataean, Roman, and Byzantine occupations, was not succeeded by more intensive occupations. Consequently, this phase should constitute the landscape that is best preserved, whereas the landscapes of the earlier periods would be expected to survive only within windows in the Roman/Byzantine landscapes. As observed by Steven Rosen, although these peaks in settlement conform roughly to periods when atmospheric moisture was more amenable to long-term sedentary settlement, climatic changes do not adequately explain the decline in post-Byzantine settlement (Rosen 1987; 2000: 54–56). This is well exemplified by recent data from Saroq Cave near Jerusalem, which suggest that although the Early Bronze Age I–II and Iron Age peaks might conform to moister conditions in the region, those of the late third millennium and Byzantine times apparently occurred under conditions that were drier than normal.

Because the Early Bronze–Middle Bronze (= Intermediate Bronze Age) was a period of collapse of urban Bronze Age civilization further

north, expansion in the Negev may be the result of the need to increase and expand extensive agro-pastoral settlement in the Negev in the wake of the urban collapse (Rosen 1987: 53; see also Finkelstein 1995). Such an interrelationship may well explain the marked growth in settlement in the Negev/Sinai deserts, where some one thousand Early Bronze IV (or Middle Bronze I) sites have been recorded (Haiman 1996; Cohen and Dever 1980). It also illustrates a key factor of landscape utilization in desert margins, namely, that human ingenuity frequently provides a variety of ways of extracting a successful way of life from what are rather reluctant environments. By employing the appropriate strategies, desert-margin communities can therefore override the limitations of the environment.

Similar principles also operate in the marginal desert steppe of northern Syria, where today agro-pastoral communities cultivate barley fields in areas subject to frequent crop failures (say one or even two years out of five). In wetter years, when a crop is produced, there is grain for humans as well as grazing on stubble for the animals and natural pasture on the steppe. On the other hand, during dry years when it is anticipated that the crop will fail to produce heads of grain, flocks of sheep and goat can graze the "failed crop," which consequently provides a bonus for the sheep (Wachholtz 1996: 97). During such years farmers can presumably sell or exchange their fattened sheep for grain. Only during the very driest years will there be insufficient growth for both humans and animals. In Syria towards the limit of viable rain-fed cultivation, agro-pastoral communities are increasingly mobile, and so they can be resident during the periods for processing of harvests and crops and preparing the fields, to return to pastoral steppelands to the south for the winter (Wachholtz 1996: 100–103). Consequently, there is no hard and

fast division between sedentary and mobile groups.

A second coping strategy entails the application of principles of runoff and water-receiving areas that are fundamental to desert ecology (see the source:sink model, above). Desert-margin communities frequently gather runoff from a large catchment zone and lead the water that is generated to fields on nearby valley floors. As a result, annual rainfall of some 100 mm may be enhanced by supplementary runoff to an amount equivalent to 300–500 mm of annual rainfall, a figure that is sufficient for a satisfactory crop (Evenari et al. 1982: 109).

The origins of such water-harvesting practices in the southern Levant are still unclear, but Levy reports a small terraced field of the Chalcolithic period at Shiqmim in the northern Negev. This field may have been supplied by water from a microcatchment on the slopes above (Levy 1987: 58). That water harvesting was practiced is supported by Arlene Rosen's (1987) studies of phytoliths in barley and wheat in the Beesheva valley, which suggest that either floodwater farming or basin irrigation were conducted. Similarly, field systems in the Uvdat valley were presumably supplied by either runoff or floodwater (Avner 1998), but the absence of secure dates as well as evidence on the precise manner of water supply renders this evidence less conclusive. Because there is a tendency to reuse valley floors for this type of agriculture, and for them to accumulate sediment, there is a strong possibility that stratigraphically datable runoff fields may eventually be found in the appropriate sedimentary contexts.

At a regional scale, detailed hydrological measurements demonstrate that wetter areas of the northern Negev shed less water as runoff than drier areas to the south, because the drier areas have a greater percentage of bedrock exposure than moister areas. Specifically, the moister northern parts of the Negev are blanketed by patches of loess or mixed soil and stone regoliths that absorb more rainfall than the rock surfaces (Yair 2001: 300). Within any lithological zone, smaller catchment basins shed a higher percentage of rainfall as runoff than larger basins because in the latter, it is more likely that rainfall will be intercepted within wadi sediments and colluvium. Moreover, the positioning of fields requires a detailed knowledge of local soil and watershed conditions because not only is it necessary to generate sufficient water for crop growth but also it is crucial to ensure that there was not too much water that could destroy field walls or damage other irrigation installations.

Further refinements to water gathering were made by the clearance of stones from slopes, so that the exposed soil could then form a smooth crusted surface that enhanced the runoff potential of the slope. Such innovations were capable of increasing mean annual runoff by between 7 and 60 percent, depending upon slope (Evenari et al. 1982: 142–147). Stone clearance has resulted in a distinctive landscape of numerous small mounds and ridges that perforate the runoff slopes above fields (Evenari et al. 1982). Although the research of Evenari and colleagues provides a convincing explanation of these landscapes, the bedouin term for such mounds (tullul al-'ainab [i.e., grape mounds]) raises the question, originally put by E. H. Palmer (1871) in the nineteenth century, that these features may in fact have been for planting grapes on the slopes. This long-standing debate has been rekindled in recent years because hydrological research suggests that parts of the midslope form a wet zone that under the right circumstances can supply sufficient moisture for the growth of bushes or vines. Moreover, such mounds when found in Yemen today are indeed used for growing vines.

Irrespective of which explanation

is accepted for the stone mounds, it is clear that by harnessing a range of runoff-harvesting techniques, the ancient farmer was capable of providing sufficient runoff for cultivated crops in areas where mean annual rainfall was 100 mm or even less.

Probably the best-studied area of ancient runoff agriculture in the world is that of the Negev desert, where pioneering studies by Kedar (1957), Evenari et al. (1982), Mayerson (1960), Bruins (1986), and others have supplied a wealth of data on the functioning of runoff agriculture. Further afield, these results can now be compared with the recently published Libyan Valleys Project devoted to Romano-Libyan runoff agriculture in the desert margins of the Sahara (Barker 1996). What is less appreciated, however, is that traditional runoff systems in the Yemen highlands (Eger 1987) provide excellent, comparable, and still functioning examples of runoff agriculture, and these are likely to date back many millennia.

The distribution of Negev runoff systems ranges from semiarid loessic landscapes of the northern Negev to arid mountains and valleys up to ca. 1,000 m above sea level in the Negev highlands to the south. As Yair (1994) has argued, the northernmost area, which is blanketed by windblown silts (loess), is less amenable to large-scale runoff farming. Instead, this area includes occasional Chalcolithic, Bronze Age, and later tells, although some valleys do contain evidence of runoff farming as well. This landscape, which features examples of radiating routes around tells (Tsoar and Yakutieli 1993), shows some similarity to the landscapes of the rain-fed farming of northern Mesopotamia discussed in chapter 6. However, to the south where rocky slopes predominate, conditions are ideal for runoff agriculture systems (Yair 1994: 220–222). Within the Avdat/Sede Boqer area, Kedar estimated that there were some 4,000 ha of runoff fields in this region, although later studies have

increased this figure considerably (Bruins 1990: 89).

The central Negev runoff systems comprise three main classes of fieldscape that mainly date from the Nabataean through Early Islamic periods (Evenari et al. 1982: 95–119).

First are terraced valleys subdivided by a series of individual cross-valley terrace walls with oblique conduits on the contributing hillsides. The latter, evident as low dry stone walls running obliquely downslope, are equivalent to the saghiyahs of Yemen. They gather water on the principle that slope runoff is less influenced by slope friction if it is gathered into deeper channel flow than by simply allowing it to flow across the surface as sheet flow. By channeling the flow into small parcels, it also becomes more manageable, and so flash floods are less likely (Evenari et al. 1982: 109).

Second are groups of terraced fields usually with an associated farmstead (fig. 8.12a). Valley–floor terraced fields, which are comparable to those described above, are surrounded by stone fences or low walls. A farmstead may be supplied with water by means of runoff water gathered from adjacent slopes and fed to a small storage cistern. Water is guided into the fields via sluice gates or drop structures, and terraces are usually equipped with drop structures that allow surplus water to flow from terrace to terrace, a feature also incorporated into the Yemeni fields analyzed by Eger (1987; see fig. 8.12). Although bedrock provides the optimum medium for slope runoff, if loess is present, this sediment can crust over, so that some 15–20 percent of annual rainfall can become runoff.

Third are larger-scale systems that divert water from wadi flash floods to fields. In terms of the ratio of water catchment area to the area of fields watered, these are less efficient, and in the Wadi Kurnab a catchment of 27 sq. km was harnessed to irrigate 10–12 ha of fields, which represents less than 2 percent runoff of

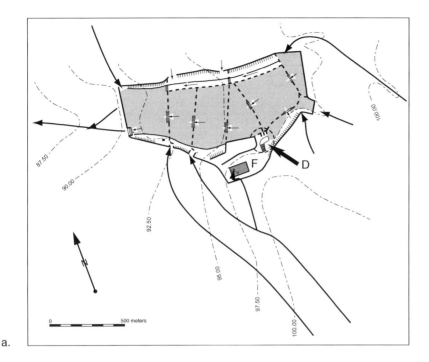

a.

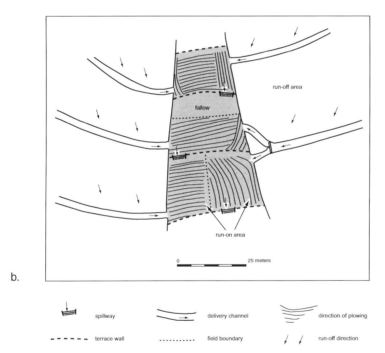

b.

| | spillway | | delivery channel | | direction of plowing |
| | terrace wall | | field boundary | | run-off direction |

Fig. 8.12 Examples of runoff agricultural systems. (a) Runoff farm in Negev desert. F = ruins of farm; D = water-distribution feature (modified from Evenari et al. 1982: fig. 72). (b) Small system of runoff irrigation in Yemen highlands to north of San ʿa (modified from Eger 1987: fig. 22).

the annual rainfall. This compares with 10–20 percent runoff expected from small watersheds (Evenari et al. 1982: 112). As in traditional Yemeni flood-diversion systems, soil bunds

often deflected floods on to fields, and of these, only the spillways were required to be built of stone (Evenari et al. 1982: 118).

Although the water-harvesting

systems discussed above primarily utilized runoff, as with any well-thought-out hydraulic system, alternative sources of supply were used where possible. Hence Bruins reports that the spring of Ein al-Qaderat was tapped by an aqueduct of stones and lime mortar that was dated by C-14 in the range 1725 to 1425 cal. B.C. (Bruins 1986: 126). In the Negev, qanats were also used where hydrological conditions allowed (Evenari et al. 1982: 173–178).

Runoff agriculture was employed particularly during the Nabataean, Roman, Byzantine, and Early Islamic periods. During the Early Islamic period in the Negev highlands (fig. 8.13; Haiman 1989: 189–191; Avni 1996), terraced runoff fields have been recorded over some 380 ha of the valley floors (Avni 1996: 14), whereas farms together with animal pens and fences, middens, cemeteries, rock shelters, cultic installations, and open-air mosques are found on adjacent higher ground. In addition, threshing floors, watch towers, and cisterns often are found closer to the fields. In contrast to Haiman, who views these Early Islamic sites as being the result of deliberate sedentarization by the Early Islamic authorities, Avni points out that these settlements coincide with the dramatic decline of the Byzantine towns of the northern Negev (Avni 1996: 86). Avni also suggests that there were two settlement zones in the Negev during the urbanization phase of the fifth–sixth centuries A.D.: first, larger permanent sites in the central Negev highlands were surrounded by a belt of villages, and second, further to the south, is found a belt of contemporaneous nomadic areas and temporary settlements the inhabitants of which maintained economic relations with the permanent settlements to the north (Avni 1996: 86; S. Rosen 2001). With the decline of the urban centers, the nomadic pastoralists lost part of their livelihood and therefore adopted a sedentary farming existence (Avni 1996: 87). If the latter

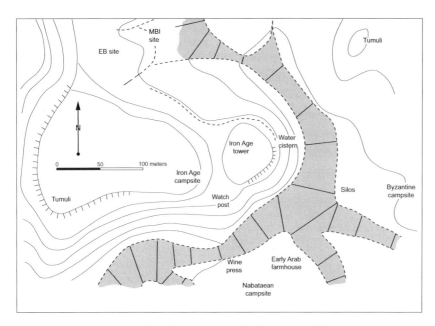

Fig. 8.13 Multiperiod landscape of wadi-floor runoff farming in central Negev (modified from Haiman 1989: fig. 2).

hypothesis is correct, it underscores both the importance of relationships between nomadic populations and the towns as well as the close link of the desert economy (both commercial and subsistence) to the larger structure of the state in the Levant as a whole (Rosen 2000: 56).

Because runoff-agricultural systems enhance the collection of water, especially in drier areas, they can blur the effect of climatic fluctuations. For example, the Early Islamic period is not known to have been climatically humid. Rather, such is the efficiency of rainwater harvesting that when the need arises (for example, when the Byzantine towns of the desert margins experienced a decline), the technology could be harnessed to provide crops and essential drinking water supplies under the most unlikely of circumstances. These technologies not only allowed the occupation of the Negev desert to take place, especially during the Nabataean–Early Islamic periods, they also enabled agriculture to extend throughout the Saharan fringe of North Africa. To the south, runoff systems form the backbone of agriculture in the Yemen highlands (Eger 1987) as well as parts of the ʿAsir

mountains of southwest Saudi Arabia (Abdulfattah 1981). Less is known about runoff-field systems in Saudi Arabia, but Khan and Mughannam (1982) report numerous Early Islamic dams in the vicinity of Taʾif, some of which show evidence of having been used to divert flood runoff to fields. One can therefore infer that the Negev and southwest Arabian systems of runoff and flood irrigation may constitute a broad zone of water capture, as was originally suggested by Roberts (1977). Similarly, further to the north, Stager (1976) reports Iron Age runoff-cultivation systems along the Jordan Valley, and the well-documented Wadi Feynan system used both springs and wadi floods to irrigate fields of at the Roman-Byzantine periods.

In the northern Fertile Crescent, runoff systems become more difficult to detect, although terraced wadis in northern Jordan may have harnessed runoff for their sustenance (Kennedy 1982). In Syria, where large areas of the desert margins are of cultivable soils, there is less evidence for runoff agriculture, but some runoff-agricultural systems may have been destroyed by recent agricultural activities or have remained on

marginal hill areas. In central Syria (e.g., to the east of Hama), numerous Roman-Byzantine towns, villages, and farmsteads were nourished by "qanat Romani" (Kobori 1980; Lightfoot 1996), which frequently supplied water for large reservoirs situated near the main settlements. These elaborate hydraulic systems probably contributed water for domestic purposes, irrigation, and the watering of flocks. Elsewhere, for example, to the east of the volcanic massif of the Jebel Arab (Druze), wadi floods provided water for an equivalent phase of Roman settlement (Sadler 1990; Newson 2000). Clearly, despite the considerable climatic impediments to settlement, during the phase of Nabataean–Early Islamic settlement dispersal, a wide range of water-gathering techniques were brought into operation, with the result that the landscape of the desert margins blossomed but in different ways, in part depending upon the practicalities of water collection.

Landscapes of the Desert Nomads

The degree of preservation of archaeological remains in deserts is partly a result of the pattern of movement of the population. Whereas in the sedentary-settled zone of the Fertile Crescent, populations tend to be fixed in one location from whence they radiate within usually a few kilometers to outlying fields or pastures, or make occasional journeys (e.g., by boat in southern Mesopotamia), in the case of pastoral nomads, trajectories of movements can be irregular or elongated and can range over as much as 300–400 km. For example, the Mutair bedouin of northeast Arabia and Kuwait traditionally would spend June until mid October camped around groups of wells near the desert edge. They then would range into the desert, where their *dirah* or tribal customary grazing lands would cover some 300 km × 250 km (Dickson 1951: 45–52). However, as Dickson points out, where grazing resources are sparser, the dirah may be larger; thus, that of the al-Murrah tribes to the north of the empty quarter extend as linear, north–south looping trajectories between 650 and 800 km in length (Cole 1975: 28–29). As a result of these huge tribal territories, both perceptions of the landscape and the impact of the communities on their landscape will be very different. Of course, because such movements are dependent upon the use of camels (probably domesticated in the late second or early first millennium B.C.), tribal territories would have been more restricted during the Bronze Age and earlier.

In the case of Arabian pastoral nomads (sing. badawi; pl. badu or bedouin), there is some degree of flexibility in the location of camps. Although water sources and pasture are of course important, it is not crucial to camp precisely by them. Therefore, settlements may develop around mud flats, on basalt plateaus, or in inconspicuous locations in side valleys, depending upon relations with neighboring tribes. This locational flexibility can contribute to the wider dispersal of archaeological features across the landscape. A key factor that differentiates mobile pastoral groups from sedentary cultivators is that except around their longer-term summer camps, there are no areas of intensive disturbance as occurs around permanent settlements or within their surrounding cultivated zones. Hence in deserts, the chances for feature preservation are much higher.

An additional factor in site recognition is the wide range of imprints that can be left by nomadic living areas. As pointed out by Cribb, the term "nomad architecture" may appear to contain an inherent contradiction (Cribb 1991: 84), but as he demonstrates, nomadic camps can contain numerous fixtures and specialized activity areas, each of which can leave a distinctive trace. Because many case studies cited by Cribb derive from rocky mountainous areas

or areas where preexisting buildings provide convenient construction materials for reinforcing tent foundations, these nomadic imprints can be remarkably durable. On the other hand, in Oman, for example, *shawawi* sheep herders often simply live beneath a convenient tree, and so traces of occupation can be much less tangible. In theory, it is possible that the camps of the same nomadic groups will leave different traces depending upon the geology and surface conditions of the camping ground and residence time in any one place. For example, for a hypothetical migration path through the sedimentary desert of sand and silt plains, stone tent foundations and architectural features will be minimal; in rocky areas, structures will be visible and often semiconstructed; in the marginal zone of the semidesert edge, periodic sedentary settlement and agriculture may mask or remove the remains of pastoral nomadic camps; in the subhumid areas of the rain-fed zone, pastoral nomadic camps will be virtually invisible because of the high background noise left by sedentary communities, especially where nomads camp on tells. In addition, mobile pastoralists make their own taphonomic contribution by taking apart standing buildings, as can be seen on aerial photographs of Roman frontier forts (see Kennedy and Riley 1990: figs. 128, 154, 155).

Such variations in the signature of pastoral nomadic groups contribute to the debate on developments of desert-fringe socioeconomic systems. According to one school of thought, the absence of physical traces of occupation implies that there was no nomadic occupation at all (Rosen 1992), whereas others contend that nomadic groups can leave different traces depending upon their position along an agro-pastoral continuum (Finkelstein 1995). Those groups whose economy is closer to sedentary agriculture will leave more tangible traces; those closer to "pure nomadism" will leave fewer or even no traces at all. Despite these differ-

ences in interpretation, what is clear is that nomadic pastoralists leave variable traces that reflect a wide range of functional, environmental, cultic, and ideational strategies.

Before examining the actual traces that remain, one must consider just what necessities were essential to life in the desert in the past and how might these make traces of nomadism different from those of sedentary groups. Such requirements are of course supplementary to obvious needs such as a source of water and forage for their animals. For example, one can subdivide the landscape of a tell into its component parts: fields, threshing floors, pits, and corrals, which are all key features of the off-site zone (see chapter 6). Of these, only corrals are crucial to nomads; fields and threshing floors are necessary only for those agro-pastoralists who adopt cultivation as part of their livelihood. Within the tell, houses, religious structures, administrative buildings, trash heaps, granaries, cemeteries, and various economic activity areas are basic features of sedentary life. Nevertheless, many nomads will minimize housing needs, ignore administration, spread trash light and wide, and have a variable, often minimal, need for granaries and economic activity areas. Religious or sacred places as well as burial areas would have been necessary, although for many traditional bedouin societies, even burial grounds can leave a minimal trace. The last two features may therefore be expected to figure strongly in the desert landscape. It is hardly surprising, therefore, that deserts furnish numerous remains of difficult-to-interpret stone structures and elaborate burial grounds.

Pasture is a key resource for nomads, and although it does not leave tangible archaeological remains, pastoral resources must be factored into our assessment of the desert landscape. Because of the importance of forage and pasture to traditional desert communities, considerable efforts are made to preserve this resource. Such efforts can, for example, take the form of the *hema* system of land management (pl. *ahmia*) in which large tracts of rangeland are conserved by the state; by customary tribal lore, which places restrictions on grazing; by the prohibition of fodder collection; or by tree cutting (Draz 1990). This is well illustrated around Taif in Saudi Arabia, where a hema area has been protected for some five hundred years. It is even possible for a hema-soil signature to be recognized in the form of a distinctive, humus-rich, mollisol soil horizon. Similar soil horizons are preserved in the Holocene stratigraphic record of highland Yemen (see chapter 9), and it is feasible that certain mollic horizons may demonstrate the existence of former pastoral preserves. In Saudi Arabia, Draz (1990) reported the former existence of three thousand ahmia, some of which provided water catchments for artificial reservoirs (Philby 1957: 10). The recent lifting of conservation law is thought to have resulted in the denudation of plant cover, soil erosion, excess floods, and even the drying up of springs (Draz 1990: 327–329). The denuded and desertic landscapes that are now evident in much of Arabia must therefore be the result of both late Holocene climatic drying and changing practices of pasture management through time.

Features of the Desert Landscape

Because of the excellent conditions for the preservation of archaeological remains, the desert includes a range of landscape features, some impressive. These are summarized on table 8.2, and their types of distributions are sketched on figure 8.14. Here some salient features are described, with emphasis upon their landscape context.

Circles. Circular, subcircular, and oval structures of stone are common throughout the deserts of Arabia.

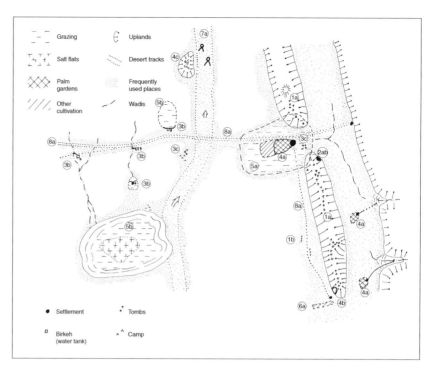

Fig. 8.14   Schematic layout of a desert landscape. Note that this represents an amalgam of periods and is therefore intended to illustrate the landscape context of frequently occurring types of sites or features. Simplified from the landscape of interior Oman and parts of Saudi Arabia. Numbers refer to table 8.2. The special function settlement (4b) at the south end of the rocky ridge is a mining settlement and its fields (6a). Only one or two examples of each site, feature, or installation are included. The two oases in the east valley are fed by the underground (*qanat*) and open channel (*ghayl*) *aflaj* respectively. The broad north–south route through 7a, along which are a number of kites, represents the migration route of wild game (such as gazelle, oryx, and ibex).

They can range in date from the period of the mid-Holocene moist interval (ca. 7000–ca. 3000 B.C.) to the recent past. Smaller circular structures may be the remains of circular huts or tent foundations, but others probably represent corrals or even burials. In eastern Jordan, Alison Betts has noted many thousands of stone circles of various dates that form loose chains along the margins of mud flats on hilltops and slopes as well as deep within the basalt (Betts 1982: 23). In Saudi Arabia, Parr and colleagues recorded a veritable village of stone enclosures of fourth millennium B.C. date (Parr et al. 1978: 38). The latter group, which comprise some fifty structures over 100 × 150 m,

represent occupation. By analogy with similar Early Bronze Age features in the Negev, these might have been used episodically over many centuries. A particularly impressive class of circular structures are the so-called jellyfish, which usually appear as two concentric circles of stones, 30–50 m in diameter, divided by radiating interior walls, with one or two centrally situated circular features (Betts 1982: 30–31). Their scale and form, together with their defensible positions on basalt hills, suggest that the jellyfish structures might be defended settlements of extended family units (Betts 1982: 31).

Overall, a compelling case can be made for associating circular dwellings with nomadic societies

(Flannery 1972). Although exceptions exist, in the Arabian cases, the lack of evidence for fields in many hut-circle localities provides support (albeit negative) for the Flannery model. Overall, it is likely that circular or subcircular huts are associated with a range of agro-pastoral practices that are not fully sedentary (de Maigret 1990; Zarins 1997; Finkelstein 1995: 94–99) but which include a range of strategies such as pastoral nomadism coordinated with seasonal cultivation, as has been suggested for the Beer Resisim area in the Negev (Cohen and Dever 1980).

Artifact Scatters. Desert surveys often recover sites in the form of artifact concentrations sometimes related to built structures. Alternatively, when group mobility is high and built remains are minimal, as with some hunter-gatherer and nomadic societies, artifacts can form extensive scatters over large areas of terrain, as described by Foley for East Africa (1981). Although most desert surveys in the Near East have not recorded off-site artifact scatters (see chapter 3 for discussion), areas that are subjected to frequent revisits, or in which the locus of occupation moves from year to year, may be expected to provide a continuum of artifacts rather than concentrations.

Kites. These form one of the more distinctive features of the desert, and they can be found in southern Syria (Echallier and Braemer 1995; Poidebard 1934), Jordan (Helms and Betts 1987, Kennedy 1982), the Negev and Sinai (Meshel 1974), and Saudi Arabia (Adams et al. 1977, Parr et al. 1978). Although kites come in a wide range of forms (Helms and Betts 1987: figs. 9–14), they basically consist of large oval, circular, or irregular enclosures of low stone walls, the perimeter walls of which are perforated by a series of stone circles. In areas such as southern Syria, these stone circles have been demonstrated to represent infilled pits. Long antennaelike walls directed toward

Table 8.2   Cultural Features Found in the Arabian Desert, according to Common Topographic Context and Broad Socioeconomic Function

Type of Feature	Physical Context	Socioeconomic Context or Function
1a. Tombs, dolmens, and tomb complexes	Rocky slopes, ridge tops, occasionally on plains	Burials for sedentary and mobile communities
1b. Triliths	Plains, often near tracks	?Commemorative monuments
1c. Standing stones, menhirs, massebot	Rocky slopes and ridges, in some cases on plains	Religious/symbolic
1d. Temples, desert mosques, sanctuaries	Frequently on routes and on hill summits	Ritual and worship
2a. Rock art	Wide range of outcrops	Places of passage, gathering points and ritual places
2b. Inscriptions	Wide range of outcrops	
3a. Water-collection devices (e.g., dams)	Wadis, basins	Water supply
3b. Cisterns and reservoirs	Wadis, runoff catchments	
3c. Wells	Plains to tap groundwater	
4a. Oases	Where groundwater table is raised or water can be gathered. Sometimes in gaps in ridges	Agricultural settlements and markets
4b. Special function settlements	Deserts (way stations), near rock outcrops (mining settlements)	To supply travelers (way stations) or minerals (mining settlements)
4c. Stone circles, jellyfish, etc.	Usually on raised ground	Settlements of agropastoral or pastoral nomads
4d. Walled enclosures	Usually on natural rock outcrops	Defensive
4e. Artifact scatters	Numerous locations; frequently visited places	Hunter-gatherer and pastoral nomadic settlements
5a. Grazing areas: Haram	Normally adjacent to villages and/or oases	Animal husbandry
5b. "Hema" areas (marah, mahmiá)	Extensive lowlands; areas of flow concentration	Restricted grazing areas
6a. Valley-floor cultivation	Along wadis	Agriculture

Table 8.2 Continued

Type of Feature	Physical Context	Socioeconomic Context or Function
6b. Slope runoff cisterns; stone mounds; saghiyas	Slopes overlooking cultivable or low ground	Agriculture
7a. Kites	Animal migration routes	Hunting
8a. Desert tracks	Various terrains	Routes for trade and transhumance of animals

Note: See figure 8.14.

References

1a: Doe 1983: 42–45; Potts 1990; Prag 1995.
1b. Doe 1983: 43.
1c. Doe 1983: 75–78; Newton and Zarins 2000.
1d. Doe 1983: 78–79.
2a. Newton and Zarins 2000.
2b. King 1990.
3b. Betts and Helms 1989; Wilkinson 1980b.
4a. Costa 1983; Orchard 1999; Frifelt 1985.
4c. Betts 1982; Zarins 1992; Cribb 1991; Bar-Yosef and Khazanov 1992.
4d. Doe 1983: 45–46.
5a. Wilkinson 1977.
5b. Draz 1990.
6d. Evanari et al. 1982; Bruins 1986.
6e. Helms and Betts 1987.
7a. Helms and Betts 1987.
8a. Al-Rashid 1979, 1980; Clapp 1998.

the enclosure extend for many hundreds of meters across the terrain (fig. 8.15) and are interpreted as being designed to funnel wild animals, usually gazelles, towards the enclosure, where they were then guided into pits or cul-de sacs for the final kill (Helms and Betts 1987).

In Jordan, kites are even linked together to form long complex "chains" dispersed along ridgelines or hills (fig. 8.15a and b; Betts 1998: 203). Early travelers in the Middle East have described the hunting techniques that were associated with similar examples (described as *misyada* [sing.] or *masāyid* [pl.]), and a tantalizing Safaitic rock-art depiction allows the technique to be traced back to the first century B.C. or A.D. (Helms and Betts 1987: 55–56). Although a dissenting view from Echallier and Braemer (1995) associated kites of southern Syria with the herding of domestic animals, the location of enormous numbers of

kites within the natural grazing and migration paths of gazelle through the steppe and desert provides contextual evidence for their association with hunting (for discussion, see Betts 1998). Kites appear to have a history extending throughout much of the Holocene (Helms and Betts 1987: 54). Remarkably, their association with Pre-Pottery Neolithic structures and artifacts suggests that some may in fact date as early as 7000 B.C. (Betts 1998). Although the preservation of such seemingly complex and fragile structures over such long spans of time may seem unlikely, their location on often rising ground in the desert is perfect for long-term preservation. Nevertheless, their very utility as hunting traps makes them ideal candidates for prolonged reuse and reconstruction, as well as occasional adaptations to corral and guide sheep when required.

Kites not only have a conspicuous

place in the landscape, they also were apparently constructed in key locations with respect to the activities of game animals. For example, in the Dhuweila area of eastern Jordan, an entire line of kites lay along a ridge that overlooked a series of mud flats to the west. The guiding walls led up the slopes in a westward direction, while the enclosures were situated just over the ridge crest downslope and out of sight of animals being driven between the antennae walls (Betts 1998: 195). Betts also cites the Austrian traveler Burckardt (1831: 220), who described a hunt in the steppe east of Damascus. In this case, the kite enclosure was positioned near a water source that attracted gazelle in summer; the herds were monitored and driven into the trap through gaps in the enclosure walls and into the pits, where hundreds were slaughtered (Betts 1998: 201). Of particular relevance to the development of the overall landscape is that kites were frequently situated in areas where obstacles or bottlenecks occurred in the annual migration paths of herds of gazelles as they moved out of the Syrian or Arabian desert toward summer pastures between Aleppo and Palmyra (Fowden 1999: 121–123). Similarly in the basalt *harra* of Jordan, linked chains of kites oriented roughly west–northwest are aligned on a range of hills and appear to have been built to intercept the regular movement of animals (Betts and Yagodin 2000).

If the majority of kites are accepted as having been used for trapping game animals and were specifically located to intercept the long-distance patterns of migratory herds, it follows that there was therefore a close relationship between the ecological patterns of the game animals and the constructed cultural landscape.

Triliths and standing stones. The architecture and distribution of kites lend themselves readily to a functionalist interpretation, but this is hardly the case for standing stones and configurations thereof for which functionalist logic only confuses the picture. Standing stones are particularly conspicuous features of the landscape. Their distinctive, sometimes anthropomorphic profile makes them ideal for marking parts of the landscape that are deemed special. In some traditional societies, especially those in which dwellings are constructed from soft, perishable materials, there is an association between stone and the ancestors (Parker-Pearson and Ramilisonina 1998: 149). Specifically in Madagascar, where standing stones are known as *vatolahy* (man stones), they can be erected to commemorate the dead, employed in tombs, or used as territorial boundary markers (Parker-Pearson and Ramilisonina 1998: 311–313).

Triliths are elongated alignments usually of triplets of stone uprights that have a surrounding collar of stones (fig. 8.16). Because of their distinctive form, they have been recorded by numerous early travelers to southeast Arabia such as Bertram Thomas (1932) and Wilfred Thesiger (1959). Triliths can be up to 25 m long, and in addition to arrangements of smaller stones between the stone uprights or to one side, they also include adjacent circular pits that appear to have been associated with burning (de Cardi et al. 1977; Doe 1983: 43; Zarins 1997: 673). Their distribution extends from the inner Omani Sharqiyah in the north to the Hadhramaut valley of Yemen in the west, and they are usually located away from agricultural areas but close to mountains. Some examples in eastern Oman were associated with areas of favorable grazing land (de Cardi et al. 1977: 29) or where nomads and settled pastoralists may have come together (Reade 2000: 133). Triliths appear to be pre-Islamic in date, and the single radiocarbon dated example was found to have been in use around cal. A.D. 100 (de Cardi 1977: 32). They do not appear to represent burial areas. The suggestion to Walter Dostal by members of the Manahil tribe that they were built to commemorate the death of a man of some importance seems reasonable but unproven. Although triliths show no common orientation, they do appear to follow the lines of wadis or of tracks (de Cardi 1977: 29), which suggests that as with kites, it is important to perceive them in terms of their landscape setting.

Standing stones, although less striking than triliths, are equally enigmatic features, and they too have enjoyed a controversial history. Their morphology varies from place to place, and examples have been recorded from the Yemeni Tihama (Keall 1998), former south Yemen (Doe 1983), Saudi Arabia (Parr et al. 1978; Zarins et al. 1979), and the Negev/Sinai deserts (Avner 1984). A related feature in northern Syria might be the monumental standing stones of Jeblet al-Beydar at the western edge of the Jebel Abd al Aziz.

Perhaps the best-known monument of standing stones in the Near East is the stone alignment of Rajajil in northern Saudi Arabia. This consists of a line of stone pillars oriented north–south and facing east, that is, toward the rising sun. Artifacts and animal bones from both the surface and excavated contexts suggest that the monument was built in the fourth millennium B.C. and was associated with a range of fauna that included equids, goat, gazelle, wild cattle, and ostrich. The impressive but equally enigmatic megalithic structure of al-Midaman recorded on the Yemeni coastal plain (the Tihama) by Ed Keall (1998) is dated to between 2400 and 1900 B.C. Its upstanding granite pillars tower some 3 m above the sand, and unlike al-Rajajil, this site is associated with cultural deposits, burials, and a cache of high-quality weapons. Given the lack of an obvious function, as well as the nature of the three child burials, a religious or ceremonial function seems appropriate for al-Midaman. Particularly impressive are decorated stelae (also known as statue-*menhirs*), recorded from eastern Yemen. These upright pillars, which are associated with tombs or arranged in alignments, can be dated to the mid third to late second millennium B.C. and are thought to be the product of nomadic groups active within the Arabian desert (Newton and Zarins 2000: 167–169). Megalith pillars are found throughout the Arabian peninsula, and as with the Levantine dolmen fields, they are thought to be the product of a pastoral elite who constructed such monuments to unify the ideology of tribal groups and to provide some central location for ritual activities (Newton and Zarins 2000: 171).

Also potentially falling into such a megalithic complex are the standing stone structures of the Negev and Sinai (*massebot*), which are of the Neolithic or later date, with several C-14 dates ranging from 6960 to 5440 B.P. (Avner 1984: 117). Most of these standing stones face east, but an example in the Wadi Zalaqa actually points toward the prominent peak of Ras el-Kalb. Their association with cultic places, altars, offering tables, and basins and their frequent orientation towards the rising sun also support a cultic explanation. Desert cultic structures also include "open sanctuaries" of mainly rectangular form, zoomorphic drawings in stone, as well as lines of cairns. The last follow along desert routes. By analogy with the traditional practices of the nomadic population, these may be interpreted as having been erected at sacred points that were visible along desert routes (Avner 1984: 127). Again, although their setting within the landscape is not always clear, there is frequently an association between standing stones, sanctuaries, and lines of cairns with route ways or with conspicuous hilltops. All the above locations could therefore be argued, but not without ambiguity, to be associated with the marking of the landscape, perhaps for commemorative reasons.

Rock art and inscriptions. Rock art can be defined as being the creation of visual images by painting or carving stone at particular places in the landscape (Bradley 2000: 65). Unfortunately, in Arabia, as with most older rock-art study areas, little attention has been paid to the landscape context of the images or to that of associated inscriptions. Consequently, as with standing stones and triliths, it can be difficult trying to understand the message that is being communicated because the crucial landscape context is missing. It is not always obvious to whom the rock art is trying to communicate, for, as Bradley has observed, unlike speech, song, or dance, rock art does not require the person who experiences it to be present at the same time (Bradley 2000: 39). In terms of the landscape, this temporal separation of artist and viewer implies that rock art is an especially useful device for communicating within or between widely separated mobile groups or alternatively perhaps for signifying boundaries in the landscape.

The Arabian peninsula is extremely rich in rock art, and major studies have been made in Saudi Arabia by the Philby-Lippens-Ryckmans expedition (Anati 1968; Newton and Zarins 2000; Nayeem 2000; Khan 1989; Kabawi et al. 1996); Negev/Sinai (Anati 1954, 1955); Jordan (King 1990); Oman (Clarke 1975; Preston 1976); and Yemen (Jung 1969). Based on Anati's analysis of rock-art styles, Newton and Zarins define two styles of rock art: The first is an earlier Realistic-Dynamic style that contains scenes of small figures actively hunting, fishing, herding cattle, dancing, and performing ceremonial activities (Newton and Zarins 2000: 155). Such carvings are not later than the second millennium B.C. and are probably significantly earlier. The succeeding Oval-headed style presents life-sized figures that emphasize body decoration, clothing, weapons, and other implements and probably mainly date to the second or early first millennium

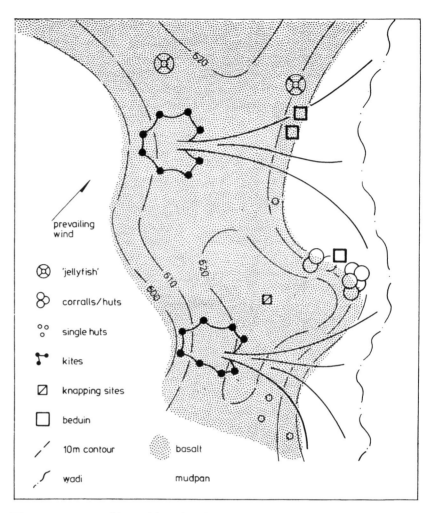

Fig. 8.15 Desert kites: (above) Schematic landscape context of kites in Jordanian desert (from Betts 1982: fig. 7, with permission). (right) Swarm of kites near Jawa in the basalt desert of Jordan (from Helms and Betts 1987: fig. 3, with permission).

B.C. (Newton and Zarins 2000). In addition, later styles associated with inscriptions in Epigraphic Old South Arabian, Thamudic, Safaitic, or early Arabic forms of writing also occur and probably relate to much more closely to bedouin cultures. This later group can be associated with images of camels and even ploughing.

Rock art or inscriptions are often made upon those types of rock that lend themselves to the carving of drawings. Hence in northern Oman, they are more likely to be associated with outcrops of Cretaceous limestone (Clarke 1975: 113); in Yemen, they are frequently on desert-varnished basalt; and in the

Hejaz, on sandstone. Nevertheless, a wide range of rock types can be used. More significant is that many examples of Omani rock art occur on major routes that cut through the mountains. Alternatively, some occur either in less visible side wadis or in remarkably inaccessible locations, the latter position implying that perhaps there was an attempt to limit access to certain individuals or groups (Bradley 2000: 69).

Overall, rock art can occupy numerous topographic locations. For example, at Jubba in the Nafud of northern Saudi Arabia (ca. 85 km northwest of Ha'il) the huge concentration of rock art and Thamudic inscriptions (the latter of the late

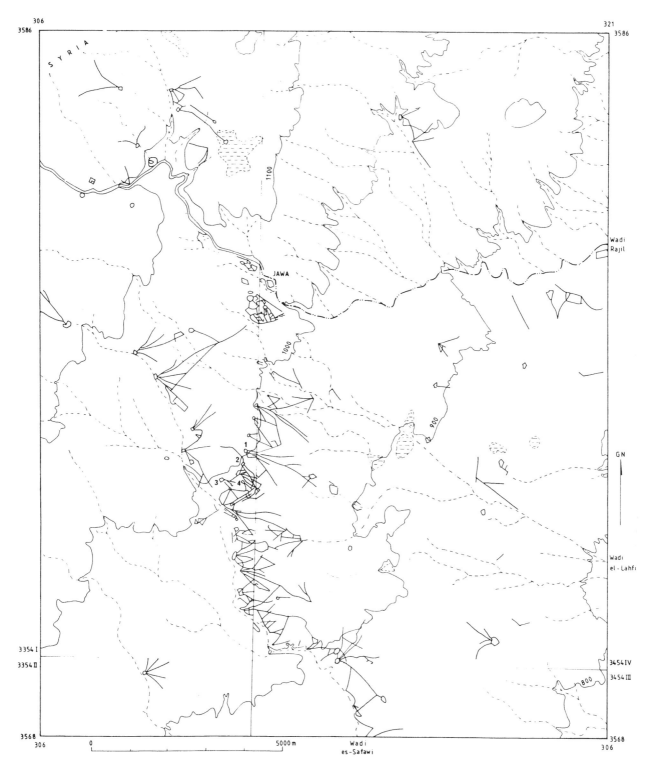

centuries B.C. and early centuries A.D.) occur on a sandstone outcrop adjacent to an important basin and watering place on a major trans-desert route (Adams et al. 1977: 39). Also in Saudi Arabia, Kabawi and colleagues note that in the southern region, rock art is frequently found near water reservoirs, springs, wells, or rainwater pools, whereas in the northern province, they occur in the vicinity of settlements (Kabawi et al. 1996). More specifically, images of females with raised arms and narrow waists are frequently found on prominent places and hilltops, as is the case for a male and female with "realistic sexual details" (Kabawi et al. 1996: 57). This pairing of figurative depictions with high places was regarded by the Saudi team as being associated with deities and presumably cultic practice. Similarly, Khan (1989: 56–57) has linked schematic

Fig. 8.16   Trilith in the desert of Dhofar, southern Oman.

rock-art features with deities and idols, which, in turn, suggests that the locations were probably sacred and perhaps represent open-air sanctuaries that were created prior to the walled temples of later sedentary settlements. Similar associations have been noted in the semiarid Yemen highlands, where studies by Joseph Daniels (2002) suggest that rock art is sometimes associated with high places that appear, according to some inscriptions, to be holy or imbued with sanctity. Other significant locations include isolated hills that lie on boundaries and are associated with possible temple sites, or rock faces located near roadside temples lying alongside major routes.

Remarkably explicit in terms of everyday life are Safaitic inscriptions and rock art recorded in the basalt *harra* of eastern Jordan. In this topographically subdued terrain, inscriptions refer to the pasturing of camels, sheep, and goats and also to topographic features such as valleys, low parts of valleys, verdant tracts of land, particular types of pasture, and springs (King 1990: 58–60). Other inscriptions relate to journeys made and named destinations visited, and in a few particularly enlightening examples, they also refer to cultic practice. For example, at one locality,

a father and son lay claim to an area of higher ground and state that they slaughtered camel(s) on it (King 1990: 61). In this case, however, the high ground referred to is simply a wadi bank, and therefore it is possible that the inscription had been dragged from its original context. Rather than simply associating rock art with the locality itself, it should also be viewed in its relationship to other prominent landscape features. Therefore, as pointed out by Julian Reade (2000), the impressive rock art on the boulder of Hasāt bin Salt in Oman (also known as "Coleman's Rock") either could have been ritually associated with hunting or trapping but equally could be seen as linked to a high phallic outcrop located just to the east.

These examples do of course provide the danger of circular argument, because so-called cultic figures on high places can endow a cultic role to that place, and other high places can therefore be interpreted as cultic as a result. Any associated images can, in turn, be declared to be cultic irrespective of their figurative content, leading to an endless circularity of interpretation. Nevertheless, when inscriptions are also present, there can be a recognizable relationship between certain types of rock-art

concentrations and high places. Similarly, the associations of rock art and inscriptions with temples on route systems where individuals may wish to stop to worship, or simply at gathering places where some form of place of worship might be expected, suggest that certain places along route systems may be imbued with long-term sanctity and consequently can be marked in the landscape. Because hunter-gatherers use rock art as a navigational device (Ross 2001: 546), desert rock art can similarly be perceived to play a crucial role in the definition and perception of the communication networks of indigenous mobile communities. Therefore, by analyzing rock art and inscriptions within their landscape context, it should be possible to breathe more meaning into these enigmatic features.

Tumuli. Positioned at the end of the human life cycle, not only are burial mounds morphologically distinctive but also they form an important component of the desert landscape. Probably the largest burial grounds are the tumulus fields of Bahrain, where some 200,000 tumuli form a vast necropolis dating from the mid third and second millennium B.C. but which continue perhaps as late as the Christian era (Ibrahim 1982). Current interpretations view such grave fields as probably having been used for the burial of local sedentary populations rather than mobile groups or outsiders. Similar large-scale necropoli also existed until the twentieth century A.D. in the region of Dhahran in eastern Saudi Arabia, where in an area of some 8x 2 km, an estimated 87,500 tumuli were noted in 1940 by Cornwall, a number that had diminished to some 2,500 or even less by 1983, as a result of urban and industrial development (Zarins et al. 1984: 25).

Equally impressive in the context of the landscape, however, are the seemingly innumerable cairn burials that are positioned prominently on hills, ridges, and mountains throughout the drylands of the Arabian peninsula. In Saudi Arabia, cairn burials have been recorded from the northwest province (Ingraham et al. 1981), the northern province (Parr et al. 1978), the central province (Zarins et al. 1979), the Nejd (Zarins et al. 1980), and the southwest province (Zarins et al. 1981; for Saudi Arabia in general, see Nayeem 1990). Cairn burial complexes are also found in Jordan (Betts 1982, Prag 1995), Oman (de Cardi et al. 1976, 1977; Gentelle and Frifelt 1989), Yemen (de Maigret 1996), and the Gulf States (summarized in Potts 1990). Particularly good examples of beehive tombs aligned along a ridge near the village of al-'Ayn in northern Oman are illustrated in de Cardi et al. 1976 (pl. 22; also this volume, fig. 8.5).

Although some cairn fields are related to settlement sites, it is evident that the scale of many tomb fields, as well as the total number of tombs, exceeds the size of nearby settlements, especially as many tombs are distant from obvious settlements. Consequently, a significant but unknown number of tomb fields may constitute burial grounds of mobile communities dating from the fourth millennium B.C. and later. Related structures are dolmens that consist of single chambers of stone slabs with a capstone, which are found along the Rift Valley of Jordan. Dolmen groups are thought to occur in areas where nomadic groups may have needed prolonged residence at either summer or winter pastures (Prag 1995: 78). It is common for archaeologists to observe that tomb fields are located in areas unsuitable for cultivation, but Reade has pointed out that this is hardly a sufficient explanation for such necropoli (Reade 2000: 136). Instead, the prominence of tomb locations implies that the individuals or clans buried within them wished to emphasize their prominent status or the ownership of territory or that such locations were of particular sanctity (Reade 2000). Unfortunately, obser-

vations of traditional burial practice among the bedouin are of little help in reconstructing such "landscapes of death" because in Islamic times, especially over the past few centuries, little attention has been paid to the construction of elaborate funerary monuments (Musil 1928; Dickson 1951: 207–215). Nevertheless, the frequent presence of graves of the third millennium B.C. and later on prominent hills does give a special significance to such locations.

Particularly impressive are a series of hilltop cemeteries in northern Yemen to the east of Marib (de Maigret 1996). These cairn burials are situated high on the ridgelines of the Jebels Ruwaik and Jidran (Steimer-Herbert 1999; Braemer et al. 2001), where they form part of a virtually uninterrupted chain around the desert of Ramlat Sabat'ayn (fig. 8.6). The tombs are found either within an uncultivated zone, but near visible traces of occupation (Steimer-Herbert 1999: 182), or along ancient roads (de Maigret 1996). Some plausibility is lent to the specific association of tombs with route ways because the tombs in questions include large "tails" that extend roughly parallel to the inferred ancient routes (fig. 8.17). Radiocarbon assay has now demonstrated that the burials range from the early third to the early second millennium cal. B.C. (Braemer et al. 2001: 41), and their location on the edge of and overlooking the deserts of Arabia suggests that they belong to the presumably mobile inhabitants of the desert rather than to the more sedentary chiefdoms of highland Yemen (fig. 8.6).

It is difficult to make generalizations about the wide range of landscape positions that tomb fields occupy in Arabia. Nevertheless, dense distributions surround and overlook the desert peripheries and also follow major route systems (Zarins et al. 1979: 25). Such locations therefore conform either to the summer pastures of mobile pastoral groups or to certain long-distance

corridors that were blessed with sufficient water supplies to make them anchor points in the trajectories of mobile groups.

Conclusions

The landscape of the deserts of the Arabian peninsula have experienced considerable environmental change during the Holocene, and despite increased aridity since the third millennium B.C., human adaptability has enabled people to continue to occupy nearly all parts of the peninsula. Although it would be tempting to declare that, as has been claimed for the Sahara, that the arid interior of Arabia operated as a large human pump, sucking people in during moist episodes and pumping them to outlying regions during arid phases (Sherratt 1997: 281), the archaeological evidence from the interior suggests that human activity did actually continue despite the drier conditions. The way of life must have changed, however, as the population had to adapt to the drying up of water sources and the desiccation of pastures. It is perhaps no coincidence that many oases were established during the third millennium B.C., when conditions were somewhat drier than during previous millennia so that former steppelands were becoming desiccated. Despite some degree of aridification during the Holocene, there are few signs of early relict fields that might relate to sedentary agriculture practiced during the mid-Holocene moist phase (cf. the Daulatabad fields, chapter 5). The wide range of archaeological features appears to relate mainly to strategies of mobile communities together with some specialized developments such as oases or various long-distance routes. Installations along the Hajj routes illustrate both a considerable degree of technological prowess on the part of the engineers and an intimate knowledge of desert ecology.

Similarly, their deep knowledge of the landscape has enabled the

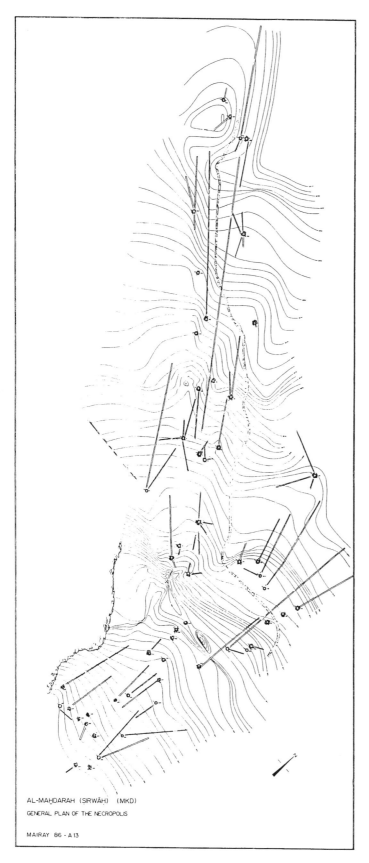

AL-MAHDARAH (SIRWĀH) (MKD)
GENERAL PLAN OF THE NECROPOLIS

MAIRAY 86 - A 13

Fig. 8.17 Bronze Age tombs with "tails" near the Ramlat Sabat 'ayn, Yemen (from de Maigret 1996: fig. 4, with permission).

inhabitants of the desert to survive and adapt. To judge by the larger size of tribal territories in dry and less-populated areas, one can infer that with late-Holocene climatic drying, desert communities probably found it necessary to range further in search of forage during their annual cycle. In contrast to pastoral nomads, the inhabitants of the oases, like their equivalents in the rain-fed Fertile Crescent, probably had a local perspective, albeit one that was tempered by a more cosmopolitan experience as a result of trade and other long-distance links. In other words, using the terminology of Tilley, whereas the oasis dweller has a more centered or concentric frame of reference, the nomads, like hunter-gatherers, probably had a more "de-centered" outlook (Tilley 1994: 36). In reality, it would seem that the nomadic pastoral groups, by ranging over vast territories, have an incremental view of many small areas of terrain, whereas those of the sedentary oasis dwellers were reinforced by constant repetitious observations.

Despite (or perhaps because of) the huge range of their migrations, the bedouin have an extraordinarily detailed knowledge of their landscape. This is built up from countless observations and much word-of-mouth lore passed down through the lineage, so that despite what might be called a "de-centered outlook," they certainly can claim to have an intimate knowledge of their landscape. In Arabia most significant geographical areas have a name, and then each smaller feature is also named so that when bedouin go out to pasture, they are traveling through an intimate landscape. Although little is known about the detailed ways of life of the pre-Islamic inhabitants of the Arabian desert, I would presume that they related to the landscape in a similar manner to the traditional bedouin, albeit perhaps within smaller territories. Consequently, the features discussed above (the cairn burials, triliths, stand-

ing stones, hut circles, kites, and so
on), although not of course contemporaneous, may well fit into such
mobile frames of reference. At this
early stage it is difficult to draw even
a general model of the development
of desert landscapes. Nevertheless,
for an undefined phase of the past,
figure 8.14 attempts to show the main
types of features and some characteristic topographic locations. Special
reference is made to those areas that
might be termed most frequently
visited places (or "persistent places":
Schlanger 1992). Such areas may be
where the inhabitants focus on areas
of better pasture as well as key water
sources such as wells or water holes.
Nevertheless, as has been noted by
Wilfred Thesiger and Donald Cole,
in most years deserts such as the
empty quarter experience some rain
somewhere. Hence by adopting a
policy of mobility, humans can survive in remarkably dry areas. In
turn, because of these relatively low
population densities, the vegetation
will become less degraded than in
moister areas further to the north in
the rain-fed Fertile Crescent.

9

Landscapes of the Highlands

Mountains in the Middle East can vary from moist ranges within otherwise desertic areas to arid highlands. In many situations, mountains provide a constraint on human settlement, either because their altitude precludes many cropping practices or because deep narrow valleys limit the prospects for cultivation. Furthermore, because of their steeper slopes, they also form very fragile environments that if misused, can be subject to rapid erosion and landscape degradation. The development of mountainous landscapes can take very different pathways, and here examples have been chosen to illustrate how seemingly similar mountainous areas can develop rather contrasting landscapes. In addition, the variable topography of mountain landscapes provides a heterogeneous framework for the development of human communities, and so economic resources may be rendered inaccessible and defensive sites can become of paramount importance. In mountains, themes such as power, symbolism, ritual, and economy therefore interact in numerous ways with the environment to provide a more richly textured cultural signature than in many of the more familiar lowland landscapes.

Because temperature decreases with increasing altitude, mountainous regions provide a wide range of potential environmental niches for human communities. In the Near East, ecological zones associated with mountains range from hot humid or hot and arid coastal plains that give way to dense forested areas and then into wooded parkland above around 2,000 m, depending upon latitude (fig. 9.1). Above this ecological boundary, permanent settlement diminishes where the highland pastures (equivalent to the Alpine zone) take over.

Highland areas have notoriously poor transport systems,[1] are known for harboring isolated (or even isolationist) communities, and also operate as barriers between large, more complex polities (McNeil 1992). In fact, in the Mediterranean sociohistorical currents have frequently been characterized as oscillations between the influence of physically dominant mountain ranges and politically and culturally prevalent plains that were frequently incapable of exerting control over their unruly or isolationist highland neighbors (Shaw 1990: 199). This isolationist tendency is well exemplified by the mountainous area of rough Cilicia in Turkey, which has a long tradition of regional autonomy and even banditry. The region is peppered with fortified residences, often located on high places, the occupants of which during the Roman empire maintained their own (Luwian) language and generally acted as a thorn in the flesh for the Romanized communities of the neighboring lowlands (Shaw 1990). Although these Isaurian/Cilician communities may provide excellent examples of highland autonomy, it would be misleading to cast this as a general model by relegating the highlands to a perpetual state of a World Systems periphery. Instead, as has been argued by Yener (1995: 119), it is more fruitful to see areas such as highland Anatolia as being not simply a "passive receiver of innovations that emanated from more sophisticated centers" but rather as a region that contributed its own innovations to the general course of development of Near Eastern civilization.

Nevertheless, it is also evident that many highland polities, if not isolated from the neighboring lowland states can, on occasion, exhibit antagonistic relationships with them. Much of the history of the highlands, and therefore their landscape history, can be seen as being partly contingent upon their relationship with lowland polities. The highlands thus play a varying role in regional interaction systems, ranging from a relationship that is strongly symbiotic to one that is antagonistic and isolationist. We also see a high degree of instability as local polities transform themselves from state peripheries with a high degree of pastoral nomadism (such as Middle Bronze Age eastern Turkey) or to regional states (such as the Himyarite state of highland Yemen contemporaneous with the Roman empire). This rapid flux from one political formation to the next can leave an interrupted but episodically indelible record on the landscape, as the following examples should illustrate.

Ecologically it is important to recognize that by penetrating higher, cooler, and frequently wetter areas, the environment can be modified in different ways, depending upon geographical location. Either highlands are more favorable for a broad range of occupation than the surrounding arid lowlands (as in the case of the Yemen highlands) or they represent cold and relatively dry uplands that

Fig. 9.1 The Taurus mountains near Kestel, Turkey, showing ecological zonation: snow/icecap, alpine meadows, treeline, eroded valley floor with agriculture.

invite more specialized modes of subsistence (as in parts of the Anatolian, Iranian, and Caucasus highlands). Overall, as one travels from Yemen in the south to the Caucasus in the north, the snow-line decreases in altitude, as do the upper limits of forests and viable settlement, and these factors all place considerable constraint on populations in the northern regions. In fact, it is important to appreciate that mountain areas may be either uninhabited or sparsely populated for long periods of time, which itself limits the development of the cultural landscape. This is well illustrated by the archaeological record for much of Northern Anatolia, which shows an apparent absence of settlement for the Neolithic. In fact, surveys by Roger Matthews in Paphlagonia (to the north of Ankara) show that apart from a few specialized sites of the Early Bronze Age, occupation

only increases in the Late Bronze Age, and not until Roman-Byzantine times is there a significant scatter of settlement (Matthews et al. 1998).

Mountains and uplands also provide considerable problems for archaeological survey because the high density of frequently steep valleys, vegetated slopes, and the overall fine-grained nature of the terrain can make survey slow and difficult. Moreover, the presence of often numerous, small, dispersed settlements (as opposed to larger nucleated sites) requires a higher intensity of survey coverage than is necessary on many plains. Because of their varied topography, in addition to ridges, high mountain peaks, and deeply incised valleys, mountain areas can include upland or intermontane plains that share characteristics with many lowland plains. Such plains, well exemplified by the Konya plain in central Anatolia and the Kur River

Basin of Iran, like their lowland counterparts can therefore be dotted by scores of mounded sites (tells).

Themes of Mountain Landscapes

Highland massifs exhibit distinct vertical ecological zones characterized by different forms of vegetation, and these, in turn, influence the various land-use zones that develop. Although the land-use zones reflect basic ecological constraints, they also result from prevailing social and economic factors such as accessibility, local population density, and the different orientation or aspect of the slopes. Slope aspect is particularly important because in highland areas, the amount of sunlight received on sun-facing or shaded slopes can result in a difference in the height of ecological and land-use zones on different sides of a valley of hundreds of meters (Peattie 1936: 85–88). In addition, it has been suggested that the subsistence economy of highlands falls into two classes: so-called peasant highland agriculture on the one hand, mobile or transhumant pastoral economies on the other, as well as a number of transitional agro-pastoral states in between. Of more analytical interest for the archaeologist, however, is the potential contrast of wealth between some highland tribal areas and neighboring lowlands. This is evident in Brian Hayden's study of Thailand, where highland tribes had a much higher proportion of well-to-do stock-holding families, versus the agriculturally productive lowlands, which were associated with a much larger but poor rural peasantry ruled over by largely urban-based noble clans (Hayden 2001: 574). Such a sharp contrast in sociopolitical structure between highland and lowland is relevant to similarly contrasting terrain types of the Near East.

As a result of their distinctive geology and often extensive woodlands, many mountainous areas become economic resource zones for adjacent lowlands. This can then result in a symbiotic relationship between the two contrasting topographic zones. Mountain resources include various metal ores, obsidian, or wood, as well as charcoal. Water might also be considered in this light because mountains act as the collection zones for water that is then distributed via natural springs or engineered distribution systems to the communities of the plains. Such products can then be exchanged for the staple products such as cereals grown in the lowlands.

Under certain social and political circumstances, highlands can become isolated from neighboring lowlands, at which time the "isolationist" highlands can gain a reputation for being inhabited by a population that not only is potentially unruly and prone to banditry but also can become an excellent source of recruitment for soldiers of the imperial

or other armies (McNeill 1992: 119). Finally, mountains play a special symbolic or religious role because many high places are sanctified locations that can then become foci of pilgrimage (Bradley 2000).

In terms of their physical landscapes, mountains can vary topographically from deep narrow valleys that have the potential to support limited populations (unless the land is built up in the form of terraces) to broad intermontain plateaus. Although the latter might be seen as being the equivalent of the classic Near Eastern tell-dotted plains discussed in chapter 6, more realistically they should be seen as potentially forming *either* a pastoral zone *or* a cultivable resource; cultivation should not automatically be assumed to be the primary land use on plains. Furthermore, the development of mining must reflect the distribution of the minerals themselves, with the result that mines, if located in isolated mountainous areas, need their source of food supply to be convenient. This results in agricultural systems developing as intrusive enclaves within mountainous areas. Finally, many mountain landscapes bear the ephemeral traces of large populations of people who are only fleetingly resident but who make their passage through as nomads (Alizadeh 1988; Cribb 1991). Such communities usually take advantage of the vertical zonation of ecological zones and in the form of so-called vertical nomads ply their way through mountain valleys on their way to the higher upland pastures that are available in late spring and summer. In such cases, the degree of landscape alteration is by no means proportional to the quantity of people who have passed through the region.

It is now appropriate to compare the mountain landscapes of southwest Arabia with those of Anatolia/Transcaucasia, to show how landscapes have developed along both similar and markedly different trajectories.

The Landscapes of Highland Yemen

In southwest Arabia, vertical ecological zonation results in distinct land-use zones, as indicated on figure 9.2. This diagram, which is representative of both the Saudi Arabian 'Asir and Yemen, shows that the desert lowlands are the realm of flood irrigation, whereas at better-watered high altitudes, localized runoff systems, terraced fields, and rain-fed cultivation predominate.

The highlands of southwest Arabia attain altitudes in excess of 3,500 m above sea level and display some of the most majestic landscapes in the Near East. In the wetter parts of the mountains, spectacular staircases of terraced fields carpet the valley sides from valley floor to mountaintop (fig. 9.3). Today a dense pattern of rural settlement in the form of thousands of small villages dot the landscape, mainly situated on rocky hills that crop out between areas of terracing. Elsewhere, broad, downfaulted intermontane basins (or *graben*) extend between semiarid fringing mountains. In these latter areas, where rainfall is less than about 300 mm per annum, cultivation is limited to the valley floors. In yet drier areas, settlement is impossible except where supplementary irrigation water emanates from wells, springs (*ghayls*), or flood runoff.

Following the dry phase of the Late Glacial Maximum, the pattern of monsoon circulation strengthened considerably, so that between 10,000 and 7,000 years B.P., increased rainfall on the highlands resulted in the growth of lakes and marshes in a number of intermontane basins (Lézine et al. 1998; Wilkinson 1997a). Between 7600 and 3000 cal. B.C., a thick black or dark brown humic palaeosol developed on hill slopes and over basin floors. This mid-Holocene soil, which continued to develop until after the lakes had dried up, can frequently be recognized as a black horizon extending over lake deposits. When found on

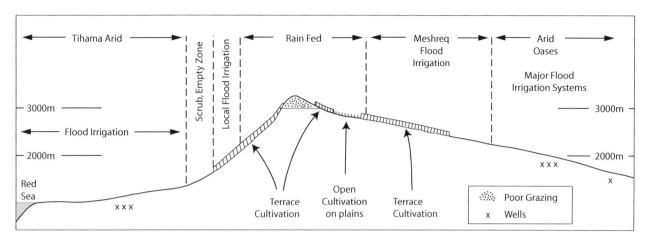

Fig. 9.2   Land-use zonation in the mountains of southwest Arabia (redrawn from Abdulfattah 1981: 68, and Fisher, 1978: fig. 16.6).

Fig. 9.3   Terraced fields at nearly 3,000 m above sea level, to the southeast of Yarim, Yemen.

hill slopes, this layer can also include Neolithic artifacts. During these earlier phases of the Holocene, the landscape appears to have been relatively stable, and although erosion occurred, it was probably insufficient to break the canopy of the ground surface. There followed after around 3,900 cal. B.C. a series of phases of soil erosion that are evident in the form of stony loams that overlie the black palaeosol and that form thick accumulations draping valley-side slopes and filling side valleys (fig. 9.4).

In some locations, this phase of soil erosion was continuous from Neolithic times, but in most places, accelerated deposition of colluvial loams did not occur until the late third or early second millennium B.C. (Wilkinson 1999a). At this time, not only was settlement rapidly increasing with resultant disturbance of the soil canopy and vegetation cover but also there was some degree of climatic drying. Rather than blaming the erosion on one or other mechanism, it seems likely that both climatic drying (which would reduce plant cover) and increased human population could both have con-

tributed to the increased evidence of erosion. This phase of erosion often resulted in the removal of any preexisting soil cover, but in areas where, for example, terraces were constructed, ground conditions then stabilized, as indicated on figure 9.4.

The record of soil erosion from the Yemen highlands is roughly comparable to that in the Horn of Africa (Bard et al. 2000). In the early Holocene the Tigray plateau of northern Ethiopia (1,000 to 3,500 m above sea level; mean annual rainfall 700–1,200 mm) had a dense vegetation cover, which probably developed under a more humid climate. In the mid/late Holocene there followed a phase of soil erosion that resulted from vegetation clearance, perhaps in combination with climatic drying. The data from Tigray supports an earlier study by Butzer (1981), which identified accelerating soil erosion from early Axumite time (100 B.C.–A.D. 400) and which showed that late-Holocene erosion resulted in part from cultural factors but was enhanced by episodic heavy rains. Although northern Ethiopia apparently lacks the dense pattern of third- and second-millennium B.C. settlement of Yemen, again it appears that during the late Holocene both human and environmental factors combined to result in increased environmental degradation and soil erosion.

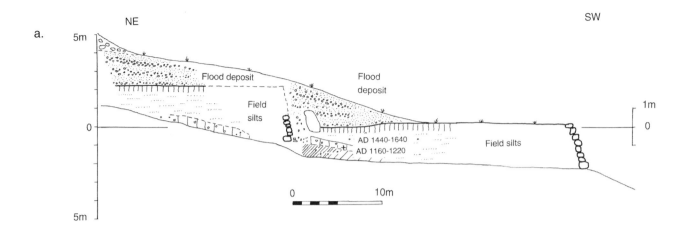

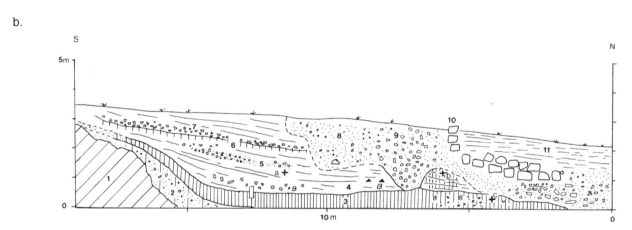

Fig. 9.4 Sedimentary sequences indicative of soil erosion in highland Yemen: (a) Section through a terrace field, near Yarim in Yemen highlands showing post-collapse gravel deposition (flood deposit) over low-energy silts accumulated behind a terrace wall. (b) Valley-floor deposits at Ghazwan (Yemen highlands): (1) decayed igneous bedrock of Yemen volcanics (Trap series); (2) late Pleistocene/early Holocene slope deposit of pale brown sandy loam with angular stones; (3) mid-Holocene palaeosol of dark reddish brown humic loam, with occasional stone artifacts and bone; (4) slope deposit of pale brown loam with stones, chert, and obsidian flakes, as well as bone fragments; (5) lens of angular stones of slope deposit; (6) weak palaeosol of pale brown silty loam representing episode of slope stability; (7) angular stones forming thin slope deposit; (8/9) moderate to high-energy wadi-gravel cut through slope deposits (4–7); subangular gravel/rubble with larger stones; (10) partly collapsed field terrace wall; (11) fine-loam, low–energy deposit accumulated behind wall 10. Radiocarbon determinations, all on charcoal: (a) 3675–3390 cal. B.C., (b) 4715–4365 cal. B.C., (c) 4940–4620 cal. B.C.

In highland Yemen, recycling of construction materials is fundamental to an understanding of the cultural landscape because it results in the attrition of earlier features and the loss of the archaeological record. Stone blocks form the basic building material for most buildings and field boundaries. When new terrace walls need to be built, the stones are fre-quently recycled from derelict struc-tures—such as houses, dams, deflec-tion walls, or other terraces—and incorporated into new walls. In areas of dense terracing or where there was much later settlement, processes of recycling can sometimes reduce ar-chaeological structures to little more than artifact scatters. In extreme cases, terraced fields even extend to the summits of hills, with the re-sult that former hilltop settlements have been dismantled and their de-bris incorporated into a mosaic of later fields. This process, when com-bined with the massive erosion that prevails in such hilltop locations, can then result in the virtual erasure of preexisting archaeological sites. Similar processes are also evident in buildings of Himyarite settlements (roughly contemporaneous with the Roman/Early Byzantine periods), elements of which can be seen incorporated into modern buildings.

An additional structural element of the Yemeni landscape derives from water-gathering systems. In the wettest areas, where summer monsoonal rainfall of between 500 and 1,200 mm per annum occurs in most years, field crops can be irrigated directly from the rain that falls on their surface. In slightly drier areas, fields benefit from a small supplement of water derived from runoff from upslope. This can be derived either from barren lands that are crossed by water gathering *saghiyas* or simply from fallowed fields upslope. In yet drier areas (between say 300 and 200 mm annual rainfall), this system is formalized, and so fields are mainly situated on valley floors and almost always receive their water from runoff areas located upslope. Although this system is a modern analogue of the well-known runoff-agricultural systems of the Negev and North Africa (chapter 8), the requirements for runoff farming in areas of summer rainfall with high-evaporation rates are more stringent than in the Negev and North Africa, where rainfall occurs within the low-evaporation cool season (Pacey and Cullis 1986: 130). In the tropical zone of southern Arabia, needs for crop water are greater, and so to be effective, the runoff systems must receive a slightly higher annual rainfall or more storms (Pacey and Cullis 1986). Finally, in the driest areas, local runoff systems are eschewed in favor of the harnessing of wadi spate flow, which is gathered behind large temporary or permanent dams (*sedd*, pl. *sedud*) and distributed on to extensive fields on valley floors. At risk of oversimplifying what is in reality a complex system of agriculture, we can see that local communities utilize water from ever-larger catchments as rainfall decreases from moist highland to arid desert fringe. In the extreme

case of the Marib Dam, which was in use during most of the first millennium B.C. and A.D., the catchment of the Wadi Dhana (Brunner 1983: 12), ca. 10,000 sq. km in area, provides the water for some 8,000 ha of irrigated fields (chapter 8). Thus it is the huge highland catchment that is the key to the development of these Sabaean irrigation systems. In reality, however, in the traditional agricultural system, there are many variations on the simple model of catchment size increasing as rainfall decreases.

In addition to this rainfall-runoff-flood irrigation continuum, other sources of water are utilized, and locally they may be of considerable importance (Varisco 1982). *Ghayl* flow is perennial flow derived either from springs or from minor pools in wadis. This is usually channeled via small open channels that lead water to irrigated fields or orchards. Well (or *bier*) supply is also locally important, although wells are useful only for the irrigation of small areas. Related to these two sources are subsurface channels that can follow valleys or less frequently occur in the form of the classic qanat or falaj system (chapter 8). Finally, there is the water tank (*ma' jil* or birkeh). The former can provide temporary storage of runoff or spring flow prior to its use for irrigation, whereas birkehs are used more for long-term storage of water for domestic or religious purposes or to supply passing travelers. Water tanks form conspicuous elements in the highland Yemeni landscape today and presumably in ancient times also, but because they remain in use for long periods of time and are frequently plastered over many times, they are difficult to date with confidence.

For the landscape archaeologist, Yemen is of exceptional interest because its terraced landscape often comprises a conspicuous palimpsest of elements the latest of which can, in the appropriate circumstances, be stripped off from earlier elements to reveal yet older landscapes. In

the most conspicuous cases, robust elements, such as the terrace walls of Himyarite estates, become enshrined within a patchwork of later landscape features (chapter 4). Also, trackways lined by desert varnished stone "fences" and locally floored by paving stones can be seen to lead between Himyarite sites and other dated features, and like their counterparts in the hill country west of the Jordan, these are demonstrably ancient features (fig. 4.8b).

Terraced Fields of Highland Yemen

At the most general level, an agricultural terrace can be defined as "any artificially flattened surface on which crops are grown subsequent to the flattening" (Spencer and Hale 1961: 3; Treacy and Denevan 1994: 93), whereas for Yemen, Varisco states that "the terrace, in essence, is an ecological response to the lack of adequate level land surface for agriculture in the mountains" (1982: 136). In many parts of the world where gently sloping land has been terraced, such land could in fact be farmed without terracing (Treacy and Denevan 1994: 93). In such cases, farmers presumably had some other motivation for terrace construction other than the creation of field space alone. These additional factors include deepening of the soil, moisture management, and the modification of microclimate (Treacy and Denevan 1994: 93). Although terraces undoubtedly reduce soil erosion (Sheng 1981), erosion reduction is generally regarded as a secondary function of field terraces rather than their primary purpose (Donkin 1979: 34; Treacy and Denevan 1994: 94).

In theory, if terraces are constructed as a response to the lack of sufficient level land, increasing population pressure in constricted highland valleys should result in the expansion of cultivation in the form of terraces on the hill slopes above. As a result of the initial disturbance arising from terrace construction, slopes would become destabilized so that the ensuing erosion could damage fields and reduce their productive capacity. On the other hand, once terraces were in place, they would trap soil from upslope and inhibit erosion. Thanks to their tendency to suppress erosion and accumulate soil, field terraces can lead to increased landscape stability (see below).

Terraced fields function as massive sediment traps because soils, when they are eroded, rather than being swept into stream channels and eventually the sea, are retained on the slope, usually by the terrace walls. In Yemen, terracing can result in complex trajectories of landscape development. On the one hand, if terraced fields completely blanket slopes, the landscape can become remarkably stable, and so both runoff and erosion are inhibited. On the other hand, terracing can result in potentially unstable landscapes if walls are not maintained properly, and so there can be a sudden loss of equilibrium, and massive sediment movement can result (Butzer 1982; Varisco 1991). In highland Yemen, such rapid erosion has been recognized within aggraded sequences of sediments associated with field terraces. In such cases, extant field terraces can become engulfed by coarse sediments transported from eroded terraced fields located further upslope. This high-energy aggradation, which partly results from the collapse of walls further upslope, is then followed by the incision of the newly formed wadis through the fields and their accumulated deposits (fig. 9.4a).

The process of construction of terraced fields results in a stepped landscape comprising dry stone walls usually built parallel to the contours, with a sediment bench behind. The combination of rainfall-absorbing terraces with the diversion of wadi flow for irrigation can reduce runoff, and so eventually wadi channels are reduced to little more than a ditch. In extreme cases, water-control features (dams, monumental cross-valley walls, and terraced fields) are so pervasive that valley floors become covered by barriers, and the valley itself will eventually become infilled by fine sediments. Because terracing can commence in the valley floors, these areas become stabilized first, and subsequently, terraces are constructed on the slopes above. Such landscapes, as long as they are maintained, can be remarkably stable, so that contrary to accepted wisdom, as population increases and more land is required, the landscape becomes more stable. The result is that the landscape is capable of supporting yet higher population levels.

The following main types of agrarian landscape occur in the archaeological record of the Yemen highlands and neighboring areas, although the variations on these classes are endless:

— Landscapes with staircases of terraced fields on the valley sides or low gradient sequences along the axes of valley floors.
— Similar landscapes of terraced fields, but with the addition of dams that supply supplementary irrigation water.
— Landscapes of wadi-flood agriculture characteristic of the desert fringes in the areas of Sabaʾ, Qataban, Hadhramaut, Ausan, and Maʿin (chapter 8).
— Flat, intermontane basins exhibiting a rectilinear patchwork of fields, sometimes weakly terraced on the downslope side. Such basins usually show little evidence for ancient sedentary settlement.

Until recently, little was known about the history of terraced agriculture in highland Yemen. Whereas in the southern Levant, terraced fields are considered to date to the Iron or Middle–Late Bronze Ages Age (chapter 7), recent investigations of Yemeni terraced fields indicate that valley-floor terraces can be traced back as far as the fourth millen-nium B.C. and valley-slope terraces probably to the third or second millennium. Whether this means that terracing in Yemen is indeed older than in the southern Levant or simply that the earliest Levantine phases have not been recognized requires further investigation.

Terraced fields, like many landscape features, are difficult to date. In the Yemen highlands the accumulated soils upslope of the terrace walls usually overlie and therefore postdate the dark gray-brown Jahran palaeosol discussed above. Some terraces evidently postdate archaeological sites, which they have disturbed and/or overlie. The best-dated field terraces are either those whose sedimentary accumulations are stratified within natural sedimentary sequences or those that exhibit buried soils that contain flecks of charcoal, which can then be dated by radiocarbon dating.

The earliest terraced fields recorded were within a sedimentary sequence 10 m deep in the valley floor upstream of a relict Himyarite Dam. It was here where a small field terrace wall or check dam, dated in the range 3955–3630 cal. B.C., was stratified within the upper horizons of the Jahran soil some 6 m below the top of late-Holocene sediments (Sedd adh-Dhraʿah II; fig. 9.5; Wilkinson 1999a: 186). This sequence suggests that valley-floor cultivation was underway during the Neolithic, and the presence of springs in the area today, as well as early-Holocene humic deposits, implies that this valley-floor terrace could have been used for simple irrigation.

Other terraces located on slopes of the valley side are dated with less confidence because they can usually only be dated "by association" with dated sites. For example, very low alignments of heavily varnished stones constructed at right angles to the slope and situated below the late third- and second-millennium B.C. site of Hammat al-Qa were excavated to reveal alternating large and small rough field stones, backed by

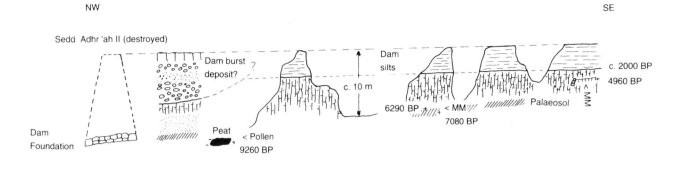

Fig. 9.5 Section through alluvial sequence, Sedd adh-Dhra'ah Yemen. The terrace wall located by the radiocarbon date 4960 B.P. was supported by fist-sized stones over which occurred a soil horizon (dated by contained charcoal to 3955–3630 cal.B.C.) accumulated against the wall. The technique of inserting stones behind a terrace wall is normal practice in the region today and is intended to drain excess water from the terrace, thereby preventing waterlogging, loss of soil strength, and ultimate collapse (see Gibson and Edelstein 1985: 143; Treacy and Denevan 1994: 95).

fist-sized stones. Only a thin lens of mid-Holocene soil remained at the base of the sequence, and the entire terrace wall and its accumulated deposits appear to have been planed parallel to the slope by prolonged erosion. Although dating by physical proximity to an archaeological site is probably the least robust form of dating (Frederick and Krahtopolou 2000: 90–91), the physical condition of the terraces and the absence of later settlement in the vicinity tentatively support a Bronze Age date. These relict terraced fields and similar examples adjacent to two other Bronze Age sites in the region therefore suggest that terraced agriculture on slopes was underway by the late third or earlier second millennium B.C. Terraces were positioned so that those below the gently sloping settlement area were higher on the slope than those to the southeast. This appears to be because the terraces to the southeast did not receive runoff from the hilltop and therefore required a greater length of slope above to generate sufficient runoff (fig. 9.6). The relict fields may therefore have been part of one system, all parts of which were carefully positioned to receive optimum runoff from the slopes and hilltop above. That these terraces appear to have functioned as an integrated system

again argues in favor of a single date of construction.

The accumulating information from highland Yemen makes it difficult to sustain one cherished belief, namely, that terracing is the result of population pressure. According to this theory, terraces on the valley side would be constructed when the population increased to a point so that there was no other available land, thereby compelling new land to be created by terracing (Semple 1941: 565). This "common sense" principal is not, however, supported by the evidence from Hammat al Qa, where the area of land required to support the estimated population of the Bronze Age hilltop settlement could be calculated (Wilkinson et al. 2001a). These estimates suggest that all staple requirements could have been derived from the surrounding plain within 1 km of the settlement. As a result, large areas of the plain would have been available as potential pasture. Probable threshing floors on adjacent spurs of land were well positioned to catch the breeze (essential for winnowing) and also were at a convenient distance to the terraced fields themselves (Wilkinson et al. 2001a). If the field terraces at Hammat al Qa were in use during the Bronze Age, there must have been plenty of land

available for cultivation. Even so, not all these areas were easily accessible. The Hammat al Qa terraces both created additional cultivable soil and provided it at a convenient location. At a still later date, soils associated with terraced fields have been dated by both radiocarbon and pottery to the first millennium B.C., at which time a significant amount of the highland Yemeni landscape appears to have been terraced. There is no compelling evidence to show that the extensive plains were fully cultivated until perhaps the last two thousand years or so.

With the rise of state-level society in the highlands during the Himyarite period (first century B.C. until sixth century A.D.), a striking new feature of the landscape appears in the form of monumental dams. These range from massive stone-built structures across highland wadis to more modest structures that can be difficult to distinguish from terrace walls except that they are equipped with sluices, spillways, and conduits that led water towards fields downslope. Four basic forms of dam can be recognized: (a) massive high dams up to 20 m high and 100 m long, (b) structures that are lower and of more modest construction, (c) low broad dams of earth and stone without obvious high-quality

Fig. 9.6 Three-dimensional reconstruction of the Bronze Age hilltop site of Hammat al-Qa, highland Yemen, showing field terraces and their potential water-catchment areas (compiled by Glynn Barratt).

masonry, and (d) low cross-valley walls up to 1 km long, superficially resembling dams known locally as "*harrah*." The masonry structures (that is, types a, b, and d) are built in a style that is regarded as Himyarite, being made of cut blocks of stone arranged in well-made horizontal courses. In addition, some dams are firmly dated to the Himyarite period by in situ inscriptions.

Dams in the Dhamar area apparently supplied supplementary water to areas that already had an agricultural base supplied by systems of terraced fields. Only occasionally are the dams in use today, in which case they appear to be irrigated according to principles in use during the Himyarite time (Barcelò et al. 2000). Other intact dams seem to have survived in the landscape either because they are exceptionally robust or because they have effectively become the walls of terraced fields. Many dams, however, have been destroyed by floods and have therefore ceased to function. Irrigation systems consist of modules comprising the following elements: (a) the dam itself and its hydrological catchment upslope. Each dam was equipped with a sluice, frequently cut through the natural rock, which fed water into irrigation channels downstream, and a passageway below the dam itself to channel the base flow (that is the perennial flow) of the wadi,

downstream, also for the purposes of irrigation; (b) long channels that led down valley towards the fields. Unlike in more arid areas where distribution channels can be conspicuous, in the subhumid highlands, continuous transformation of the landscape has frequently resulted in these features being incorporated into the modern fields or in the agricultural soils being built up above the channels thereby obscuring them. Nevertheless, irrigation channels are frequently known to the local inhabitants, and channels are occasionally evident on air photographs where they form sinuous features following the boundaries of terraced fields; (c) finally, the channels must have distributed water to ancient fields located within the irrigated plains. But because such features must have been constructed within a matrix of preexisting fields, and equally such fields will have continued in use, even after the irrigation system had been abandoned, the irrigated fields are difficult to distinguish from those that simply were fed by rainfall. Additional complications are evident where water from one water-collection system is diverted into another by means of low, masonry damlike structures (Barcelò et al. 2000).

Rather than replacing existing agricultural systems, dams and their irrigated fields probably supple-

mented terraced agriculture, thereby providing a dual system of economic support for Himyarite society. The basis of that support probably continued to be terraced agriculture and small runoff fields, both of which could be built and managed at the level of either the household or groups of cooperating households. Supplementary provisioning then came from the dams, which supplied irrigation water to fields often located some distance out on the plains. Whether this means that former pasture areas were converted to cultivation is not clear, but the provisioning of irrigation water to areas that would otherwise have only received water from rainfall probably means that dams increased the total productivity of the terrain. Each major dam therefore probably formed the focal point of either a Himyarite estate or a module that consisted of a small town, its dam(s), irrigation system, cross-valley walls and monumentally terraced fields, in addition to the conventional small-scale terraced fields (fig. 9.7). The planning and construction of such modules was almost certainly at a larger scale than the household, and inscriptions hint that some dams were administered from the Himyarite capital of Zafar (Norbert Nebes personal communication).

Harrah (monumental cross-valley walls) add an interesting dimen-

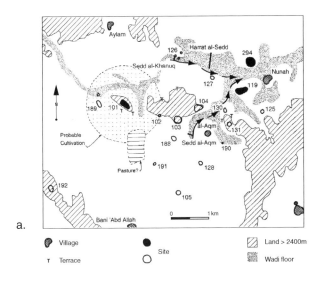

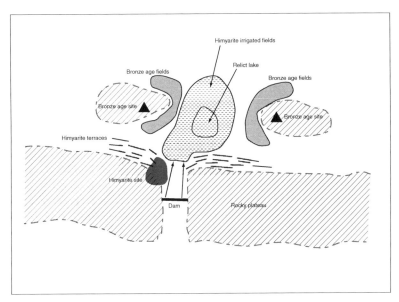

b.

Fig. 9.7 Agricultural landscapes of highland Yemen: (a) A Bronze Age site (DS 101 = Hammat al-Qa) with its estimated cultivated area and a possible relict lake/marsh remaining as pastoral enclave. During the Himyarite period, water was collected by the two dams (*sedds*) and conducted downstream (arrows) beyond *Harrat al-Sedd*, towards the main Himyarite town of Nunah (DS 294) (based on Wilkinson et al. 2001). (b) Modular Bronze Age/Himyarite landscape for highland Yemen, showing Bronze Age sites on plateau overlooking a relict lake and marsh that was then encroached upon and covered during the Himyarite period by silts deposited by waters conducted from the Himyarite dam.

sion to the landscape because of their hybrid function that incorporates the attributes of both dams and terrace walls. Some harrah are relatively modest in scale, being little more than 100 m in length, whereas others are up to 900 m long and can span entire valleys (fig. 9.8a). Unlike dams, harrah were not sited at narrow choke points of valleys but instead were built where valleys become wide and where down-valley

water flow becomes dispersed and of low power, thereby favoring the deposition of sediment. Although harrah formed terraces, they appear to have been constructed in one phase, which implies that some of the fill upstream may have been introduced from elsewhere. Unlike traditional terraces, they are of monumental landscape scale, and according to local tradition, each has its own apparently ancient name.

Harrah appear to be a local Yemeni analogue of the *khadin* of Rajastan, which function as traps for silt and water, thereby building up fertile patches of land upslope (Pacey and Cullis 1986: 134–135). In such cases, runoff accumulates behind the cross-valley wall, and excess water may then flow via spillways to a second feature further downslope. An important feature of the khadin, and perhaps the Yemeni harrah, is that prolonged moisture accumulation upslope can promote soil microbial activity and the accumulation of humus, which together promote fertility and increase the moisture-holding capacity of the soils upstream of these features (Pacey and Cullis 1986: 140).

The massive harrah also performed supplementary roles in the landscape. Some provide ways across the valley, for example, the ancient Himyarite road from Marib to Zafar crosses the head of the valley of the Wadi Shalalah via a harrah 900 m long (fig. 9.8a), and the same feature also acts as a traditional tribal boundary. Dams and cross-valley harrah in the landscape of the Himyarite highlands combine elements of the flood-irrigation system of the desert fringe (namely, dams) with the check dam or terraced landscape of the highlands. These elements then became formalized to a monumental scale not apparent in the landscape prior to the Himyarite period.

Following the fall of the Himyarite kingdom, some of the larger dams failed (fig. 9.8b) and were replaced either by locally administered flood (or sayl) agriculture or by a more

Fig. 9.8 Monumental hydraulic structures in the landscape of highland Yemen: (top) View of cross-valley wall (*harrah*) in the Wadi Shalalah, Yemen. (bottom) Large Himyarite dam of Sedd al-Ajmar, now breached as a result of a major flood.

extensive network of terraced fields. The continued use of some smaller dams in the well-controlled and geomorphologically stable Zafar valley also testifies to the extraordinary longevity of traditional landscape practice in parts of Yemen (Barceló et al. 2000).

Model of Settlement and Land Use for a Highland Basin

During the mid Holocene (ca. 8000–3000 B.C.) the central parts of many basins in highland Yemen held freshwater lakes or marshes (Wilkinson 1997a). There is little evidence for either Neolithic or Bronze Age settlement within them or their surrounding plains. Because Bronze Age sites on the nearby hilltops would have required cultivated areas of less than 1 km radius to provision their relatively modest populations (Wilkinson et al. 2001a), it would have been unnecessary to cultivate the basin centers (fig. 9.7a). Therefore, the basin centers probably remained as open space in the form of grassland or marsh into the third and second millennia B.C., thereby providing valuable pastoral reserves. During the Iron Age and Himyarite periods, cultivation probably then crept towards the central parts of basins and encroached upon the pastoral reserves (fig. 9.7b).

The archaeological landscapes of the montane plains of Yemen are thus virtually an inversion of those of the Fertile Crescent, which were, for much of the Bronze Age and later, characterized by tells located predominantly on plains. In these landscapes of tells, settlements avoided hilltops except under specific circumstances (chapter 6). The preliminary model for the intermontane plains underscores two fundamental points concerning the landscapes of semiarid Near Eastern plains. First, the development of tells should not be assumed; second, extensive plains should also be regarded as ideal areas of pasture, not simply as a

resource to be cultivated. Such valuable pastoral resources would then be expected to persist through time, thereby forming a conservative element in the landscape that would be maintained through local tradition.

In Yemen, although a wide range of agricultural strategies have operated within the landscape through time, three main systems of land use were in operation during the first millennia B.C. and A.D.

(a) In the highlands, family-maintained terrace fields probably provided the long-term mode of sustenance until the introduction of formal monumental irrigation works in the Himyarite period. Terraced fields, runoff cultivation, and local floodwater-farming systems could have been constructed and maintained by the family or small cooperative groups of families. They were sustained either by the rain that fell on them or by a bonus of excess water from upslope or upstream. This system was flexible, resilient, and extendable as long as there was more land that could be made into terraces.

(b) Production from irrigation systems supplied by monumental dams was supplementary to that of terraced agriculture. This entailed the collection of flood-runoff water from tributary valleys and the conduction of that water via a system of distribution canals downstream to irrigate the edge of the adjacent area of lowlands (the Qa). This system provided water for a significant area of lowland but not for the entire population of the region in question. In many cases, irrigation could have supplied estates that in addition to small-scale terraced fields also included more formal fields with monumental terrace walls. Although the precise date and details of the administration of

such systems remain unknown, rock-cut commemorative inscriptions in epigraphic Old South Arabian, when present, suggest that most were in use during the last centuries B.C. and first centuries A.D. Unfortunately, occasional peak floods destroyed many of the larger dams. When such failures occurred, that part of agricultural production vested in terraced agriculture was able to continue. Therefore, although vulnerable to high floods, this system had a built-in safety net.

(c) In contrast, the massive high dams of the Sayhad (chapter 8) were vulnerable to high floods; if a breach occurred, the entire crop supply system was threatened. Consequently, management and mobilization of large quantities of labor were crucial to both the construction and the repair of these systems.

The large-scale flood agriculture of the Sayhad was therefore brittle and inflexible and also required a larger component of management and administration than the dual systems of the highlands. Collapse of the polities of the desert fringe, when it came at various times during the late first millennium B.C. and early first millennium A.D., was not simply the result of any specific dam burst but was probably a complex downward spiraling resulting from shifts and eventually a decline in incense trade, lack of investment in irrigation systems, siltation in the field areas, decline in local population (and therefore labor), sociopolitical disruptions, and major flood events. Fortunately, the more flexible agricultural strategies of the highlands enabled most communities to absorb or avoid such catastrophes.

Highland Anatolia

On first impression, the high plains of Anatolia resemble the Upper

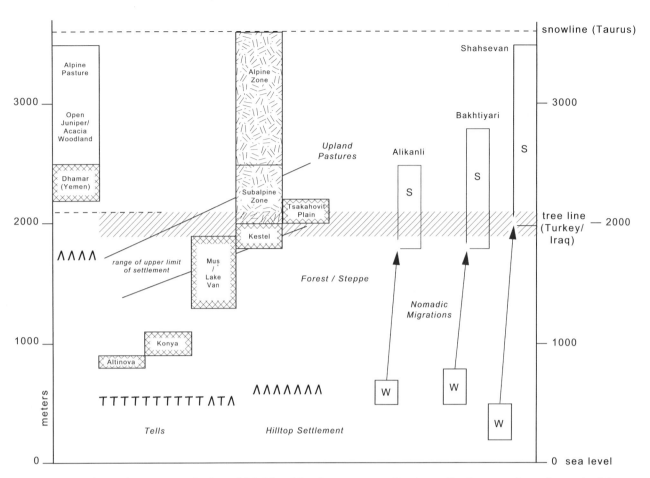

Fig. 9.9   Ecological contexts of selected highland landscape types for Anatolia, Iran, and southern Arabia, according to altitude. Note that the Shirak plain is also known as the Tsakahovit plain.

Mesopotamian plains described in chapter 6, being scattered with occasional prominent tells dating from Neolithic until Ottoman times. At higher elevations and further to the east in parts of easternmost Turkey, Georgia, and Armenia, however, except in restricted localities usually at lower elevations, mounded settlements form a less prominent feature of the landscape (Sagona 1984: 25).

That there is a general relationship between mounded settlement and altitude is evident from figure 9.9, which shows the altitudinal range of various landscape types with respect to ecological zones, the upper limits of permanent settlement, as well as selected patterns of transhumance. Ever since the classic studies of von Humbolt (1769–1859), geographers have been aware that the vertical distribution of vegetational zones re-

flects changes in climatic parameters with increased altitude. Similar relationships also hold, at a general level, for zones of land use and human occupation. Equally, however, because socioeconomic and political factors are fundamental to patterns of human settlement and land use in mountain areas (Funnell and Parrish 2001), it is hardly surprising that human adaptation to ecological constraints is remarkably flexible and contingent on a range of historical, socioeconomic, and political factors. In turn, the archaeological record may equally be expected to show a marked degree of variation through time. Nevertheless, that there is some relationship between settlement and ecology should be evident from the following cases.

The Altinova plain (ca. 850 m above sea level; fig. 9.9) along the

upper Murat river in eastern Turkey is punctuated with tells that were occupied within a temporal range that spanned from early Chalcolithic to medieval times (Whallon 1979). Although there were significant declines in population during the Chalcolithic/Early Bronze Age transition, Early Bronze III, and the Late Iron Age, Whallon saw no reason to posit that there were fluctuations between sedentary and nomadic settlement. Rather, he argued that sedentary settlement continued through time, albeit with high points being coincident with periods when the area was engaged heavily in trade with neighboring empires or when the region itself was incorporated within such empires (Whallon 1979: 278).

Similarly, surveys in the Konya plain, located at some 1,000 m above sea level, show a dense pattern of tells unrivaled elsewhere in Turkey (Mellaart 1961: 159). In fact, some tells even attain sizes of 40–60 ha, scales not far short of those in northern Syria and Iraq (Mellaart 1963; French 1972; Baird 2000). A significant increase in nucleated tell-type settlement during Early Bronze I/II times (i.e., earlier third millennium B.C.) was followed by a virtual cessation of sedentary settlement during the late third and second millennium B.C., after which repopulation of the plains occurred during the Iron Age. This pattern then persisted until the present day. Because this dense distribution of tells occurs in an area regarded as the "granary of Turkey," it appears that the production of staple crops (mainly, grains and legumes) was a significant factor in the local economies as well as in settlement development.

Superficially, the third area, the Lake Van/Muş area in eastern Anatolia, is similar to the Konya and Altınova plains. However, these plains are significantly higher, being between 1,300 m and more than 1,900 m above sea level. In this region, snow blankets the ground from four to six months of the year (Rothman 2000: 431; Burney 1957), and rainfall is low, so that crops benefit from irrigation (Erinç and Tunçdilek 1952: 189). This harsh climate is reflected today in a much lower population density than, for example, in neighboring Malatya, located at some 800–900 m. Not only is the Lake Van/Muş region one of resource abundance (forest, iron, copper, lead, and obsidian), but it is also well endowed with extensive pastures. Ecologically, this region is therefore well suited to pastoralism. In the twentieth century A.D., about 80 percent of the rural economy was based upon animal husbandry and 20 percent on cultivated agriculture, although large areas are also regarded as nonagricultural land (Zimansky 1985: 15; Yakar 2000: 402).

Focused around Lake Van itself is a series of highland oases devoted to orchard crops and to irrigated and rain-fed grain fields (Erinç and Tunçdilek 1952: 189–191; Zimansky 1985: 16–17). During the major episode of sedentary settlement of the Kura-Araks period (early third millennium B.C.; Burney 1957), many settlements in the Muş area were ideally situated in relation to both pastures and transport arteries (Rothman 2000). Reliance on pasture then probably increased during the hiatus or decline in settlement that occurred during the second millennium B.C., a period that arguably relates to a resurgence of nomadic pastoral activity (for pros and cons of this case, see Edens 1995). As in highland Yemen, there is no reason to assume that upland plains continued as a long-term cultivated resource.

Unlike the Konya and Altınova plains, the Van/Muş area exhibits a mixed pattern of settlement that comprises both tells in pockets of upland plain as well as hilltop settlements on the surrounding uplands. In the first millennium B.C., the region then witnessed a dramatic change in the pattern of settlement with the appearance of numerous Urartian fortifications (some with well-developed lower towns) concentrated around the fertile highland oases (Burney 1957; Burney and Lang 1971: 5; Zimansky 1985: 16–17). To counteract the dry summers, Urartians invested in complex, monumental irrigation systems that, according to their inscriptions, transformed the landscape from what had been a "wilderness." Although the main agricultural products to benefit from the irrigation were vineyards, orchards, and grain fields (Burney 1977), Assyrian records suggest that meadows also were irrigated. This strategy of irrigating pastures could have increased the amount of feed for the large number of horses and presumably other domestic animals that were raised and that ultimately found there way into the records of tribute (Luckenbill 1927: 160; Burney 1977: 4). That animals formed a mainstay of the economy is suggested by inscriptions listing large numbers of animals destined to be sacrificed, lists of booty taken by the Assyrians, as well as the huge number of skeletons of sheep, goats, and cattle that have been recorded, such as those from the citadel of Anzaf located at 1995 m above sea level (Zimansky 1985: 15, 95; Yakar 2000: 418).

Clearly, pastoral resources played an important role in the landscape of Urartu, but precisely how the inhabitants managed such large flocks and herds during the harsh winters remains less well understood. Observations by Xenophon in the fifth century B.C. and by nineteenth-century travelers suggest that the village animals were wintered underground or in houses, where they would have been fed on forage supplied by the cultivated lands. Although shared accommodation between man and beast provides the benefit of the added winter warmth from the animals, such an arrangement may have proved inconvenient because of both the smell and the likelihood of diseases being transmitted from the animals to humans. On the other hand, the unpredictability of the onset of winter and the difficulty of passage through the narrow valleys to the south of the Van/Muş area would, according to Zimansky, have mitigated against transhumance to lowland winter pastures (Zimansky 1985: 15). Clearly, the brutal environment of eastern Anatolia constrained the agricultural economy and contributed to a landscape that differed from those at lower altitudes. This apparently influenced both land use and the form and patterning of sites through time, a point to which I will return below.

Yet more extreme environmentally are the high plains of Transcaucasia, which comprise an area of virtually treeless mountain steppe located around 2,000 m above sea level, rising to alpine summits beyond (fig. 9.9). In Armenia where the landscape is virtually bereft of tells, archaeological surveys undertaken in the Tsakahovit plain by Adam Smith and Armenian colleagues demonstrate that settlement sites tend to be restricted to the rocky hills around the basins and plains. Archaeological features include occupational sites with wall traces, faint lines of irrigation channels, circles of stones resembling animal corrals, as well as 144 discrete cemeteries (Avetisyan et al. 2000: 32). The cemeteries, which seem to exceed the number of people that could be accommodated by the contemporaneous settlements, extend up the hillsides to 2,500 m above sea level (Avetisyan et al. 2000: 43), that is, probably into the subalpine pastures.[2] Breaks in the distribution of cemeteries suggest that they may have related to some form of territorial boundaries. Sedentary settlement, which is confined to the surrounding hills, occurred mainly in the Early Bronze Age, Late Bronze/Early Iron Age, and Urartian/Achaemenid periods, with some classical occupation as well (Avetisyan et al. 2000: 32). Typically during the Late Bronze Age/Early Iron Age, settlement took the form of isolated hilltop fortress defended by walls of cyclopean masonry (Smith 1999: 48) positioned in areas remote from the main lowlands and in areas where slopes were remarkably steep. There followed during the main phase of Urartian imperial settlement a shift of individual sites from the less accessible summits towards hilltops closer to the plains, or as in the lower Ararat plain, to the south towards the main routeways. In contrast to the rather well populated hillsides, the valley floors appear to have been without artifacts, settlement sites, or landscape features, except for some (undated) possible corrals (Avetisyan et al. 1999: 32; Smith 1999: 48–55).

When examined together, these cases demonstrate that landscapes of tells predominate in lower areas such as the Altinova and Konya plains, both of which, despite summer aridity, are blessed with long growing seasons and relatively short winters. Such areas are well suited to cereal growing, and such staples probably formed a significant component of their subsistence economies. In contrast, the Tsakahovit plain in Armenia is situated near the upper limit of tree growth, where although the valley floors are cultivated today, the growing season is commensurately brief. This area of high pastures falls within the range of elevations of the higher summer pastures of vertical pastoral groups such as the Shahsevan and Bakhtiyari nomads in northern and western Iran and the Alikanli of eastern Turkey.

Finally, the Van/Muş area represents a transitional landscape between the Altinova/Konya plains and those of the Transcaucasian plateau (see below for Kestel). This landscape exhibits both tells and hilltop settlements, showing the potential as well for pastoral nomadism and sedentary cultivation.

Examination of land-use strategies through time provides insights into some of the factors that underlie these variations in landscape type. The emphasis of the Urartian economy on large animal holdings is logical, given the environmental constraints on the cultivation of crops. As is evident from the traditional strategies of the region's inhabitants, one of the most effective ways of increasing wealth and capital would have been by the accumulation of large numbers of livestock (Cribb 1991: 34). Such strategies, as have been demonstrated for highland Thailand, can lead to the growth of a large, relatively affluent stockholding elite (Hayden 2001). It is clear, however, that the long, cold, and snowy winters would have made grazing on pastures impossible and would have put a tremendous burden on the production of sufficient winter feed for the animals and on indoor stalling. To avoid such constraints, tribes could have migrated to neighboring enclaves of lower pastures in the winter (de Planhol 1966), but if that was impossible, the highland communities would have been forced to greatly increase winter feed and indoor stalling. Under normal circumstances, a transhumance strategy would have been possible because, as has been recorded by the Turkish anthropologist Ismail Beşikçi during the twentieth century A.D., highland tribes such as the Alikanlı migrated to winter pastures located to the south along and near the Tigris valley (cited in Cribb 1991: 197). To resolve the problem of overwintering and stall-feeding large hungry flocks on the highlands, a logical strategy would therefore have been for part of the community to move for the winter to the pastures along the Tigris, located around 500–700 m above sea level (fig. 9.9). During the Urartian period, large-scale movements of humans could have proved problematic, however, if such winter pastures lay within the boundaries of Assyrian provinces such as Tushan. Despite the incorporation of part of the Tigris Valley incorporated into the Neo-Assyrian empire, archaeological surveys suggest that much land immediately beyond the Tigris and between the Garzan and Bohtan Su rivers actually fell beyond the reach of Assyrian administration (Parker 1997: 236; Parker 2001; Algaze et al. 1991: 183). Because the Garzan/Bohtan area falls within the zone of winter pastures of several nomadic tribes of eastern Anatolia (Beşikçi cited in Cribb 1991: fig. 10.5), such lowlands could have provided ideal winter pastures for Urartian communities. As has been suggested by Liverani (1992), transhumance was therefore probably part of the way of life of the inhabitants of the mountains of eastern Anatolia and neighboring areas (see also Khazanov 1984 for early evidence of vertical nomadism in the region). Consequently, it is to be expected that population cycles and land-use patterns in the uplands that formed the summer pastures would be expected to undergo marked cycles between sedentary mixed farming and dominantly pastoral regimes.

Fig. 9.10   Deserted Luri campsites within deserted fields west of the Saimarrah River, near Kermanshah, Iran (view looking to west; by Eric F. Schmidt in November 1937; see Schmidt 1940: pl. 117; courtesy of the Oriental Institute of the University of Chicago). The campsites are evident as small, well-defined groups of stone-walled, subrectangular features, one of which is visible at the base of the image just left of center. A total of 11 occur within the more subtle and faint images of the terracelike relict fields. For an interpretive sketch of this photograph, see Cribb 1991: fig. 8.1.

Although little is known about the landscape of early pastoral nomadic communities (but see Hole 1978; Cribb 1991), according to recent studies of Anatolian nomads, these should leave distinctive signatures, albeit not necessarily in places that are frequently surveyed by archaeologists (fig. 9.10). Not only would seasonal movements of part of the community have been an economic necessity, but the process of transhumance would have given the kings or their families a broad knowledge of large areas of landscape. Such mental maps could have aided them at times of an external threat such as when the Assyrian army approached. Consequently, rather than fleeing into the unknown at the approach of the Assyrian armies (as the Neo-Assyrian texts imply), the flight of the Urartians may simply have represented a tactical withdrawal through areas that were well known because they fell well within their patterns of transhumance (Liverani 1992: 149). Thus, whereas the Assyrians were rooted to the plains or to campaign routes that led them through hostile territories, for the Urartians even remote valleys within the highland landscapes were part of their cognitive sphere. Consequently, the mountain landscapes would have been perceived very differently by the Urartians and the Assyrians.

Site Locations: Economy versus Power

The topographic diversity of the Anatolian and Armenian highlands results in substantial differences in potential agricultural productivity. Around Lake Van a wide range of orchard and grain crops can be grown, whereas at higher elevations to the east and in Transcaucasia, much of the land was probably best devoted to pasture. In some areas, even apparently "cultivable" valley floors would have provided pasture rather than being given over to cultivation. This dichotomy between cultivable land and potential pasture is exemplified by the fertile and eminently cultivable Amuq plain in southern Turkey. During the eighteenth and nineteenth centuries A.D., it provided ideal pasturelands for nomadic groups, especially during periods when the area was deserted of sedentary settlement and when the central government was weak (Aswad 1971: 10, 18). In most other periods, however, the plain formed a major cultivated lowland. This example shows that as was the case in Yemen, land with high cultivation potential may not necessarily have been cultivated.

Similarly, in eastern Anatolia and Transcaucasia, the tradition of valley-floor pasturelands could have extended through long periods of time. One should not therefore assume that landscapes underwent a complete and "logical" reorganization during each phase of settlement. Instead, key land-use zones such as pasture may have been retained in use even while settlement patterns changed around them. For example, in Middle Bronze Age Transcaucasia, valley floors could have been used by mobile transhumant pastoralists, as has been suggested by Burney and Lang 1971 (but see Edens 1995 for a more cautious view). Then, during the Late Bronze Age and Iron Age, they could have reverted either to the exclusive use of local sedentary communities or to a combination of local sedentary occupation integrated with periodic seasonal visits by mobile groups from outside.

In contrast to Transcaucasia, the Altinova and Konya plains, although situated within the orbit of present day transhumant groups, are landscapes dominated primarily by tells or smaller mounded sites located within largely cultivable terrain. Such locations imply that proximity to one's fields was of greater significance than considerations of security, a situation that parallels that of the Syrian/Iraqi Jazira discussed in chapter 6, where tells were rendered defensible by fortification walls. Episodes of nomadism may have interrupted phases of sedentism, but

it appears that cultivation and storage of staple products were more significant factors in site location than pastoralism.

In those areas where settlement was predominantly upon hill summits, it seems that other circumstances were of importance to the inhabitants. First, hilltop settlements are not confined only to eastern Turkey and the Caucuses; surveys in other parts of Turkey demonstrate that settlement also occurred elsewhere on hilltops, at least during certain periods (Haspels 1971; von der Osten 1929). In eastern Turkey and Transcaucasia, the possession of large flocks that could be pastured either on the subalpine steppe or on the valley floors would not have required a valley-floor location for settlement. Therefore, the lifting of this constraint would have freed settlement so that considerations (such as defense or political oversight of low-lying lands, pastures, fields, irrigation systems, and settlements) would have been of greater importance than proximity to one's cereal fields. The specific selection of hilltop settlements is evident in traditional Yemeni settlements, where it is common (although by no means exclusively so) for houses of high-status individuals, fortified administrative areas, and other loci of power to be located on hilltops over looking places of lesser status. In such positions, the interests of status, power, and defensibility frequently coincide.

Parallel trends in settlement can be observed in the Anatolian/Transcaucasian and Yemeni highlands during phases of increased social complexity and the rise of regional polities. In highland Yemen there appears to have been a tension between the prestige, defensibility, latent power, and symbolism of hilltop sites on the one hand and the advantages of a pragmatic location at lower elevations that provide greater access to fields and routes on the other. The Yemen highlands show more evidence for political integra-

tion with the desert-fringe polities of the incense trading cities during the first millennium B.C. Consequently, in many locations, Bronze Age strongholds on more isolated hills were progressively replaced by settlements at lower elevations located in convenient proximity to cultivable lands or route ways. As a result, by the Iron Age and Himyarite periods, although hilltop fortresses continued to be occupied in select localities, many larger settlements had moved to locations closer to fields, irrigation systems, and route systems.

An equivalent shift occurred in the Ararat plain during the imperial Urartian period, when sites were relocated towards (but not on) the plain, which as noted by Smith, provided greater political oversight of the valley-floor resources (1999: 55). The sheer variety of settlement patterns that can be observed in the highland areas discussed above indicates (as the above simplifications do not) that settlement and landscape can be remarkably fluid. Although framed to a certain degree by ecological constraints, such settlement and landscapes are highly contingent upon antecedent conditions (such as traditions of retention of pastoral rights), political circumstances, longterm social practice, and investments in the form of technologies such as irrigation. As a result of such changing circumstances, land-use strategies would have varied through time, but the emphasis can be expected to have shifted from pastoralism to rain-fed cultivation, to irrigation, and perhaps back to pastoralism through time.

It is also evident that especially in the higher altitude areas of Armenia and eastern Turkey, the landscape does not represent an imprint that reflects a long-term adaptation to any given environmental regime. Rather, land-use practices, although partly conditioned by the ecological requirements of high altitudes, are equally (more or less) contingent upon the political economy of highland society as well as practices that have been inherited from earlier generations or populations.

Not only did ecological conditions impose a constraint on the societies of the eastern Anatolian highlands and Armenia; conversely, those societies appeared to have had some impact on the ecology. Thus, the pollen sequence from Söğütlü, at the west end of Lake Van, shows a dramatic decrease in oak woodland, specifically that of Quercus cerris type, during the first millennium B.C. (Bottema 1995: fig. 3). This oak decline is paralleled by faunal evidence from Horum in Armenia that shows a significant diminution of antlers of red deer between the Early Iron Age and Urartian time (Smith 1996: 96). These species, which are associated with a woodland or woodland steppe, suggest that what is virtually a treeless area today must have been well wooded in the early Iron Age but rather less endowed with woodland during Urartian times (Badaljan et al. 1994: 18–22). Such decreases in woodland through time may be blamed on increased demand for fuel and cultivable land by the expanding Urartian and later states, as well as perhaps in increased bronze and iron production.

Alternatively, because the Iron Age is also a period of relatively dry conditions in eastern Anatolia (Lemcke and Sturm 1997), this woodland decline may, in part, result from climatic drying. Certainly, the two factors acting together (climatic drying and the expansion of the dynamic mountain state of Urartu) could be expected to have exerted a significant impact on the amount of local forest. In addition, the presence of significant amounts of poplar and willow from probably around 2950 B.P. (equivalent to approximately to the Late Bronze/Early Iron Age; Bottema 1995) suggests that it was at this time that the foundations of the irrigated landscape were laid rather than during the Urartian period, as the inscriptions would have us believe.

Irrigation technologies are in fact particularly well developed on the plateaus around Lake Van, where the fringing highlands provide water-gathering areas in the form of masonry canals and reservoirs for extensive canal systems. Commemorative inscriptions emphasize the role of Menua the king (ca. 810–786 B.C.) in subduing the wilderness and constructing canals for the benefit of the populace (Belli 1994, 1999). For example, the 51 km Menua canal, which followed a circuitous course to irrigate the southern part of the Van plain, was endowed with some fifteen cuneiform building inscriptions along its route. In addition to recording that the canal was indeed the canal of Menua, the inscriptions threatened that the gods would punish anyone who might damage it (Belli 1999: 16, based on König 1955–1957). Also noteworthy is the complexity of some Urartian irrigation systems that provided integrated systems of water management. In the case of the canals that directed water towards the Van plain from Lake Rusa, water was transported from one watershed to another, presumably to direct water to locations where it was most needed and to offset shortfalls in the pattern of distribution (Belli 1999: fig. 6).

Probably the most eloquent description of the role of irrigation in the landscape of eastern Anatolia can be found in this statement from Sargon II:

The city of Ulhu, a stronghold at the foot of Mount Kishpal . . . . Ursâ, their king and counselor, following [his heart's] desire . . . . showed [them] where the waters gushed forth. A ditch, carrying these flowing waters, he dug and . . . . brought plenty, like the Euphrates. He made numberless channels lead off from its bed . . . . . . and irrigated the orchard. Its waste land, which from days of old . . . . and made fruit and grapes as abundant as the rain. Plane trees, exceedingly high (?), of the riches of his palace

. . . . . like a forest, he made them cast their shadows over its plain, and in his uncultivated fields. . . . like god, he made its people raise their glad songs. 300 homers of seed land, planted (?) in grain, he in [by] . . . the crop gave increased return of grain at the gathering. The ground of his uncultivated areas he made like a meadow, flooding it abundantly in springtime, [and] grass and pasturage did not fail [cease], winter and summer; into stamping grounds [corrals] for horses and herds he turned it. The camels in (?) all of his submerged country he trained (?) and they pumped [lit., poured] [the water into] ditches. (D. D. Luckenbill 1927 [1968]: 86–87)

Although inscriptions such as one from Argishti I state explicitly that prior to the construction of such canals the area was a wilderness (Melikishvili inscription no. 137, cited in Smith 1999: 46), in the Ararat plain, less-monumental irrigation canals are associated with Early Iron Age fortresses. This implies that earlier communities were also engaged in canal building, a point that is supported by the pollen analysis from Söğütlü, which suggests that a landscape with irrigated waterways had developed by the Late Bronze/Iron Age. The presence of possibly earlier Transcaucasian irrigation systems implies that Urartian irrigation technology was not developed in a vacuum but instead built upon an earlier stage of technology.

Intrusive Landscapes of Extraction in the Highlands

Industrial and mining landscapes provide a stark contrast with the landscapes that surround them, but their presence underscores just how human endeavors can create a life-support system under the least promising of circumstances. Because minerals and metal-bearing rocks frequently crop out in inaccessible mountains, the extraction of such minerals results in the development of distinctive mining landscapes (Knapp 1999). Moreover, the need to provision miners and ancillary workers with food, fuel, mining supplies, and so on frequently resulted in the development of self-contained land-use modules in the vicinity of mines where, however, both cultivable soil and water resources may have been limited. Nevertheless, the application of appropriate agricultural technologies (which are often not far removed from those applied to mining) can render even the most unlikely setting into a verdant garden. Given the marginal nature of such environments, following the withdrawal of mining, one would then expect their agricultural and industrial areas would be abandoned, to remain as small windows of landscapes of survival.

Because of their high demand for fuel and other resources, mines exert considerable stress on a mountain environment: wood is required for fire-setting within the mines, as well as for pit props and for the manufacture of large quantities of charcoal for smelting; clay is needed for the manufacture of crucibles and furnaces; mineral fluxes aid in the smelting process itself; fibers are used for ropes for evacuating the ore; and food is obviously essential for the miners as well as fodder for the draft animals. The procurement of these commodities places a considerable burden on the infrastructure of what would otherwise be an isolated region. Thus, what may have once been an austere or serene mountain environment could, within a few years, become a denuded, polluted, slag-heap infested, industrial landscape, pockmarked with mine workings. Unfortunately, because archaeological investigations often concentrate on archaeometallurgical issues, the landscape itself is often neglected. Nevertheless, it is clear from environmental studies near the mines of the Wadi Feynan in Jordan that industrial pollution from the nearby mines must have

been considerable during the Roman period (Barker et al. 1999: 262–269). Furthermore, the presence of certain minerals in the soil or patterns of waste dumping (such as mine tailings and slag heaps) can result in distinctive botanical patterns and geochemical traces (Brooks and Johannes 1990).

Mining Landscapes of the Taurus Mountains

The impact of ancient mining can be gauged from the Bolkardağ mining district in the Turkish Taurus mountains, where more than eight hundred mine remains have been reported (Yener and Özbal 1987). These occur between 1,950 and 3,000 m above sea level in an area that is today well wooded with coniferous trees up to altitudes of around 2,000 m. Most sites are unmounded, in part because the component buildings were probably of wood, and most were sited on hill slopes and summits. Other features of this mining landscape include both natural and artificial caves and tunnels, the latter penetrating to as much as 4 km into the mountains (Yener 2000: 77), as well as fields of mine slag and "tailings" of mine waste. Because this region is well endowed with lead, zinc, silver, gold, iron, and tin, it must have been constantly in demand for ores because as one source was used up, or an alternative source came into use, other ores would be discovered or be in demand. Traditionally there was a tendency to locate smelters close to the forests because of the demand for enormous quantities of wood or charcoal to smelt the ore. Consequently, as soon as fuel resources were depleted, smelting installations would be shifted to where wood was available (Yener 2000: 78). In this way, deforestation occurred as a moving patchwork, and smelting extended over larger spatial areas than a single location might dictate.

Within the Taurus mineralization zone the best evidence for

a mining landscape comes from Kestel/Göltepe, an Early Bronze Age tin mine located on the northern edge of the main range of the Taurus mountains at around 1,800 m above sea level (figs. 9.1, 9.11). Here the mining site of Kestel and neighboring tin processing village (Göltepe) are situated near the edge of the Niğde massif in narrow but fertile valleys, where it is possible to grow legumes, fruit, and wheat (Yener 2000: 83). Despite the high elevation and thin soils, relict field systems are evident in the form of small embanked, enclosed parcels, sometimes with low terrace scarps. In one case to the southwest of the Kestel mine, an entire slope was covered in a patchwork of low terraced fields bounded on one side by a relict linear stone alignment, possibly a boundary wall. On the stony hill summit at some 2,000 m above sea level were relict stone-clearance mounds, 2 to 5 m in diameter and often as little as 3 to 4 m apart (figs. 4.5, 9.11). Relict fields are a relatively common feature in the area (fig. 9.11). In addition to patchworks of long-abandoned fields and clearance mounds, they also include terraced fields that are still in use. Soils accumulated upslope of the terrace walls exhibited sparse field scatters of battered pottery. Although none of the fields can be dated directly, many may have been in use at the time of the Early Bronze Age mining, this being arguably the period of greatest settlement and demand for food crops. Analysis of carbonized grains plant remains by palaeobotanist Mark Nesbitt demonstrated the presence of the typical Bronze Age crop husbandry of the Anatolian plateau, namely, two-row hulled barley, bread wheat, lentil, and grape. If these were locally grown, their presence implies that despite the altitude, farming was not so close to the climatic margin of cultivation that it was necessary to grow an especially narrow economic range of crops.

It is clear from the relict fields that farming was pursued within the

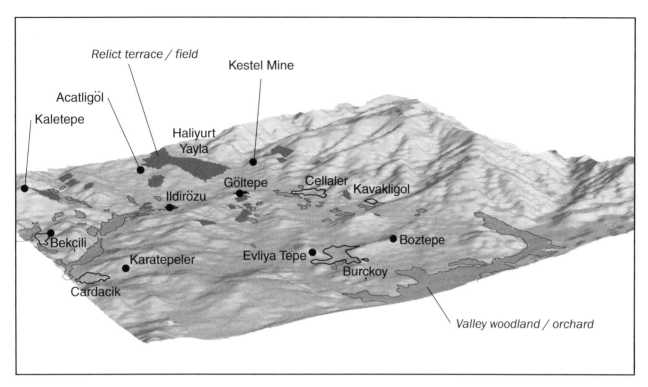

Fig. 9.11 Three-dimensional image showing relict fields just below the bare upland steppe near the Early Bronze Age mine of Kestel and the mining settlement of Göltepe (Turkey). Relict fields: dark shading; present-day valley-floor woodland: light shading; modern villages: in outline. Note that the highest fields extend to ca. 2,000 m above sea level (based on Yener 2000: pl. 3).

main area of lowlands around the habitation and mineral processing site of Göltepe and that cultivation spread up hillsides within the massif itself to elevations approaching 1,900 m above sea level. Computer simulation of growth and regeneration cycles of woodland in the area suggest that the combined effect of mining and domestic fuel demands could have had a significant effect on the local landscape (Chadderton cited in Redman 1999: 181–182). To what degree the uplands above the mine of Kestel were wooded during the third or fourth millennium B.C. remains unclear, however, because vegetation reconstructions simply suggest that this was naturally a partly wooded steppe forest that was subsequently replaced by a secondary xeromorphic dwarf shrub (TAVO map A VI 4). Moreover, the practice of coppicing of trees[3] may have been practiced to conserve woodland. This practice would have resulted in selected areas of woodlands being

managed rather than entire areas being totally deforested. Despite the high demand for wood, the abundance of charcoal in archaeological deposits and the virtual absence of carbonized dung (or carbonized seeds therefrom) suggest that there was still sufficient woodland in the area so that there was no need to burn large quantities of dung. This and the possibility that coppicing may have been practiced suggest that there may not have been too much stress on local supplies of fuel.

Therefore, despite the environmentally marginal location of Kestel/Göltepe and the high demand for fuel, the landscape may have included more cultivable land than exists in the region today. Although demand for fuel would have been high, there was apparently sufficient woodland in the area, perhaps because woodland was managed by means of coppicing, to provide a sustainable supply for both mining and domestic requirements. Loss of

woodland from the hills was sufficient to register in the landscape as charcoal-clearance horizons and associated colluviation, but these are no more in evidence than in nonmining areas. Although the database is sparse, there is nothing to suggest that mining had exerted a massive stress on the local environment, as is implied in parts of Jordan (chapter 7). This is contrary to what one might expect from an intensive extractive industry established in a marginal environment. This enigma may be explained by the nature of the pattern of residence and the labor regime, both of which may have been seasonal. As has been suggested by Yener, the present-day inhabitants of the area were originally Yörük nomads who wintered in the lowlands of Cilicia and neighboring areas and then traveled through the Taurus passes up to their summer pastures in the Niğde massif at 1,600–2,000 m above sea level (Yener 2000: 84). If a similar pattern of human movement prevailed in Early Bronze Age times, this would have reduced the winter population in the mines, and winter fuel demands would have lessened the impact of local populations on resources. As in Urartu, there is no reason to assume that there was either a fixed year-round population in the highlands or a total seasonal migration to the lowlands. Rather, a minority of the population could have remained to perform key tasks, whereas a majority could have departed for more hospitable climates in the lowlands.

Mining Landscapes in Oman

As an alternative to adapting to the local ecological circumstances (as may have been practiced in the Taurus mountains), mining communities can override local shortfalls in agricultural potential by introducing appropriate technology. This approach is evident in the mining landscapes of the Hajar mountains of northern Oman, where extensive copper resources, usually in the form of sulphide ores, occur sporadically throughout the sullen mass of the dark ultrabasic ophialitic rocks that form the backbone of northern Oman (Ibrahim and al-Mahi 2000). That the ancient copper workings in Oman are truly landscape features is evident from both the circumstances of their discovery and the role they played in the recycling of earlier mining features. The mine workings and smelters were initially discovered by modern mining engineers, not archaeologists. In their search for workable ore fields, the engineers scrutinized air photographs that showed the presence of early mines (located near ore bodies) in the form of extensive concentrations of black copper slag, which were sometimes adjacent to reddened oxidized "iron hats" or gossans that form at the ore body itself (Goettler et al. 1976). On investigation, the smelting areas were evidently ancient, but despite earlier suggestions that Oman might have

been the land of Magan known from Akkadian sources as a supplier of copper to Sumer and Akkad (for review see Weisgerber 1983), most of the mines and smelting areas proved to be Early Islamic in date. Although third millennium B.C. mining sites have been recognized since the mid 1970s (Hastings et al. 1975), the general lack of evidence for pre-Islamic mines can be explained by reference to landscape taphonomy. In other words, Early Islamic mining and smelting operations were so extensive and destructive that earlier installations appear to have been either erased or obscured by those of later date, unless they had survived by chance. Despite the destruction of Islamic mining, a number of early mining areas have been recognized, and the following example illustrates how by the employment of water-extraction technologies that resulted in a shift in the locus of smelting, it was possible for some earlier mining landscapes to have escaped destruction.

The mines of Arja/Baydha within the foothills of the Hajar mountains were situated immediately north of a major route that linked the interior oasis of Buraymi with the coastal port of Sohar (fig. 9.12). This provided an optimum location for the availability of fuel (in the form of a savanna of acacia trees), copper, water, and flux, as well as being conveniently positioned in relation to transport routes through the mountains (Weisgerber 1987). Settlement and early smelting initially developed at Zahra 1 in the broad open Wadi Bani Umar al-Gharbi during the second half of the third millennium B.C. Following a gap during the second millennium B.C., settlement then resumed during the early first millennium B.C. at Zahra 2 (fig. 9.12; Costa and Wilkinson 1987: 95–105). During the early phases of settlement at Zahra, agriculture relied on a combination of wells and water-diversion dams. These small-scale schemes were capable of extracting or diverting the relatively small

amounts of water that were required to sustain the modest-sized Bronze and Iron Age populations. Landscape transformations at Bronze Age Zahra were minor and were similar in scale to the flood-irrigation systems that supplied the Bronze Age mining settlement of Maysar in the Wadi Samad of eastern Oman. The fields at Maysar were surrounded by low boundary mounds and were associated with water-gathering systems that resembled the traditional garbarband systems of Iran and Pakistan (Weisgerber 1983: 274). These Maysar systems probably represent the oldest well-developed fields in southeast Arabia.

At Arja, Iron Age smelting and ore processing took place between the two ore bodies southeast of the wadis, whereas the miners and their families lived in the small village of Zahra 2 on the Wadi Bani Umar adjacent to the Bronze Age smelting settlement (fig. 9.12; Costa and Wilkinson 1987). During the Sasanian/Early Islamic period (between the fifth and tenth centuries A.D.), the system was totally re-oriented and, a new water-supply system, 7 km long, was constructed to conduct water from the wadi directly to the area of the mines. This took the form of a small, deep, open channel of waterproof plaster (saruj), ca. 35 cm wide × 30 cm, which collected water from permanent pools in the wadi bed and cut through the watershed into a neighboring wadi catchment to transport water to a point midway between the two mines. En route the channel powered a water mill and irrigated fields. For the latter, water filled a broad, shallow cistern, which retained water until there was sufficient to irrigate a single field. Fields were surrounded by low stone walls, provision being made for the passage of flocks across the valley and between the fields (fig. 4.4). Within the field boundaries, the exposed soils were scattered with Early Islamic sherds, probably resulting from the spreading of ash and compost as fertilizer

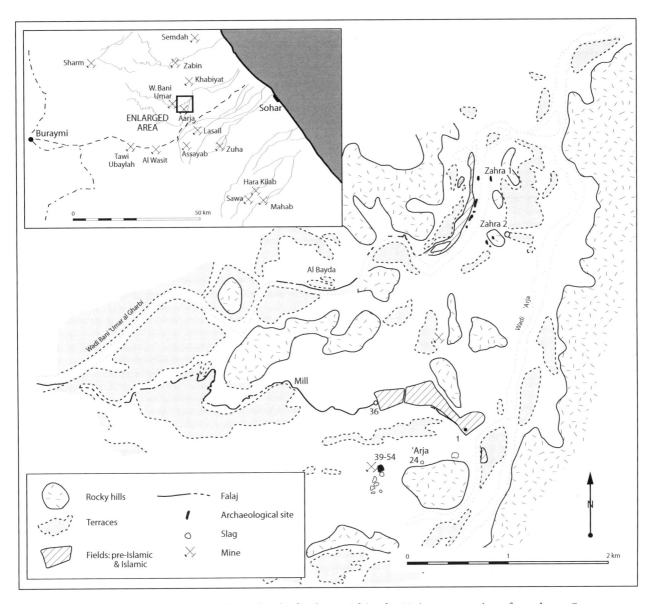

Fig. 9.12   Inset: Mining sites in the hinterland of Sohar, within the Hajar mountains of northern Oman (from Weisgerber 1987: fig. 64). Below: mining landscapes at Arja. The main reorientation of the landscape was from the Wadi Bani Umar al-Gharbi in the Bronze and Iron Ages (Zahra 1 and 2), to a location to the southeast near Arja and away from the Wadi (in the vicinity of the mine at Arja) during the Early Islamic period (from Costa and Wilkinson 1987: fig. 33).

(Costa and Wilkinson 1987: 118–119). On one or two of the surrounding hills were situated the foundations of threshing floors and praying areas (*masallahs*).

The mining landscape consisted of mine shafts and patchy scatters of black copper slag strewn over the surface, particularly around the main ore-bearing area at Arja. Each slag field was associated with a single production unit comprising a roast-

ing pit (for burning off sulphur prior to smelting), a smelting furnace, and a small hut (Weisgerber 1987: 158). Living areas comprised two distinct settlements: to the south, a "mining camp" of buildings surrounding an enclosed area with a small mosque, and to the north, a courtyard building atop a small gabbro hill within the relict gardens that appears to have functioned as the dwelling of a member of the local

elite (perhaps a sheikh). Between the two settlement areas an Early Islamic cemetery (24) was sited on an Iron Age ore-preparation area. The entire agricultural/mining enclave was overseen by a single hilltop fort. Population estimates from the mining settlement itself suggests that some 90–140 people represented the long-term resident population of the site, a figure that conforms roughly with an estimated 102 to 157 people that could be supported by the products of the fields. Nevertheless, temporary or short-term populations could have been larger and been accommodated in outlying buildings or even outside, given the mild winters and hot summers.

By the Early Islamic period at Arja, the use of sophisticated engineering techniques enabled a new industrial landscape to be created close to the source of ore itself. Whether it was of any real advantage for the mining engineers, families, or workers to live immediately adjacent to a smoky, noisy, and ugly extraction and smelting area is difficult to say, but by diverting the water to valleys by the mine, a larger area of cultivable land was exploited at a convenient distance from the main place of work. As with other major water systems in the Sohar region, this canal, 7 km in length, with its water mill and other installations, represents an investment, perhaps by one of the shareholders located in the city of Sohar who then benefited in the form of rents received (J. C. Wilkinson 1979: 892). Furthermore, the sophisticated engineering of the water channel and the orderly layout of the mining settlement hint at, but do not prove, that the entire project may have been planned and engineered as a single contained mining camp.

Whereas the Arja area provides a good example of a complex mining landscape, other Early Islamic mines in the region show less well preserved landscapes. At nearby Lasail, ore extraction and processing occurred within a more restricted valley area, and so houses became inextricably mixed with the slag fields, and agricultural areas were apparently forced to develop a few kilometers away from the mine in the Wadi Jizzi. Particularly striking was that the scale of extraction (some 100,000 tons of slag have been estimated within this single complex) resulted in large sections of the hill being dug away. This apparently initiated the collapse of the

surrounding rock to form a large waste-filled basin. Similar collapsed depressions, which have been noted at other sites such as Semdah to the north of Arja, provide a distinct and unnervingly modern aspect to these Islamic mining landscapes.

Certainly, the enormous scale of the Early Islamic mining must have placed a considerable stress on the wood resources of what is naturally an acacia savanna with very sparsely vegetated hill slopes and wadi terraces. Weisgerber has estimated that the total amount of slag generated by the Omani mines in the Early Islamic period amounted to some 200,000–240,000 tons. This, in turn, required some 280,000 tons of charcoal, which required around 1,400,000 tons of wood (Weisgerber 1980: 119). If estimates of household fuel consumption are factored in as well and it is assumed that there was around 100 kg of wood per tree, such consumption would have required that some 20 million trees be cut down. In such an arid area as northern Oman (mean annual rainfall varying around 100 mm), these demands on woodland would have resulted in a massive loss of wood cover, unless special efforts were made to manage tree cutting by means such as coppicing. It is therefore quite possible that the amount of mineral extraction was limited by the availability of wood, much more so than in the Taurus mines discussed above.

Mountains and Sanctity

In addition to their role in providing sustenance or mineral wealth for the inhabitants, mountains play a vital role in many religions. For example, as Sir William Ramsay has observed for Hittite Anatolia, uncultivated mountain lands are thought to have been regarded as God's land (hence the name Allah Dagh = Mountain of God). As such, they both provided a focus for religious activity and formed boundaries between polities. As a result of this sanctity,

mountains and high places in general can be seen to form their own sacred landscapes (Bradley 2000). The role of high places is particularly evident in the location of eastern Roman temples, which are frequently situated on natural eminences, and even if they lack temples themselves, these sacred high points were often made accessible by rock-cut ways leading up to them (Ball 2000: 346–348). As Ball points out, the sacred high places of Syria have predecessors extending back into early Syrian and Arabian religious ritual, and similar arguments for early religious places can be made for the hilltops of Hittite Anatolia and Zoroastrian Iran.

Evidence for a long history of religious continuity is apparent in cases where the Hellenistic, Roman, or Byzantine religious monuments are simply a formalization of earlier sanctified high places. For example, the majestic Mount Kasios (Jebel al-Akra), located some 65 km southwest of Antioch (Antakya in Turkey), towers some 1,728 m above the adjacent Mediterranean Sea. Mount Kasios is primarily known for its Roman/Byzantine religious monuments, but cult practice on this mountain can be traced back to the Hittite period, at which time it was dedicated to the local deity of Baal Shamin (Djobadze 1986:4). Although virtually denuded of vegetation today, this eminence was thickly wooded (except for the top 25 percent) until the nineteenth century A.D., which implies that worshipers must have made their way through woodland and mountain forest rather than through the open vegetation evident today.

The role of mountains and other ritually "pure" high places is made evident from the Hittite cult inventories of the thirteenth century B.C. These inventories, which collected information about shrines and their condition in the Hittite lands, provide numerous insights into ritual practice and indirectly their landscape context. Hence a priest would carry presumably a statue of the mountain god Halwanna up to the mountain and place the god on a special stone under a tree. Offerings of meat, beer, and bread would then be made, and at sunset, the god would be returned to the temple in the settled lands (Gurney 1977: 28).

That related rituals also took place in Phrygia (between the eighth and fourth centuries B.C.) is evident from a wide range of natural rock places in the Anatolian highlands. For example, to the east of Ankara, the artificially flattened peak of Kara Hissar near Alaca Höyük with its Phrygian rock-cut altars on a "bare isolated, double peaked rock" provides a distinctive mountain sanctuary (von der Osten 1929: 98–99). Related features are the cult façades of the Phrygian highlands west of Ankara, into which were cut niches for the placement of statues of the mother (or mountain) goddess Kybele. This concentration of sanctuaries cut from the local volcanic tuffs is partly conditioned by the nature of the terrain. It provides a record in concrete form of cult practice, which complements the local fortified hilltop (kale-type) settlements on the surrounding hills (Haspels 1971). The spiritual role of high places and ridges is particularly well exemplified in the region of Alishar Höyük in the Anatolian heartland, originally surveyed by von der Osten (1929). Here, Scott Branting has illustrated how tumuli of the Bronze and Iron Ages concentrate on visible ridgelines and highlands overlooking adjacent valleys (Branting 1996). In contrast, the valleys are occupied by strings of Chalcolithic and Bronze Age höyüks and presumably their adjacent fields, which provide a conspicuous example of landscapes of the living.

Among the large number of holy mountains in Syria/Anatolia are Nemrud Daği (Turkish Euphrates), Mount Casios (southern Turkey), Mount Sinai (Jebel Musa), Mount Hermon/Jebel esh-Sheikh (Israel, Syria, Lebanon), and Jebel Sheikh Barakat (Syria). In some of these, the landscape is by no means dominated by cult practice. Witness the mix of domestic, cult, and mining (for cosmetic kohl) around Mount Hermon (Dar 1993), but elsewhere, such as at Nemrud Daği and Mount Sinai, religious practice dominates the landscape.

At the peak of the monastic movement, Mount Sinai probably housed less than one thousand monks. Nevertheless, this arid landscape of granitic valleys and mountain peaks (rainfall in the range 65–80 mm; maximum elevation 2,273 m above sea level) provided a distinct and locally verdant habitat. Elements of the landscape included monastic settlements of various sizes, the cells of individual hermits, prayer niches, small agricultural plots used for orchards and vegetables, pathways sometimes paved or built-up, lime kilns, and wine presses (Dahari 2000). For those who prefer their ideational landscapes in a quantified form, each monk is calculated to have lived in an area of 4–5 sq. m, had access to 4.4 sq. km of land, but only had some 323 sq. m of cultivated plots, which according to Dahari (2000: 152), was, however, sufficient to live on.

Movement through this sanctified terrain seems to have been highly structured, so that the visitor would arrive out of the desert into an oasis with a monastery. Within the monastery was a church, within the east end of which was a relic of a burning bush, which constituted the lowest, innermost part of the monastery. Pilgrims would then ascend the mountain to a summit church, after which they would then descend to a cave where Moses is thought to have received tablets and experienced a vision of God (Coleman and Elsner 1994). Prayer niches formed an important element of this highly sanctified landscape by providing places to pray, sometimes in locations from which pilgrims might glimpse the peak of the holy mountain itself (Coleman and Els- ner 1994). Pilgrims would therefore experience this sanctified area not so much as an intellectual process but through their physical action (Coleman and Elsner 1994: 84).

Similarly, Nemrud Daği required of the visitor certain physical action, by requiring them to experience the arduous climb and often bitter cold of this 2,150 m high peak, which dominates the kingdom of Commagene along the Turkish Euphrates. Although some neighboring mountains are higher, Nemrud Daği is the only peak that is clearly visible from all directions, with prominent views across spectacular scenic vistas (Goell, in Sanders 1996: 2). Excavated by Theresa Goell between 1953 and 1973, this peak formed the place of gods as well as the final resting place of Antiochus I of Commagene (69–34 B.C.). The Hittite architectural parallels suggest that Nemrud Daği may have already been a sacred high place in the second millennium B.C., but the removal of some three hundred thousand tons of rock to erect the tumulus may have easily (and perhaps deliberately) expunged any earlier cultic activity (Sanders 1996: 8). The tomb sanctuary consisted of guardian animals and statuary raised on terraces around the rubble tumulus. It formed the focal point of the landscape, and processional ways led to it from all directions. These included deliberately cut (or worn) processional ways that led past stelae to the northeast and southwest, as well as to springs and settlements in the surrounding lowlands. Therefore, not only did Antiochus, in death, continue metaphorically to command his territory, but also the web of formal and informal ways provided a continuing link between the sanctified tomb sanctuary and the surrounding landscape.

It should not be assumed that all sacred high places occupy physically striking and visible locations. The sanctuary of Zeus Baetocaece, located in the mountains of northwest Syria, remains nestled in an elevated basin, the only landmark hinting at its presence being a neighboring peak that looms above it (Steinsapir 1998: 20). Although not forming a prominent peak, the sanctuary incorporated both a spring and a sacred rock. As with Nemrud Daği, processional routes from lowland population centers to the cultic buildings played an important role linking the religious center with the fertile agricultural lands that form its hinterland.

This bald summary of what is a large and undercontextualized field of research hints at the important role that sacred high places played in the landscape. As with the economic landscapes that formed the earlier part of this chapter, religious landscapes show evidence for landscape transformation that have sometimes expunged earlier phases of use. Whereas in some cases these sacred landscapes stand apart from the economic landscape because there is no requirement for agricultural systems of sustenance (as is the case for Nemrud Daği), in other cases (such as the Phrygian highlands and Mount Sinai), the cultic landscape continues to be part of a living patchwork of agricultural supply and cult practice. Consequently, as with many centers of pilgrimage, the sanctuary of Zeus Baetocaece played an economic role in the community. In addition to being physically linked with the lowlands, such sanctuaries can be seen as having intertwined economic relationships with them as well. It would therefore be misleading to draw an arbitrary boundary between religious and economic landscapes.

Conclusions

Despite the overlap with landscapes of irrigation and those dominated by tells, mountains can be seen to exhibit their own distinctive archaeological signatures. The configuration of ecological zones appears to result in landscapes that are more suitable for pastoral activities with increased altitude. In addition, at higher elevations, hilltop settlements become more common, and pastoral strategies are more likely to be incorporated into patterns of long-distance transhumance. Hilltop locations often become the choice of settlements during certain phases in parts of Anatolia and southwest Arabia, specifically during times of conflict and raiding. Similar patterns have also been observed both in the New World at Oaxaca (Reynolds 1999) and in Italy (Potter 1976), especially during phases of increased local conflict. As the settlement record from areas like the Muş plain clearly demonstrates, there is no long-term adaptation towards any given settlement-landscape signature. Rather, there is frequently a switch from one pattern to another, depending upon the combined effects of environmental constraints (or opportunities) and the contingencies of political, social, and economic circumstances. Traditionally, processual models have often assumed that patterns of land use change in concert with changes in settlement. Although this may partly be true, some components of the landscape, such as large pastoral reserves, must have continued to be used through long periods of time, even though the settlements and other communities that relied upon them may have changed.

A common feature of the highland landscapes of both Anatolia and Yemen are the irrigation systems that appear to be supplementary to the existing agricultural economy. For example, the desert-fringe oasis at Marib discussed in the previous chapter contrasts with agricultural systems of highland Yemen, where irrigation systems not only were of a much smaller scale but were evidently incapable of supporting the populations of the modest-sized Himyarite capitals. The well-watered highlands had complex agricultural economies that appear to have been reliant on family-managed terraced cultivation and only in part on a system of large-scale irrigated cultivation. Consequently, the highland systems, with their dual economy, were much more adapted to cope with environmental stress than were the lowland systems. In the desert-fringe oases, one major flood could sweep the entire support system away; in the highlands, even though dam bursts did occur, it was possible for agriculture to continue, using both rain-fed terraced agriculture and an adapted form of low-investment sayl agriculture. Such tactics ensured the continuity of the resilient and sustainable highland systems of settlement long after the decline of the "brittle" flood-irrigation systems of the lowlands.

Terraced agriculture is a common feature of mountain landscapes, but it is not necessarily a product of population pressure. Although the construction of terraced fields is a natural response to the restricted availability of space within narrow mountain valleys, in parts of highland Yemen many early terraces developed at a time when there was abundant cultivable land to be had. Not only is it more convenient to have fields on the hill slope below one's house than a kilometer away on the plain, customary rights to verdant long-term grazing land on the valley floor would probably take priority over the replacement of such land with cultivated fields. Through time, the circumstances that influence such trade-offs must change, but because traditional rights would dictate the pace of change, such practices would appear to exert a cultural glue that would deflect the development of landscapes from purely economic trajectories.

Terracing also played a major role in the development of the physical landscape because of its contribution to landscape stability. Nowhere is this more evident than in the landscapes of highland Yemen, where high rural population densities and terraced agriculture coexist to produce a landscape that exhibits remarkable physical stability. This calls into question one of the enduring myths of highland landscapes, namely, that with increasing population, landscapes must become more degraded so that greater erosion necessarily results.[4] Nevertheless, if demographic circumstances changed, then the situation could dramatically switch: for example, if the population declined, the result could be less labor available for the maintenance of terraces. Once the terraces collapsed, the entire landscape could become rapidly mobilized, with terraces being eroded by gullies, to produce deep valley fills (Butzer 1982: 130–133; Varisco 1991). Landscape stability is therefore contingent on a number of social factors that are sometime invisible to the archaeologist but are deeply embedded in the social matrix of the region.

Although, in theory, mining landscapes should result in the appearance of landscapes of preservation within otherwise marginal areas, as the examples show, this is not always the case. In the Taurus mining area the preliminary archaeological record hardly indicates a stressed economy at the environmental margin. The case of copper-mining sites in Oman is rather more extreme, and here we do get a clear signature of a true industrial wasteland, complete with collapsed landscapes and pollution. Although such landscapes must have provided some degree of annoyance for the original inhabitants, especially to the poor souls that were sent down narrow mines shafts to depths of more than 100 m to extract the ore, archaeologically their desolate signature is truly informative.

Mountainous areas therefore accommodate a distinctive range of landscape dynamics but certainly no simple set of landscape signatures. Such landscapes can be seen to be contingently unstable: stable terraced landscapes can convert rapidly to gully-eroded hillsides, landscapes of tells can be transformed by the adoption of transhumant pastoral systems, and shifts in patterns of economics and trade can result in the sudden growth or decline of mining areas. Although all these contingencies are relevant to other landscapes as well, they are particularly applicable to mountains areas.

10 Landscape Trajectories in Time and Space

No single theoretical perspective can bring coherence to the broad range of landscape configurations evident in the Near East, but a number of themes deserve emphasis. These include structural properties of the landscape such as patterns of settlement and communication systems that provide information on how populations were aggregated or dispersed and how goods and information might have flowed between them. In addition, dynamic properties refer to the manner in which landscapes changed through time from one state to another. Both of these properties relate to large-scale patterns, namely, systems of settlement or land use. It is also necessary, however, to appreciate that land-use systems are managed by people, families or communities, and where appropriate, I point out how specific social groups relate to landscape features and how individual management strategies may have influenced the dynamics of landscape.

Rain-Fed Upper Mesopotamia versus the Irrigated South

Comparison of the settlement landscapes for irrigated southern Mesopotamia and the rain-fed north (fig. 10.1) indicate that landscape structure may influence the potential ways that goods and information would be moved and power may have been exercised in the two regions. In the rain-fed north, administration and religion were probably vested in a scatter of roughly equivalent settlements (in terms of size and population) so that no one center was able to totally dominate any of

the others. Similarly, although some places may have had a minor advantage over neighboring centers, perhaps because they were located on, for example, a particularly successful overland route or at nodal points where several such networks met, there is no evidence that any particular site had an overwhelming situational or demographic advantage. Therefore, despite the fact that cities such as Brak (Nagar) and Tell Mardikh (Ebla) administered large areas of northern Syria during the mid third millennium B.C., the landscape record of settlement patterns and radial linear hollows suggests that probably the underlying long-term pattern of production and administrative units comprised a large number of semi-autonomous centers. Each of these was probably administered by its own ruler. Under certain circumstances, perhaps as a result of the efforts of charismatic leaders or an invasive empire (such as the Akkadian Empire), such patterns could then be rapidly transformed into a unitary state or empire (Marcus 1998; also Stein 1994). As described in chapter 6, the Bronze Age system of large centers distributed at intervals across the plains may have been an emergent property of a self-organizing settlement system in which both positive and negative feedback mechanisms balanced out to produce a system in which settlements could not readily exceed 100–150 hectares. More specifically and explicitly tied to social processes is the practice of holding land in common already noted in chapter 6. If this practice was indeed widespread in Upper Mesopotamia,

it seems likely that the large, nucleated, tell-based settlements with their radial hollow-way systems so characteristic of parts of northeast Syria and northwest Iraq formed a patchwork of agro-towns surrounded by 3–5 km zones of commonly held fields reminiscent of fields of the *musha'a* system of the Levant and medieval common fields of Britain (cf. Adams 1982: 2, 8).

Although practices of landholding in the south may have been different from those in the rain-fed north, it is difficult from the archaeological landscape to detect whether land has been allocated to communities or households or whether it was held by larger entities such as palaces and temples. Structurally, however, southern Mesopotamia presents a very different landscape from that of the rain-fed north. This is not simply because of the higher level of productivity that results from irrigation but also because of the opportunities for exercising power. Such opportunities are provided by the process of channel management, especially those occurring at bifurcation points in the major alluvial channels. As described in chapter 5, the process of crevasse-splay management and eventual channel avulsion, if well managed, would have provided an opportunity for Mesopotamian communities to extend their irrigation and agricultural potential to increase agricultural production. The main branches in the dynamic pattern of anastomosing river networks would have provided the predominant points of control so that any political leaders situated at those points, or in a position to administer them,

a.   b.

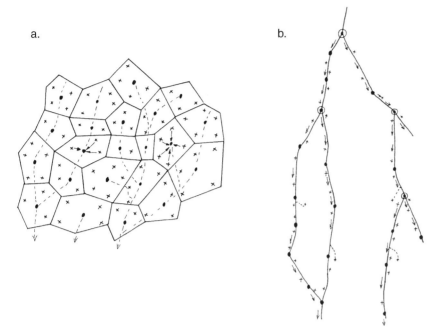

Fig. 10.1 Modular settlement patterns (a) for Upper Mesopotamia and (b) for irrigated southern Mesopotamia, to show the contrasting structures of the two landscapes. Solid circles represent central settlements: crosses, minor settlements.

exerted a degree of control over that part of the settlement and land-use system located downstream.

Interestingly, this hierarchy of potential power may not have been the same as the hierarchy of settlement scale.[1] In fact, in both northern and southern settlement systems there is no guarantee that hierarchies of settlement scale were coterminous with those of potential power relationships. As a result, a dual hierarchy or heterarchical pattern may have existed in which a major center and its satellite communities downstream either could have been held hostage by a smaller upstream neighbor situated at a potentially changeable channel bifurcation or alternatively could have administered such a control point, even though there is no hint from the settlement pattern itself. Thus the laconic comment of Sin-iddinam, king of Larsa, about restoring the course of the Tigris (chapter 5) may actually have heralded the end of a long period of turf wars over suzerainty over a particular channel system.

To sum up, the rain-fed north had a landscape structure that balanced positive and negative feedback mechanisms to constrain settlements from growing beyond a certain size. In southern Mesopotamia, however, there was a greater chance of these mechanisms being out of balance. Population influxes into cities would result from the increased presence of traders, growth of the palace and temple personnel, increased craft specialization, and so on. Moreover, when it was necessary to mobilize labor for canal construction, this could lead to positive feedback because the mobilized labor force would contribute (either permanently or temporarily) to population growth. On the other hand, mechanisms that would serve to limit growth would be less constraining in the south. Instead, increased land-use productivity resulted in larger surpluses, a network of channels allowed for the efficient mobilization of goods to growing settlements (Weiss 1986; Algaze 2001a), and channel bifurca-

tions provided opportunities for the exercising of power. Together, these factors must have provided opportunities for settlements in the south to grow more than in the north.[2] The existence of such differences in landscape structure must therefore have contributed to the rapid rise of state power during the third millennium and resulted in southern settlements becoming significantly larger than those in the north.

Settlement Dispersal during Territorial Empires

Although Mesopotamian canal systems were clearly being excavated and administered during the third millennium B.C., the control and extension of such systems appears to have increased through time so that by the first millennium B.C., one can discern the emergence of entire landscapes that show evidence for the exercising of power by an individual authority. Interregional canal systems attained their apogee in the Sasanian period, when substantial areas of the Iranian borderlands and southern Mesopotamia were irrigated and laid out under single irrigation systems of enormous scale (fig. 10.2). At a roughly comparable scale is the deliberate resettlement of communities in dispersed systems of rural settlement that were administered from the newly founded capitals of the Assyrian heartland (chapter 7). Although most of these settlement schemes relied upon rainfed cultivation, marginal areas were also subjected to considerable investments in canal construction during the Middle or Late Assyrian periods (Ergenzinger et al. 1988; Ergenzinger and Kühne 1991; Morandi 1996a). Such "blueprint landscapes" were by no means universal, however, and in many parts of the Assyrian steppe, spontaneous settlement may account for similar dispersed settlement landscapes.

The dispersal of settlement that was evident in the Fertile Crescent and parts of Anatolia from the Iron

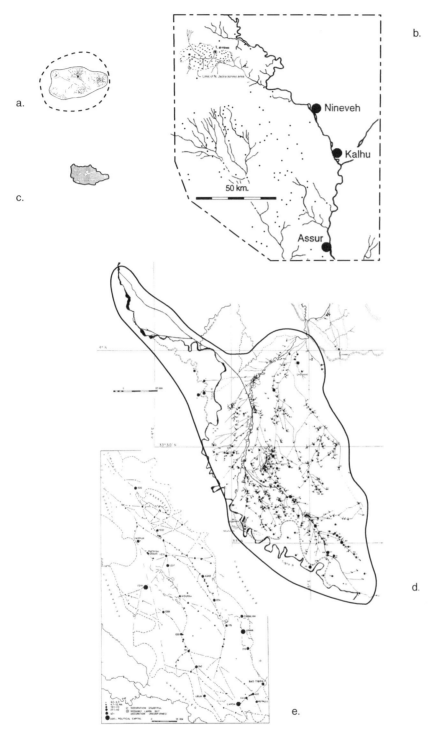

Fig. 10.2 Landscape in the Near East, showing potential increases in the scale of administered landscapes through time (all at the same scale): (a) Third-millennium B.C. settlement system around central tell in northern Iraq (based upon Wilkinson and Tucker 1995). (b) Pattern of dispersed first-millennium B.C. rural settlement west of the Tigris in relation to the Neo-Assyrian capitals (from Barbanes 1999). Note boundary is arbitrary because Neo-Assyrian administration during the ninth–seventh centuries B.C. extended well beyond this limit. (c) The cultivated Sabaean oasis of Marib (Yemen). (d) The extent of irrigation in the Diyala area of Iraq (including the Nahrawan canal) during the Sasanian period (Adams 1965). (e) Ur III–Isin Larsa settlement pattern on the Mesopotamian plains. In this case, it is difficult to estimate system boundaries because of the high degree of linkage provided by the channel systems (based on Adams 1981).

Age through Byzantine/Sasanian periods can be ascribed to a number of causes, some of which can be seen as spontaneous settlement, others (for example, those associated with the development of the Roman frontier) being imposed. At the same time, the pattern of urban settlement appears to have shifted so that in the

early first millennium B.C. within the Assyrian heartland, major administrative centers increased in scale and in the Syro-Hittite realm of western Syria and southern Turkey large new urban centers also appeared (Mazzoni 1994). Although imposed landscape patterns are not as clear as in the zone of Sasanian irriga-

tion, the recognition of centuriation in parts of western Syria suggests that Hellenistic/Roman landscapes showed evidence for imperial re-organization. Overall, the dispersal of rural settlement was a widespread phenomenon throughout much of the Fertile Crescent during the Iron Age; therefore, terms such as "Neo-

Assyrian" or "Israelite" settlement provide a spurious level of specificity for what must be seen as a more wide-ranging phenomenon.

On first impression it appears that these dispersed rural settlement systems of the first millennium B.C. and later may provide a "signature" of territorial empires. The structure of settlement pattern may therefore correspond to a range of underlying process that prevailed when large territories came under a single overarching administrative control. Although the actual processes that ushered in these changes after around 1200 B.C. are beyond the scope of this volume, it is likely that with the decline of the small-scale polities of the Bronze Age there were substantial changes in the type of land holdings, demographic composition of the local populations as well as the commercialization of the economy, the last attaining its climax during the Roman-Byzantine period.

Landscapes, Climate, and Human Activity

Because a wide range of factors contributes to landscape degradation, there appears to have been only a general correlation between valley fills and human/environmental variables. Overall, in many parts of the Near East during the Holocene there has been an increase in human population in the face of climatic drying as well as an extension of settlement into more erodable terrain types. The cumulative stresses resulting from these factors may therefore account for the increased degradation that is evident. In addition, as more vegetation was lost from the region, surface conditions (albedo, retention or loss of soil moisture) must have changed, thereby feeding back into the local climate, which itself may have changed as a result (Kutzbach et al. 1996).

Altogether, it is still difficult to recognize precisely when human factors became more significant in the denudation of the Near Eastern land-

scape than climate. Table 7.2 sums up some of the salient trends for the Levant, and a wider geographical universe would provide a similar view, with human impacts starting early in the Holocene. To what degree the Neolithic impacts suggested by Köhler-Rollefson and Rollefson (1990) for Jordan and McCorriston (1992) for Syria can be extrapolated across the entire Fertile Crescent is less clear, but such early impacts are supported by a Pre-Pottery Neolithic decline in deciduous oak recorded in the recent Ghab pollen cores (Yasuda et al. 2000: 131). In Yemen, soil erosion apparently resulting from human impact is clearly evident by the fourth millennium B.C. and continues thereafter (chapter 9). In the Near East, overall, localized human impacts appear to have been underway as early as the Neolithic. Although such impacts probably strengthened considerably in the third millennium B.C., it was probably not until the first millennium B.C., with the widespread extension of settlement on to erodable uplands, that landscape denudation and soil erosion really became significant and perhaps irreversible.

The response of individual hydrological catchments to human activity will, of course, have varied depending upon catchment morphology and soils, as well as the sensitivity of the land to erosive, high-intensity rainfalls (for the importance of deluges, see Bintliff 1992; Grove and Rackham 2001). Once ecosystems had been destabilized and the landscape was depleted of its protective cover of vegetation, the effect of climatic events of especial severity would have been amplified, and so their effects would have been considerably more damaging in terms of erosion. Consequently, the apparent increased severity of soil erosion described, for example, in southern Turkey and Yemen may reasonably be ascribed to the combined effects of high-energy rainfall events, in the context of a reduced vegetation cover, the latter resulting from both

human activity and perhaps a drier climate.

Ecology and Marginal Environments of the Highland and Desert

The low rainfall of the deserts and the short growing seasons at high elevations both place constraints on human communities that are less evident in other parts of the Near East. The coping strategies that have been devised for the desert margins clearly demonstrate that humans are capable of overriding the limitations of a dry climate and that these strategies (runoff agriculture, qanat construction, or specific agro-pastoral strategies) have been applied over a wide area of desert margins from Syria as far south as southern Arabia. There is therefore no reason to assume that there would ever have been a distinct line between the desert and the sown. Rather the transition zone would fluctuate in breadth depending upon prevailing social, political, and environmental circumstances as well as the application of technologies of hydraulic management.

Similarly, there is no single adaptation to mountainous areas. Within any given upland area to a certain altitudinal limit, one finds at different periods agrarian land dominated by tells, landscapes of irrigation, and pastoral-nomadic land-use strategies, or of course, as was pointed out in chapter 9, no significant occupation whatsoever.

The apparent increased significance (or at least survival) of religious places in mountains and deserts is partly a result of these areas being situated within the landscape of preservation. Nevertheless, written texts of various types are persuasive in demonstrating that many uplands did possess sanctity and provided numerous opportunities for cultic activity, which set them apart from the everyday life of the agricultural lowlands. By way of contrast, in agricultural lowlands, religious places either appear to be concentrated in existing settlements or they lack the characteristics that make them conspicuous. For example, many small, mounded sites may have had more of a religious function than is appreciated, but such features are difficult to detect from archaeological surveys and instead require the application of focused and problem-oriented excavation.

Signature Landscapes and Landscape Sequences

One organizing concept of this book has been that "signature landscapes" can be recognized within certain geographical zones. It is quite clear, however, from the examples discussed that there are numerous deviations from the norms expressed in these models. In all parts of the Near East, landscapes are dynamic and can switch from one state to another (e.g., cultivation to pasture) through time. Nevertheless, key land-use types can be recognized. Table 10.1 summarizes some of the main relationships between the signature archaeological landscapes and the inferred type of land use. As with all models, these simplify a complex reality, but it is hoped that they provide a basis for deeper analysis.

By way of example, the commonly cited notion that communities that lived in landscapes of tells must have relied to a significant degree upon staple production in the form of rain-fed cultivation seems eminently reasonable. Moreover, that these systems frequently employed some form of communal land management can be suggested for certain time periods. These land-use strategies may, in turn, have each been related to different forms of storage, but whether this took the form of domestic, communal, or redistributive storage systems (Pfälzner 2002) remains to be seen. Nevertheless, by recognizing key landscape modalities it should eventually be possible to forge linkages between the landscape and certain features of the material

culture and archaeology recorded on the archaeological sites, as well, of course, to the biological record derived from on-site palaeobotany and faunal analysis.

Archaeological surveys demonstrate that marginal areas of the Fertile Crescent were subject to marked population cycles, which resulted in phases of settlement being punctuated by episodes of abandonment or substantial decline (S. Rosen 1987). Detailed surveys in Upper Mesopotamia suggest, however, that such abandonments were often patchy in their spatial expression, with large areas being abandoned while others experienced apparent growth (Algaze 1999; Wilkinson 2000b). The pattern of third-millennium settlement and abandonment in the Jazira, although still poorly understood, appears to have been variegated. Whereas some posit an abrupt phase of prolonged drought as being the culprit for regional collapse (Weiss et al. 1993), others see such declines as being a result of the failure of the network of interregional trade and exchange linkages (Butzer 1997b). In many cases, "collapse" is manifested simply by a dispersal of population into smaller village-sized settlements (Wilkinson 1990a; Peltenburg 1999; Algaze 1999). In some climatically marginal settlements, occupation apparently continued after the postulated collapse (e.g., Tell Brak), or settlements even increased in size (e.g., Tell Sweyhat). Although it is not yet possible to resolve any of these arguments satisfactorily, the application of landscape analysis must play a significant role in framing and understanding such cyclical changes.

As has been argued by Finley (1985) and most recently David Schloen (2001: 101), early cities (especially those in the rain-fed zone) were heavily reliant upon agriculture for their economic sustenance. Moreover, this sector must have been vulnerable to climactic fluctuations. There is, however, no reason to assume that all Bronze Age

tells were blessed with precisely the same balance of economic sectors, so that there is no reason to assume that external factors would have had equal impacts on all settlements. An alternative to viewing climate, social processes, or economy as forcing mechanisms behind settlement and landscape change is to examine the areas of vulnerability of different economic sectors for any given site. Whereas some settlements would have received most of their sustenance from the production of staple crops such as cereals (with trade and animal husbandry playing minor roles), other settlements (such as those on trade routes or in areas that favored exchange with pastoral groups) would have had an economy more reliant on the accumulation of wealth.

Certainly, powerful cities such as Ebla generated considerable wealth from tribute, taxes, gift exchange, or plunder, and this must have made them well positioned to override climatic fluctuations but vulnerable to economic perturbations. A third group, namely agro-pastoralists, may have held a significant part of their wealth in the form of animals, usually sheep and goats. The contribution of these different sectors to the economy would therefore result in a patterned response to any external stress. For example, a significant drought would severely impact the economy of sites dominated by staple production or agro-pastoral production but might leave settlements with more of their wealth derived from trade, exchange, or tribute relatively unscathed because the latter could to some degree import food from elsewhere (Wilkinson 2000a: 6–16).

The Dynamics of Successive Landscapes

It is clear from the distribution of archaeological sites that much of Upper Mesopotamia and the eastern Mediterranean has been in agricultural use for millennia, and in such

Table 10.1 Signature Landscapes and Basic Categories of Land Use

Signature Landscape	Primary Land Use	Secondary Land Use
Ch. 5: Landscapes of irrigation (fig. 5.12)	In Mesopotamia, linear zones of palm gardens with understory of annuals.	Cereal fields beyond palm gardens; pasture beyond that.
Ch. 6: Landscapes of tells (figs. 6.13, 6.17)	Extensive and intensive cereal cultivation. Perhaps significant amount of commonly held fields.	Pasture beyond and on semiarid steppe.
Ch. 7: Landscapes of dispersal. Mode (a), Mediterranean zone and Levant	In addition to staple production on fields, increased tendency toward olive and vine cultivation in the Levant and the subhumid Fertile Crescent.	
Landscapes of dispersal. Mode (b), the Jazira of Upper Mesopotamia (fig. 7.3b)	Extensive cultivation of staple products around small, dispersed settlements. Vines and olives in subhumid areas.	Irrigated cultivation along rivers in the desert margins.
Ch. 8: Landscapes of the desert, mode (a).(figs. 8.3, 8.8, 8.14)	Oasis cultivation of date palms with understory of vegetables.	Cereal fields and pasture on oasis perimeter and downstream.
Landscapes of the desert, mode (b). Cross-desert routes (fig. 8.10)	Way stations with water-supply features and occasional minor agricultural areas.	Large pasture reserves.
Landscapes of the desert, mode (c) (fig. 8.14)	Mobile pasture on the semiarid and arid steppe.	Use of markets on edge of desert and (in some cases) ownership of fields in oases.
Landscapes of the desert, mode (d) (figs. 8.12, 8.13)	Transitional agro-pastoralist strategies with runoff fields and marginal cultivation.	
Chapter 9: Landscapes of the highlands. Mode (a)	Landscapes of tells with staple production.	
Landscapes of the highlands. Mode (b)	Mixed cropping on terraced fields in highland valleys.	Localized runoff or flood agriculture irrigated with dams.
Landscapes of the highlands. Mode (c)	Hilltop settlements with agro-pastoral strategies.	
Landscapes of the highlands. Mode (d) (fig. 9.9)	Pastoral nomadic strategies, sometimes with transhumance to lower pastures.	
Landscapes of the highlands. Mode (e) fig. 9.12)	Mixed farming to supply specialized mining sites.	

areas low-yield production appears to have been sustainable for long periods of time (Butzer 1996: 145). The heavy use of soils around tells during the fourth and third millennia probably reduced their nutrient capacity as well as moisture-holding humus. This would have been particularly true if crop residues were not returned to the soil, as would occur, for example, if straw from the annual crop was used for the tem-

per of mudbricks for major building programs. Such nutrient losses must have reduced crops yields as well as the support base for rising populations unless the situation could be counteracted by switching to annual cropping. Such a strategy, however, by withdrawing more moisture from the soil, would then increase the potential for crop failures in low-rainfall years (Wilkinson 1994). Such a delicate balance was exacerbated

by the fodder requirements of sheep, which may have placed further demands on agricultural production systems (Danti 2000).

Overall, in densely populated and climatically marginal areas the local subsistence economy was very vulnerable to runs of drier years, the impact of which could have been absorbed by more extensive farming systems. By depleting both the nutrient base and the moisture retention of the soil, high-intensity farming systems developed inherent weaknesses, which then made their agricultural production systems more vulnerable to episodes of drier climate. Even during dry years, however, valley floors, by virtue of their raised levels of soil moisture, could have continued to supply some grain production. Moreover, in valleys occupied by permanent streams, drier conditions could have been offset by irrigation. In such cases, however, increased withdrawal of water by upstream communities would lead to those positioned downstream (in the Jazira in drier areas) being deprived of essential water.

Major religious centers may have been able to override environmental perturbations because their sanctity would have meant that unlike more secular locations, they would not have been allowed to collapse. One problem inherent in persistent urbanization is that such population concentrations must have encouraged the spread of infectious disease (Redman 1999: 174–175). This situation can only have been exacerbated if the site was surrounded by water-filled brick pits that may have become transformed into fetid swamps as a result of the contamination from domestic or animal wastes.

In sum, cycles of settlement growth and decline must therefore be seen as resulting from a complex range of factors. These cycles must, in turn, have exerted a considerable influence on the pattern of successive landscapes.

In some cases, changes in settlement and landscape did not simply show linear responses to physical, social, or economic determinants. Instead, landscapes sometimes apparently switched from one state to another rather than attaining long-term static equilibrium. The complexity of such landscape dynamics has already been sketched by B. K. Roberts, who recognizes two fundamental categories of settlement pattern: stable and unstable as well as four main developmen-

tal processes (Roberts 1996: 127): continuity; rapid, often cataclysmic change; impact of colonization; and the existence of changing economic systems.

Alternatively, landscapes can be envisaged to behave in the manner of complex adaptive systems. The patterns outlined in the next paragraph echo the picture expressed by human ecodynamics in which environment and cultural systems are viewed as interacting. Such theoretical developments represent an escape from the limitations of concepts such as adaptation and equilibrium (McGlade 1995). Although a system will retain its apparent stability until acted upon by external forces, there is often a nonlinear and complex response to any perturbation, and so rare and perhaps extreme events can suddenly exceed the resilience of the system. As a result, perturbations can cause cascades of responses throughout the system. Moreover, feedback processes play a key role in complex systems (e.g., chapters 6 and 8) by either amplifying changes or suppressing them. A much-commented-on feature of such systems is the existence of "attractors" (regions to which all points of the universe of possibilities converge), self-organization, or "emergent" behaviors (chapter 1; also McGlade 1995: 120).

Complex adaptive systems and agent-based modeling provide attractive models for assessing landscape developments because they are capable of dealing with a wide range of inputs of social and environmental data, all of which interact to produce complex, occasionally unanticipated outcomes. Sometimes there will even be two outcomes to the same scenario, with the result that what appears to have been a fairly simple trajectory of landscape development will suddenly split to form a so-called bifurcation, which results in a critical instability followed by the creation of a divergent pathway of development (see the second case discussed below). Although it is all

too easy to apply these models in an inappropriate manner to qualitative data sets such as the landscape, the following examples should suffice to show that Near Eastern landscapes have undergone complex life cycles through the millennia with often unanticipated outcomes. Consequently, rather than witnessing a "chest of drawers" succession of landscapes, landscape change appears to proceed through time as a chronological succession of kaleidoscopes.

For example, in the Jazira of northwest Iraq and northeast Syria, the succession from tell-based agrarian landscapes with more distant pasture lands of the fourth, third, and early second millennia B.C. was followed by a distinct dispersal of rural settlement that commenced in the late second millennium and continued during the first millennium B.C. Elsewhere, for example, in the western Khabur basin, widespread desertion of sedentary settlement in the late third or second millennium B.C. was followed by first-millennium resettlement, whereas along river valleys, a shift toward agricultural intensification took the form of lengthy Middle or Late Assyrian canals resulting from major imperial investments (Kühne 1990; Morandi 1996a). Over large areas of the Jazira, the configuration of mainly dispersed rural settlement persisted through the first millennium B.C. and A.D., after which there followed patchy desertion and renewed pastoral activity during the second millennium A.D. Overall, a characteristic switch from landscape to landscape appears to have taken place in many parts of upper Mesopotamia. A common attribute of these landscapes appears to have been that phases of medium-term system stability (tells) were interrupted by desertion and renewed pastoral activity or by phases of colonization, in conjunction with either rain-fed agriculture or irrigation (cf. Roberts 1996: fig. 6.4).

Such cyclicity is captured in a rather two-dimensional manner by demographic proxy curves based on aggregate settlement area through time. These curves, although giving an impression of broad-scale population cycles, probably understate the spatial and temporal complexities of the record. Unfortunately, because each successive landscape removes part or all of the previous one, many parts of the record will be missing, especially if they include more lightly etched landscapes such as those of pastoral nomads. Only under particularly favorable circumstances is the landscape record preserved. For example, the distinctive "landscapes of tells" of Upper Mesopotamia described in chapter 6 seem to have been preserved by a taphonomic fluke in a similar manner that the remarkable fossilized lime-cemented canals of the Tehuacan valley of Mexico have been preserved as a result of the precipitation of travertine from calcium carbonate-saturated groundwaters that fed this system of canals (Woodbury and Neely 1972).

Traditional studies of ancient agricultural systems frequently assume agricultural strategies will be economically rational, but in reality, farmers (or agricultural administrators) can adopt a wide range of strategies that range from conservative to radical (e.g., maximizing production) depending upon their circumstances or point of view. This is illustrated for a Jazira rain-fed farming economy by conservative farmers who could elect to continue biennial fallow to conserve soil moisture and ensure stability of production. More radical farmers (or administrators) could seek to maximize production by dispensing with fallow so as to produce a crop every year. The latter strategies would provide higher short-term yields but would be less stable (as discussed in chapter 6). In terms of the landscape record, such relatively short-lived strategies of intensification might result in the extensive field scatters recorded at various times and places in the Fertile Crescent. Because decisions on when and how frequently

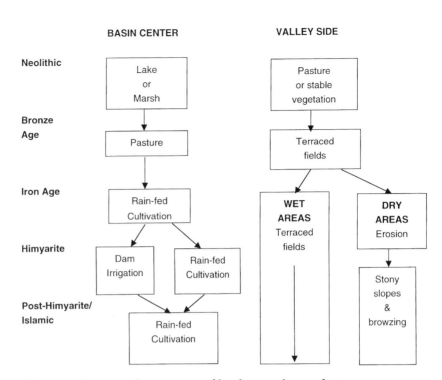

Fig. 10.3   Suggested sequences of landscape change for two topographic locations in part of the Yemen highlands.

to crop would be a function of individual perceptions and the desire to replicate (or avoid) neighbor's success (or failure), the actual outcome would be difficult to predict and contingent on a range of social and cognitive factors. Consequently, the decision to adopt a different agricultural strategy may itself be conditioned by changing economic circumstances and itself could lead to a range of outcomes depending upon the individual farmer and his decision-making circumstances. An indeterminate factor must therefore be included in our models of agro-ecosystems to allow for such contingencies.

In highland Yemen, as in Upper Mesopotamia, settlement-landscape trajectories followed a succession of different states (fig. 10.3). The postulated dichotomy between Bronze Age cultivation of near-site fields and basin-floor pastoralism gave way during the Iron Age to the gradual encroachment of cultivation onto basin floors. The transformation of this patchwork of fields or terraces during the Himyarite period

towards a dual economy with a supplementary layer of high-investment dam irrigation appears ultimately to have been unsustainable in many localities. This is because many dams were vulnerable to high floods and were swept away to be replaced by simple flood cultivation systems (*sayl* cultivation) or a reemphasis on terraced agriculture. In turn, terraced cultivation showed an interesting bifurcation. Where rainfall was higher and terraced agriculture was maintained over many centuries or millennia, the landscape often became remarkably stable, and so erosion and runoff were minimized. In contrast, in drier areas where terraced agriculture had been transitory and probably restricted to the Bronze Age, slopes suffered heavy erosion, and landscapes (apart from the cultivated valley-floor lands) underwent considerable instability and erosion.

Similar flips in landscape systems may be suggested for highland Anatolia, where at elevations close to the upper limit of cultivation, ecological constraints must have placed severe limitations on staple food production, and alternative economic strategies represented viable options. Although one such option was to focus on pastoral production, winter cold and limitations of fodder must have severely restricted the scale of pastoral systems, and so transhumance would represent the most appropriate solution. Such responses to altitudinal zonation may, in turn, result in the development of long-distance exchange networks such as are well known in traditional society in the Andes (Moran 2000). Not only does transhumance enable upland pastures to be used more effectively, it also allows for a dual use of the land, one by intrusive mobile communities and a second by local more sedentary groups, as well as a wide range of mutual interactions in between to allow for differences in plant and animal production. Overall, long-term patterns of land use may therefore have alternated between a dominantly cultivation-based land use on the one hand and pastoralism on the other, with a wide range of strategies in between.

Not only do transhumant strategies influence the highlands, they also impact neighboring lowlands that would have supplied seasonal grazing lands. Probably the best examples occur within the Upper Khabur basin, which fall within the range of the winter grazing of highland nomadic groups, as well as the summer grazing of bedouin. Such areas may therefore have experienced triple land usage during any one year: (1) year-round cultivation and pasture from local sedentary communities; (2) winter grazing for transhumant groups who arrived from the neighboring Anatolian highlands; (3) summer grazing from the nomads of the Arabian steppe to the south. If such triple usage was in operation at any time during history, this may have contributed to social stress among the local inhabitants because of conflicts over pasturage rights. Moreover, multiple land usage would have exerted considerable physical stress on eco-

systems, which may account for the highly degraded appearance of these landscapes today.

Landscape Management

The management of natural resources appears to have been a key factor in landscape development in the ancient Near East. On the one hand, a close relationship with the environment could have made communities vulnerable to environmental fluctuations, whereas on the other, this would have armed them with the appropriate techniques to override many social or climatic perturbations. The management of riverine environments in Mesopotamia (chapter 5), the use of runoff agriculture in the desert margins (chapter 8), and terraced agriculture in the uplands (chapter 9) all appear to result from the formalization and management of natural processes. In each case, early farming communities had a sufficiently intimate knowledge of the land and its biological resources. Simply by managing available resources, such as by controlling the flow through a levee break or guiding normal floodwaters on to the land, it was possible to enhance production and take the first steps towards the development of a "cultural" landscape. This of course is not a new concept (see Sherratt 1980; Roberts 1998). Nevertheless, it is significant that in southern Mesopotamia, such management may have led to increases in the scale of agricultural systems with simple levee-break irrigation leading (geomorphologically at least) towards fully fledged avulsion and channel bifurcation that enabled the irrigation system to expand and an entirely new set of land-use patterns and/or power relations to emerge.

The concept of resource management neither is deterministic nor does it necessarily lead to the landscape attaining a long-term static equilibrium. Because landscapes result from the action of social groups within a physical environment that

itself has been altered by earlier social groups, it is crucial to identify social aspects of landscape management. By analogy with modern-day societies, many archaeological landscape features can be inferred to have been operated and administered by either families or small communities (Netting 1993). In other words, the day-to-day operation and management of the agrarian landscape was done at a local level, and growth was probably effected by incremental investment when new fields or installations were required. In many cases, this probably resulted in the piece-meal extension of fields or irrigation systems that ultimately produced the "organically evolved" landscapes that are so common throughout the Near East.

The operation of such local rules can result in a deceptive degree of apparent landscape organization. For example, in Yemen during the first millennium B.C. and A.D. there was probably a transition from rain-fed terrace fields in the moist highlands, through small-scale runoff cultivation in semiarid areas, to massive flood-runoff systems along the desert margins. Each land-use system appears well configured and adjusted to its local environment so as to give the impression that each local configuration forms a component part of one large system. Clearly, however, each land-use system developed over long periods of time as a result of local actors obeying local rules of behavior. Only in the largest systems around sites like Marib was any large-scale coordination required. In a similar manner, the radial agrarian landscapes around tells in Upper Mesopotamia and many of the bifurcating channel systems of lowland Iraq could have been managed at the local level without the necessity of being coordinated by a centralized administration. Such fundamental configurations may again be emergent properties of localized processes of land-use control.

If investment exceeds the incremental input provided by local communities, however, then a more formalized landscape may have resulted because a greater area of land could be developed and laid out at one time. In Iran when landlords supplied high levels of investment to enable new qanats to be constructed, these systems were capable of supporting entire villages. At its most extreme, such investment resulted in the laying out of entire landscapes, either as a result of deliberate colonization, such as was epitomized by some Neo-Assyrian settlement policies, or as occurred during the Sasanian period in parts of western Iran and Iraq. Such administered systems, however, were of such a large scale that they failed to be sensitive to local soil and hydrological environments, with the result that extensive waterlogging and salinization could result (Adams 1981).

What we see when natural resources are managed to provide enhanced land-use productivity is a classic case of "we shape the environment, and it shapes us" (or vice versa):

— By managing the environment, humans become reliant upon it.
— Human communities therefore become vulnerable to environmental perturbations.
— Alternatively, management strategies also enable people to override environmental perturbations.
— If pursued at a sufficiently large scale (as in large-scale irrigation systems) or at a sufficient intensity (e.g., by violating fallow), societies then become vulnerable to an entirely new set of environmental problems such as salinization, reduced soil moisture, more pests, and so on, which makes them more vulnerable to catastrophic declines in production.

Clearly, there is no single trajectory along which human-environment interactions develop. Neither does the environment simply drive human agricultural practices. Rather, climatic and human factors are intimately related, with each influencing the landscape in a complex pattern of intertwined relationships. The cultural landscape that remains is therefore frequently the result of these complex interactive processes. To sort out which factor was the causal mechanism behind change can be extremely difficult.

Future Prospects

The record of landscape development in the Near East is clearly complex, and the technical and theoretical tools for dealing with such a range of variables are not yet fully developed. Nevertheless, it should be clear that landscape archaeology has a major role to play in an understanding of the development of ancient Near East society and culture because it provides a unique and geographically broad view of large regions through extended periods of time. At the outset, it is essential to examine the archaeological record in terms of its likelihood of being preserved. Without some idea of how much of the landscape has been lost as a result of taphonomic processes, we cannot even start to understand the landscape that survives. This issue is particularly urgent today because vast areas of the Middle Eastern landscape and its archaeological sites are being irretrievably lost as a result of flooding behind major dams, highway and urban development, and new levels of intensive agriculture. Virtually every survey or landscape project now entails some degree of salvage archaeology. Unless steps are taken to halt the destruction (or at least to record what is being destroyed), very little of the ancient landscape and archaeological sites will remain for future generations to study.

Because the landscape is both a physical and a cultural entity, landscape studies should necessarily develop on a broad front. In the future, phenomenological approaches will play an important role in the development of the field of Near Eastern landscape archaeology because the landscape in its entirety is experienced by the human population, either directly or indirectly, and therefore plays an ideational or cognitive role in everyday life. More specifically, many landscapes contain natural features that have played a long-term religious role in the lives of both local people and entire cultures. Such perceptions are often underrepresented in conventional studies of "economic" landscapes or subsistence economies. By mapping both economic and ideational landscapes, it should be possible to reconstruct compound landscapes in which both types of features can be recognized, probably as complex and intertwining palimpsests, to provide a deeper understanding of landscapes than has been sketched herein.

Rather than leading to the development of a new subfield, the study of ideational landscapes should be integrated with those of economic landscapes because, as Lansing (1987) has shown for Balinese water temples, the economic and ideational facets of life tend to be deeply intertwined.

Complex adaptive systems and dynamic agent-based modeling will surely play an important role in any future understanding of the dynamics of landscape development, a point well made by recent studies by Kohler and Gumerman (2000) and Adams (2001). A start has already been made in applying such principles to ancient Egypt (Lehner 2000). Nevertheless, the results from such exercises can provide only some loose guidelines to potential developmental trajectories, and as Jim Doran has pointed out, modeling will probably be used more to generate "sets of trajectories" rather than single solutions (Wright 2000: 380). That such multiple trajectories may be detectable is perhaps starting to become evident from the examples illustrated above. By harnessing the powers of agent-based modeling, a

wider range of landscape scenarios
should become evident.

Despite the appeal of employing
the modeling capabilities of complex adaptive systems, it is advisable
to recognize that more traditional
evolutionary models such as chiefdom, state, and territorial empire
can be perceived in the landscape
record, possibly because these stages
relate to stable "emergent" states
of complex systems. Moreover, it
is necessary to place the development of such sociopolitical configurations and their settlement
landscapes within a larger framework to incorporate the full range
of settlement/landscape variation
that is recognizable from recent regional studies. Finally, although the
complexity of the landscape can be
captured within broad theoretical
frameworks, much more fieldwork is
required to test the proposed models
and to provide more detail at both
the local and regional level.

Notes

Chapter 2. Environmental Context

1. This proxy climatic curve has yet to be published with radiocarbon dates as control. Recent analyses suggest that it might be as much as one thousand years in error (Roberts 2002). Consequently, this must be regarded as a preliminary result.

2. Whether the large Hellenistic city of Thaj is actually ancient Gerrha' has been much debated, but the presence of a relict arm of the sea in this location raises the possibility that the *sabkha* may have originally been the bay of Gerrha'. This provides some support for Thaj being ancient Gerrha' (Barth 2001; see also Potts 1990: 89 for archaeological and historical discussion of Gerrha').

3. For a critical discussion of this issue, see Grove and Rackham (2001: 328–350), who point out that delta expansion in the Mediterranean cannot be demonstrated to always have resulted from human-induced accelerated erosion.

4. This summary of data is from various sites around the Mediterranean basin. Deviations from the illustrated patterns are quite common, and overall, the relationship between climate, land use, and sediment yield is very complex. They do, however, serve to illustrate some salient trends.

Chapter 3. Recording the Ancient Near Eastern Landscape

1. The new monographs provide a summary of the archaeological remains according to individual 1:20,000 map sheets. Following introductory sections on the environment, the reports record existing and ancient roads; an archaeological overview of each significant period, together with a summary of individual features such as sites, cairns, lime kilns, reservoirs, bell-shaped cisterns, and threshing floors; and an outline of the current population of the area.

Chapter 4. Elements of Landscape

1. Nevertheless, steep-sided aqueducts do exist. For example, the Humeima aqueduct in Jordan has, in places, a gradient of between 10 and 45 degrees (Oleson 1991: 49).

2. Near Eastern examples have been recorded from Samosata, Perge, and Aspendos in Turkey (Hodge 2000).

3. They normally exhibit sparse scatters of pottery with a narrower range of types than is found on sedentary sites (Cribb 1991: 76).

4. These are microscopic calcium carbonate spheres that occur in the stomachs of ruminant animals and that also can be found in dung as well as in a range of archaeological sediments (Canti 1998).

Chapter 5. Landscapes of Irrigation

1. The Samarran period dates from ca. 6000 B.C. until around 5400 B.C.

2. These site areas were suitably corrected to variable lengths of ceramic periods using Dewar's methodology (Neely and Wright 1994: 210–213).

3. These are very low rises of land contained within the plains. These are thought to be islands of ancient (i.e., Pleistocene) sediments surrounded by the younger sediments of the plain (Pournelle in press 2001b).

4. Note that according to Paepe and Baeteman (1978), the main early- to mid-Pleistocene channels were through the Tharthar depression, as well as the Habbaniyah-Abu Dibis depressions along the west side of the plains.

5. Usually, organic matter occurs at less than 1 percent, according to Buringh (1960: 253); see also Mabbutt and Floret (1980: 194–196).

6. E-mail communication from Robert Adams 23/1/01; see also the southernmost channel on figure 5.11 and Wright 1981: 327–328.

7. Morony (1994), however, suggests a more nuanced scenario. Rather than there being a reduction in settlement in Early Islamic times, Morony sees instead a reorientation towards a newly commercialized economy in the Early Islamic period. These various interpretations are based around details of dating Sasanian and Early Islamic pottery, which are beyond the scope of this book.

8. For pre-Sargonic to Old Babylonian periods, Powell (1985) has argued that the evidence is equivocal for a major shift from wheat to barley cultivation as well as for a decline in yields.

Chapter 6. Landscapes of Tells

1. For settlements in Upper Mesopotamia there is less evidence for temples occupying central and highly visible locations as in southern Mesopotamia. Although northern cities of the third millennium B.C. did function as religious centers, in many cases, temples appear to have been scattered through different neighborhoods. According to Stein, their context implies that they functioned for lineage-based groups rather than being ritual centers for an entire community (Stein 2001). Nevertherless, at Alalakh a sequence of temples did remain in virtually the same location for much of the second millennium B.C. This implies some degree of religious continuity on this site.

2. This is compared to the 70–95 percent of the Negev loessic soils (Tsoar and Yekutlieli 1993; Buringh 1960: 220; Mulders 1969).

3. Where rain fell between 200 and 400 mm per annum, although normal yields would have sufficed to feed a family (either nucleated or a fairly small extended family) and perhaps some craft specialists or nonagricultural personal, in dry years (or areas) there would have

been insufficient food to cover both sets of needs. Moreover, the lower the yield, the less each agricultural unit (be it family or palace based) would be able to supply as a surplus. In other words, for every additional dependent individual, more agricultural producers would be required to support them.

high productivity of irrigation and the presence of numerous channels for the transportation of bulk goods must have contributed considerably to the growth of southern cities. The latter factor, especially, would have counteracted the limits placed on settlement growth by virtue of their limited agricultural hinterlands of these southern cities.

Chapter 7. The Great Dispersal

1. The photographs were made in 1953 (by Hunting Surveys) for the Jordanian southern Hauran (Kennedy 1995: 276) and in 1929–1930 for the Syrian Hauran (Gentelle 1985).

Chapter 9. Landscapes of the Highlands

1. Albeit, the difficulty of communicating may be ameliorated by high levels of investment in roads or paths as can be found in the system of Inka roads (Trombold 1991) as well as in parts of the Yemen highlands.

2. Owing to the absence of trees in the Tsakahovit plain, the elevation of the boundary between the tree line and subalpine pastures is difficult to estimate, but in neighboring Iran, Bobek (1968) estimates this limit at varying elevations between ca. 1,980 m and 2,743 m above sea level. This suggests that the fortress sites (at elevations between 2,000 and 2,400 m) developed in the transition zone between the upper limit of woodland and the subalpine pasture above.

3. That is, the cutting of trees down to a stub, which then sprouts a series of new stems in future seasons (Grove and Rackham 2001: 48–49).

4. For alternative views of this "Himalayan dilemma," see Ives and Messerli (1989) and Haigh (1994).

Chapter 10. Landscape Trajectories in Time and Space

1. This is well illustrated by Ebla, which during the mid third millennium B.C. ruled over a large part of western and central Syria, but at ca. 56 ha was relatively modest in scale compared to sites such as Qatna, Leilan, Hamoukar, Mozan, or Kazane Höyük. In these cases, there is no obvious correlation between a settlement's size and its political clout (cf. Marcus 1998).

2. As noted in chapter 6, both the

Glossary

'ayn. Arabic for spring of water.

aggradation. The accumulation and building up of sediments, frequently on a valley floor.

albedo. The proportion of incident light reflected from the earth's surface.

allocthonous. Materials derived from or processes occurring outside the system.

alluvial. Deriving from a river.

AMS (Accelerator Mass Spectrometry) dating. Method of radiocarbon dating that entails the direct measurement of the ratio of different carbon isotopes. Important for landscape studies because this method can be applied to very small samples.

anaerobic (or anoxic). Without oxygen.

anastomosing. A river with multiple channels the major distributaries of which branch from and rejoin the main channel.

anthrosol. A soil whose main characteristics are the result of human activity.

aquifer. Water-bearing stratum of permeable rock, sand, or gravel.

archaeozoology. The study of faunal remains from archaeological sites to reconstruct the environment, the subsistence economy, or human diet.

assemblage. Group of artifacts or biological materials occurring together at a particular time and place.

augering. The use of a drill (operated by hand or machine) to determine the depth, stratigraphy, and nature of sediments.

autochthonous. Opposite of allocthonous. Materials produced in situ or by processes occurring within a system.

avulsion. An abrupt shift of a river channel in favor of a new course. This frequently, but not necessarily, entails the abandonment of an earlier channel.

basalt. Dense igneous rock, usually gray or black in color and containing basic plagioclase and augite.

bedload. The sedimentary material, usually coarse, transported along the bed of a river.

bedouin, *bedu* (or *badw*). Tribal nomads.

bioclastic. Adjective for a rock or mineral that has attained its present form through the action of living organisms.

bioturbation. The churning and mixing of deposits by organisms.

bir. Arabic for water well.

birkeh. Arabic for water tank or cistern.

braided channel. A multiple river channel with numerous branches around intervening bars or islands of sand or gravel. Braided channels are less sinuous, are wider, and exhibit steeper long profiles than so-called single-thread channels.

calcic xerosol. One of the characteristic soils of the Fertile Crescent, occurring where rainfall is between 300 and 500 mm per annum. Usually developed on calcareous sedimentary rocks. Reddish brown in color, usually with a horizon enriched in calcium carbonate soft concretions, locally becoming a hardened calcrete-type horizon. These are fertile soils normally suitable for wheat and legumes; barley predominates near the margins of rain-fed cultivation.

calcrete. A deposit of calcium carbonate that can include powdery to nodular states but frequently is cemented into a hard mass as a result of the redeposition of calcium carbonate from solution. Also known as caliche.

carrying capacity. The number of humans or animals that can be supported in a specific ecological or economic situation.

central places. Administrative or economic centers with dependent hinterlands.

centuriation. A regular grid of square plots of land subdivided according to Roman systems of land measurement and laid out as a result of Roman policies of land allotment. Usually assigned to colonists or veterans.

chiefdom. A ranked society ruled by a chief; usually a small-scale polity with a permanent ritual and ceremonial center.

collective burial. Grave in which large numbers of inhumations or parts of bodies have been collected within one burial chamber.

colluvial. Slope deposits accumulated by gravity flow, overland flow, and soil wash.

complex adaptive system. Systems consisting of interacting entities or agents that adopt rules of behavior also based upon those of other agents. Agents' behaviors can adapt to those of other agents as experience accumulates so that the systems behavior can attain an emergent or self-organized state (see also *self-organization*).

core (ocean). Cores drilled through sediments underlying the seabed. Microfossils and geochemical data derived from the cored sediments provide a proxy record of long-term climate change.

CORONA. Satellite photographs of the CORONA program taken by U.S. missions for intelligence purposes during the late 1960s and early 1970s.

crevasse splay. The breach of a river levee by a minor channel (crevasse channel) that results in the accumulation of a fan- or tongue-shaped accumulation on the flood plain.

C-transforms. Term coined by Michael Schiffer to describe formation processes of the archaeological record attributable to cultural processes.

cultural-historical approach. Archaeological investigation that emphasizes description and empirical testing rather than explanation and process.

dar. Tribal territory also known as *dira*.

deflation. The removal of sediments by strong winds, frequently associated with arid environments.

demography. The study of the structure and dynamics of populations.

dendrochronology. Dating by counting the annual growth rings in trees and old timbers.

desert varnish. A black or brown coating of iron, manganese, and clay that coats the surface of building stones, surface stones of a desert pavement, or bedrock surfaces and that appears to darken with age.

diachronic. Through time.

early state module. Political unit that forms a building block in state formation and considered to be of roughly similar size wherever it occurs.

ecological determinism. A form of explanation in which it is assumed that changes in the environment have determined changes in human society.

endogenous. Derived from within.

ENSO (El-Niño–Southern Oscillation). An oscillation of weather patterns that relates to the strength of the atmospheric pressure gradient across the South Pacific.

eustatic. Changes of sea level that occur worldwide, primarily as a result of the melting or growth of ice sheets, which provides a rise and fall, respectively, of sea level.

exogenous. Transformations originating from outside the system.

falaj. A system for distributing water; in Oman these are usually underground channels equivalent to the *qanat*. Note that the term can also refer to open channels.

field scatter. Extensive scatters of artifacts, usually small potsherds, scattered across the ground surface, frequently on the surface of fields. Field scatters are usually found off site, and are often associated with the spreading of organic waste on the land as fertilizer in antiquity.

flotation. The technique of separating carbonized plant materials from their soil matrix by immersion in water.

garrigue. Plant communities of the Mediterranean area, usually characterized by undershrubs or "dwarf shrubs."

geoarchaeology. The study of sediments and soils in association with archaeological sites or features; or archaeological research using the methods and concepts of earth sciences.

geomorphology. The study of the formation of landforms and their associated sedimentary formations.

geo-referencing. Refers to the location of a thematic layer of a GIS in space as defined by a coordinate system.

ghayl. Arabic term for perennial flow in a dry streambed (wadi).

GIS (Geographic Information System). A computerized system for integrating, viewing, and analyzing spatial data related to the surface of the earth.

gley. A soil characterized by blue, gray, or olive colors, usually resulting from chemical reduction (and localized oxidation) of iron compounds in the soil matrix under anaerobic and waterlogged conditions.

gossan. A mining term referring to iron oxides created by weathering in association with a sulfide mineral deposit. Often associated with ancient mines.

GPS (Geographic Positioning System). A small hand-held device for fixing geographical locations.

hadhar. Arabic term (*hādāar*) referring to settled peoples.

hajj. The Muslim pilgrimage to Mecca.

hectare (ha). 100 × 100 m or 2.471 acres.

hema, hima. Areas of the semiarid or arid steppe in which grazing, wood gathering, and other activities are restricted. Grazing can only take place during part of the year.

hollow way. See *linear hollow.*

Holocene. The postglacial period of the geological record beginning some 10,000 radiocarbon years ago, or 11,500 years cal. B.P.

homeostatic. The process by which negative feedback occurs so that the system remains in its equilibrium state.

homer. A measure of ancient capacity used in the Near East. Ultimately, a natural unit that defines approximately the weight that a donkey can carry, namely, some 90 kg. This works out at approximately 150 liters of barley or 120 liters of wheat.

horizon (of soil). Horizontal features of a soil profile defined either by weathering or by the accumulation (usually within the soil matrix) of humus, iron, clay, calcium carbonate, and so on. Soil horizons are not to be confused with sedimentary deposits or layers.

hunter-gatherers. A term for small-scale mobile or semisedentary societies whose subsistence needs mainly derive from hunting wild game and gathering plant products (R and B 488).

ice cores. Borings through the Arctic and Antarctic ice caps. Analysis of geochemical indicators contained within layers of ice, or voids within the ice, provides a sensitive record of long-term climate change.

ideational. According to the *Oxford English Dictionary*, either the formation of ideas or mental images of things not present to the senses or culture based on spiritual values or ideas. In terms of landscapes, ideational can relate to landscapes of the mind or mental landscapes.

IKONOS. Commercially available satellite imagery first launched in 1999 with a resolution of 1 m.

inorganic. Derived from molecules based primarily on elements other than carbon.

intensification. The derivation of increased production from the land by the investment of increased labor and other inputs.

isostatic. Changes in the earth's crust in which compression and unloading, usually by large masses of ice, result in land masses becoming depressed or elevated. Specifically, this results in local sea-level changes in contrast to more region-wide sea-level changes characteristic of eustatic changes.

isotope. Forms of an element whose nuclei contain the same number of protons but different numbers of neutrons.

jabal/jebel. Arabic: mountain.

khirbeh. Low mound or series of mounds of cultural debris. Arabic for ruin.

kranzhügel. German term for a class of tells surrounded by a circular mound representing a defensive wall within which occurs a flat, usually circular, city mound. Originally recorded by Max von-Oppenheim in the steppe regions of northern Syria between the Balikh and Khabur river valleys.

kurkar. Low ridges made of a cemented calcareous sandstones, usually formed parallel to the coast of Israel.

LANDSAT. Satellite images taken from the earth resource satellites of NASA. First launched in 1972 (Landsat 1) these multispectral images were taken from satellites orbiting the globe along north–south orbits at a nominal altitude of 900 km.

Late-glacial maximum. A brief phase of the last glacial period between about 17,000 and 20,000 years before present, representing the phase of minimum global temperature.

levee. Low ridge on top of which a river flows. Mainly consists of the sands and silts deposited on the flood plain immediately adjacent to the channel and on the neighboring flood plain. Levee can also refer to sediments cleaned out of and dumped beside a natural or artificial channel.

limes. A term that refers to the administered border region of the Roman empire, sometimes including military roads and other military installations.

lineage. Group claiming descent from a common ancestor.

linear hollow. Usually a shallow, fairly straight valley that runs between sites or radiates from sites and is frequently discordant to the natural drainage. Often difficult to discern on the ground, hollow ways (or linear hollows) are most evident on air photographs or high-resolution satellite images, where they can also be evident in the form of soil or vegetation marks.

lipid. A large class of water-insoluble organic substances found in living cells, primarily including fats, oils, and waxes.

locational analysis. Usually refers to the quantitative analysis of the distribution of settlements and land-use zones, frequently employing principles of economic geography.

loess. Fine-grained sediments mainly comprising wind-blown silt and very fine sand.

magnetic susceptibility. The propensity of a sediment to become magnetized, usually determined by the abundance of ferro-magnetic minerals.

maquis. Mediterranean vegetation dominated by shrubs or small trees (often less than 5 m in height); also referred to as *macchia.*

matrix. Relatively fine-grained mass of the soil within which the coarser particles are embedded.

micromorphology. The microscopic study of thin sections or slices made through soils hardened by the impregnation of a resinlike material.

midden. The accumulation of domestic waste, ash, and other materials, often around the edge of a settlement or individual houses. When dominated by marine shells, these are termed shell middens.

model. An idealized representation of reality.

mollisol. Soils with a thick, dark, base-rich, humus-rich horizon (mollic horizon). The mollic horizon develops close to the surface, but it can also form a distinctive subsoil horizon of a palaeosol.

multispectral (MSS). Refers to satellite sensors that can receive electromagnetic radiation from the earth in the form of discrete narrow wavebands. The wide range of spectral radiation received by multispectral sensors enables various types of vegetation, soil moisture, soil classes, and geological features to be recognized. It is also possible to distinguish between ashy archaeological materials and the surrounding natural soils.

negative feedback. A process that acts to dampen the potentially disruptive effects of external inputs; acts as a stabilizing mechanism in a complex system.

North Atlantic Oscillation. An index of the periodic fluctuation of pressure conditions in the North Atlantic, represented by the difference between sea-level pressure in the Azores and Iceland. High values of the NAO are associated with stronger mid-latitude westerly circulation over Europe.

N-transforms. Term coined by Michael Schiffer to describe formation processes of the archaeological record attributable to natural or noncultural processes.

obsidian. Natural glass formed from cooled lava.

off-site survey. A form of archaeological survey that recognizes the importance of recording features and artifact scatters that occur beyond the limits of conventional archaeological sites (see also *field scatters*).

ophiolite. A dark ultra basic igneous rock often emplaced into the earth's crust along mid-oceanic ridges.

optical luminescence dating. A technique of dating sediments in which trapped electrons within the minerals are activated to emit light in proportion to their age. The range of dates obtainable is from between a few years and roughly one million years.

organic. Derived from molecules based primarily on the element carbon.

oxidation. An increase in the formal charge of an atom by removal of electrons. In soils, this manifests itself as reddened or orange forms of iron.

palaeoethnobotany. The study of plant remains (usually in the form of carbonized seeds or charcoal) from archaeological contexts.

palaeosol. An ancient soil that is no longer actively forming today. In some cases, these form a sequence of buried soil horizons; in other circumstances, a palaeosol can be exposed at the present ground surface but exhibits evidence that it includes relict features inherited from earlier phases.

palimpsest. Literally, a parchment that has traces of several phases of writing on it. When applied to landscapes, palimpsest refers to many phases of a landscape of greater or lesser visibility that show evidence for the history of that landscape.

palynology. The analysis of fossil pollen to reconstruct the history of vegetation.

parna. An Australian term referring to silt-clay aggregates that form aeolian dunes. In the Middle East these particles are frequently derived from the erosion of preexisting soils, marshes, lakes, or clay beds.

path dependence. The tendency of an earlier state of a system to influence subsequent stages of the development of the system.

penstock. A built feature along a water channel for regulating flow. For water mills, this specifically refers to a large masonry structure that raises the channel to an appropriate elevation before the water is led into a vertical pipe to power the mill.

phenomenology. According to *Webster's Dictionary*, the study of the development of human consciousness and self-awareness. In terms of the landscape, the term refers to how people experience and move about the social landscape.

phosphate. An organic compound of phosphoric acid.

phytolith. Microscopic particles of silica (SiO_2) derived from the cells of plants. These remain in the soil and can provide information on the general types of vegetation present plus information on past land-use practices.

pilgrim routes. Regularly used routes by pilgrims to reach major religious centers.

playa. The floor of an enclosed basin usually in an arid region. Playa floors are flat, are usually of clay, and can contain salt flats or temporary lakes.

Pleistocene. The geological period that covers the glacial and interglacial cycles from around 2 million years ago until the beginning of the Holocene period some 11,500 years ago.

pluvial. Period of increased wetness, often reflected in higher lake levels and resulting from a combination of increased precipitation and decreased evaporation.

point bars. Sedimentary deposit on the inside of a meander bend where flow velocity is usually lower than in the main channel.

polity. Political unit or group, usually of large scale.

positive feedback. In systems theory, refers to a state of a system in which changing output of the system results in further growth of the system.

post-processual. A range of schools of archaeological thought that developed as a reaction to the functionalist-processual school. As with post-modernist thought, this school emphasizes individual action, subjectivity, diversity, and relativism.

processual. In contrast to post-processualism, this school emphasizes the dynamic relationship between social and economic aspects of culture and the environment as the basis for understanding the process of culture change.

qanat. Underground channel that collects water from the groundwater table, often within an alluvial fan, and leads it towards the ground surface, where it supplies water to a settlement and its irrigated fields.

Quaternary. The period of geological time corresponding to roughly the last 2 million years and comprising the Pleistocene and Holocene.

radiocarbon dating. A technique of radiometric dating for estimating the age of organic materials based on the incorporation and decay of the radioactive isotope ^{14}C within organic materials. Effective for approximately the last 40,000 years.

reduction. In soils, this relates to a deficit of oxygen usually during waterlogged conditions.

regression. The withdrawal of water from the land mass, usually associated with a lowering of sea level.

remote sensing. A range of techniques that provide a view of the earth's surface or its immediate subsoil levels using either satellites or aircraft or by means of geophysical instrumentation, the last being used at ground level to "see beneath the soil."

rendzina. Shallow soils, usually fairly rich in organic matter developed on limestones and other calcareous parent materials.

roasting. Chemical change resulting from an ore being heated in air to convert a sulphide ore to an oxide.

rock varnish. See *desert varnish.*

sabkha. Salt flat (Arabic).

sayl. Ephemeral flow or flood in a wadi bed.

sedd or *sadd.* Dam (Arabic).

sedentism. Refers to communities that remain in one place for the entire year.

self-organization. A process in which pattern at the global level of a system emerges solely from numerous interactions among the lower-level components of the system.

settlement pattern. The distribution of occupation sites across the landscape, often referred to as nucleated (where most people live within a single center) and dispersed (where settlement is primarily within numerous small settlements).

shaikh. Head of a tribe (Arabic).

shawawi. In Oman, nomads of the mountain fringes; elsewhere, often mobile groups of sheep and goat herders.

shrine. A place in which devotion is paid to a religious deity, or more generally, a place that is hallowed by its associations.

site. Usually a concentration of artifacts or buildings in the landscape; sometimes in the Near East these are mounded to form tells. In some cases, individual sites are difficult to define, and instead, sites merge into off-site artifact scatters to form part of the continuous landscape.

site-catchment analysis. The analysis of the subsistence economy through the analysis of the exploitation territory of an individual site. The site catchment is that region from which most of the materials used within a settlement were derived; often synonymous with the agricultural territory of a site.

slag. Glassy waste product of silicates, iron oxides, and other materials derived from the smelting of ores.

soil resistivity. The measurement of changes in soil resistance or its converse electrical conductivity to detect subsurface features.

SPOT (System Pour l'Observation de la Terre). Satellite images developed by the French government at a ground resolution of 10 and 20 m.

staple finance. Mobilization and redistribution of part of subsistence food production to support parts of population such as craft specialists.

steatite. Soapstone or soft stone for carving stone bowls or other artifacts.

subsistence economy. The basic production of an agricultural community required to support human habitation and without the mobilization of a significant marketable surplus.

taphonomy. The study of processes that have resulted in the dispersal or mixing of organic materials such as bone, shell, and plant remains after their initial deposition. Here the term landscape taphonomy is enlarged to encompass processes that have resulted in the reworking and attrition of landscape features such as settlement sites, field walls, and canals.

TAVO (Tübinger Atlas des Vorderen Orients). A major series of maps, accompanying texts and monographs describing the distribution of archaeological sites, cultural resources, and natural/ecological resources in the Near East and adjacent areas.

tectonic movements. Displacement of the earth's surface along fault lines, often associated with the movement of terrestrial plates.

tell. Vertical accretions of settlement debris in the form of ash middens, mudbrick buildings, and other cultural debris to form mounds that vary in size from less than one hectare to one hundred hectares or more.

terra rossa. A red Mediterranean soil comprising A and B horizons of reddish iron-enriched clay over limestone. According to the classification UNESCO soil map of the world, this soil group is known as chromic luvisols.

terrace (field). A field bench normally formed on a hill slope as a result of the construction of a wall or similar barrier usually parallel to the contours. Soil accumulates upslope, either as a result of natural slope wash or by deliberate infilling, to form an over-deepened soil profile ideal for cultivation.

terrace (river). A bench next to a river or stream that represents the deposits of earlier stages of the river. The terrace then becomes raised relative to the riverbed as a result of the incision of the channel into its bed.

Thiessen polygons. A method for estimating site territories according to the principle that the mutual boundary between any two adjacent and contemporaneous settlements can be represented by a line drawn orthogonally from the halfway point between the two sites. The boundaries represented by these orthogonal lines meet to form polygons known as tesselations (see fig. 7.4).

trace-element analysis. The use of chemical analytical techniques such as neutron activation analysis or X-ray fluorescence spectrometry to determine the trace-element signature of sediments or archaeological materials.

transgression. The spread or encroachment of the sea over a previously dry area of land, usually associated with a rise in sea level.

transhumance. The movement of mobile groups of people, usually in response to the changing seasons. In the Near East, transhumance frequently entails people residing with their flocks during the summer in the uplands and moving to the plains during the winters.

varves. Annually layered lake or marine deposits usually evident as thin light and dark couplets of sediment. Because these accumulate annually, they can be counted to provide a varve chronology.

viewshed. GIS-based analysis using topographic data to visualize the area of land that is visible from any given point on the landscape. This can be used, for example, to reconstruct the perceived universe of an ancient community.

viticulture. The cultivation of grapes specifically for the production of wine.

wadi. Valley or drainage channel found in dry regions of the Middle East.

wakil. Arabic term for an Islamic agent.

wealth finance. The use of some form of currency or metals to finance state activity such as production by craft specialists.

world-systems model. Theory of economic relationships in which areas larger than individual polities are linked and integrated by various levels of exchange and in which an exploited periphery becomes dependent on an exploiting core.

xerophytic. Drought-tolerant plants.

Younger Dryas. A cool, usually dry phase of the earth's climate between 13,000 and 11,500 cal. B.P.

Younger fill. A term coined by Claudio Vita-Finzi to describe sedimentary deposits of the last two thousand years accumulated in valleys around the Mediterranean Sea.

Bibliography

Abdulfattah, Kamal. 1981. *Mountain Farmer and Fellah in 'Asir, South-west Saudi Arabia: The Conditions of Agriculture in a Traditional Society.* Erlangen: Erlanger Geographische Arbeiten, Sonderband 12.

Abu Dayyah, Abdel Sami. 2001. "Selected Roman stone quarries in central Jordan: A cultural resource." *Studies in the History and Archaeology of Jordan* 7: 521–530.

Adams, Richard E. W., Walter Brown Jr., and T. Patrick Culbert. 1981. "Radar mapping, archaeology and ancient Maya land use." *Science* 213: 1557–1563.

Adams, Robert, McC. 1962. "Agriculture and urban life in early southwestern Iran." *Science* 136: 109–122.

———. 1965. *Land behind Baghdad.* Chicago: University of Chicago.

———. 1972. "Settlement and irrigation patterns in ancient Akkad." Pp. 182–208 in *The City and Area of Kish,* ed. McG. Gibson. Miami: Field Research Projects.

———. 1974. "Historic patterns of Mesopotamian irrigation agriculture." Pp. 1–6 in *Irrigation's Impact on Society,* ed. Theodore E. Downing and McGuire Gibson. Tucson: University of Arizona.

———. 1981. *Heartland of Cities.* Chicago: University of Chicago.

———. 1982. "Property rights and functional tenure in Mesopotamian rural communities." Pp. 1–14 in *Societies and Languages of the Ancient Near East. Studies in Honour of I.M. Diakonoff,* ed. M. A. Dandamayev, I. Gershevitch, H. Klengel, G. Komoróczy, M. T. Larsen, and J. N. Postgate. Warminster, UK: Aris and Phillips.

———. 2001. "Steps toward regional understanding of the Mesopotamian plain." Paper presented at the meetings of the American Oriental Society, Toronto, April 2001.

———. 2001. "Complexity in Archaic states." *Journal of Anthropological Archaeology* 20: 345–360.

Adams, Robert, McC., and Hans Nissen. 1972. *The Uruk Countryside.* Chicago: University of Chicago.

Adams, Robert McC., P. J. Parr, M. Ibrahim, and A. S. al-Mughannum. 1977. "The preliminary report on the first phase of the comprehensive archaeological survey program (eastern and northern provinces)." *Atlal* 1: 21–40.

Aharoni, Y. 1962. *The Land of the Bible: A Historical Geography.* Philadelphia: Westminster.

Åhlström, G. 1978. "Wine presses and cup-marks of the Jenin-Megiddo Survey." *Bulletin of the American School of Oriental Research* 231: 19–49.

Aitken, Martin J. 1997. "Luminescence dating." Pp. 183–216 in *Chronometric and Allied Dating in Archaeology,* ed. R. E. Taylor and M. J. Aitken. New York: Plenum.

Akkermans, Peter M. M. G. 1993. *Villages in the Steppe.* Ann Arbor: International Monographs in Prehistory.

Akkermans, Peter M. M. G., J. Limpens, and R. H. Spoor. 1993. "On the frontier of Assyria: Excavations at Tell Sabi Abyad 1991." *Akkadica* 84–85: 1–52.

Aksu, A. E., R. N. Hiscott, P. J. Mudie, A. Rochon, M. A. Kaminski, T. Abrajano, and D. Yaşar. 2002. "Persistent Holocene outflow from the Black Sea to the Eastern Mediterranean contradicts Noah's flood hypothesis." *GSA Today* May 2002: 4–10.

al-Asfour, Taiba. 1978. "The Marine Terraces of the Bay of Kuwait." Pp. 245–254 in Brice.

Alcock, Susan E. 1993. *Graecia Capta: The Landscapes of Roman Greece.*

———. 1994. "Breaking up the Hellenistic world: Survey and society." Pp. 171–190 in *Classical Greece: Ancient Histories and Modern Archaeologies,* ed. Ian Morris. Cambridge: Cambridge University.

Alcock, Susan E., John F. Cherry, and Jack L. Davis. 1994. "Intensive survey, agricultural practice and the classical landscape of Greece." Pp. 137–170 in *Classical Greece: Ancient Histories and Modern Archaeologies,* ed. Ian Morris. Cambridge: Cambridge University.

Algaze, Guillermo. 1989. "A new frontier: First results of the Tigris-Euphrates Archaeological Reconnaissance Project, 1988." *Journal of Near Eastern Studies* 48: 241–281.

———. 1999. "Trends in the archaeological development of the Upper Euphrates basin of southeastern Anatolia during the Late Chalcolithic and Early Bronze Ages." Pp. 535–572 in *Archaeology of the Upper Syrian Euphrates: The Tishrin Dam Area,* ed. G. del Olmo Lete and J.-L. Montero Fenollós. Barcelona: Editorial Ausa, Aula Orientalis Supplement 15.

———. 2001a. "Initial social complexity in southwestern Asia: The Mesopotamian advantage." *Current Anthropology* 42: 199–233.

——— (ed.). 2001b. "Research at Titris Höyük in southeastern Turkey: The 1999 season." *Anatolica* 24: 23–106.

Algaze, Guillermo, R. Breuninger, C. Lightfoot, and M. Rosenberg. 1991. "The Tigris-Euphrates Archaeological Reconnaissance Project: A preliminary report of the 1989–1990 seasons." *Anatolica* 17: 175–240.

Algaze, Guillermo, A. Misir, and T. J. Wilkinson. 1992. "Şanli Urfa Museum/University of California Excavations and Surveys at Titrish Hoyuk, 1991: A preliminary report." *Anatolica* 18: 33–60.

Algaze, Guillermo, R. Breuninger, and J. Knutstad. 1994. "The Tigris-Euphrates Archaeological Reconnaissance Project: Final Report of the Birecik and Carchemish Dam survey areas." *Anatolica* 20: 1–96.

Alizadeh, Abbas. 1988. "Mobile Pastoralism and the Development of Complex

Societies in Highland Iran." Ph.D. dissertation, Department of Near Eastern Languages and Civilizations, University of Chicago.

Allen, John R. L. 1965. "A review of the origin and characteristics of recent alluvial sediments." *Sedimentology* 5: 89–101.

Al-Rashid, Sa'ad. 1979. "Ancient water tanks on the Hajj route from Iraq to Mecca and their parallels in other countries." *Atlal* 3: 55–62.

———. 1980. *Darb Zubayda: The Pilgrim Route from Kufa to Mecca*. Riyadh: Riyadh University Libraries.

———. 1986. *al-Rabadah: A Portrait of Early Islamic Civilization in Saudi Arabia*. Riyadh, Saudi Arabia: King Sa'ud University, and London: Longman.

Al-Rawi, G. J., and C. Sys. 1967. "A comparative study between Euphrates and Tigris sediments in the Mesopotamian flood plain." *Pedologie* 17: 187–209.

Alsharhan, A. S., K. W. Glennie, G. L. Whittle, and C. G. St. C. Kendall (eds.). 1998. *Quaternary Deserts and Climatic Change*. Rotterdam: Balkema/Brookfield.

Al-Tikriti, W. Y. 2002. "The origins of the *falaj*: Further evidence from the United Arab Emirates." Pp. 339–355 in *Of Pots and Plans: Papers on the Archaeology and History of Mesopotamia and Syria Presented to David Oates in Honour of His 75th Birthday*, ed. Al-Gailani-Werr, J. Curtis, H. Martin, A. McMahon, J. Oates, and J. Reade. London: Nabu.

Anati, E. 1954. "Ancient rock drawings in the Negev." *Bulletin of the Israel Exploration Society* 18: 245–254.

———. 1955. "Rock engravings in the central Negev." *Archaeology* 8: 31–42.

———. 1968. *Rock Art in Central Arabia*. Vol. 1: *The "Oval-Headed" People of Arabia*. Louvain: Bibliothèque du Muséon.

Anderson, J. D. 1998. "The impact of Rome on the periphery: The case of Palestina-Roman period (63 B.C.E-324 CE). Pp. 446–468 in Levy.

Anderson, P., and J. Chabot. 2001. "Functional analysis of glossed blades from northern Mesopotamia in the Early Bronze Age." Pp. 257–276 in *Journée d'étude du Groupe de recherches en archéométrie du Celat, 1997 and 1999*, ed. Michel Fortin. Quebec: CELAT.

Anschuetz, Kurt F., R. H. Wilshusen, and C. L. Scheick. 2001. "An archaeology of landscapes: Perspectives and directions." *Journal of Archaeological Research* 9 (2): 157–211.

Aqrawi, A. A. M. 1995. "Correction of Holocene sedimentation rates for mechanical compaction: The Tigris-Euphrates delta, lower Mesopotamia." *Marine and Petroleum Geology* 12 (4): 409–416.

———. 2001. "Stratigraphic signatures of climatic change during the Holocene evolution of the Tigris-Euphrates delta, lower Mesopotamia." *Global and Planetary Change* 28: 267–283.

Archi, Alberto. 1990. "The city of Ebla and the organization of the rural territory." Pp. 15–19 in *The Town as Regional Economic Centre in the Ancient Near East*, ed. Erik Aerts and Horst Klengel. Leuven: Leuven University.

Armstrong, James A., and Margaret C. Brandt. 1994. "Ancient dunes at Nippur." Pp. 255–263 in *Cinquante-deux relexions sur le Proche-Orient Ancien, offertes en hommage à Léon De Meyer*, ed. Hermann Gasche, Michel Tanret, C. Janssen, and A. Degraeve. Leuven: Peeters.

Ashmore, Wendy, and A. Bernard Knapp. 1999. *Archaeologies of landscape: Contemporary perspectives*. Oxford: Blackwell.

Aspaturian, Heidi. 1992. "The Road to Ubar." *Caltech News* 26 (2): 1–7.

Aston, Michael. 1985. *Interpreting the Landscape: Landscape Archaeology and Local History*. London: Routledge.

Aswad, Barbara. 1971. *Property Control and Social Strategies in Settlers in a Middle Eastern Plain*. Ann Arbor: Publications of the Museum of Anthropology.

Avetisyan, Pavel, Ruben Badalyan, and Adam T. Smith. 2000. "Preliminary report on the 1998 archaeological investigations of Project ArAGATS in the Tsakahovit Plain, Armenia." *Studi Micenei ed Egeo-Anatolici* 42 (1): 19–59.

Avitsur, S. 1960. "On the history of the exploitation of water power in Eretz-Israel." *Israel Exploration Journal* 10: 37–45.

Avner, Uzi. 1984. "Ancient cult sites in the Negev and Sinai deserts." *Tel Aviv* 11: 115–131.

———. 1998. "Settlement agriculture and palaeoclimate in 'Uvda valley,

southern Negev Desert, sixth–third millennia B.C." Pp. 147–202 in Issar and Brown.

Avni, Gideon. 1996. *Nomads, Farmers and Town Dwellers: Pastoral-sedentist Interaction in the Negev Highlands, Sixth–Eighth Centuries C.E.* Jerusalem: Israel Antiquities Authority.

Badaljan, R., P. L. Kohl, D. Stronach, and A. V. Tonikjan. 1994. "Preliminary report on the 1993 excavations at Horom, Armenia." *Iran* 32: 1–29.

Bagg, Ariel M. 2000. *Assyrische Wasserbauten*. Mainz: Verlag Philipp von Zabern (Baghdader Forschungen 24).

Bailey, Donald M. 1999. "Sabakh, sherds and survey." *Journal of Egyptian Archaeology* 85: 211–218.

Baird, Douglas. 2000. "Konya Plain Survey." *Anatolian Archaeology* 6: 15.

Ball, Warwick. 2000. *Rome in the East: The Transformation of an Empire*. London: Routledge.

Banning, Edward B. 1986. "Peasants, pastoralists and *Pax Romana*: Mutualism in the southern highlands of Jordan." *Bulletin of the American Schools for Oriental Research* 261: 25–50.

———. 1996. "Highlands and lowlands: Problems and survey frameworks for rural archaeology in the Near East." *Bulletin of the American Schools for Oriental Research* 301: 25–45.

———. 2002. *Archaeological Survey*. Dordrecht: Kluwer Academic.

Barbanes, Eleanor. 1999. "Heartland and Province: Urban and Rural Settlement in the Neo-Assyrian Empire." Ph.D. dissertation, Department of Near Eastern Studies, University of California, Berkeley.

Barceló, Miquel, Helena Kirchner, and Josep Torró. 2000. "Going around Zafar (Yemen), the Banū Ru 'ayn field survey: Hydraulic archaeology and peasant work." *Proceedings of the Seminar for Arabian Studies* 30: 27–39.

Bard, K. A., M. Coltorti, M. C. DiBlasi, F. Dramis, and R. Fattovich. 2000. "The environmental history of Tigray (northern Ethiopia) in the middle and late Holocene: A preliminary outline." *African Archaeology Review* 17: 65–86.

Barker, Graeme. 1996. *Farming the Desert: The UNESCO Libyan Valleys Archaeological Survey*. Tripoli and London: UNESCO/Society of Libyan Studies.

———. 1996. "Regional archaeological projects: Trends and traditions in

Mediterranean archaeology." *Archaeological Dialogues* 2: 160–175.

———. 1997. "Writing landscape archaeology and history." *Topoi* (Orient-Occident) 7/1: 267–281.

———. 2002. "A tale of two deserts: Contrasting desertification histories on Rome's desert frontiers." *World Archaeology* 33 (3): 488–507.

Barker, Graeme W., O. H. Creighton, David D. Gilbertson, C. O. Hunt, D. J. Mattingly, S. J. McLaren, and D. C. Thomas. 1997. "The Wadi Faynan Project, Southern Jordan: A preliminary report on geomorphology and landscape archaeology." *Levant* 29: 19–40.

Barker Graeme W., R. Adams, O. H. Creighton, D. D. Gilbertson, C. O. Hunt, D. J. Mattingly, S. J. McLaren, and D. C. Thomas. 1998. "Environment and land use in Wadi Faynan, southern Jordan (1997)." *Levant* 30: 5–26.

Barker, Graeme W., R. Adams, O. H. Creighton, D. Crook, D. D. Gilbertson, J. P. Gratton, C. O. Hunt, D. J. Mattingly, S. J. McLaren, H. A. Mohammed, P. Newson, C. Palmer, F. B. Pyatt, T. E. G. Reynolds, and R. Tomber. 1999. "Environment and land use in the Wadi Faynan, southern Jordan: The third season of geoarchaeology and landscape archaeology (1998)." *Levant* 31: 255–292.

Barker, Graeme W., R. Adams, O. H. Creighton, P. Daly, D. D. Gilbertson, J. P. Gratton, C. O. Hunt, D. J. Mattingly, S. J. McLaren, P. Newson, C. Palmer, F. B. Pyatt, T. E. G. Reynolds, H. Smith, R. Tomber, and A. J. Truscott. 2000. "Archaeology and desertification in the Wadi Faynan: The fourth (1999) season of the Wadi Faynan landscape survey." *Levant* 32: 27–52.

Barker, Graeme, and David Mattingly (eds.) 2000. *The Archaeology of the Mediterranean Landscape* (5 volumes). Oxford: Oxbow.

Bar-Matthews, M., A. Ayalon, and A. Kaufman. 1997. "Late Quaternary paleoclimate in the Eastern Mediterranean region from stable isotope analysis of speleothems at Soreq Cave, Israel." *Quaternary Research* 47: 155–168.

Bar-Matthews, M., A. Ayalon, and A. Kaufman. 1998. "Middle to late Holocene (6,500 yr. period) paleoclimate in the eastern Mediterranean region from stable isotopic composition of speleothems from Soreq Cave, Israel." Pp. 203–214 in Issar and Brown.

Bar-Matthews, M., A. Ayalon, A. Kaufmann, and G. J. Wasserburg. 1999. "The eastern Mediterranean paleoclimate as a reflection of regional events: Soreq Cave, Israel." *Earth and Planetary Science Letters* 166: 85–95.

Barth, Hans Jörg. 1999. "Desertification in the Eastern Province of Saudi Arabia." *Journal of Arid Environments* 43: 399–410.

———. 2001. "Understanding of coastal fluctuations at the Arabian Gulf leading to the 'lost city' of Gerrha'?" *Palaeoecology of Africa and the Surrounding Islands* 27: 291–303.

Bartl, Karin. 1996. "Balih Valley Survey. Settlements of the Late Roman/early Byzantine and Islamic period." Pp. 333–348 in *Continuity and Change in Northern Mesopotamia from the Hellenistic to the Early Islamic Period*, ed. Karin Bartl and Stephan Hauser. Berlin: Berliner Beitrage zum Vorderen Orient Band 17.

Baruch, Uri. 1986. "The late Holocene vegetational history of Lake Kinneret (Sea of Galilee), Israel." *Paléorient* 12 (2): 37–48.

———. 1990. "Palynological evidence of human impact on the vegetation as recorded in Late Holocene lake sediments in Israel." Pp. 283–293 in Bottema et al.

Baruch, Uri, and Sytze Bottema. 1999. "A new pollen diagram from Lake Hula: Vegetational, climatic and anthropogenic implications." Pp. 75–86 in *Ancient Lakes: Their Cultural and Biological Diversity*, ed. H. Kawanabe, G. W. Coulter, and Anna C. Roosevelt. Belgium: Kenobi.

Bar-Yosef, Ofer, and A. Khazanov (eds.). 1992. *Pastoralism in the Levant: Archaeological Materials in Anthropological Perspective*. Madison: Prehistory Press.

Bar-Yosef, Ofer, and Renee S. Kra. 1994. *Late Quaternary Chronology and Paleoclimates of the Eastern Mediterranean*. Tucson, AZ: Radiocarbon.

Bawden, Garth, and Richard Martin Reycraft (eds.). 2000. *Environmental Disaster and the Archaeology of Human Response*. Albuquerque, NM: Maxwell Museum of Anthropology, University of New Mexico.

Beaumont, Peter. 1989. "The qanat: A means of water provision from groundwater sources." Pp. 13–31 in Beaumont et al.

Beaumont, Peter, M. Bonine, and Keith McLachlan. 1989. *Qanat, Kariz and Khattara: Traditional Water Systems in the Middle East and North Africa*. Wisbech, Cambridgeshire: MENAS.

Beaumont, Peter, Gerald H. Blake, and J. Malcolm Wagstaff. 1976. *The Middle East: A Geographical Study*. London: John Wiley.

Beazeley, G. A. 1919. "Air photography in archaeology." *Geographical Journal* 53: 330–335.

Becker, H., and J. G. Jansen. 1994. "Magnetische Prospektion 1993 der Unterstadt von Troia und Ilion." *Studia Troica* 4: 105–114.

Bell, Martin, and M. J. C. Walker. 1992. *Late Quaternary Environmental Change: Physical and Human Perspectives*. New York: Longmans/John Wiley.

Belli, Oktay. 1994. "Urartian dams and artificial lakes recently discovered in eastern Anatolia." *Tel Aviv* 21: 77–116.

———. 1999. "Dams, reservoirs and irrigation channels of the Van plain in the period of the Urartian kingdom." *Anatolian Studies* 49: 11–26.

Benoist, A., J. Cordoba, and M. Mouton 1997. "The Iron Age in al-Madam (Sharjah, UAE): Some notes on three seasons of work." *Proceedings of the Seminar for Arabian Studies* 27: 59–73.

Benvenisti, Meron. 2000. *Sacred Landscape: The Buried History of the Holy Land Since 1948*. Berkeley: University of California.

Bernbeck, Reinhard. 1993. *Steppe als Kulturlandschaft*. Berlin: Dietrich Reimer.

Bernbeck, Reinhard, Susan Pollock, and Cheryl Coursey. 1999. "The Halaf settlement at Kazane Höyük: Preliminary report on the 1996 and 1997 seasons." *Anatolica* 25: 109–147.

Betts, Alison V. G. 1982. "Prehistoric sites at Qa'a Mejalla, eastern Jordan." *Levant* 14: 1–34.

———. 1998. *The Harra and Hamad: Excavations, and Surveys in Eastern Jordan, Volume 1*. Sheffield: Academic.

Betts, Alison V. G., S. Eames, S. Hulka, M. Schroder, J. Rust, and B. McLaren. 1996. "Studies of Bronze Age occupation in the Wadi al-'Ajib, southern Hauran." *Levant* 28: 27–39.

Betts, Alison, and Svend W. Helms. 1989. "A water harvesting and storage system at Ibn el-Ghazzi in eastern Jordan: A preliminary report." *Levant* 21: 3–11.

Betts, Alison V. G., and V. N. Yagodin. 2000. "A new look at desert kites." Pp. 31–43 in Stager et al.

Bevan, Bruce. 1994. "Remote sensing of gardens and fields." Pp. 70–90 in Miller and Gleason.

Biagi, Paolo. 1994. "A radiocarbon chronology for the aceramic shell middens of coastal Oman." *Arabian Archaeology and Epigraphy* 5: 17–31.

Bilal, Bey, Bernt Schroder, and Ünsal Yalcin. 1997. "Human impact on the Holocene landscape evolution in the lower course of the Buyuk Menderes (W. Anatolia)." Paper presented at the Inqua meeting, Ankara, Turkey, 1st–4th April 1997.

Bintliff, John. 1992. "Erosion in the Mediterranean lands: A reconsideration of pattern, process and methodology." Pp. 125–131 in *Past and Present Soil Erosion: Archaeological and Geographical Perspectives*, ed. Martin Bell and John Boardman. Oxford: Oxbow.

———. 2000. "The concept of 'site' and 'off-site' archaeology in surface artefact survey." Pp. 200–215 in *Non-destructive Techniques Applied to Landscape Archaeology*, ed. Marinella Pasquinucci and Frédéric Trément. Oxford: Oxbow.

Bintliff, John, and Anthony Snodgrass. 1988. "Off-site pottery distributions: A regional and inter-regional perspective." *Current Anthropology* 29: 506–513.

Bintliff, John, B. Davies, C. Gaffney, A. Snodgrass, and A. Waters. 1992. "Trace Metal Accumulations in soils on and around ancient settlements in Greece." Pp. 9–24 in *Geoprospection in the Archaeological Landscape*, ed. Paul Spoerry. Oxford: Oxbow Monograph 18.

Black, Jeremy A., H. Gasche, A. Gautier, R. G. Killick, R. Nijs, and G. Stoops. 1987. "Habl as-Sahr 1983–1985: Nebuchadnezar II's cross-country wall north of Sippar." *Northern Akkad Project Reports* 1: 3–42. Ghent: University of Ghent.

Blanton, Richard E. 2000. *Roman and Byzantine Settlement Patterns of the Coast Lands of Western Rough Cilicia*. Oxford: Archaeopress, BAR (International Series) 879.

Bloch-Smith, E., and B. Alpert Nakhai.

1999. "A landscape comes to life: The Iron Age I." *Near Eastern Archaeology* 62 (2): 62–92, 101–127.

Bobek, H. 1968. "Vegetation." Pp. 280–293 in *The Land of Iran*. Cambridge History of Iran, vol. 1. Cambridge: Cambridge University.

Bonine, Michael E. 1989. "Field systems and morphology: Rectangularity on the Iranian plateau." Pp. 35–58 in Beaumont et al.

Borowski, Oded. 1987. *Agriculture in Iron Age Israel*. Winona Lake, IN: Eisenbrauns.

Boserup, Ester. 1965. *The Conditions of Agricultural Growth*. Aldine: Chicago.

———. 1981. *Population and Technology*. Oxford: Blackwell.

Bottema, Sytze. 1995. "Holocene vegetation of the Van area: palynological and chronological evidence from Söğütlü, Turkey." *Vegetation History and Archaeobotany* 4: 187–193.

Bottema, Sytze, G. Entjes-Nieborg, and W. Van Zeist (eds.). 1990. *Man's Role in the Shaping of the Eastern Mediterranean Environment*. Rotterdam: AA Balkema/Brookfield.

Bottema, Sytze, and Henk Woldring. 1990. "Anthropogenic indicators in the pollen record of the eastern Mediterranean." Pp. 231–264 in Bottema et al.

Boucharlat, Rémy. 2001. "Les galeries de captage dans la péninsule d'Oman au premier millénaire avant J.-C.: Questions sur leurs relations avec les galeries dur plateau iranien." Pp. 157–183 in *Irrigation et drainage dans l'antiquité, qanāts et canalisations souterraines en Iran, en Égypte et en Grèce*, ed. Pierre Briant. Paris: Collège de France-Thotm Éditions.

Bowen, Richard LeB. 1958. "Irrigation in ancient Qataban." Pp. 43–131 in *Archaeological Discoveries in South Arabia*, ed. Richard LeB. Bowen and Frank P. Albright. Baltimore: Johns Hopkins University.

Bradford, John. 1957 (1980). *Ancient Landscapes. Studies in Field Archaeology*. Westport, CT: Greenwood.

Bradley, Richard. 2000. *An Archaeology of Natural Places*. London: Routledge.

Braemer, Frank, J.-C. Echallier, and A. Teraqji. 1996. "Khirbet al-Umbashi (Syrie), rapport préliminaire sur les campagnes 1993 et 1994." *Syria* 43: 117–127.

Braemer, F., T. Steimer-Herbet, L. Bu-

chet, J. F. Saliége, and H. Guy. 2001. "Le Bronze ancien du Ramlat as-Sabatayn (Yémen): Deux nécropoles se la première moitié du IIIᵉ millénaire à la bordure du désert: Jebel Jidran et Jebel Ruwaiq." *Paléorient* 27 (1): 21–44.

Braidwood, Robert J. 1937. *Mounds in the Plain of Antioch*. Chicago: Oriental Institute.

Braidwood, Robert J., and Linda S. Braidwood. 1960. *Excavations in the Plain of Antioch I: The Earlier Assemblages, Phases A–J*. Chicago: Oriental Institute Publications 61.

Brandt, Margaret C. 1990. "Nippur: Building an environmental model." *Journal of Near Eastern Studies* 49 (1): 67–73.

Branting, Scott A. 1996. "The Alişar region survey 1993–1994: A preliminary report." *Anatolica* 22: 145–158.

Breasted, James Henry. 1933. *The Oriental Institute*. Chicago: University of Chicago.

Breton, Jean-Francois. 1998. *Arabia Felix from the Time of the Queen of Sheba: Eighth Century B.C. to First Century AD*. Notre Dame, IN: University of Notre Dame.

Breton, Jean-Francois, J.-C. Arramond, B. Cique-Delhuille, and P. Gentelle. 1998. *Une vallée aride du Yémen antique: Le wadi Bayhân*. Ministère des Affaires Etrangères. Éditions Recherche sur les Civilisations, Paris.

Bretschneider, Joachim. 1997. "Die Unterstadt (Feld J)." Pp. 209–243 in *Tell Beydar, Three Seasons of Excavations (1992–1994), A Preliminary Report*, ed. Marc Lebeau and Antoine Suleiman. Subartu 2. Brussels: Brepols.

Brice, William C. 1978. *The Environmental History of the Near and Middle East since the Last Ice Age*. London: Academic.

Brinkman, John A. 1984. "Settlement surveys and documentary evidence: Regional variation and secular trend in Mesopotamian demography." *Journal of Near Eastern Studies* 43 (3): 169–180.

Brinkmann, Robert. 1996. "Pedological characteristics of anthrosols in the al-Jadidah basin of Wadi al-Jubah, and native sediments in Wadi al-Ajwirah, Yemen Arab Republic." Pp. 45–211 in *The Wadi Jubah Archaeological Project*. Vol. 5: *Environmental Research in Support of Archaeological Investigations in the Yemen Arab Republic, 1982–1987*, ed. Maurice J. Grolier, Robert Brinkmann, and James A. Blakely. Washington, DC: American Foundation for the Study of Man.

Brizga, S. O., and B. L. Finlayson. 1990. "Channel avulsion and river metamorphosis: The case of the Thompson River, Victoria, Australia." *Earth Surface Processes and Landforms* 15: 391–404.

Broeker, William, and T. Liu. 2001. "Rock varnish: Recorder of desert wetness?" *GSA Today* August 2001: 4–10. Boulder, CO: Geological Society of America.

Brooks, Robert R., and Dieter Johannes. 1990. *Phytoarchaeology*. Portland, OR: Dioscorides.

Broshi, Magen, and Israel Finkelstein. 1992. "The population of Palestine in Iron Age 2." *Bulletin of the American Schools of Oriental Research* 287: 47–60.

Brothwell, Donald R., and A. Mark Pollard (eds). 2001. *Handbook of Archaeological Sciences*. Chichester, UK: Wiley.

Brown, A. G. 1997. *Alluvial Geoarchaeology: Floodplain Archaeology and Environmental Change*. Cambridge: Cambridge University.

Brück, Joanna, and M. Goodman (eds.). 1999. *Making Places in the Prehistoric World: Themes in Settlement Archaeology*. London: UCL.

Brückner, Helmut. 1996. "Geoarchäologie an der türkischen Ägäisküste." *Geographische Rundschau* 48: 568–574.

Bruins, Hendrik J. 1986. *Desert Environment and Agriculture in the Central Negev and Kadesh-Barnea during Historical Times*. Nijkerk Netherlands: Midbar Foundation.

———. 1990. "The impact of man and climate on the central Negev and northeastern Sinai deserts during the Late Holocene." Pp. 87–99 in Bottema et al.

Brunner, Ueli. 1983. *Die Erforschung der antiken Oase von Marib mit Hilfe geomorlogischer Untersuchungsmethoden*. Deutsches Archäologisches Institut, San ʿa. Mainz am Rhein: Phillip von Zabern.

———. 1997. "Geography and human settlements in ancient south Arabia." *Arabian Archaeology and Epigraphy* 8: 190–202.

Brunner, Ueli, and H. Haefner. 1986. "The successful floodwater farming system of the Sabaens, Yemen

Arab Republic." *Applied Geography* 6: 77–86.

Brunswig, Robert H. 1989. "Cultural history, environment and economy as seen from an Umm an-Nar settlement: Evidence from test excavations at Bāt, Oman, 1977–78." *Journal of Oman Studies* 10: 9–50.

Buccellati, Georgio. 1990. "'River bank', high country, and 'pasture land': The growth of nomadism in the middle Euphrates and the Khabur." Pp. 47–66 in *Tall al-Hamidiya 2: Recent Excavations in the Khabur Region*, ed. S. Eichler, Marcus Wäfler, and David Warburton. Freiburg: Universitätsverlag.

Bull, Ian D., P. B. Betancourt, and R. P. Evershed. 2001. "An organic geochemical investigation of the practice of manuring at a Minoan site on Pseira Island, Crete." *Geoarchaeology* 16 (2): 223–242.

Bull, Ian D., I. A. Simpson, P. F. van Bergen, and R. P. Evershed. 1999. "Muck 'n' molecules: Organic geochemical methods for detecting ancient manuring." *Antiquity* 73: 86–96.

Burckardt, John Lewis. 1831. *Notes on the Beduins and Wahabys*. London: Colburn and Bentley.

Buringh, Peter. 1957. "Living conditions in the lower Mesopotamian plain in ancient times." *Sumer* 13: 30–46.

———. 1960. *Soils and Soil Conditions in Iraq*. Baghdad: Republic of Iraq, Ministry of Agriculture.

Buringh, Peter, and C. H. Edelman. 1955. "Some remarks about the soils of the alluvial plain of Iraq, South of Baghdad." *Netherlands Journal of Agricultural Science* 3: 40–49.

Burney, Charles A. 1957. "Urartian fortresses and towns in the Van region." *Anatolian Studies* 7: 37–53.

———. 1972. "Urartian irrigation works." *Anatolian Studies* 22: 179–186.

———. 1977. "The economic basis of settled communities in north-west Iran." Pp. 1–7 in *Mountains and Lowlands: Essays in the Archaeology of Greater Mesopotamia*, ed. Louis D. Levine and T. Cuyler Young Jr. Malibu: Undena.

Burney, Charles, and D. M. Lang. 1971. *The People of the Hills: Ancient Ararat and Caucasus*. London: Weidenfeld and Nicholson.

Butler, Howard Crosby. 1929. *Early Churches in Syria, Fourth to Seventh Centuries*, ed. E. Baldwin Smith.

Princeton, NJ: Department of Art and Archaeology, Princeton University.

Butzer, Karl W. 1958. *Quaternary Stratigraphy and Climate in the Near East*. Bonner Geographische Abhandlungen 24: 1–157.

———. 1971. *Environment and Archeology: An Ecological Approach to Prehistory*. Chicago: Aldine-Atherton.

———. 1974. "Accelerated soil erosion: A problem of man-land relationships." Pp. 57–78 in *Perspectives on Environment*, ed. Ian R. Manners and Marvin Mikesell. Washington, DC: Association of American Geographers, Publication no. 13.

———. 1981. "Rise and fall of Axum, Ethiopia: A geoarchaeological interpretation." *American Antiquity* 46: 471–495.

———. 1982. *Archaeology as Human Ecology*. Cambridge: Cambridge University.

———. 1995. "Environmental change in the Near East and human impact on the land." Pp. 123–151 in *Civilizations of the Ancient Near East*, vol. 1, ed. Jack Sasson. New York: Scribners, Macmillan.

———. 1997a. "Environmental archaeology." Pp. 244–252 in Meyers.

———. 1997b. "Sociopolitical discontinuity in the Near East c. 2200 B.C.E.: Scenarios from Palestine and Egypt." Pp. 245–296 in Dalfes et al.

———. 1996. "Ecology in the long view: Settlement histories, agrosystemic strategies, and ecological performance." *Journal of Field Archaeology* 23: 141–150.

Callot, Olivier. 1984. *Huileries antiques de Syrie du nord*. Paris: Institut Française D'Archéologie de Beyrouth Bibliothèque Archéologique et Historique 118.

Calvet, Yves, and Geyer, B. 1992. *Barrages antiques de Syrie*. Lyon: Collection de la Maison de l'Orient Méditerranéen 21.

Camazine, Scott, J.-L. Deneubourg, N. R. Franks, J. Sneyd, G. Theraulaz, and E. Bonabeau. 2001. *Self-Organization in Biological Systems*. Princeton, NJ: Princeton University.

Campbell, Stuart. 1992. "The Halaf period in Iraq: Old sites and new." *Biblical Archaeologist* 55 (December): 182–187.

Campbell, Stuart, E. Carter, E. Healey, S. Anderson, A. Kennedy, and S. Whitcher. 1999. "Emerging complexity on the Kahramanmaraş Plain, Turkey: The Domuztepe Project, 1995–1997." *American Journal of Archaeology* 103 (3): 395–418.

Canti, Matthew. 1998. "The micromorphological identification of faecal spherulites from archaeological and modern materials." *Journal of Archaeological Science* 25: 435–444.

Casana, J. In press. "The archaeological landscape of Late Roman Antioch." In *Culture and Society in Late Roman Antioch*, ed. J. A. R. Huskinson and Bella Sandwell. Oxford: Oxbow.

Caton-Thompson, Gertrude, and E. W. Gardner. 1939. "Climate, irrigation and early man in the Hadramaut." *Geographical Journal* 93: 18–38.

———. 1944. *The Tombs and Moon Temple of Hureidha (Hadhramaut)*. Oxford: Reports of the Research Committee of the Society of Antiquaries of London 13.

Chabot, J. 2001. "Persistance des outils en pierre taillée à l'Age du Bronze ancien en Syrie du Nord (3000–2500 av. J.-C.)." Pp. 61–68 in *Canadian Research on Ancient Syria*, ed. Michel Fortin. Toronto: Canadian Society for Mesopotamian Studies (Bulletin no. 36).

Chapman, John. 1997. "Places as Timemarks—The social construction of prehistoric landscapes in eastern Hungary." Pp. 31–45 in *Semiotics of Landscape: Archaeology of Mind*, ed. George Nash. Oxford: BAR (International Series) 661.

Charles, Michael P. 1988. "Irrigation in lowland Mesopotamia." *Bulletin for Sumerian Agriculture* 4: 1–39.

Cherry, John F. 1983. "Frogs round the pond: Perspectives on current archaeological survey projects in the Mediterranean area." Pp. 375–416 in *Archaeological Survey in the Mediterranean Area*, ed. Donald R. Keller and David W. Rupp. Oxford: BAR (International Series) 155.

Cherry, John F., J. L. Davis, and E. Mantzourani. 1991. *Landscape Archaeology as Long-term History: The Keos Survey*. Los Angeles: UCLA Institute of Archaeology.

Christensen, Peter. 1993. *The Decline of Iranshahr: Irrigation and Environments in the History of the Middle East 500 B.C. to AD 1500*. Copenhagen: Museum Tusculanem.

Civil, Miguel. 1994. *The Farmer's Instructions*. Barcelona: Aula Orientalis.

Clapp, Nicholas. 1998. *The Road to Ubar: Finding the Atlantis of the Sands*. New York: Houghton Mifflin.

Clark, Geoffrey, D. I. Olszewski, J. Schuldenrein, N. Rida, and J. A. Eighmey. 1998. "Survey and excavation in the Wadi al-Hasa: A preliminary report of the 1993 field season." Pp. 165–175 in *The Archaeology of the Wadi al-Hasa, West-central Jordan*, vol. 1, ed. Nancy R. Coinman. Tempe: Arizona State University, Anthropological Research Papers no. 50.

Clark, I., and Fontes J.-C. 1990. "Palaeoclimatic reconstruction in northern Oman based on carbonates from hyperalkaline groundwater." *Quaternary Research* 33: 320–336.

Clarke, Christopher. 1975. "The rock art of Oman." *Journal of Oman Studies* 1: 113–115.

Cleere, Henry. 1995. "Cultural landscapes as world heritage." *Conservation and Management of Archaeological Sites* 1: 63–68.

Cleuziou, Serge. 1996. "The emergence of oasis towns in eastern and southern Arabia." Pp. 159–165 in *The Prehistory of Asia and Oceania*, vol. 16, ed. Gennadii E. Afanas'ev, Serge Cleuziou, John R. Lukacs, and Maurizio Tosi. Forlì, Italy: International Union of Prehistoric and Protohistoric Sciences.

———. 1997. "Construire et protéger son terroir: Les oasis d' Oman à l' Age du Bronze." In *La dynamique des paysages protohistoriques, antiques, médiévaux et modernes*. XVIIᵉ Rencontres Internationales d'Archéologie et d'Histoire d'Antibes. Éditions APDCA, Sophia Antipolis.

Cleuziou, Serge, M. L. Inizan, and B. Marcolongo. 1992. "Le Peuplement pre et protohistorique systeme fluviatile fossile du Jawf-Hadramaut au Yemen." *Paléorient* 18 (2): 5–29.

Cohen R., and Dever William. 1980. "Preliminary report of the third and final season of the 'Central Negev Highlands Project.'" *Bulletin of the American Schools of Oriental Research* 243: 57–77.

Cole, Donald P. 1975. *Nomad of the Nomads: The Āl Murrah Bedouin of the Empty Quarter*. Chicago: Aldine.

Cole, Steven W. 1994. "Marsh formation in the Borsippa region and the course of the lower Euphrates." *Journal of Near Eastern Studies* 53: 81–109.

Cole, Steven W., and H. Gasche. 1998. "Second and first millennium B.C. rivers in northern Babylonia." Pp. 1–64 in Gasche and Tanret.

Coleman, Simon, and J. Elsner. 1994. "The pilgrim's progress: Art, architecture and ritual movement at Sinai." *World Archaeology* 26 (1): 73–89.

Cooke, Ronald U., and R. W. Reeves. 1976. *Arroyos and Environmental Change in the American South-west*. Oxford: Clarendon.

Cooper, J. 1983. *Reconstruction History from Ancient Inscriptions: The Lagash-Umma Border Conflict*. Sources from the Ancient Near East 2 (1). Malibu: Undena.

Cordova, Carlos. 1999. "Landscape transformation in the Mediterranean-steppe transition zone of Jordan: A geoarchaeological approach." *The Arab World Geographer* 2 (3): 182–201.

———. 2000. "Geomorphological evidence of intense prehistoric soil erosion in the highlands of central Jordan." *Physical Geography* 21 (6): 538–567.

Costa, Paolo M. 1983. "Notes on settlement patterns in traditional Oman." *Journal of Oman Studies* 6: 247–268.

———. 2000. "Adaptation of man to the environment: The Arabian experience." *Journal of Oman Studies* 11: 75–81.

———. 2001. *Historic Mosques and Shrines of Oman*. Oxford: BAR (International Series) 938.

Costa, Paolo M., and Tony J. Wilkinson. 1987. "The hinterland of Sohar: Archaeological surveys and excavations within the region of an Omani seafaring city." *Journal of Oman Studies* 9: 1–238.

Courty, Marie-Agnes. 1994. "Le cadre paléogéographique des occupations humaines dans le bassin du Haut-Khabur (Syrie du nord-est): Premiers Résultats." *Paléorient* 20 (1): 21–59.

Courty, Marie-Agnes, Paul Goldberg, and Richard I. MacPhail. 1989. *Soils and Micromorphology in Archaeology*. Cambridge: Cambridge University.

Crawford, O. G. S. 1923. "Air survey and archaeology." *Geographical Journal* 23: 324–366.

———. 1954. "A century of air photography." *Antiquity* 28: 206–210.

Cribb, Roger. 1991. *Nomads in Archaeology*. Cambridge: Cambridge University.

Cullen, Heidi M., and Peter B. de Menocal. 2000. "North Atlantic influence on Tigris-Euphrates streamflow."

International Journal of Climatology 20: 853–863.

Cullen, Heidi M., P. B. de Menocal, S. Hemming, G. Hemming, F. H. Brown, T. Guilderson, and F. Sirocko. 2000. "Climate change and the collapse of the Akkadian Empire: Evidence from the deep Sea." *Geology* 28: 379–382.

Curvers, H. H. 1991. "The Balikh Drainage in the Bronze Age." Ph.D. dissertation. University of Amsterdam, Faculty of Letters.

Dabbagh, A. E., K. G. al-Hinai, and M. A. Khan. 1998. "Evaluation of the Shuttle imaging radar (SIR-C/X-SAR) data for mapping paleo-drainage systems in the Kingdom of Saudi Arabia." Pp. 483–493 in Alsharhan et al.

Dahari, Uzi. 2000. *Monastic Settlements in South Sinai in the Byzantine Period: The Archaeological Remains.* Jerusalem: Israel Antiquities Authority.

Dalfes, H. Nüzhet, George Kukla, and Harvey Weiss. 1997. *Third Millennium B.C. Climate Change and Old World Collapse.* NATO ASI Series: Global Environmental Change, vol. 49. Berlin: Springer.

Daniels, Joseph. 2002. "Landscape graffiti in the Dhamar Plains and its relation to mountaintop religious practice." Paper presented at the annual meeting of the Seminar for Arabian Studies, London, July 19.

Danti, Michael. 2000. "Early Bronze Age Settlement and Land Use in the Tell es-Sweyhat Region, Syria." Ph.D. dissertation, Department of Anthropology, University of Pennsylvania.

Danti, Michael, and Richard L. Zettler. 1998. "The evolution of the Tell es-Sweyhat (Syria) settlement system in the 3rd millennium B.C." *Bulletin of the Canadian Society for Mesopotamian Studies* 33: 209–228.

Dar, Shimon. 1986. *Landscape and Pattern.* Oxford: BAR (International Series) 308.

———. 1993. *Settlements and Cult Sites on Mount Hermon, Israel.* Oxford: BAR (International Series) 589.

———. 1999. *Sumaqa: A Roman Byzantine Jewish Village on Mount Carmel, Israel.* Oxford: BAR (International Series) 815.

Davidson, Donald A., and I. A. Simpson. 2001. "Archaeology and soil micromorphology." Pp. 167–178 in Brothwell and Pollard.

al-Dayel, Khalid, and Salah al-Helwah.

1978. "Preliminary report on the second phase of the Darb Zubayda reconnaissance 1397–1977." *Atlal* 2: 51–64.

Dearing, John. 1994. "Reconstructing the history of soil erosion." Pp. 242–261 in *The Changing Global Environment*, ed. Neil Roberts. Oxford: Blackwell.

de Cardi Beatrice, S. Collier, and D. B. Doe. 1976. "Excavations and survey in Oman 1974–75." *Journal of Oman Studies* 2: 101–187.

de Cardi, Beatrice, D. B. Doe, and S. Roskams. 1977. "Excavations and survey in Oman 1976." *Journal of Oman Studies* 3: 17–70.

de Maigret Alessandro. 1990. *The Bronze Age Culture of Hawlan at Tiyal and al-Hada (Republic of Yemen): A First General Report* (2 vols.). Rome: ISMEO.

———. 1996. "New evidence from the Yemenite "turret graves" for the problem of the emergence of the south Arabian states." Pp 321–337 in *The Indian Ocean in Antiquity*, ed. Julian Reade. London: Kegan Paul.

de Menocal, Peter, B. 2001. "Cultural responses to climatic change during the Late Holocene." *Science* 292: 667–673.

De Morgan, Jaques. 1900. "Étude géographique sur la Susiane." *Mémoires de la Délégation en Perse* 1: 4–32.

Denevan, William M. 1987. "Terrace abandonment in the Colca valley, Peru." Pp. 1–43 in *PreHispanic Agricultural Fields in the Andean Region*, ed. William M. Denevan, K. Matthewson, and G. Knapp. Oxford: BAR (International Series) 359.

de Planhol, X. 1966. "Aspects of mountain life in Anatolia and Iran." Pp. 291–308 in *Geography as Human Ecology*, ed. S. R. Eyre and G. R. Jones. New York: St. Martins.

Dever, William G. 1969. "The water systems at Hazor and Gezer." *Biblical Archaeologist* 32: 71–78.

———. 1992. "Pastoralism and the end of the urban early Bronze Age in Palestine." Pp. 83–92 in *Pastoralism in the Levant: Archaeological Materials in Anthropological Perspective.* ed. Ofer Bar-Yosef and A. Khazanov. Madison, WI: Prehistory.

de Vries, Bert (ed.). 1998. *Umm al Jemal 1.* Portsmouth, RI: *Journal of Roman Archaeology* Supplementary vol. 26.

Dewar, Robert E. 1991. "Incorporating variation in occupation span into

settlement-pattern analysis." *American Antiquity* 56 (4): 604–620.

Dewdney, J. C. 1971. *Turkey, An Introductory Geography.* New York: Praeger.

Dickson, Harold R. P. 1951. *The Arab of the Desert.* London: George Allen and Unwin.

Djobadze, Wachtang. 1986. *Archaeological Investigations in the Region West of Antioch On-the-Orontes.* Stuttgart: Franze Steiner.

Dodinet, M., J. Leblanc, J.-P. Vallat, and F. Villeneuve. 1990. "Le paysage antique en Syrie: L'exemple de Damas." *Syria* 67: 339–355.

Doe, Brian. 1983. *Monuments of South Arabia.* New York and Cambridge: Oleander.

Donkin, R. A. 1979. *Agricultural Terracing in the Aboriginal New World.* Tucson: University of Arizona, Viking Fund Publications in Anthropology no. 56.

Donoghue, Daniel N. M. 2001. "Remote Sensing." Pp. 555–563 in Brothwell and Pollard.

Doolittle, William E. 1990. *Canal Irrigation in Prehistoric Mexico: The Sequence of Technological Change.* Austin: University of Texas.

Doose-Rolinsky, H., U. Rogalla, G. Scheeder, A. Lückge, and U. von Rad. 2001. "High-resolution temperature and evaporation changes during the late Holocene in the northeastern Arabian Sea." *Paleoceanography* 16: 358–367.

Downing Theodoer, and McGuire Gibson. 1974. *Irrigation's Impact on Society.* Tucson: University of Arizona.

Draz, Omar. 1990. "The hema system in the Arabian peninsula." Pp. 321–331 in *The Improvement of Tropical and Subtropical Rangelands.* Washington, DC: National Academy.

Dunnell R. C., and W. S. Dancey. 1983. "The siteless survey: A regional scale data collection strategy." *Advances in Archaeological Method and Theory* 6: 267–287.

Dutton, Roderic W. 1989. "Aflaj renewal in Araqi: A village case study from Oman." Pp. 237–256 in Beaumont et al.

Eastwood, William J., N. Roberts, and H. F. Lamb. 1998. "Palaeoecological and archaeological evidence for human occupance in SW Turkey: The Beyshahir occupation phase." *Anatolian Studies* 48: 69–86.

Echallier, J. C., and Braemer, F. 1995.

"Nature et fonctions des 'desert kites,' données et hypothèses." *Paléorient* 21 (1): 35–63.

Edelstein, Gershon, and Shimon Gibson. 1982. "Ancient Jerusalem's food basket: The new archaeology looks for an urban center's agricultural base." *Biblical Archaeology Review* 8: 46–54.

Edelstein, Gershon, and M. Kislev. 1981. "Mevasserat Yerushalayim: The ancient settlement and its agricultural terraces." *Biblical Archaeologist* Winter: 53–56.

Edens, Christopher. 1982. "Towards a definition of the western ar-Rub al Khali 'Neolithic.'" *Atlal* 6: 109–123.

———. 1988a. "The Rub al-Khali 'Neolithic' revisited: The view from Naqdan." Pp. 17–43 in *Araby the Blest*, ed. Daniel Potts. Copenhagen: Carsten Niebuhr Institute Publications 7.

———. 1988b. "Archaeology of the sands and adjacent portions of the Sharqiyah." Pp. 113–130 in *The Scientific Results of the Royal Geographical Society's Wahiba Sands Project 1985–1987*, ed. Roderic Dutton. Muscat, Oman: *Journal of Oman Studies* Special Publication no. 3.

———. 1995. "Transcaucasia at the end of the Early Bronze Age." *Bulletin of the American Schools of Oriental Research* 299/300: 53–64.

Edens, Christopher, and T. J. Wilkinson. 1998. "Southwest Arabia during the Holocene: Recent archaeological developments." *Journal of World Prehistory* 12 (1): 55–119.

Edens, Christopher, T. J. Wilkinson, and G. Barratt. 2000. "Hammat al-Qa: An early town in southern Arabia." *Antiquity* 74: 854–862.

Eger, Helmut. 1987. "Runoff agriculture: A case study about the Yemeni highlands." *Jemen Studien* 7: 1–238. Wiesbaden: Ludwig Reichert.

Eidt, Robert C. 1977. "Detection and examination of anthrosols by phosphate analysis." *Science* 197: 1327–1333.

Eismer, D. 1978. "Stream deposition and erosion by the eastern shore of the Aegean." Pp. 67–81 in Brice.

El-Faiz, Mohammad. 1995. *L'agronomie de la Mésopotamie antique*. Leiden: Brill.

El-Samarraie, Husam Q. 1972. *Agriculture in Iraq during the Third Century AH*. Beirut: Librarie du Liban.

Ergenzinger, Peter J. 1991. "Geomorphologische Untersuchungen im Unterlauf des Habur." Pp. 35–50, 163–190

in *Die Rezente Umwelt von Tall Šeh Hamad und Daten zur Umweltrekonstruktion der Assyrischen Stadt Dur Katlimmu*, ed. Hartmut Kuhne. Berlin: Dietrich Reimer.

Ergenzinger, Peter J., and H. Kühne. 1991. "Ein regionales Bewässerungssystem am Hābur." Pp. 163–190 in *Die Rezente Umwelt von Tall Šeh Hamad und Daten zur Umweltrekonstruktion der Assyrischen Stadt Dur Katlimmu*, ed. Hartmut Kühne. Berlin: Dietrich Reimer.

Ergenzinger, P. J., W. Frey, H. Kühne, and H. Kurschner. 1988. "The reconstruction of environment, irrigation and development of settlement on the Habur in North-east Syria." Pp. 108–128 in *Conceptual Issues in Environmental Archaeology*, ed. John Bintliff, D. A. Davidson, and E. G., Grant. Edinburgh: Edinburgh University.

Erinç, Sirri. 1978. "Changes in the physical environment in Turkey since the end of the last glacial." Pp. 87–110 in Brice.

Erinç, S., and N. Tunçdilek. 1952. "The agricultural regions of Turkey." *Geographical Review* 42: 179–203.

Evenari, Michael, L. Shanan, and N. Tadmor. 1982. *The Negev: The Challenge of a Desert*. Cambridge, MA: Harvard University.

Evershed, Richard P., P. H. Bethell, P. J. Reynolds, and N. J. Walsh. 1997. "5ß Stigmastanol and related 5ß Stanols as biomarkers of manuring: Analysis of modern experimental material and assessment of the archaeological potential." *Journal of Archaeological Science* 24: 485–495.

Everson, Paul, and T. Williamson (eds). 1998. *The Archaeology of Landscape*. Manchester: Manchester University.

Falconer, Steven E., and Patricia Fall. 1995. "Human impacts on the environment during the rise and collapse of civilization in the eastern Mediterranean." Pp. 84–101 in *Late Quaternary Environments and Deep History: A Tribute to Paul S. Martin*, ed. David W. Steadman and J. I. Mead. Hot Springs, SD: The Mammoth Site of Hot Springs Scientific Papers.

Falconer, Steven E., and S. H. Savage. 1995. "Heartlands and hinterlands: Alternative trajectories of early urbanization in Mesopotamia and the southern Levant." *American Antiquity* 60 (1): 37–58.

Fales, Mario. 1990. "The rural landscape

of the Neo-Assyrian empire: A survey." *State Archives of Assyria, Bulletin* 4/2: 81–142.

Fales, Mario, and J. N. Postgate. 1995. *Imperial Administrative Records, Part 2: Provincial and Military Administration*. State Archives of Assyria, vol. 11, Helsinki.

Feinman, Gary M. 1999. "Defining a contemporary landscape approach: Concluding thoughts." *Antiquity* 73: 684–685.

Fernea, Robert A. 1970. *Shaykh and Effendi: Changing Patterns of Authority among the El Shabana of Southern Iraq*. Cambridge, MA: Harvard University.

Fincke, Jeanette. 2000. "Transport of agricultural produce in Arrapne." Pp. 147–170 in Jas (ed.).

Finkelstein, Israel. 1988. *The Archaeology of the Israelite Settlements*. Jerusalem: Israel Exploration Society.

———. 1995. *Living on the Fringe: The Archaeology and History of the Negev, Sinai, and Neighboring Regions in the Bronze Age*. Sheffield: Sheffield Academic.

———. 1998. "The great transformation: The 'conquest' of the highlands frontiers and the rise of the territorial states." Pp. 349–365 in *The Archaeology of Society in the Holy Land*, ed. Thomas E. Levy. Leicester: Leicester University.

Finkelstein, Israel, and R. Gophner. 1993. "Settlement, demographic and economic patterns in the highlands of Palestine in the Chalolithic and early Bronze and the beginnings of urbanism." *Bulletin of the American Schools of Oriental Research* 289: 1–22.

Finkelstein, Israel, and Z. Lederman. 1997. *Highlands of Many Cultures: The Southern Samaria Survey*. Tel Aviv: Institute of Archaeology, Tel Aviv University, Report no. 14.

Finley, Moses, I. 1985. *The Ancient Economy*. Berkeley: University of California.

Finster, Barbara. 1978. "Die Reiseroute Kufar-Sa'udi Arabien in Fruhislamischier zeit." *Baghdader Mitteilungen* 9: 53–91.

Fischer, Moshe, Benjamin Isaac, and Israel Roll. 1996. *Roman Roads in Judaea II*. Oxford: BAR (International Series) 628.

Fisher, C. T., and T. L. Thurston. 1999. "Dynamic landscapes and sociopolitical process: The topography of anthropogenic environments in global perspective." *Antiquity* 73: 630–631.

Fisher, W. B. 1978. *The Middle East: A Physical, Social and Regional Geography.* London: Methuen.

Flannery, Kent V. 1972. "The origins of the village as a settlement type in Mesoamerica and the Near East: A comparative study." Pp. 25–53 in *Man, Settlement and Urbanism,* ed. Peter J. Ucko, Ruth Tringham, and Geoffrey W. Dimbleby. London: Duckworth.

Flannery, Kent V., and Joyce Marcus. 1976. "Formative Oaxaca and the Zapotec cosmos." *American Scientist* 64: 374–383.

Flemming, Nicholas C. 1983. "Preliminary geomorphological survey of an early Neolithic submerged site in the Sporadhes, N. Aegean." Pp. 233–268 in Masters and Flemming.

———. 1998. "Archaeological evidence for vertical movement of the continental shelf during the Palaeolithic, Neolithic and Bronze Age periods." Pp. 129–146 in *Coastal Tectonics,* ed. Ian Stewart and Claudio Vita-Finzi. London: Geological Society Special Publication no. 146.

Foley, Robert. 1981. *Off-site Archaeology and Human Adaptation in Eastern Africa.* Oxford: BAR (International Series) 97.

Fontugne M., C. Kuzucuoğlu, M. Karabiyikoğlu, C. Hatté, and J.-F. Pastre. 1999. "From Pleniglacial to Holocene: A 14C chronostratigraphy of environmental changes in the Konya Basin." *Quaternary Science Reviews* 18: 573–592.

Forbes, Robert James. 1955. *Studies in Ancient Technology.* Leiden: Brill.

Forman, Richard T. T. 1995. *Land Mosaics: The Ecology of Landscapes and Regions.* Cambridge: Cambridge University.

Foss, Clive. 1995. "The Near Eastern countryside in late antiquity: A review article." *Journal of Roman Archaeology,* Supplementary Series 14: 213–234.

———. 1997. "Syria in Transition, A.D. 550–750: An Archaeological Approach." *Dumbarton Oaks Papers* 51: 189–269.

Foster, Benjamin R. 2001. *The Epic of Gilgamesh.* New York: W. W. Norton.

Fowden, G. 1999. "'Desert Kites': Ethnography, archaeology and art."

Pp. 107–136 in *The Roman and Byzantine Near East.* Vol. 2: *Some Recent Archaeological Research,* ed. J. H. Humphrey. *Journal of Roman Studies* Supplementary Series no. 31.

Fowler, Peter. 1998. "Moving through the landscape." Pp. 42–66 in Everson and Williamson.

Fox, Cyril. 1923. *The Archaeology of the Cambridge Region.* Cambridge: Cambridge University.

Frankel, Rafael. 1994. "Upper Galilee in the Late Bronze–Iron I transition." Pp. 18–34 in *From Nomadism to Monarchy: Archaeological and Historical Aspects of Early Israel,* ed. Israel Finkelstein and N. Na'aman. Jerusalem: Israel Exploration Society.

———. 1999. *Oil and Wine Presses in Israel and adjacent Mediterranean Lands.* Sheffield: Sheffield Academic.

Frayne, Douglas. 1990. *Royal Inscriptions of Mesopotamia: Early Periods.* Vol. 4: *2003–1595 B.C.).* Toronto: University of Toronto.

Frederick, Charles. 2000. "Evaluating causality of landscape change: Examples from alluviation." Pp. 55–76 in *Earth Sciences and Archaeology,* ed. Paul Goldberg, V. T. Holliday, and C. Reid Ferring. New York: Academic/Plenum.

Frederick, Charles, and A. Krahtopoulou. 2000. "Deconstructing agricultural terraces: examining the influence of construction method on stratigraphy, dating and archaeological visibility." Pp. 79–94 in Halstead and Frederick.

French, David. 1972. "Settlement distribution on the Konya Plain, south central Turkey." Pp. 231–238 in *Man, Settlement and Urbanism,* ed. Peter J. Ucko, R. Tringham, and G. W. Dimbleby. London: Duckworth.

———. 1981. *Roman Roads in Asia Minor.* Oxford: BAR (International Series) 392.

Frey, W., C. Jagiella, and H. Kürschner. 1991. "Holzekohlefund in Dūr katlimmu/ Tall Šeh Hamad und ihre Interpretation." Pp. 137–161 in *Die rezente Umwelt von Tall Šeh Hamad und Daten zur Umweltrekonstruktion der assyrischen Stadt Dūr Katlimmu,* ed. Hartmut Kuhne. Berlin: Dietrich Reimer.

Frifelt, Karen. 1976. "Evidence of a third millennium B.C. town in Oman." *Journal of Oman Studies* 2: 57–73.

———. 1985. "Further evidence of the

third millennium B.C. town of Bāt in Oman." *Journal of Oman Studies* 7: 89–104.

Frumkin, Amos, I. Carmi, I. Zak, and M. Magaritz. 1994. "Middle Holocene environmental change determined from the salt caves of Mount Sedom, Israel." Pp. 315–332 in Bar-Yosef and Kra.

Frumkin, Amos, I. Carmi, A. Gopher, D. C. Ford, H. P. Schwartz, and T. Tsuk. 1999. "A Holocene millennial-scale climatic cycle from a speleothem in Nahal Qanah Cave, Israel." *The Holocene* 9 (6): 677–682.

Fulford, Michael G., T. Champion, and A. Long (eds.). 1997. *England's Coastal Heritage: A Survey for English Heritage and the RCHME.* London: English Heritage, Royal Commission on the Historical Monuments of England, Archaeological Report 15.

Funnel, Don, and Romola Parish. 2001. *Mountain Environments and Communities.* London: Routledge.

Gaffney, Vince L., J. Bintliff, and B. Slapsak. 1991. "Site formation process and the Hvar survey project, Yugoslavia." Pp. 59–77 in *Interpreting Artefact Scatters: Contributions to Ploughzone Archaeology,* ed. A. J. Schofield. Oxford: Oxbow Monograph no. 4.

Gaffney, V., Z. Stančič, and H. Watson. 1995. "The impact of GIS on archaeology: A personal perspective." Pp. 211–230 in *Archaeology and Geographical Information Systems: A European Perspective,* ed. Gary Lock and Z. Stančič. London: Taylor and Francis.

Galili, Ehud, and M. Weinstein-Evron. 1985. "Prehistory and paleoenvironments of submerged sites along the Carmel coast of Israel." *Paléorient* 11 (1): 37–52.

Galili, Ehud, M. Weinstein-Evron, I. Hershkovitz, A. Gopher, M. Kislev, O. Lernau, L. Kolska-Horwitz, and H. Lernau. 1993. "Atlil-Yam: A prehistoric site on the sea floor off the Israeli coast." *Journal of Field Archaeology* 20: 133–157.

Galili, Ehud, D. J. Stanley, J. Sharvit, and M. Weinstein-Evron. 1997. "Evidence for earliest olive-oil production in submerged settlements off the Carmel coast, Israel." *Journal of Archaeological Science* 24: 1141–1150.

Gardiner M., and Alison McQuitty. 1987. "Water mill in Wadi el-Arab, north

Jordan and water mill development." *Palestine Exploration Quaterly* 119: 124–132.

Garrard, Andrew, and C. P. D. Harvey. 1981. "Environment and settlement during the Upper Pleistocene and Holocene at Jubba in the Great Nafud, Northern Arabia." *Atlal*: 5: 137–148.

Gasche, Hermann, and M. Tanret (eds.). 1998. *Changing Watercourses in Babylonia: Towards a Reconstruction of the Ancient Environment in Lower Mesopotamia.* Ghent: University of Ghent, and Chicago: Oriental Institute.

Gasche, Hermann, M. Tanret, S. W. Cole, and K. Verhoeven. 2002. "Fleuves du temps et de la vie. Permanence et instabilité du réseau fluviatile baylonien entre 2500 et avant notre ère." *Annales Histore, Sciences Sociales* 57 (3): 531–544.

Gawlikowski, M. 1997. "The Syrian desert under the Romans." Pp. 37–54 in *The Early Roman Empire in the East*, ed. Susan E. Alcock. Oxford: Oxbow.

Gelb, Ignace J. 1986. "Ebla and Lagash: Environmental contrast." Pp. 157–167 in *The Origins of Cities in Dry-farming Mesopotamia in the Third Millennium B.C.*, ed. Harvey Weiss. Guilford, CT: Four Quarters.

Gentelle, Pierre. 1985. "Elements pour une histoire des paysages et du peuplement de Djebel Hauran septentrional, en Syrie du sud." Pp. 19–59 in *Hauran 1*, ed. J.-M. Dentzer, Paris: Institut Français D' Archéologie du Proche Orient, Librairie Orientaliste Paul Geuthner.

———. 1991. "Les irrigations antique à Shabwa." *Syria* 68: 5–54.

———. 1998. "La nature et l'irrigation." Pp. 75–125 in Breton et al.

Gentelle, Pierre, and Karen Frifelt. 1989. "About the distribution of third millennium graves and settlements in the Ibra area of Oman." Pp. 119–126 in *Oman Studies: Papers on the Archaeology and History of Oman*, ed. Paolo M. Costa and Maurizio Tosi. Rome: Istituto Italiano per il Medio Estremo Oriente.

Geyer, Bernard (ed.). 1990. *Techniques et practiques hydro-agricoles.* Paris: Bibliothèque Archéologique et Historique CXXXVI.

———. 1998. "Géographie et peuplement des steppes arides de la Syria du nord." *Bulletin of the Canadian Society for Mesopotamian Studies* 33: 1–8.

Geyer, Bernard, and Paul Sanlaville. 1996. "Nouvelle contribution à l'étude géomorphologique de la région de Larsa-Oueili (Iraq)." Pp. 391–408 in *Oueli: Travaux de 1987 et 1989*, ed. J.-L. Huot. Paris: Éditions Recherche sur les Civilisations.

Gibson, McGuire. 1972. *The City and Area of Kish.* Miami: Field Research Projects.

———. 1973. "Population shift and the rise of Mesopotamian civilisation." Pp. 447–463 in *The Explanation of Culture Change: Models in Prehistory*, ed. Colin Renfrew. London: Duckworth.

———. 1974. "Violation of fallow and engineered disaster in Mesopotamian civilization." Pp. 7–19 in *Irrigation's Impact on Society*, ed. Theodore E. Downing and McGuire Gibson. Tucson: University of Arizona.

Gibson, Shimon. 1984. "Lime kilns in north-east Jerusalem." *Palestine Exploration Quarterly* 116: 94–102.

———. 2001. "Agricultural terraces and settlement expansion in the highlands of early Iron Age Palestine: Is there any correlation between the two?" Pp. 113–146 in *Studies in the Archaeology of the Iron Age in Israel and Jordan*, ed. Amihai Mazar. *Journal for the Study of the Old Testament* Supplement Series 331. Sheffield: Sheffield Academic.

Gibson, Shimon, and G. Edelstein. 1985. "Investigating Jerusalem's rural landscape." *Levant* 17: 139–155.

Gibson, Shimon, B. Ibbs, and A. Kloner. 1991. "The Sataf Project of landscape archaeology in the Judaean Hills." *Levant* 23: 29–54.

Gibson, Shimon, S. Kingsley, and J. Clarke. 1999. "Town and Country in the southern Carmel: The LAPD Project." *Levant* 31: 71–121.

Gillings, Mark, and Alicia Wise. 1999. *GIS Guide to Good Practice.* Oxford: Oxbow.

Gillings, Mark, D. Mattingly, and J. van Dalen (eds.). 2000. *Geographical Information Systems and Landscape Archaeology.* Oxford: Oxbow.

Given, Michael. 2001. "From density counts to ideational landscapes: Intensive survey, landscape archaeology and the Sydney Cyprus Survey Project." Paper presented at the meetings of the Society for American Archaeology, New Orleans, April 20, 2001.

Gleason, Katherine L. 1994. "To bound and to cultivate: An introduction to the archaeology of gardens and fields." Pp. 1–24 in Miller and Gleason.

———. 1997. "Gardens in Preclassical, Hellenistic and Roman times." Pp. 383–387 in Meyers, vol. 2.

Glennie, Kenneth W. 1998. "The desert of SE Arabia: A product of Quaternary climatic change." Pp. 279–292 in Alsharhan et al.

Glover, Emily. 1998. "Mangroves, molluscs and man: Archaeological evidence for biogeographical changes in mangrove around the Arabian Peninsula." Pp. 63–78 in *Arabia and Its Neighbours: Essays on Prehistorical and Historical Developments*, ed. Carl S. Phillips, Daniel T. Potts, and Sarah Searight. Leuven: Brepols.

Glueck, Nelson. 1934. Explorations in Eastern Palestine I. *Annual of ASOR* 14.

———. 1935. "Air reconnaisance in South Jordan." *Bulletin of the American Schools of Oriental Research* 66: 2–28.

———. 1959. *Rivers in the Desert: A History of the Negev.* New York: Farrar, Strauss, and Cudahy.

Goettler, G. W., N. Firth, and C. C. Huston. 1976. "A preliminary discussion of ancient mining in the Sultanate of Oman." *Journal of Oman Studies* 2: 43–56.

Goetze, A. 1953. "An Old Babylonian itinerary." *Journal of Cuneiform Studies* 7: 51–72.

Goldberg, Paul. 1998. "The changing landscape." Pp. 40–57 in Levy.

Goldberg, Paul, and Ofer Bar-Yosef. 1990. "The effect of man on geomorphological processes based upon evidence from the Levant and adjacent areas." Pp. 71–86 in Bottema et al.

Goodfriend, Glenn A. 1990. "Rainfall in the Negev desert during the middle Holocene, based on ^{13}C of organic matter in land snail shells." *Quaternary Research* 34: 186–197.

———. 1991. "Holocene trends in ^{18}O in land snail shells from the Negev desert and their implications for changes in rainfall source areas." *Quaternary Research* 35: 417–426.

Gophner, Ram, and J. Portugali. 1988. "Settlement and demographic processes in Israel's coastal plain from the Chalcolithic to the Middle Bronze Age." *Bulletin of the American Schools of Oriental Research* 269: 11–28.

Goudie, Andrew, and John Wilkinson.

1977. *The Warm Desert Environment.* Cambridge: Cambridge University.

Göyünç, Nejat, and Wolf-Dieter Hütteroth. 1997. *Land an der Grenze: Osmanische Verwaltung im heutigen türkisch-syrisch-irakischen Grenzgebiet im 16. Jahrhundert.* Istanbul: Eren.

Graf, David F. 2001. "First millennium AD: Roman and Byzantine periods landscape archaeology and settlement patterns." *Studies in the History and Archaeology of Jordan* 7: 469–480.

Greene, Joseph A. 1997. "Necropoli." Pp. 118–119 in Meyers.

Greene, Kevin. 1986. *The Archaeology of the Roman Economy.* Berkeley: University of California.

Gregory, Sheila, and David Kennedy. 1985. *Sir Aurel Stein's Limes Reports.* Oxford: BAR (International Series) 272.

Griffiths, Huw I., A. Schwalb, and L. R. Stevens. 2001. "Environmental change in southwestern Iran: The Holocene ostracod fauna of Lake Mirabad." *The Holocene* 11 (6): 757–764.

Groenman-van Waateringe, W., and Mark Robinson (eds.). 1988. *Man-made soils.* Oxford: BAR (International Series) 410.

Grolier, Maurice J., Robert Brinkman, James Blakeley. 1996. *The Wadi al-Jubah Archaeological Project.* Vol. 5: *Environmental Research in Support of Archaeological Investigations in the Yemen Arab Republic, 1982–1987.* Washington, DC: American Foundation for the Study of Man.

Groom, Nigel. 1981. *Frankincense and Myrrh.* London: Longman.

Grossman, David, and Z. Safrai. 1980. "Satellite settlement in western Samaria." *Geographical Review* 70: 446–61.

Grove, A. T., and Oliver Rackham. 2001. *The Nature of Mediterranean Europe: An Ecological History.* New Haven, CT: Yale University.

Guérin, Alexandrine. 1997. "Terrois, territoire et peuplement en Syrie Méridionale à la période Islamique (VIIe siècle–XVI siècle)." (3 volumes). Ph.D. thesis, Depart. Archéologie et Histoire Islamique, Université Lumièr Lyon 2.

Gurney, Oliver R. 1977. *Some Aspects of Hittite Religion.* Oxford: Oxford University.

Haigh, Martin J. 1994. "Deforestation in the Himalaya." Pp. 440–462 in *The Changing Global Environment*, ed. Neil Roberts. Oxford: Blackwell.

Haiman, Mordechai. 1989. "Preliminary report of the western Negev Highlands Emergency Survey." *Israel Exploration Journal* 39: 173–191.

Haiman, Mordechai. 1996. "Early Bronze Age IV settlement pattern of the Negev and Sinai Desert: A view from small marginal temporary sites." *Bulletin of the American Schools of Oriental Research* 303: 1–32.

Hallo, William W. 1964. "The road to Emar." *Journal of Cuneiform Studies* 18: 57–88.

Halstead, Paul, and Charles Frederick. 2000. *Landscape and Land Use in Postglacial Greece.* Sheffield: Sheffield Academic.

Hanns, C. 1998. "Predominant features of the Quaternary relief development seawards of the Oman Mountains as reflected in wadi and coastal terraces and other coastal features." Pp. 17–28 in Alsharhan et al.

Harlan, Jack R. 1982. "The garden of the Lord: A plausible reconstruction of natural resources of southern Jordan in the Early Bronze Age." *Paléorient* 8/1: 71–78.

Harris, S. A., and Robert Mc. Adams. 1957. "A note on canal and marsh stratigraphy near Zubediyah." *Sumer* 13: 157–162.

Harrison, Timothy P. 1997. "Shifting patterns of settlement in the highlands of central Jordan during the Early Bronze Age." *Bulletin of the American Schools of Oriental Research* 306: 1–37.

Harverson, M. 1993. "Watermills in Iran." *Iran* 31: 149–177.

Haspels, C. H. Emilie. 1971. *The Highlands of Phrygia: Sites and Monuments.* Princeton, NJ: Princeton University.

Hassan, Fekri A. 2000. "Holocene environmental change and the origins and spread of food production in the Middle East." *Adumatu* 1: 7–28.

Hastings, Ann, J. H. Humphries, and R. H. Meadow. 1975. "Oman in the 3rd millennium B.C.E." *Journal of Oman Studies* 1: 9–56.

Hauptmann, Andreas, and Ü. Yakin. 2000. "Lime plaster, cement and the first puzzolanic reaction." *Paléorient* 26 (2): 61–68.

Hauser, Stefan. 1999. "Ecological limits and political frontiers: The 'kingdom of the arabs' in the eastern Jazira in the Arsacid period." Pp. 187–201 in Milano et al.

Hayden, Brian. 2001. "The dynamics of wealth and poverty in the transegalitarian societies of Southeast Asia." *Antiquity* 75: 571–581.

Hehmeyer, Ingrid. 1989. "Irrigation farming in the ancient Oasis of Marib." *Proceedings of the Seminar for Arabian Studies* 19: 33–44.

———. 1998. "Mosque, bath and garden: Symbiosis in the urban landscape of Sana'a, Yemen." *Proceedings of the Seminar for Arabian Studies* 28: 105–115.

Hehmeyer, Ingrid, and J. Schmidt. 1991. *Antike Technologie—Die Sabäische Wasserwirtschaft von Marib, 1.* Deutsches Archäologisches Institut, San 'a. Mainz: Verlag Philipp von Zabern.

Heimpel, W. 1990. "Ein zweiter Schritt zur Rehabilitierung der Rolle des Tigris in Sumer." *Zeitschrift fur Assyriologie* 80: 204–13.

Helbaek, Hans. 1972. "Samarran irrigation agriculture at Choga Mami." *Iraq* 34: 35–48.

Helms, Svend W. 1981. *Jawa: Lost City of the Black desert.* Ithaca: Cornell University.

Helms, Svend W., and A. Betts. 1987. "The desert 'kites' of the Badiyat esh-Sham and northern Arabia." *Paléorient* 13 (1): 41–67.

al-Helwah, Saleh, A. A. al-Shaikh, and A. S. Murad. 1982. "Preliminary report on the sixth phase of the Darb Zubayda reconnaissance 1981 (1401)." *Atlal* 6: 39–62.

Heron, Carl. 2001. "Geochemical prospection." Pp. 565–574 in Brothwell and Pollard.

Hester, J., R. Hamilton, A. Rahbini, K. M. Eskoubi, and M. Khan. 1984. "Preliminary report on the third phase of ancient mining survey of southwestern province-1403AH 1983." *Atlal* 8: 115–141.

Higgs, Eric S., and Claudio Vita-Finzi. 1972. "Prehistoric economies: A territorial approach." Pp. 27–36 in *Papers in Economic Prehistory*, ed. Eric S. Higgs. Cambridge: Cambridge University.

Hijjara, Ismael. 1997. *The Halaf Period in Northern Mesopotamia.* London: Nabu Publications.

Hirschfeld, Y. 1997. "Jewish rural settlement in Judaea in the early Roman period." Pp. 72–88 in *The Early Roman Empire in the East*, ed. Susan E. Alcock. Oxford: Oxbow.

Hirschfeld, Y., and R. Birger-Calderon. 1991. "Early Roman and Byzantine estates near Caeseria." *Israel Exploration Journal* 41: 81–111.

Hodge, A. Trevor. 2000. "Aqueducts." Pp. 39–66 in Wikander.

Hoelzmann, P., D. Jolly, S. P. Harrison, F. Laarif, R. Bonnefille, and H.-J. Pachur. 1998. "Mid-Holocene land-surface conditions in northern Africa and the Arabian peninsula: A data set for the analysis of biogeographical feedbacks in the climatic system." *Global Biogeochemical Cycles* 12 (1): 35–51.

Hoelzmann, P., B. Keding, H. Berke, S. Kröpelin, and H. J. Kruse. 2001. "Environmental change and archaeology: Lake evolution and human occupation in the eastern Sahara during the Holocene." *Palaeogeography, Palaeoclimatology, Palaeoecology* 169: 193–217.

Højlund, F., and H. H. Andersen. 1997. *Qala'at al-Bahrain, volume 2.* Aarhus, Denmark: Jutland Archaeological Society.

Hole, Frank (ed.). 1977. *Studies in the Archaeological History of the Deh Luran Plain: The Excavation of Chagha Sefid.* Ann Arbor: Memoirs of the Museum of Anthropology, University of Michigan, no. 9.

———. 1978. "Pastoral nomadism in western Iran." Pp. 127–167 in *Explorations in Ethnoarchaeology,* ed. R. A. Gould. Albuquerque, NM: University of New Mexico.

———. 1980. "Archaeological survey in southwest Asia." *Paléorient* 6: 21–44.

———. (ed.). 1987. *The Archaeology of Western Iran: Settlement and Society from Prehistory to the Islamic Conquest.* Washington, DC: Smithsonian Institution.

———. 1996. Intermittent settlement in the Jebel Abd al-Aziz region. Paper prepared for the international colloquium: The Syrian Djezireh: Cultural Heritage and Interrelations, Deir ez-Zor, April 22–25, 1996.

———. 1997a. "Evidence for mid-Holocene environmental change in the western Khabur drainage, northeastern Syria." Pp. 67–106 in Dalfes et al.

———. 1997b. "Palaeoenvironment and human society in the Jezireh of northern Mesopotamia 20,000–6,000 B.P." *Paléorient* 23 (2): 39–49.

Hole, Frank, K. V. Flannery, and J. A. Neely. 1969. *Prehistory and Human Ecology of the Deh Luran Plain.* Ann Arbor: Memoir no. 1 University of Michigan, Museum of Anthropology.

Hole, Frank, and N. Kouchoukos. In press. "Preliminary report on an archaeological survey in the western Khabur basin, 1994." *Annales Archéologiques Arabes Syriennes.*

Honari, M. 1989. "Qanats and human ecosystems in Iran." Pp. 61–86 in Beaumont et al.

Hopkins, David C. 1985. *The Highlands of Canaan: Agricultural Life in the Early Iron Age.* Decatur, GA: Almond/ASOR.

Horowitz, Aharon. 1979. *The Quaternary of Israel.* New York: Academic.

Hoskins, W. G. 1955. *The Making of the English Landscape.* London: Hodder and Staughton.

Hötzl, H., A. R. Jado, H. Moser, W. Rauert, and J. G. Zötl. 1984. "Climatic fluctuations in the Holocene." Pp. 301–314 in *The Quaternary Period in Saudi Arabia,* vol. 2, ed. Abdul R. Jado and Josef G. Zötl. New York: Springer-Verlag.

Hughes, K. J. 1999. "Persistent features from a palaeo-landscape: The ancient tracks of the Maltese Islands." *Geographical Journal* 165 (1): 62–78.

Hunt, Robert C. 1988. "Hydraulic management in southern Mesopotamia in Sumerian times." *Bulletin on Sumerian Agriculture* 4 (1): 189–206.

Huot, Jean-Luis. 1989. "'Ubaidian villages of lower Mesopotamia. Permanence and evolution from 'Ubaid 0 to 'Ubaid 4 as seen from Tell el' Oueili." Pp. 19–42 in *Upon This Foundation: The 'Ubaid Reconsidered,* ed. Elizabeth F. Henrickson and Ingolf Thuesen. Copenhagen: Carsten Niebuhr Institute Publications 10.

———. 1996. *Oueli: Travaux de 1987 et 1989.* Paris: Éditions Recherche sur les Civilisations.

Hütteroth, Wolf-Dieter. 1990. "Villages and tribes of the Gezira under early Ottoman administration (16th century), a preliminary report." *Berytus* 38: 179–184.

Ibach, R. D. 1987. *Archaeological Survey of the Hesban Region.* Berrien Springs, MI: Andrews University.

Ibrahim, Jabir Khalil. 1986. *Pre-Islamic Settlement in Jazira.* Baghdad, Republic of Iraq: Ministry of Culture and Information, State Organisation of Antiquities and Heritage.

Ibrahim, Moawiyah. 1982. *Excavations of the Arab Expedition at Sar el-Jisr.* Bahrain: Bahrain Ministry of Information.

Ibrahim, Moawiyah, and Ali Tigani al-Mahi. 2000. "Metallurgy in Oman during the Early Islamic period." Pp. 207–220 in *The Archaeology of Jordan and Beyond: Essays in Honor of James A. Sauer,* ed. Lawrence E. Stager, Joseph A. Greene, and Michael D. Coogan. Winona Lake, IN: Eisenbraun.

Ilan, D. 1997. "Dolmen." Pp. 167–168 in Meyers.

Inbar, M. 1992. "Rates of fluvial erosion in basins with a Mediterranean type climate." *Catena* 19: 393–409.

Ingraham, Michael L., T. D. Johnson, B. Rihani, and I. Shatler. 1981. "Preliminary report on a reconnaisance survey of the northwest province." *Atlal* 5: 59–84.

Innes, J. L. 1985. "Lichenometry." *Progress in Physical Geography* 9: 187–254.

Ionides, M. G. 1937. *The Regime of the Rivers Euphrates and Tigris.* London: E. and F. Spon.

Iraq Department of Antiquities. 1976. *Archaeological Atlas of Iraq.* Baghdad, Republic of Iraq: Department of Antiquities.

Issar, Arie, and Neville Brown (eds.) 1998. *Water, Environment and Society in Times of Climatic Change.* Dordrecht: Kluwer.

Ives, Jack D., and Bruno Messerli. 1989. *The Himalayan Dilemma: Reconciling Development and Conservation.* New York: Routledge.

Jacobsen, Thorkild. 1958. "Summary of a report by the Diyala Basin Archaeological Project, June 1, 1957 to June 1, 1958." *Sumer* 14: 79–89.

———. 1960. "The waters of Ur." *Iraq* 22: 174–185.

———. 1969. "A survey of the Girsu (Telloh) region." *Sumer* 25: 103–109.

Jacobsen, Thorkild, and Seton Lloyd. 1935. *Sennacherib's Aqueduct at Jerwan.* Chicago: Oriental Institute Publications 24.

Jacobsen, Thorkild, and R. McC. Adams. 1958. "Salt and silt in ancient Mesopotamian agriculture." *Science* 128: 1251–1258.

Jager, S. W. 1985. "A prehistoric route and ancient cart tracks in the Gement of Anloo (Netherlands)." *Palaeohistoria* 27: 185–202.

Jas, Remko. 2000. "Land tenure in northern Mesopotamia." Pp. 247–263 in Jas (ed.).

———— (ed.). 2000. *Rainfall and Agriculture in Northern Mesopotamia*. Leiden: Nederlands Historisch-Archaeologisch Instituut te Istanbul.

Joffe, Alexander H. 1993. *Settlement and Society in the Early Bronze Age I and II, Southern Levant*. Sheffield: Sheffield Academic.

Johns, C. H. W. 1901. *An Assyrian Domesday Book*. Leipzig: J. C. Hinrichs.

Johnson, Gregory J. 1973. *Local Exchange and Early State Development in Southwestern Iran*. Ann Arbor: Anthropological Papers no. 51, University of Michigan, Museum of Anthropology.

Jones, L. S., and Stanley A. Schumm. 1999. "Causes of avulsion: An overview." *Special Publications of the International Association of Sedimentology* 28: 171–178.

Jones, Martin. 1987. *England before Domesday*. Totowa, NJ: Barnes and Noble.

Jung, Michael. 1991. *Research on Rock Art in North Yemen*. Napoli Istituto Universitario Orientale.

Kabawi, A. B., M. K. H. Khan, A. al-Zahrani, A. Y. al-Mubarak, M. H. as-Sumer, and M. A. al-Shawati. 1996. "Comprehensive rock art and epigraphic survey (1990)." *Atlal* 14: 55–72.

Karastathis, V., and S. P. Papamarinopoulos. 1997. "The detection of the Xerxes canal by the use of shallow reflection and refraction seismics: Preliminary results." *Geophysical Prospection* 45: 389–401.

Kayan, Ilhan. 1999. "Holocene stratigraphy and geomorphological evolution of the Aegean coastal plains of Anatolia." *Quaternary Science Reviews* 18: 541–548.

Keall, Edward J. 1998. "Encountering megaliths on the Tihāmah coastal plain of Yemen." *Proceeding of the Seminar for Arabian Studies* 28: 139–147.

Kedar, Y. 1957. "Water and soil from the Negev: Some ancient achievements in the central Negev." *Geographical Journal* 123: 179–187.

Kennedy, David L. 1982. *Archaeological Explorations on the Roman Frontier in North-east Jordan*. Oxford: BAR (International Series) 134.

————. 1995. "Water supply and use in the southern Hauran, Jordan." *Journal of Field Archaeology* 22: 275–290.

————. 1998. "Declassified satellite photographs and archaeology in the Middle East: Case studies from Turkey." *Antiquity* 72: 553–561.

————. 2001. "History in depth: Surface survey and aerial archaeology." *Studies in the History and Archaeology of Jordan* 7: 39–48.

————. 2002. "Aerial archaeology in the Middle East: The role of the military—past, present and future?" Pp. 33–48 in *Aerial Archaeology: Developing Future Practice*, ed. Robert H. Bewley and W. Raczkowski. Berlin: NATO and IOS.

Kennedy, David L., and Derek Riley. 1990. *Rome's Desert Frontier from the Air*. Austin: University of Texas.

Kennedy, David L., and P. Freeman. 1995. "Southern Hauran Survey, 1992." *Levant* 27: 39–73.

Kennedy, David L., H. I. MacAdam, and D. N. Riley. 1986. "Preliminary report on the Southern Hauran Survey, 1985." *Annual of the Department of Antiquities of Jordan* 30: 145–153 and 452–455.

Khan, M. 1989. "Art and religion: Sacred images of the metaphysical world." *Atlal* 12: 55–57.

Khan, M., and A. al-Mughannam. 1982. "Ancient dams in the Taif area 1981 (1401)." *Atlal* 6: 125–135.

Khazanov, Andrei M. 1984. *Nomads and the Outside World*. Madison: University of Wisconsin.

King, Geraldine. 1990. "The basalt desert rescue survey and some preliminary remarks on the Safaitic inscriptions and rock drawings." *Proceedings of the Seminar for Arabian Studies* 20: 55–79.

Kingsley, Sean. 2001. "The economic impact of the Palestinian wine trade in late Antiquity." Pp. 44–68 in *Economy and Exchange in the East Mediterranean during Late Antiquity*, ed. Sean Kingsley and Michael Decker. Oxford: Oxbow.

Kloner, Amos. 1996. "Stepped roads in Roman Palestine." *Aram* 8: 111–137.

Knapp, A. Bernard. 1999. "Ideational and industrial landscapes on prehistoric Cyprus." Pp. 229–252 in *Archaeologies of landscape: contemporary perspectives*, ed. Wendy Ashmore and A. Bernard Knapp. Oxford: Blackwell.

Knudstad, James. 1977. "The Darb Zubayda Project, 1396–1976: Preliminary report on the first phase." *Atlal* 1: 41–68.

Kobori, Iwao (ed.). 1980. *Qanawat Romani of Taibe Oasis*. University of Tokyo: Department of Geography, The Tokyo University Scientific Mission for the Comparative Study of the Foggara Oasis: Report no. 1.

Kohler, Timothy A., and George J. Gummerman (eds.). 2000. *Dynamics in Human and Primate Societies: Agent-Based Modeling of Social and Spatial Processes*. New Mexico, Santa Fe Institute and Oxford University.

Köhler-Rollefson I., and G. O. Rollefson. 1990. "The impact of Neolithic subsistence strategies on the environment: The case of 'Ain Ghazal, Jordan." Pp. 3–14 in Bottema et al.

Kolars, John F., and W. A. Mitchell. 1991. *The Euphrates River and Southeast Anatolia Development Project*. Carbondale: Southern Illinois University.

Kosmas, C., N. Danalatos, L. H. Cammeraat, M. Chabart, J. Diamantopoulos, R. Farand, L. Gutierrez, A. Jacob, H. Marques, J. Martinez-Fernandez, A. Mizara, N. Moustakas, J. M. Nicolau, C. Oliveros, G. Pinna, R. Puddu, J. Puigdefabregas, M. Roxo, A. Simao, G. Stamou, N. Tomasi, D. Usai, and A. Vacca. 1997. "The effect of land use on runoff and soil erosion rates under Mediterranean conditions." *Catena* 29: 45–59.

Kouchoukos, Nicholas. 1998. "Landscape and Social Change in Late Prehistoric Mesopotamia." Ph.D. dissertation, Department of Anthropology, Yale University.

————. 2001. "Satellite images and near eastern landscapes." *Near Eastern Archaeology* 64: 80–91.

Kouchoukos, Nicholas, R. Smith, A. Gleason, P. Thenkabail, F. Hole, Y. Barkoudah, J. Albert, P. Gluhosky, and J. Foster. 1998. "Monitoring the distribution, use, and regeneration of natural resources in semi-arid southwest Asia." In *Transformations of Middle Eastern Natural Environments: Legacies and Lessons*, ed. J. Albert, M. Bernhardsson, and R. Kenna. Yale School of Forestry and Environmental Studies 103: 467–489.

Kozlowski, Stefan K. 1999. *The Eastern Wing of the Fertile Crescent: Late Prehistory of Greater Mesopotamian Lithic Industries*. Oxford: BAR (International Series) 760.

Kraft, John C., I. Kayan, and O. Erol. 1982. "Geology and paleogeographic reconstructions of the vicinity of Troy." Pp. 11–41 in *Troy, the Archaeo-*

logical Geology, ed. George Rapp and John A. Gifford. Princeton, NJ: Princeton University.

Kramer, Carol. 1979. *Ethnoarchaeology: Implications of Ethnography for Archaeology*. New York: Columbia University.

Kuhne, Hartmut. 1990. "The effects of irrigation agriculture on Bronze Age and Iron Age habitation along the Khabur, eastern Syria." Pp. 15–30 in Bottema et al.

Kutzbach, John, G. Bonan, J. Foley, and S. P. Harrison. 1996. "Vegetation and soil feedbacks on the response of the African monsoon to orbital forcing in the early to middle Holocene." *Science* 384: 623–626.

Kwasman, Theodore, and Simo Parpola (eds.). 1991. *Legal Transactions of the Court of Nineveh, Part I*. Helsinki: University of Helsinki Press, State Archives of Assyria VI.

Lafont, Bertrand. 2000. "Irrigation agriculture in Mari." Pp. 129–146 in Jas (ed.).

Lamb, Hubert H. 1977. *Climate Past, Present and Future*. London: Methuen.

Lambeck, Kurt. 1996a. "Sea-level change and shoreline evolution: Aegean Greece since the Upper Palaeolithic." *Antiquity* 70: 588–611.

———. 1996b. "Shoreline reconstruction for the Persian Gulf since the last Glacial Maximum." *Earth and Planetary Science Letters* 142: 43–57.

Lambton, Ann K. S. 1989. "The origin, diffusion and functioning of the qanat." Pp. 5–12 in Peter Beaumont et al.

Lancaster, William, and Fidelity Lancaster. 1999. *People, Land and Water in the Arab Middle East. Environments and Landscapes in the Bilad ash-Sham*. Amsterdam: Harwood Academic Publishers.

Lanfranchi, G. B., and S. Parpola. 1990. *The Correspondence of Sargon II, Part II: Letters from the Northern and Northeastern Provinces*. State Archives of Assyria, vol. 5. Helsinki: Helsinki University.

Langbein, W. B., and S. A. Schumm. 1958. "Yield of sediment in relation to mean annual precipitation." *American Geophysical Union Transactions* 39: 1076–1084.

Lansing, J. Stephen. 1987. "Balinese 'water temples' and the management of irrigation." *American Anthropologist* 89: 326–341.

Lapp, P. W. 1969. "The 1968 excavation at Tell Ta 'annek." *Bulletin of the American Schools of Oriental Research* 195: 12.

Larsen, Curtis E. 1983. *Life and Land Use on the Bahrain Islands: The Geoarchaeology of an Ancient Society*. Chicago: University of Chicago.

Larsen, Curtis E., and G. Evans. 1978. "The Holocene geological history of the Tigris-Euphrates-Karun delta." Pp. 227–244 in *The Environmental History of the Near and Middle East since the Last Ice Age*, ed. William C. Brice. London: Academic.

Layard, Austen H. 1849. *Nineveh and Its Remains*. London: John Murray.

Lees, G. M., and N. L. Falcon. 1952. "The geographical history of the Mesopotamian plains." *Geographical Journal* 118: 24–39.

Lehmann, Gunnar. 2001. "Phoenicians in Western Galilee: First results of an archaeological survey in the hinterland of Akko." Pp. 65–112 in *Studies in the Archaeology of the Iron Age in Israel and Jordan*, ed. Amihai Mazar. Sheffield: Sheffield Academic; *Journal for the Study of the Old Testament* Supplement Series 331.

Lehner, Mark. 2000. "The fractal house of Pharaoh: Ancient Egypt as a complex adaptive system, a trial formulation." Pp. 275–254 in *Dynamics in Human and Primate Societies: Agent-based Modeling of Social and Spatial Processes*, ed. Timothy Kohler and George Gumerman. Santa Fe Institute and Oxford University.

Lemcke, Gary, and M. Sturm. 1997. "^{18}O and trace element measurements as proxy for the reconstruction of climate changes at Lake Van (Turkey): Preliminary results." Pp. 653–678 in Dalfes et al.

Le Strange, Guy. 1905. *Lands of the Eastern Caliphate*. London: Frank Cass.

Letts, Sally. 1978. *Water*. Department of Geography, University of Durham, UK. Vol. 2 of Research and Development Surveys in Northern Oman, Final Reports.

Levy, Thomas E. 1998. *The Archaeology of Society in the Holy Land*. Leicester: Leicester University.

Levy, Thomas E., and D. Alon. 1987. "Settlement patterns along the Nahal Beersheva-Lower Nahal Besor: Models of subsistence in the northern Negev." Pp 45–138 in *Shiqmim I: Studies Concerning Chalcolithic Societies in the Northern Negev Desert, Israel (1982–1984)*, ed. Thomas E. Levy. Oxford: BAR (International Series) 356.

Levy, Thomas, E., and A. Holl. 2002. "Migrations, ethnogenesis and settlement dynamics: Israelites in Iron Age Canaan and Shuwa-Arabs in the Chad Basin." *Journal of Anthropological Archaeology* 21: 83–118.

Lev-Yadun, S. 1997. "Flora and climate in southern Samaria: Past and present." Pp. 85–102 in Finkelstein and Lederman.

Lev-Yadun, S., Y. Mizrachi, and M. Kochari. 1996. "Lichenometric studies at Rogem Hiri." *Israel Exploration Journal* 46: 196–207.

Lewis, Norman. 1987. *Nomads and Settlers in Syria and Jordan, 1800–1980*. Cambridge: Cambridge University.

Lézine, A.-M., J.-F. Saliège, C. Robert, F. Wertz, and M.-L. Inizan. 1998. "Holocene lakes from Ramlat as-Sab'atayn (Yemen) illustrate the impact of monsoon activity in southern Arabia." *Quaternary Research* 50: 290–299.

Lézine, A.-M., J.-F. Saliège, R. Mathieu, T.-L. Tagliatela, S. Mery, V. Charpentier, and S. Cleuziou. In press. "Late Holocene mangroves of Oman: Climatic implications and impact on human settlements." *Vegetation History and Archaeobotany*.

Lightfoot, Dale R. 1996. "Syrian qanat Romani: History, ecology, abandonment." *Journal of Arid Environments* 33: 321–336.

———. 2000. "The origin and diffusion of qanats in Arabia: New evidence from the northern and southern peninsula." *Geographical Journal* 166 (3): 215–266.

Lillesand, Thomas M., and Ralph W. Kiefer. 1999. *Remote Sensing and Image Interpretation*. New York: Wiley.

Littauer, M. A., and J. H. Crouwel. 1990. "Ceremonial threshing in the ancient Near East." *Iraq* 52: 19–23.

Liverani, Mario. 1992. *Studies on the Annals of Ashurnasirpal II: 2: Topographical Analysis*. Rome: Quaderni di Geografica Storica 4.

———. 1996. "Reconstructing the rural landscape of the ancient Near East." *Journal of the Social and Economic History of the Orient* 39: 1–49.

Lloyd, J. 1991. "Conclusion: Archaeological survey and the Roman landscape." Pp. 233–240 in *Roman Landscapes: Archaeological Survey in the Mediter-*

ranean Region, ed. Graeme Barker and J. Lloyd. Rome: British School at Rome, Archaeological Monograph no. 2.

Lloyd, Seton. 1954. "Mound surveys." *Antiquity* 28: 214–220.

———. 1963. *Mounds of the Near East.* Edinburgh: Edinburgh University.

Lock, Gary, and Z. Stančič (eds.). 1995. *Archaeology and Geographical Information Systems: A European Perspective.* London: Taylor and Francis.

Luckenbill, Daniel D. 1927 (1968). *Ancient Records of Assyria and Babylonia.* New York: Greenwood.

Lyon, Jerry D. 2000. "Middle Assyrian expansion and settlement development in the Syrian Jazira: The view from the Balikh Valley." Pp. 89–126 in Jas (ed.).

Lyonnet, Bertille. 1998. "Le peuplement de la Djéziré occidentale au début 3ᵉ millénaire, villes circulaires et pastoralism: Questions et hypothèses." *Subartu* 4: 179–193.

Mabbutt, J. A., and C. Floret. 1980. "Desertification in the Greater Mussayeb Project, Iraq." Pp. 176–213 in *Case Studies on Desertification*, ed. J. A. Mabbutt and C. Floret. Paris: UNESCO and United Nations Environmental Programme.

MacDonald, Burton. 1992. *The Southern Ghors and Northeast 'Arabah Survey.* Sheffield: J. R. Collis.

MacKenzie, Neil D., and Salah al-Helwah. 1980. "Darb Zubayda 1979: A preliminary report." *Atlal* 4: 37–50.

Magee, Peter. 2000. "Patterns of settlement in the southeastern Arabian Iron Age." *Adumatu* 1: 29–39.

Mainguet, Monique. 1999. *Aridity: Droughts and Human Development.* Berlin: Springer.

Maizels, Judith. 1990. "Raised channel systems as indicators of palaeohydrological change: A case study from Oman." *Palaeogeography, Palaeoclimatology, Palaeoecology* 76: 241–277.

Makaske, Bart. 2001. "Anastomosing rivers: A review of their classification, origin and sedimentary products." *Earth Science Reviews* 53: 149–196.

Marcolongo, Bruno, and D. Morandi Bonocossi. 1997. "L'abandon du système d'irrigation Qatabanite dans la vallée du wadi Bayhan (Yemen): Analyse géo-archéologique." *Sciences de la terre et des planetes* 325: 79–86.

Marcus, Joyce. 1998. "The peaks and valleys of ancient states, an extension of the dynamic model." Pp. 59–94 in *Archaic States*, ed. Gary M. Feinman and Joyce Marcus. Santa Fe, NM: School of American Research.

Marfoe, Leon. 1978. "Between Qadesh and Kumidi: A History of Frontier Settlement and Land Use in the Biqaʿ, Lebanon." Ph.D. dissertation, Department of Near Eastern Languages and Civilizations, University of Chicago.

———. 1979. "The integrative transformation: Patterns of sociopolitical organization in southern Syria." *Bulletin of the American Schools of Oriental Research* 234: 1–42.

Masry, Abdullah H. 1997. *Prehistory in Northern Arabia: The Problem of Interregional Interaction.* London: Kegan Paul International.

Masters, Patricia M., and Nicholas C. Flemming. 1983. *Quaternary Coastlines and Marine Archaeology: Towards the Prehistory of Land Bridges and Continental Shelves.* New York: Academic.

Matthers, John (ed.). 1981. *The River Qoueiq, Northern Syria and Its Catchment: Studies Arising from the Tell Rifa'at Survey 1977–79.* Oxford: BAR (International Series) 98.

Matthews, V. H. 1978. *Pastoral Nomadism in the Mari Kingdom (ca. 1830–1760 BC).* Cambridge, MA: ASOR.

Matheson, Sylvia A. 1976. *Persia: An Archaeological Guide.* London: Faber and Faber.

Matney, Timothy, and Guillermo Algaze. 1995. "Urban development at mid-late Early Bronze Age Titriş Höyük in southeastern Anatolia." *Bulletin of the American Schools of Oriental Research* 299/300: 33–52.

Matsutani T., and Y. Nishiaki. 1998. "Bedrock Pits from Pottery Neolithic Sites in North Mesopotamia: Reconsideration of the Function of Pit 9 from Tell Kashkashok II, Syria." *Subartu* 4 (1): 31–37.

Matthews, Roger. 2000. *The Early Prehistory of Mesopotamia 500,000 to 4,500 B.C.* Subartu 5.

Matthews, Roger, T. Pollard, and M. Ramage. 1998. "Project Paphlagonia: Regional survey in northern Anatolia." Pp. 195–206, in *Ancient Anatolia. Fifty Year's Work by the British Institute of Archaeology at Ankara*, ed. Roger Matthews. London: British Institute of Archaeology at Ankara.

Mattingly, David J. 1996. "First fruit? The olive in the Roman World." Pp. 213–253 in *Human Landscapes in Classical Antiquity. Environment and Culture*, ed. Graham Shipley and J. Salmon. London: Routledge.

Mayerson, Philip. 1960. *The Ancient Agricultural Regime of Nessana and the Central Negeb.* Jerusalem: British School of Archaeology in Jerusalem.

Mazzoni, Stefania. 1994. "Aramaean and Luwian new foundations." Pp. 319–339 in *Nuove fondazioni nel Vicino Oriente antico: realta e ideologia*, ed. Stefania Mazzoni. Pisa: Giardini Editori.

McClellan, Thomas L. 1998. "Tell Banat North: The White Monument." *Subartu* 4 (1): 243–269.

McClellan, Thomas L., R. Grayson, and C. Oglesby. 2000. "Bronze Age water harvesting in north Syria." *Subartu* 7: 137–155.

McClure, Harold A. 1978. "Ar-Rub' Al Khali." Pp. 252–263 in *The Quaternary Period in Saudi Arabia. v. 1*, ed. Saad S. Al-Sayari and Josef G. Zötl. New York: Springer-Verlag.

McCorriston, Joy. 1992. "The Halaf environment and human activities in the Khabur drainage, Syria." *Journal of Field Archaeology.* 19: 315–333.

McCorriston, Joy, and S. Weinberg. 2002. "Spatial and temporal variation in Mesopotamian Agricultural practices in the Khabur Basin, Syrian Jazira." *Journal of Archaeological Science* 29: 485–498.

McDonald, R. A. 1995. "CORONA: Success for space reconnaissance: A look into the Cold War, and a revolution for intelligence." *Photogrammetric Engineering and Remote Sensing* 61: 689–720.

McGlade, James. 1995. "Archaeology and the ecodynamics of human-modified landscapes." *Antiquity* 69: 113–132.

———. 1997. "Archaeology and the evolution of cultural landscapes: Towards an interdisciplinary research agenda." Pp. 458–482 in *The Archaeology and Anthropology of Landscape*, ed. Peter J. Ucko and Robert J. Layton. London: Routledge.

McNeill, John R. 1992. *The Mountains of the Mediterranean World: An Environmental History.* Cambridge: Cambridge University.

Meijer, Diederik J. W. 1986. *A Survey in Northeastern Syria.* Leiden: Netherlands Historical-Archaeological Institute, Istanbul.

Mellaart, James. 1961. "Early cultures

of the South Anatolian plateau I." *Anatolian Studies* 11: 139–184.

———. 1963. "Early cultures of the South Anatolian plateau II." *Anatolian Studies* 13: 199–236.

Meshel, Z. 1974. "New data about the 'desert kites.'" *Tel Aviv* 1: 129–143.

Metheny, Karen B. 1996. "Landscape archaeology." Pp. 384–385 in *The Oxford Companion to Archaeology*, ed. Brian Fagan. Oxford: Oxford University.

Meyers, Eric M. (ed.). 1997. *The Oxford Encyclopedia of Archaeology in the Near East* (5 volumes). Oxford: Oxford University.

Mikesell, Marvin. 1969. "The deforestation of Mount Lebanon." *Geographical Review* 59: 1–28.

Milano, Lucio, S. de Martino, F. Mario Fales, and G. B. Lannfranchi (eds.). 1999. *Landscapes, Territories, Frontiers and Horizons in the Ancient Near East.* Padova, Italy: Sargon srl.

Miller, J. Maxwell. 1991. *Archaeological Survey of the Kerak Plateau.* Atlanta: SOR, Archaeological Reports 1.

Miller, Naomi, F. 1997a. "Sweyhat and Hajji Ibrahim: Some archaeobotanical samples from the 1991 and 1993 seasons." Pp. 95–122 in Zettler.

———. 1997b. "Farming and herding along the Euphrates: Environmental constraint and cultural choice (fourth to second millennia B.C.)." Pp. 123–132 in Zettler.

———. 1998. "The macrobotanical evidence for vegetation in the Near East, c. 18000/16000 B.C. to 4000 B.C." *PaléOrient* 23/2: 197–207.

Miller, Naomi F., and Katherine L. Gleason. 1994. *The Archaeology of Garden and Field.* Philadelphia: University of Pennsylvania.

Miller, Naomi F., and Tristine L. Smart. 1984. "Intentional burning of dung as fuel: A mechanism for the incorporation of charred seeds into the archeological record." *Journal of Ethnobiology* 4: 15–28.

Miller, Robert. 1980. "Water use in Syria and Palestine from the Neolithic to the Bronze Age." *World Archaeology* 11 (3): 331–41.

Moore, Andrew M. T., G. Hillman, and A. J. Legge. 2000. *Village on the Euphrates: From Foraging to Farming at Abu Hureyra.* Oxford: Oxford University.

Moore, Jerry D. 1988. "Prehistoric raised field agriculture in the Casma valley, Peru." *Journal of Field Archaeology* 15: 265–276.

Moortgat-Correns, Ursula. 1972. *Die Bildewerke vom Djebelet el Beda in Ihren Räumlichen und Zeitlichen UmWelt.* Berlin: Walter de Gruyter.

Moran, Emilio. 2000. *Human Adaptability: An Introduction to Ecological Anthropology.* Boulder, CO: Westview.

Morandi, Daniele Bonacassi. 1996a. *Tra il fiume e la steppa: insediamento e uso del territorio nella bassa valle del fiume Habur in epoca neo-assira.* Padova: Sargon srl.

———. 1996b. "'Landscapes of power.' The political organisation of space in the lower Habur Valley in the Neo-Assyrian period." *Bulletin of the State Archives of Assyria* 10 (2): 15–49.

———. 2000. "The Syrian Jazireh in the Late Assyrian period: A view from the countryside." Pp. 349–396 in *Essays on Syria in the Iron Age*, ed. Guy Bunnens. Louvain: Peeters.

Morony, Michael T. 1994. "Land use and settlement patterns in late Sasanian and early Islamic Iraq." Pp. 221–230 in *The Byzantine and Early Islamic Near East.* Vol. 2: *Land Use and Settlement Patterns*, ed. Geoffrey R. D. King and Averil Cameron. Princeton, NJ: Darwin.

Morozova, G. S., and N. D. Smith. 1999. "Holocene avulsion history of the lower Saskatchewan fluvial system, Cumberland Marshes, Saskatchewan-Manitoba, Canada." *Special Publications of the International Association of the International Association of Sedimentology* (28): 231–249.

Mortimore, Michael. 1989. *Adapting to Drought: Farmers, Famines, and Desertification in West Africa.* Cambridge: Cambridge University.

el-Moslimany, Ann P. 1994. "Evidence of early Holocene summer precipitation in the continental Middle East." Pp. 121–130 in Bar-Yosef and Kra.

Mulders, Michel A. 1969. *The Arid Soils of the Balikh Basin (Syria).* Rotterdam: Drukkerij.

Musil, Alois, 1928. *Northern Neğd. A Topographic Itinerary.* New York: American Geographical Society.

Nanson, G. C., and H. Q. Huang. 1999. "Anabranching rivers: Divided efficiency leading to fluvial diversity." Pp. 477–494 in *Varieties of Fluvial Form*, ed. A. J. Miller and A. Gupta. Chichester, UK: John Wiley.

Nasif, Abdullah A. 1988. *al-'Ula: An Historical and Archaeological Survey with Special Reference to Its Irrigation System.* Riyad: King Saud University.

Al-Nasser, Ali Nasser, Abd al-Aziz Hameed al-Ruwaite, and Mohammad Abdul Aziz. 1988. "A preliminary study of Darb al-Feel: 'Road of the Elephants.'" *Atlal* 11: 87–92.

Nayeem, Mohammed A. 1990. *Prehistory and Protohistory of the Arabian Peninsula.* Vol. 1: *Saudi Arabia.* Hyderabad: Hyderabad.

———. 2000. *The Rock Art of Arabia.* Hyderabad: Hyderabad.

Neely, James, A. 1974. "Sassanian and early Islamic water-control and irrigation systems on the Deh Luran plain, Iran." Pp. 21–42 in Downing and Gibson.

Neely, James A., and H. T. Wright. 1994. *Early Settlement and Irrigation on the Deh Luran Plain. Village and Early State Societies in Southwestern Iran.* Ann Arbor: University of Michigan Museum of Anthropology, Technical Report 26.

Nelson, H.S. 1962. "An abandoned irrigation system in southern Iraq." *Sumer* 18: 67–72.

Nemet-Nejat, Karen R. 1998. *Daily Life in Ancient Mesopotamia.* Westport, CT: Greenwood.

Netser, Michael. 1998. "Population growth and decline in the northern part of Eretz-Israel during the historical period as related to climatic changes." Pp. 129–145 in *Water, Environment and Society in Times of Climatic Change*, ed. Arie Issar and Neville Brown. Dordrecht: Kluwer.

Netting, Robert McC. 1993. *Smallholders and Householders: Farm Families and the Ecology of Intensive, Sustainable Agriculture.* Stanford: Stanford University.

Newson, Paul. 2000. "Differing strategies for water supply and farming in the Syrian Black Desert." Pp. 86–102 in *The Archaeology of Drylands*, ed. Graeme Barker and David Gilbertson. London: Routledge.

Newton, Lynne S., and Juris Zarins. 2000. "Aspects of Bronze Age art of southern Arabia: The pictorial landscape and its relation to economic and socio-political status." *Arabian Archaeology and Epigraphy* 11: 154–179.

Nieuwenhuyse, Olivier. 2000. "Halaf settlement in the Khabur headwaters."

Pp. 151–260 in *Prospection Archéologique du Haut-Khabur Occidental (Syrie du N.E.)*, ed. Bertille Lyonnet. Beirut-Damascus: Institut Français D'Archéologie du Proche-Orient.

Nissen, Hans J. 1988. *The Early History of the Ancient Near East 9000–2000 B.C.* Chicago: University of Chicago.

Northedge, Alistaire. 1990. "The racecourses at Samarra." *Bulletin of the School of Oriental and African Studies* 53: 31–56.

Northedge, A., T. J. Wilkinson, and R. Falkner. 1990. "Survey and excavations at Samarra.'" *Iraq* 52: 121–148.

Oates, David. 1968. *Studies in the Ancient History of Northern Iraq.* London: British Academy.

Oates, David, and Joan Oates. 1976. "Early irrigation agriculture in Mesopotamia." Pp. 109–135, in *Problems in Economic and Social Archaeology* ed. G. de G. Sieveking, Ian H. Longworth, and K. E. Wilson. London: Duckworth.

———. 1990. "Aspects of Hellenistic and Roman settlement in the Khabur Basin. Pp. 227–248, in *Resurrecting the Past: A Joint Tribute to Adnan Bounni.* ed. Paolo Matthiae, M. van Loon, and H. Weiss. Leiden: Nederlands Historisch-Archaeologische Instituut te Istanbul.

Oates, Joan. 1969. "Choga Mami, 1967–68: A preliminary report." *Iraq* 31: 115–152.

———. 1982. "Archaeological evidence for settlement patterns in Mesopotamia and eastern Arabia in relation to possible environmental conditions." Pp. 359–398 in *Palaeoclimates, Palaeoenvironments and Human Communities in the Eastern Mediterranean Region in Later Prehistory*, ed. John L. Bintliff and W. van Zeist. Oxford: BAR (International Series) 133.

Oded, Bustanai. 1979. *Mass Deportations and Deportees in the Neo-Assyrian Empire.* Wiesbaden: Ludwig Reichert.

Oleson, John Peter. 1991. "Aqueducts, cisterns, and the strategy of water supply at Nabataean and Roman Auara (Jordan)." Pp. 45–62 *Future Currents in Aqueduct Studies*, ed. John Peter Oleson. Leeds: Francis Cairns.

Oppenheim, A. Leo, and Erica Reiner (eds.). 1958. *Chicago Assyrian Dictionary: "E."* Chicago: Oriental Institute Publications.

Orchard, Jocelyn. 1982. "Finding the ancient sites in southern Yemen." *Journal of Near Eastern Studies* 41: 1–21.

Orchard, Jeffery. 1999. "The layout and Monuments of an al-Hajar Oasis town at Besya in the Wadi Behla, Oman (Late 4th–Late 3rd millennium B.C.)." Pp 213–232 in Milano et al.

Overstreet, William, Maurice J. Grolier, and Michael R. Toplyn. 1988a. *Geological and Archaeological Reconnaissance in the Yemen Arab Republic, 1985.* Washington, DC: American Foundation for the Study of Man.

Overstreet, William C., R. C. Eidt, R. Brinkmann, D. E. Detra, and T. T. Chao. 1988b. "Orientation survey using phosphate fractionation to distinguish anthrosols from native sediments in the Wadi al-Jubah archaeological area, Yemen Arab Republic." Pp. 121–154 in Overstreet et al.

Pacey, Arnold, and Adrian Cullis. 1986. *Rainwater Harvesting: The Collection of Rainfall and Runoff in Rural Areas.* London: Intermediate Technology.

Paepe, R. 1971. "Geological approach of the Tell ed-Der area, Mesopotamian plain, Iraq." Pp. 9–27 in *Tell ed-Der I*, ed. Leon de Meyer. Leuven: Editions Peeters.

Paepe, R., and C. Baeteman. 1978. "The fluvial system between Tell ed-Der and Abu Habba. Pp. 37–56 in *Tell ed-Der III*, ed. Leon De Meyer: Leuven: Editions Peeters.

Page, Stephanie. 1968. "A stela of Adad Nirari III and Nergel Eres from Tell al-Rimah." *Iraq* 30: 139–53.

Palmer, E. H. 1871. *The Desert of the Exodus.* Cambridge: Cambridge University.

Parker, Bradley J. 1997. "The northern frontier of Assyria: An archaeological perspective." Pp. 217–214 in *Assyria 1995*, ed. Simo Parpola and Robert M. Whiting. Helsinki: Publications of the State Archives of Assyria Project.

———. 2001. "The colonizer, the colonized, and the colonists: Empire and settlement on Assyria's Anatolian frontier." UTARP web page: www.utarp.org.

Parker, S. Thomas. 1986. *Romans and Saracens: A History of the Arabian Frontier.* Winona Lake, IN: Eisenbrauns.

Parker-Pearson, Michael, and Ramilsonina. 1998. "Stonehenge for the ancestors: The stones pass on the message." *Antiquity* 72: 308–326.

Parr, Peter J., J. Zarins, M. Ibrahim, J. Waechter, A. Garrard, C. Clarke, M. Bidmead, and H. al-Badr. 1978. "Northern Provinces survey." *Atlal* 2: 29–50.

Peattie, Roderick. 1936. *Mountain Geography: A Critique and Field Study.* Cambridge, MA: Harvard University.

Peleg, Y. 1991. "Ancient pipelines in Israel." Pp. 129–140 in *Future Currents in Aqueduct Studies*, ed. A. Trevor Hodge. Leeds: Francis Cairns.

Peltenburg, Edgar. 2000. "From nucleation to dispersal: Late third millennium B.C. settlement pattern transformations in the Near East and Aegean." *Subartu* 7: 183–206.

Peltenburg, Edgar, D. Bolger, S. Campbell, M. A. Murray, and R. Tipping. 1996. "Jerablus Tahtani, Syria, 1995: Preliminary report." *Levant* 28: 1–125.

Peltenburg, Edgar, S. Colledge, P. Croft, A. Jackson, C. McCartney, and M. A. Murray. 2000. "Agro-pastoral colonization of Cyprus in the 10th millennium BP: Initial assessments." *Antiquity* 74: 844–853.

Petersen, Andrew. 1994. "The archaeology of the Syrian and Iraqi Hajj routes." *World Archaeology* 26 (1): 47–56.

Pfälzner, Peter. 2002. "Modes of storage and the development of economic systems in the Early Jezirah period." Pp. 259–286 in *Of Pots and Plans: Papers on the Archaeology and History of Mesopotamia and Syria Presented to David Oates in Honour of His 75th Birthday*, ed. Al-Gailani-Werr, J. Curtis, H. Martin, A. McMahon, J. Oates, and J. Reade. London: Nabu.

Pfeiffer, R. H., and E. A. Speiser. 1936. "One hundred new selected Nuzi texts." *Annual of the American Schools of Oriental Research* 16: 1–168.

Philby, H. St. John. 1957. *The Land of Midian.* London: Ernest Benn.

Philip, Graham, D. Donoghue, A. Beck, and N. Galiatsatos. 2002a. "CORONA satellite photography: An archaeological application from the Middle East." *Antiquity* 76: 109–118.

Philip, Graham, F. Jabour, A. Beck, M. Bshesh, J. Grove, A. Kirk, and A. Millard. 2002b. "Settlement and landscape development in the Homs region, Syria: Research questions, preliminary results 1999–2000 and future potential." *Levant* 34: 1–23.

Poidebard, Antoine. 1934. *La trace de*

Rome dans le désert de Syrie; le limes de Trajan à la conquête arabe; recherches aériennes (1925–1932). 2 vols. Paris: P. Geuthner.

Pollock, Susan. 1999. *Ancient Mesopotamia*. Cambridge: Cambridge University.

Pope, Kevin, O., and Bruce H. Dahlin. 1989. "Ancient Maya wetland agriculture: New insights from ecological and remote sensing Research." *Journal of Field Archaeology* 16: 87–106.

Porter, Anne. 2000. "Mortality, Monuments and Mobility Ancestor Traditions and the Transcendence of Space." Ph.D. dissertation, Department of Near Eastern Languages and Civilizations, University of Chicago.

———. 2002. "The dynamics of death: Ancestors, pastoralism, and the origins of a third-millennium city in Syria." *Bulletin of the American Schools of Oriental Research* 325: 1–36.

Postgate, J. Nicholas. 1974. "Some remarks on the conditions in the Assyrian countryside." *Journal of the Economic and Social History of the Orient* 17 (3): 232–240.

———. 1979. "The economic structure of the Assyrian empire." Pp. 209–220 in *Power and Propagander*, ed. M. Trolles Larsen. Copenhagen: Akademisk Forlag.

———. 1992a. *Early Mesopotamia: Society and Economy at the Dawn of History*. London: Routledge.

———. 1992b. "The land of Assur and the yoke of Assur." *World Archaeology* 23 (3): 247–263.

Potter, T. W. 1976. "Valleys and settlement: Some new evidence." *World Archaeology* 8 (2): 207–219.

Potts, Daniel T. 1990. *The Arabian Gulf in Antiquity* (2 vols). Oxford: Clarendon.

———. 1997. *Mesopotamian Civilization: The Material Foundations*. Ithaca, NY: Cornell University.

Pournelle, Jennifer. 2001a. "Titris and its hinterlands: The EBA landscape of the city." Pp. 58–106 in "Research at Titris Höyük in southeastern Turkey: The 1999 season." *Anatolica* 24: 23–106.

Pournelle, Jennifer, 2001b. "Founded on sand: Using satellite photography toward a new understanding of 5th/4th millennium B.C. landscapes in the Warka survey area, Iraq." Paper presented at the annual meeting of the American Anthropological Association annual meetings, November 2001, Washington, DC.

Powell, Marvin. 1985. "Salt, seed, and yields in Sumerian agriculture: A critique of the theory of progressive salinization." *Zeitschrift fur Assyriologie* 75: 7–38.

Prag, Kay. 1995. "The Dead Sea dolmens: Death and the landscape." Pp. 75–84 in *The Archaeology of Death in the Ancient Near East*, ed. Stuart Campbell and Anthony Green. Oxford: Oxbow Monograph 51.

Preston, Keith. 1976. "An introduction to the anthropomorphic context of the rock art of Jebel Akhdhar." *Journal of Oman Studies* 2: 17–28.

Preucel, Robert, and Ian Hodder. 1996. "Nature and culture." Pp. 23–38 in *Contemporary Archaeology in Theory*, ed. Robert Preucel and Ian Hodder. Oxford: Blackwell.

Prickett, Martha. 1986. "Settlement during the early periods." Pp. 215–246 in *Excavations at Tepe Yahya, Iran 1967–1975: The Early Periods*, ed. Thomas W. Beale. Cambridge: American Society for Prehistoric Research.

Radner, Karen. 2000. "How did the Neo-Assyrian king perceive his land and resources?" Pp. 233–246 in Jas (ed.).

Raikes, Robert. 1967. *Water, Weather and Prehistory*. London: John Baker.

Rawat, J. S., G. Rawat, and S. P. Rai. 2000. "Impact of human activities on geomorphic processes in the Almora region, central Himalaya, India." Pp. 285–299 in *Geomorphology, Human Activity and Global Environmental Change*, ed. Olav Slaymaker. Chichester, UK: John Wiley.

Reade, Julian E. 1978. "Studies in Assyrian geography, parts I and II." *Revue d'Assyriologie* 72: 47–72 and 157–180.

———. 1983. *Assyrian Sculpture*. London: British Museum.

———. 2000. "Sacred places in Ancient Oman." *Journal of Oman Studies* 11: 133–138.

Redman, Charles L. 1999. *Human Impact on Ancient Environments*. Tucson: University of Arizona.

Reichel, Clemens. 1997. "Changes in the plain levels of Babylonia and the Diyala region from 6000 B.C. onwards: A view from excavated sites." Paper presented at the 44th Rencontre Assyriologique Internationale in Venice, July 1997.

Reifenberg, A. 1936. *The Soils of Palestine*. London: Thomas Murby.

Renger, J. M. 1990. "Rivers, watercourses and irrigation ditches and other matters concerning irrigation based on Old Babylonian sources (2000–1600 B.C.)." *Bulletin on Sumerian Agriculture* 5: 31–46.

———. 1995. "Institutional, communal, and individual ownership or possession of arable land in Ancient Mesopotamia from the end of the fourth to the end of the first millennium B.C.." *Chicago-Kent Law Review* 71 (1): 269–319.

Reynolds, Robert G. 2000. "The impact of raiding on settlement patterns in the northern valley of Oaxaca: An approach using decision trees." Pp. 251–274 in Kohler and Gumerman.

Riehl, Simone. 1999. *Bronze Age Environment and Economy in the Troad: The Archaeobotany of Kumtepe and Troy*. Tübingen: Mo Vince.

Rimmington, J. N. 2000. "Soil geochemistry and artefact scatters in Boeotia, Greece." Pp. 190–199 in *Nondestructive Techniques Applied to Landscape Archaeology*, ed. M. Pasquinucci and F. Trément. Oxford: Oxbow.

Roaf, Susan. 1989. "Settlement form and qanat routes in the Yazd province." Pp. 59–60 in Beaumont et al.

Roberts, Brian K. 1987. "Landscape archaeology." Pp. 77–95 in *Landscape and Culture: Geographical and Archaeological Perspectives*, ed. J. Malcolm Wagstaff. Oxford: Blackwell.

———. 1996. *Landscapes of Settlement: Prehistory to the Present*. London: Routledge.

Roberts, Neil. 1977. "Water conservation in ancient Arabia." *Proceedings of the Seminar for Arabian Studies* 7: 134–146.

———. 1982. "Lake levels as an indicator of Near Eastern Palaeoclimates: A preliminary appraisal." Pp. 235–267 in *Palaeoclimates, Palaeoenvironments and Human Communities in the Eastern Mediterranean Region in Later Prehistory*, ed. John L. Bintliff and W. van Zeist. Oxford: BAR (International series) 133.

———. 1990. "Human-induced landscape change in south and southwest Turkey during the later Holocene." Pp. 53–67 in Sytze Bottema et al.

——— (ed.). 1994. *The Changing Global Environment*. Oxford: Blackwell.

———. 1998. *The Holocene*. Oxford: Blackwell.

———. 2002. "Did Neolithic landscape management retard the post-glacial spread of woodland in Southwest Asia?" *Antiquity* 76: 1002–1010.

Roberts, Neil, and Herbert E. Wright Jr. 1993. "Vegetational, lake-level and climatic history of the Near East and Southwest Asia." Pp. 194–220 in *Global Climates since the Last Glacial Maximum*, ed. Herbert E. Wright Jr., J. E. Kutzbach, T. Webb III, W. F. Ruddiman, F. A. Street-Perrott, and P. J. Bartlein. Minneapolis: University of Minnesota.

Roberts, Neil, S. Black, P. Boyer, W. J. Eastwood, H. Griffiths, H. F. Lamb, M. Leng, R. Parish, J. M. Reed, D. Twigg, and H. Yiğitbaşioğlu. 1999. "Chronology and stratigraphy of Late Quaternary sediments in the Konya Basin Turkey: Results from the KOPAL project." *Quaternary Science Reviews* 18: 611–630.

Roberts, Neil, M. E. Meadows, and J. R. Dodson. 2001. "The history of mediterranean-type environments: Climate, culture and landscape." *The Holocene* 11 (6): 631–634.

Roberts, Neil, J. M. Reed, M. J. Leng, C. Kuzucuoğlu, M. Fontugne, J. Bertaux, H. Woldring, S. Bottema, S. Black, E. Hunt, and M. Karabıyıkoğlu. 2001. "The tempo of Holocene climatic change in the eastern Mediterranean region: New high-resolution crater-lake sediment data from central Turkey." *The Holocene* 11 (6): 721–736.

Ron, Z. 1966. "Agricultural terraces in the Judaean mountains." *Israel Exploration Journal* 16: 33–49, 111–122.

Rosen, Arlene Miller. 1986. *Cities of Clay: The Geoarchaeology of Tells*. Chicago: University of Chicago.

———. 1987. "Phytolith studies at Shiqmim." Pp. 243–249 in Thomas E. Levy.

———. 1998. "Early to Mid-Holocene environmental changes and their impact on human communities in southeastern Anatolia." Pp. 215–240 in *Water, Environment and Society in Times of Climatic Change*, ed. Arie Issar and Neville Brown. Dordrecht: Kluwer.

Rosen, Arlene M., and P. Goldberg. 1995. "Palaeoenvironmental investigations." In "Titrish Hoyuk, A Small Urban Center in SE Anatolia: the 1994 season." ed. Guillermo Algaze *Anatolica* 21: 32–37.

Rosen, Steven A. 1987. "Demographic trends in the Negev Highlands: Preliminary results from the emergency survey." *Bulletin of the American Schools of Oriental Research* 266: 45–58.

———. 1992. "Nomads in archaeology: A response to Finkelstein and Perevoltsky." *Bulletin of the American Schools of Oriental Research* 287: 75–85.

———. 2000. "The decline of desert agriculture: A view from the classical period Negev." Pp. 44–62 in *The Archaeology of Drylands*, ed. Graeme Barker and David Gilbertson. London: Routledge.

Ross, Mairi. 2001. "Emerging trends in rock-art research: Hunter-gatherer culture, land and landscape." *Antiquity* 75: 543–548.

Rossignol, Jacqueline. 1992. "Concepts, methods and theory building: A landscape approach." Pp. 3–16 in Jacqueline Rossignol and LuAnn Wandsnider.

Rossignol, Jacqueline, and LuAnn Wandsnider (eds.). 1992. *Space Time and Archaeological Landscapes*. New York: Plenum.

Rossignol-Strick, M. 2002. "Holocene climatic changes in the Eastern Mediterranean and the spread of food production from southwest Asia to Egypt." Pp. 157–169 in *Droughts, Food and Culture: Ecological Change and Food Security in Africa's Later Prehistory*, ed. Fekri A. Hassan. New York: Kluwer.

Rothman, Mitchell S. 2000. "Environmental and cultural factors in the development of settlement in a marginal, highland zone." Pp. 429–433 in Stager et al.

Rowton, Michael. 1967. "The woodlands of ancient western Asia." *Journal of Near Eastern Studies* 26: 261–277.

Ryan, Walter B. F., W. C. Pitman, C. O. Major, K. Shimkus, V. Moskalenko, G. A. Jones, P. Dimitrov, N. Gorur, M. Sakinç, and H. Yuce. 1997. "An abrupt drowning of the Black Sea Shelf." *Marine Geology* 138: 119–126.

Sader, Helen. 2000. "The Aramaean kingdoms of Syria: Origin and formation processes." Pp. 61–76 in *Essays on Syria in the Iron Age*, ed. Guy Bunnens. Louvain: Peeters.

Sadler, S. 1990. "Le terroir agricole de Diyateh, l'irrigation comme condition d'existence de ce terroir." Pp. 421–451 in *Techniques et Practiques Hydro-Agricoles Traditionelles en domaine irrigué* ed. Bernard Geyer.

Paris: Bibliotèque Archéologique et Historique CXXXVI.

Safar, Fuad, M. A. Mustafa, and S. Lloyd. 1981. *Eridu*. Baghdad: Department of Antiquities.

Safrai, Ze'ev. 1994. *The Economy of Roman Palestine*. London: Routledge.

Safriel, Uriel N. 1999. "The concept of sustainability in dryland ecosystems." Pp. 117–137 in *Arid Land Management: Toward Ecological Sustainability*, ed. Thomas W. Hoekstra and Moshe Shachak. Chicago: University of Illinois.

Saggs, H. W. F. 1959. "The Nimrud letters, 1952–Part 5." *Iraq* 21: 158–180.

Sagona, Antonio G. 1984. *The Caucasian Region in the Early Bronze Age*. Oxford: BAR (International Series) 214 (3 volumes).

Sanders, Donald H. 1996. *Nemrud Daği: The Hierothesion of Antiochus I of Commagene: Results of the American Excavations Directed by Theresa B. Goell*. Winona Lake, IN: Eisenbrauns.

Sanlaville, Paul. 1989. "Considerations sur l'evolution de la basse Mesopotamie au cours des derniers millenaires." *Paleorient* 15 (2): 5–27.

———. 2000. *Le Moyen-Oriente arabe: Le milieu et l'homme*. Paris: Armand Colin.

Sarris, A., and R. E. Jones. 2000. "Geophysical and related techniques applied to archaeological survey in the Mediterranean: A review." *Journal of Mediterranean Archaeology* 13 (1): 3–75.

Schaloske, Michael. 1995. *Untersuchungen der Sabäischen Bewässerungsanlagen in Marib*. Deutsches Archäologisches Institut, San ʿa. Mainz am-Rhein: Philipp von Zarbern.

Schama, Simon. 1995. *Landscape and Memory*. New York: Knopf.

Schiffer, Michael B. 1987. *Formation Processes of the Archaeological Record*. Albuquerque: University of New Mexico.

Schioler, T. 1989. "The water mill at the crocodile river: A turbine dated to 345–380 A.D." *Palestine Exploration Quaterly* 121: 133–143.

Schlanger, S. H. 1992. "Recognizing persistent places in Anasazi settlement systems." Pp. 91–112 in Rossignol and Wandsnider.

Schlesinger, W. H., J. F. Reynolds, G. L. Cunningham, L. F. Huenneke, W. M. Jarrell, R. A. Virginia, and W. G. Whitford. 1990. "Biological feedbacks in global desertification." *Science* 247: 1043–1048.

Schloen, J. David. 2001. *The House of the Father as Fact and Symbol: Patrimonialism in Ugarit and the Ancient Near East*. Cambridge, MA: Harvard Semitic Museum Studies in the Archaeology and History of the Levant.

Schmidt, Erich F. 1940. *Flights over Ancient Cities of Iran*. Chicago: University of Chicago.

Scholte, P., Abdu Wali al-Khuleidi, and J. J. Kessler. 1991. *The Vegetation of the Republic of Yemen (Western Part)*. San'a Yemen: Agricultural Research Authority and DHV Consultants.

Schulz, E., and J. W. Whitney. 1986. "Upper Pleistocene and Holocene lakes in the an-Nafud, Saudi Arabia." *Hydrobiologia* 143: 175–190.

Schumm, Stanley A. 1992. "Great alluvial rivers and ancient civilizations: Stability, flux, catastrophe." Unpublished manuscript 1992.

Schwartz, Glenn M., H. H. Curvers, F. A. Gerritsen, J. A. MacCormack, N. F. Miller, and J. A. Weber. 2000. "Excavation and survey in the Jabbul Plain, Western Syria: The Umm al-Marra Project 1996–1997." *American Journal of Archaeology* 104: 419–462.

Semple, Ellen C. 1941. *Influences of Geographic Environment: On the Basis of Ratzel's System of Anthro-Geography*. New York: Henry Holt.

Serjeant, Robert B. 1988. "Observations on irrigation in Southwest Arabia." *Proceedings of the Seminar for Arabian Studies*, 18: 145–153.

Shachak, M., S. T. A. Pickett, B. Boeken, and E. Zaady. 1999. "Managing patchiness, ecological flows, productivity, and diversity in drylands: Concepts and applications in the Negev Desert." Pp. 117–137 in *Arid Land Management: Toward Ecological Sustainability*, ed. Thomas W. Hoekstra and Moshe Shachak. Chicago: University of Illinois.

Shaw, Brent, D. 1990. "Bandit highlands and lowland peace: The mountains of Isauria-Cilicia." *Journal of Economic and Social History of the Orient* 33: 199–233, 237–270.

Shell, Colin A. 1996. "The magnetometric survey at Çatalhöyük East." Pp. 101–113 in *On the Surface: Çatalhöyük 1992–1995*, ed. Ian Hodder. Cambridge: McDonald Institute Monographs.

Sheng, T. C. 1981. "The need for soil conservation structures for steep cultivated slopes in the humid tropics." Pp.

357–372 in *Tropical Agricultural Hydrology*, ed. R. Lal and E. W. Russell. Chichester, UK: John Wiley.

Sherratt, Andrew. 1980. "Water, soils and seasonality in early cereal cultivation." *World Archaeology* 11 (3): 313–330.

———. 1997. "Climatic cycles and behavioural revolutions: the emergence of modern humans and the beginning of farming." *Antiquity* 71: 271–287.

Sirocko, Frank. 1996. "The evolution of the monsoon climate over the Arabian Sea during the last 24,000 years." *Palaeoecology of Africa* 24: 53–69.

Slingerford, R., and N. D. Smith. 1998. "Necessary conditions for a meandering-river avulsion." *Geology* 26 (5): 435–438.

Smith, Adam. 1996. "Imperial Archipelago: The Making of the Urartian Landscape in Southern Transcaucasia." Ph.D. dissertation, Department of Anthropology, University of Arizona.

———. 1999. "The making of an Urartian landscape: A study of political architectonics." *American Journal of Archaeology* 103: 45–71.

Snodgrass, Anthony, M. 1994. "Response: The archaeological aspect." Pp. 197–200 in *Classical Greece: Ancient Histories and Modern Archaeologies*, ed. Ian Morris. Cambridge: Cambridge University.

Snyder, Jeffrey A., K. Wasylik, S. Fritz, and H. E. Wright Jr. 2001. "Diatom-based conductivity reconstruction and palaeoclimatic interpretation of a 40-ka record from Lake Zeribar, Iran." *The Holocene* 11 (6): 737–745.

Sodini, J. P., G. Tate, B. Bavant, S. Bavant, J.-L. Biscop, and D. Orssaud. 1980. "Déhès (Syrie du Nord), Campagnes I–III (1976–1978)." *Syria* 57: 1–304.

Spencer, J. E., and G. A. Hale. 1961. "The origin, nature and distribution of agricultural terracing." *Pacific Viewpoint* 1: 1–40.

Stager, Lawrence E. 1975. "Ancient Agriculture in the Judaean Desert: A Case Study of the Buqe'ah Valley in the Iron Age." Ph.D. dissertation, Department of Near Eastern Languages and Civilizations, Harvard University.

———. 1976. "Farming in the Judaean Desert during the Iron Age." *Bulletin of the American Schools of Oriental Research*. 221: 145–158.

Stager, Lawrence E., J. A. Greene, and M. D. Coonan (eds.). 2000. *The Ar-

chaeology of Jordan and Beyond, Essays in Honor of James A. Sauer*. Winona Lake, IN: Eisenbrauns.

Steimer-Herbert, T. 1999. "Jabal Ruwaik: Megaliths in Yemen." *Proceedings of the Seminar for Arabian Studies* 29: 179–182.

Stein, Gil J. 1994. "Segmentary states and organizational variation in early complex societies: a rural perspective." Pp. 10–18 in *Archaeological Views from the Countryside. Village Communities in Early Complex Societies*, ed. Glenn M. Schwartz and Steven E. Falconer. Washington, DC: Smithsonian Institution.

———. 2000. *Rethinking World Systems: Diasporas, Colonies, and Interaction in Uruk Mesopotamia*. Tucson: University of Arizona.

———. 2001. "Structural parameters and socio-cultural factors in the economic organization of north Mesopotamian urbanism in the third millennium B.C." Paper presented at a meeting on "The Economies of Ancient States" in Snowbird, Utah, October 20–21, 2001.

Stein, Mark, Aurel. 1919. "Air photography of ancient sites." *Geographical Journal* 54: 200.

———. 1921. *SerIndia* (5 volumes). Oxford: Clarendon.

———. 1938. "Note on the remains of the Roman limes in north western Iraq." *Geographical Journal* 95: 428–438.

Steinkeller, Piotr. 2001. "New light on the hydrology and topography of southern Babylonia in the third millennium." *Zeitschrift fur Assyriologie* 91: 22–84.

Steinsapir, Ann I. 1998. "Rural Sanctuaries in Roman Syria: The Dynamics of Architecture in the Sacred Landscape." Ph.D. dissertation, Department of Near Eastern Studies, University of California, Los Angeles.

Steinsapir, Ann I. 1999. "Landscape and the sacred: The sanctuary dedicated to holy, heavenly Zeus Baetocaece." *Near Eastern Archaeology* 62 (3): 182–194.

Stevens, L. R., H. E. Wright Jr., and E. Ito. 2001. "Proposed changes in seasonality of climate during the Lateglacial and Holocene at Lake Zeribar, Iran." *The Holocene* 11 (6): 747–755.

Stoddart, Simon, and Ezra Zubrow. 1999. "Changing places." In C. T. Fisher and T. L. Thurstone (eds.). *Antiquity* 73: 686–688.

Stone, Elizabeth C. 1995. "The development of cities in ancient Mesopotamia." Pp. 235–248 in *Civilizations of the Ancient Near East*, vol. 1, ed. Jack M. Sasson. New York: Charles Scribner's Sons.

Stone, Elizabeth C., and P. Zimansky. 1994. "The Tell Abu Duwari Project, 1988–1990." *Journal of Field Archaeology* 21: 437–455.

———. Forthcoming. *The Anatomy of a Mesopotamian City: Survey and Soundings at Mashkan-shapir*. Winona Lake, IN: Eisenbraun.

———. 2001. "Ten year's excavations at Rusahinili Eiduru-kai." Pp. 355–376 in *Ayanis I*, ed. Altan Cilingiroğlu and Mirjo Salvini. Rome: Istituto per gli Studi Micenei ed Egeo-Anatolici, Documenta Asiana.

Stone, Glenn Davis. 1996. *Settlement Ecology: The Social and Spatial Organization of Kofyar Agriculture*. Tucson: University of Arizona.

Stouthamer, E., and H. J. A. Berendsen. 2000. "Factors controlling the Holocene avulsion history of the Rhine-Meuse delta (The Netherlands)." *Journal of Sedimentary Research* 70: 1051–1064.

Sumaka'i Fink, Amir. 2000. "Quarries and quarrying methods at Ramat Hanadiv." Pp. 628–636 in *Ramat Hanadiv Excavations: Final Report of the 1984–1998 Seasons*, ed. Yizhar Hirschfeldt. Jerusalem: Israel Exploration Society.

Summers, Geoffrey, and F. Summers. 1998. "Kerkenes Dağ Project." Pp. 177–194 in *Ancient Anatolia*, ed. Roger Matthews. Oxford: British School of Archaeology at Ankara.

Sumner, William M. 1990. "Full coverage regional archaeological survey in the Near East: An example from Iran." Pp. 87–115 in *The Archaeology of Regions: A Case for Full-Coverage Survey*, ed. Susan K. Fish and Stephen A. Kowelewski. Washington, DC: Smithsonian Institution.

Sweet, Louise E. 1974. *Tell Toqaan: A Syrian Village*. Ann Arbor: University of Michigan, Museum of Anthropology Anthropological Papers no. 14.

Tate, Georges. 1992. *Les campagnes de la Syrie du Nord (Tome 1)*. Paris: Librairie Orientaliste Paul Geuthner.

———. 1997. "The Syrian countryside during the Roman era." Pp. 55–72 in *The Early Roman Empire in the East*, ed. Susan E. Alcock. Oxford: Oxbow.

TAVO Map A VI 1 Middle East Vegetation; and A VI 4 Middle Taurus (Turkey) Vegetation.

TAVO Map A IX 11 Nomadism in the Middle East.

TAVO Map A X 4 Mesopotamia: Land Utilization.

TAVO Map A X 1 The Near East: Land Utilization.

Taylor, Christopher C. 1972. "The study of settlement pattern in pre-Saxon Britain." Pp. 109–114 in *Man, Settlement and Urbanism*, Peter J. Ucko, Ruth Tringham, and G. W. Dimbleby (eds.). London: Duckworth.

Taylor, J. 2000. "Soil phosphate survey." Pp. 182–189 in *Non-destructive Techniques Applied to Landscape Archaeology*, ed. M. Pasquinucci and F. Trément. Oxford: Oxbow.

Tchalenko, Georges. 1953. *Villages antique de la Syrie du Nord II*. Paris: Librairie Orientaliste Paul Geuthner.

Teller, J. T., K. W. Glennie, N. Lancaster, and A. K. Singhvi. 2000. "Calcareous dunes of the United Arab Emirates and Noah's flood: The postglacial reflooding of the Persian (Arabian) Gulf." *Quaternary International* 68–71: 297–308.

Thenayian, Mohammed, A. R. 1999. "An Archaeological Study of the Yemeni Highland Pilgrim Route between San 'a and Makkah." Kingdom of Saudi Arabia: Ministry of Education, Deputy Ministry of Antiquities and Museums.

Thesiger, Wilfred. 1959. *Arabian Sands*. New York: Dutton.

Thomas, Bertram, 1932. *Arabia Felix: Across the "empty quarter" of Arabia*. New York: C. Scribner's and Sons.

Thomas, Julian. 1993. "The politics of vision and the archaeologies of landscape." Pp. 19–48 in *Landscape: Politics and Perspectives*, ed. Barbara Bender. Oxford: Berg.

Thompson, R., G. M. Turner, M. Stiller, and A. Kaufman. 1985. "Near East secular variation recorded in sediments from the Sea of Galilee (Lake Kinneret)." *Quaternary Research* 23: 175–188.

Tilley, Christopher. 1994. *A Phenomenology of Landscape*. Oxford: Berg.

Toplyn, Michael, R. 1988. "The 1984 geological probes GP1-GP3 in Wadi al-Jubah, Yemen Arab Republic." Pp. 85–104 in Overstreet et al. 1988a.

Tosi, Maurizio. 1985. "Archaeological activities in the Yemen Arab Republic, 1985: Tihamah coastal archaeological survey." *East and West* 35: 363–369.

Treacy, J. M., and William M. Denevan. 1994. "The creation of cultivable land through terracing." Pp. 91–110 in Miller and Gleason.

Trimble, S. W. 1981. "Changes in sediment storage in Coon Creek basin in the Driftless Area, Wisconsin 1853–1975." *Science* 214: 181–83.

Trombold, Charles D. (ed.). 1991a. *Ancient Road Networks and Settlement Hierarchies in the New World*. Cambridge: Cambridge University.

———. 1991b. "An introduction to the study of ancient New World road networks." Pp. 1–9 in Charles D. Trombold (ed.).

Tsoar, Haim, and Y. Yekutieli. 1993. "Geomorphological identification of ancient roads and paths on the loess of the northern Negev." *Israel Journal of Earth Sciences* 41: 209–216.

UNEP. 1992. *World Atlas of Desertification*. London: Edward Arnold.

Ur, Jason. 2002. "Settlement and landscape in Northern Mesopotamia: The Tell Hamoukar Survey 2000–2001." *Akkadica* 123 (2002): 57–88.

———. 2003. "CORONA satellite photography and ancient road networks: A northern Mesopotamian case study." *Antiquity* (295): 102–115).

van Andel, Tjeerd, and E. Zangger. 1990. "Landscape stabilty and destabilisation in the prehistory of Greece." Pp. 139–158 in Bottema et al.

Van De Mieroop, Marc. 1999. *The Ancient Mesopotamian City*. Oxford: Oxford University.

Van Driel, G. 1988. "Neo-Babylonian agriculture." *Bulletin for Sumerian Agriculture* 4: 121–151.

Van Lerberghe, Karel. 1996. "The Beydar tablets and the history of the Northern Jazira." *Subartu* 2: 119–122.

van Liere, W. J. 1958–1959. "Ager centuriatus of the Roman colonia of Emesa (Homs)." *Les Annales Archéologique Arabes Syriennes* 8–9: 55–58.

van Liere, W. J., and J. Lauffray. 1954. "Nouvelle prospection archeologique dans la Haute Jazireh Syrienne." *Les Annales Archéologique Arabes Syriennes* 4/5: 129–148.

van Zeist, Willem, and Sytze Bottema. 1977. Palynological Investigations in Western Iran. *Palaeohistoria* 19: 19–85.

van Zeist, Willem, and Sytze Bottema. 1991. *Late Quaternary Vegetation of the Near East*. Wiesbaden: Dr. Ludwig

Reichert Verlag, TAVO Atlas, Natur-wissenschaften 18.

van Zeist, W., H. Woldring, and D. Sta-pert. 1975. "Late Quaternary vege-tation and climate of southwestern Turkey." *Palaeohistoria* 17: 55–143.

van Zeist, Willem, and W. Waterbolk-van Rooijen. 1989. "Plant remains from Tell Sabi Abyad." Pp. 325–335 in *Ex-cavations at Tell Sabi Abyad*, ed. Peter M. M. G Akkermans. Oxford: BAR (International Series) 468.

Varisco, Daniel. 1982. "The Adaptive Dynamics of Water Allocation at al-Ahjur, Yemen Arab Republic." Ph.D. dissertation, Department of Anthro-pology, University of Pennsylvania.

———. 1991. "The future of terrace farming in the Yemen: A development dilemma." *Agriculture and Human Values* 8: 166–172.

Verhoeven, Kris. 1998. "Geomorpho-logical research in the Mesopotamian floodplain." Pp. 159–245 in Gasche and Tanret 1998.

Verhoeven, Kris, and L. Daels. 1994. "Remote sensing and Geographi-cal Information Systems (GIS) for archaeological research (applied in Mesopotamia)." *Mesopotamian His-tory and Environment* II, pp. 519–539. Ghent: Peeters.

Vermore, M., E. Smets, M. Waelkens, H. Vanhaverbeke, I. Librecht, E. Palis-sen, and L. Vanhecke. 2000. "Late Holocene environmental change and the record of human impact at Gragaz near Sagalassos, Southwest Turkey." *Journal Archaeological Science* 27: 571–595.

Vermore, M., S. Bottema, L. Van-hecke, M. Waelkens, E. Paulissen. and E. Smets. 2002. "Palynological evidence for late-Holocene human occupation recorded in two wetlands in sw Turkey." *The Holocene* 12 (5): 569–584.

Vidale, F. S. 1978. "Utilization of surface water by Northern Arabian Bedouins." Pp. 111–126 in *Social and Technologi-cal Management in Dry Lands. Past and Present, Indigenous and Imposed*, ed. Nancy L. González. Boulder, CO: Westview.

Villeneuve, F. 1985. "L'economie ru-rale." Pp. 63–136 in *Hauran 1*, ed. J.-M. Dentzer, Paris: Institut Fran-çais D'Archéologie du Proche Orient, Librairie Orientaliste Paul Geuthner.

Vita-Finzi, Claudio. 1969. *The Mediter-ranean Valleys: Geological Changes in Historical Times*. Cambridge: Cam-bridge University.

von der Osten, Hans H. 1929. *Explo-rations in Central Anatolia Season of 1926*. Chicago: Oriental Institute Publications 5.

———. 1929. *Explorations in Hittite Asia Minor 1927–28*. Chicago: Oriental Institute Communications 6.

Wachholtz, Rolf. 1996. *Socio-Economics of Bedouin Farming Systems in Dry Areas of Northern Syria*. Kiel, Germany: Wissenschaftsverlag Vauk Kiel.

Waelkens, M., N. Herz, and L. Moens. 1992. *Ancient Stones: Quarrying, Trade and Provenance*. Leuven: Leuven University.

Wagner, Winfried. 1993. *Bodenkundliche Untersuchungen in der Oase Marib*. Deutsches Archäologisches Insti-tut, San ʿa. Mainz am Rhein: Verlag Philipp von Zabern.

Wagstaff, J. Malcolm. 1981. "Buried as-sumptions: Some problems in the interpretation of the 'Younger Fill' raised by recent data from Greece." *Journal of Archaeological Science* 8: 247–264.

———. 1985. *The Evolution of Middle Eastern Landscapes*. London: Croom Helm.

Walker, D., and G. Singh. 1993. "Earliest palynological records of human im-pact on the world's vegetation." Pp. 101–108 in *Climate Change and Human Impact on the Landscape*, ed. F. M. Chambers. London: Chapman and Hall.

Wallèn, C. C. 1967. "Aridity definitions and their applicability." *Geografiska Annaler* 49A: 367–384.

Walling, D. E. 1996. "Erosion and sedi-ment yield in a changing environ-ment." Pp. 43–56 in *Global Continental Changes: The Context of Palaeo-hydrology*, ed. J. Branson, A. G. Brown, and K. J. Gregory. Geological Society of London Special Publication 115.

Waters, Michael R. 1992. *Principles of Geoarchaeology, a North American Perspective*. Tucson: University of Arizona.

Waters, Michael R., and J. J. Field. 1986. "Geomorphic analysis of Hohokam settlement patterns on alluvial fans along the western flank of the Tortolita Mountains, Arizona." *Geoarchaeology* 1: 329–345.

Wazana, N. 2001. "Border descriptions and cultural barriers." Pp. 696–710 in *Akten des IV. Internationalen Kongress für Hethitologie*, ed. Gernot Wilhelm. Wiesbaden: Harrassowitz.

Weaver, T., and D. Dale. 1978. "Tram-pling effects of hikers, motorcycles and horses in meadows and forests." *Journal of Applied Ecology* 15: 451–457.

Weisgerber, Gerd. 1980. "Patterns of Early Islamic metallurgy in Oman." *Proceedings of the Seminar for Arabian Studies* 10: 115–126.

———. 1983. "Copper production dur-ing the 3rd millennium B.C. in Oman and the question of Makkan." *Journal of Oman Studies* 6: 269–276.

———. 1987. "Archaeological evidence of copper exploitation at Arja." Pp. 145–172 in Costa and Wilkinson.

Weiss, Harvey. 1986. "The origins of Tell Leilan and the conquest of space in 3rd millennium Mesopotamia." Pp. 71–108 in *The Origins of Cities in Dry-farming Syria*, ed. Harvey Weiss. Guilford, CT: Four Quarters.

Weiss, H., M. A. Courty, W. Wetterstrom, F. Guichard, L. Senior, R. A. Meadow, and A. Curnow. 1993. "The gene-sis and collapse of third millennium north Mesopotamian civilization." *Science* 261: 995–1004.

Wenke, Robert J. 1975–1976. "Imperial investment and agricultural devel-opment in Parthian and Sasanian Khuzestan: 150 B.C.–AD 640." *Mesopo-tamia* 10–11: 31–221.

Wenke, Robert, J. 1987. "Western Iran in the Partho-Sasanian period: The imperial transformation." Pp. 251–281 in Hole.

Whallon, Robert. 1979. *An Archaeo-logical Survey of the Keban Reservoir Area of East-Central Turkey*. Ann Arbor: Memoirs of the Museum of Anthropology University of Michigan no. 11.

Wheatley, Paul. 2001. *The Places Where Men Pray Together: Cities in Islamic Lands: Seventh through the Tenth Cen-turies*. Chicago: University of Chicago.

Whitcomb, Donald. 1978. "The archae-ology of al-Hasa oasis in the Islamic period." *Atlal* 2: 95–113.

Wiggermans, F. A. M. 2000. "Agriculture in the northern Balikh valley: The case of Middle Assyrian Tell Sabi Abyad." Pp. 171–231 in Jas (ed.).

Wigley, T. M. L., and G. Farmer. 1982. "Climate of the Eastern Mediter-ranean and Near East." Pp. 3–37 in *Palaeoclimates, Palaeoenvironments and Human Communities in the East-ern Mediterranean Region in Later Pre-*

history, ed. John L. Bintliff and Willem van Zeist. Oxford: BAR (International Series) 133.

Wikander, Orjan. 2000. *Handbook of Ancient Water Technology.* Leiden: Brill.

Wilkinson, John C. 1977. *Water and Tribal Settlement in Oman: A Study of the Aflaj of Oman.* Oxford: Clarendon.

———. 1979. "Suhār (Sohar) in the Early Islamic period: The written evidence." Pp. 887–908 in *South Asian Archaeology* 4 (1977), ed. M. Taddei. Naples: Naples Istituto Universitario Orientale.

———. 1983. "Traditional concepts of territory in south east Arabia." *Geographical Journal* 149: 301–315.

Wilkinson, Tony J. 1980a. "Water mills of the Batina coast of Oman." *Proceedings of the Seminar for Arabian Studies* 10: 127–132.

———. 1980b. "Darb Zubayda-1979: The water resources." *Atlal* 4: 51–67.

———. 1982. "The definition of ancient manured zones by means of extensive sherd-sampling techniques." *Journal of Field Archaeology* 9: 323–333.

———. 1988. "The archaeological component of agricultural soils in the Middle East: The effects of manuring in antiquity." Pp. 93–114 in *Man-made soils,* ed. W. Groenman-van Waateringe and Mark Robinson. Oxford: BAR (International Series) 410.

———. 1990a. *Town and Country in SE Anatolia.* Vol. 1: *Settlement and Land Use at Kurban Höyük and Other Sites in the Lower Karababa Basin.* Chicago: Oriental Institute Publications 109.

———. 1990b. "Early channels and landscape development around Abu Salabikh, a preliminary report." *Iraq* 52: 75–83.

———. 1990c. "Soil development and early land use in the Jazira region, Upper Mesopotamia." *World Archaeology* 22 (1): 87–102.

———. 1993. "Linear hollows in the Jazira, Upper Mesoptamia." *Antiquity* 67: 548–562.

———. 1994. "The structure and dynamics of dry farming states in Upper Mesopotamia." *Current Anthropology* 35 (1): 483–520.

———. 1995. "Late-Assyrian settlement geography in Upper Mesopotamia." Pp. 139–159 in *Neo-Assyrian Geography,* ed. Mario Liverani. Rome: University di Roma, Quaderni di Geografia Storica, 5.

———. 1997a. "Holocene environments of the high plateau, Yemen: Recent geoarchaeological investigations." *Geoarchaeology* 12 (8): 833–864.

———. 1997b. "The history of the lake of Antioch: A preliminary note." Pp. 557–576 in *Crossing Boundaries and Linking Horizons: Studies in Honor of Michael C. Astour on His 80th Birthday,* ed. Gordon Young, M. Chavalas, and R. Averbeck. Bethesda, MD: CDL.

———. 1998. "Water and human settlement in the Balikh Valley, Syria: Investigations from 1992–1995" *Journal of Field Archaeology* 25: 63–87.

———. 1999a. "Settlement, soil erosion and terraced agriculture in highland Yemen: A preliminary statement." *Proceedings of the Seminar for Arabian Studies* 29: 183–191.

———. 1999b. "Holocene valley fills of southern Turkey and NW Syria: Recent geoarchaeological contributions." *Quaternary Science Reviews* 18: 555–572.

———. 2000a. "Settlement and land use in the zone of uncertainty in upper Mesopotamia." Pp. 3–35 in Jas (ed.).

———. 2000b. "Regional approaches in Mesopotamian archaeology." *Journal of Archaeological Research* 8: 219–267.

Wilkinson, Tony J., and Eleanor Barbanes. 2000. "Settlement patterns in the Syrian Jazirah during the Iron Age." Pp. 397–422 in *Essays on Syria in the Iron Age,* ed. Guy Bunnens. Louvain: Peeters.

Wilkinson, T. J., Belinda Monahan, and D. J. Tucker. 1996. "Khanijdal East: A small Ubaid site in northern Iraq." *Iraq* 58: 17–50.

Wilkinson, Tony J., C. Edens, and M. Gibson. 1997. "The archaeology of the Yemen high plains: A preliminary chronology." *Arabian Archaeology and Epigraphy* 8: 99–142.

Wilkinson, T. J., C. Edens, and G. Barratt. 2001. "Hammat al Qā': An early town in southern Arabia." *Proceedings of the Seminar for Arabian Studies* 31: 249–59.

Wilkinson, T. J., C. A. I. French, W. Matthews, and J. Oates. 2001. "Geoarchaeology, landscape and the region." Pp. 1–14 in *Excavations at Tell Brak.* Vol. 2: *Nagar in the Third Millennium B.C.,* ed. David Oates, Joan Oates, and Helen McDonald. Cambridge: British School of Archaeology in Iraq and McDonald Institute of Archaeological Research.

Wilkinson, Tony J., and David J. Tucker.

1995. *Settlement Development in the North Jazira, Iraq: A Study of the Archaeological Landscape.* Warminster, UK: Aris and Phillips.

Willcox, George. 1999. "Charcoal analysis and Holocene vegetation history in southern Syria." *Quaternary Science Reviews* 18: 711–716.

Williamson, Tom. 1987. "Early coaxial field systems on the East Anglian boulder clays." *Proceedings of the Prehistoric Society* 53: 419–431.

———. 1998. "Questions of preservation and destruction." Pp. 1–24 in *The Archaeology of Landscape: Studies Presented to Christopher Taylor,* ed. Paul Everson and Tom Williamson. Manchester: Manchester University.

Willey, G. R. 1953. *Prehistoric Settlement Patterns in the Virù Valley, Peru.* Bureau of American Ethnology Bulletin 155. Washington, DC: Smithsonian Institution.

Wilson, Andrew. 2000. "Industrial uses of water." Pp. 127–150 in Orjan Wikander (ed.).

Wilson, D. R. 2000. *Air Photo Interpretation for Archaeologists.* Stroud, UK: Tempus.

Wirth, Eugen. 1971. *Syrien, eine geographische Landeskunde.* Darmstadt: Wissenschaftliche Buchgesellschaft.

Woldring, Henk. 2002. "Climate change and the onset of sedentism in Cappadocia." Pp. 59–66 in *The Neolithic of Central Anatolia: Internal Developments and External Relations during the 9th–6th Millennia Cal B.C.,* ed. Frédéric Gérard and Laurens Thissen. Istanbul: Ege Yayınları.

Woodbury R. B., and J. A. Neely. 1972. "Water control systems of the Tehuacan Valley." Pp. 81–153 in *The Prehistory of the Tehuacan Valley.* Vol. 4: *Chronology and Irrigation,* ed. Richard S. MacNeish and Frederick F. Johnson. Austin: University of Texas.

Wright, Katherine, M. Najjar, J. Last, N. Moloney, M. Flinder, J. Gower, N. Jackson, A. Kennedy, and R. Shafiq. 1998. "The Wadi Faynan Fourth and Third Millennium Project 1997: Report on the first season of test excavations at Wadi Faynan 100." *Levant* 30: 33–60.

Wright, Henry T. 1969. *The Administration of Rural Production in an Early Mesopotamian town.* Ann Arbor: Museum of Anthropology, University of Michigan, Anthropological Papers no. 38.

———. 1981. "The southern margins of Sumer: Survey of the area of Eridu and Ur." Pp. 295–345 in Adams 1981.

———. 1994. "Pre-state political formations." Pp. 67–84 in *Chiefdoms and Early States in the Near East: The Organizational Dynamics of Complexity*, ed. Gil Stein and Mitchell Rothman. Madison, WI: Prehistory.

———. 2000. "Agent-based modeling of small scale societies: State of the art and future prospects." Pp. 373–385 in *Dynamics in Human and Primate Societies. Agent-based Modeling of Social and Spatial Processes*, ed. Timothy Kohler and George Gumerman. Santa Fe, NM: Santa Fe Institute, and Oxford: Oxford University.

Yair, A. 1994. "The ambiguous impact of climate change at a desert fringe: northern Negev, Israel." Pp. 199–227 in *Environmental Change in Drylands: biogeographical and geomorphological perspectives*, ed. Andrew C. Millington, and Kenneth Pye. New York: John Wiley.

Yair, A. 2001. "Water-harvesting efficiency in arid and semi-arid areas." Pp. 289–302 in *Sustainable Land Use in Deserts*, ed. S.W. Breckle, M. Veste, and W. Wucherer. Berlin: Springer.

Yakar, Jak. 2000. *Ethnoarchaeology of Anatolia. Rural Socio-economy in the Bronze and Iron Ages*. Tel Aviv: Tel Aviv University.

Yasuda, Y., H. Kitagawa, and T. Nakagawa. 2000. "The earliest record of major anthropogenic deforestation in the Ghab Valley, northwest Syria: a palynological study." *Quaternary International* 73/74: 127–36.

Yener, K. Aslıhan. 1995. "The archaeology of empire in Anatolia: Comments." *Bulletin of the American Schools of Oriental Research* 299/300: 117–121.

———. 2000. *The Domestication of Metals: The Rise of Complex Metal Industries in Anatolia*. Leiden: Brill.

Yener, K. A., and H. Özbal. 1987. "Tin in the Turkish Taurus Mountains: The Bolkardağ mining district." *Antiquity* 61: 220–226.

Yener, K. A., C. Edens, T. P. Harrison, J. Verstraete, and T. J. Wilkinson. 2000. "The Amuq Valley Regional Project 1995–1998." *American Journal of Archaeology* 104: 163–220.

Yule, Paul (ed.). 1999. *Studies in the Archaeology of the Sultanate of Oman*. Rahden, Westfalia: Marie Leidorf.

Zaccagnini, Carlo. 1979. *The Rural Landscape of the Land of Arraphe*. Rome: Quaderni di Geografia Storica.

Zammit, T. 1928. "Prehistoric cart tracks in Malta." *Antiquity* 2 (5): 18–25.

Zangger, E., M. E. Timpson, S. Yazvenko, and H. Leiermann. 1999. "Searching for the ports of Troy." Pp. 89–103 in *Environmental Reconstructions in Mediterranean Landscape Archaeology* (Populus series), ed. P. Leveau, F. Trément, K. Walsh, and G. Barker. Oxford: Oxbow.

Zarins, Juris. 1992. "Pastoral nomadism in Arabia: Ethnoarchaeology and the archaeological record: a case study." Pp. 219–240 in *Pastoralism in the Levant: Archaeological Materials in Anthropological Perspective*, ed. Ofer Bar-Yosef and Anatoly M. Khazanov. Madison, WI: Prehistory.

———. 1997. "Persia and Dhofar: Aspects of Iron Age international politics and trade." Pp. 615–689 in *Crossing Boundaries and Linking Horizons: Studies in Honor of Michael C. Astour on His 80th Birthday*, ed. Gordon Young, M. Chavalas, and R. Averbeck. Bethesda, MD: CDL.

———. 2000. "Environmental disruption and human response: An archaeological-historical example from South Arabia." Pp. 35–50 in *Environmental Disaster and the Archaeology of Human Response*, ed. Garth Bawden and Richard M. Reycraft. Albuquerque: University of New Mexico, Maxwell Museum of Anthropology.

Zarins, J., M. Ibrahim, D. Potts, and C. Edens. 1979. "Preliminary report on the third phase of the comprehensive archaeological survey project: The central provinces." *Atlal* 3: 9–42.

Zarins, J., N. Whalen, M. Ibrahim, A.J. Mursi, and M. Khan. 1980. "Preliminary report on the central and southwestern province survey, 1979." *Atlal* 4: 9–36.

Zarins, J., A. Murad, and K. al-Yaish. 1981. "The second preliminary report on the southwest province." *Atlal* 5: 9–42.

Zarins, J., Ali S. Mughannum, and Mahmoud Kamal. 1984. "Excavations at Dhahran South–the tumulus field." *Atlal* 8: 25–54.

Zarins, J., and A. Zahrani. 1985. "Recent archaeological investigations in the southern Tihama plain, 1404/1984." *Atlal* 9: 65–107.

Zeder, Melinder A. 1995. "The archaeobiology of the Khabur Basin." *Bulletin of the Canadian Society for Mesopotamian Studies* 29: 21–32.

———. 1998. "Environment, economy and subsistence on the threshold of urban emergence in northern Mesopotamia." *Bulletin of the Canadian Society for Mesopotamian Studies* 33: 55–67.

———. 1999. "The role of pastoralism in the development of specialized urban economies in the ancient Near East." Paper presented at the Annual Meetings of the Society for American Archaeology, Chicago, March 1999.

Zettler, Richard, L. 1989. "Field plans from the Ur III Temple of Inanna at Nippur," *Acta Sumerologica* 11: 305–113.

——— (ed.). 1997. *Subsistence and Settlement in a Marginal Environment: Tell es-Sweyhat, 1989–1995 Preliminary Report*. MASCA Research Papers in Science and Archaeology 14. Philadelphia: University of Pennsylvania, University Museum, MASCA.

Zimansky, Paul. 1985. *Ecology and Empire: The Structure of the Uratian State*. Chicago: Oriental Institute, Studies in Ancient Oriental Civilization 41.

Zohary, D. 1973. *Geobotanical Foundations of the Middle East*. Stuttgart: Fischer.

Zonneveld, K. A. F., G. Ganssen, S. Troelstra, G. J. M. Versteegh, and H. Visscher. 1997. "Mechanisms forcing abrupt fluctuations of the Indian Ocean summer monsoon during the last deglaciation." *Quaternary Science Reviews* 16: 187–201.

Index

About the Author

Tony Wilkinson was trained as a geographer at Birkbeck College, London University, and at McMaster University in Hamilton, Ontario. At McMaster his research focused upon the hydrology of overland flow in the Canadian High Arctic. From Canada he then moved into archaeology where he worked on regional landscape projects in the United Kingdom and the Middle East. Within those areas his special interests have included landscapes of dry lands (deserts) and wetlands (specifically those submerged beneath the sea). He has undertaken landscape fieldwork in Oman, Yemen, Saudi Arabia, Iraq, Syria, Turkey, and Iran, as well as various places in the United Kingdom.

He was formerly Assistant Director of the British Archaeological Expedition to Iraq, in Baghdad, Research Associate (Associate Professor) at the Oriental Institute, University of Chicago, as well as Lecturer and Professor in the Department of Archaeology, University of Edinburgh. He is a Fellow of the British Academy, and since 2006 has been a Professor in the Department of Archaeology, Durham University, U.K.

Since 2002 he has been principal investigator of an NSF-funded project to model ancient settlements in greater Mesopotamia, and his most recent project is the Fragile Crescent Project funded by the Arts and Humanities Research Council (UK). This four-year project is analyzing settlement and landscape trends across northern Syria, southern Turkey, and northwestern Iraq during the Chalcolithic and Bronze Ages.